FIREARMS *of the* AMERICAN WEST
1866–1894

FIREARMS OF THE

AMERICAN WEST
1866–1894

LOUIS A. GARAVAGLIA

CHARLES G. WORMAN

University of New Mexico Press • Albuquerque

Library of Congress Cataloging in Publication Data
(Revised for vol. 2)

Garavaglia, Louis A., 1940–
    Firearms of the American West.

    Includes bibliographies and indexes.
    Contents: [1] 1803–1865 — [2] 1866–1894.
    1. Firearms, American—History.   I. Worman, Charles G.,
1933–   . II. Title.
TS533.2.G36   1984   vol. 1   683.4'00973   83-12528
ISBN 0-8263-0720-5 (set)
ISBN 0-8263-0792-2 (v. 2)

Designed by Whitehead & Whitehead

CONTENTS

PREFACE

Between 1865 and 1900 the American frontier changed radically. In the pre–Civil War period, threats to the white frontiersman came most often from Indians or wild animals, and less frequently from other settlers. Certainly there were exceptions to this; the violence in California during the gold rush is but one example. Yet prior to 1865 the vast expanse between the Missouri River and the West coast was largely a void, inhabited principally by Indians, bears, and wolves.

After 1865 all this began to change. Great numbers of settlers pushed toward the sunset, often following courses pointed out by the iron fingers of the new Pacific-bound railroads. And as the numbers of westerners grew, so did violence. Now, increasingly, white clashed with white: the lawful clashed with the lawless. Peace officers and judges were few and far between, and even when they were within reach, frontier dwellers often chose to dispense justice themselves. As a ranch foreman in central Texas stated in 1879: "The fear of the law is not half so great as the fear of a bullet with the characters we have to deal with." Swords and pikes had long since been laid aside; now it was the firearm that either broke or enforced the law. And as the frontier experience was an integral and important part of our national experience, so firearms were an integral and important part of the frontier experience.

Our first volume on this subject covered the years between 1803 and 1865. This volume begins, logically enough, with 1866 and ends (technically, at least) with 1894. We chose 1894 as a cut-off date for two reasons. First, that year saw the initial army issues of a new high-velocity bolt-action rifle designed for smokeless-powder cartridges. Second, the Winchester Model 1894, a civilian arm adapted for smokeless-powder ammunition, also appeared at that time. Thus, for all practical purposes, 1894 marks the beginning of the modern era in firearms. In a few instances, however, we have allowed ourselves the latitude of extending the narrative to about 1900.

Within this time span we have attempted to deal with all the important military and civilian firearms used in the settling of the West, as well as the guns favored by Indians. As far as the quality of our work is concerned, we will again leave that to the reader to judge.

Louis A. Garavaglia and Charles G. Worman
Colorado Springs, Colorado

To my children, Heather and Matt.
L. A. G.

To Carol, Liz, Paul, and Rob,
for their patience and support.
C. G. W.

ACKNOWLEDGMENTS

As with our first volume, this book could not have reached completion without the help of numerous individuals and institutions. Again hoping we have not left too many out, we list these individuals and institutions below:

Individuals:

Gene Ball
Tom Barr
Ann Berry
Robert V. Bell
Nick Bleser
Sidney B. Brinckerhoff
Emory Cantney, Jr.
Pierce A. Chamberlain
Donald Chaput
Malcolm Collier
Barry B. Combs
Hollis N. Cook
Gary L. Delscamp
Merrilee Dowty
John Dutcher
Jim Earle
Harry B. Elliott
Norm Flayderman
Dr. Lawrence A. Frost
Herb Glass, Jr.
Neil Gutterman
Ashley Halsey, Jr.
Charles E. Hanson, Jr.
Dr. Vance Haynes
Wesley Henry
Charles L. Hill, Jr.
Roy G. Jinks
Tom Keilman
Alan S. Kelly
Gerald Kelver
John A. Kopec
E. Dixon Larson
Holli Locke
Gerald Lytle
Roy Martin Marcot

Gordon Matson
Samuel L. Maxwell, Sr.
C. H. McKennon
Calvin Moerbe
Burton R. Nelson
The late Willis E. Neuwirth
Ross Osborne
Lt. Col. William R. Orbelo, U.S.A. (ret.)
Maj. Charles W. Pate
Pam Patrick
Norman Paulson
Mrs. Sandy Perlman
David R. Phillips
Don L. Reynolds
Jim Roller
Steve Romanoff
Konrad F. Schreier, Jr.
Charles Schreiner, III
William B. Secrest
Lawrence P. Shelton
Mrs. Nancy Sherbert
Jan R. Shrader
Joseph W. Snell
A. W. F. Taylerson
The late M. D. "Bud" Waite
Paul Weisberg
Michael Winey
Dr. Robert L. Woolery

Special thanks to the following:

William Francis Deverell, Jr.
E. Lee Manning, Jr.
Robert E. McNellis, Jr.
Herb Peck, Jr.
Frank M. Sellers
Russell E. Thornton
Bleecker R. Williams, Jr.
The late H. Paul Wilson

Organizations:

Arizona Historical Society, Tucson, Ariz.

Amon Carter Museum of Western Art, Fort Worth, Tex.

Richard A. Bourne Co., Inc., Hyannis, Mass.

Buffalo Bill Historical Center, Cody, Wyo.

California State Library, Sacramento, Calif.

Colorado State Historical Society, Denver, Colo.

Connecticut State Library, Hartford, Conn.

Custer Battlefield Historical and Monument Assn., Inc., Crow Agency, Mont.

Denver Public Library, Western History Dept., Denver, Colo.

Ft. Laramie Historical Assn., Ft. Laramie, Wyo.

Harrah's Automobile Collection, Reno, Nev.

Hastings Museum, Hastings, Neb.

Kansas State Historical Society, Topeka, Kan.

Library of Congress, Washington, D.C.

Los Angeles County Museum of Natural History, Los Angeles, Calif.

Milwaukee Public Museum, Milwaukee, Wis.

Montana Historical Society, Helena, Mont.

Museum of New Mexico, Santa Fe, N. Mex.

Museum of the American Indian, New York City, N.Y.

Museum of the Fur Trade, Chadron, Neb.

Museum of the Great Plains, Lawton, Okla.

National Cowboy Hall of Fame, Oklahoma City, Okla.

National Park Service

Nebraska Historical Society, Lincoln, Neb.

Nevada State Museum, Carson City, Nev.

Northfield Historical Society, Northfield, Minn.

Oregon Historical Society, Portland, Ore.

Ohio State University Library, Columbus, Ohio

Panhandle-Plains Historical Museum, Canyon, Tex.

Pioneers' Museum, Colorado Springs, Colo.

Rutherford B. Hayes Presidential Center, Fremont, Ohio

Saint Joseph Museum, St. Joseph, Mo.

Smithsonian Institution, Washington, D.C.

Sotheby Park-Bernet, Los Angeles, Calif.

State Historical Society of North Dakota, Bismarck, N. Dak.

State Historical Society of Wisconsin, Madison, Wisc.

Union Pacific Museum, Omaha, Neb.

United States Army Military History Institute, Carlisle Barracks, Pa.

University of Oklahoma Library, Norman, Okla.

W. H. Over Museum, Vermillion, S. Dak.

Wells Fargo Bank History Room, San Francisco, Calif.

West Point Museum, West Point, N.Y.

Wyoming State Archives and Historical Dept., Cheyenne, Wyo.

We also wish to thank Luther Wilson and the staff of the University of New Mexico Press for smoothing the final stretch of the road toward publication. Finally, we must thank Karen McAuliffe Garavaglia for typing the polished version of a lengthy and often-altered manuscript.

·PART I·

MILITARY ARMS

THE REGULAR MOUNTED UNITS that had marched eastward in 1861 to fight the Civil War returned to the frontier in 1865 with new names: the First and Second Dragoons had become the First and Second Cavalry, the Mounted Rifles had become the Third Cavalry, and the First and Second Cavalry had become the Fourth and Fifth. A new regiment, the Sixth, had taken the field beside them. Designations of the infantry units stayed the same, but to the existing ten regiments Congress had added nine more.

By 1866 it was apparent that despite the increase in the army's strength, there were too few soldiers for the jobs required of them. Federal officials judged that the unreconstructed states of the South would need garrisons amounting to nearly a third of the military's manpower; yet the frontier, with its ceaseless Indian wars and the westward press of thousands of new homesteaders, subjected the army to even greater demands. In July of 1866, therefore, the army's authorized strength made another jump: the number of cavalry units went from six to ten; the infantry regiments went from nineteen to forty-five, only to drop to twenty-five in 1869.

The men who made up these regiments were a diverse lot. Some were former slaves, organized into one of four black regiments led by white officers. Many others were immigrants from Europe, who looked upon a five-year enlistment as a way to learn the language and customs of their new country. Additional enlistees included young men lured to the army by adventure and by the opportunity to see the West. And others, enlisting under an alias, were hiding from the law.

Whatever their backgrounds, a high proportion of the enlisted men in this postwar army were raw recruits, who knew nothing of military life and who found little in the way of training programs awaiting them. Prior to the mid-1870s, for example, an entire year's worth of marksmanship instruction might involve the firing of only ten or twelve cartridges. Essential to the army's success, therefore, was the experience and guidance provided by seasoned non-commissioned officers, many of whom had held commissions on one side or the other during the Civil War. (Sgt. William McCall, who participated in the desperate Battle of Beecher's Island in 1868, had during the war commanded a Pennsylvania regiment as a brevet brigadier general.)

Besides the lack of training, the enlisted man faced other difficulties. He had to contend with a rigid caste system and the prospect of harsh punishment for minor violations of strict rules. If wounded or ill in the field, he could rarely expect trained medical assistance. Frequent exposure to dampness promoted rheumatism, while inadequate diet and poor sanitation produced a high rate of disease. Through the 1870s there was no regular rotation of troops, so the same men and officers might serve for years at one remote post. Thus desertion in most of the white regiments was common. (Those who enlisted in the fall merely to gain winter shelter before deserting in the spring were known as "snow birds.") Among the most reliable troops were the blacks, whose regiments generally had the lowest desertion rates.

The Indian-war army offered little more inducement to officers than it did to enlisted men. Low pay and inferior social standing, the possibility of extended service far from "civilization," bleak quarters, and extremely slow promotion were all factors which discouraged a military career. Not until the late 1870s, after Indian campaigning had passed its zenith, did significant improvements in frontier living conditions become common.

In addition to the trouble faced by individual soldiers, the army as a whole had problems, some of which had persisted since troops first crossed the Mississippi. There were often inadequate numbers of soldiers for the jobs at hand. Geographical barriers caused difficulty in communication and transportation. The government's Indian policy vacillated: the lenient Quaker "peace policy" of "conquest by kindness," adopted during the Grant administration, stood in sharp contrast to the policy advocated by William Tecumseh Sherman:

> The more we can kill this year, the less will have to be killed the next war, for the more I see of these Indians the more convinced I am that they all have to be killed or maintained as a species of paupers. Their attempts at civilization are ridiculous.

The question of which policy to follow was confused by the fact that there was often no obvious line distinguishing peaceful from hostile elements of a tribe.

These problems were the more pressing because, at almost any given time between 1866 and 1886, the army was involved in a campaign against hostiles somewhere on the frontier. And yet, few soldiers saw much fighting other than skirmishes. The main reason for this was the philosophy of warfare held by most of the tribes. Raiding was virtually a form of sport. Successfully stealing another tribe's horses or other property brought much individual honor, particularly if it was accomplished without loss or injury to the raiders. If cornered or if defending village or family, Indians could be savage foes, willing to fight to the death. In open battle, however, warriors typically fought not as disciplined members of a united force, but rather as individuals. As such they were free to withdraw from combat without any accusation of cowardice if they felt the advantage over an enemy had disappeared. They usually attacked suddenly, relying on surprise and superior numbers, then scattered as soon as resistance stiffened. Experienced frontiersmen knew that even if they were outnumbered by hostile Indians, a show of determined resistance on their part could often discourage an attack. As a consequence of the Indian view of warfare, soldiers found that lengthy, hard-fought battles were rare. Without a clear advantage the Indians declined to fight, evading the troops pursuing them with frustrating ease. The army's many futile efforts to bring warriors to bay helped initiate winter campaigns, in which, with little actual combat, troops were able to destroy Indian villages and food supplies. Such losses, coupled with the start of the buffalo slaughter by professional hide hunters, sometimes put the tribes in a surrender-or-starve position.

Again, Indians usually chose to fight if they enjoyed superiority in numbers, and they enjoyed just that advantage in upper Wyoming in 1866. There thousands of Sioux under the redoubtable Red Cloud were plaguing the Bozeman Trail and the Eighteenth Infantrymen who occupied the posts built to defend it. An especially harsh blow fell on the troops in December of 1866, when warriors lured into ambush and annihilated Captain William J. Fetterman and the eighty men with him. During the following summer two smaller detachments barely escaped a similar fate, chiefly because they were armed with new fast-firing breech-loading rifles. The war for the Bozeman Trail lasted until mid-1868, when the army reluctantly abandoned the posts guarding it in exchange for Red Cloud's signature on a peace treaty.

This agreement, however, brought no peace to the plains of western Kansas and eastern Colorado, where Cheyenne and Arapaho raided without letup. Repeatedly they attacked settlements, stagecoach lines, and construction crews on the Kansas Pacific railway. To bring them to terms Gen. Philip Sheridan fielded a major offensive during the winter of 1868/69, a time when the Plains Indians were most vulnerable. Sheridan's campaign was largely successful, due in part to a strike at the Cheyenne on the Washita by George Custer's Seventh Cavalry in November of 1868. Just as successful was a second strike in the summer of 1869, when, at Summit Springs in northeastern Colorado, Fifth Cavalrymen and a battalion of Pawnee scouts won a notable victory over the Cheyenne Dog Soldiers.

After Summit Springs a temporary peace settled over the central plains, but this was not the case in other regions. Between 1871 and 1873, for example, Lt. Col. George Crook (who had given the Paiutes a sound drubbing in 1867–68) used elements of the First and Fifth Cavalry and the Twenty-third Infantry to wage an effective war against the Apaches in Arizona's Tonto Basin. In this war Crook made extensive use of Indian scouts and mobile pack-mule trains, both of which he would employ again, with equal success.

Late in 1872, when Crook was still pressing the Apaches, another war broke out with the Modocs who lived along the California-Oregon border. Withdrawing to the easily defended lava beds south of Tule Lake, fewer than seventy-five Modoc warriors held off troops of the First Cavalry and Twenty-first Infantry for five months, before new commanders and as many as fourteen hundred men finally subdued them and sent them to a reservation in Kansas.

Less than a year after the Modoc War the army mounted a broad offensive in Texas against some of the most warlike Indians on the continent: the Kiowas, Comanches, and Southern Cheyennes. Through the summer and fall of 1874 soldiers from the Fourth, Sixth, Eighth, and Tenth Cavalry, and the Fifth and Eleventh Infantry, chased the hostiles across the Texas panhandle, fighting several major engagements and over a dozen small actions. Besides their casualties the Indians were worn down by the weather—first a scorching drought, then torrential rains, finally a bitter winter—and began surrendering en masse early in 1875.

Almost a year earlier a military expedition under

George Custer had left Fort Abraham Lincoln to explore the Black Hills of Dakota. The treaty that Red Cloud had signed in 1868 had guaranteed this land to the Sioux in perpetuity; but the discovery of gold there and the resultant influx of miners brought about yet another Indian war. In the spring of 1876 the army launched a three-pronged offensive, designed to force all hostile Sioux and Cheyenne to stand and fight somewhere in southeastern Montana. Stand and fight they did: first they battled George Crook's command of Second and Third Cavalrymen and Fourth and Ninth Infantrymen to a standstill on the Rosebud, and then, in a blow that shook the country itself, wiped out George Custer and five troops of the Seventh Cavalry on the Little Bighorn. After the Little Bighorn the Indians, flushed with success, simply evaded the huge columns sent after them. But between October of 1876 and May of 1877 Nelson A. Miles's Fifth Infantry and Ranald MacKenzie's Fourth Cavalry, marching back and forth across the Yellowstone country, dealt them a series of defeats which convinced most of them to return to the reservation.

Less important than the Sioux War of 1876–77, but equally tense for those involved, were the actions that occupied the army from 1877 to 1879. In the former year the Nez Percé of Idaho, reacting against a government attempt to remove them from a favorite hunting ground, bested the troops sent against them in three separate engagements, then fled toward Canada. When finally intercepted and surrounded by Nelson Miles's Fifth Infantrymen and elements of the Second and Seventh Cavalry, they were a mere fifty miles from the international boundary and safety. In the spring of 1878 a new war erupted with Idaho's Bannock Indians and some Paiutes who joined them. This time the army fought with grim efficiency, and by late summer the war was over. Idaho again became the scene of hostilities in May of 1879 when, following the murder of five Chinese miners, troops of the First Cavalry and Second Infantry pursued Shoshoni "Sheepeaters" over the fastnesses of the rugged Salmon River Range and drove them to the point of surrender. More serious

than the Sheepeater affair was the uprising by the Utes in western Colorado in September of 1879, resulting from Agent Nathan Meeker's overzealous efforts to convert them to farmers. More than twenty soldiers and civilians died, Meeker among them, before additional troops and the mediation of peaceful Indians and government officials ended the hostilities.

After the Ute rebellion the army turned most of its attention to the Southwest. Here, some three years earlier, the Apaches had again started raiding. Riding hard and striking fast, they were terrorizing settlements on both sides of the international border. For a time Victorio and his Warm Springs Apaches posed the principal threat, leading troops of the Sixth, Ninth, and Tenth Cavalry on long pursuits across Texas, New Mexico, Arizona, and even into Mexico itself. But after Victorio's death in Mexico in 1880, other leaders equally capable—Nana, Chato, and especially the Chiricahua chief Geronimo—rose to take his place. In September of 1882, however, George Crook resumed command of Arizona. Using his Apache scouts and mobile pack-mule trains, Crook and a Sixth Cavalry detachment tracked the hostiles deep into Mexico and, after one sharp fight in May of 1883, persuaded them to return to the Arizona reservations. They bolted in 1885 and again in 1886; but in September of 1886 Geronimo surrendered with finality, this time to Nelson A. Miles and a detachment of Fourth Cavalrymen.

One last Indian outbreak was yet to come. In 1890 a "Ghost Dance" movement swept through tribes in the West, impelling the Teton Sioux to a brief, bloody, and disastrous stand-up fight with the Seventh Cavalry at Wounded Knee Creek in South Dakota.

Besides fighting Indians, the army had other responsibilities on the frontier. Between 1867 and 1879 it participated in two major surveys of the West, one under Clarence King and the other under Lt. George Wheeler. It also surveyed railroad routes, guarded construction crews, built roads, and performed similar tasks. But to most observers, combat remained the army's most visible task.

· 1 ·

LONG ARMS

BREECH-LOADING INFANTRY ARMS: THE SPRINGFIELDS OF 1865 AND 1866

TRAGIC AS IT WAS, the Civil War did provide a first-rate testing ground for new designs and concepts in weapons and tactics. For Ordnance men, the principal lesson learned in connection with small arms was that in the heat of battle a good breechloader was superior to even the best muzzle-loader. As utterly simple and rugged as the Minie rifle was, it was no better than the soldier who used it, as shown graphically by an Ordnance survey taken after the Battle of Gettysburg. Following Lee's retreat from the field, Union ordnance personnel recovered some 27,500 abandoned muzzle-loaders, of which at least 24,000 were still charged. Of this number about half had two loads rammed down the barrel, and a fourth contained from three to ten loads each. Furthermore, "twenty-three loads were found in one Springfield rifle-musket, each loaded in regular order. Twenty-two balls and sixty-two buckshot with a corresponding quantity of powder all mixed up together were found in one percussion smooth-bore musket." If a soldier rammed down a ball without first pouring in the powder, his gun was useless until he pulled out the bullet with the ball screw on the end of his rammer. In the grip of excitement or terror, he might forget to cap the nipple, and instead merely go through the motions of loading and firing, piling one load on top of another. As reliable as the Minie rifle was, therefore, it had no control over the reliability of the soldier who carried it into combat.[1]

On the other hand, a breechloader by its very design mitigated some of the disastrous effects resulting from the use of muzzle-loaders by inexperienced troops in battle. Chief among its advantages was its speed of reloading, which saved the soldier the frantic twenty seconds or so it took to charge a muzzle-loader. As one veteran, who termed the muzzle-loader a "bungling, slow-shooting gun," described his feelings in 1864:

Let [those who champion the muzzle-loader] come to the front armed with one Springfield musket, and oppose themselves to an equal number of Rebs. armed with repeaters or breechloaders. If they can stand that, let them go to the picket line, and while fumbling for a cap and trying to get it on the cone one of these cold days, offer themselves as a target to some fellow on the other side who has nothing to do but cock his piece and blaze away. . . . The objection has been urged that we fire too many shots with our present muzzle-loaders, and consequently it would be folly to add to the waste of ammunition by affording us greater ease or facility in loading. Do our good friends ever reflect that the loss of time in loading is the great *cause* of haste, and consequent inaccuracy in firing?

Moreover, during the loading process the man armed with a breechloader could not force more than one round into the chamber, and could load his weapon easily in the prone position, thereby protecting himself from the effects of enemy fire.[2]

During most of the 1850s the Ordnance Department had shown no reluctance to arm its mounted troops with breech-loading carbines, and by 1858 had demonstrated a willingness to consider the breechloader for infantry as well as cavalry. In that year Ordnance contracted with two inventors, George W. Morse and William Mont Storm, for the rights to apply their breech-loading designs to infantry arms. Patented in October of 1856 and June of 1858, Morse's system involved a short longitudinally sliding breechbolt backed by a long upward-pivoting locking block. What was really important, however, was that Morse designed his gun around a center-fire metallic cartridge. Like the Joslyn carbine of 1855, Mont Storm's arm, patented in July of 1856, incorporated a "trap-door" breechblock, in which a transverse pivot passing through the block's upper front corner allowed it to swing upward and forward to expose the chamber for loading. Although the Mont Storm used a paper cartridge instead of the advanced ammunition of the Morse, its breechblock did incorporate an efficient gas-sealing

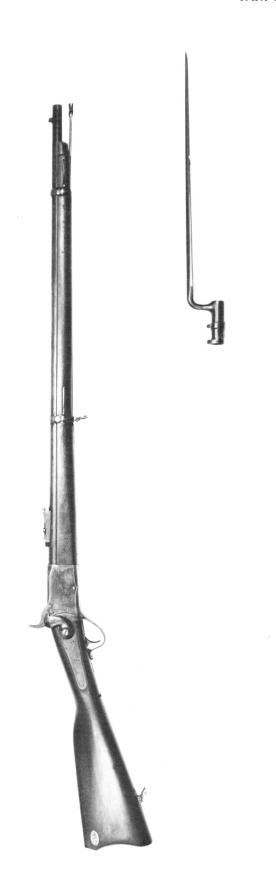

Peabody single-shot breech-loading rifle. (Courtesy National Park Service, Fuller Gun Collection, Chickamauga and Chattanooga National Military Park)

sleeve, and Ordnance men regarded both designs as worthy of test: between the fall of 1858 and mid-1860 Springfield Armory converted a number of rifled muskets to Morse breechloaders, while Harper's Ferry converted at least 300 Mississippi rifles to Mont Storm's design. Late in 1860 John B. Floyd, the secretary of war, predicted that "as certainly as the percussion cap has superseded the flint and steel, so surely will the breech-loading gun drive out of use those that load at the muzzle."[3]

The outbreak of war temporarily interrupted the government's experiments with breech-loading infantry rifles, but within three years military planners were again looking hard in that direction. Late in 1864 General A. B. Dyer, chief of ordnance, reported that:

The use of breech-loading arms in our service has, with few exceptions, been confined to mounted troops. So far as our limited experience goes, it indicates the advisability of extending this armament to our infantry also, and this experience is corroborated by that of several foreign nations. . . . It is therefore intended to make this change of manufacture at our national armories as soon as the best model for a breech-loader can be established by full and thorough tests and trials. . . . The alteration of our present model of muzzle-loading arms is also a very desirable measure, both on account of economy and improvement in the character of these arms.

In December of 1864 Dyer invited anyone having a method for converting the army's thousands of muzzle-loading rifle-muskets to breechloaders to submit a sample for trial, but he had also directed Erskine S. Allin, master armorer at Springfield, to come up with a conversion system of his own. To get the best gun possible, Dyer further instructed Allin to use features from any existing patent, regardless of who held it.[4]

In January of 1865 a board of officers convened at Springfield to examine what would eventually be a total of sixty-five breech-loading designs. Testing continued until early April when, with the outcome of the war no longer in doubt, the board abruptly concluded that the Spencer lever-action repeater and a single-shot rifle patented by Henry O. Peabody in July of 1862 were both superior to any of their competitors. Due to the termination of hostilities, however, the Ordnance Department took no action on the board's findings.[5]

Then, in September of 1865, Allin patented his method of converting the army's muzzle-loaders to breechloaders. Employing a breechblock hinged at its upper front corner, the Allin action was yet another trapdoor design, already well known to the military because of the Mont Storm and 1855 Joslyn. Thus Allin's patent did not claim the basic design, but instead dealt principally with two of its features—the extractor and an arrangement for both locking the breechblock and preventing accidental discharge.

This system comprised a rotating, convex-faced "cam latch" in the rear of the breechblock, which engaged a concave recess in the face of the breechplug for locking. The cam latch was rigidly connected to an external thumbpiece at the right rear of the block; once the hammer was cocked, an upward and forward push on the thumbpiece rotated the cam latch through the same arc, disengaging it from its recess in the breechplug and allowing the breechblock to pivot upward and foward for loading. The thumbpiece itself acted as a safety feature; when the cam latch was not fully seated in its recess, the thumbpiece lay between the firing pin and the hammer nose, precluding discharge until the block was completely locked. With the latch fully seated the hammer nose overrode the thumbpiece, and by preventing the thumbpiece from rising, the hammer thus acted as a secondary lock to keep the block closed.

While the hammer-blocking, hammer-locked thumbpiece was a clever idea, the extractor was a frail, needlessly complex rack-and-pinion affair which constituted the weakest part of the conversion, and which gave way within a year to a simpler type. Poor as the extractor was, the chief of ordnance saw promise in Allin's overall design, and late in 1865 ordered 5000 rifle-muskets converted to the Allin system. The conversion itself involved milling away the upper part of the barrel at the breech, making the necessary cuts in the barrel wall and breechplug to accommodate the extractor and cam latch, chambering the barrel for a .58 rimfire cartridge, and bolting to the top of the barrel, just in front of the breechblock mortise, a "hinge strap" which carried the hinge pin for the breechblock. Although it had its weaknesses, the trapdoor design lent itself admirably to the conversion of a muzzle-loader; as Allin phrased it in his patent:

> It is particularly adapted to the alteration of the Springfield rifle-musket, (or any other,) as it can be done without changing the feature of the musket or without throwing away any of its parts. All that is necessary is to cut away the barrel on the top at the breech and add the [breechblock] and shell-[extractor], cut the recess in the breech-screw, and modify the hammer. All other parts remain the same.[6]

This first-model government conversion, now called the Model 1865 Springfield but known to Ordnance men as "Allin's Alteration," also acquired an unofficial but widely used nickname, the "needle gun," stemming from the long slender firing pin which extended

First Model .58 Allin conversion (1865) of the Springfield .58 percussion rifle musket. (Courtesy National Park Service, Fuller Gun Collection, Chickamauga and Chattanooga National Military Park)

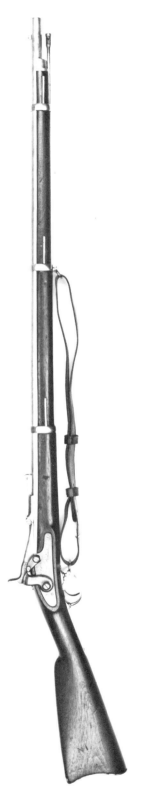

U.S. Model 1866 .50-70 Springfield (Second Model Allin conversion). (Courtesy Mr. Richard K. Halter)

diagonally through the entire length of the breechblock. The short copper-cased cartridge detonated by this needle-like pin had a 500 grain bullet backed by a 60 grain powder charge, roughly the equivalent in power of the paper cartridge for the .58 muzzle-loader.[7]

Early in 1866, while a quantity of M1865 Springfields went to a battalion of the Twelfth Infantry for field trials, a board of officers met in Washington for additional small-arms testing. This time more than forty designers submitted their guns for trials, which lasted from mid-March until early June. Some of the arms were already well known: there were several Sharps models chambered for metallic cartridges; Henry rifles in both .44 and .50 caliber; three types of Remingtons; and a Maynard designed for a self-priming cartridge. Although the first-model Allin underwent testing with all the other guns, three weeks before the trials ended Allin submitted a new rifle, described by the board as "Allin's plan for modification of Springfield musket, with tube reducing the calibre from fifty-eight to fifty." Officially termed the Springfield Model 1866, Allin's second design was still based on a .58 caliber muzzle-loading barrel, but in this case the barrel was reamed out to .64 caliber for the insertion of a rifled .50 caliber liner, held in place by brazing. Colonel T. T. S. Laidley, who had guns of his own entered in the trials, had come up with this idea, but the mechanical skill required to execute it was considerable, and its successful application was a real credit to Springfield artisans.[8]

Other new features of the M1866 included a longer, more easily manufactured breechblock, a longer hinge strap more rigidly secured to the barrel, and a new extractor. While the new breechblock retained the cam latch and hammer-blocking, hammer-locked thumbpiece of the 1865 Allin, it had another safety device as well. Called a "hammer guard," this was an integral transverse ridge, projecting from the rear of the block just below the firing pin; like the thumbpiece, the hammer guard prevented the hammer nose from striking the firing pin until the breechblock was fully closed. The 1866 breechblock also incorporated additional refinements, in the form of coil springs for the cam latch and firing pin.[9]

Although the new extractor was a notable improvement over the rack-and-pinion type of 1865, it may have been something of an embarrassment to Allin; it was a close copy of the extractor used in a hammer-locked trapdoor carbine patented in November of 1864 by Edward S. Wright, whose gun was an entry in both the 1865 and 1866 trials. In the Wright and the Allin systems, the integral hinge-pin sleeve at the upper front corner of the breechblock had at its front a vertical metal lip, called an "extractor hook"; when the trooper swung the breechblock upward and forward for loading, the extractor hook rotated downward and backward, catching the rim of the fired case and pulling it a fraction of an inch from the chamber. As the case began sliding backward a powerful U-shaped spring, one arm of which had engaged the rim during loading, flung the case clear of the chamber and out of the gun. The extractor hook, which afforded the 1866 Springfield its "primary extraction," was a well-thought-out design, but a problem developed with the U-shaped spring: it was under tension whenever the breechblock was closed, regardless of whether there was a cartridge in the chamber, and for this reason it soon lost its elasticity, or simply broke.[10]

In all, however, the 1866 Allin conversion was a much better service arm than its predecessor, although there were other guns entered in the 1866 trials which offered it strong competition. In testing the arms submitted to it the board was to make three distinct choices: the best breech-loading action for the conversion of muzzle-loaders, the best breech-loading action for a completely new gun, and the best breech-loading action for use by mounted troops. When the trials ended the board presented, as its clear choice for a conversion system, a trapdoor action patented in February of 1866 by Hiram Berdan, of "Berdan's Sharpshooters" fame. The best of the completely new guns was the Peabody, with the Remington a close second. The board was reluctant to name a carbine, but tentatively recommended the Spencer, which had experienced extraction troubles during the tests. Another matter to be decided was the best caliber for small arms, which the board determined to be .45 instead of .50 or .58.[11]

By the time the board's report reached the secretary of war, however, both the chief of ordnance and General U. S. Grant had added their own opinions. Dyer suggested that the Allin was worthy of consideration, noting that "a battalion of the 12th infantry has been armed with this musket for several months, and the report of the commanding officer upon them is highly favorable." Grant further suggested that:

There being such a large number of arms on hand capable of economical alteration, it seems unnecessary at present to experiment with new arms. . . . The superiority of the .45 calibre in accuracy, range, and penetration seems to have been placed beyond a doubt, but a uniformity of calibre being so desirable, and there being such a large number of arms of caliber .50 on hand, it may be advisable to adopt this calibre.

So at the expense of the Berdan, the Peabody, and the relatively efficient .45 caliber, the army's standard infantry weapon became the M1866 Allin conversion, chambered for a new .50-70 centerfire cartridge. In July of 1866 the secretary of war ordered the conversion of 25,000 muzzle-loaders to the M1866 system, following this with a second order for another 25,000, all of which Springfield completed by March of 1868. Others assembled sporadically thereafter boosted the total to more than 52,500 arms.[12]

The .50-70 cartridge, firing a 450 grain slug at a muzzle velocity of about 1250 feet per second, was a worthwhile improvement over the .58. In July of 1867 Dyer reported that firing tests at Springfield had shown the .50 caliber M1866 to be nearly twice as accurate at 500 yards as was the M1865, whose .58 rimfire cartridge had a muzzle velocity of only 960 feet per second. Philadelphia's Frankford Arsenal produced the Martin bar-anvil-primed .50-70 copper-cased cartridges from October of 1866 until March of 1868, when the arsenal began using the Benet cup primer instead of the Martin type. Both primers were set into the case from the mouth and held in place against the head by "stab crimps"; as a result, the .50-70 military loads looked like rimfire rounds. Because they were "inside primed," they could not be reloaded. Moreover, they were of "folded head" contruction, in which the case head was no thicker than the body; heavy powder charges fired in such cases sometimes caused the heads to bulge or rupture, which led to jamming or extraction problems.[13]

Frankford Arsenal issued the .50-70 cartridges in packages of twenty rounds each, "which are of such size that two packages will easily fit into the service cartridge-box after the tin cases [liners] have been removed." Not all troops bothered to remove these liners, however, and this, curiously enough, led to a different method of carrying the cartridges. When the future brigadier general Anson Mills led two infantry companies into Fort Bridger, Wyoming, in 1866, he found the volunteer garrison there armed with Spencer carbines:

[Mills] turned in my muzzle-loading Springfields and equipped my two companies with the Spencers which . . . had heavy metallic cartridges, Cal. .50. Our equipment consisted of the regular old-fashioned cartridge box for paper cartridges to be carried in tin cases inside the leather boxes, and were wholly unsuited for metallic cartridges. I furnished mounted guards and patrols to the daily Overland Mail, and the metallic ammunition carried in these tin boxes rattled loudly, and were even noisier when carried by men afoot.

To correct this situation Mills devised a leather waist belt, made by the post saddler, which had loops for fifty cartridges. This belt proved to be much more comfortable and efficient than the cartridge box, and when sutler W. A. Carter traveled to Washington,

D.C., he filed patent papers on Mills's behalf. This patent proved to be the basis of Mills's other cartridge-belt patents, which resulted in changes in methods of carrying ammunition not only within the U.S. Army but also in armies throughout the world. (Mills "eventually made an independent fortune.")[14]

From the end of the Civil War through mid-1866, while all the development work was going on at Springfield, arsenals and depots held thousands of serviceable breechloaders purchased prior to the surrender at Appomattox. Apparently, however, the army preferred to keep most of its breechloaders in storage, and until mid-1867 a majority of the infantry units garrisoning the frontier continued to rely on muzzle-loading Springfield and Enfield rifle-muskets. As of mid-1866 the Third U.S. Infantry (stationed in Kansas and New Mexico), the Fifth Infantry (in New Mexico, Texas, and Arizona), the Ninth (in California and Nevada), and the Tenth (in Minnesota and Dakota) all carried .58 Springfield muzzle-loaders, while elements of the U.S. Colored Infantry (in Texas and New Mexico) had either .58 Springfields or .577 Enfields. Omaha Scouts at the Omaha Agency in Nebraska also had Enfields, while the First Arizona Infantry still carried some .54 caliber Mississippi rifles alongside its Springfields. Shortly after the war western states and territories such as Kansas and Colorado received small quantities of .58 Springfields from the federal government; Kansas stamped its guns "Property Of The State Of Kansas" on the barrels, while the Colorado arms had "U.S./Col. Ter." branded in large letters on the buttstocks. Although these guns typified the arms issued to the regular army, state troops, particularly cavalrymen, were sometimes even better armed than the regulars; certain Kansas and Colorado units, for example, managed to get Spencer rifles and carbines. Colonel Henry B. Carrington, who with the Eighteenth Infantry had the unenviable task of building posts along the Bozeman Trail in Wyoming in 1866, repeatedly referred to the obsolete arms carried by most of his men. When C Company of the Second Cavalry reported to him for duty in November, Carrington wrote that the cavalrymen—most of whom were green recruits—were "poorly armed with old Springfield rifles and Star carbines." About fifty cavalrymen exchanged their Starrs for Spencers carried by the regimental band, but the Spencer-armed recruits were of little help when, in late December, a Sioux war party attacked a wood train near Fort Phil Kearny. The warriors successfully decoyed a relief force of eighty-one men, sent out by Carrington under the command of Captain William J. Fetterman, into an ambush from which no white man escaped. Aside from his recruits, Fetterman's force carried muzzle-loading Springfields. However, two civilian employees of the Quartermaster Department who accompanied the relief force owned Henry repeaters, and at least managed to sell their lives dearly, as the pile of empty .44 rimfire cases at their position revealed. The lesson was not lost on Carrington, who after the Fetterman massacre urgently cabled for reinforcements: "Only the new Spencer arms should be sent; the Indians are desperate; I spare none, and they spare none."[15]

Between late 1866 and mid-1867 the state of affairs for other infantry units on the frontier began to change. By mid-1867 the Third and Thirty-seventh infantrymen (stationed in Kansas and New Mexico) had Civil War breechloaders: there were Spencer rifles with the Third and .52 caliber Sharps rifles with the Thirty-seventh. Rather than take a standard-issue arm, Lieutenant Philip Reade of the Third Infantry carried a handsome octagon-barreled Spencer sporting rifle, inscribed on the frame with his name, rank, and unit. The M1866 Springfield had also reached the West: the Fourth and Thirtieth Infantry (in Dakota and Colorado) and the Thirty-eighth (in Kansas) were armed exclusively with such guns. There was also a scattering of 1866s among other infantry units, but not enough to displace their muzzle-loaders: the Twenty-second Infantry (in Dakota), the Twenty-seventh (in Dakota and Montana), the Thirty-sixth (in Dakota, Utah, and Nebraska), and companies of the Eighteenth (in Dakota) all had .58 muzzle-loaders in addition to their .50-70s. Elements of the Eighteenth at Fort Casper, Dakota, also had a few .58-rimfire Allin conversions on hand. But all other infantry regiments, as well as all the artillery units, still carried muzzle-loaders. Even those units with access to breechloaders continued to use muzzle-loaders. Describing military life in Dakota in 1867, Philippe Regis de Trobriand wrote:

> It is always necessary to go armed when venturing out on the prairie, and since the hunting gun is loaded at the muzzle—the breech-loaders would be useless if we exhausted the supply of cartridges, which are impossible to replenish for months—prudence demands that a revolver be carried in the belt.[16]

Issues of the M1866 continued steadily, however, and by October of 1867 General Dyer could report that:

> All of the converted arms have been issued to troops, and nearly all of the infantry serving in the departments of the Missouri and the Platte have been armed with them. . . . In a campaign against the Indians during the past summer these arms have done excellent service, and very few have been rendered unserviceable.

The fighting during the summer of 1867 had involved two of the most dramatic encounters between soldier and Indian in the history of the postwar frontier—the

These men of the Seventh Infantry photographed in 1866 would
soon exchange their .58 muzzle-loading U.S. rifle muskets for .50
Springfield breechloaders. (Courtesy Ft. Laramie Historical Assn.)

Hayfield and Wagon Box fights. On the first of August a large party of Sioux attacked a detail of twenty soldiers and six civilians cutting hay near Fort C. F. Smith, another of the Bozeman Trail outposts. Only a week before, the permanent garrison at the post had been reinforced by the arrival of two companies of the Twenty-seventh Infantry, escorting a wagon train loaded not only with supplies for the post sutler but also with a quantity of M1866 Springfields and .50-70 cartridges. During the all-day fight the six civilians relied principally on Spencer and Henry repeaters, except for one man with a muzzle-loading Enfield; while the repeaters did more than their share of damage, the soldiers used their new breechloaders with equally telling effect. So decimated were the Indians by the unexpected firepower that the whites, after withstanding repeated assaults, were finally able to reach safety. In his official report of the fight, Captain T. B. Burrowes accorded the 1866 a good deal of credit because it permitted the hard-pressed soldiers to fire faster and expose themselves less than did a muzzle-loader. Furthermore, the weapon's firing rate and accuracy "tends to keep [the men] calm, composed, and confident under fire."[17]

An infantry contingent, armed with .50 Springfield M1866 trap-door rifles, stands witness to the historic linking of the transcontinental railroad at Promontory, Utah, in 1869.

One day after the Hayfield fight, in a separate but coordinated attack, another force of Sioux under the personal leadership of Red Cloud jumped a detachment of twenty-six infantrymen from Fort Phil Kearny commanded by Captain James Powell, who had been at the fort during the Fetterman disaster. With four civilian woodcutters Powell's men took cover behind some wooden wagon boxes which had been removed from the running gear, and reinforced them with bags of corn and barrels of salt and beans. Like the troops at the Hayfield fight, Powell's men had exchanged their muzzle-loaders for the new 1866 Springfields only a few weeks before, in early July, when the breech-loaders had come in with an ox train again escorted by the Twenty-seventh Infantry. However, there had been little chance to practice with the guns, and this point—plus the fact that Powell's men could see several hundred Sioux massing for attack—gave the troops grave doubts about their chances for survival. As Sergeant Samuel Gibson of the Twenty-seventh Infantry remembered it:

When I took my place in the wagon box occupied by Sergeant McQuiery and Private John Grady, both of them had their shoes off, and were fixing their shoestrings into loops to fit them over the right foot and from thence to the triggers of their rifles, for the same purpose that Sergeant Robertson had done—to kill themselves when all hope was lost, in the event the Indians passed over our barricade by an overwhelming force of numbers, when every man would stand erect, place the muzzle of his loaded rifle under his chin and take his own life, rather than be captured and made to endure the inevitable torture. I had just taken off my own shoes and made loops in the strings when the firing began.

Private Frederic Claus said that once the fighting started "the air was so full of smoke from our guns that it was seldom that we could see further than a few rods." And Sergeant Gibson recalled that:

After we had commenced firing, a great number of Indians rode in very close—probably within a hundred and fifty yards, and sitting on their ponies waited for us to draw ramrods for reloading, as they supposed we were yet using the old muzzle-loaders but, thanks to God and Lieutenant-General Sherman, the latter had listened to the appeals of Colonel Carrington, commanding Fort Phil Kearny the previous year, and we had just been armed with the new weapon, and instead of drawing ramrods and thus losing precious time we simply threw open the breech-blocks of our new rifles to eject the empty shell and slapped in fresh ones. This puzzled the Indians, and they were soon glad to withdraw to a safe distance.

Some of the poorer shots reloaded for the better marksmen; one civilian, a former trapper and reportedly a crack shot, admitted that he had "kept eight guns pretty well het up for mor'n three hours." Teamster Smyth had two Spencer carbines and a pair of Colt revolvers and fired through a hole drilled in the wooden wagon box. Sergeant Max Littmann recalled that in addition to their Springfields, each soldier was armed with a revolver, "but we did not use them—not, at least to my knowledge."[18]

THE SPRINGFIELDS OF 1868 AND 1870 VERSUS THE REMINGTON, THE SHARPS, AND THE WARD-BURTON

Its performance in the hard service of the frontier earned the 1866 Springfield a good reputation. General C. C. Augur's official report from the Department of the Platte in September of 1867 included this note:

The new breech-loading rifle (altered Springfield) issued this year to the troops in this department has increased their efficiency wonderfully. All reports concur in regarding this arm as nearly perfect for infantry, and the ammunition with it as the best ever furnished to troops.

An Ordnance board which met in January of 1868 also had high praise for the arm, noting that:

The Springfield rifle musket, altered to a breech loader, on the plan of 1866, has been in the hands of troops for the past eighteen months. A careful examination of more than two hundred monthly reports of Company commanders shows that it is considered a very powerful, accurate, and serviceable infantry arm.

And in October of 1869, the chief of ordnance reported:

All the infantry, heavy artillery, and engineer troops have been provided with the Springfield breech-loading rifled musket. Many of them have had these arms for more than two years. The reports from the different branches of the service in all parts of the country have been highly favorable to this arm and its ammunition.

After thus commending the 1866, however, the ordnance chief added diplomatically that:

The slight defects developed in the arm by long usage in the field have, from time to time, been reported to the bureau. The new model arms now being made at Springfield Armory, it is thought, will be free from any and all the defects heretofore found. In comparison with other breech-loading arms, it is confidently believed that this new pattern musket, and the ammunition made for it at the Frankford Arsenal, will stand unsurpassed.

The "new pattern musket" had resulted from the recommendations of the 1868 Ordnance board, which among other changes suggested housing the breech-block in a separate receiver, shortening the barrel, adopting a new type of extractor, and increasing the size of the cam latch "to better secure [it] in its place."[19]

Although the Model 1868 used a few Civil War components, such as lockplates, lock parts, and screws, Springfield had to build most of the arm from the ground up, and it took the armory time to tool up for its manufacture. As a result armory workmen did not complete any of the new guns until the first quarter of 1869. In its production form the M1868 had a $32^5/8$ in. round barrel with new long-range sights, threaded into a separate receiver; most of the barrels were newly

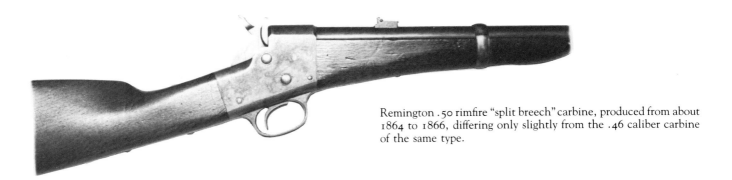

Remington .50 rimfire "split breech" carbine, produced from about 1864 to 1866, differing only slightly from the .46 caliber carbine of the same type.

made, but some were shortened muzzle-loader barrels, relined to .50 caliber. While retaining the basic features of the 1866 breechblock, the new block had a high arch milled into its underside to reduce weight and to allow the block to close even if dirt accumulated in the bottom of the receiver well. The receiver itself had long shallow cuts on either side to permit the escape of powder gas in the event of a ruptured case head.[20]

Another new point in the M1868 was its extractor. Pivoting on the hinge pin for the breechblock, the new extractor had a short upper leg, projecting above the top of the receiver, and a long lower leg which engaged the case rim. When the breechblock swung upward and forward for loading, its top struck the extractor's upper leg and forced it forward, whereupon the lower leg, with the assistance of a powerful coil spring, quickly rotated backward, pulling the case from the chamber and throwing it out of the receiver. This extractor was quite strong and positive in its operation—a little too strong, as events would prove, for a folded-head copper cartridge. However, the M1868 was not the only rifle Springfield worked on during that period: between March and June of 1868, even before production of the new trapdoor model began, the armory assembled 504 "Breech-loading rifle muskets, 'Remington.'" Already on its way to becoming a phenomenal commercial success, the Remington "rolling block" rifle was the ultimate refinement of a hammer-locked breechloader initially patented by Leonard Geiger in January of 1863. Geiger's basic idea, altered and improved by Joseph Rider, first came to commercial and military notice as the Remington "split breech" pistol and carbine, but not until Rider's final patent, in January of 1865, did the rolling-block arm assume its nearly perfected form. Both the split-breech and rolling-block carbines were entries in the 1866 Ordnance trials, but it was the latter arm with which Remington made its bid for an uncertain postwar arms market.[21]

One of the simplest and strongest of all the postwar breechloaders, the Remington rolling block—described in detail in the *Army and Navy Journal* in October of 1866—comprised only two major parts, a breechblock pivoted at its lower front corner and, behind that, a locking block with the hammer integrally mounted atop it; both breechblock and locking block swung on massive pivot pins passing transversely through the frame. Pulling the hammer/locking-block unit to the full-cock position allowed the breechblock to rotate backward and downward for loading, an action which gave the rifle its popular "rolling block" nickname. When the shooter closed the block and pulled the trigger, the locking block, lying below and projecting well ahead of the hammer nose, swung forward into engagement with the underside of the breechblock, and had it securely locked by the time the hammer reached the firing pin. The system was so simple as to be almost foolproof, and strong not only because of the basic design but also because of the large bearing surfaces of its working parts. Impressed by this gun, a board of navy and marine officers chose it for use by the sea services in 1869, after the usual competitive trials.[22]

Largely because of the navy's action, still another army ordnance board began small-arms tests in St.

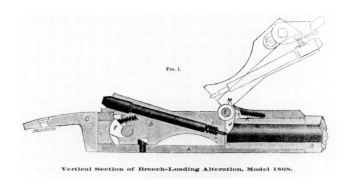

Breech mechanism of the Springfield M1868 rifle.

Louis in March of 1870, examining not only infantry weapons but carbines and handguns as well. Of the different types of infantry arms submitted to the board, including the Berdan, the Roberts, and several variations of the Peabody, the board actually tested only six: the Remington, the Springfield, the Sharps, the Morgenstern, the Martini-Henry, and the Ward-Burton, recommending them in that order. But the board's final judgment reduced these six candidates to three:

Only the first three systems named possess such superior excellence as warrants their adoption by the Government for infantry and cavalry without further trial in the hands of troops. Of these three, considering all the elements of excellence and cost of manufacture, the board are unanimously and decidedly of the option that the Remington is the best system. . . .

Evidently some of the 504 Remington rifles made by Springfield in 1868 had gone into the hands of troops for field trials well before the St. Louis board convened, because in July of 1870 the chief of ordnance, expressing skepticism at the board's choice, wrote that:

serious defects existed in the Remington arms, not observable in the Springfield or the Sharps, such as frequent failures to explode the cartridges, occasional sticking of the empty shell in the chamber, and the difficulty of moving the hammer and breechblock after firing with heavy charges. The first two of these defects, and also the objection arising from the arm being loaded only at a full-cock, have been brought to the notice of this bureau by the commanding officers of all companies using this arm. These defects show that the Remington arm should not be adopted before being thoroughly tested in service.

Field trials, in fact, would be a fair requirement for any arm the St. Louis board considered worthwhile, and with that in mind the Chief of Ordnance concluded that:

the Remington, the Springfield, and the Sharps systems are decidedly superior to all other systems which have been brought to (the board's) notice, and I recommend that one thousand muskets and three hundred carbines be prepared according to each of the three systems, and issued for comparative trial in the service. . . . This department is now making the Springfield musket, and is preparing to make the Remington musket for the Navy; and it can readily have some of the Sharps rifles on hand converted into muskets.[23]

By March of 1871 the national armory had completed 1001 experimental Remingtons, 1020 Model

Model 1871 .50 rifle, made at the Springfield Armory under a royalty agreement with the Remington firm. (Courtesy National Park Service, Fuller Gun Collection, Chickamauga and Chattanooga National Military Park)

1870 Springfields, and 501 Sharps "muskets," all of which were on their way to troops for trial within two months. The Sharps, another 500 of which Springfield finished by June, were converted for the trials at the armory by the addition of new 32½ in. barrels chambered for the .50-70 cartridge, with new full-length forestocks held to the barrels by two bands. The Remington barrels were of the same length.[24]

Externally the Model 1870 Springfield differed from the M1868 chiefly in having a shorter receiver, but internally the new rifle incorporated some subtle mechanical changes, made necessary by the folded-head government cartridge. Ordnance officers sometimes went out of their way to point out what a good cartridge the copper-cased .50-70 was: in his 1870 report, for example, General Dyer stated that "our ammunition for [the M1868] has been proven to be very superior—unsurpased by any that has ever been made." Understandable as his fondness for the cartridge was, his statement was something less than accurate. By the early 1870s commercial manufacturers were abandoning copper for their centerfire cartridge cases and using brass in its place.[25]

There was a good reason for this choice. At the instant of firing any cartridge case would expand tightly against the chamber walls, but when the bullet left the muzzle and the pressure in the bore dropped, the case had to contract slighty to allow for extraction. Brass cases, made with the right proportions of copper and zinc, had enough elasticity to regain their original shape after firing, but copper was an uncertain material in this respect; as a result copper cases were prone to stick in the chamber, especially a chamber heated and fouled from previous shooting. Even if the case body contracted enough to free itself from the chamber walls, the case head was liable to swell or ruture; this could keep enough pressure on the front face of the breechblock to cause friction between the locking surfaces, which in turn would make the action difficult to open. Major friction problems were avoided in the trapdoor Springfield, however, because everything about its rotating cam latch, including the contours and locking angle, was designed specifically to prevent the latch from sticking or jamming under any circumstances.[26]

This led to another problem. In a majority of trapdoor designs, including the 1866 and 1868 Springfields, the hinge pin for the breechblock lay well above the bore axis and immediately behind the cartridge head. Because of this, the backward thrust of the cartridge case at the instant of firing tended not so much to push the breechblock straight back as it did to rotate the block upward around its hinge pin, into the open position. And because the cam latch was designed to disengage easily, it was not well suited to resist the

upward push of the block when the arm was fired.

Ordnance officers were well aware of the tendency of the block to swing open under pressure, and to eliminate it they used a variation of a technique employed in previous trapdoor designs (including two Berdan models): the hinge-pin hole in the M1870 breechblock was slightly elongated, to become a short slot instead of a simple hole. The reason for this was that if the front of the hinge-pin hole could not touch the front of the hinge pin at the moment of discharge, there was no tendency for the block to pivot open from the strain of firing. Thus in the M1870 and later Springfields, as the trooper snapped the breechblock shut the cam latch, rotating downward under spring pressure into its fully locked position, forced the block to slide forward a fraction of an inch, thereby preventing contact between the hinge-pin hole and the pin itself.[27]

However, this system gave rise to still another problem, which did not become immediately apparent. Because the cam latch forced the breechblock to side forward during locking, it did not allow the rear face of the block to bear against the rear face of its mortise in the receiver. A solid bearing at that point, in concert with the elongated hinge-pin hole, would have given the Springfield action a great deal of added strength. But there was still the matter of the copper cartridge: a badly bulged case head could cause enough friction between the rear of the block and the receiver to make the block hard to open. Thus the cam latch alone, its front face bearing against a recess in the rear of the breechblock and its rear face bearing against a recess in the face of the breechplug, took up the shock of firing. But even when fully locked, the latch, with its easy-opening contours, lay at an upward angle to the bore axis instead of parallel to it; because of this, the pressure of a heavy powder charge against the front face of the block tended to force the latch farther upward, into its open position. If that happened only the hammer nose, lying over the cam-latch thumbpiece, could keep the latch from popping open.[28]

Years would pass before this problem became apparent, and then it would present itself only during the testing of special loads. As it was, the trapdoor design, as embodied in the 1870 and later Springfields, was amply strong for repeated firings of any round loaded with 70 or 80 grains of black powder. And when used with the copper cartridge, the trapdoor Springfield offered a major advantage: regardless of what went wrong with the cartridge, it was practically impossible to jam the Springfield action in the closed position. In almost every respect, in fact, this rifle was better suited to handle the service load than were most competing designs.

The field trials of 1871–73 confirmed this point. At

the close of 1870 the principal infantry arm among troops stationed on the frontier was the M1866 Springfield, supplemented by a limited number of M1868s and a few hundred Remingtons, which were probably part of the lot made by Springfield in 1868. By May of 1871, however, as the 1866s were gradually being withdrawn and more 1868s were going into service, the experimental Springfield, Remington, and Sharps rifles were reaching posts in the departments of the Platte, the Missouri, the Pacific, and the Gulf, with about eighteen to twenty of each issued to selected companies.[29]

The monthly reports from company commanders reflected a general dislike for the Sharps. From Company G, Third Infantry, came the opinion that the rifle "[requires] a trigger-guard; does not eject; [and] clogs. . . ." Captain George Choisy, commanding Company A of the Eleventh Infantry, rendered a confirming opinion, noting that the Sharps "does not always eject." And Captain E. E. Sellers of Company D, Tenth Infantry, regarded the Sharps as "inferior to Springfield, being heavier, not so accurate, and more complicated."

The Remington earned somewhat better marks. The commander of Company A, Eighth Infantry, found it "most durable and most unlikely to get out of order." A company commander in the Sixth Infantry wrote that "as a mechanical proposition the Remington [is] superior," but added that "the men are inclined to prefer the Springfield." Complaints against the Remington reflected the objections raised by the chief of ordnance in July of 1870: officers thought it should "load at half-cock" and invariably noted that it "does not always eject." There was an additional comment from the Ninth Infantry: "Dust and rust prevent hammer from working freely." And from the Eleventh Infantry: "The Remington cannot be loaded and fired as rapidly as the Springfield."

Few derogatory comments were directed toward the Springfield. A Third Infantry company considered it "the best arm, less complicated and less liable to get out of order." A captain of the Thirteenth Infantry regarded it as "more easily handled and kept clean; efficient in dust and rain." And the commander of Company A, Twenty-fifth Infantry, "prefers Springfield over Remington and Sharps for strength of stock, rapidity of fire, ejection of shells, and ability to stand rough usage . . ."[30]

Although the St. Louis board's recommendations had stopped with these three guns, there were others worth examining. Late in 1871 Springfield Armory converted 1108 Spencer carbines to infantry rifles, using the same 32½ in. barrels previously fitted to the experimental Sharps and Remingtons. But because the Spencer action was too short to handle the .50-70 cartridge, the converted rifles took the Spencer .56-.50 rimfire round, a load notably inferior to the .50-70.[31]

Another design that deserved consideration was the Ward-Burton, sixth on the St. Louis board's list of choices but worth investigating because it was a bolt-action arm. Although anything but popular in the early 1870s, the bolt-action rifle would eventually become the standard military arm for almost all countries. And the Ward-Burton—from a design standpoint, at least—was a good example of its type. Based primarily on patents issued to Bethel Burton in December of 1859 and August of 1868, the rifle had a cylindrical, longitudinally sliding breechbolt common to other arms of its type, but its locking arrangement was unusual; on either side of the bolt body at the rear were integral screw threads, which locked into corresponding threads inside the receiver walls. Rotating the bolt handle upward and to the left through a 90 degree arc disengaged the threads and allowed the bolt to slide straight back to expose the chamber for loading. In lieu of a hammer, the Ward-Burton employed a longitudinally sliding striker, housed in the bolt body and powered by a coil spring. When the shooter pushed the bolt forward, the sear caught the striker and held it to the rear against spring pressure. Cocking was therefore automatic, requiring no conscious effort on the shooter's part; as soon as he rotated the bolt handle downward into locking position, the arm was ready to fire. While this self-cocking feature was practically a prerequisite for all later bolt-action rifles, it was to prove a drawback with the Ward-Burton.[32]

Springfield Armory itself undertook the manufacture of this rifle, completing 1015 between late 1871 and early 1872, and by March of 1872 the first of them were reaching troops for field trials. A captain of the Thirteenth Infantry described the new gun as "a very good arm, preferable to Remington or Sharps." More conservatively, the commander of Company H, Fifth Infantry, characterized it as "a good arm in the hands of careful men." The problem, however, was that most of the troops who carried the Ward-Burton were anything but careful. Because the forward push on the bolt automatically cocked the striker, the rifle was prone to accidental discharge when used by men unfamiliar with it. Opinions from the Tenth Infantry such as "dangerous, because cocked by action of loading" and from the Third Infantry, "a dangerous arm in the hands of green troops," were common. Captain A. L. Hough of the Thirteenth Infantry wrote that: "in consequence of the number of accidents occurring in using the Ward-Burton arm the men of my company are afraid to use them . . . As my reports have shown, I would prefer the Springfield." Aside from the probability of accidental discharge, which was primarily

Model 1871 .50 Ward-Burton bolt action carbine. (Courtesy National Park Service, Fuller Gun Collection, Chickamauga and Chattanooga National Military Park)

the fault of the men and not the gun, the Ward-Burton suffered a greater percentage of broken parts than any of its competitors.[33]

Field trials of the Ward-Burton, the Springfield, the Remington, and the Sharps continued through 1872, with reports on their performance coming in constantly. As originally proposed by the chief of ordnance, the reports from the field would go to a board of officers, which after studying them would select one of the arms for general issue. This board, presided over by Gen. A. H. Terry, met in New York City early in September of 1872, both to study the reports and to examine any new arms inventors might submit.

At about the same time, due to the reasonably good performance of the Remington rolling-block arm, Springfield Armory began the manufacture of 10,000 "Remington locking rifles." As its name implied, this rifle was designed to overcome the common objection that the Remington could be loaded only at full-cock. Externally the "locking" rifle was no different from the earlier rolling-blocks issued for field trials, but it did incorporate a mechanical change. To load, the trooper full-cocked the hammer, swung the breechblock backward and downward, and slipped a cartridge into the chamber: when he pushed the block upward and forward to close the breech, however, the hammer automatically fell forward to the half-cock position, and stayed there until the trooper again pulled it to full cock.

With or without the locking feature, the Remington was one design that the New York board looked upon favorably. But in March of 1873, with the field trials over and all the reports tabulated, the Remington came in a distant second to the M1870 Springfield; eighty-four commanders preferred the Springfield, ten the Remington, one the Sharps, and none the Ward-Burton. Aside from these four, however, the board had a host of other guns to consider: during the eight months it was in session, in fact, more than eighty domestic arms came to its attention, as well as nine foreign types. From all these guns, the board was to select a single breech-loading action which would serve both for an infantry rifle and for a cavalry carbine.[34]

CAVALRY CARBINES: THE SPENCER, THE SHARPS, AND OTHERS

In general the search for a suitable carbine had followed the same course as that for a rifle. The two big favorites immediately after the war were the seven-shot Spencer repeater and the single-shot Sharps. Other guns, of course, were still in use: between mid-1866 and mid-1867 most companies of the Second Cavalry, then in Colorado and Kansas, carried .54 caliber Starrs, while Companies B and L of the First Cavalry, stationed in Nevada and Arizona, had .50 caliber Maynards. Nevertheless, as the officers who conducted the 1866 trials remarked:

> The board is not decided in the opinion whether it would be best to have only magazine carbines in the cavalry service [, but] The experience of the late war, as well as all experiments by this board, prove that the Spencer magazine carbine is the best service gun of this kind yet offered.

(During the war the Ordnance Department had purchased just over 1700 Henry rifles from the New Haven Arms Company, but such quantities were too small to allow the Henry to offer the Spencer any real competition.) Although difficulties with the Spencer's extractor showed up during the 1866 tests, the board suggested a modified type, "producing, in the opinion of the manufacturers themselves, a decided improvement in the arm, and one that will lessen much the liability to become disabled in the service." Although Sharps breechloaders adapted to take metallic cartridges did quite well in these trials, the board passed them over in favor of three other single-shot carbines—the Remington, the Laidley, and the Peabody. In the main, however, the board was less than enthusiastic about adopting any new carbines, and as a result the Spencer remained the more or less official arm for mounted troops.[35]

But during the course of the war the Union government had purchased more than 80,000 Sharps carbines, whose only real drawback by 1866 was their percussion ignition system. In November of 1867, therefore, the Ordnance Department signed a contract with the Sharps concern "to alter Sharp's carbines" for the .50-70 cartridge. Sharps completed delivery of the first 1000 in February of 1868, ultimately furnishing the War Department with more than 30,000 such arms by the close of 1869.[36]

Initially, however, it was the Spencer which bore the brunt of the cavalry's postwar Indian fighting. Although the Spencers carried by Fetterman's Second Cavalry recruits had done little to stave off their impending massacre, that had been the fault of the men and not the guns, and frontier commanders such as Carrington continued to press the War Department to issue Spencers to their units. Some posts, however, did not get the repeaters until two years after the Civil War. In July of 1867 Major W. B. Lane of the Third Cavalry, then at Fort Union, New Mexico, wrote this letter to the adjutant general:

> I have the honor to state, that Spencer Carbines for the Regiment have arrived at this Post. I would therefore respectfully request that I be furnished with fifty (50) copies of the Manual, for this Carbine, for distribution, there being none on hand in the Regiment, or to my knowledge in the District.[37]

Many of the Spencers which went into postwar service were Model 1865s, first delivered under contract by Spencer and by the Burnside Rifle Company in April of the model year. The M1865 Spencer differed from the original in having a smaller caliber and a magazine cutoff; in addition, those made by Burnside had 20 in. barrels, 2 in. shorter than standard. The magazine cutoff, invented by Edward M. Stabler of Maryland, stopped the backward and downward movement of the breechblock/carrier assembly just before it could pick up a fresh cartridge from the magazine, thereby allowing the cavalryman to use his Spencer as a single-shot breechloader. After considerable discussion regarding the proper caliber for the new carbine, with some arguing in favor of the .56-.46, the original .56-.56 Spencer cartridge was replaced by a new .56-.50 round, in which the .56 rimfire case was elongated and its neck diameter reduced to hold a .50 caliber bullet.[38]

Many of the older Spencers which had seen active Civil War service remained in use on the plains alongside the M1865s, although some of them were badly in need of an overhaul. Pawnee scouts, organized to guard railroad crews working on the Union Pacific, were first equipped with muzzle-loading Springfields and Colt percussion revolvers, but in the spring of 1867 they were sent to Fort Sedgwick in northeastern Colorado to exchange the Springfields for Spencers. As Luther North remembered it:

> The carbines that we got in exchange for the muzzle loaders were old guns, and a good many of them were defective, so we had to examine each one to see that all were right. The ordinance sergeant would hand me a carbine, I would put a cartridge in the breech, then throw down the lever of the breechblock, and if the shell slipped through all right I would pull the lever up and the shell would be forced into the barrel of the gun. Many of the guns would not work and the shells would not go in. When I found one of those, I would hand it back and try another. General Emory was in command at Fort Sedgewick at this time, and he came over to the stock house where we were getting the carbines. When I got one of the guns that the cartridge stuck in and handed it back to the sergeant, he said: "What is the matter with that gun." I told him the shell stuck. He said: "Let me see it," and I handed it to him. The shell was about half way into the chamber. He took hold of the lever and gave a quick jerk and the breechblock struck the cartridge—they

Sharps .50-70 carbine (#91828) and .44 Remington New Model (#113680), each with Company K, Ninth Cavalry markings. Ordnance returns confirm use of these models by the Ninth Cavalry while serving in Texas in the mid-1870s.

were rim fire—with so much force that it exploded and the whole charge of powder blew out into his face. Fortunately he was wearing glasses and they saved his eyes, but the blood spurted from his face in streams. He did not have anything further to say, and left us to select our own guns. . . .[39]

During the late 1860s Spencer rifles and carbines flooded onto the frontier, not only with the troops but also with the tide of civilian emigrants. And the role of the Spencer in the hands of soldiers was as dramatic as that of the 1866 Springfield. The most prominent engagement in which the Spencer played a decisive part occurred in 1868, when Brevet Colonel George

Close-up of regimental stamping on .44 Remington #113680. The same die seems to have been used to stamp both the Remington and the Sharps carbine.

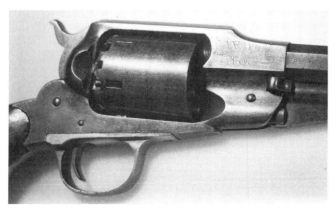

A. Forsyth, with Lieutenant Beecher and fifty frontiersmen, took up the trail of a large Sioux and Cheyenne war party north of Fort Wallace, Kansas. According to Forsyth:

Our equipment was simple: A blanket apiece, saddle and bridle, a lariat and picket pin, a canteen, a haversack, butcher knife, tin plate, tin cup, a Spencer repeating rifle . . . a Colt's revolver (army size), and a hundred and forty rounds of rifle and thirty rounds of pistol ammunition per man—this carried on the person.

The command also had three Springfield breechloaders and one or two Henrys, but it was the Spencer that was to prove decisive. In mid-September Forsyth's men became the hunted rather than the hunters; the Indians, led by Roman Nose and Pawnee Killer, turned on the small party, forcing it to "fort up" on a low island on the Arikara Fork of the Republican River. Only the Spencers' rapid fire broke up the Indians' repeated charges, finally driving them off without the mortally wounded Roman Nose. When a relief column from the Tenth Cavalry reached the scene nine days later, the surviving scouts on the island—later named Beecher's Island—had been reduced to eating the flesh of their dead horses and pack mules, after liberally sprinkling it with gunpowder to mask the sickening flavor.[40]

Later the same year Gen. Philip H. Sheridan inaugurated plans for a winter campaign against hostile Indians in what is now Oklahoma. A member of a volunteer unit recruited for this campaign, the Nineteenth Kansas Cavalry, wrote that in early November of 1868:

Henry .44 rifle reputedly used at the Battle of Beecher's Island. Several civilian scouts used Henry repeaters during the engagement although the soldiers carried Spencers plus several Springfield rifles. (Courtesy Kansas State Historical Society)

We drew our guns and twenty rounds of ammunition. . . . Our guns are the Spencer carbine, thirty inches long with a cartridge magazine holding seven cartridges. These are thrown into the barrel by a lever which is also a guard over the small trigger underneath. They are carried on horseback by a strap over the shoulder that holds them diagonally across our backs, making them easy to carry and not in the way while riding. No sabres or revolvers were issued.

Because the Seventh Cavalry under George Amstrong Custer was to take part in the operation, Custer, with Sheridan's support, instituted a system of target practice at Camp Supply, involving two drills daily. The troops fired their Spencer carbines at ranges of 100, 200, and 300 yards, and for more than a month scorekeepers carefully recorded each shot. The incentive for accurate shooting was that the forty best marksmen out of the eight-hundred-man command would be organized as an elite company of sharpshooters, exempt from guard and picket duty and permitted to march with the column as a separate unit.[41]

There proved to be a more practical incentive, for late in November of 1868, as the shivering regimental band played "Garry Owen," the Seventh struck Black Kettle's Cheyenne camp on the Washita, with the sharpshooters pouring in fire from their Spencers. At first the volume of fire stunned the Indians, but as their resistance stiffened it became apparent that Custer had hit what was only one of a number of camps along the river valley. Feigning an offensive maneuver, Custer burned many of the Indians' belongings, slaughtered the pony herd, and successfully withdrew his force under cover of approaching darkness. (His official report cited Indian casualties at more than 100, plus losses of 875 horses and mules, more than 1100 buffalo robes and skins, 35 revolvers, 47 rifles, 535 pounds of powder, 1350 pounds of lead and bullets, 4000 arrows and arrowpoints, 75 spears, and 35 bows and quivers.)[42]

In spite of the creditable record compiled by the Spencer, the Sharps carbine converted to take a metallic cartridge was coming into increasing favor with the military. Late in 1869 the chief of ordnance reported that:

The cavalry have been supplied with Spencer carbines, or with Sharp's carbines altered to receive the musket metallic cartridges caliber .50. About 30,000 of these latter arms have been altered. The Spencer carbine at the end of the war was generally regarded with favor, and as being the best arm that had been in service, and it continues to be regarded as a superior arm by the cavalry. The altered Sharp's carbine gives great satisfaction, and is preferred by some of the cavalry regiments to the Spencer. In some respects—particularly in the ammunition, which is the same as the breech-loading musket ammunition—it is decidedly superior to the Spencer carbine.[43]

At the meeting of the St. Louis board early in 1870, other carbines besides the Spencer and Sharps also came under consideration. Final recommendations for carbines followed those for rifles: the Remington rolling-block was the board's first choice, followed by the Springfield and the Sharps, but the board "regarded as essential for cavalry service that the Remington carbine be so modified as to load at the half-cock."[44]

Lt. Col. George A. Custer near Ft. Dodge, Kansas, in 1868 with his hunting dogs and a pet pelican. The Spencer he holds may be the sporting rifle, which an 1866 letter from the factory indicates he special-ordered. Another Spencer owner was Lt. (later brigadier general) Edward S. Godfrey who served under Custer in the 7th Cavalry and participated in the Battle of the Washita in 1868 and the fight at the Little Bighorn in 1876. Godfrey's M1860 Spencer carbine (#30313) exists today in a private collection. (Courtesy Custer Battlefield Historical and Monument Assn., Inc.)

By order of the chief of ordnance 300 samples of each carbine were to be made and distributed to companies of cavalry for testing. Accordingly, the national armory assembled 341 Model 1870 Springfield carbines, 313 Remingtons, and 308 Sharps, finishing them all by June of 1871. Within three months, limited numbers of all three of the new carbines were serving with elements of the First, Second, Sixth, Eighth, and Ninth Cavalry, then scattered through Arizona, Nebraska, Kansas, New Mexico, and Texas.

Moreover, late in 1871 armory workmen put together 317 carbines using the Ward-Burton action, and by June of 1872 small quantities of the guns were on duty with the Second, Third, Fourth, Sixth, Seventh, and Ninth Cavalry. Others subsequently reached the Fifth Cavalry.[45]

Although field reports concerning the new guns were not unanimous, most again favored the trapdoor Springfield. In fact such was the fondness for the Springfield that in November of 1871 the chief of ordnance sent this note to the commanding officer of Springfield Armory: "You will please make twenty Springfield Breech-loading Carbines Cal. 50 like the 300 experimental Model 1870 recently made . . . and send them to San Antonio Arsenal. . . . These twenty are intended for sales to Officers." In May of 1872 Lt. Charles Larned of the Seventh Cavalry observed that:

> the piece seemingly requiring the least attention in manipulation of loading was the government Springfield carbine . . . For rapidity of fire there appears to be little choice between the Ward-Burton and the Springfield, both of which excel in that respect the Remington, as their facilities for ejecting cartridges are superior to those of the latter. This superiority appears to rise from the fact, first, of their greater leverage, by which a tight cartridge is withdrawn without difficulty, the same also affecting its insertion; second that in the [Remington] the thumb, in drawing back the breech-block, is generally in the way of the falling cartridge. . . .

And in a special report, Captain Elijah Wells of the Second Cavalry stated that:

> I have used the experimental arms a long time, and find that the Sharps' carbine fouls in the breech by use, and, after being fired a number of times, the lever-bar does not work smoothly; also, the extractor does not extract the shells properly. The Remington, also, does not extract the shells properly. The extractor only draws the shell a short distance, when they have to be taken out with the fingers. Sometimes they expand, and cannot be withdrawn without considerable difficulty. The Ward-Burton fails often to explode the cartridge, which is caused

U.S. M1870 .50 Springfield carbine. (Courtesy National Park Service, Fuller Gun Collection, Chickamauga and Chattanooga National Military Park)

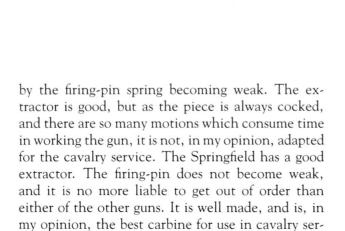

A Tenth Cavalry–marked Sharps .50-70 carbine (#71068), a New Model 1863 converted from percussion. The regimental stamping is located on the right side of the barrel. A photo of a similarly marked Colt M1860 revolver appears in the chapter on military handguns. Also known to the authors is a Springfield M1873 carbine (#29383) bearing a probable Tenth Cavalry stamping, "A. 10 CAV.Y./NO 73" on the trigger guard plate at the rear.

by the firing-pin spring becoming weak. The extractor is good, but as the piece is always cocked, and there are so many motions which consume time in working the gun, it is not, in my opinion, adapted for the cavalry service. The Springfield has a good extractor. The firing-pin does not become weak, and it is no more liable to get out of order than either of the other guns. It is well made, and is, in my opinion, the best carbine for use in cavalry service.[46]

Besides the four carbines issued for field trials, many of the older converted Sharps and veteran Spencers remained in service among mounted units. Between mid-1871 and mid-1873, in fact, the Ordnance Department issued more than 6600 Sharps and 1400 Spencers to the regulars.

Moreover, carbines abandoned by the regulars at the end of the war continued to see action in the hands of the volunteers. In 1866, for example, elements of the First Nevada and Eleventh Ohio carried, in addition to their Sharps and Spencers, a quantity of rimfire Joslyns. In the spring of 1869 Ordnance officials issued 1000 Smith carbines and 10,000 Smith cartridges to the Territory of Dakota, following this in 1870 with an issue of 35 Burnsides. Other areas in the West were somewhat more fortunate: in 1870 210 .50 caliber Spencers went to Nebraska, while Arizona received 250 Spencer .50s and 250 Sharps. Sharps carbines adapted for metallic cartridges saw additional use by the Lone Star State; from 1872 through 1874 the Ordnance Department sent Texas more than 1200 such guns.[47]

Having arms of different calibers within a single regiment might cause problems for Ordnance sergeants and supply officers, but in one incident involving the First Cavalry it did prove advantageous. During the Modoc campaign of 1872–73, fought through the lava

"L TROOP 1ST CAVALRY" stamped in the butt stock of this Spencer M1865 carbine indicates possible usage by that unit during the campaign against the Modoc Indians in 1872–73. (Courtesy Mr. Irvin D. Baer)

Spencer-armed Warm Springs Indian scouts during the Modoc campaign. (Courtesy National Archives)

beds of northeastern California, a company armed with Spencers encountered a defective lot of rimfire cartridges. As an enlisted man of another unit recalled it: "Several men of that troop told me that the failure of so many cartridges almost caused a panic, and would have . . . had it not been for the fact that other troops with them had Sharp's carbines that never missed fire." The trooper further recalled that when a cartridge stuck fast in the chamber of his Sharps, he nearly panicked himself until he managed to remove it.[48]

In decreasing numbers the Spencer carbine stayed with troops in the West through 1873, with a few still on hand as late as September of 1874. The last major

military role played by the seven-shooter occurred in the summer of 1873, when it accompanied a large number of cavalrymen under General David S. Stanley on an escort mission with Northern Pacific railroad surveyors along the Yellowstone River. In 1889, while noting that other arms had long since replaced the Spencer, a former Sixth Cavalry sergeant summed up his opinion of the weapon in these words: "It had many good features, among which its strength and durability were prominent." To the Ordnance officers of the early 1870s, the Spencer's drawback was its short rimfire cartridge; although the gun could have been converted to handle centerfire ammunition, it

An Indian scout aims his Spencer carbine from behind a barricade of lava rock. The lava beds formed a natural fortress which the Modocs used to good advantage. (This view was the genesis of the effort resulting in this and the authors' preceding volume on frontier guns.) (Courtesy National Archives)

could not be altered to take cartridges as long as the .50-70.[49]

Thus the Spencer repeater was not among the guns presented to the Ordnance board which convened in New York in September of 1872. Out of the over eighty domestic arms submitted for trials, in fact, most were single-shot weapons. Some of these were merely slight variations of others, a few were wooden models, and a few more were merely examined by the board and not test-fired, but the number of arms actually subjected to trial was impressive enough. Among the better-known were guns by Springfield, Remington, Peabody, Sharps, Whitney, Winchester, Berdan, Ward-Burton, and a newly designed single-shot rifle by Spencer; lesser-known arms included those by Evans, Broughton, Lee, Dexter, Elliot, Milbank, Freeman, Gardner, and Joslyn-Tomes.[50]

Conducting its business concurrently with the small-arms board was a caliber board, appointed to determine the best caliber for rifles and carbines. This board limited its options to cartridges of .40, .42, .45, and .50 caliber, testing them with various powder charges at ranges up to a thousand yards. It finally decided that for all purposes the optimum caliber was .45, the same caliber, ironically enough, chosen by the 1866 Ordnance board.[51]

Cavalrymen with Sharps carbines stand in formation with lava beds in the background during the Modoc War. (Courtesy National Archives)

One of the most important facts to emerge during the small-arms trials concerned not the guns themselves but the copper-cased service cartridge: its tendency to bulge and stick in a heated chamber could make an otherwise-serviceable arm look bad. For example, after testing the Broughton No. 45, a modified trapdoor design, the board noticed that:

> [it] Worked easily, except when firing service cartridges . . . The trouble found in this gun arose from the head of the cartridge swelling back against the breech and thus keeping it tightly pressed against the firing-bolt, by which it is locked in place. . . . When service-cartridges were used, the breech-block generally required a sharp blow with a stick to start it. With brass shells it worked freely.

After tests of another gun, the Updegraff rolling-block rifle, the board noted that "toward the last of the trial [with service cartridges] the piece opened very hard, a fact which was not observed when the Berdan brass shells were afterward tried."[52]

The guns that made it through the regular tests,

severe enough even without the problems caused by the copper cartridge, then underwent "supplementary tests," which included the firing of a special cartridge loaded with 120 grains of powder and a 1200 grain bullet. After the supplementary tests only nine American and two foreign guns still worked, with some functioning more efficiently than others: two Springfields, two Remingtons, a Peabody, an Elliot, a Broughton, a Freeman, a Ward-Burton repeater, the British Martini-Henry, and the Austrian Werndl. Taking the results of the 1871–73 field trials into consideration, a majority of the board members voted to select the Springfield No. 99, a Model 1870 action fitted with a .45 caliber barrel. However, the other arms had done too well to be overlooked completely, especially the Ward-Burton bolt-action repeater and the Elliot, a modified Peabody design. In the board's opinion:

> the Elliot system has exhibited remarkable facility of manipulation in requiring but one hand to work it, [which renders] it especially adapted to the

mounted service . . . the experiments before the board with the magazine-carbine, made upon the Ward-Burton system at the Springfield Armory and using the Metcalfe cartridge, have so impressed the Board with the merits of this gun that they consider it as more nearly fulfilling the conditions [of a suitable repeater] than any other magazine-gun tried by them or of which they have any knowledge. . . .

But in recommending field trials of these two guns the board ran afoul of an unusual law promulgated in June of 1872, which stated expressly that the gun formally adopted—in this case the trapdoor Springfield—"shall be the only one to be used by the Ordnance Department in the manufacture of muskets and carbines for the military service."

As good as they were, then, neither the Elliot nor the Ward-Burton reached the hands of troops for trial. An indication that the board was not completely happy with its choice of the single-shot Springfield lies in a resolution it adopted when the testing was over:

Resolved, That, in the opinion of the Board, the adoption of magazine-guns for the military service, by all nations, is only a question of time; that whenever an arm shall be devised which shall be as effective [when used as a single-shot rifle] as the best of the existing single breech-loading arms, and at the same time shall possess a safe and easily manipulated magazine, every consideration of public policy will require its adoption.[53]

THE SPRINGFIELD .45-70s OF 1873

But for the time being the Springfield No. 99 became the standard U.S. shoulder arm for both infantry and cavalry, a position it was to hold for twenty years. The official approval for its manufacture, given in July of 1873, stipulated that manufacturing preference would go to the carbine instead of the rifle, "so that the cavalry service, now armed with inferior weapons, may this fall receive a carbine of an improved pattern."[54]

Put into service as the Springfield Model 1873, the rifle had a 32⅝ in. barrel chambered for a new .45-70 cartridge, with a 405 grain bullet driven out of the muzzle at a velocity of about 1350 feet per second. The 22 in. barrel of the carbine would also chamber this round, but for mounted use the cartridge contained only 55 grains of powder, to become the .45-55, with a muzzle velocity of just over 1100 feet per second. Externally, however, both rifle and carbine cartridges were identical, and a practical joke which soon became a favorite among cavalrymen was to slip a rifle cartridge into a comrade's ammunition during practice and watch his expression as he experienced the jolt from the unexpected recoil. Production of the Benet-cup-primed carbine cartridges started at Frank-

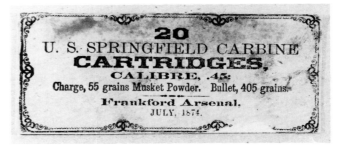

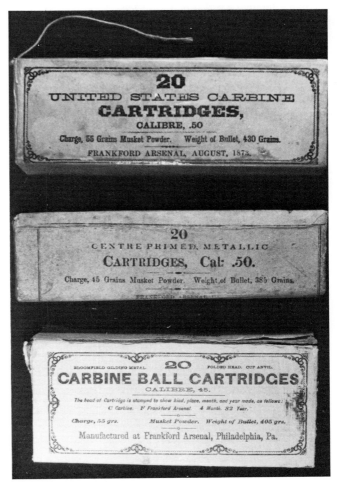

Labels from 20-round cardboard boxes of .45 and .50 carbine and .50 rifle cartridges.

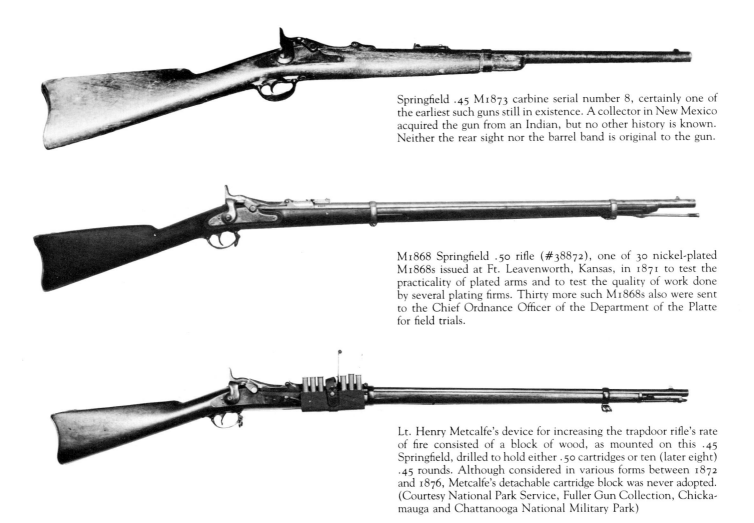

Springfield .45 M1873 carbine serial number 8, certainly one of the earliest such guns still in existence. A collector in New Mexico acquired the gun from an Indian, but no other history is known. Neither the rear sight nor the barrel band is original to the gun.

M1868 Springfield .50 rifle (#38872), one of 30 nickel-plated M1868s issued at Ft. Leavenworth, Kansas, in 1871 to test the practicality of plated arms and to test the quality of work done by several plating firms. Thirty more such M1868s also were sent to the Chief Ordnance Officer of the Department of the Platte for field trials.

Lt. Henry Metcalfe's device for increasing the trapdoor rifle's rate of fire consisted of a block of wood, as mounted on this .45 Springfield, drilled to hold either .50 cartridges or ten (later eight) .45 rounds. Although considered in various forms between 1872 and 1876, Metcalfe's detachable cartridge block was never adopted. (Courtesy National Park Service, Fuller Gun Collection, Chickamauga and Chattanooga National Military Park)

ford Arsenal in September of 1873; four months later Frankford began the manufacture of .45-70 rifle ammunition.[55]

Although the M1873 incorporated minor changes in the contours of various parts to facilitate manufacture, its big external difference from earlier service rifles was its blued finish. With one notable exception, all previous trapdoors had been finished in "National Armory bright." The exception was a special lot of Model 1868s, which had been nickel plated by three different firms for field trials. In 1871 30 of these guns had gone to Omaha for distribution to troops in the Department of the Platte; another 30 had gone to Leavenworth for issue in the Department of the Mis-

souri. The field trials were evidently unsuccessful, resulting in the blued finish for the Model 1873.[56]

Because the 1873 Springfield was so similar to the model of 1870, Springfield Armory did not require much time to tool up for its manufacture. As a result just over 10,000 of the new carbines and 18,000 new rifles were completed between late 1873 and mid-1874. Initial issues of the carbine took place between January and March of 1874, with the bulk of them going to troopers of the Tenth Cavalry, then stationed in Texas. The immediate delivery of the carbines to Texas may have been due to a letter sent to the Ordnance Department in December of 1873 by the commandant of San Antonio Arsenal. He asked whether San An-

Demonstrating the use of the Metcalfe loading block (c. 1876).
(Courtesy West Point Museum)

tonio could expect the new guns within thirty days, since the troops would need them for spring operations against the Indians. (If the Springfields were to be unavailable, he requested 200 .50-70 Sharps carbines in their stead.) Rifles were first issued in the spring of 1874, when large numbers went to the first five regiments of infantry, all of which except the Second were on duty in the West. Within a year the infantrymen also received new broad-bladed "trowel bayonets," designed to serve as both weapon and entrenching tool.[57]

The prompt issue of 1873 Springfields did not extend to all units on the frontier, however, and as usual the older guns remained in service in the more remote locales for many months after the appearance of the

.45-70. In fact, late in 1873 Springfield Armory made up 500 M1870 .50-70 rifles fitted with "Metcalfe's detachable cartridge-holder." Lt. Henry Metcalfe's "cartridge-holder" was probably the best-known attempt to increase the Springfield's rate of fire without altering its mechanism. It comprised a rectangular wood block with eight or ten vertical holes which held a like number of .50 or .45 caliber cartridges. When snapped into special fittings on the rifle stock just in front of the lockplate, Metcalfe's block gave the soldier ready access to his cartridges, and Ordnance tests showed that a Springfield equipped with the device would fire ten shots in twenty-five seconds. The idea seemed good enough for general issue, and in February of 1874

Springfield M1873 .45 carbine (#17025) found at the Little Big-horn battlefield following Custer's defeat there. (Courtesy Smithsonian Institution)

George A. Custer's .50-70 sporting rifle, a modified M1866 Springfield. Armory alterations included shortening the forestock, adding a white metal forearm tip, reducing the buttstock width, and adding set triggers, a fancy trigger guard, and a sling swivel to the buttstock. This specimen is similar to other sporting rifles prepared at Springfield prior to the production of the .45 Officer's Model rifles. No records are known to exist regarding Custer's order for such a rifle, but the weapon can be traced back to the Custer family. There is little doubt that it is the same weapon that appears in the accompanying photo of Custer and Grand Duke Alexis. (Photo by and courtesy of Dr. Vance Haynes)

a quantity of Metcalfe-equipped .50 caliber M1870s went to selected companies of the Tenth, Eleventh, Twenty-fourth, and Twenty-fifth Infantry regiments, all stationed in Texas, for field trials.[58]

Besides the M1870s, considerable numbers of M1868s continued in service in the West. This was especially true for the volunteers, who besides their M1868s still relied in part on the Model 1866. In 1870 the Ordnance Department had issued 60 M1866s to Oregon, following this three years later with an issue of 500 M1866s to Washington Territory. In 1872, two years after supplying 100 M1868s to Wyoming Territory, Ordnance issued 80 M1868s to Colorado, 100 to Nebraska, 596 to Nevada, and fully 1000 to Montana. Texas, in contrast, received 499 Remington .50 caliber "locking" rifles in 1874. With the coming of 1875, 1500 new .45-70s were on their way to California, with lesser numbers going to Texas, Nevada, and Kansas.

By mid-1875 all regular army units had at least a few 1873 Springfields on hand—even the men of the two artillery companies stationed in far-off Alaska, who had earlier patrolled that region with M1868s and a few M1870s. The M1868, carried primarily by the Third, Tenth, and Fifteenth Infantry stationed in the Southwest, remained in evidence throughout 1875, and as late as March of 1876 a company of the Fifteenth Infantry in New Mexico still had some M1868s

in service alongside its .45-70s. One M1868, displayed at Philadelphia's Centennial Exposition in 1876, was probably unique: it had been "struck by lightning when in the hands of a sentinel at Fort Shaw, Montana. Point of bayonet, rear of guard-plate, and lock-plate melted and butt-stock split. Sentinel and two prisoners knocked down without injury."[59]

Older arms stayed on duty with the cavalry as well as with the infantry. Although the Ordnance Department sent out only about 3700 M1873 carbines between mid-1874 and mid-1875 (compared to more than 12,000 rifles), distribution of the cavalry arms was apparently more efficient; by September of 1874 all cavalry regiments except the Fifth and the Eighth had received their first issues of the .45 caliber carbine. George Custer made sure his Seventh Cavalry got the new guns by delaying the departure of his 1874 reconnaissance expedition into the Black Hills until the arms reached him. Other mounted units were less fortunate. Through mid-1874 the Fifth Cavalry, stationed in Arizona, had relied principally on Sharps, Ward-Burton, and M1870 Springfield carbines; it was still heavily equipped with the Sharps by the end of that year. Moreover, by June of 1875 the Ordnance Department had replaced only half the unit's Sharps with 1873 Springfields. The Fifth was not the only regiment to use obsolescent arms in mid-1875: at that time the First and Third Cavalry still had fair numbers

Lt. Col. George A. Custer (left) with his .50 Springfield rifle. The revolver at Grand Duke Alexis of Russia's waist may be the Smith & Wesson .44 No. 3 presented to him at the S&W factory in December 1871 during his visit there to review production of revolvers for the Russian government. Factory records place the cost of the presentation No. 3 at $400, including $100 for carved pearl grips and $100 for a case. Each man holds a buffalo tail as a trophy. (Courtesy Custer Battlefield Historical and Museum Assn., Inc.)

of .50 caliber Springfields to supplement their new .45s.[60]

Besides concentrating on production of the standard 1873 rifles and carbines, the national armory put together 10 "Springfield rifles, officers'," early in 1875. These arms resulted from the occasional requests of officers for sporting-style rifles, made up on the trap-door Springfield action, which they could purchase for their own use. Prior to 1875 Springfield had assembled fewer than 20 officers' rifles, in part because the cost was so high. General Grenville M. Dodge, builder of the Union Pacific Railroad, ordered a Springfield M1868 sporter which when delivered early in 1870 cost him $70.00 (including a screwdriver), $56.50 more than the cost of a standard M1868 infantry rifle. An equally famous owner of a Springfield

William H. Jackson, famed western photographer, poses for his photo in 1872. His rifle is a .50-70 Springfield, typical of those half-stocked rifles fabricated at that armory on special order. (U.S. Geological Survey photo, courtesy National Archives)

Springfield M1875 Type II .45 Officer's Model. (Courtesy National Park Service, Fuller Gun Collection, Chickamauga and Chattanooga National Military Park)

An Apache scout holds the bridle of Lt. Britton Davis's white riding mule. Davis apparently preferred the comfort of a civilian saddle over the regulation McClellan. Suspended from the pommel is a holstered Colt Single Action revolver and what appears to be an Officer's Model .45 Springfield, recognizable by the fold-ing front sight and what seems to be a wiping rod beneath the barrel. The cartridge belt holds both rifle and revolver cartridges. Davis, like Gen. George Crook and others, found a mule to be a better mount than a horse during the rugged Apache campaigns. (Courtesy National Archives)

sporter was George Armstrong Custer: in a photograph taken during the Russian grand duke Alexis's American tour in 1872, Custer is holding a M1866 sporter with a half stock and double set triggers. Writing to his wife Elizabeth from the field in June of 1873, he praised the peformance of his "new Springfield rifle," presumably the same weapon, and mentioned that it had dropped an antelope at 280 yards:

Poor Fred and Tom [Custer]! They have accompanied me frequently . . . and yet neither of them has been able thus far to kill a single antelope. I tease them a great deal, for they use the Winchester rifle. It is remarkably accurate up to one hundred yards, and not beyond that distance. You know when Tom takes a notion to get anything of mine how very persistent he is. Well, his latest dodge is to obtain possession of my Springfield rifle, which I allow my orderly, Tuttle, to carry. Night before last he carried it off to his tent without saying anything about it; but Tuttle slipped down while Tom was at breakfast and recaptured the rifle! Tuttle killed two antelope at one shot with my Springfield at pretty long range.

Later that summer Tuttle was killed in a skirmish in Montana, apparently while using Custer's sporter. In Custer's words:

I had mounted my command and formed it in line close under the bluffs facing from the river, where we waited the attack of the Indians in our front. The Sharp-shooting across the river still continued, the Indians having collected some of their best shots—apparently armed with long-range rifles—and were attempting to drive our men back from the water's edge. It was at this time that my standing orderly, Private Tuttle, of "E" troop, 7th Cavalry, one of the best marksmen in my command, took a sporting Springfield rifle and posted himself, with two other men, behind cover on the river bank, and began picking off the Indians as they exposed themselves on the opposite bank. He had obtained the range of the enemy's position early in the morning, and was able to place his shots wherever desired. It was while so engaged that he observed an Indian in full view near the river. Calling the attention of his comrade to the fact, he asked him "to watch him drop that Indian," a feat which he succeeded in performing. Several other Indians rushed to the assistance of their fallen comrade, while Private Tuttle, by a skilful and rapid use of his breech-loading Springfield, succeeded in killing two other warriors. The Indins [sic], enraged no doubt at this rough handling, directed their aim at Private Tuttle, who fell pierced through the head by a rifle-bullet. He was one of the most useful and daring soldiers who ever served under my command.[61]

Custer acquired another sporting rifle in 1873, this one a .50 caliber Remington rolling-block. The gun accompanied him on the Yellowstone Expedition of 1873, as he mentioned in a letter to the Remington firm in October of that year:

With the expedition were professional hunters, employed by the Government to obtain game for the troops. Many of the officers and men also were excellent shots, and participated extensively in hunting along the line of march. I was the only person who used one of your Rifles, while, as may properly be stated, there were pitted against it breech-loading Rifles of almost every description, including many of the Springfield breech-loaders altered to Sporting Rifles. With your Rifle I killed far more game than any other single party, professional or amateur, while the shots made with your Rifle were at longer range and more difficult shots than were those made by any other Rifles in the command.[62]

Despite Custer's fondness for the Remington (which he carried with him to the Little Bighorn three years

later), the Springfield sporting rifle was, as his letter suggested, becoming fairly popular among officers stationed on the frontier.

Of the ten officers' rifles completed early in 1875, 6 went to Camp Supply, Indian Territory, as the result of an order from Lt. Gardener of the Nineteenth Infantry. The rifles cost Gardener and his five fellow officers $41.27 each. (Slightly less expensive was the Winchester Model 1866 repeating carbine purchased at about the same time by Lt. William B. Wetmore of the Sixth Cavalry.)[63]

Annoyed by the intermittent requests from officers for custom-made rifles, Brigadier General Stephen Vincent Benet, the new chief of ordnance, ordered Springfield Armory in May of 1875 to make "a rifle suitable for [sporting] purposes which will hereafter serve as a model from which to manufacture and sell to officers. A model being adopted, no sporting arms differing from it will be made at the Armory." The Model 1875 officers' rifle was characterized by a 26 in. round barrel, half stock, wood cleaning rod under the barrel, and scroll engraving on the action. Besides an open rear sight on the barrel, there was an adjustable peep sight mounted on the stock wrist, plus the additional refinement of a single set trigger. An improved version of the officers' rifle, introduced in April of 1877, had a detachable wood pistol grip and "an additional spring in setting [the] trigger."[64]

The rifle's initial price of $36, reduced to $27 in August of 1879, probably helped limit its sale; in any event the production of the standard infantry rifle and cavalry carbine was far more important. By the close of 1875 every unit on the frontier was equipped exclusively, or very nearly so, with the new .45-70s. A cavalryman who fought under General George Crook against the Sioux and Cheyenne at Rosebud Creek in June of 1876 recalled that:

The Springfield 1873 Model was our rifle equipment. . . . It would shoot and kick hard, carrying up to 500 yards very well. The infantry had the same kind of gun, except theirs had a longer barrel. Our form of the rifle was known as the "carbine," theirs was known as the "Long Tom." Their gun would carry farther as its cartridge held 70 grains of powder.[65]

The 1873 Springfield figured even more prominently in another engagement later that same month—the most famous soldier-Indian encounter of the postwar West, the Battle of the Little Bighorn. After George Custer's Seventh Cavalry went down to a disastrous defeat, a wave of criticism swept over the Springfield, much of it thoroughly justified.

Most of the criticism resulted from the difficulty of extracting the copper cartridge, a problem already well known to Ordnance officers. Field manuals issued with every trapdoor Springfield from the Model 1866 through the Model 1873, in fact, had warned of this problem. The manual for the M1866 noted that "should the extractor hook cut through the rim of the shell, and thereby fail to withdraw it, draw the ramrod and drive it out." The 1873 manual was even more detailed, warning that "should the head of a cartridge come off in the act of firing," the trooper was to pull the bullet from an unfired cartridge, force it into the muzzle, and drive it down the bore with the cleaning rod until it struck the case mouth and pushed the case from the chamber. Not addressed in these instructions was the fact that the carbine did not have a cleaning rod.[66]

Besides printing warnings in the manuals concerning the extraction problem, the Ordnance Department tried dealing with it in other ways. As early as 1873 Springfield Armory had started manufacturing cartridge cases with "solid heads," turning out more than 21,000 by mid-1875. Although a solid-head cartridge case was far stronger than the folded-head type, Ordnance officers regarded it chiefly as an experiment, and issues to troops in the field, if any, were limited. Another solution to the extraction problem was the design of a "headless shell extractor," the manufacture of which started early in 1876. This extractor comprised a cylindrical metal body with three spring-tempered steel "fingers" at the front; if the head of a cartridge case tore off during extraction, the trooper could either push the extractor down the bore from the muzzle, or open the breechblock and slip it through the case from the rear, permitting him to knock the case loose. Unfortunately the headless shell extractor could not prevent a ruptured case head; it could only deal with the problem after it had occurred. It was an adequate measure only as long as combat casualties were few.[67]

But the Custer disaster, which was first-page news even in the New York papers, brought the shortcomings of the trapdoor Springfield and its copper cartridge into sharp focus. Less than a month after the battle Major Marcus Reno wrote to the chief of ordnance, stating that six of his carbines had malfunctioned due to:

> failure of the breech block to close, [thus] leaving a space between the head of the cartridge and the end of the block, and when the piece was discharged and the block thrown open, the head of the cartridge was pulled off, and the [rest of it] remained in the chamber, whence with the means at hand it was impossible to extract it. . . . In the manufacture of the gun the breech block is in many instances so made that it does not fit snug up to the head of the cartridge after the cartridge is sent home, and it has always been a question in my mind whether

the manner in which it revolves into its place does not render a close contact almost impossible to be made; another [problem] is, that the dust, always an element to be considered on the battle-field, prevents the proper closing of the breech block, and the same result is produced. . . . I also observed another bad fault of the system, although it did not render the guns unserviceable, viz., the weight of the breech block is such that the hinge on which it revolves is very soon loosened, giving to the block a lateral motion that prevents its closing. I can also state that the blowing up of the breech block was a contingency that was patent to members of the Board which adopted the system, and induced strong opposition to it on the part of a minority. . . . An Indian scout, who was with that portion of the regiment which Custer took into battle, in relating what he saw in that part of the battle, says that from his hiding place he could see the men sitting down under fire, and working at their guns—a story that finds confirmation in the fact that officers, who afterwards examined the battle-fields as they were burying the dead, found knives with broken blades lying near the dead bodies. . . .[68]

Although other officers called Reno's conduct during the battle into question, he had plenty of supporters for his opinion of the Springfield carbine. Trooper William C. Slaper, who fought with Reno's companies on the bluffs overlooking the river, described the actions of Captain French during the engagement: "He would extract shells from guns in which cartridges would stick, and pass them loaded, then fix another. . . ." An *Army and Navy Journal* correspondent wrote that:

> In the ravines, during Colonel Mills' late fight with Crazy Horse's band, twenty-one persons were completely concealed, and four more were dragged from them dead. . . . One of [the] squaws showed a fearful gunshot wound through both thighs, and probably received in the Custer massacre. With the carbines was a loaded Henry rifle, and only one other cartridge was found near. In each carbine was discovered an exploded shell, which the piece had failed to eject. With this gun our cavalry are armed, and the sooner the Government makes a change the better for its frontier soldiers, whose lives are at the mercy of a fickle steel [ejector] spring.

Still another correspondent, who signed himself "Fort M——," penned this dramatic account of the Springfield's deficiencies, which he entitled "Cavalry Board":

> Two cavalry soldiers are ordered to carry a despatch from one command to another in Montana. Half

the distance having been made, they are discovered and pursued by twenty or more hostile Sioux. The pursuit is kept up for miles. . . . As the Indians still gain upon them, and as their horses show signs of exhaustion, they dismount and prepare to fight for their lives. Lying down in a buffalo wallow this board now tests the carbine. They have no resources of skilled workmen and tools to aid them, as some of the other boards had. They are alone on the plains. Their ammunition is not packed in cotton, fresh from the factory, but has been carried for months. It has been worn for days and weeks through dust and rain. The firing begins. At the fifth shot from Tom's carbine his ejector spring pulls the head of the cartridge off and leaves the empty shell in the barrel, he turns and exclaims: "For God's sake, Bill, hand me your knife quick, my carbine has gone up." Cold drops of perspiration roll down his forehead as he realizes his utter helplessness and thinks how often the carbine has proved worthless in times of great exigency. . . . He thinks of this as he cuts and cuts, trying to get the shell out. Seconds seems hours. At last he succeeds. But his comrade is already badly wounded, while his gun has also been disabled. The Indians come closer to the wallow as the fire slackens. The wounded man cuts feebly away with his knife at the headless shell in his carbine, but finally succeeds in getting it out. He fires as rapidly as possible with his failing strength, but he desparingly sees that his ejector spring has become bent and disabled by his knife striking it while trying to cut out the headless shell. Meanwhile, his comrade's carbine has again failed him. A few revolver shots are given, and the board adjourns, never more to meet until the final roll call shall sound.[69]

Other letters of a similar nature published in the *Journal* forced a reaction from the Ordnance Department. In mid-August of 1876 Captain J. W. Reilly, Ordnance officer with the Military Division of the Missouri, wrote to the chief of ordnance:

As telegraphed to you to-day, Colonel Mackenzie requested Winchester rifles for the Fourth Cavalry. . . . I quote this as an illustration of the dissatisfaction with the carbine; and while it is impossible to gratify all the caprices of officers, yet the very general complaints at the inefficiency of the carbine must be based on some real grounds. . . .

Reilly, however, missed the point, adding that the carbine's defects were "inaccuracy and short range." Regarding the all-important extraction problem, he noted only that the carbine "should also be provided with a ramrod, to remove cartridge shells which the extractor fails to eject."[70]

Reilly's letter appeared in the *Journal* accompanied by a summary of firing tests conducted at Springfield Armory, which pitted the cavalry carbine against the 1873 Winchester. Expressed in terms of "mean deviation," the results of the accuracy tests, in which the carbine was fired with both its original 55 grain cartridge and the 70 grain rifle cartridge, were:

	100 yds.	300 yds.	500 yds.
Springfield Carbine			
(with rifle cartridges):	3.17″	8.36″	14.03″
(with carbine cartridges):	2.48″	7.97″	19.05″
Winchester Rifle:	2.27″	12.27″	21.56″

At a range of 900 yards the Winchester scattered its shots too widely to be detected. In the penetration tests, fired into white pine at a range of 100 yards, bullets from the carbine plunged 10 in. into the wood, twice as deeply as those from the Winchester, and more deeply than bullets from .50 caliber Spencer and Sharps carbines fired for comparison.[71]

Again, however, the real issue was reliability, not power or accuracy, and the Ordnance Department tests brought forth even more criticism. As "an officer of General Terry's command" phrased it:

Poor Mackenzie! he has requested to be furnished with a magazine carbine, for active field service this winter, to be used at *close quarters*. However, the Chief of Ordnance informs him that the Springfield carbine has a greater range, and therefore is the best weapon. Who knows best what the cavalry soldier wants, the officer at his desk in Washington or the soldier in the field? Is it not time for a reform, or must we still *advance backwards?*

In support of this opinion, another writer suggested that "the Ordnance Department be compelled to go out into the field and use the weapons they believe in so implicitly."[72]

In spite of the scathing criticism, the trapdoor Springfield did have its defenders. Captain Guy V. Henry, who fought with Crook's force on Rosebud Creek, commented that: "I see some papers about the carbines [which] failed to 'eject' cartridges at Rosebud—I had no such trouble—other companies may have had." General John Gibbon thought the rifle was "first-rate . . . and probably the best that was ever placed in the hands of troops." Writing in January of 1877, a cavalry officer stated that with the original .45-55 cartridge the accuracy of the carbine was "perfect at 500 yards . . . with the rifle, or 70 grain cartridge, the carbine is perfectly accurate at 800 yards." He noted further that his company had used the weapon constantly since receiving it in late September of 1874,

In a training exercise, men of the Sixth Cavalry accustom their mounts to gunfire from their .45 Springfield "trapdoor" carbines at Ft. Bayard, New Mexico Territory. (Courtesy National Archives)

"and as for mud, water, sand, and hard knocks, I know of no arm that will stand anything like as much as the Springfield carbine will, and that can be as easily cleaned as it can."[73]

Other officers expressed their approval of the arm by spending thirty-six of their hard-earned dollars for a new officers' rifle. Between May of 1876 and October of 1878 the Ordnance Department sold at least 10 such guns to officers in the Department of Texas, among whom were Col. Benjamin H. Grierson, commander of the Tenth Cavalry, and Lt. John L. Bullis of the Twenty-fourth Infantry, who commanded a detachment of Seminole-Negro scouts. Those officers who wanted to save money bought the standard cavalry carbine instead of the officers' model: as early as February of 1874, in fact, the commandant of San Antonio Arsenal had requested 50 carbines for sale to officers in his department. Individual buyers of carbines in 1876 included Lt. Bullis, Captain Charles Bentzoni of the Twenty-fifth Infantry, and Lt. William Paulding of the Tenth Infantry. Evidently these guns were no different from the standard-issue model, but

in February of 1879 Lt. R. E. Safford of the Tenth Cavalry paid $15.50 for a special-order carbine, with a silver front sight and without the sling bar. Captain J. M. Clons of the Twenty-fourth Infantry wanted neither a carbine nor an officers' rifle, buying instead a standard infantry rifle.[74]

Even the Springfield's advocates, however, were generally aware of its shortcomings. Aside from the extraction problem, there were complaints about the carbine's rear sight and lack of a ramrod. Thus in 1877 a modified carbine appeared, incorporating a redesigned rear sight and a recess in the buttstock which housed a three-piece ramrod and the headless shell extractor. Instead of shipping entirely new guns to frontier units, the Ordnance Department sometimes sent out only the new components, which the company armorer installed on existing arms. In mid-1878, for example, San Antonio Arsenal sent a quantity of M1877 carbine stocks to Captain John See of the Fourth Cavalry, then stationed at Fort Clark, to replace the stocks on carbines already in the hands of his men.[75]

Chasing renegade Indians near Willcox, Arizona Territory, in the fall of 1885. The trackers carry Springfield M1884 carbines with the Buffington adjustable rear sight. (Courtesy Arizona Historical Society)

To facilitate extraction in the Springfield, the Ordnance Department could have modified the arm itself, by the addition of dual extractors; this was never done. Besides, the problem that really needed correction was the folded-head copper cartridge. The 1877 Ordnance report alluded to this by quoting the findings of a U.S. Ordnance commission which examined the small arms and ammunition of all the major European powers. The commission's report stated in part that:

The general mode of priming the metallic cartridge in Europe is that known as "outside-center fire," which permits the empty shells to be reprimed and reloaded several times. . . . The material generally employed for cartridge-shells is brass; this material possesses more elasticity than copper; it therefore is generally preferred for reloading shells, as they retain their form and can be more easily inserted into the chamber of the gun when reloaded. The heads of all cartridge-shells firing large charges of powder are either made solid, or with a folded flange

which is afterward re-enforced with a thin lining of metal or a wad of paper. . . .

In spite of this report, no changes were made in the .45 Springfield cartridge case until 1882.[76]

Although improvements in the cartridge were slow in coming, the Ordnance Department constantly experimented with the rifle and carbine in attempts to upgrade them. The Springfield models of 1879, for example, were the culmination of a series of minor changes begun early in 1878, which included a wider receiver with all inside corners rounded, the stiffening of the breechblock by the filling in of the high arch in its underside, and the addition of a new "buckhorn" rear sight. The rifle also acquired two features already used in the carbine—a recess in the buttstock and a three-notch tumbler. To help the rifle deliver all its potential accuracy, Ordnance officers kept experimenting with the rear sight; between January of 1877 and July of 1880, for instance, it underwent no fewer than six separate changes.[77]

Even with simple sights, however, the Springfield

Their .45 M1873 Springfield rifles nearby, some of Brig. Gen. George Crook's men butcher one of the horses slaughtered for food during the 1876 campaign against the Sioux. The months of campaigning following the Indian victories over Crook and Custer in June of that year were brutal ones for animals and men. (Courtesy W. H. Over Museum, University of South Dakota)

was an accurate weapon. As Capt. O. E. Michaelis of the Department of Dakota remarked:

I have seen Capt. D. W. Benham, of the Seventh Infantry, now on the Equipment Board in Washington, hit a tree-stump three times in five shots, standing and firing from the shoulder without muzzle rest, at a distance of 1,000 yards, with [a] caliber .45 Springfield rifle taken at haphazard from his company rack. On the Yellowstone in 1876, General Terry, at a range of 400 yards, with a similar arm outshot both the Sharp's Creedmoor and Winchester guns.

Any inaccuracy, then, was due not so much to the rifle as it was to the soldier behind it. A trooper who served with the Eighteenth Infantry in 1866 recalled that his company had engaged in no target practice at all during that year because of shortages of ammunition. A year later a Seventh Cavalry lieutenant was given temporary command of two new Gatling guns escorting Indian peace commissioners to a meeting at Medicine Lodge, Kansas; after mentioning his intention to give his gun crews some practice, he was quickly informed that he would have to pay for any practice ammunition out of his own pocket![78]

Yuma Indian scouts attached to M Troop of the Tenth Cavalry during a campaign against the Apaches. The arms are .45-70 Springfield rifles and a Richards conversion of the Colt M1860 .44 revolver. (Courtesy Smithsonian Institution)

By the late 1860s there was enough of a demand for marksmanship training to bring about a general order, issued in May of 1869, calling for the establishment of a general system of rifle practice—with the allocation of a mere 10 ball cartridges per man per month for practice. In 1874 the secretary of war reaffirmed the issuance to each soldier of only 120 rounds annually for practice, due to the cost involved. An officer with lengthy frontier experience subsequently wrote that:

Compared with the white hunter of the plains, the Indian is a wretched shot. He is about equal to the

United States soldier, being deficient for the same reason—lack of practice. The Government and the Indian are each too poor to afford to waste more than ten cartridges a month on drill, and no man ever became an expert marksman on that allowance. . . .

A few years later the chief of ordnance would emphatically concur with this opinion:

In an Indian fight the best marksman is the strongest man. Victory is not for the man of muscle, but the result of the quick eye and cool nerve of the fine shot. If our soldiers can pick off an Indian at one thousand yards, or even at five hundred yards, with unerring certainty, the Indian's occupation is gone. But we can make marksman of our soldiers only by continued practice, and by a constant expenditure of ammunition. This costs money, but our Army is very small, and lack of numbers must be compensated [for] by the greatest efficiency possible.[79]

A goodly number of officers and men were firm believers in this logic. While preparing for the Black Hills Expedition of 1874, George Custer wired General Terry that his men were badly in need of firing practice. The Seventh Cavalry then discontinued morning drill and, using all the cartridges it could find, began intensive training on the firing range. General Gibbon, bemoaning the fact that such training did not always extend to other units, thus described an engagement with the Nez Percé Indians: "At almost every shot of their rifles one of our men fell, and this, too, when our men were at a distance from the enemy, such as rendered it utterly impossible for them to compete with the Indians in their accuracy of fire."[80]

By the late 1870s, however, this situation was beginning to change. When young Lt. Stephen Mills arrived at Benecia Barracks, California, in December of 1877, he found that:

Target practice was practically unknown. I think the allowance of ammunition was twenty rounds a year . . . Guy Howard and I, with the enthusiasm of extreme youth, rigged up a hundred-yard range on the east side of [Angel] Island, and gave the recruits a smattering of an idea of how to handle the rifle. As I remember, our efforts were regarded with an amused toleration by the seniors of the garrison.

In March of 1878 the Department of the Pacific issued the following circular:

The commanding officer of Benecia Arsenal reports that there are muzzle-loading S. B. muskets, cal. 58, and cartridges for them, and also Colt's and

Indian scouts and Lt. McDonald, armed with .45 Springfields, pose in a ravine during a campaign against the Apaches in New Mexico Territory in the 1880s. The civilian scout carries a lever action repeating rifle and the Indians display various articles of army clothing and gear including an enlisted man's dress helmet. After 1866, most Indian scouts were formally enlisted directly into the army and until 1891 served almost exclusively in a scouting role. But beginning in 1891, Troop L of each frontier cavalry regiment and Company I of each frontier infantry regiment were composed of Indian recruits. Exceptions were the Ninth and Tenth Cavalry and the Twenty-fourth and Twenty-fifth Infantry regiments, these being black units. (Courtesy Smithsonian Institution)

Remington pistols, breech loaders, for paper cartridges, at the Arsenal . . . post commanders will immediately make requisition for ten muzzle loading rifles for each artillery and infantry company, and for twenty muzzle loading rifles and twenty Colt's or Remington pistols for paper cartridges for each cavalry company at their posts (if they are not already on hand . . .) and ammunition therefor to the extent of 400 rounds per man. So soon as possible, target practice with these arms, commencing with the worst marksman in each company, will proceed daily, taking precedence over all other duty.[81]

In line with the increased emphasis on marksmanship training, three Thirteenth Infantry teams met at Baton Rouge Barracks in April of 1878 for a shooting match with the .45-70 service rifle. One Private Thomas Marriott walked off with top individual honors and a ten-dollar meerschaum pipe. A year later the War Department detailed Col. T. T. S. Laidley to work out a complete program of rifle training. Suggestions in his book on the subject, *Laidley's Rifle Firing*, were incorporated in a new Springfield "Long Range" rifle, designed to help army marksmen compete in national matches on an equal footing with other shooters, who often used finely accurate Sharps, Remington, or Peabody rifles. Except for its detachable pistol grip and special sights, some of which were inspired by Laidley, the long-range rifle was externally almost identical to the service rifle, but its bore had six grooves instead

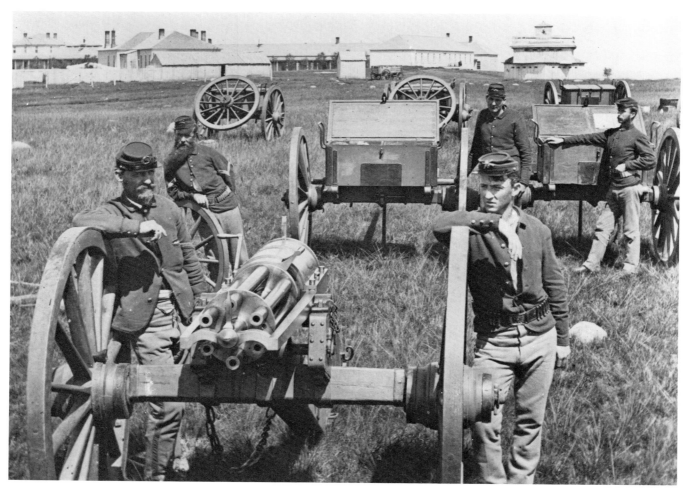

Men of the Twentieth Infantry and a Gatling gun at Ft. McKean, Dakota Territory in 1877. These hand-cranked "machine guns" were used most frequently by the army in the West for the defense of fixed positions such as frontier posts. In the spring of 1876, 34 army posts within the Division of the Missouri, bordered roughly by the Mississippi River, the Rockies, Canada, and Mexico, tallied

54 Gatling guns in a listing of artillery on hand. By caliber, these included one .45, thirty-four .50, and nineteen 1.00-inch guns. (As seen in this view, frontier forts were seldom guarded by perimeter walls despite common television portrayals.) (Courtesy Custer Battlefield Historical and Museum Assn., Inc.)

of three, with the slightly faster twist of one turn in $19^3/8$ in. Between July of 1879 and January of 1880 Springfield made at least 30 of these rifles, assembling just over 150 more by mid-1881.[82]

With the rifle came a special cartridge, the .45-80-500, which in large part was the result of extensive firing tests begun by the Ordnance Department in 1877. Initially Ordnance officers tried packing this load into the service case, but with 80 grains of powder there was barely enough room left to seat the bullet, a situation which brought about a new $2^4/10$ in. case, made especially for the long-range rifle. The cartridge case for the standard-issue rifle and carbine remained at its original $2^1/10$ in., but between mid-1880 and

mid-1881 Frankford Arsenal began replacing the 405 grain bullet with the ballistically better 500 grain size, loading the newer bullet in all cartridges intended for the service arms. Then, in July of 1882, Frankford scrapped the weak inside-primed folded-head case and started manufacturing a solid-head outside-primed type. The external primer allowed the case to be reloaded, a job which often fell to the troops themselves. (In some units the task of reloading was rotated as regular duty among the men; in others it became a form of off-hours, extraduty punishment.) The solid-head cases did help solve the extraction problem: A. O. Neidner, who served with the Sixth Cavalry during the 1880s, recalled that he seldom saw a malfunction among the

Cavalry carbine practice with .45 Springfield trapdoor carbines (c. 1880). (Courtesy National Archives)

Certificate issued at Vancouver Barracks, Washington Territory, in 1887 to Pvt. Louis Dunsing after qualifying for the rating of marksman. He was scored at ranges of 200, 300, 500, and 600 yards. (From the U.S. Army Military History Research Collection, Carlisle Barracks, Pa.)

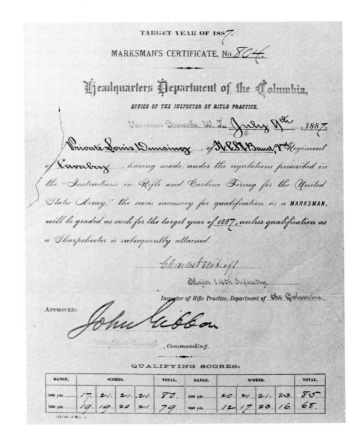

Springfields due to faulty ammunition. Frankford, however, continued using copper for the case material, not changing to brass until 1888.[83]

Some of the Springfield long-range rifles and special ammunition found their way to frontier posts, used there by army marksmen to practice for the national matches. Although a few of these rifles may have been used on the skirmish line, they were not intended for combat but for formal target shooting. Nevertheless, the real purpose of the army's marksmanship program was to develop battlefield troopers capable of hitting what they aimed at, especially at long distances. When faced with hostile Indians, experienced soldiers usually tried to get to open ground, where the long-range fire

Contestants in an army rifle match in the Department of Dakota, probably in the 1880s, using .45 Springfield service rifles. (Courtesy National Archives)

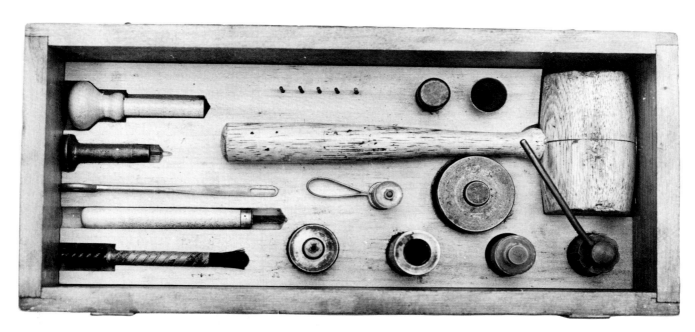

Rare Frankford Arsenal–made field reloading kit for .45 rifle cartridges. The primer setter, loading and crimping die, and primer extractor are all marked "FRANKFORD ARSENAL" while most of the other components are stamped "US" with "OEM" inspector's initials. (Photo by Mr. Hugo G. Poisson, courtesy Richard A. Bourne Co., Inc.)

Men of the Seventh Infantry demonstrate the reclining "Texas position" while firing on the 600 yard range with .45 trapdoor rifles in the 1880s. (Courtesy National Archives)

from their Springfields could keep the attackers at a distance well beyond their capability as marksmen. An officer who served in Dakota advised anyone caught in the open by Indians to "beat a careful and deliberate retreat, arms ready, and the moment the enemy comes in range, draw a bead on him." One requirement for a skilled long-range shot was the ability to estimate distance, and in combat the men who had this ability often showed their companions the appropriate sight setting. Men unable to estimate the range to the target were generally ordered to shoot low, since a ricochet might do as much damage as a direct hit. When expert marksman on frontier duty were not traveling to or from the national matches, they often acted as "sharpshooters" during Indian fights; it was their job to advance and initiate firing, thus giving the men behind them time to form a skirmish line and move their horses to the rear. A. O. Neidner of the Sixth Cavalry drew three dollars a month extra and a rifle, or "Long Tom," instead of the usual carbine while serving as a sharpshooter in Arizona. In his opinion, "a sharpshooter got paid $3 extra for being shot at." The issue

of rifles instead of carbines to mounted troops was not confined to the Sixth Cavalry. In 1879 Capt. Reilly wrote that each company in the Fifth Cavalry had "five Springfield rifles for [use by] selected marksmen, and in the Seventh Cavalry . . . ten rifles per company for the same purpose." When firing at ranges greater than 600 yards, sharpshooters occasionally used the "Texas" position, a popular one in the national matches, which involved lying on the back or side and resting the rifle inside the thigh or on the hip.[84]

NEW SINGLE-SHOT SPRINGFIELDS, REPEATING RIFLES, AND SHOTGUNS

The constant attention Ordnance officers devoted to perfecting the trapdoor Springfield as a long-range rifle did not prevent them from considering other rifles as possible replacements for it. As the 1872–73 Ordnance board had stated, "the adoption of magazine-guns for the military service, by all nations, is only a question of time." Early in 1878 no less prominent a figure than General Phil Sheridan wrote that: "I be-

"The Longhorns," a winning army rifle team in an 1887 competition at the Bellevue Rifle Camp in Dakota Territory. Participants are armed with the .45 trapdoor service rifle. (From the U.S. Army Military History Research Collection, Carlisle Barracks, Pa.)

lieve in the magazine gun. It will be the gun of the future, and all that is now wanting is some inventive genius to produce an acceptable gun which will fire from seven to ten loads in quick succession."[85]

Thus in April of 1878, only five years after the conclusion of the 1872–73 trials, another Ordnance board convened to test repeating rifles designed for the service cartridge. Among the lever-action arms which came to the board's attention were a Winchester and a Whitney-Burgess, but neither did very well in the firing tests, partly because gun designers at that time were having trouble adapting such an action to a cartridge of the .45-70's length. Two trapdoor Springfields, converted to repeaters by the insertion of tubular magazines in their buttstocks, also underwent testing, but did even more poorly than the lever actions. However, all the major armsmakers, including Winchester, entered bolt-action rifles in the trials, and as a class they acquitted themselves fairly well.[86]

Although it was a controversial system through much of the 1870s, the bolt action was basically simple and easy to make, was adaptable to cartridges of almost any length, was readily applicable to both single-shot and repeating rifles, and was inherently reliable because the major functions of opening and closing were performed manually rather than mechanically. Of the bolt actions submitted by the major manufacturers—the Winchester-Hotchkiss, the Remington-Keene, the Colt-Franklin, and the Sharps-Vetterli—the winning entry was the Hotchkiss, which had come to Winchester's attention during the Philadelphia Centennial Exposition of 1876. Based primarily on U.S. patents issued to B. B. Hotchkiss in August of 1869 and February of 1870, the original action had been modified to include a tubular magazine in the buttstock, loaded through the open action, and, of course, a magazine cutoff to allow the gun to be used as a single-shot arm. Like many other bolt actions of the time, the Hotchkiss had a three-piece bolt, comprising head, body, and cocking piece; there was only one locking surface, the rear face of the integral guide rib on the bolt body,

Hotchkiss .45 M1878 rifle. (Courtesy National Park Service, Fuller Gun Collection, Chickamauga and Chattanooga National Military Park)

which in locked position rested against a shoulder on the right side of the receiver. Cocking was somewhat unusual: raising the bolt handle to unlock the action cammed back the striker, but the striker spring was not fully compressed until the shooter pushed the bolt handle down into locked position.[87]

Manufacture of the Hotchkiss was a joint venture, with Winchester supplying the actions and Springfield Armory the balance of the arm. Between late 1878 and mid-1879 Springfield assembled just over 500 rifles and a like number of carbines; both types had five-shot magazines, but the barrel for the rifle was 28⁵/₈ in. long, that for the carbine 24 in. long. Because of the interest in long-range target rifles, at least two Hotchkiss actions were fitted with the special six-groove barrels made for the long-range Springfield.[88]

Early in 1879 the Ordnance Department issued 201 carbines and 202 rifles to the regulars for field tests, forwarding the rest of the guns to additional troops within a year. By mid-1879 some of the carbines were in use among elements of the Tenth Cavalry at Fort Davis, Texas, reaching members of the Eighth Cavalry, also stationed in Texas, shortly afterward. Near the close of 1880 the commander of the Sixteenth Infantry, on duty at Fort Concho, requested a number of Hotchkiss rifles for his men, but in January of 1881 the chief of ordnance informed him that the guns were then being exchanged with Winchester for improved models; and since the Hotchkiss was an experimental arm, the Sixteenth Infantry would be able to get only 8 or 10 of them in any event. Cavalrymen evidently had an easier time getting the gun; the 1881 Ordnance report recorded the issue of another 490 Hotchkiss carbines to the regulars.[89]

In no way did the experimental issue of the Hotchkiss stop Ordnance officers from working on the trapdoor Springfield. In 1878 and again in 1879 the chief of ordnance had suggested abolishing the bayonet and the saber; while unwilling to go quite that far, General of the Army William T. Sherman did recommend "shaping and strengthening the present ram or cleaning rod to the uses of a bayonet." Thus between mid-

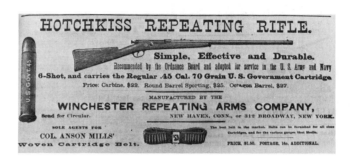

Forest and Stream, November 1881.

1880 and mid-1881, while still working on its long-range rifle, Springfield Armory manufactured 1014 trapdoors incorporating a triangular rod bayonet housed in the forestock, a device not seen in the army since the days of the Hall carbine. After completion, many of the rod-bayonet Springfields went to troops stationed in Wyoming, Dakota, and Texas for field trials. A report on the guns from Cheyenne Ordnance Depot in 1882 stated that "in almost every instance when they have had a fair and extensive trial they have been received with favor." But response from Fort Abraham Lincoln was not so enthusiastic: "the man must be standing still to readily fix and unfix this bayonet"; the report recommended replacement of the arms with a "ram-rod gun of improved pattern."[90]

No sooner had the armory finished these rod-bayonet rifles than it started work on two new models, one of which was a "Marksman's Rifle," intended to be awarded to the army's top target shooters. With its 28 in. round barrel, engraved action, and half stock with integral pistol grip, the marksman's rifle strongly

Soldiers and scouts at a water hole during one of the Apache campaigns in the 1880s. The Indian scouts carry Springfield .45 trapdoor rifles, their companions Second Model Winchester-Hotchkiss bolt action .45-70 carbines with a six-shot tubular mag- azine in the buttstock. The two men standing at left and third from left appear to carry nonregulation Colt M1878 double action revolvers in civilian-style holsters. (Courtesy Arizona Historical Society)

resembled the officers' rifle and was every bit as hand-some, but the troops qualified to receive it apparently preferred medals to guns, and Springfield made only 11 of them before stopping production.[91]

The other new model that came out of Springfield in 1881 was not a rifle at all, but a special single-barreled shotgun based on the trapdoor action. This gun, however, was not the first breech-loading shotgun to be issued by the Ordnance Department; as early as 1874, in fact, the national armory had put together "1 breech-loading shot-gun," and within a year Ord-nance had issued "25 breech loading shot-guns, dou-ble-barrel, No. 10 bore," purchased from commercial channels, to the regulars. Such acquisitions resulted from appeals similar to that from San Antonio Arsenal in November of 1876:

At the request of the Commanding General, De-partment of Texas, I have the honor to request that (16) sixteen double barrelled, centre-fire breech-loading shot-guns, short barrelled, 10 gauge, with 1,000 cartridge cases and 2,000 wads for the same and 100 lbs. of buckshot, may be sent to this arsenal for the use of escorts to paymasters on duty in this Department. Gen'l Ord desires me to state [that] the recent frequent stage robberies in Texas and notices of plans to rob paymasters, makes it nec-essary to provide that arm for escort duty of this kind which will be most certain and destructive at short range, and that for this service he would much prefer shotguns to the service carbines.

The Ordnance Department agreed that short-barreled, large-bore shotguns were "decidedly more effective and more dreaded by road agents" at close range than was the carbine, and as a result issued more than 80 such guns to regular army units between 1875 and 1881. Although the annual Ordnance reports usually failed

A rare Springfield prototype or pattern piece for the M1881 Marksman rifle, of which only about a dozen were produced. The butt plate is stamped "BY ORDER OF COL. BENTON FEB. 18, 1881," and the rifle displays such unusual features as a checkered pistol grip and foreend, a tang peep sight, and an integral Schnable-type foreend cap. The round barrel is 32 1/2 in. long; the oval silver presentation plate at the bottom of the pistol grip is uninscribed. (Photo by Mr. Hugo G. Poisson, courtesy Richard A. Bourne Co., Inc.)

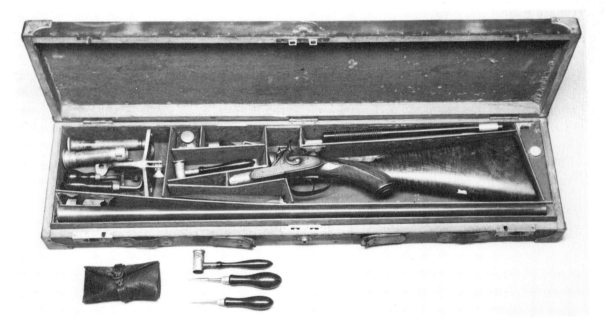

Cased 10-gauge breech-loading shotgun by J. P. Clabrough & Bros. of Birmingham, England. It was owned by Capt. Cyrus A. Earnest, who was stationed at Benicia Barracks near San Francisco from 1879 until 1886. He probably purchased it from the Clabrough & Golcher gun store in San Francisco. The gun has 32 in. barrels and is extensively engraved and embellished with gold and platinum inlays. (Courtesy Mr. Lawrence P. Shelton)

to specify the maker of these guns, at least 16 of them, bought in November of 1876, were 10-gauge Parkers. In March of 1879 the commandant of San Antonio wrote the chief of ordnance soliciting:

> for use with Escorts for Paymasters travelling in the Department of Texas, Six (6) double barreled shot guns, 10 gauge, of a pattern similar to those sent here in January 1877, from the Springfield Armory. Those are of the "Parker" Manufacture and have stood the hard service required of them remarkably well.[92]

On the plains the life of the shotgun was often rough and hard. In November of 1880 the commandant of San Antonio Arsenal noted that paymasters sometimes returned the guns issued to them with broken stocks or bent barrels, and suggested that since they were in short supply, they be issued only to paymasters traveling by stage, as it did not appear necessary to loan them to paymasters who had a regular escort. Finally, in May of 1882, the commandant wrote a Pay Department clerk at Galveston that: "I am drawing in all the Parker shot-guns heretofore issued to Paymasters for use on pay-trips, it having been decided by the Dept. Commander that their issue is no longer necessary."[93]

Other commercially made double guns remained in use at frontier garrisons because they were personally owned arms. General John Gibbon carried a shotgun during his pursuit of the Nez Percé in 1877, as did General Crook in his later campaigns against the Apaches. In the fall of 1879 officials at the Sharps Rifle Company received this letter from Fort Davis, Texas: "I have a breech-loading shot gun of W. & C. Scott & Son manufacture & I have gotten the stock broken & I desire to have the same restocked & to have a Sole leather box made to put the gun in, will you restock the same & make the box[?]"

After its appearance in 1878 a new double barreled breech-loading Colt shotgun became a popular item among army officers serving in the West. Orders for this gun came from military posts in such diverse locations as Arizona, Montana, Nebraska, and Indian Territory. One incentive for such orders was that by the 1880s the Colt concern was offering a 25 percent discount to officers who purchased their guns directly from the company. In September of 1879 Lt. F. B. Taylor of the Ninth Cavalry, then in New Mexico, ordered from Colt a 12-gauge with 30 in. barrels, as did Lt. L. J. Hearn of Fort Lapwai, Idaho, in October of 1882. In that year Assistant Surgeon Leonard Y. Loring, then at Fort Dodge Kansas, requested a somewhat fancier arm, a Colt 10-gauge with line-engraved rebounding locks and checkered "half-grip" stock. But even this gun could not compare with the 10-gauge double bought by Captain Cyrus Earnest of Benecia Barracks from J. P. Clabrough & Bros. of San Francisco. Earnest's gun had a fully engraved frame with gold and platinum inlays, and was cased with appropriate accessories.[94]

Despite the competition from other guns, the popularity of the Parker never waned. When Lieutenant C. H. Murray of Fort Stanton, New Mexico, ordered a 12-gauge Colt in 1887, he added this note to his letter:

> In purchasing a "Colt" gun, I must frankly state that I do so against the advice of many of my shooting friends at this post, who are almost unanimously in favor of the "Parker," but so great is my faith in the Colt's arms in general, that I am confident "my gun" will hold its own against any "Parker" of like or even higher grade. Any way I stand committed to prove it.[95]

Officially, however, the Parker had been replaced by the single-barreled Springfield, which began arriving at posts in the West in 1882.

These Springfield shotguns took shape largely at the hands of Col. J. C. Kelton, assistant adjutant-general of the Military Division of the Pacific, based at the Presidio in San Francisco. In January of 1881 Kelton wrote the division commander that "the Ordnance Department has converted some caliber .58 breech-loading Ordnance rifles into shotguns for Army use. Two have been sent to these headquarters for trial, experiment, and report." The test results were promising enough to prompt another letter to the chief of ordnance, in which Kelton stated that the guns would be a means "of educating at least a few men in every company in a way that will make them invaluable on the scout and in war." The chief of ordnance then informed General Sherman that Springfield Armory could easily make the guns "by using discarded parts of the .58 caliber muzzle-loading muskets, reaming out the barrel, and applying a modified breech-loading system." Sherman concurred with the idea, recommending in mid-February of 1881 that 250 shotguns be assembled and "sent to the posts in the West, where hunting is practicable and usual, at the rate of two per company . . . for the use of hunters and scouts to kill deer and large birds." Springfield completed the 250 guns early in October of 1881, and put together another 1100 or more between that time and mid-1885. The gun had a 26 in. round barrel bored to 20-gauge, and a straight-grip half stock secured to the barrel by a screw instead of a band.[96]

In March of 1882 the Ordnance Department authorized the arsenal at San Antonio and the depots at Fort Leavenworth, Fort Abraham Lincoln, and Cheyenne to supply two guns and two boxes of ammunition to each infantry company within their jurisdiction, with instructions that each company commander receiving them "encourage [his] men to use them freely for hunting game, birds, ducks, and anything else that will contribute to their comfort and increase their skill in quick shooting."[97]

The Springfield smoothbores were in evidence all across the frontier by the close of 1882, when 18 more went to various First Infantry companies stationed in Arizona Territory. There were a few problems at first, such as the bending or breaking of extractors, but in general the guns proved a very worthwhile addition to the arms racks, remaining in use among units in the West, especially those in Alaska, for some twenty years after their introduction. (The special 20-gauge all-brass shotshells made for these guns at Frankford Arsenal turn up in field finds and archeologial digs at practically every western military post of the period.)[98]

In 1882 still another new Springfield came out of the armory, this one an experimental "short rifle" designed for both infantry and cavalry. Although full-stocked, the Model 1882 had a barrel only 28 in. long, with sling swivels bent to conform to the stock cur-

Springfield M1881 shotgun. (Courtesy National Park Service, Fuller Gun Collection, Chickamauga and Chattanooga National Military Park)

Springfield M1882 infantry-cavalry rifle with triangular rod bayonet. (Courtesy National Park Service, Fuller Gun Collection, Chickamauga and Chattanooga National Military Park)

Remington-Lee M1879 .45 rifle. (Courtesy National Park Service, Fuller Gun Collection, Chickamauga and Chattanooga National Military Park)

vature. Of 52 rifles made, some had the triangular rod bayonet of the M1880 and others took the standard socket bayonet. Sent to the new School of Application for Infantry and Cavalry at Fort Leavenworth for trial, the guns evidently did not offer enough advantages over the standard models to warrant adoption.[99]

The Ordnance board that suggested this infantry and cavalry rifle had convened in July of 1881, primarily to test a new series of repeaters. Lasting for more than a year, the trials encompassed not only a host of bolt actions, but also a Model 1881 lever-action Marlin and a slide-action Spencer-Lee, both of which did surprisingly well. As in the 1878 trials, however, the bolt-action rifles generally turned in the best performances. But the increasing favor the bolt action was finding with the Ordnance Department did not deter two inventors living on the frontier from entering arms of a different type: J. Sheridan Jones of Menno, Dakota, submitted a trapdoor Springfield converted to a tubular-magazine repeater, and Private Charles Dean of the First Cavalry, stationed at Fort

Walla Walla in Washington Territory, offered a lever-action rifle with two magazines, one in the forestock and the other in the buttstock.

Of a total of forty rifles entered in the trials, however, no fewer than thirty were bolt guns. Remington submitted five such rifles, Winchester four; three more came from a then little known designer named James P. Lee. Additional bolt guns were entered by the partnership of R. S. Chaffee and General J. N. Reece, W. G. Burton (who had earlier been connected with the development of the Ward-Burton rifle), and Lieutenant A. H. Russell of Fort Union, New Mexico. When the tests ended in September of 1882, the board recommended not one rifle but three: the Lee No. 36, the Chaffee-Reece No. 33, and the Winchester-Hotchkiss No. 34, in that order.[100]

For some twenty years James Lee had been trying to sell his rifles to the government. During the Civil War he had arranged to sell the Ordnance Department a single-shot breechloader, only to see it rejected because of a misunderstanding about chamber dimen-

Soldiers in the Southwest armed with M1883 Third Model Winchester-Hotchkiss rifles, distinguishable from earlier versions by the two-piece stock. One Indian scout carries a Springfield trapdoor rifle while the "Apache Kid" at far right is armed with what appears to be a Winchester M1876 with a half-length magazine.

Cartridge belts are the M1881 "prairie style" and replaced earlier leather belts which caused metallic cartridge cases to corrode, sometimes a factor contributing to extraction difficulties with Springfield trapdoor arms. (Courtesy Arizona Historical Society)

sions. He entered two rifles in the 1872–73 trials, one of which was based on a modified Peabody action; it looked promising enough for limited testing in the field, and Springfield Armory made 145 of them in 1874–75, but Ordnance officers soon dropped the gun from consideration.[101]

The bolt-action rifles Lee entered in the 1881–82 tests were merely refinements of an arm he had originally submitted to the 1878 Ordnance Board; he withdrew this arm shortly after the 1878 trials started, but officers on an army equipment board which met in December of that year took special note of it:

The magazine of the Lee gun is a small metallic case containing five cartridges, which can be attached or removed at pleasure, and in the time

required to load a single cartridge. . . . When detached the gun may be used as a single loader. In the breech mechanisms there are but twenty-two parts, the recoil is taken up on both sides of the bolt, and the gun can be fired with accuracy twenty times in thirty seconds. . . .[102]

Patented in November of 1879, the principal feature of the Lee was its "box magazine," a readily detachable sheet-metal box which held five .45-70 cartridges, one on top of the other. Lee's magazine snapped into the underside of the stock just in front of the trigger guard, and fed its cartridges upward by spring pressure through a slot in the bottom of the receiver, into the path of the bolt.[103]

In contrast to the Lee, both the Winchester-Hotch-

kiss and the Chaffee-Reece employed a tubular magazine in the buttstock. While basically the same as
earlier models, the new Hotchkiss had a deep flat-
sided receiver which necessitated a two-piece stock.
Its magazine pushed cartridges into the path of the
bolt by spring pressure, just as in previous models.

Rather than using a spring to feed its cartridges, the
Chaffee-Reece employed the positive action of two
long ratchet bars in either side of the magazine tube.
The ratchet teeth in each bar were about 3 in. apart,
with each tooth resting against the head of a .45-70
cartridge. The bar on the left was capable only of
moving a slight distance outward or inward, but the
bar on the right was linked to the bolt and traveled
back and forth with it. A forward push on the open
bolt to chamber a round also pulled this right-hand
bar forward, thereby advancing the train of cartridges
in the magazine tube; as the shooter opened the bolt
after firing, the left-hand bar prevented the cartridges
still in the magazine from sliding backward. A third
short bar in the magazine assembly spread the two
long bars apart to allow a fresh supply of cartridges to
be loaded through a gate in the buttplate. Because of
its method of feeding cartridges, the Chaffee-Reece
had a different "feel" from other bolt actions: as the
trooper pushed the bolt forward to chamber the first
round, he was also pulling forward all the cartridges
remaining in the magazine.

Aside from their magazine systems, there were various other differences among the Hotchkiss, the Chaffee-Reece, and the Lee. The Hotchkiss, for example,
had a three-piece bolt, while the Chaffee-Reece had
the simpler two-piece type. In this respect it was similar to the Lee, but the Lee bolt had a distinct advantage over those of both its competitors. The bolts
in each of the other two guns had only one locking
surface, the rear face of the guide rib; the Lee bolt,
however, had two—the rear face of the guide rib and
a separate lug on the opposite side of the bolt body,
a point which Ordnance officers noted with approval.[104]

When the Ordnance Department indicated a desire
to begin field trials, both Lee and the Chaffee-Reece
partnership found themselves in an awkward position,
because neither had the facilities to manufacture the
required quantity of guns. Although the Sharps Rifle
Company had made the first few Lee rifles, the firm's
failure in 1881 temporarily left Lee without a backer.
However, the Remington concern had been interested
in this weapon since its inception, and quickly took
up the option to make it. Colt offered to manufacture
the Chaffee-Reece, but at the staggering price of $150
each. Ordnance officers quickly concluded that

U.S. M1882 Chaffee-Reese bolt action .45-70 magazine rifle, pro-
duced at the Springfield Armory. (Courtesy National Park Service,
Fuller Gun Collection, Chickamauga and Chattanooga National
Military Park)

Springfield Armory could make the gun for about one-third of that, using some of the machinery earlier employed in the fabrication of the Ward-Burton. By mid-1884 Springfield had completed 753 Chaffee-Reece arms, but neither Remington nor Winchester were able to complete delivery of a like number until later in the year, when field trials finally got under way.[105]

Distribution of the bolt actions was especially heavy among frontier units: troops in the departments of California, Arizona, Dakota, Texas, the Columbia, the Platte, and the Missouri all received a quantity of the guns for test. Contrary to the usual custom, no carbines were issued; rifles were sent to cavalry units as well as to the infantry.

Despite the good performances the three rifles had given in the Ordnance trials, the reports from the field, which began reaching the Ordnance Department early in 1886, were sharply critical. Mounted units judged the bolt system "unfitted for cavalry service; too easily fouled with dust," or termed it a "complicated mechanism liable to accident in field service . . . [subject] to fouling, injury, jamming, rust, & c." Other comments, such as "difficulty with reloaded ammunition" and "reloaded ammunition works badly," pinpointed the real problem, caused not so much by the guns as by the copper-cased cartridges. When the Ordnance Department tabulated the test results, it found that in "comparing the magazine guns and the Springfield for *all* uses, the preference is: For the Lee, 10; Chaffee-Reece, 3; Hotchkiss, 4, and the Springfield, 46. . . ." A few units sent no reports in: Companies A and F of the Fourth Cavalry, armed with the Hotchkiss and the Lee respectively, were in the field against hostile Apaches at the time their reports were due.[106]

While not commenting on the rifle's vices or virtues, Contract Surgeon Leonard Wood mentioned a Hotchkiss in connection with an incident that occurred during surrender negotiations with Geronimo's band of Apaches in the summer of 1886:

Geronimo came to me and asked to see my rifle. It was a Hotchkiss and he had never seen its mechanism. When he asked me for the gun and some ammunition, I must confess I felt a little nervous, for I thought it might be a device to get hold of one of our weapons. I made no objection, however, but let him have it, showed him how to use it, and he fired at a mark, just missing one of his own men, which he regarded as a great joke, rolling on the ground, laughing heartily and saying "good gun."[107]

By mid-1886 troop units on the frontier had turned in most of the repeaters, but even as the arsenals received them they were busy issuing new experimental trapdoor Springfields for field trials. (Ironically, the Lee would eventually become a phenomenal military success in the hands of the British, and both it and the Hotchkiss did achieve limited commercial success; but the Chaffee-Reece, although appearing briefly once more as a .30 caliber rifle, soon dropped from sight.)

In 1884 the venerable trapdoor Springfield had changed again, this time by the adoption of a new long-range rear sight designed by Col. A. R. Buffington; there were a few other changes as well, such as the elimination of the recess in the buttstock of the rifle. The Buffington sight soon proved itself unsuited for rough service. One military critic called it "a sight for peace and not for war . . . fit for target shooting and not for battle." But because it was a good target sight, it fit in very well with the arm's marksmanship program. So commonplace did marksmanship training become at posts in the West that in 1886 a self-made poet at Fort Custer penned these lines:

The target practice days have come,
    and like a chanticleer
At early dawn til day is done,
    the rifle's bang we hear.
So when the Scorer calls your name,
    Quick answer back your "page."
And sit down on a cactus plant
    To adjust your weather gauge.
Now to the shoulder bring the piece.
    Be sure it isn't "canted,"
Get your head between your knees
    And both feet firmly planted.
Draw in your breath as still as death.
    And call out the white disc,
"I've got a five as I'm alive,"
"No! Brown, another miss."[108]

An issue of the *Fort Custer News* in 1886 gave less poetic but more specific information about the training of cavalry troopers:

Twenty-four shapes of men made of iron frames covered with target paper, were placed in the different positions presumed to be natural for an enemy to assume, either standing, lying or kneeling, about five yards apart. At the command "commence firing" the exercise assumed all the details of a genuine skirmish. The bugle sounded "Advance," "Retreat," until each trooper had fired ten shots. Then the markers counted the holes in the figures and declared the total. when another troop arrived to beat the score if possible. B Troop, 1st Cavalry, made the highest score last year: 258 hits out of a possible 300.[109]

F. W. Flopfer (in buckskins) of Troop H, Fourth Cavalry with a group of Mescalero Apache scouts at Ft. Stanton, New Mexico Territory, in 1885. The weapons are a mixture of old and new— bows and arrows, single-shot Springfield trapdoor carbines, and a repeating Winchester M1873 rifle in the hands of the seated scout. (Courtesy National Archives)

(There were other rewards for skillful marksmanship besides recognition in print. One such prize, an engraved Winchester Model 1886 lever-action .45-70 with serial number in the 5000 range, has a silver plaque in the buttstock inscribed: "Awarded by J. F. Schmelzer & Son at 7th annual meeting Rifle Marksmen. Department of the Missouri. Leavenworth, Kansas.")[110]

Although the M1884 rifle and carbine were considered regulation and not experimental arms, they had barely gone into production when experimental versions of them appeared. In the summer of 1885, for example, Springfield Armory fitted just over 1000 M1884 rifles with new round rod bayonets and detachable front-sight covers; the latter soon became standard issue. As usual many of these rod-bayonet rifles went west, some finding their way to the Department of the Platte. Still another experimental Springfield came out early in 1886, this one a special carbine with 24 in. barrel and full-length forestock, held by one band near the muzzle. Of 1000 carbines made, a fair number again went west; in September of 1886, for instance, 185 were ordered sent to elements of the Third and Eighth Cavalry stationed in Texas.[111]

Two more experimental Springfields were yet to appear: a "positive cam" rifle in 1888 and a .30 caliber model in 1889. Both, however, were assembled primarily for the testing of special high-pressure cartridges and were not intended for general issue.[112]

The last of the regulation trapdoor Springfields resulted from a suggestion by Colonel A. R. Buffington, made late in 1888, that the rod bayonet be used for all future infantry arms. Reports from the field concerning the use of the experimental M1884 rod-bayonet rifle came before an army tactical board meeting at Fort Leavenworth, which in May of 1889 officially concurred with Buffington's suggestion. Although manufacture of the new gun did not start until 1890, the Ordnance Department termed it the Model 1888. Still a .45-70, the M1888 had a round rod bayonet like that of the experimental M1884, plus a new trigger guard forged in one piece with its tang. Between mid-1890 and mid-1893 Springfield made more than 64,000 of these rifles, but initial issues were very limited, with a mere 1102 sent to the regulars in the same period.[113]

Army paymaster and escort, armed with Springfield .45 trapdoor carbines, near Deadwood, South Dakota, in 1888. (Courtesy Library of Congress)

In October of 1890 a modification for the carbine appeared, a new "sight-protector" barrel band with a wide backward-slanting projection on its top to shield the front end of the Buffington rear sight. Carbine manufacture had actually stopped early in 1889, and Ordnance sergeants simply installed the new band on existing weapons.[114]

Like the old M1840 flintlock musket, the M1888 rod-bayonet rifle and the modified carbine of 1890 were obsolete even before they were adopted, but they and guns like them would continue to serve troops stationed on the frontier until the mid-1890s. A summary of arms on hand at the Ordnance depots at Cheyenne, Fort Leavenworth, and Vancouver Barracks, compiled in April of 1890, gives a good idea of the various models available to soldiers in the West near the close of the frontier period: the three depots held a total of 598 M1884 rifles and 755 M1884 carbines, plus 59 additional carbines "with ramrod in butt"; Cheyenne had 11 officers' rifles and five Springfield shotguns as well, and there were 2 long-range

rifles at Vancouver. Four years later, with the addition of the M1888 rifle and the 1890 carbine, this summary would still be representative of the arms carried by troops in the West.

Although the Springfield shotgun was generally satisfactory, there were periodic calls from the frontier for a shotgun with a bigger bore; in 1890 and again in 1892, in fact, the chief Ordnance officer for the Department of the Platte noted that a 10-gauge gun would be more useful on the plains than the 20-bore Springfield. Perhaps as a consequence, the Ordnance Department issued 66 new 12-gauge slide-action Spencer repeating shotguns to the regulars in 1892–93.

Ordnance officers had first tested this gun in January of 1886, and it had performed so well that an order for 240 samples followed immediately. All 240 went to the militia, but by mid-1889 the army had purchased another 48 for the regulars. These guns undoubtedly passed their field tests successfully, resulting in the issue of the additional 66 in 1892–93. At that time, however, the Ordnance Department also issued

Interior of a cavalry barracks at Ft. Robinson, Nebraska, about 1893. The arms racks hold Colt .38 double-action revolvers and Springfield .45 carbines. (Courtesy National Archives)

the regulars 72 20-gauge Springfields, so the Spencer served as an adjunct to the Springfield rather than as a replacement for it.[115]

THE HIGH-VELOCITY, SMALL-BORE RIFLE

Two developments, both occurring before 1890, had rendered the trapdoor Springfield obsolete. One, of course, was the availability of reliable repeating rifles. In October of 1887, little more than a year after the field trials of the Lee, Hotchkiss, and Chaffee-Reece, the chief of ordnance wrote that "an effective and simple magazine gun has become a necessity." But to be truly reliable a repeater had to use cartridges with brass instead of copper cases; not until July of 1888 did Frankford Arsenal begin the manufacture of brass

cases, plating them with tin to resist corrosion around the primer pocket.[116]

The other development, embodied in a new French service rifle of 1886, was to have a profound influence on small arms all over the world. In itself, the French Lebel rifle—a bolt-action repeater with a tubular magazine mounted under the barrel—was unremarkable; the innovation lay in its small-caliber high-velocity cartridge, which had a long, heavy bullet of only .32 caliber, driven out of the muzzle at the seldom-attained velocity of some 2000 feet per second. This velocity resulted from the newly developed "smokeless powder" used in the cartridge, the real secret of the rifle's success.[117]

When U.S. ordnance officers heard rumors of the

A forecast of future mechanized army development. With their Krag .30 rifles slung across their backs, members of the black Twenty-fifth Infantry bicycle platoon were photographed near Ft. Missoula, Montana, in 1896 on a march to Missouri. (Courtesy Ft. Laramie Historical Assn.)

Lebel rifle's performance, they began work on a "reduced caliber" of their own. The effectiveness of a small bullet for military use depended heavily on its velocity, however, and since the French guarded the secret of smokeless powder carefully, the Ordnance Department had to find another means of reaching an adequate velocity level. There were experiments with special propellants such as compressed and perforated black powder, but as the 1888 Ordnance report explained, "as yet the powder makers have not succeeded in producing a satisfactory powder, the desired velocity being accompanied by too great a pressure." For the trapdoor Springfield, at least, the pressure was indeed too great. Writing in the late 1890s, Ordnance Colonel Joseph P. Farley went so far as to say that "an increase of the black powder charge (70 grains) now used, by about 10 grains, will exceed the safety limit in the Springfield." Col. Edward S. Farrow subse-

quently wrote: "Eighty grains was the limit powder charge that could be used, as the cam latch worked loose with a greater charge." The problem stemmed from the easy-opening contours of the latch and the fact that, even in its fully locked position, it lay at an upward angle to the bore axis instead of parallel to it. Because of this, severe pressure against the front face of the breechblock could drive it back just far enough to force the cam latch farther upward, into its open position.[118]

To prevent this from happening, Ordnance officers devised a "positive cam," equipping 100 Springfields with it by mid-1888. Somewhat obliquely the Ordnance Department described the new locking arrangement as "a modification in the cam and shaft by which, in addition to its former motion of rotation as the latch is lifted, it is also given a motion of translation at right angles to the axis of the receiver." The first

100 positive-cam rifles were .45-70s, but late in 1889, in keeping with the desire for a smaller caliber, Springfield Armory assembled a .30 caliber trapdoor, complete with rod bayonet. Because of its positive cam, the rifle proved "perfectly safe" during the firing of cartridges loaded with "powders giving great velocity," but there was a problem with the breechblock, which sometimes jammed in the closed position from the pressures involved.[119]

Nevertheless, the Ordnance Department was not yet ready to abandon the trapdoor design. At the close of 1890 an Ordnance board convened to test a new series of small-caliber high-velocity magazine rifles, and at the special request of the chief of ordnance, three .30 caliber trapdoor Springfields underwent testing with the repeaters. All three rifles had positive cams, and, in addition, two had wider, heavier receivers and larger extractors. During firing tests of the rifle with the old extractor, Ordnance officers noted that "in 10 cases, near latter part of these sets of 50 [rounds], as gun had become heated, the extractor tore through head, leaving shell in chamber." Furthermore, the positive cam would sometimes fail to lock properly; with another .30 caliber Springfield, "as the fouling and unburnt powder accumulated . . . at seat of cam, pressure on the thumb piece was necessary to close the latch. In the 500 shots this assistance had to be given 142 times." Moreover, after the trials "the gun was examined and a very noticeable impression of the cam observed on the face of recess in breech screw." These tests involved high-pressure smokeless-powder cartridges, for which the Springfield was never designed, and it was a credit to the rifle that it did not fly apart under the shock of such loads. But as Ordnance officers concluded after the trials, the trapdoor Springfield embodied "a system which, though found efficient for a larger caliber at lower pressures, is not well adapted to this reduced caliber and the high pressures caused by smokeless powder."[120]

With these words, the long history of the trapdoor Springfield officially came to a close. Since the appearance of the all-new .50-70 model of 1868, the infantry rifle had passed through no fewer than five standard variations: the M1868, M1873, M1879, M1884, and M1888. Besides these standard versions there were the two types of officers' rifles, plus the experimental models of 1870, 1880, 1882, and 1884. The long-range rifle, the short-lived marksman's rifle, and thousands of scaled-down arms made for the use of cadets extended the list.

Aside from the experimental model of 1870 the trapdoor carbine had also passed through five standard variations—1873, 1877, 1879, 1884, and 1890—plus the experimental type of 1886. The last of the single-shot Springfields, the .30 caliber positive-cam rifle, dropped from sight soon after it appeared. Although thousands of .45-70 trapdoors went to volunteer troops during the Spanish-American War of 1898, only two models remained in the hands of the regulars through the turn of the century: at least one officers' rifle was sold in 1900, and small numbers of Springfield 20-gauge shotguns were still being issued at that time.[121]

About 1900 one of the Springfield's former users, looking back fondly on his experience with the arm, composed an ode to it which reads in part:

I was nothing too light on your shoulder,
You were glad when you stacked me o' nights,
But I'd drill an Apach'
From the thousand-yard scratch
If you'd only hold straight on the sights—old sights!
My trusty old Buffington sights! . . .
For I led every march on the border,
And I taught every rookie to fight;
Though he'd curse me in close marching order,
Lord!—he'd hug me on picket at night. . . .[121]

Ironically enough, the small-bore repeating rifle that replaced the Springfield in the hands of the regular army was to have a much shorter service life than its predecessor; only eleven years after its adoption an even newer rifle would supersede it.

The magazine-rifle trials that resulted in the new repeater started in December of 1890 and continued until August of 1892. Of fifty-three arms entered, almost all were designed for small-caliber high-velocity cartridges. Many of the entries were, of course, American: the Blake, Bruce, Chaffee-Reece, Hampden, Lee, Savage, and a rifle from a California inventor named Durst, among others. Numerous other guns, however, came from overseas, including the Berthier, Krag-Jorgensen, Kropatschek, Lee-Speed, Mannlicher, Mauser, and Schmidt entries. A few of the arms, such as the Savage, the Larsen, and the Schulhof, were lever-actions, but most were bolt-actions. As the official report of the trials stated:

the bolt system of breech closure as developed in the last few years, and particularly for arms of the reduced caliber, is superior as a single-loader, in ease of manipulation, facility of loading, and rapidity of fire, to an arm on the block system like the Springfield, and has the additional advantage that without sacrificing any of its features it is also adaptable to use as a magazine arm.

(While still classed as bolt guns, two of the Mannlichers and the Schmidt did not employ the conven-

Seventh Infantry target practice with Krag .30 bolt action rifles
(c. 1896). (Courtesy Denver Public Library, Western History Dept.)

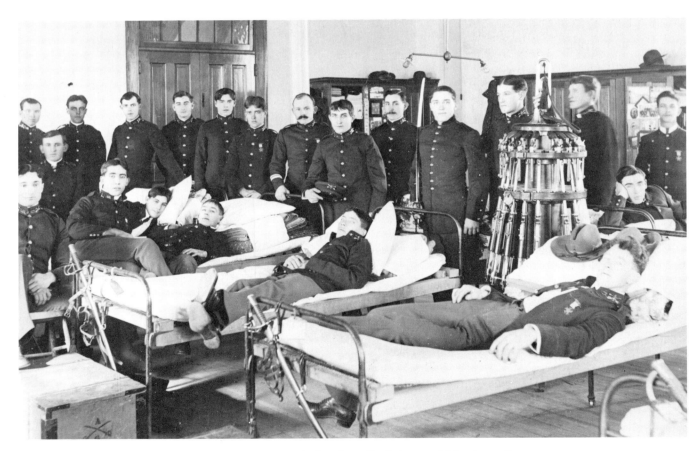

Men of Troop A, Sixth Cavalry at Ft. Robinson, Nebraska, with
their Krag carbines and .38 double-action Colts stored under lock
and key (c. 1898). (Courtesy Ft. Laramie Historical Assn.)

tional rotating and sliding bolt, but instead incorporated "straight-pull" actions, in which only a rearward pull and a forward push on the bolt handle were necessary for operation.)

Ordnance officers found especially interesting "those in which the magazine can be charged and then held in reserve while single fire is delivered, magazine fire being, however, available at any moment." In other words, the same considerations that had influenced the small-arms trials of 1878 and 1882 were in effect. This qualification—a repeating rifle that would serve equally well as a single-shot arm—was to have an important bearing on the final selection.

The trials included the usual phases: rapid fire, 500-round endurance, dusting, rusting, and firing with defective cartridges and excessive charges. Since the means for measuring the pressures of the variouus types of smokeless powders used in the tests were not always adequate for the purpose, some of the excessive charges were excessive indeed. By the time the tests were over, only three American arms—the Bruce No. 2, the Hampden No. 2, and the Lee No. 3—were in acceptable working order. The lever-action Savage No. 2 was also able to function, but it "worked stiffly." Among the surviving foreign guns, a straight-pull Mannlicher carbine, the Mauser No. 3, and four slightly different version of the Krag-Jorgensen "worked well," while the British Lee-Speed "opened with difficulty."

Again, in making its final choice the board had to select an arm that: "[showed] itself to be an efficient single-loader, [and] a rapid magazine arm, holding meanwhile that magazine in reserve, with a cut-off plainly indicating to the officers which class of fire is being delivered. . . ." Faced with these considerations, the board recommended the adoption of the Krag-Jorgensen No. 5, which, besides its other qualities, had demonstrated that "as a single-loader it is the best arm presented."[124]

Already the standard service rifle in Denmark, the new U.S. Model 1892 had been designed by two Norwegians, Captain Ole Krag and Erik Jorgensen. In many respects it was a conventional bolt-action, but was noticeably fast and smooth in operation. The bolt itself had a single locking lug at its head, with a long guide rib on its side and a well-positioned handle lying just above the trigger. Concerning the action's strength, the manual issued with the rifle indicated that: "The locking lug will sustain any powder pressure liable to occur, but if worn by usage or upset by excessive pressures the rear end of the guide rib will bear on the locking shoulder of the receiver, permitting the continued use of the arm with safety."[125]

The rifle's most unusual feature was not its action but its magazine system. A long loading gate, resting

Model 1896 Krag .30 carbine. (Courtesy National Park Service, Fuller Gun Collection, Chickamauga and Chattanooga National Military Park)

Camp scene in Yosemite National Park. Arms are Krag .30-40 carbines and a holstered Colt .38 double action. (Courtesy Kansas State Historical Society)

on a longitudinal hinge, was positioned on the right side of the receiver below the bolt. After opening the gate the trooper could push from one to five rounds individually into the magazine, where they lay one beside the other, parallel to the bore. With the loading gate closed, a strong follower spring housed inside it pressed the cartridges from right to left and up an inclined plane inside the left wall of the magazine, so that they entered the bolt path from the lower left. The cartridge itself, soon to be known as the .30-40 Krag, had a rimmed bottlenecked case, loaded with about 40 grains of smokeless powder, and a jacketed 220 grain bullet which left the muzzle at some 2000 feet per second.[126]

There were the usual delays before production actually commenced, caused in part by the complaints of inventors whose arms had fared poorly in the trials. By the spring of 1894 the Krag was still not ready for general issue, but at that time the Ordnance Department did send a few individual samples to various military departments. In late June of 1894 the Ordnance officer for the Department of the Platte reported that:

The new rifle has been on exhibition in my office and at Fort Omaha for about two months and has been examined by many officers and civilians. There has been no opportunity to try it at the range as I have no ammunition for it, but its general appearance and action have found much favor.[127]

The rifles which finally came off the line had 30 in. barrels, adapted for a new knife bayonet with a 12 in. blade. The first sizable shipment of these arms left Springfield in October of 1894, slated for the Fourth Infantry Division, then assigned to the Department of the Columbia. Distribution was brisk enough thereafter so that by January of 1895 roughly half the army's infantry regiments had received their quotas. With

A frontier cavalryman in the 1890s. His new Krag carbine in its saddle scabbard contrasts with his obsolete Model 1860 cavalry saber, a weapon of little practical value to the post–Civil War mounted trooper in the West. (Although this saber has long been known by collectors as the M1860, initial quantities were ordered by the army as early as 1858.) (Courtesy Western History Collections, University of Oklahoma Library)

manufacture of the rifle well under way, the Ordnance Department laid plans for a carbine. The 1895 Ordnance report noted that "a few carbines have been made and the preparations for manufacture advanced so that the issue of this arm to the cavalry can be commenced at an early date."[128]

The adoption of a small-caliber smokeless-powder magazine rifle put the U.S. Army on a par with the military establishments of most other powers. Ironically, however, the Krag's magazine system, which at first counted so heavily in its favor, soon proved to be a drawback; it was much slower to reload than were the clip-loaded magazines of competing rifles. As a result, the Krag was officially replaced by a Mauser-type rifle in 1903. Even as they issued the Krag, Ordnance officers were considering alternatives. As early as 1895, in fact, they conducted experiments with military rifles having calibers as small as .20 and .22. Truly, a new era had begun.[129]

·2·

HANDGUNS

PERCUSSION VERSUS
CARTRIDGE REVOLVERS

Through the late 1860s and well into the 1870s, the frontier cavalryman's principal sidearm was a .44 caliber percussion revolver. By 1866, of course, Ordnance officers were thoroughly familiar with metallic-cartridge handguns; foreign-made cartridge revolvers—the LeFaucheux, the Perrin, and the so-called Raphael made by Pidault & Cordier—had seen considerable use by Union forces during the Civil War, especially those in the West. At the end of the war, in fact, an Ordnance inventory found 622 Le-Faucheux revolvers at Vancouver Arsenal, and another 539 at San Antonio Arsenal. The wartime use of privately purchased cartridge handguns by officers and enlisted men included many American models as well: Smith & Wesson .22s and .32s; Sharps pepperboxes; evasions and infringements of the Smith & Wesson design, such as the teat-fire Moore and the rimfire Warner; and a number of similar arms. But with the possible exception of the Smith & Wesson .32, none of the domestic handguns were seriously regarded as practical military weapons, primarily because of their low-powered ammunition.[1]

Although the Ordnance Department had displayed a keen interest in metallic-cartridge shoulder arms even before the end of the war, this interest—officially, at least—did not extend to handguns until several years later. The revolver's period of military supremacy had been brief, reaching from the latter part of the Mexican War to the latter part of the Civil War, when the widespread use of breech-loading and repeating carbines toppled it from its lofty position. By the close of 1867 infantrymen and cavalrymen were using metallic-cartridge rifles and carbines almost exclusively; but an Ordnance memorandum of 1868 stated specifically that "the urgency of the service" did not demand the immediate introduction of pistols "adapted to the use of metallic primed cartridges."[2]

There was another reason for the lack of official interest in cartridge pistols: Smith & Wesson's rigidly enforced control of the Rollin White patent on bored-through chambers. Those Ordnance officers and arms designers aware of the need for a big-bore cartridge revolver could do little about it because of the restrictions posed by this patent, which would not expire until 1869.

Shortly after the end of the war the Ordnance Department called in most of the Whitney, Savage, and LeFaucheux revolvers remaining in its frontier arsenals. The handguns left for the use of regular troops garrisoning the West were thus chiefly Model 1851 Navy and Model 1860 Army Colts, Remington New Models, and a sprinkling of .44 caliber Starrs. Volunteers, of course, continued to use other types; in November of 1867, for instance, the Ordnance Department issued a thousand Whitneys to Dakota Territory. Despite the gradually increasing competition from cartridge pistols, the percussion Colt and Remington .44s represented two of the best arms of their type, and as such found ready buyers among civilians living near frontier posts. In January of 1866 Captain James R. Kemble, stationed at Fort Union, New Mexico, requisitioned 55 Remington revolvers to make up deficiencies in his company; the unit had originally received 88 handguns, but some of the men had apparently sold their revolvers, which cost them twelve dollars if lost, to settlers willing to pay fifty dollars or more for such weapons.

Troopers in more dangerous areas did not have the luxury of selling their six-shooters because they needed them for self-defense. Early in December of 1866 Indians attacked a wood train outside Ft. Phil Kearny; Col. Henry Carrington and a cavalry detachment attempted a rescue, but Carrington saw that he was riding into a trap and hastily sounded a recall:

That left Lieutenant Bingham, Sergeant Bowers, and John Donovan cut off by the Indians. They dismounted for a short time, but decided that their only chance was to run the gauntlet, as their commander had retreated to a higher point. Lieutenant Bingham and Sergeant Bowers were pulled off their horses by the Indians. John Donovan was armed

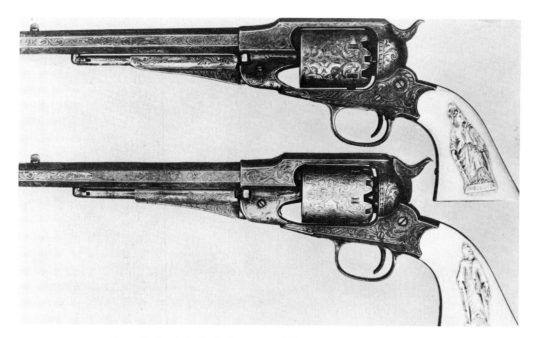

Gen. Richard I. Dodge's engraved Remington .44 New Model percussion revolvers. Dodge spent three decades on the frontier during his military career. (Courtesy Arizona Historical Society)

Colt M1851 (#1299??) inscribed on the butt "H. B. Carrington Col. 18th Inf. U.S.A." Carrington laid out the Bozeman Trail defensive line in Montana Territory in 1866, building or improving and garrisoning Forts Reno, Phil Kearny, and C. F. Smith, posts which were later abandoned under the Ft. Laramie Treaty of 1868. (Courtesy Mr. Norm Flayderman, New Milford, Conn.)

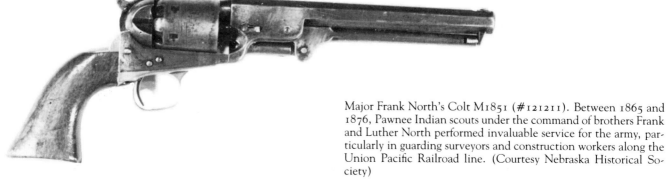

Major Frank North's Colt M1851 (#121211). Between 1865 and 1876, Pawnee Indian scouts under the command of brothers Frank and Luther North performed invaluable service for the army, particularly in guarding surveyors and construction workers along the Union Pacific Railroad line. (Courtesy Nebraska Historical Society)

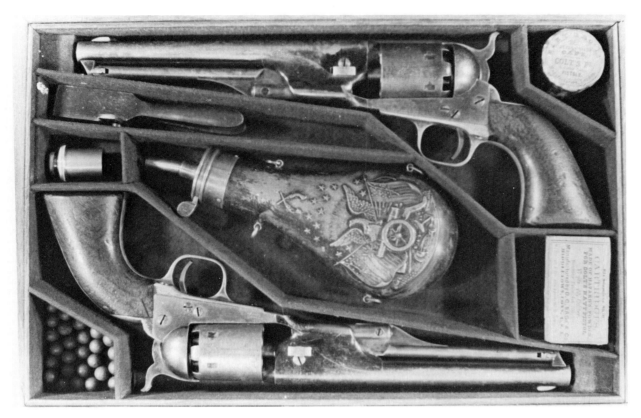

Cased Colt M1861 .36 percussion revolvers (#s 29387 and 29536) once owned by Lt. William L. Sherwood and possibly presented to him upon his promotion to 1st lieutenant on July 22, 1872. Sherwood served in Arizona with the Twenty-first Infantry from 1869 until 1873 when he was transferred to the District of the Lakes in California. He died on April 14, 1873, of wounds received from Modoc Indians who shot him three days earlier while meeting with him under a flag of truce. (Courtesy Mr. Jim Roller)

with a Colt army revolver and a single shot Star carbine using a copper cartridge, the same as the Spencer carbine. The revolver . . . was all that saved him when the Indians were on each side of him trying to pull him off his horse, for just in the nick of time he shot one on each side.[3]

Besides the issue arms, numerous cap-and-ball revolvers were the private property of army officers. General Grenville Dodge owned a cased .44 Remington, while George Custer possessed both a .44 Remington and a Colt Model 1860. Colonel Henry B. Carrington of the Eighteenth Infantry, and Luther North of the Pawnee Battalion, both owned Model 1851 Navy Colts. Another Colt owner was young Alson B. Ostrander, an "army boy of the sixties." When he passed through Omaha in the spring of 1866 en route to the Powder River country, Ostrander bought "a latest improved Colt's six [shot] revolver. George Lanthier, the leading saddler of the city and a warm personal friend of mine,

had made and presented me an elegant belt and an embossed and handcarved holster." The gun and belt were stolen shortly afterward when Ostrander stopped at Ft. Sedgwick, and, "to console me, Lieutenant Arnold offered to let me have his Spencer rifle whenever I wanted to hunt." Ostrander, however, did have a back-up handgun in the breast pocket of his vest: "a small Smith & Wesson twenty-two caliber pistol." One day, soon after his arrival at Ft. Laramie,

my vest happened to be open [and] the butt of the pistol was exposed. [Old Nick Janis] saw it and asked, "What's that?"

I took the little revolver out and showed it to him. The minute he got it in his hands he just roared with laughter, and exclaimed, "Oh, look at the play toy!" Then he broke open the gun, and taking out the cylinder looked through the barrel, chuckling as he did so. Finally, handing it back to me, he said, "Boy, if you shoot me with dat and I

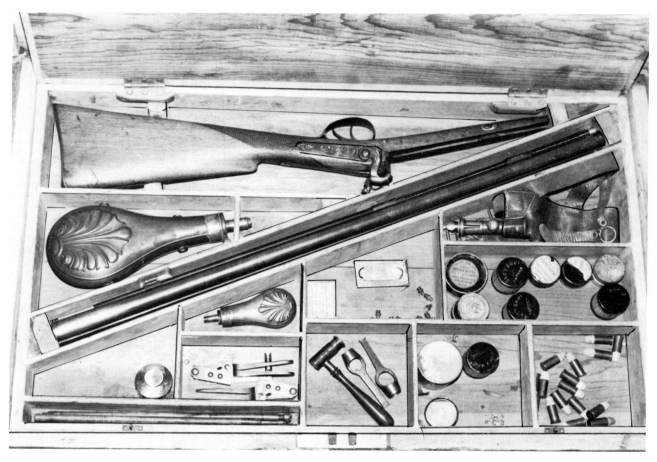

Lieutenant Sherwood's 15-gauge percussion shotgun made by the Joseph Manton firm of England. A silver inlay is inscribed with Sherwood's initials. Inside the officer's foot locker is a tray fitted to hold the shotgun and various shooting accessories such as powder and shot flasks; wad cutters; percussion caps; nipple wrench, spare nipples, packet of .36 skin cartridges, and two bullet molds for his pair of Colt M1861 revolvers; plus a handful of .44 rimfire cartridges for his M1866 Winchester rifle. The front of the locker is painted in script "Lieut. W. L. Sherwood/21st U. S. Infantry." (Courtesy Mr. Gerald H. Lytle)

find out, I put you across my knee and spank hell outen you!"

Nearly every day after that he would ask to see that "play toy," and then comment on it before the men. He acted like a kid with a new plaything; so one day I said to him, "Nick, do you want that?"

"Me?" he asked.

"Yes," I replied. "I'll give it to you if you want it."

He hesitated for a moment; then, patting me on the shoulder, he said: "You good boy. Ol' Nick your frien'. I make it all ri' sometime."

Now without a handgun of any kind, Ostrander found that Colonel Bullock, the sutler at Laramie, "kept a good line of guns and revolvers, and I looked them over longingly. Finally I selected a Colt revolver of thirty-eight caliber and asked the price. 'Twenty dollars,' he told me, and he would throw in fifty car-

tridges." Ostrander bought it, and later, in a conversation with the famous Jim Bridger, told him about the little Smith & Wesson. Bridger said: "Yep, I've seen that kind, but never handled 'em. Was afeard I'd break it."

A more unusual weapon was the "old-fashioned 'pepper-box' seven shooter pistol" carried by Chaplain David Wright. During an Indian fight on the Powder River near Crazy Woman Creek in 1867, Wright and another soldier charged up a ravine to drive some Indians from their position; soon listeners heard a strange volley of shots, which turned out to be all the barrels of Wright's pepperbox going off at once.[4]

By 1867 the more vocal military men were arguing for metallic-cartridge sidearms, and in March of that year the following letter appeared in the *Army and Navy Journal*:

We want a pistol of the size and weight of the present Army pistol to use the metallic cartridge,

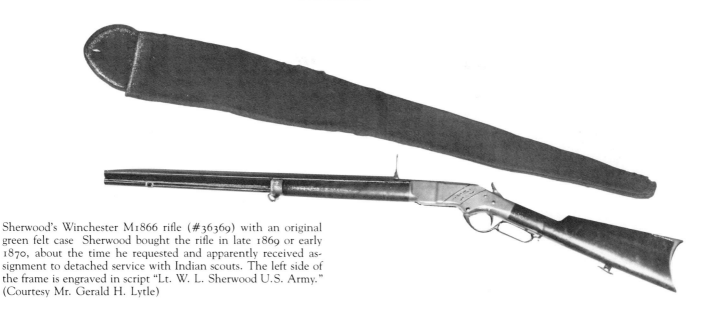

Sherwood's Winchester M1866 rifle (#36369) with an original green felt case Sherwood bought the rifle in late 1869 or early 1870, about the time he requested and apparently received assignment to detached service with Indian scouts. The left side of the frame is engraved in script "Lt. W. L. Sherwood U.S. Army." (Courtesy Mr. Gerald H. Lytle)

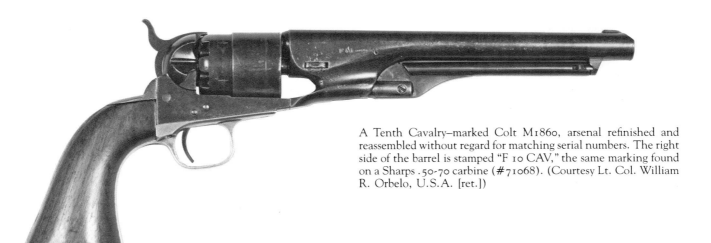

A Tenth Cavalry–marked Colt M1860, arsenal refinished and reassembled without regard for matching serial numbers. The right side of the barrel is stamped "F 10 CAV," the same marking found on a Sharps .50-70 carbine (#71068). (Courtesy Lt. Col. William R. Orbelo, U.S.A. [ret.])

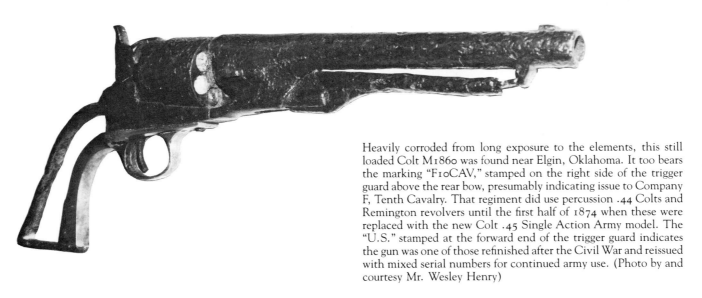

Heavily corroded from long exposure to the elements, this still loaded Colt M1860 was found near Elgin, Oklahoma. It too bears the marking "F10CAV," stamped on the right side of the trigger guard above the rear bow, presumably indicating issue to Company F, Tenth Cavalry. That regiment did use percussion .44 Colts and Remington revolvers until the first half of 1874 when these were replaced with the new Colt .45 Single Action Army model. The "U.S." stamped at the forward end of the trigger guard indicates the gun was one of those refinished after the Civil War and reissued with mixed serial numbers for continued army use. (Photo by and courtesy Mr. Wesley Henry)

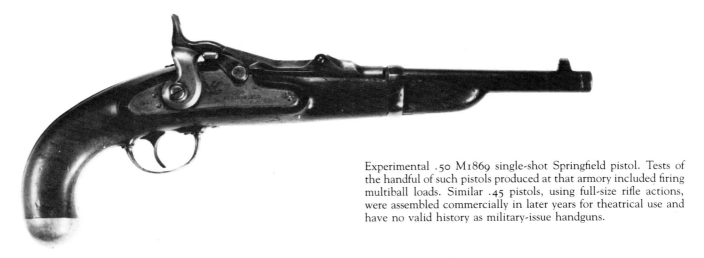

Experimental .50 M1869 single-shot Springfield pistol. Tests of the handful of such pistols produced at that armory included firing multiball loads. Similar .45 pistols, using full-size rifle actions, were assembled commercially in later years for theatrical use and have no valid history as military-issue handguns.

of the calibre to be adopted for the new carbines (.45 or 50); or the Colt and Remington pistols might be altered to use metallic explosive cartridges, by cutting off the rear of the cylinder, so as to make it similar to Smith and Wesson's pistol cylinders. . . . Every one in the Army knows the great inconvenience of loading and capping an Army pistol while in motion on horseback, and also the great number of pistol cartridges [of paper or skin] that are destroyed in the cartridge box, and in loading.[5]

Still, there was the matter of the Rollin White patent. One attempt to get a cartridge handgun to troops in the field without infringing upon this patent resulted in the experimental assembly of at least two single-shot trapdoor pistols at Springfield Armory in 1868, but the idea went no further. Then, in October of 1868, Colt treasurer Hugh Harbison sent the chief of ordnance a new Colt Model 1860, converted to a front-loading metallic-cartridge revolver by the Thuer method. Again, however, no official action resulted.[6]

While Colt's Thuer revolver found no military and few civilian buyers, Remington solved the problem of marketing large-caliber cartridge handguns, at least in part, by coming to terms with Smith & Wesson. In February of 1868 Smith & Wesson authorized Remington to convert its New Model .44s to cartridge arms by the substitution of new five-shot cylinders, chambered for a copper-cased .46 caliber rimfire load. Some of these conversions, or Remingtons altered to cartridge guns by different means, may have reached the Ordnance Department. On his way to the battle at the Washita in November of 1868, Capt. Albert Barn-

tiz "lost my Remington pistol, Breech-Loader, on the march." An 1869 editorial in the *Army and Navy Journal* noted that:

Officers of cavalry regiments stationed in the Indian country, complain that many of the arms issued by Government to their commands do not come up to that standard of efficiency which the peculiar nature of frontier service demands . . . the Remington revolver, adopted as the standard arm of the service, also comes in for its share of censure; at least those belonging to the first and imperfect issue of several years ago . . . while some companies of a regiment are armed with the Spencer and Henry [?] carbine and the improved Remington revolver, others are compelled to use the old Sharpe carbine and the unimproved Remington. . . . The Remington revolver of the recent issue is an undeniably good weapon. Its range is great and it can be relied on for accuracy. It is the old issue to which exceptions are taken.[7]

Officers and enlisted men unwilling to rely on "old-issue" arms could, of course, buy their own guns. As might be expected, there was an assortment of personally owned cartridge handguns among soldiers on frontier duty. Lt. Alexander Wishart, stationed in Wyoming during the late 1860s, owned a Smith & Wesson .32, a much better weapon than Alson Ostrander's little .22. A pair of Smith & Wesson .32s, engraved and cased, were presented to George Custer in October of 1869 by one J. B. Sutherland. Custer received still another metallic-cartridge arm that year, as did

Engraved Remington .44 New Model percussion revolver with carved ivory grips, presented to Lt. Col. George A. Custer by E. Remington & Sons. (Courtesy Custer Battlefield Historical and Monument Assn., Inc.)

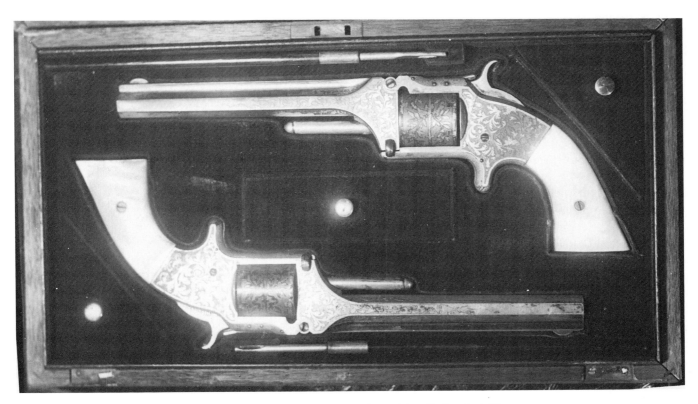

Cased pair of silver-plated, engraved, pearl-handle Smith & Wesson .32 No. 2 revolvers (#s 20757 and 20615) presented to Lt. Col. Custer in 1869 by J. B. Sutherland. (From *The Custer Album*, courtesy Dr. Lawrence A. Frost)

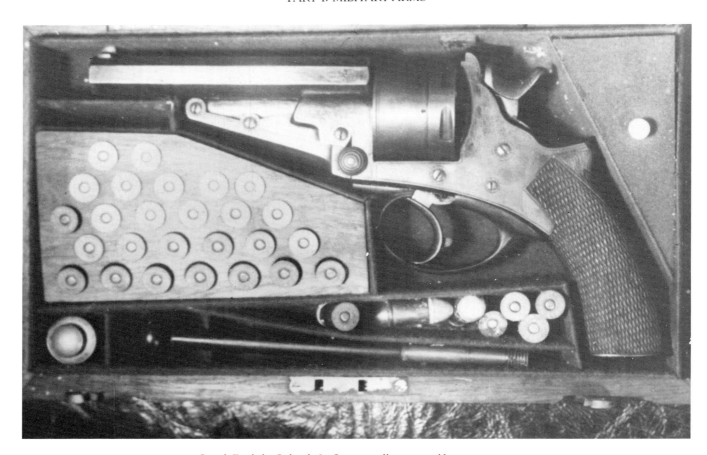

Cased English Galand & Sommerville .450 self-extracting revolver presented by Lord Berkley Paget to Capt. Thomas Custer
in remembrance of time spent buffalo hunting in Kansas in September 1869. Paget presented George A. Custer with a similar
Galand & Sommerville in a compartmented case. (Courtesy Col.
Charles A. Custer via Custer Battlefield Historical and Monument
Assn., Inc.)

his brother Tom: a visiting English sportsman presented each Custer with a Galand & Sommerville .45
centerfire double-action revolver, "in remembrance of
the very happy time spent at Fort Hayes while Buffalo
hunting in Kansas in Sept. 1869." Patented in England
in October of 1868, the Galand & Sommerville was
an early, well-made example of a "self-extracting" revolver; unlatching a lever under the barrel and swinging it downward and forward pulled the barrel and
cylinder forward as a unit along the cylinder pin, while
a separate extractor plate (also riding on the cylinder
pin) held the fired cases to the rear.[8]

The Galand & Sommerville would probably have
proved quite adequate as a service weapon, but with
the expiration of the Rollin White patent in April of

1869, the requirement for troopers to purchase metallic-cartridge handguns with their own money rapidly disappeared. Later that year Springfield Armory
experimentally converted two Colts and two Remingtons to cartridge arms, and while this effort was
small in itself, it was a forerunner of things to come.
In the meantime Smith & Wesson, well aware of how
easily such conversions could be effected, labored diligently on a new self-extracting .44; by the spring of
1870 they had a prototype ready to submit to the
Ordnance board then meeting in St. Louis.[9]

Besides the new Smith & Wesson, the St. Louis
board had other handguns to consider: five .44 caliber
Remingtons (one of which came from Springfield Armory); two Remington .50 caliber single-shot pistols;

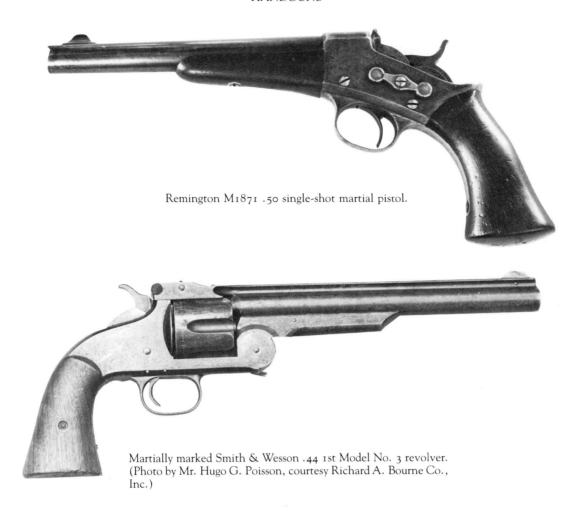

Remington M1871 .50 single-shot martial pistol.

Martially marked Smith & Wesson .44 1st Model No. 3 revolver.
(Photo by Mr. Hugo G. Poisson, courtesy Richard A. Bourne Co.,
Inc.)

two .44 caliber Whitney revolvers (one with a "revolving breech," the other with a "stationary breech");
and a .45 caliber front-loading National revolver. After
studying the guns, the board selected "the following
six in the order of relative merit":

First.	The Remington single-barrelled pistol, with guard, centre fire.
Second.	The Smith Wesson revolver.
Third.	The Remington revolver No. 2.
Fourth.	The Remington revolver No. 5.
Fifth.	The Remington revolver No. 3.
Sixth.	The Remington revolver No. 4.

The Remington is the only single-barrelled pistol
submitted. It is an excellent weapon, but should be
so modified as to load at the half-cock. The Smith
Wesson is decidedly superior to any other revolver
submitted. It should be modified as follows, viz.:
made centre fire; the cylinder lengthened . . . and
countersunk to cover the rim of the cartridge; calibre increased to the standard.

The mainspring of the Remington arm should be
strengthened, so as to increase the certainty of fire;
also the plunger should be made to strike more
accurately the centre of the base of the cartridge.[10]

Following his review of the board's findings, the
chief of ordnance asked for authority to purchase:

one thousand Remington single-barrel pistols, calibre 50, and one thousand Smith & Wesson re-

Lt. William B. Wetmore, Sixth Cavalry, served on the frontier in Kansas and Colorado in 1872–75. On September 10, 1873, he thwarted an attempted robbery of an army paymaster and in the struggle shot the leader of the desperadoes to death. Wetmore later earned a citation for gallantry in an engagement with Indians on the Red River on August 30, 1874. The revolver he carries butt forward appears to be a nickeled S&W .44 No. 3. (Courtesy Mr. David R. Phillips)

volvers of same calibre as our Army revolvers . . . and to have one thousand Remington revolvers altered after the plan of revolver No. 2; these pistols to be issued for comparative trial in service, as in the case of the muskets and carbines. If the revolver is to be retained in service, as I believe it should be, I do not think that the calibre should be increased to 50, which is the established calibre for muskets and carbines.[11]

The board's first choice, the Remington .50 caliber pistol, had a rolling-block action identical to that of the rifle; it was therefore rugged and dependable. But it was still a single-shot arm, and its selection may have resulted, at least in part, from the favoritism accorded the rolling-block system even before the trials started.

The second choice, the new Smith & Wesson "No. 3," differed considerably from the firm's earlier revolvers. In the new gun (which was based on no fewer than five patents issued to various designers between July of 1860 and August of 1869), the barrel was hinged at the front of the bottomstrap, with the cylinder pin rigidly attached to the rear of the barrel lug. Releasing a catch at the rear of the topstrap allowed the muzzle to swing downward and the cylinder, in see-saw fashion, to swing upward, above the standing breech, thereby exposing all its chambers for loading. In itself this arrangement was not new, but the gun did incorporate a real innovation in the form of its extractor, which was recessed into, and formed part of, the rear face of the cylinder. When the shooter broke the gun open for loading, a rack and pinion assembly automatically forced this extractor rearward, away from the cylinder, thus pulling out the fired cases; with the revolver fully open, a coil spring surrounding the extractor stem jerked the extractor back into its place in the rear face of the cylinder.[12]

The advantages of this design—fast loading and even faster ejection—were obvious, and in late December of 1870 the Ordnance Department contracted with Smith & Wesson to suppy 1000 No. 3s, chambered for a .44 centerfire cartridge. Since the firm was then manufacturing the gun in quantity for the civilian market, deliveries to the army began promptly, in March of 1871. Inspectors from the Ordnance Department accepted all but four of these guns, and issues to cavalrymen in the field followed shortly. Late in March, in fact, the chief of ordnance ordered a special issue of 80 Smith & Wessons and 20 Springfield carbines sent to Lieutenant George M. Wheeler, then at Halleck's Station on the Central Pacific Railroad.[13]

As supplied to the military, the No. 3—later to be termed the "American"—had an 8 in. barrel and a six-chambered cylinder, adapted to a new .44 center-

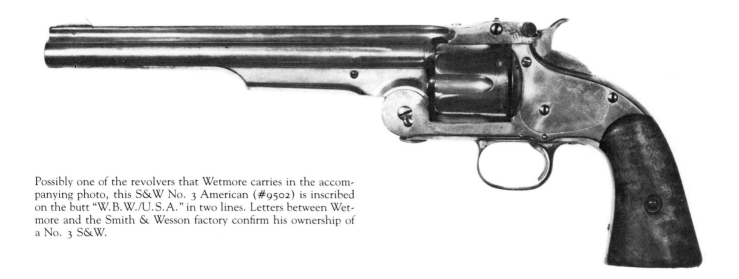

Possibly one of the revolvers that Wetmore carries in the accompanying photo, this S&W No. 3 American (#9502) is inscribed on the butt "W.B.W./U.S.A." in two lines. Letters between Wetmore and the Smith & Wesson factory confirm his ownership of a No. 3 S&W.

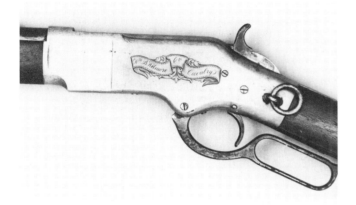

Close-up of the left sideplate of Lt. Wetmore's Winchester M1866 carbine (#101215), almost certainly the same '66 he holds in the photo of him. (Courtesy Mr. Herb Glass, Jr.)

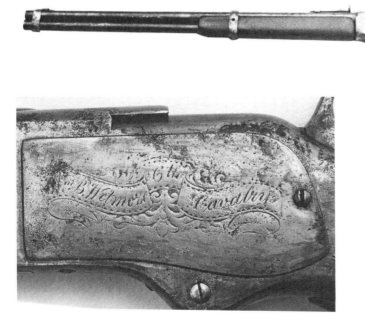

Lt. Wetmore's M1873 Winchester .44 carbine (#2875). Although the gun has been abused during the last century, his name and regiment are still visible inscribed on the left sideplate.

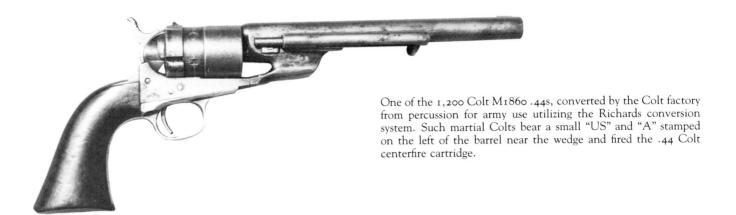

One of the 1,200 Colt M1860 .44s, converted by the Colt factory from percussion for army use utilizing the Richards conversion system. Such martial Colts bear a small "US" and "A" stamped on the left of the barrel near the wedge and fired the .44 Colt centerfire cartridge.

Frame, cylinder, and loading gate from a Colt M1860 Richards conversion, found on the site of the post dump at Ft. Bliss, Texas.

fire load which carried a 205 grain bullet and a 25 grain powder charge. Aside from the general break-open design, the revolver differed from earlier Smith & Wessons in various details: the hammer-activated cylinder bolt, for instance, was housed within the frame instead of the topstrap, and a conventional trigger and guard replaced the usual sheath trigger.[14]

An Ordnance Department order in May of 1871 stipulated that a preponderance of the .44s go to Omaha, Leavenworth, and Benecia for distribution in the departments of the Platte, the Missouri, and the Pacific respectively. The first units to receive the new guns were J Company of the First Cavalry, then at Medicine Bow, Wyoming Territory: J Company of the Third, en route to Camp McDowell, Arizona; and L Company of the Fifth, stationed at Fort McPherson, Nebraska; a quantity also went to the Fourth Cavalry adjutant at Fort Richardson, Texas. By the fall of 1871 limited numbers of the new .44s were in use by selected companies of all cavalry regiments except the Eighth, Ninth, and Tenth. In many instances both blued and nickeled revolvers were issued to the same company for side by side testing. During the summer of 1871, for example, Companies A, B, C, D, J, and K of the Fourth Cavalry in Texas each had one nickeled and five blued revolvers for trial.[15]

Government sales of the Smith & Wesson American to individual troopers evidently began in June of 1871, with the blued arms bringing $14.25 and the nickeled $15.25. Omaha Depot sold a total of 26 in 1871 and 1872, and an "O. O. Howard," probably General Oliver Otis Howard, brought two in July of 1872 from the Ordnance Agency in New York.[16]

In the last quarter of 1871 a new cartridge arm, officially listed as "Colt's, for metallic ammunition, cal. .44," began reaching units stationed on the frontier. Although Colt's front-loading Thuer conversion had encountered little more than official disinterest, the expiration of Rollin White's patent allowed the Hartford firm to work on a conversion using conventional cartridges loaded from the rear, and this conversion was to prove far more successful with the military. Designed by C. B. Richards of Colt and patented in July of 1871, this system involved cutting away the rear of the cylinder, thus exposing the rear of the chambers, and fitting into the empty space a circular "breech-plate" which carried the firing pin and loading gate. A spring-loaded ejector-rod assembly, positioned along the lower right side of the barrel, replaced the percussion loading lever. Internal changes included recutting the ratchet at the rear of the cylinder and installing a new pawl with two bearing surfaces instead of one. The cartridge this conversion chambered was another .44 centerfire load, termed the ".44 Colt"; it held a 210 grain bullet and 23 to 28 grains of powder, but with its longer, fatter case it was not interchangeable with the .44 Smith & Wesson.[17]

In January of 1871, some six months before Richards got his patent, the Colt firm submitted a prototype of his conversion to the Ordnance Department, which soon ordered 1000 Model 1860 Army Colts altered accordingly. Ultimately just over 1200 Colts went to the factory at Hartford for conversion, 50 of which had a "Locke Safety notch" added to the hammer.[18]

The first of the converted .44s were issued late in 1871 to companies of the Second Cavalry, scattered through Nebraska and Wyoming, and to the Sixth Cavalry in Kansas. By February of 1872 additional conversions had gone to A and D Companies of the Ninth Cavalry and B and L Companies of the Fourth, all serving in Texas. In April of that year the commandant of San Antonio Arsenal requested 20 such guns for sale to officers in his department. Within six months still more Colt conversions had reached various companies of the Third and Fifth Cavalry.[19]

It was undoubtedly this conversion that a first sergeant in the Fifth Cavalry was referring to when he wrote to the Colt concern from Camp Verde, Arizona Territory, in January of 1873:

In regard to your improved Army Revolver it is superior to all other Pistols used here and it is considered the best arm of the kind ever invented by every Person that has used them in this Territory, as far as I have used them I can say without the least hesitation they are the strongest and most accurate shooting pistol I have ever used and I have been useing different modeled pistols in the army for 12 years. I consider them equal if not superior to the Winchester Rifle and when they become better known I would not wonder if they would supercede all Rifles that carry a ball under Cal. 44. they have not up to this time become introduced to the Miners Packers Scouts Teamsters and others in the remote Territories and when the above parties see them in the hands of Soldiers they offer such fabulous prices that the soldiers as a general rule sell them although they have to pay the Government $50.00 for them if lost.

The only trouble I have noticed by close observation in your Pistol for Army use is haveing to carry it at a half cock now the U.S. Government have on hand a large amount of pistol belt Holsters which was made for the old pattern Colts pistol and Remmington which is still issued to Troops and will be for years to come and it is impossible to button the flap of the Holster with one of your new modeled

pistols in it when at half cock to obviate this I have the men to carry only 5 loads in their pistols and let the hammer down so the firing bolt will enter the empty chamber . . .[20]

Curiously the Remington .50 caliber rolling-block pistol, first choice of the St. Louis Ordnance Board, was the last of the three experimental handguns to reach the troops. Instead of paying cash for this arm, the Ordnance Department sent 5000 unused Remington New Model .44s to the home factory in Ilion, and got 5000 single-shot pistols in return. By March of 1872 48 of them had gone to F Company of the Fourth Cavalry, but the unit had no cartridges to fit; the big .50 caliber rounds, loaded with 320 grain bullets and 30 grains of powder, were even slower in coming than the pistols. In fact, appreciable numbers of the guns did not get to frontier garrisons until the final three months of 1872. At that time there were 329 in use among four companies of the First Cavalry, then in Washington Territory, with another 83 assigned to G Company of the Fifth in Arizona, and 82 more with M Company of the Sixth. Supply officers for the Sixth probably greeted the Remingtons with mixed emotions, for they then had to contend with providing ammunition not only for the big single-shots, but also for the Colt conversions, the Smith & Wesson .44s, and the numerous .44 Colt and Remington percussion revolvers already in service. Although the chief of ordnance had recalled most of the .36 caliber Navy Colts in the spring of 1871, there were still enough of them left in service to require periodic issues of their ammunition.[21]

In the spring of 1873 many additional single-shot Remingtons went to the frontier; by the end of June just over 1500 of the big pistols were in use, principally by the First, Second, Fifth, and Sixth regiments. The Fifth and Sixth also had substantial numbers of Smith & Wessons, as did the Fourth and Seventh. By the close of 1873, however, the days of the experimental handguns were numbered.[22]

THE COLT AND SMITH & WESSON .45s

More than a year earlier, in September and October of 1872, three new Smith & Wesson .44s and a new cartridge Colt with open-top frame had come to the Ordnance Department for trial. Tests of the Smith & Wessons had barely concluded when, in November of 1872, still another new Colt arrived for trial; with its solid frame this arm was a distinct departure from the company's well-established but less rugged open-top guns. The solid-frame Colt was chambered for the .44 Smith & Wesson Russian cartridge, a load which would prove one of the most accurate of its era. But the Ordnance Department required that any new hand-

First Cavalry troopers conduct saber drill, probably in the early
1870s. Accounts of army campaigns against Indians in the 1850s
contain fairly frequent mention of the use of sabers, but the weapon
was seldom used in campaigns in the West after the Civil War.
(Courtesy National Archives)

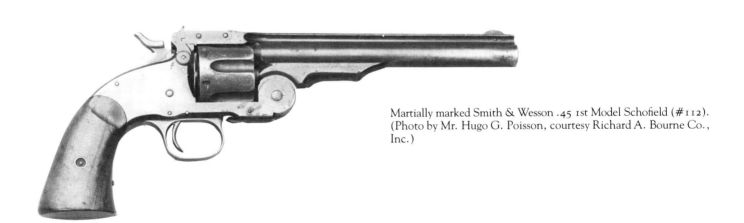

Martially marked Smith & Wesson .45 1st Model Schofield (#112).
(Photo by Mr. Hugo G. Poisson, courtesy Richard A. Bourne Co.,
Inc.)

guns submitted be chambered for the .44 American
round, so the Colt went back to the factory for the
installation of another cylinder.[23]

When tests of the solid-frame Colt ended in late
December, Ordnance Captain John R. Edie, comparing it to the three Smith & Wessons, reported that:

the better working of the Colt's is noticeable
throughout. No difficulty has been found with it,
while the Smith & Wesson has several times clogged
to such an extent as to render it almost impossible

to cock it. This clogging is most liable to occur in
cold and dry weather, when the fouling is allowed
to harden on the piece. . . . A great objection to
this arm is the difficulty of dismounting for cleaning
and reassembling it. Though [recently] improved in
this respect . . . soldiers generally would still find
it complicated. The only superiority it can claim
over the Colt's, is the greater rapidity of ejecting
the empty cases. I think that in case of poor ammunition and the bursting of the heads of cartridges
in the two arms, the Smith & Wesson could more

readily be relieved from the consequent clogging than the Colt's.

[But] In the Colt's the number of the parts is less, they are more simple and stronger, and are not subjected to as great strains as those in the Smith & Wesson. It can be dismounted for cleaning by drawing one screw and slipping out the base-pin, and reassembled with the same ease . . . I have no hesitation in declaring the Colt's revolver superior in most respects, and much better adapted to the wants of the Army than the Smith & Wesson.

Edie also found the Colt more accurate: at 50 yards the arm gave an absolute mean deviation of 3.11 in., in contrast to the 4.39 in. given by one of the Smith & Wessons.[24]

Such a report would normally have prompted an immediate contract for the Colt, but proponents of the Smith & Wesson had yet another gun to offer for consideration, one put together by Major George W. Schofield of the Tenth Cavalry. Impressed with the American model's rapid ejection, Schofield had acted as sales agent for it, purchasing at least 111 from the factory between September of 1870 and April of 1871; in all likelihood he sold a goodly number of these to fellow officers as personal sidearms. Then, in June of 1871, Schofield patented one of two modifications to the Smith & Wesson design: a barrel catch mounted on the frame instead of on the top strap. His simplified ejection system was protected by a second patent, issued in April of 1873.[25]

By the spring of 1873 official opinion leaned heavily toward the solid-frame Colt, but the Ordnance Department was still willing to examine Schofield's arm and any other new revolvers that might come to hand. In fact, Captain Edie tested a Sharps revolver and a Smith & Wesson of variant design in March, but neither proved promising enough for further experiment. By May of 1873, however, two of Schofield's revolvers had reached Edie's hands for trial. At least one of them had a newly designed double ratchet for rotating the cylinder which Edie noted with approval, but as he expressed it in his report, the Schofield was nevertheless:

a revolver with a goodly number of small parts, always liable to be broken and lost. The number of parts, as compared with the Smith & Wesson, is reduced by one only in the whole revolver, still leaving it objectionable for troops, in comparison with a weapon of a less number and more simple ones.[26]

Although Schofield would be heard from again, Edie's unfavorable report removed the last objection to the purchase of the solid-frame Colt. Thus in late July of 1873 Ordnance and Colt officials signed a contract for 8000 samples of the handgun destined to become the most famous of its time—the Colt Single Action Army revolver. Government inspectors accepted delivery of the first 1000 in November of 1873, and by late March of 1874, when Colt completed its contract, 671 were in the hands of the Tenth Cavalry, 168 were assigned to the Second, and 80 to the Fourth.[27]

As initially issued the Single Action Army had a 7 1/2 in. barrel, a side-rod ejector, and a fluted six-shot cylinder, chambered for a new .45 caliber centerfire cartridge recommended by the Ordnance board conducting the long-arms trials of 1872–73. The load was a potent one, comprising 30 grains of powder behind a 250 grain bullet. Internally the arm was much the same as the 1860 Army, but it did have the double-bearing-surface pawl and, more important, a bushing between the cylinder and cylinder pin to allow free and easy rotation. Due to its grip contour and long, low hammer spur, the Colt was easy to handle and fast to cock; the gun's handling qualities, in fact, constituted one of its most obvious advantages over the Smith & Wesson. As Edie had written early in 1873 after comparing one with the other, the Colt was "a much pleasanter weapon to handle [and] its working appears freer and easier."[28]

Additional numbers of the new Colts went to frontier regiments between March and June of 1874; by mid-year the Sixth and Seventh Cavalry were using them almost exclusively. As was the case with long arms, however, older handguns remained in service well after the arrival of newer arms. In June of 1874, for example, cavalry troops on frontier duty still carried large numbers of Colt and Remington .44 percussion revolvers, plus more than 1400 Remington single-shot pistols and lesser numbers of Smith & Wesson Americans and Colt .44 conversions. By March of 1875 one company of the First Cavalry and three companies of the Fifth were still carrying the .50 caliber single-shot Remingtons, while two more companies of the Fifth relied upon Colt conversions. Fewer than 100 Smith & Wesson Americans remained in use at that time, scattered throughout several regiments. A year later Ordnance returns for all ten cavalry regiments included only negligible quantities of the experimental handguns; the 49 Colt M1860 and 60 Remington percussion .44s still carried on the books probably lay unused in the arms racks. In short, the Colt .45 and the Schofield had effectively displaced the older guns.[29]

For the adverse report on Schofield's revolver in May of 1873 had not deterred him from pressing for a War Department order. In January of 1874 an Ordnance board found itself confronted with yet another arm of Schofield's design, and this time the major

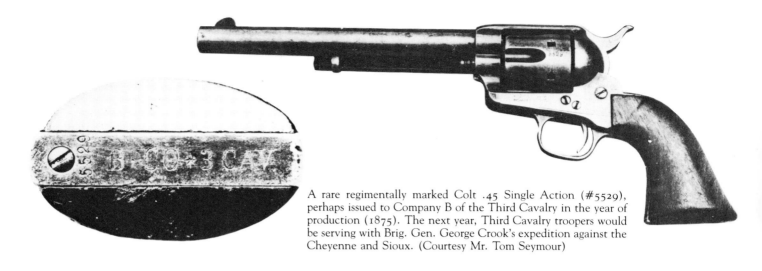

A rare regimentally marked Colt .45 Single Action (#5529), perhaps issued to Company B of the Third Cavalry in the year of production (1875). The next year, Third Cavalry troopers would be serving with Brig. Gen. George Crook's expedition against the Cheyenne and Sioux. (Courtesy Mr. Tom Seymour)

"Private Jeremiah J. Murphy/3rd U.S. Cavalry/1876" is inscribed between the rings on the scabbard accompanying this U.S. M1860 cavalry saber, made by Ames in 1864. Murphy was awarded the Medal of Honor for his action on 17 March 1876 when, during an engagement with the Sioux on Powder River, he made a heroic effort to rescue a wounded companion from within enemy lines. (Although known to collectors as the M1860, government purchases of this light cavalry saber began as early as 1858.) (Courtesy Mr. Charles L. Hill, Jr.)

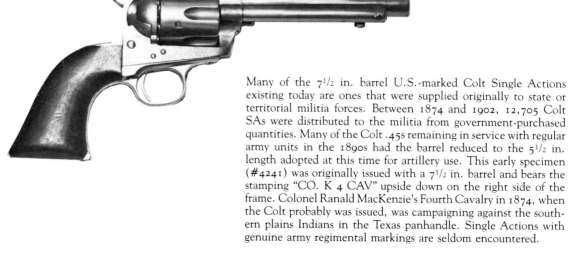

Many of the 7½ in. barrel U.S.-marked Colt Single Actions existing today are ones that were supplied originally to state or territorial militia forces. Between 1874 and 1902, 12,705 Colt SAs were distributed to the militia from government-purchased quantities. Many of the Colt .45s remaining in service with regular army units in the 1890s had the barrel reduced to the 5½ in. length adopted at this time for artillery use. This early specimen (#4241) was originally issued with a 7½ in. barrel and bears the stamping "CO. K 4 CAV" upside down on the right side of the frame. Colonel Ranald MacKenzie's Fourth Cavalry in 1874, when the Colt probably was issued, was campaigning against the southern plains Indians in the Texas panhandle. Single Actions with genuine army regimental markings are seldom encountered.

This view of Lt. Col. George Custer (seated) and several of his Indian scouts has been cited as evidence supporting the theory that scouts were issued nickel-plated Colt Single Actions rather than ones with the standard blued and case-hardened finish. But recent study has refuted this theory quite conclusively. It's far more likely that existing nickled U.S.-marked Colt SAs were once militia guns or were specimens purchased by officers for personal use. The rolling-block rifle in the foreground may be Custer's Remington sporter. (Courtesy Montana Historical Society)

would not be put off. In presenting his case to the board Schofield found support in the opinions of several line officers: although Captain Miles Keogh of the Seventh Cavalry termed the Smith & Wesson "too complicated and constantly out of repair," Captain George Yates of the same unit, whose company was testing Remington single-shot pistols, declared that for a campaign against hostile Indians he would choose "the new Springfield carbine and the Smith & Wesson revolving breech loading pistol calibre .44, and feel that I was as well armed as any company in the world." Other officers were willing to buy Smith & Wessons with their own money, testimony enough of their faith in the design. Aside from the preference of individual officers for the Smith & Wesson, Schofield enjoyed considerable influence with the War Department. His brother, Major General John Schofield, was a close associate of General Sherman's, had served as acting secretary of war in the late 1860s, and was subsequently to command the Division of the Missouri.[30]

Thus in June of 1874, after giving Schofield every opportunity to "explain, correct, withdraw and introduce modifications in his plans," the board rendered a favorable opinion of his weapon:

> Major Schofield's revolver is well suited to the military service, and [the board recommends] that a limited number of these pistols be placed in the hands of troops for comparative trial with the Colt and Smith & Wesson revolvers now in service; and that, as far as possible, the different pistols be tried side by side in the same commands.[31]

As a result of this report the Ordnance Department contracted with Smith & Wesson in September of 1874 for 3000 Schofields at $13.50 each. A second contract for another 3000 was signed in March of

Capt. Frederick W. Benteen's 7¹/₂ in. Colt .45 (#60991) inscribed on the backstrap "F. W. Benteen, 9th Cav." It originally had a blued and case-hardened finish and was one of 20 Colt .45s delivered to the government inspector at the Colt plant on December 6, 1880, but it bears no "U.S." stamp on the frame. It may have been nickel plated to fill Benteen's special order for a personal sidearm, or he may have had it plated at a later date. Benteen previously had served with the Seventh Cavalry under Custer during the regiment's ill-fated 1876 campaign against the Sioux and Cheyennes. Service revolver cartridges for the Colt Single Action, S&W .44 No. 3, and S&W .45 Schofield were issued in cardboard packages containing 12 rounds, as shown here. (Courtesy the Spaulding Collection)

1875, even before Smith & Wesson had completed delivery of the first lot.[32]

The fact that Ordnance officers were taking delivery of the new Colt .45s, and would soon be accepting shipments of Schofields, did not prevent them from testing other revolvers submitted as possible service arms. In December of 1874, for instance, officers at Springfield Armory had occasion to test samples of a .44 caliber solid-frame single-action revolver made by Forehand & Wadsworth, successors to Ethan Allen & Co. The design was basically sound, but the ejector proved unsuitable for cavalry use; as the official report phrased it, the arm's other defects were "not so much in kind as in degree: feeble springs . . . shallow stop notches . . . backward rotary motion of the cylinder . . . defective working of the breech gate . . . no safety notch."[33]

Obviously the Forehand & Wadswoth posed no threat to the Schofield. Late in February of 1875 the chief of ordnance noted that the first few Schofields would be ready for issue by April; these went to 45 troopers of F Company, Ninth Cavalry, stationed at Fort Clark, Texas, and 95 more went to men of the Tenth Cavalry. By mid-1875 Ordnance officers had issued more than 550 to the regulars. Colonel Ranald MacKenzie of the Fourth Cavalry took an immediate liking to Schofield's design and requested 1000 for use by his regiment. By September of 1875 his troops, then scattered through Texas and Indian Territory, had joined men of the

Ninth and Tenth in field-testing Schofield's arm alongside the Colt .45. In addition Ordnance depots in the West sold a total of 12 Schofields to individual officers between May and December of 1875. Government sale of the single-action Colt was more brisk; western depots sold a total of 37 in that year.[34]

Although the Schofield was a .45 caliber arm, it had a shorter cylinder than the Colt and would not accept the long and powerful .45 Colt cartridge. Because of this Frankford Arsenal had begun production of a shorter round early in 1875 which would chamber in both revolvers. Somewhat less potent than the Colt load, the .45 Schofield cartridge contained 28 grains of powder behind a 230 grain bullet. Initially the Ordnance Department issued the longer Colt and shorter Schofield rounds side by side, but this soon led to problems. As Captain Charles King showed in his semifictional *Trials of a Staff Officer*:

X. had been ordered to send [Captain Egan] five thousands rounds of Colt's revolver ball-cartridges, and he did so. One blissful June morning the telegraph operator at the post darted in to X. with a dispatch from the chief ordnance officer at Omaha. "Captain Egan reports that the cartridges you sent him will not fit his pistols. . . ." Ten minutes after came another from "Teddy" himself: "Cannot use the cartridges; all too long." Then in came the colonel with a dispatch from department head-quarters, and a perturbed expression on his face. "Mr. X., what is the matter with the cartridges sent Captain Egan? The adjutant-general is after us with a sharp stick."

X. meantime summoned the ordnance-sergeant, and that veteran glances over the papers and explains the matter in a dozen words. "He's been trying to use Colt's revolver cartridges in his Smith & Wessons, sir," and so it proved. The "revolver ball-cartridge" is made to fit both the Colt and the Smith & Wesson, whereas the "Colt's revolver ball-cartridge" can be used only in the Colt. This information was telegraphed at once to the captain in the field and the explanation wired to Omaha, but meantime head-quarters had been racked to its foundation at a discovery of so alarming a nature. Dispatches had been sent all over the country to cavalry company commanders directing them to test their cartridges in Smith & Wesson pistols. . . .[35]

Whether Schofield or Colt, the army's revolvers proved difficult to keep in service. In November of 1875 the War Department issued the following circular:

> The Chief of Ordnance reports that during the past fifteen months the loss of revolvers in the Cavalry service has been at the rate of one out of every thirteen of those in the hands of Cavalry soldiers, and that about two thirds of those lost have been carried off by deserters, and have not been paid for, thus entailing heavy expense upon the United States. The attention of commanders of regiments, companies, and posts is therefore called to the necessity of taking the most stringent measures possible to correct this evil, and they are enjoined to adopt the best possible method within reach to avoid leaving these arms in the possession of the men, except at such times as they are required for actual use.[36]

For Ordnance officials the controversy surrounding the relative merits of the Colt and Schofield designs was as much a cause for concern as was the theft of government arms. When Remington submitted its new Model 1875 Army revolver to the military for trial in February of 1876, the Ordnance Department took advantage of the opportunity to test not only the Remington but the Colt and Schofield as well. Presumably a formal comparative test—Colt versus Schofield—would yield a clear indication of which revolver was better suited for combat duty. The single-action solid-frame Remington was mechanically much like the Colt and, as the trials would demonstrate, performed much the same.

While the Schofield showed itself capable of being reloaded much faster than the Colt and the Remington, it suffered most in the rust test, after which it was impossible to bring the hammer to full-cock. The board withheld a final opinion of the Schofield since it was then undergoing field trials, but did make this comment: "The Board finds that in point of workmanship, delicacy and nicety of adjustment and ingenuity of mechanism, this arm presents great recommendations, and believes that it would be in demand by a large class of commissioned officers in time of war." Its conclusion, however, was that "taking all things into consideration, the Board expresses its decided preference for the Colt Army revolver, as the one best adapted to meet all the requirements of the military service."[37]

The second-model Schofields, delivered later in 1876 under the contract of 1875, differed from the first models only in minor details. In most respects—the simple, hook-activated extractor, the frame-mounted barrel catch, and the trigger-activated cylinder bolt—the two models were the same. No army order for the Model 1875 Remington was forthcoming, although the Bureau of Indian Affairs obtained a quantity in the early 1880s for issue to Indian police.[38]

Among cavalrymen a rivalry soon developed regarding the merits of the Schofield and the Colt. The pages of the *Army and Navy Journal*, for example, carried letters on the subject from partisan readers: one correspondent, who signed himself "Veritas," noted in May of 1876 that it took as long to prepare the Colt for loading as it did to actually load the Schofield. In contrast, "Pine Butts" later pointed out that when one wanted to reload only one or two chambers in the Schofield, one still had to eject all six rounds. "How much time has been saved and how much is the advantage now?" he asked. "Will this offset the advantage of a solid frame?"[39]

One comparison of the two revolvers came from Captain O. E. Michaelis, Ordnance officer for the Department of Dakota. In 1877 the captain wrote that:

> The experience of the past year, has shown that the Colt's calibre .45 pistol is a reliable weapon. The Schofield Smith and Wesson Revolvers used in the field, have not proved themselves acceptable to Cavalry officers.
>
> Of course their only claim to superiority over the Colt's, is founded upon their capability of automatic extraction. This feature, however, is attained at the expense of simplicity of mechanism and strength.

Other officers disagreed with Michaelis's statement. Between 1876 and 1878 officers stationed in Texas purchased at least 9 Schofields.[40]

NONSTANDARD HANDGUNS AND CARTRIDGES

Some officers avoided the controversy between the two government revolvers by procuring commercial handguns of their own choice. These commercial arms were usually revolvers, but on occasion a different type of pistol—the derringer—made an appearance. In My Life on the Plains George Custer described his preparations for entering an Indian camp for a parley:

So confident did one of the most prudent officers of my command feel in regard to our annihilation by the Indians, that in bidding me good-by he contrived to slip into my hand a small pocket Derringer pistol, loaded, with the simple remark, 'You had better take it, General; it may prove useful to you.' As I was amply provided with arms, both revolvers and rifle, and as a pocket Derringer may not impress the reader as being a very formidable weapon to use in Indian warfare, the purpose of my friend in giving me the small pocket weapon may not seem clear. It was given to me under the firm conviction that the Indians would overwhelm and massacre my entire party; and to prevent my being captured, disarmed, and reserved for torture, that little pistol was given to me in order that at the last moment I might become my own executioner—an office I was not seeking, nor did I share in my friend's opinion.

In his letter to Colt in January of 1873, a first sergeant in the Fifth Cavalry, then in Arizona Territory, noted that: "in regard to the Derringers I wanted made . . . I have now ordered a pair of your Cal. 41 from Messrs Schuyler Hartley & Graham of New York which will suit me just as well except it will not be quite so easy to get ammunition." (Presumably the sergeant had earlier requested a specially made pair of .44 caliber derringers, chambering the same cartridge as that for the converted Colt revolvers.) Writing in 1876 William Blackmore, in his introduction to Col. Richard Irving Dodge's The Plains of the Great West, noted that:

Even officers of the United States have not disdained when engaged in Indian warfare to carry with them a small pocket Derringer pistol, loaded, to be used in the event of capture as a dernier ressort, so as to escape by self-inflicted death the torture to which captives are invariably subjected.[41]

Privately purchased revolvers, however, were more in evidence than were derringers. And whatever they were, the revolvers George Custer carried with him into the valley of the Little Bighorn were not standard issue. Lt. Edward S. Godfrey of K Company, who was with Benteen's column during the fight, later described Custer's handguns as "two Bulldog, self-cocking, English, white-handled pistols, with a ring in the butt for a lanyard." And Sergeant Windolph of H Company specifically mentioned Custer's "two short 'bull-dog' revolvers." Manufactured by P. Webley & Sons of Birmingham, England, the "British Bull Dog" enjoyed brisk sales in the West during the 1870s. It was a solid-frame, five-shot, double-action, pocket-size revolver with a 2½ in. barrel and parrot-beak butt. However, the genuine Webley Bulldog had no provision for a lanyard ring, so Custer may have carried another type of British double-action, such as Webley's "Royal Irish Constabulary" revolver. On the market by 1868, the Webley R.I.C. had a square butt with lanyard ring and an unfluted six-shot cylinder, usually adapted for the .442 Webley or .450 centerfire loads. Aside from its lanyard ring, the distinguishing external feature of this arm was that the locking notches were near the front of the cylinder rather than the rear. Although a 4½ in. barrel was standard, shorter barrels were evidently available. Custer's preference for a nonstandard firearm may be explained in part by his comment to Capt. James W. Reilly, chief ordnance officer at Lt. Gen. Philip Sheridan's headquarters, in which he cited the "shortness of our revolver handle" in apparent reference to the Colt Single Action and the better proportions of English revolvers.[42]

Custer was hardly the only officer to carry nonissue weapons. In 1877, a trader claimed he had seen in the hands of one of the refugee Sioux braves in Canada a handsome English pattern revolver with the name of Miles W. Keogh, Seventh Cavalry, inscribed on the grip. Captain Keogh lost his life on the Little Bighorn with Custer. (Years ago a heavily rusted Moore open-top .32 rimfire revolver, its barrel broken off and several of its chambers still loaded, was dug up on the bluffs overlooking the Little Bighorn.) Captain Michaelis owned a double-action Colt Lightning, introduced early in 1877. Even more popular as an item of private purchase was the bigger Colt double-action Frontier revolver of 1878, which, unlike the Lightning, would accept the government's .45 caliber service load. Some of these purchases probably resulted from the large display advertisements for the arm that appeared in the Army and Navy Journal. In September of 1879 surgeon George C. Moran, writing from Camp Thomas in Arizona, ordered from the factory a nickel-plated gun with 7½ in. barrel and "walnut or hard rubber stock—whichever you think will stand this excessively dry climate best." Three months later Lt. M. H. Kendall of the Sixth Cavalry, also in Arizona, ordered a pair of the same. A man of more expensive tastes was Lt. William H. Smith of the Tenth Cavalry, who wrote the company early in 1884 to ask for the price of a pair of silver-plated and engraved double-actions with checkered ivory grips.[43]

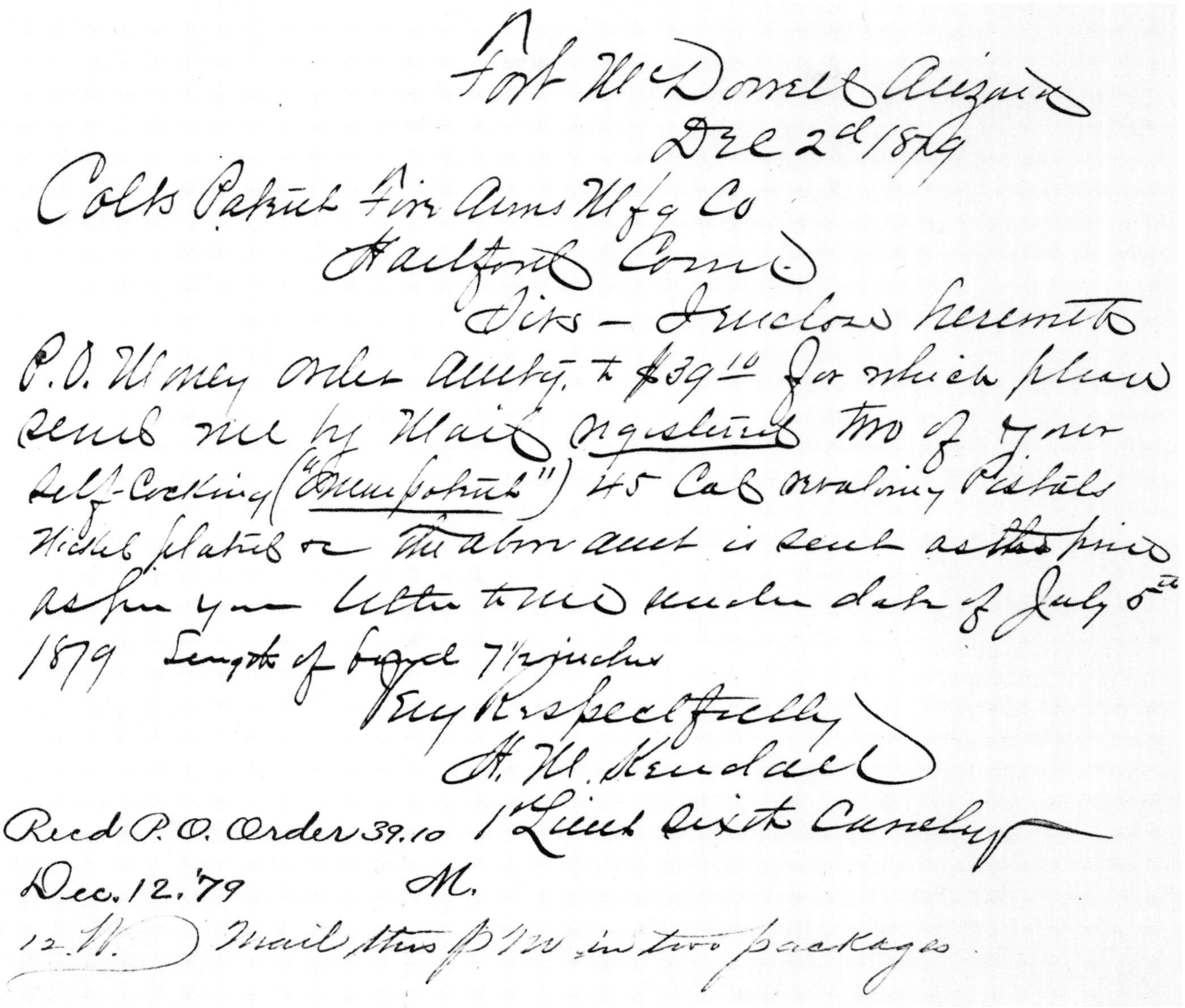

[handwritten letter reproduction]

Fort McDowell Arizona
Dec 2d 1879

Colts Patent Fire Arms Mfg Co
Hartford Conn)
Sirs — I inclose herewith
P.O. U/ money order amtg. to $39.10 for which please
send me by Mail registered two of your
Self-Cocking ("Omnipotent") 45 Cal revolving Pistols
Nickel plated or the above amt is sent as the price
as per your letter to me under date of July 5th
1879 Length of barrel 7½ inches
Very Respectfully
H. M. Kendall
1st Lieut Sixth Cavalry

Recd P.O. Order 39.10
Dec. 12.79   M.
12.W.   ) Mail these p/m in two packages.

Lieutenant Kendall's letter from Arizona ordering a pair of nickeled .45 M1878 Colts with 7½ in. barrel length. The nickname "Omnipotent" for this model was coined by the firm of B. Kittredge of Cincinnati, but was not widely used. A very few M1878s are known with the word etched on the side of the barrel. (Courtesy Connecticut State Library)

Army officers undoubtedly owned other types of handguns as well, among which may have been a few examples of the self-extracting Merwin & Hulbert. This revolver was based on a number of patents issued between 1874 and 1877, the most important of which was that granted to the well-known Daniel Moore in December of 1874. The distinctive feature of this patent, and of the arm itself, was the powerful extraction system, a desirable advantage in the days of copper cartridges. In the Merwin & Hulbert the interlocked barrel-cylinder assembly rested on a long cylinder pin, with the cartridge rims engaged by a fixed ring on the face of the standing breech. Pulling back a latch at the front of the bottomstrap permitted the shooter to rotate the barrel on the cylinder pin; as the barrel rotated, screw threads on the pin automatically forced barrel and cylinder to slide forward a short distance, thereby starting the fired cases from the chambers. The shooter then pulled the barrel straight forward to allow the cases to fall free.[44]

The revolver was actually manufactured by Hopkins & Allen, but was stamped with the distributor's name, "Merwin Hulbert & Co.," and was generally known as such. Merwin & Hulbert displayed a prototype of this arm at the Philadelphia Exposition of 1876, where it first attracted the attention of the military. Not until the close of 1877, however, did a sample of the arm reach the Ordnance Department for formal tests. The official report of the trials, published in January of 1878, concluded with the statement that "on the whole, the Board regards this as a very good pistol, it having endured the tests in a fairly satisfactory manner." Although the Ordnance Department did not purchase any of the guns for field trials, Merwin & Hulbert subsequently advertised it in the *Army and Navy Journal.*[45]

One major reason for the Merwin & Hulbert's failure to gain military acceptance was that cavalrymen and Ordnance officials were satisfied with the Colt single-action; the few complaints directed toward it from the field came principally from those favoring the Smith & Wesson. With any of these revolvers, however, the owner who persisted in loading all six chambers rather than five was risking serious accident. Newspaper correspondent John Finerty, who accompanied George Crook's column against the Sioux and Cheyenne in 1876, learned this lesson the hard way: while remounting after a rest halt, Finerty's carbine muzzle struck the hammer of his revolver, which had been resting on a live cartridge. "An explosion followed. I felt as if somebody had hit me a vigorous blow with a stick on the right rear of my pantaloons, and my horse . . . reeled under the shock." Captain Guy Henry galloped back: "Is the bullet in your person?" he asked. "I don't know," the Irishman replied. "Then, by Jove, it is about time you found out," Henry answered, and rode away laughing.[46]

By the late 1870s another dimension had been added to the question of cavalry armament. The situation was perhaps best summed up by a correspondent of the *Journal*, "Cavalry Man," who wrote in 1878 that:

The "Colt's Improved" and the "Smith and Wesson Schofield improved," are both good, both have their advocates, and no serious complaints can be brought against either, and I think that in a fight one is just as good as the other . . . [but] the pistol for a cavalry man is the one suggested by Capt. J. W. Reilly, Ord. Dept., viz.: A Pistol that will throw buck shot— or buck and ball. Such a pistol, a six shooter, would be the *ne plus ultra* for a cavalry man. . . .[47]

Multi-ball loads came under official consideration largely because the average cavalryman was a poor shot with a handgun. Target practice, which would have done much to change this fact, was all too infrequent during the 1870s. The difference target practice could make in the cavalryman's effectiveness was demonstrated by an account from the pen of a Seventh Cavalry enlisted man, describing the training he received in 1877:

Mounted target practice is fascinating. The target is made from pieces of hard-tack boxes shaped to resemble a man standing erect. The company is formed in a right front into line, and then the men file off from the right of the line, with horses at a walk. They do not stop their horses, but as they pass the target they try to see how many bullets they can put through the tack man, firing from the shoulder; that means having the muzzle of your revolver held on a level with the shoulder, and then firing as soon as the arm is extended.

As soon as the men get so that they can hit the target with their horses on a walk, at thirty paces from it, they go into a trot, then lope, and at last as fast as their horses can run. It is very exciting . . . and it is considered good shooting to hit a target and load and hit it again, in a distance of not more than forty yards, and your horse on a dead run all the time.

Still, such practice was infrequent. During 1878, in attempts to increase soldiers' chances of striking enemies in close combat, Captain E. M. Wright devoted much effort to the subject of multiball loads. He altered a single-action Colt .45 to a five-shot "buckshot revolver," achieving creditable results with cartridges containing three buckshot; later in the year he devised a lighter two-ball load which would fit the standard Colt and Schofield cylinders. With less powder and lighter projectiles, these new loads were less satisfactory:

With regard to dispersion of fire, which is the true *raison d'etre* of these cartridges . . . at short ranges there is none at all, the bullet hole of each shot nearly coinciding. At longer ranges—75 to 100 yards—there is a considerable dispersion of balls; but they have too little power to do much execution.[48]

Somewhat more promising were the multiball loads developed for the Springfield rifle and carbine, since the longer cases would hold much more powder and lead than those adapted to the revolver. The Ordnance Department sent 10,000 of these multiball rifle cartridges to San Antonio Arsenal in September of 1878.[49]

The army was still not ready to give up on multiball handgun loads, and in December of 1878 an equipment board reported on the following:

Two patterns of smooth bore revolvers for firing multiball or buckshot cartridges . . . one, self cock-

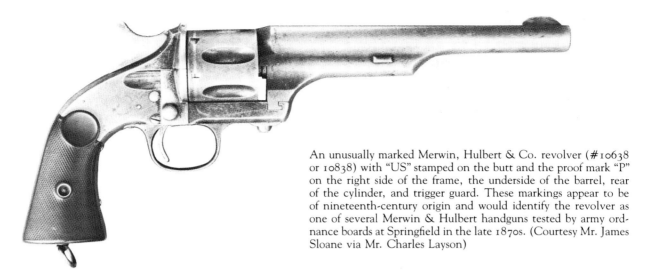

An unusually marked Merwin, Hulbert & Co. revolver (#10638 or 10838) with "US" stamped on the butt and the proof mark "P" on the right side of the frame, the underside of the barrel, rear of the cylinder, and trigger guard. These markings appear to be of nineteenth-century origin and would identify the revolver as one of several Merwin & Hulbert handguns tested by army ordnance boards at Springfield in the late 1870s. (Courtesy Mr. James Sloane via Mr. Charles Layson)

Outfitted for winter campaigning, these men constituted a portion of the troops that put down the final Sioux uprising in the battle at Wounded Knee Creek in South Dakota in December 1890. The revolvers are Colt .45 Single Actions, the cannon a Hotchkiss breechloader, and the knives are M1880 army hunting knives, designed as a camp utility tool rather than as a weapon. (Courtesy Denver Public Library, Western History Dept.)

ing, presented by Messrs. Remington and Co., New York, and the other by Mr. W. C. Dodge, of Washington. While the mechanism of the pistols seems to be good their general merits were not fully tested by the Board. They were the means of demonstrating, however, that at effective distances the destructive power of the pistol is greatly increased by the "multiball" or buckshot cartridges, and the Board is so much impressed with the value of that kind of ammunition that it recommends that it be manufactured and adapted to the Army revolver.

Smith & Wesson agreed to manufacture 1000 .58 caliber smoothbore revolvers of Dodge's design, but nothing came of the board's tests, and production never began. However, another board convened at Springfield in May of 1879 to test a multiball cartridge submitted by Merwin & Hulbert. As in earlier trials the conclusion drawn was that multiball cartridges for both revolver and shoulder arm, at least in .45 caliber, showed too little dispersion at short range, and at long range too little power, accompanied by erratic dispersion. Obviously a larger caliber, suited for a larger-capacity case, would have helped to solve the problem, but the army was unwilling to revert to a larger caliber simply to accommodate a multiball load. By the close of 1879 the Ordnance Department had dropped the whole idea.[50]

For about ten years afterward, while Ordnance officers experimented constantly with the trapdoor Springfield, they did little with the service revolvers. In 1887 a few Schofields were fitted with a safety device and sent to Fort Leavenworth for trial, but this was an isolated and inconsequential incident. The 6000 Schofields the army had ordered between September of 1874 and March of 1875 were later supplemented by over 2000 more, bringing the total Schofield purchase to slightly more than 8000 arms. However, government orders for the Colt single-action .45, extending from 1873 through 1890, amounted to more than 35,000 guns. Issues of this arm, moreover, were not confined to the army, but also spread to the militia, the Treasury Department, the Post Office, and other government agencies. The Colt was obviously the preferred sidearm.[51]

THE .38s

In March of 1889 Capt. William Hall of the Fifth Cavalry wrote the chief of ordnance, requesting 12 Smith & Wesson .38 caliber five-shot hammerless revolvers for use by his troops. His letter went on to say that he had carried "two of these arms for more than a year, 'fired two or three thousand rounds from them and snapped them over five thousand times, without either getting out of repair a single time, and has carried them on his saddle in the field for two months of the time.'" Since Hall was a well-known pistol marksman, his letter prompted the meeting of an Ordnance board in April to test the new Smith & Wesson.

The board also decided to test a new Colt revolver at the same time. This arm, another double-action .38, had been adopted by the navy in 1888. Like the Smith & Wesson hammerless it was a sharp departure from anything the firm had previously made.[52]

To Ordnance officers, of course, double-action revolvers were no novelty. Besides the Starr, Massachusetts Arms, and other double-action revolvers used in the Civil War, later models had, on occasion, found their way to the Ordnance Department for testing. In the summer of 1878, for example, Colt representatives had attempted to interest the military in their double-action Frontier revolver; the attempt failed primarily because of the frequency of misfires, amounting in one instance to seven out of one hundred rounds.[53]

As in the case of the bolt-action rifle, however, what first appeared to be an unsuitable design for service use passed through various modifications and improvements until it could compete successfully with older arms. While the lockwork of Colt's new Navy revolver retained some of the features used in the 1878 Frontier, it also incorporated certain improvements, borrowed in part from earlier European military revolvers. The feature of the new Colt that army officers found most interesting was not its double-action mechanism, but its swing-out cylinder. In principle the Colt swing-out cylinder design was no different from that patented by Charles Hopkins in May of 1862. A vertical arm, or crane, projected downward from the front of the cylinder pin to a longitudinal pivot housed in the bottomstrap; pulling back a spring-loaded latch at the left rear of the frame allowed the cylinder-crane assembly to swing outward and downward on the pivot, through a 90 degree arc, exposing the chambers for loading. The extractor, recessed in the rear face of the cylinder as in the Smith & Wessons, was manually operated by a rearward push on a spring-loaded, centrally positioned rod projecting from the front of the cylinder. The appeal of this design lay in the fact that it permitted loading and reloading at a speed comparable to that of a hinged-frame revolver, but still retained the important advantage of a solid frame.[54]

Daniel Wesson was still pleased with his hinged-frame design, and used it as a basis for the hammerless revolver announced in the spring of 1887. The frame of this arm completely enclosed the hammer, thereby keeping dirt and other foreign matter out of the lockwork. But like the percussion Pettengill revolver, the Smith & Wesson hammerless could only be fired by a long pull on the trigger. To give the shooter the advantage of a short single-action trigger pull, Wesson designed into his lockwork a "hesitation" feature, involving a jointed, two-piece sear; the shooter pulled the trigger in double-action fashion until the lower arm of this sear came into contact with the upper arm, causing additional resistance which the shooter could feel through the trigger. He could then align the sights and squeeze the trigger carefully, exactly as he would with a single-action revolver.

Equally as important was the gun's "grip safety," which constituted its real selling point in the civilian market. A long bar, positioned vertically in the backstrap, had to be forced forward by the heel of the shooting hand before it would allow the hammer to move. When the gun was not grasped in the usual manner for shooting, the bar locked the hammer and prevented the lockwork from functioning. Accidental discharges seldom occurred with this arm.[55]

While members of the Ordnance board that convened in 1889 to test the Colt and Smith & Wesson duly noted the latter's safety feature, they concluded that "by its use accidents will only be partially avoided. A great number of premature discharges take place when the handle of the revolver is grasped by the soldier." The board found the enclosed-hammer design and the hesitation lockwork more important. Regarding the Colt, the board noted that it had "the great advantage of possessing a solid frame, and this is combined with the feature of simultaneous ejection of cartridges, though the ejection is not automatic, as in the Smith & Wesson." Performance of both revolvers in tests for velocity, penetration and recoil, accuracy, rapidity of loading and firing, endurance, and fouling ranged from fair to good. The dust test, however, disabled the Colt as a double-action arm, although it would still function as a single-action weapon. Dust presented no problem for the Smith & Wesson, but the rust test completely disabled it. The board's final opinion was that:

the issue of a limited number of each of these arms would be advantageous, as affording a comparison between the double-acting system and the single-action system in use in the service. Each of the revolvers possesses advantages peculiar to itself, and a competitive test in service would be necessary to determine definitely which is the superior.

Because both arms were .38s instead of .45s, the board took note of a factor which would later assume major importance: "Whether these arms have the necessary stopping power, the board has no means of determining." Where the Colt .45 was concerned, there were no questions about stopping power. A. C. Gould related this incident:

After the Wounded Knee fight, the body of Captain [George] Wallace was found at the entrance of an Indian lodge, and there was every evidence that the officer had sold his life very dearly. Five Indian warriors lay dead around him, each of them with a single bullet wound. The captain had a six-chambered revolver in his hand empty, and it is therefore presumed that, before he was overpowered by the savages, he had a desperate fight, and emptied the revolver upon his adversaries, each shot having fatal effect. The revolver used by Captain Wallace was a Colt .45 army pattern. . . .[56]

Early in 1890 the Ordnance Department ordered 100 Colts and 100 Smith & Wessons for the recommended field trials. Shortly afterward Col. Elmer Otis of the Eighth Cavalry, inquiring about the availability of hammerless Smith & Wessons for his unit, was informed by the chief of ordnance that no new re-

volvers would be issued on a broad scale without being thoroughly field-tested first.[57]

Delivered in the late spring of 1890, the trial revolvers—94 of each were actually issued—went to nine troops of the First, Third, Fifth, Sixth, Eighth, and Ninth cavalry regiments. After some fourteen months of hard field testing, the units turned in the sidearms for study by an Ordnance board which convened in November of 1891. The board's report, filed in January of 1892, left little doubt as to which gun was preferred:

Of the thirteen cavalry officers to whom these revolvers were [issued], eleven express an unqualified preference for the .38 caliber Colt, one for the .38 caliber Smith & Wesson, while one, favoring the .38 caliber Colt above the .38 caliber Smith & Wesson, prefers to either of the smaller calibers the present .45 caliber Colt on account of its heavier bullet and consequent greater stopping power. . . . Of the ninety-four Smith & Wesson so tested seven were unserviceable and could not be fired; of these seven . . . the main springs of two were broken and the remaining five failed through the effect of rust about the cylinder or the safety device. Three others, while not unserviceable, were worked with much difficulty. . . . Of the ninety-four Colts so tested but one was found unserviceable, due to rust on the cylinder. Of the others, the rebound spring in one worked poorly and in two the cylinder was revolved at first with difficulty.[58]

Even so, the Colt was not without defects. One of the features of the Model 1889, carried over from the double-action Frontier of 1878, was a pawl which also served as a cylinder bolt. That part of the pawl which bolted the cylinder had a small bearing surface, subject to battering and wear. The board specifically noted this fact, commenting on the Colt's "insecure locking of the cylinder at the time of firing." As a result Colt submitted a modified revolver in March of 1892, which incorporated a trigger with integral cylinder bolt and a separate "cylinder lock," designed to prevent cylinder rotation when the action was at rest. The rebound spring, which forced the trigger back to its rest position after firing, was also strengthened.[59]

Officially termed the Model 1892, the modified revolver earned the army's approval and a consequent order for 5000 samples. As purchased and issued, the Model 1892 had a 6 in. barrel and a six-shot cylinder which took the .38 Long Colt cartridge. In contrast to the Model 1889, whose cylinder had no locking notches, the cylinder of the M1892 had two sets of notches, which readily distinguished it from the earlier arm. The cartridge carried a 150 grain bullet and 18

.38 Smith & Wesson New Departure (#41401) with 6 in. barrel and martial markings, one of those field tested by the army. (Courtesy Maj. Charles W. Pate)

grains of powder, a notably lighter load than that for the single-action .45s.[60]

By August of 1893 the commander of the Department of the Platte, in referring to the new Colt, could report that "the new revolver has been issued during the year to all the cavalry in the department except the Indian troop. It is very handsome, convenient, and apparently well made, and a decided improvement over the old caliber (.45)." He added, however, that "some defects were developed during the recent competition. These will be investigated. . . ." The subsequent investigation showed that some line officers regarded the mainspring as too weak, but a more general complaint centered on the method used to mount the cylinder in the frame. In the swing-out-cylinder Colts of 1889, 1892, 1894, and several later models, the cylinder rotated to the left and also swung out to the left for loading. In the cavalry, however, the trooper was taught to hold the reins in his left hand and his revolver in his right. To reload, it was easier for the

trooper to switch the revolver to his left hand, which held the reins, than to switch the reins to the hand that held the revolver. A gun held in the left hand was naturally easier to reload if its cylinder swung outward to the right. A majority of cavalry officers, therefore, wanted the cylinder to open to the right. But their collective opinion carried little weight with the Ordnance Department; although the direction of cylinder rotation was later changed from left to right, the cylinder of later models continued to swing open to the left for loading.[61]

Another problem that presented itself in 1893 was that the Model 1892 could be cocked and fired even when the cylinder was not properly locked into the frame. To preclude this eventuality, F. B. Felton of Colt designed and patented an interlock which jammed the trigger unless the cylinder latch was fully seated in its recess in the center of the ratchet. Ordnance officers labeled this improved revolver the Model of 1894, and in April of 1896 sent circulars to San An-

Tenth Cavalry troopers, armed with Colt .38 revolvers and Springfield .45 carbines, take a noon break while escorting Gen. Wesley Merritt's party near St. Marys, Montana, in 1894. (Courtesy Montana Historical Society)

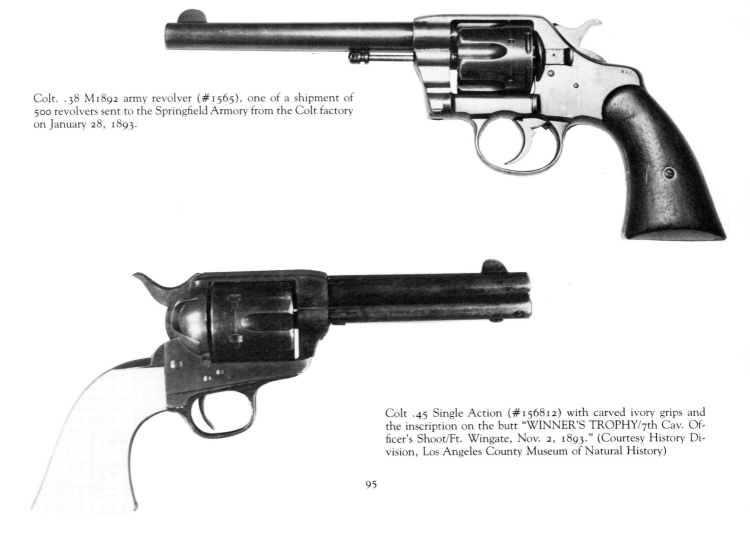

Colt. .38 M1892 army revolver (#1565), one of a shipment of 500 revolvers sent to the Springfield Armory from the Colt factory on January 28, 1893.

Colt .45 Single Action (#156812) with carved ivory grips and the inscription on the butt "WINNER'S TROPHY/7th Cav. Officer's Shoot/Ft. Wingate, Nov. 2, 1893." (Courtesy History Division, Los Angeles County Museum of Natural History)

Troopers of the Sixth Cavalry pose with Springfield .45 trapdoor carbines and Colt .38s in D. Rodocker's photo studio in Winfield, Kansas, in the 1890s.

only 651 single-action Colts and only 3 Schofields to the regulars, but in his annual report for 1895 the chief of ordnance stated that:

> Light [artillery] batteries will be provided with 25 Colt's revolvers to each battery for arming noncommissioned officers and drivers. These revolvers are the caliber .45 pattern recently in service, but have the barrel shortened from 7½ inches (the old length) to 5½ inches.[63]

The Colt single-action .45 was to see even more service during the Philippine Insurrection, when the light bullets from the army's .38s proved incapable of stopping Moro attackers. For Ordnance officers the Philippine experience settled once and for all the question of a suitable caliber for service pistols; the handguns subjected to the trials of 1907 were all of .45 caliber.[64]

Hampered by various mechanical problems, the Colt Model 1892 and subsequent variations never proved entirely satisfactory, and for purposes of commercial sales the Colt concern gladly abandoned the design in favor of the New Pocket–New Police–New Service series of 1894–98. And during the 1890s a new type of handgun appeared which seriously threatened the revolver's half-century of dominance as a military sidearm—the self-loading or semiautomatic pistol. Between mid-1897 and mid-1902 the Ordnance Department tested semiauto pistols by Borchardt, Mannlicher, Mauser, Colt, Luger, and Bergmann, with some interesting results. For example, the report of a test of a .38 caliber Colt-Browning pistol in the spring of 1900, which involved the firing of some 5800 rounds, concluded with this statement:

> The test to which this pistol was subjected was in every way more severe than that to which revolvers have been heretofore subjected, and the endurance of this pistol appears to be greater than that of the service revolver. It possesses further advantages as follows: Very simple construction. It is easy to operate. It is not liable to get out of order. It is capable of a very high rate of fire. It can be conveniently loaded with either hand. It gives a high initial velocity and flat trajectory. It is more accurate than a revolver.

From that time on, the revolver's days as a military sidearm were numbered.[65]

tonio Arsenal and other western outposts directing them to send all the M1892s on hand back to Springfield for conversion to M1894s.[62]

The widespread issue of the double-action Colt .38s during and after 1893 did not put the older single-action .45s completely out of business. Between mid-1892 and mid-1893 the Ordnance Department issued

·PART II·

CIVILIAN ARMS

IN THE MONTHS FOLLOWING the Civil War America shifted its attention to the frontier, where, in quick succession, a number of factors interacted to promote settlement: railroad construction, the elimination of the buffalo as a hindrance and the Indian as a threat, discoveries of new precious-metal deposits, the development of the range-cattle industry, and the movement of farmers onto the Great Plains.

No engineering feat of nineteenth-century America was more significant than the construction of the transcontinental railroad. Army engineers had surveyed potential routes through the West as early as 1853, but sectional rivalries and then the Civil War had delayed actual construction. By the close of 1865, in fact, the Union Pacific had laid only some forty miles of track west of Omaha. But under the direction of engineer General Grenville Dodge and of brothers Jack and Dan Casement, who put track laying on a production-line basis, work progressed rapidly; by the close of 1866 the U.P. rails were nearing the Nebraska-Wyoming border. In the meantime the Central Pacific, building eastward from Sacramento to meet the Union Pacific, had to dig and blast its way through the mighty Sierra Nevadas, a challenge it met largely with the vitality of thousands of Chinese laborers. Finally, in May of 1869, seventy miles northwest of Salt Lake, the two lines were joined with a symbolic golden spike; within a week of the ceremonies, trains were running on the new line daily.

Other railroads were soon pushing their way across the plains. Running out of Kansas City south of the U.P. was the Kansas Pacific, which reached Denver in 1870. Below the K.P. line was the route of the Atchison, Topeka, and Santa Fe, whose rails clambered into Dodge City, Kansas, in 1872. Far above the U.P. was the Northern Pacific, which by mid-1873 extended from St. Paul to Bismarck in the Dakotas.

During construction of the railroads across the prairies the workers had subsisted mainly on buffalo meat brought in by company hunters. In fact, young Bill Cody had earned the nickname "Buffalo Bill" while shooting buffalo for workers on the Kansas Pacific in 1867. In 1871, however, after the improvement in methods for producing leather goods from buffalo hides, the killing of the bison began in earnest. Carried out by professional hide hunters, the slaughter was such that in 1872–73 alone the rails hauled some 1.25 million hides to the East. The railroads themselves promoted this slaughter by offering excursion trips for "sport hunters." One observer described an 1872 excursion thus: "The car windows are opened, and numerous breech-loaders fling hundreds of bullets among the densely crowded and flying masses. . . . Immense carcases of wantonly slain buffalo . . . line the Kansas Pacific Railroad for two hundred miles."

The professional hunters were interested only in the hides: after they stripped them from the carcasses, they left countless tons of meat to rot on the plains. (General Philip Sheridan once remarked that the hide hunters deserved medals for depriving the Indians of their means of subsistence.) But farmers and others found profit in the gathering of buffalo bones for sale to fertilizer factories; in one year, 1874, the Santa Fe shipped 3500 tons of bones east.

The shooting of buffalo on the Overland Trail and along the routes of the western railroads effectively split them into two great herds, the northern and the southern. Gradually the southern herd shifted southward, the hide hunters hounding it through Kansas and Indian Territory into the Texas panhandle, often at considerable peril. As one Kansan wrote in October of 1874: "There has not been any buffalo herds on [the north] side of the Arkansaw since long in July, when the Indians went out on the war path. The south side of the Arkinsaw the Indians try to hold as their hunting grounds. It is dangerous for any buffalo hunters to go south of that river." Nevertheless they persisted, and by 1878 the southern herd had all but disappeared. The bankruptcy of the Northern Pacific during the financial panic of 1873 forestalled, but did not prevent, a similar fate for the northern herd.

The railroads also had their effect on the cattle

business. Civil War veterans returning to Texas found large numbers of rangy longhorn cattle wandering free; in 1866, with no local market for them, Texans started driving them north and east along the Shawnee Trail to Missouri. The following year, however, the Pacific-bound railroads offered the drovers more practical access to the beef-hungry East. In the summer of 1867 Illinois cattle buyer Joseph McCoy built new shipping facilities on the Kansas Pacific line, at the tiny hamlet of Abilene, Kansas. Soon a veritable flood of longhorns was moving north, along a route later famous as the Chisholm Trail.

At the height of the trail-driving season a herd in open country was seldom out of sight of other herds. In the peak year of 1871, an estimated 600,000 cattle plodded north to Kansas. Not all of them went to Abilene; another boom town, Ellsworth, was now on the K.P. route west of Abilene, and south of Ellsworth, on the rival Santa Fe line, the town of Newton was established. In 1872 a spur line joined Newton to Wichita, which sat on the Arkansas River thirty miles to the south. For a few years thereafter Ellsworth and Wichita competed briskly with one another for the bulk of the longhorn trade. But in mid-1875 a new cowtown—Dodge City, on the Santa Fe route in southwestern Kansas—began to claim its share of Texas cattle. Drovers soon blazed a different trail to Dodge, called the Western because it lay a hundred miles west of the Chisholm.

Lying at the end of the long road from Texas, the Kansas cowtowns offered the bored, dusty drovers all the pleasures the trail lacked. The nature of these is suggested by such contemporary comments as "Hell is still in session in Ellsworth," and "Everything goes in Wichita." Just as descriptive was Dodge City's nickname—"Gomorrah of the Plains." Violence was often evident; in a single incident in a Newton dance hall in 1871, four men died by gunfire and four more were wounded. The lawmen hired to keep order in these towns—Hickok, Earp, Masterson, and others—gained wider fame than did such cattle-industry pioneers as McCoy, Charles Goodnight, and John Chisum.

Violence, of course, was not the exclusive property of the cowtowns. It was also prevalent in some of the mining camps which sprang up in the 1870s and 1880s. The discoveries on which these camps rose involved not only gold and silver, but also major copper deposits in Arizona and Montana. During 1875 and 1876, however, the big rush was to the gold-laden Black Hills of Dakota. Gunfire crackled continually; the stage lines that began plying the routes from the railheads at Cheyenne and Bismarck to the Black Hills mining towns found themselves plagued by both highwaymen and Sioux warriors, who regarded the Black Hills as sacred ground. There was violence within the towns as well; in 1876 Wild Bill Hickok was shot in the back in a Deadwood saloon.

Another mining town with violent beginnings was Tombstone, Arizona, built on the site of an 1877 silver strike. Here, in 1881, occurred the famous face-to-face gunfight between the Earps and the Clantons at the OK Corral. Wyatt Earp was no stranger to frontier violence; he had earlier worked as a lawman in both Wichita and Dodge City.

By 1880 Dodge City was one of the two principal Kansas shipping points for Texas longhorns. The other was Caldwell, built near the Kansas-Oklahoma border astride the old Chisholm Trail and now linked to the Santa Fe by a spur line. Herds from Texas continued to come north through the summer of 1885; within two years, however, they almost vanished from the trails. Coincidentally, the years between 1880 and 1885 also witnessed the destruction of the northern buffalo herd. After recovering from the bankruptcy of 1873 the Northern Pacific again started laying rails across the upper plains, reaching the Dakota-Montana line in 1880 and Miles City in 1881. With the railroad came the professional hide hunters, and within four years the Montana herd was little more than a memory.

As the country's railroad network expanded, and as cattlemen found that their herds could survive the winters on more northerly ranges, Texas's prominence as a major beef source diminished. But there were other factors involved in the end of the long trail drives. One was the westward march of farmers who, with their barbed-wire fences, made it increasingly difficult for Texans to find an open road to the north.

The Homestead Act of 1862 had offered farmers 160 acres of government land on the plains at little or no cost. To encourage railroad construction through the area the government had granted large tracts of land to railroad companies, which in turn sold this land to American and European immigrant farmers. Added encouragement for plains farming came with the Timber Culture Act of 1873, which permitted the acquisition of additional land if some of it was used for the cultivation of trees. In most cases, then, the land did not cost much. But even after the buffalo and the Indian were no longer threats, farmers faced other problems. Because of the lack of wood they had to build their houses and barns with blocks of prairie sod. Dried grass and buffalo dung had to serve as fuels. Devastating invasions of grasshoppers periodically ate everything except the mortgage. Working in the farmers' behalf, however, were new inventions and techniques. Improved plow design eased the task of turning the heavy sod, while improved reapers and binders facilitated the gathering of the harvest. Such inventions, coupled with drought-resistant grains and cultivation methods which conserved soil moisture, made great-plains farming not only possible but profitable.

Another invention, designed for farmers by a farmer in 1873, roused the anger of the cattleman—barbed wire. Now farmers and small ranchers could enclose their crops, pasture lands, and water cheaply and effectively. In so doing, however, they cheaply and effectively closed off the open range upon which the cattlemen depended, and also blocked off their routes to rail shipping points. Cattlemen reacted by fencing off large expanses of public grazing land, and by the mid-1880s "fence-cutting wars" were part and parcel of frontier life.

In part these fence-cutting wars were the result of an overcrowded range. With the great buffalo herds and the hostile Indians gone, the cattle barons who had once dominated the prairies had to contend for grass not only with newcomers to the cattle business, but also with sheepmen and farmers. The most telling blow against the open-range cattle empires, however, came from nature itself. The summer of 1886 brought with it a severe drought, and the winter which followed was one of the harshest on record; it wiped out entire herds, bankrupting small ranchers and giant corporate concerns alike. Cattlemen who survived the winter of 1886/87 still had to struggle against the press of farmers, a conflict which flared into violence most noticeably in Wyoming's Johnson County in 1892. Ending in a victory for the homesteaders, the Johnson County war was symbolic of the waning influence of the cattlemen.

But even as farmers had learned to adapt, so did the cattle ranchers. They reduced their huge herds to more manageable numbers and controlled them better, now themselves using barbed wire freely for the purpose. They adopted breeding programs to improve the quality of their beef, and also joined stockmen's protective associations to reduce lawlessness.

By the mid-1890s the Wild West was fast disappearing. Plains and mountains were now crisscrossed by railroads, cut up by fences, and roamed by prospectors. Gradually cattlemen, sheepmen, and farmers were learning to live peacefully with one another.

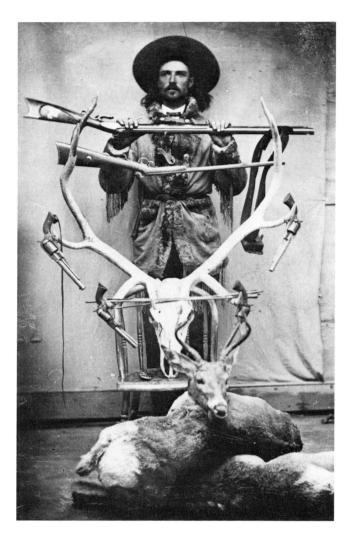

A tintype view of a neatly garbed western hunter. The elk skull makes a convenient rack for a sturdy plains-type percussion rifle with a double-keyed barrel (top) and a Frank Wesson carbine. The revolvers are New Model Remingtons (at top), a Colt M1851 or contemporary copy thereof (lower left), and what appears to be a .38 rimfire E. A. Prescott (lower right). The small pocket revolver on the chair can't be identified. (Courtesy Mr. Herb Peck, Jr.)

Rocky Mountain News (Denver), May 1865.

·3·

RIFLES

Even before the end of the Civil War, arms dealers in the West were able to offer their customers a variety of breech-loading and repeating rifles. But despite the availability of reliable repeaters, another kind of weapon would soon rise to a dominant position on the plains, and maintain that dominance for some fifteen years after the war: the heavy single-shot rifle designed for truly powerful metallic cartridges.

Until the close of the 1860s, however, the long guns most commonly used in the West were muzzle-loaders and moderately powered breechloaders. With the surrender at Appomattox, military-surplus breechloaders reached gun houses on the frontier in great numbers. In 1865 alone, dealers from St. Louis to San Francisco were selling such up-to-date metallic-cartridge arms as the Maynard, the Wesson, the Ballard, the Spencer, and the Henry.[1] Other breechloaders, including the Sharps, the Joslyn, and the Burnside, had reached the frontier before the war, and still others came West immediately afterward, in the hands of discharged veterans.[2]

MUZZLE-LOADERS

Faced with such competition, the popularity of the muzzle-loading rifle declined steadily between 1865 and 1870; yet certain factors kept the muzzle-loader alive even after that time. For some users the choice of a muzzle-loader resulted from personal taste or simple conservatism; for some, it stemmed from economic considerations; and for others (chiefly experienced, far-ranging frontiersmen) it originated in the necessity for dealing with situations peculiar to life on the plains.

Many of the settlers who came west after the war preferred to spend what little money they had on livestock and farm equipment rather than on weapons. To them the muzzle-loading rifle was attractive not only because of its low selling price, but also because of the low prices for powder, caps, and lead. In contrast far-ranging frontiersmen needed a weapon not only simple and easy to repair, but one for which they could get ammunition even in the most remote locations. In addition they needed an arm with enough power and range to deal with almost any emergency. With the notable exception of the .44-77 Sharps and the .50-70 government rounds, the ammunition for most of the breechloaders of the late 1860s was of low or medium power, not really suitable for all-around use on the frontier. The .56-.56 Spencer round, for instance, was usually loaded with a 360 grain bullet and 45 grains of powder; as a consequence it was unable to match the .58 or .69 Minie bullets, backed by 60 to 80 grain powder charges.[3]

This point was vividly demonstrated to Lt. Eugene Ware of the Seventh Iowa Cavalry during his stay at Fort McPherson, Nebraska, in 1865. Ware described his personal long gun variously as a "target rifle, Smith & Wesson, caliber .44," or simply as a "Smith & Wesson carbine," terms often used in the 1860s to denote the Frank Wesson two-trigger single-shot cartridge rifle. One day in early February Ware noticed a lone Indian sitting motionless on his horse on the far side of the Platte River. Since a major war with the Sioux, Cheyenne, and Arapaho was then raging all along the Platte, Ware decided:

> [to] see what effect I could make on him with my target rifle. . . . By throwing up the sights on my target, I pulled on him, but the bullet fell short, as I could see by the dust which rose where it struck. I had scarcely fired my gun when the Indian fired and a bullet went whizzing over my head in a way so familiar that I knew it to be a Belgian rifle-musket. I had heard them often down South. I then made three quick shots, to see if I could reach the Indian, but my rifle would not carry to him. I began to march obliquely back to the post, going somewhat to the left, so as to change the Indian's line of fire, but he got in two shots on me before I got back to the post, to which I went in a leisurely but somewhat interested way. The Indian had a better gun than I had, that is to say, one that would shoot farther. . . . This man had been standing out there

"Beaver Dick," photographed about 1872 by William H. Jackson in front of his tepee with his family. He holds a halfstock muzzle-loading rifle. A half-breed hunter and trapper, he helped guide the Hayden expedition into present Yellowstone National Park in 1872. (Courtesy State Historical Society of Wisconsin)

Charles S. Stobie, handsomely attired for a photo taken in Colorado in 1866. The muzzle-loading fullstock rifle appears sufficiently sturdy for frontier use. (Courtesy Denver Public Library, Western History Dept.)

Two frontiersmen, probably photographed in the late 1860s. Both carry two-key half-stock muzzle-loading rifles. (Courtesy Mr. Herb Peck, Jr.)

Harry Yount, first Yellowstone National Park ranger, photographed north of Berthoud Pass, Colorado, about 1874. His rifle appears to be a percussion over-and-under muzzle-loader. (U.S. Geological Survey photo, courtesy National Archives)

A classic interior view at the Sawtell Ranch in Idaho (1872). The myriad of guns displayed includes Spencer and Sharps carbines, Remington and Colt M1851 and M1860 revolvers, Springfield .50 rifles (one with a commercial capbox inset in the buttstock), what seems to be a British Enfield rifle musket, a muzzle-loading sporting rifle, and others. The three revolvers on the mantel are, from left, a Moore's patent .32 teat-fire, a large-frame Remington, and a Smith & Wesson .44 No. 3. (U.S. Geological Survey photo, courtesy National Archives)

making a target of himself so as to get somebody to come out and fire at him, and I had done exactly what he wanted me to do, and he had got three good shots at me before I was through with him. And I had to thank my stars that it was no worse.[4]

Minie rifles came west in considerable numbers after the Civil War, many of them brought by returning veterans. According to government records, discharged soldiers from California, Colorado, Dakota, Kansas, Nebraska, Nevada, New Mexico, Oregon, and Washington Territory took with them a total of 2115 Springfield "rifled Muskets" (presumably in both .58 and .69 caliber), 157 Enfield rifled muskets, 53 "Har-

per's Ferry Muskets," 24 Whitney rifles, and 14 "United States Rifles" when they left the service. Moreover, the actual number of muzzle-loaders taken from the government by westerners probably far exceeded the official figures.[5]

One veteran, in a letter in which he explained the merits of a telescopic sight, noted the use of muzzle-loading rifles in a remote corner of the Rocky Mountains in 1866–67:

In the year 1865—after the war—I crossed the plains to the Rockies, carrying with me a Sharps rifle, .52-caliber linen cartridge, government caps. The rifle was fitted with a fine Malcolm telescopic sight. The

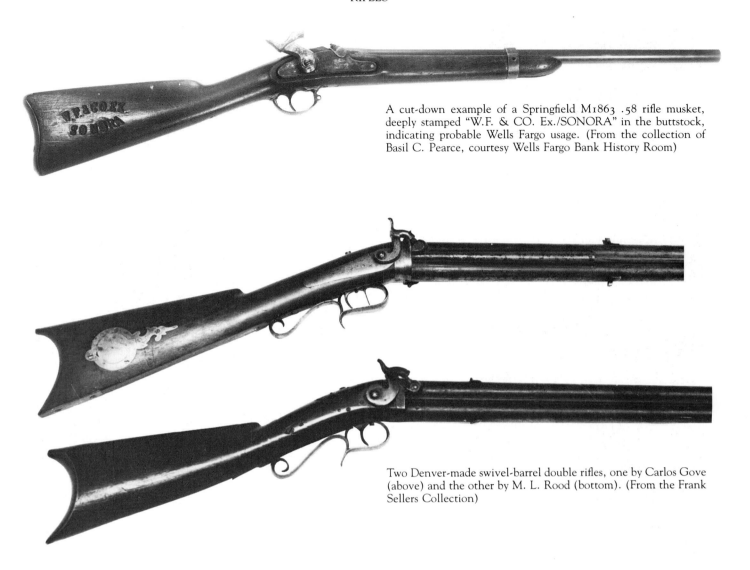

A cut-down example of a Springfield M1863 .58 rifle musket, deeply stamped "W.F. & CO. Ex./SONORA" in the buttstock, indicating probable Wells Fargo usage. (From the collection of Basil C. Pearce, courtesy Wells Fargo Bank History Room)

Two Denver-made swivel-barrel double rifles, one by Carlos Gove (above) and the other by M. L. Rood (bottom). (From the Frank Sellers Collection)

following year found me, with this rifle, camped with a band of hunters and trappers in the Wind River Mountains, at that time a paradise for large game, and scalping Indians. The rifle itself, as well as the telescope, was something of a novelty in that region in those days, and much was the discussion as to the merits and demerits of the telescopic sight. Within a year from the time I joined the band, every one of that little company of hunters and trappers procured, and had fitted, the best Malcolm telescopic sights to their muzzle-loading rifles.[6]

The Malcolm scopes acquired by the trappers may have come from Carlos Gove of Denver, who handled a large assortment of firearms and related items. Although his stock included breechloaders and repeaters, Gove was presumably most proud of his personally manufactured single- and double-barreled muzzle-loading rifles. Advertising in the *Rocky Mountain News* in 1866, Gove repeated an earlier advertisement of 1865, styling himself a "Manufacturer and Dealer in every description of Fire-Arms. . . . P.S.—I keep the Hawkin's Rifle; also, manufacturer of Double, Single and Telescope Rifles which I warrant in point of power and accuracy second to none." At the same time Morgan L. Rood, Gove's chief competitor in Denver, advertised his own "Single, Double and Three Barrel Gain Twist Rifles . . . target rifles and telescopes made to order and warranted." Whether made by Gove or Rood, these single- and double-barreled arms, as well as Rood's three-barrel, were manufactured on a gradually decreasing scale well into the 1870s.[7]

One factor that may have hindered the sale of commercial muzzle-loaders was the ready availability of surplus military arms. In the famous Hayfield Fight of

Rocky Mountain News (Denver), September 1865.

Rocky Mountain News (Denver), April 1866.

1867, during which twenty soldiers and six civilian haycutters held off several hundred Sioux, Zeke Colvin, one of the civilians present, used the .577 Enfield muzzle-loader he had carried through the Civil War. James Lockwood, another participant, wrote later that during the battle an Indian crawled up to a wagon and stealthily took from it a panful of molasses;

> He was seen by a teamster, who, still having one of the old Springfield muzzle-loaders, and being short of ammunition for it, had loaded into it a handful of thirty-two calibre pistol cartridges, copper shells and all. It is hardly necessary to state that this dose did the business for the brave who possessed such an inordinate fondness for sweets.[8]

The arms sold at Leavenworth in 1867 included 320 Enfields and 86 Prussian rifles, as well as 78 Colt revolving rifles; San Antonio Arsenal sold just over 800 Enfields in 1868; and a year later Camp Douglas, Utah, sold 193 "Jaegers."[9]

During the 1868 Indian troubles in eastern Colorado Irving Howbert, a resident of that area, noted that:

> The contest [with the Indians] had been an unequal one from the start. The settlers possessed only a miscellaneous lot of guns, most of which were muzzle-loading rifles, while the Indians were armed with breech-loading Government guns, using metal cartridges. . . . The only assistance we received was from the Territorial authorities at Denver, who supplied our county with a limited number of old Belgian [other accounts say Austrian] muskets, together with the necessary ammunition. These guns were so much inferior to those in the hands of the Indians that they added little to our security.[10]

Watching participants in a Kansas murder trial in 1869, John Cook noticed a mixture of military and civilian arms:

> These men were walking arsenals. Nearly all were carrying two six-shooters, and among them were rifles of many different patterns. One man could be seen with a long-barreled Hawkins rifle, while his neighbor carried an army Enfield, one a Springfield, and one man an old brass-band American musket.[11]

When Richard Townshend came to Colorado from England in the same year, he brought a heavy Greener double-barreled muzzle-loading smoothbore, suitable for shot or ball. For a hunting expedition, however, "Godfrey let me use his rifle, an old-fashioned small-bored muzzle-loader with a heavy octagon barrel nearly four feet long, I should say." And in the early 1870s Frank Collinson, a newcomer to the frontier, "discovered that my ten-pound, forty-caliber, muzzle-

A ranch scene in the late 1880s in Carbon County, Montana.
While his companions prefer lever action repeating rifles, the man
at left is armed with a double-barrel rifle, fitted with a bayonet,
in addition to a revolver at his waist and a knife in a boot sheath.
(Courtesy Montana Historical Society)

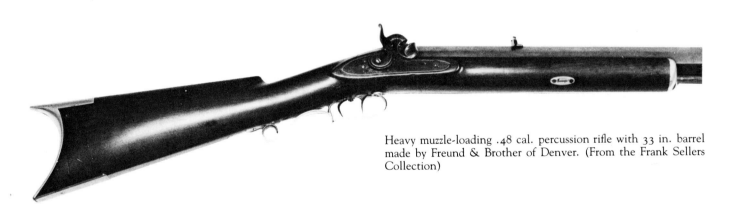

Heavy muzzle-loading .48 cal. percussion rifle with 33 in. barrel
made by Freund & Brother of Denver. (From the Frank Sellers
Collection)

loading rifle was too long and too heavy for a saddle
gun. I sold it to an Arkansas wagon-maker. With the
money received I bought a first model centerfire Winchester carbine, which turned out to be a good
gun. . . ."[12]

As Collinson's account indicates, the muzzle-loading rifle's popularity in the West declined still further
after 1870, due to the increasing use of repeaters and
single-shot rifles chambering long, powerful cartridges,

such as the .44-77 Sharps and the .50-70. Nevertheless, a small number of makers and dealers continued
offering front-loading guns to the frontier market. Rifles of about the same caliber as Collinson's muzzle-
loader were furnished to the Texas market by Schmidt
& Kosse of Houston. Schmidt himself had made copies
of the Deringer pocket pistol about the time of the
Civil War; in the Houston directories of 1866 and
1867–68 his firm was still listed as E. Schmidt & Co.,

The sign in front of Carlos Gove's gunshop in Denver aided illiterates and others to identify the lines of merchandise he offered. (Courtesy Denver Public Library, Western History Dept.)

Martin Holje, a member of the San Francisco Schuetzen Club of target shooters, holds a rifle made by Slotter & Co. of Philadelphia (c. 1870). (Courtesy California State Library)

German muzzle-loading hunting/target rifle publicized as having been used by Louis Buerman to kill a member of the James gang named McDaniel, who in 1875 escaped from the Douglas County, Kansas, jail. (Courtesy Kansas State Historical Society)

but in the 1870–71 directory it became Schmidt & Kosse, and remained so through 1873. Half-stocked rifles stamped with this trademark were similar in outside dimensions to the prewar plains rifle, but had somewhat smaller bores, usually ranging from .40 to .44.[13]

More closely resembling the large-caliber plains rifle were the big muzzle-loaders made in the late 1860s and early 1870s by two brothers, Frank and George Freund. Soon to rank among the most famous armsmakers and dealers in the West, the Freund brothers described themselves in an 1871 Colorado directory as makers and importers of "Breech and Muzzle Loading Shot Guns and Rifles . . . Manufacturers of Shot Guns and Rifles of all kinds." Muzzle-loading rifles with the "Freund & Bro." mark were typically heavy-barreled, big-bore, half-stocked arms, somewhat Hawken-like in appearance.[14]

Another frontier maker of big-bore half-stock plains rifles during the early 1870s was A. E. Rudolph of Canon City, Colorado. One of his rifles, its heavy octagon barrel dated "1872," its stock bleached, weathered, and broken through the wrist, was found years ago near Fremont Peak, half-concealed under the skeletons of a human and a bear.[15]

Nor had the legendary Hawken rifle disappeared. After Sam and William Hawken went to Colorado during the Pike's Peak rush, other gunmakers took over the business in St. Louis and continued making heavy-caliber plains rifles, often stamped with the Hawken name, well into the 1870s. Describing conditions around Fort Phil Kearny in 1866 and 1867, Margaret Carrington wrote that:

Rifles, both English and American, abound. The Hawkins is a favorite, carrying what is called the trade ball, and requiring a patch; but many of the old guides, trappers, and half-breeds still cling to their use as in the days of Pathfinder and other heroes of Cooper.

In the 1872–73 Omaha directory, A. D. McAusland advertised not only breechloaders but the "Hawken Mountain Rifle" as well.[16]

An arm less typical of the prairies than the Hawken turned up in a Colorado hunt in the fall of 1874. One of the hunters, Jim Brinkerhuf, carried "a long muzzle loader which was built with the hammer on the under side."[17]

In the early 1870s Carlos Gove gradually reduced his output of muzzle-loading rifles; although he occasionally made such guns through the mid-1870s, he began devoting more and more of his time to breechloaders. Morgan Rood, however, briskly advertised his one-, two-, and three-barreled arms in the *Rocky*

Mountain News through 1875. Both men offered "Breech and Muzzle-loading Rifles and Shot Guns" in a Denver directory of 1876, and in that same directory John P. Lower advertised "Leman's Indian Rifles," repeating this listing in the 1877 directory. In 1878 a large band of Cheyennes passed through Kansas on their way north; one of a group of settlers who gathered for mutual protection noted that although their arms included a Sharps, a Starr, and one or two Spencers, "most of the men were armed with muzzle loading rifles."[18]

WAR-SURPLUS BREECHLOADERS

Even after that incident, the muzzle-loading rifle continued to be used for hunting and target shooting. But as an all-purpose arm suitable for self-defense as well as for recreation, it had all but disappeared from the West by the mid-1870s. To a majority of those bound for the postwar frontier, the muzzle-loader was unacceptable because of the time required to reload it.

For the less-than-wealthy buyer an inexpensive alternative to the muzzle-loader was one of the many types of Civil War breechloaders, sold by the government and by dealers for considerably less than their initial cost. When they left the service, veterans from ten states and territories west of the Missouri River—California, Colorado, Dakota, Kansas, Nebraska, Nevada, New Mexico, Oregon, Texas, and Washington Territory—retained a total of 1169 Spencers, 683 Sharps, 193 Maynards, 135 Joslyns, 84 Smiths, 19 Gallaghers, and a few Cosmopolitans, Starrs, and Merrills. The Smith was fairly popular on the plains during the late 1860s: between 1862 and 1865 the government had accepted delivery of 30,000, and its promoters, Poultney & Trimble, had also sold it commercially. In 1921 ex-bullwhacker Bill Hooker and an old friend wandered through the ruins of Ft. Laramie:

In the old sutler's store we rummaged among the debris . . . and found on a top shelf, covered with fully one-half inch of dust, two boxes of cartridges, where they had been placed, Mr. Hunton believed, by some former clerk more than 50 years ago—these are Poultney's patent metallic for Smith's breech-loading carbine—50–100 calibre, and were made in Baltimore. . . .

Those westerners who had not actually fought in the war still found it easy to get government breechloaders. In 1866, for example, Denver Arsenal sold varying quantities of Starr, Gallagher, and Joslyn carbines, at prices ranging from $1.00 to $4.60. Moreover, a major government sale of surplus arms at Fort Leavenworth in November of 1867 included not only

Sharps M1863 percussion carbine (#C, 23499) with Wells Fargo stamping on barrel and butt stock. (Courtesy Wells Fargo Bank History Room and the Ordnance Chest)

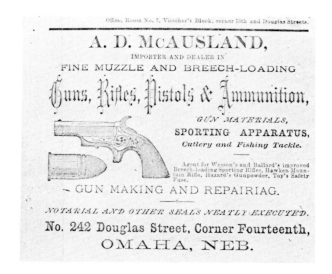

FOR SALE CHEAP.

35 entirely new breech loading Carbine Rifles (Star patent), and 3,000 rounds of fixed ammunition to suit. Address
S. R. KIRBY, Supt. M. M. L. & M. Co.
oc6-111-123-w *

Montana Post (Helena), October 1866.

Office, Room No. 7, Visscher's Block, corner 13th and Douglas Streets.

A. D. McAUSLAND,
IMPORTER AND DEALER IN
FINE MUZZLE AND BREECH-LOADING
Guns, Rifles, Pistols & Ammunition,
GUN MATERIALS,
SPORTING APPARATUS,
Cutlery and Fishing Tackle.

Agent for Wesson's and Ballard's improved Breech-loading Sporting Rifles, Hawken Mountain Rifle, Hazard's Gunpowder, Toy's Safety Fuse.

GUN MAKING AND REPAIRIAG.

NOTARIAL AND OTHER SEALS NEATLY EXECUTED.
No. 242 Douglas Street, Corner Fourteenth,
OMAHA, NEB.

Briggs & Lowry's 1872–73 *Omaha* (Nebraska) *Directory.*

Warner single-shot carbine. (Courtesy National Park Service, Fuller Gun Collection, Chickamauga and Chattanooga National Military Park)

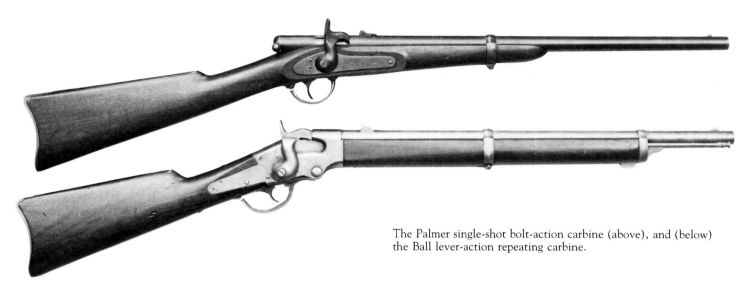

The Palmer single-shot bolt-action carbine (above), and (below) the Ball lever-action repeating carbine.

foreign and domestic muzzle-loaders, but quantities of Burnside, Cosmopolitan, Greene, Hall, and Wesson carbines as well. In the main, these arms were purchased by large gun houses for subsequent resale; a good many of the 311 Burnsides sold by San Antonio Arsenal in 1868, however, were bought by individuals.[19]

Frontier photographer William Henry Jackson got his carbine from a different source. When he passed Fort Kearny in 1866 on his way to Salt Lake, "they furnished me a Sharp's carbine & I had a Colt's revolver of my own." In October of that year an enterprising mining superintendent inserted the following notice in the *Montana Post:* "FOR SALE CHEAP— 35 entirely new breech loading Carbine Rifles (Star patent), and 3,000 rounds of fixed ammunition to suit."[20]

One of the most active distributors of breechloaders in the postwar Southwest was J. Miller & Co. of Galveston. In 1867, for example, Miller's firm offered not only shotguns, revolvers, and Kentucky rifles, but also Sharps, Maynard, Ballard, and Henry rifles, plus "Ball's Patented nine [shot] Repeater [and] Palmer's single Breech-Loading Carbines, (A splendid arm for Frontier Service.)." Late in the war the Ordnance Department had ordered 1000 Palmer and 1000 Ball carbines, but the war ended before officials could issue either gun. Patented in December of 1863, the Palmer was a single-shot bolt-action arm similar to the Ward-Burton; its bolt was locked at the rear by interrupted screw threads on either side. Unlike the Ward-Burton, however, the Palmer had an outside hammer and chambered the .56-.50 rimfire cartridge. For service on horseback the gun was especially useful because, with its short 20 in. barrel, it weighed a mere 4½ pounds.[21]

In contrast to the light single-shot Palmer, Albert Ball's carbine, patented in 1863 and 1864, was a lever-action repeater. Among its features were an integral breechblock-carrier and a tubular magazine under the barrel, loaded through the open action and concealed by a full-length forestock. Although most of the guns were .56-.50s, a few took the .44 rimfire round.[22]

During a stay in Wyoming in 1868, John Chisholm described his equipment as "a small hatchet and a butcher knife slung to my side [and] a Starr breach loader hanging from the horn of the saddle." Although some of the men attending an 1869 Kansas murder trial carried muzzle-loaders, "some had the Gallagher, some the Spencer, and some the Sharp's carbine." While working as a Kansas drover in 1871, C. W. "Doc" Shores also carried a Gallagher; during a stampede, Shores "raised my single-loading Galagher rifle and took a shot at a yearling . . . [then] I broke open the rifle at the breach, removed the spent shell, and shoved in a new cartridge."[23]

A brass-frame carbine that saw little if any use in the West during the war, but came to the frontier soon afterwards, was patented by James Warner in February and December of 1864. Besides its brass frame, Warner's carbine featured a manually operated extractor and a breechblock which swung upward and to the right on a longitudinal hinge mounted on the right side of the action. Between January of 1864 and March of 1865 the government purchased a total of 4001 Warners, and after the war distributed quantities of them to states and territories in need of arms. During the Indian fighting in Colorado in 1868, officials reported that the territorial weapons supply amounted to only a few hundred obsolete Austrian rifles and fewer than 100 Warner carbines; the officials distributed these guns to settlers living at points most ex-

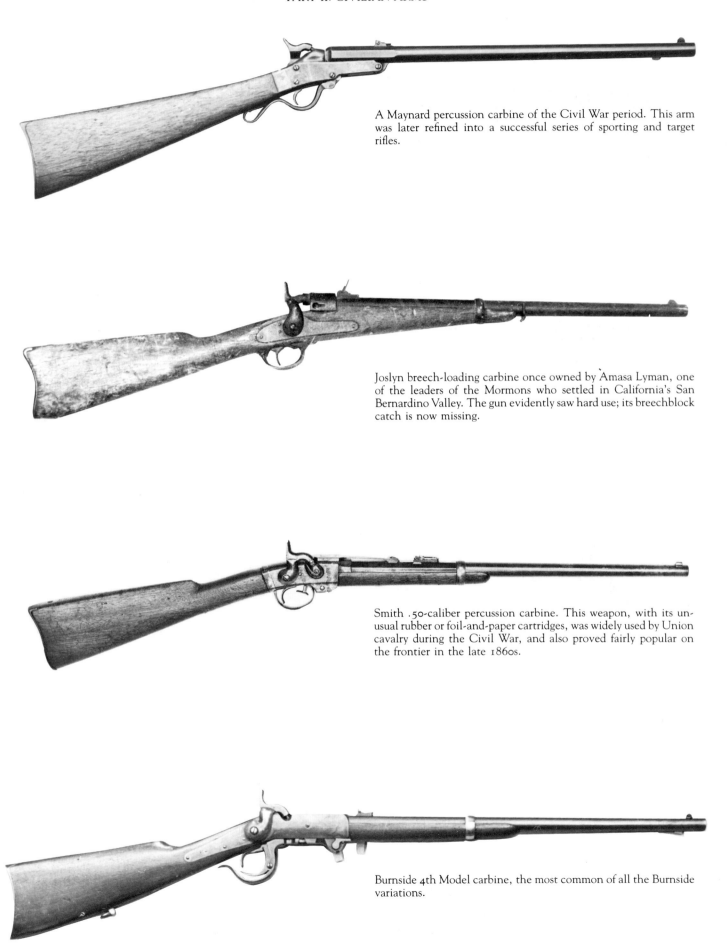

A Maynard percussion carbine of the Civil War period. This arm was later refined into a successful series of sporting and target rifles.

Joslyn breech-loading carbine once owned by Amasa Lyman, one of the leaders of the Mormons who settled in California's San Bernardino Valley. The gun evidently saw hard use; its breechblock catch is now missing.

Smith .50-caliber percussion carbine. This weapon, with its unusual rubber or foil-and-paper cartridges, was widely used by Union cavalry during the Civil War, and also proved fairly popular on the frontier in the late 1860s.

Burnside 4th Model carbine, the most common of all the Burnside variations.

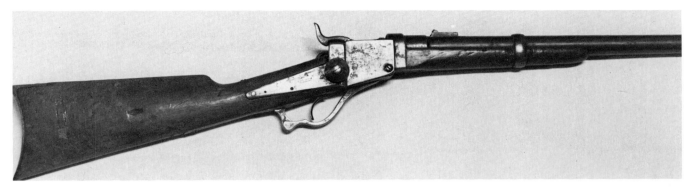

Starr .52 rimfire carbine, #32223, used in a Colorado stagecoach robbery in 1892. (Courtesy Colorado Springs Pioneers' Museum)

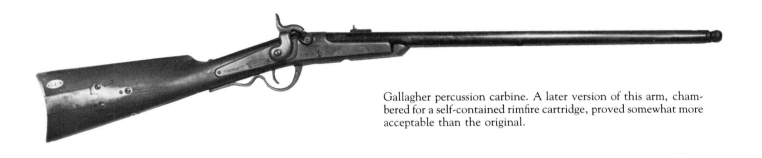

Gallagher percussion carbine. A later version of this arm, chambered for a self-contained rimfire cartridge, proved somewhat more acceptable than the original.

Sharps & Hankins navy model carbine, little different from the army model except for the presence of the leather barrel covering to reduce salt-water corrosion. (Courtesy National Park Service, Fuller Gun Collection, Chickamauga and Chattanooga National Military Park)

posed to attack. Two years later Richard Townshend encountered a Warner in a restaurant near the site of Colorado Springs: "I heard Mrs. Binney rummaging under the bed, and presently she emerged with a very dusty firearm; it was a Warner carbine, an early form of breechloader, rimfire, .50 calibre." More searching by Mrs. Binney brought forth seven copper cartridges, "some of them a good deal bent and bulged." After cleaning the dirt-choked bore, Townshend fired the gun at a dry-goods box twenty yards away—and missed![24]

Still another Civil War carbine which saw frontier service was the sliding-barrel Sharps & Hankins, characterized (in the navy version) by its leather-covered barrel. John Nelson, who accompanied Richard Hughes's party into the Black Hills in 1876, carried such a gun, and probably regretted it:

[Nelson's] gun was what he termed a Sharps navy rifle; the only one of the kind I ever saw. The most distinguishing feature of this firearm was a leather covering that had been shrunken onto the barrel. Poor Nelson and his "leather gun" furnished the butt of many a joke for a good while thereafter.[25]

More widely used in the West than the Sharps & Hankins were two lever-action repeaters, the Spencer and the Henry, and the Colt side-hammer revolving rifle. The Colt, of course, had reached the frontier before either of the other two; although it was a percussion arm, western dealers such as Curry and Liddle & Kaeding of San Francisco, and Henderson & Co. of Prescott, Arizona, continued advertising it through the late 1860s. For an expedition against the Indians in Colorado late in 1868, one Mr. Hall loaned Irving Howbert:

an excellent horse and a Colt's rifle, a kind of gun that I had not seen before nor, for that matter, have I seen one like it since. It was a gun built exactly on the principle of a Colt's revolver. The trouble with it was that one never knew just how many shots might go off at once.

Ten years later one of the men trailing Dull Knife's band of Cheyennes northward, Sol Rees, found that "in trying to work the cylinder of my revolver, the last cartridge had slipped back, and the cylinder would not work . . . I then went back to a man named Ingalls, and got a Colt's repeating rifle."[26]

Owing to the success of metallic-cartridge repeaters with tubular magazines, the popularity of the revolving rifle was fast disappearing. And yet by 1865 Remington had seen fit to introduce a revolving rifle of its own, basically a New Model handgun fitted with buttstock and long octagon barrel. Made initially as a .36 or .44 percusson arm, and later modified to take metallic cartridges, the Remington was available with barrel lengths from 24 to 28 inches. Advertisements for this rifle and other Remington arms, which appeared in the *Arizona Miner*, *Dallas Herald*, *Elko Independent*, and other western papers through the late 1860s, usually referred potential purchasers to the Remington agencies in St. Louis and San Francisco rather than to individual dealers; evidently the sales of the firm's revolving rifle never equaled those of Colt's. Even less popular was the cylinder rifle made by Morgan Rood of Denver; although Rood advertised this gun from the early 1860s through the mid-1870s, the demand, if one existed at all, was extremely limited.[27]

THE SPENCER AND THE HENRY

Sales of the Spencer and the Henry far outstripped those of any revolving rifle used in the postwar West. While the Spencer had been the clear choice of the military, the Henry proved a strong competitor in the civilian market of the late 1860s; from 1865 through 1871 dealers in California, Oregon, Nevada, Arizona, Colorado, Nebraska, and undoubtedly in other parts of the West as well, sold both guns, and one saw about as much use on the plains as the other. Soon after Edward Ordway arrived in Denver in the spring of 1866, he wrote,

I met Riley in Groves' [Gove's?] Gunshop. We met there for the same purpose—gun cleaning. He had a Henry and I a Spencer carbine. As there were some other men there . . . conversation turned to a discussion of the merits and defects of firearms in general. The majority were of the opinion that they would not lay down a muzzle-loader for any machine gun. One man insisted that given a hundred and fifty yards start he could outrun all the sixteen shots in a Henry. Another fellow would not take the gift of a Spencer carbine for the good reason that the luckiest man on the earth was never known to hit anything he shot at. Others offering their testimony along the same line, caused us to adjourn to a corral outside of town that was built of pine lumber with plenty of knots in the boards. I offered to bet a ten dollar hat that I could knock out seven knots that I would mark at thirty yards off hand, and do the trick in less than twenty seconds with the seven shots in my gun. One skeptic in the crowd gleefully accepted the bet and sorrowfully paid it. Riley asked me if I could do that every time, and I told him that with a fair amount of luck I could. Then he told me that he was [boss and] part owner of a bull train . . . and if I was game enough to take the chances he would take me on as an extra, naming a renumeration that struck me as so very liberal that I did not hesitate to accept it. . . .

While William Breakenridge was in eastern Colorado about 1867:

a band of six Indians ran through the edge of town close to the soldiers' barracks and attempted to cut the ropes on several horses that were picketed there. . . . The men all ran out and one of them took my Springfield . . . [I] had to stop to get another. It was a Spencer carbine which loaded in the stock with seven cartridges, held in by a spring . . . I fired at one [Indian] . . . I felt sure that I had hit him and tried to throw another shell into the gun, when I found that the spring that held the cartridges in the breech had come out and all the shells had fallen out of the gun.[28]

After traveling through Kansas in the early summer of 1867, William Bell, another Spencer user, wrote a graphic description of a fortified stage station near Fort Wallace:

Standing side by side, and built of wood and stone, are the stables and the ranche in which the drivers and the ostlers live. Behind is a coralle, or yard, divided off from the plain by a wall of stones . . . A little subterranean passage, about five feet by three, leads from the stables to the house. Another one leads from the stables to a pit dug in the ground, about ten yards distant. This pit is about eight or ten feet square, is roofed with stone supported on wood, and just on a level with the ground portholes open on all sides. The roof is raised but little above the general level of the ground; more, however, at this station than at most of them. Another narrow subterraneous passage leads from the house to a second pit, commanding the other side of the station; while a third passage runs from the coralle to a larger pit, commanding the rear. In both houses, many repeating Spencer and Henry breech-loading rifles—the former carrying seven, and the latter eighteen [sic] charges—lie loaded and ready to hand; while over each little fort a black flag waves, which the red-men know well means "no quarter" for them. When attacked, the men creep into these pits, and, thus protected, keep up a tremendous fire through the portholes, Two or three men, with a couple of breech-loaders each, are a match for almost any number of assailants. I cannot say how many times these little forts have been used since their construction, but during the three weeks we were in the neighbourhood, the station was attacked twice. . . .[29]

Some of the civilians at the Hayfield Fight of 1867 also used the Spencer, as did teamsters on the wagon trains hauling freight up the Bozeman Trail in 1868. The reports of army officers who inspected these trains included the following notes:

No Guns: 4 Spencer and 7 Muskets—Am 150 Rounds.

No Arms: 7 Spencer and 7 Enfield Rifles. Ammunition: 200 Rounds Spencer Cartridges.

No Arms: 7 Spencer and 9 other Rifles—Ammunition—200 Rounds Spencer and 75 Rounds Musket Cartridges.

Arms—24 Spencer Carbines—7 Springfield Muskets—Ammunition—1300 Rounds Spencer Cartridges—Arms Unserviceable—3 Spencer and 2 Springfield Rifles.[30]

The chief competitors of the stagecoach lines—the railroads—also made use of the Spencer. Union Pacific

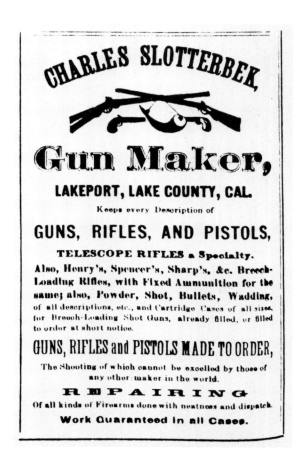

L. A. Paulson's Handbook and Directory of Yolo, Solano, Napa Lake, Sonoma, and Marin Counties [California] 1878–79, p. 196. (Courtesy Bancroft Library, University of California)

workers had them, as did the crewmen of other roads; in the summer of 1870, as the last stretch of Kansas Pacific track went down east of Denver, young John Armor visited the site and noted that "the government had furnished about thirty-five Spencer repeater rifles (seven shots), mostly carbines (the short rifles), and plenty of government ammunition for defense against the Indians."[31]

Individual users of the Spencer were numerous, but one of the more interesting was a mysterious stranger who rode into a Colorado camp late in 1871:

He . . . was neatly and rather stylishly dressed. . . . His only ornament was a short, magazine rifle known as the Spencer carbine, a weapon of large calibre and carrying eight cartridges . . . during the time he was with us, never for a single instant was he

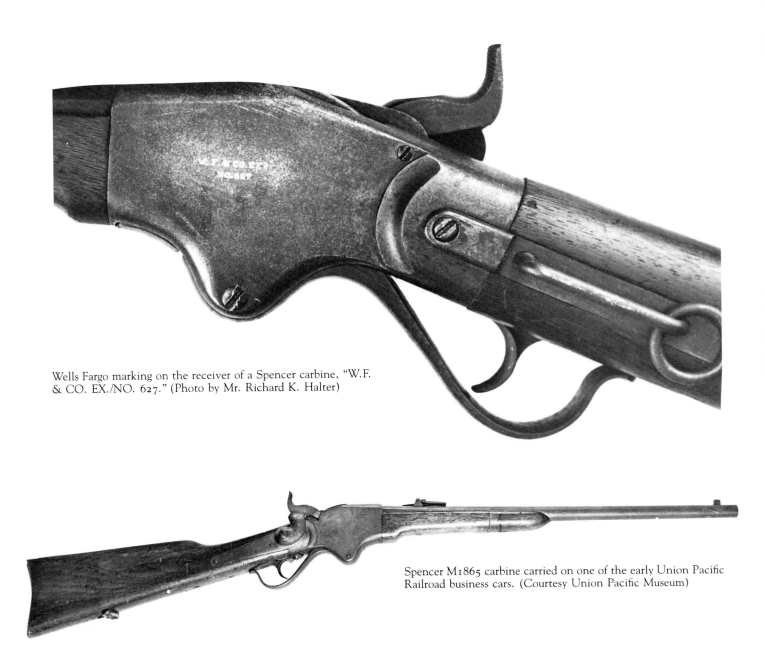

Wells Fargo marking on the receiver of a Spencer carbine, "W.F. & CO. EX./NO. 627." (Photo by Mr. Richard K. Halter)

Spencer M1865 carbine carried on one of the early Union Pacific Railroad business cars. (Courtesy Union Pacific Museum)

without that gun in his possession. Awake or asleep, it was always in his hand. . . .[32]

Only slightly less popular was the Henry. Edward Ordway left a stirring account of the Henry's use by a bull train on the Bozeman Trail in 1866:

We scouted the hills and creek but no signs of Indians did we see, not even the wave of a feather or glitter of a mirror on distant hills. But that was not considered a favorable sign, for as the old timers put it all in one terse sentence, "You are never safe from Indians until you can see them." After crossing the divide between Cheyenne and Powder Rivers,

one morning pony tracks were seen near a small creek some distance above where the road crossed. The sign proved that a small party of Indians had been there the day before . . . and Riley was too old a hand in the game to take a needless chance. One of his wagons had for a part of its load, arms and ammunition, and among the lot were some cases of Henry rifles. I do not suppose at this late day that there are now living many who remember anything about that long ago discarded firearm, nor that it was the legitimate parent of all the magazine guns in use now. It was short ranged and could do but little damage beyond two hundred yards, but it

Prospectors, probably in the southwestern U.S. A Spencer military-style rifle is hung from the saddle on the mount at far right. (Courtesy Arizona Historical Society)

was as near mechanically perfect as any machine gun could be made, and in the hands of men of that day sixteen shots could be fired with astonishing rapidity. Riley broke open some boxes and dealt out two rifles and ammunition to each man in the outfit. [Then,] about ten o'clock [our Pawnee scouts] discovered a war party of seventy five or eighty quietly waiting in a small valley, and [their] telescopic eyes soon made out another party coming to join the others. The Pawnees knew that they were planning to make a surprise attack and they lost no time in getting back to the train. A few words from them to Riley and the order was given, "Corral!" The bull teams swung around into place with the mules and horse teams in the center. The wagons [were] chained together, wheels locked and everything made fast, with but a short space of time to spare until the Indians came in sight, and but few seconds elapsed until the men were under the wagons, each with his rifle at rest through a wheel. They did not come on in a bunch, but scattered out over a wide space. When they saw that everything was arranged for their reception they all rounded up and appeared to be holding a council of war. They had evidently planned to make the attack while the train was strung out on the road, and perhaps, but for the daring of our scouts, it might have happened that way. As the case then stood they had to change their tactics, which they did in short order and began the offense in the old way by

From a photograph taken by Charles T. Smith, Topeka, Kansas. At left, an M1860 Spencer carbine, and at right a Colt M1855 percussion revolving rifle. (Courtesy Mr. Herb Peck, Jr.)

Hunters in South Park, Colorado, probably in the 1880s. The man at left holds a Spencer carbine, while the man third from right has a Sharps. (Courtesy Mr. Malcolm Collier)

Gold Hill (Nevada) *Daily News*, July 1865.

circling around, making feints at charging, and all the tricks wherein they were devilishly proficient, for the purpose of drawing our fire at a long range, and then charging in on empty guns. That they got no reply from the old muzzle-loaders, and not knowing the rod we had in pickle for them, was positively a puzzle they could not solve, but [they] kept drawing a little nearer until perhaps their patience became exhausted and [with] no resistance against their maneuvers, they made a simultaneous dash on all sides, and coming within the limits of the rifle range the Henrys began to play a tattoo the like of which they had never heard before. . . . To say that the Indians were astonished at the storm of lead that met them would be but a weak expression. A gatling gun would not have surprised them more. It was but a very few minutes after we began to fire until they were gathering up their dead and wounded and nothing short of total annihilation would have stopped them from doing that—and they were scurrying away toward the shelter of the hills, wiser if not happier Indians. The magic of the white man's guns was a long way past their understanding. They let us alone while in their territory. In less than an hour after the last shot was fired the train was rolling along as merrily as though nothing had happened.[33]

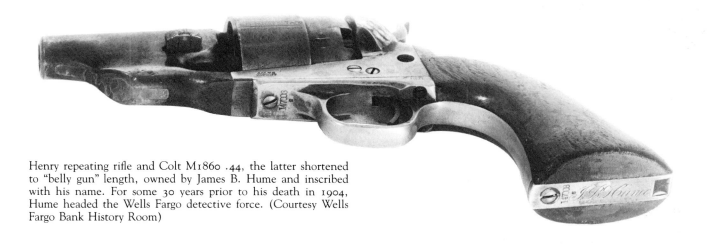

Henry repeating rifle and Colt M1860 .44, the latter shortened to "belly gun" length, owned by James B. Hume and inscribed with his name. For some 30 years prior to his death in 1904, Hume headed the Wells Fargo detective force. (Courtesy Wells Fargo Bank History Room)

When Andrew Simmons and his party traveled down the Missouri by Mackinaw boat in the summer of 1866, they were well equipped with Henrys. Simmons told of others who were less well armed, and who paid dearly for it:

Toward evening we descried a party of white men on the right bank, hove to, and went ashore. They proved to be a party of seven, engaged in chopping wood for steamboats. . . . These men were armed with Hawkins rifles, which, being muzzle-loading, were greatly inferior to the breech-loading cartridge guns then in use. We warned them of their danger, but with [their] energy and enterprise they possessed also the courage and recklessness of all pioneers. They said they were ready to take chances. Poor fellows! The chances were too strong for them, for only a few days afterwards a body of Sioux Indians

came upon them. They made a desperate defence, but were overpowered and every one of them massacred.

A short distance downriver Simmons and his companions encountered their own problems:

It was evident we had come up with a large party of Sioux who were about to attack us, and we must make the best of the situation. Despite our labor at the oars, the current swept us down in direct range of the spot occupied by the Indians, who, before we had finished fastening our boat, opened fire upon us with about fifty shots, which fortunately whistled over our heads . . . Before they could correct their aim for another fire, we were behind a breastwork hastily extemporized by throwing up our blankets and baggage against the exposed gunwale of the boat. This they pierced with bullets thick as hail, but the protection it afforded us was ample, and we soon got ready to return their leaden compliments. Each of our Henry rifles contained sixteen cartridges when we opened fire, and the distance being about one hundred and fifty yards to the bluff, which was literally swarming with savages, not more than ten minutes elapsed until every one of them had disappeared. The fearful death howl, however, assured us that our fire had not been in vain.[34]

The two scouts killed in the Fetterman Massacre in December of 1866 also carried Henrys, and probably took a heavy toll of their attackers before they fell. Ironically, a Henry rifle was to help avenge the Fetterman disaster. After the Hayfield Fight of 1867, Finn Burnett, a Spencer-wielding participant of that battle, wrote:

I don't believe there is another man living, or that ever lived, who has killed as many Indians in a day as [D. A.] Colvin did on the occasion of the hayfield fight. He was armed with a sixteen-shot repeating rifle, and had a thousand rounds of ammunition. He was a dead shot, and if he missed an Indian in that fight none of us ever knew it. He fired about three hundred shots that day. . . . As he did most of his shooting at distances of from twenty to seventy-five yards, it was almost impossible for him to miss. . . . He was shooting steadily from nine-thirty in the morning until five o'clock in the afternoon, and the ground around where he was stationed was literally covered with empty shells from his rifle.[35]

Members of the Davy Expedition, which left Minnesota for Montana in the same year, brought along various carbines, shotguns, revolvers, and more than 30 Henry rifles. Philippe Regis de Trobriand took note of the Henry carried by a Dakota scout, and even the famous journalist Henry M. Stanley mentioned the arm: "It has been impressed on us . . . that when travelling in this wild [Kansas] country we should carry slung to our waist a museum of arms, such as a bowie knife, a brace of revolvers, and a Henry rifle." In 1868 the well-known scout Luther "Yellowstone" Kelly paid about fifty dollars for a Henry at Fort Berthold: "With the Henry and the stubby little .44 caliber cartridges that went with it I killed many a buffalo, as well as other game, and it stood me in good hand when I was forced to defend myself in encounters with hostile Indians." One of these encounters involved a sudden meeting with two Sioux, who got off the first shot:

One was armed with a good double-barreled gun; the other had only a bow and some arrows . . . my horse began to kick and jump. I knew that he had

been shot, and that it would be impossible to hold him still, so I had to jump to the ground. In jumping, I fell full length, and while I was trying to get on my feet, one of the Sioux ran up to within six feet of me, took aim, and fired, I would be dead now if the gun had gone off; but since the percussion cap missed fire, I did not lose any time in firing back, and my enemy fell dead, a bullet through his head. Then it was like a duel with the other one who kept under cover behind a tree trunk, where he shot arrows at me. . . . Since I could still fire fifteen shots without reloading . . . I started to fire carefully at my man. The last tree he hid behind was not big enough to cover him. . . .

Walter Trumbull, who lived near Fort Ellis about 1870, wrote that "we citizens carried an assorted armory, consisting of Henry, Ballard, and Spencer rifles, revolvers, and bowie knives."[36]

Not all the Henry's owners were enthusiastic about it. Frank Canton, whose party traveled through Indian Territory in 1869, noted later that their arms comprised "some old Henry rifles, which were rim fire and not much good, but we all had good six-shooters."[37]

James Cook, however, had a different opinion. When he first came to the plains after the war he bought a muzzle-loader, which he later traded for a Spencer. On one occasion, while he was working for Texas cattleman Ben Slaughter, Slaughter told him to shoot a cow for camp meat:

[Cook] pulled the Spencer carbine which I was carrying, pointed it toward the heifer, and exclaimed, "There is a good one." Mr. Slaughter started his horse toward me, fairly yelling, "Hold on, young man; don't you see that's a T-Diamond?" "Yes," I replied, "What brand is that?" "I reckon that's my brand," was the answer. "We don't kill that kind in this country. Kill an LOW or a WBG"—meaning anyone's brand but his own. "They taste better."

But Cook did not like his Spencer because of its low-velocity ammunition; he termed it "a real 'humdinger'; the person using it could often hear its bullet hum as it whirled end-over-end through the air." Then, one summer day in the early 1870s:

a Mexican rode into camp with an almost new Henry rifle on his saddle. He wanted to buy some cartridges for it. We had no Henry rifle shells, but did have some Spencer ammunition, and I succeeded in trading him, for his Henry, my Spencer carbine and what cartridges I had. . . . This rifle proved to be a most accurate shooting piece, and I had the sat-

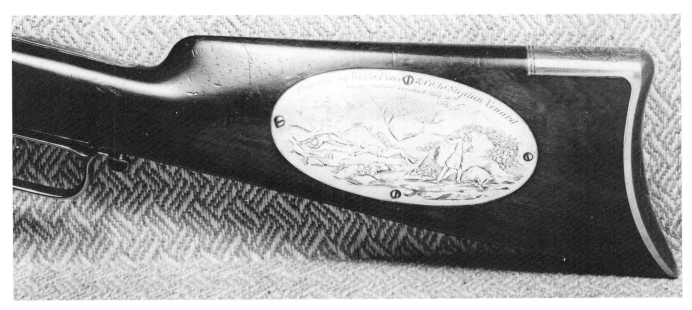

About 4 A.M. on May 16, 1866, three armed bandits held up a Wells Fargo stagecoach near Nevada City, Calif. Former Nevada City town marshal Stephen Venard took up the robbers' trail alone and by noon had recovered the stolen money, killing the three bandits with only four shots from his Henry repeating rifle. A grateful Wells Fargo presented Venard with a $3000 reward and this new engraved Henry. The plaque set in the stock is inscribed "Presented by WELLS FARGO & CO. to Stephen Venard for his gallant conduct May 16th 1866." (Courtesy Wells Fargo Bank History Room)

isfaction of knowing that nobody in Texas had a better shooting iron than I.[38]

Both the Henry and the Spencer were used in the West well into the 1880s. Christopher Spencer's real success, however, had come during the war, with the sale of more than 100,000 of his military arms to the Union and state governments. When these guns flooded the civilian market in the late 1860s, they greatly hindered the sales of Spencer's .56-.46 sporting rifles, which sold for higher prices than his military-surplus arms. Some Spencer sporters did reach the frontier; from 1867 through 1871, for example, Curry of San Francisco advertised the Spencer in both military and sporting versions. In addition to the factory-made sporters, frontier gunsmiths sometimes fitted Spencer actions with heavy octagon barrels, barrels which occasionally bore the names of Hawken, Dimick, Robert Liddle, or A. J. Plate. The modification did not always stop there, however, and often included double set triggers and graceful stocks which, like the barrels, were reminiscent of the muzzle-loading plains rifle.[39]

But in making thousands upon thousands of guns for the military, Spencer had simply produced himself out of the postwar arms market. By 1869 his company had failed, its remaining assets bought by none other than Oliver Winchester, head of the firm which had manufactured the Henry. Into Winchester's hands, in fact, was to fall the biggest share of the West's repeating-rifle market.

THE FIRST WINCHESTER

Winchester did not conquer the market with the Henry rifle. Despite its commercial success, the arm's drawbacks—the long open slot in the underside of the

Edward L. Schieffelin's pick and Henry rifle (#2197), displayed with a contemporary canteen at the Tombstone (Arizona) Courthouse State Historical Park. Prospecting for silver in 1877 in the Apache-occupied San Pedro Valley, he was warned that all he would find would be his tombstone. That warning inspired the name for one of his silver strikes and, two years later, the name for the town that grew from the miners' camp. He sold his silver claims in the area in 1880 for $300,000, but instead of living comfortably he grew restless and resumed prospecting elsewhere in the West and Alaska until his death in 1897. (Photo by Mr. James L. Kidd, courtesy Mr. Hollis N. Cook)

Portland *Oregonian*, October 1867.

One identifying characteristic of a stagecoach robber being sought in 1875 was the rifle he carried. The Henry had a popular nickname of "sixteen shooter," a term sometimes applied as well to the M1866 Winchester, although the '66 rifle had a magazine capacity of 17 cartridges. (Photo by Mr. Richard K. Halter, courtesy the late Mr. Willis E. Neuwirth)

Frontiersman Jeremiah "Liver Eating" Johnson's 11-pound sporting rifle, combining a Spencer action and a barrel stamped "S. Hawken St. Louis." It is not clear whether such converted Spencers were produced in the old Hawken shop or by others using Hawken-marked barrels. The Museum of the Fur Trade at Chadron, Nebraska, has a similarly converted Spencer with a barrel stamped "P. Gemmer St. Louis." Gemmer, a former Hawken employee, took over operation of the Hawken shop in 1865. (Courtesy Museum of the Fur Trade)

A trio of Winchester .44 M1866 rifles used by Union Pacific Railroad special agents. The barrel of the top specimen has been cut to a nonstandard length, even shorter than the usual 20 in. length of the carbine. (Courtesy Union Pacific Museum)

magazine tube, and the requirement for loading the tube from the front—started Winchester and his engineers working on improvements as early as mid-1865. Although several loading systems came under consideration, the design finally adopted was that patented by Nelson King, Winchester's new superintendent, in May of 1866. Positioned under the barrel as in the Henry, King's magazine tube was open only at the rear, where it entered the receiver, and was partially protected by a wood forestock. To load, the shooter simply pushed the cartridges, one after another, inward and forward through a spring-tempered loading gate in the right side of the receiver.[41]

The commercial success of a rifle employing the new magazine system seemed to be assured, and in May of 1866, at the time King patented his magazine,

An 1872 scene at Major Pease's ranch on the Yellowstone River in Montana. The tamed elk calf's mother was perhaps killed with the Winchester M1866 rifle leaning against the corner of the sod-roofed cabin. (U.S. Geological Survey photo, courtesy National Archives)

Winchester changed the name of his firm from the Henry Repeating Rifle Company (previously the New Haven Arms Company) to the Winchester Repeating Arms Company.

Aside from its vastly improved magazine, the first rifle to bear the Winchester name—later called the Model 1866—had a brass receiver, which housed the same toggle-link action used in the Henry. Moreover, it chambered the same cartridge, a .44 rimfire round with a bullet of about 200 grains and a 28 grain powder charge. Two standard versions of the 1866 Winchester were available: a rifle with a 24 in. octagon barrel, and a carbine with a 20 in. round barrel. A little extra money, however, would buy a fancy stock, fancy sights,

Winchester M1866 rifle used by a driver on the stagecoach line between Cheyenne, Wyoming Territory, and Deadwood, Dakota Territory. (Courtesy Union Pacific Museum)

Directors of the Union Pacific Railroad meet in Thomas C. Durant's private car, lavishly furnished with crystal chandeliers, fancy mirrors, and china spittoons, as well as a pair of Winchester M1866 rifles and a pair of Colt-type percussion revolvers, probably M1851 Navies (c. 1868). (Courtesy Union Pacific Museum)

Winchester Repeating Rifles !

Firing Two Shots a Second, as a Repeater, and Twenty Shots a Minute as a Single Breach-Loader.

These powerful, accurate, and wonderfully effective weapons, carrying eighteen charges, which can be fired in nine seconds, are now ready for the market, and are sold by all responsible Gun Dealers throughout the country. For information send for circulars and pamphlets to the WINCHESTER REPEATING ARMS CO., New Haven, Conn.   oct7w229

Leavenworth (Kansas) *Times and Conservative*, October 1868.

Dupont's Gunpowder, Safety Fuse,
—AND—
WINCHESTER REPEATING ARMS.

DUPONT'S Superior Mining Powder (saltpetre), F FF-FFF.

DUPONT'S Blasting Powder, in air-tight corrugated Iron Kegs, C-F-FF-FFF.

DUPONT'S Celebrated Brand, Diamond Grain, Nos. 1, 2, 3 and 4, in 1 lb. and ½ lb. canisters.

DUPONT'S Unrivalled Brands, Eagle Duck and Eagle Rifle, Nos. 1, 2, 3, in half kegs, qr. kegs, 5 lb. tins, and in 1 lb. and ½ lb. canisters.

DUPONT'S Standard Rifle, Fg-FFg-FFFg, in kegs, half kegs and qr. kegs, and in 1 lb., ½ lb., and ¼ lb. canisters.

DUPONT'S Superior Rifle, A. F. & Co., F-FF-FFF, in kegs, half kegs, qr. kegs, and in 1 lb., ½ lb. and ¼ lb. canisters.

DUPONT'S Cannon, Musket, Meal and Fuse Powder.

EAGLE SAFETY FUSE (manufactured near Santa Cruz, Cal. by the L. S. & P. Co.) Constantly on hand full supplies of their Celebrated Brands, Waterproof and Submarine, Triple Taped, Double Taped, Single Taped and Hemp Fuse. Fuse made especially to explode the Giant Powder and Hercules Powder Caps.

The above named Fuse are warranted equal to any made in the world.

WINCHESTER REPEATING ARMS (Henry's Improved) and FIXED AMMUNITION.

A large and complete stock of these celebrated arms constantly on hand, to wit :

Repeating Sporting Rifles—Oiled Stocks.

Repeating Sporting Rifles—Varnished Stocks.

Gold, Silver and Nickle-plated Rifles—beautifully Engraved.

Repeating Carbines—Oiled Stocks.

Repeating Carbines—Gold, Silver and Nickel-Plated and Engraved.

Muskets—Angular or Sword Bayonets.

Full stock constantly on hand of all the different parts of the Winchester Arms.

Cartridges in cases (Brand H), manufactured by the W. R. A. Co. expressly for their arms.

A full and complete stock of the above named merchandise always on hand and for sale by

JOHN SKINKER, Sole Agent,

5v24-6m lmtr   108 Battery street, S. F.

San Francisco Mining and Scientific Press, March 1872.

or fancy metalwork such as plating and engraving. With the magazine fully loaded and a round in the chamber, the rifle would hold a maximum of eighteen cartridges; similarly loaded, the carbine would hold fourteen. Because the Winchester and the Henry were sometimes used side by side on the frontier, the Henry might be mistakenly called an "eighteen shooter," or the Winchester a "sixteen shooter," by a casual observer.[42]

Although manufacture of the arm began in 1866, there were evidently no domestic sales until 1867. Company officials recalled that, except for one or two sample arms, the first two carbines sold in this country went to Major H. G. Litchfield, adjutant for the Department of the Platte, in late August of 1867. However, a small quantity may have left the factory before that: in the spring of 1867 a cavalry detachment in Wyoming surprised a band of Indians about to attack a wagon train on the Platte River; Finn Burnett and two soldiers chased one Indian into a hollow, where he put up a stiff fight before going down. Burnett "took from him the first Winchester rifle I had ever seen."[43]

Apparently neither Winchester nor its dealers made much of an effort to promote the new arms until 1868. They were advertised in Galveston and Brownsville papers in February of that year, and in March the Freund brothers, with large advertisements in the *Cheyenne Leader* and the *Frontier Index*, proclaimed

themselves "Sole Agents For the Whole West For the Celebrated Winchester's Patent Repeating Rifle And Carbine." A. D. McAusland of Omaha also advertised the Winchester in 1868, and in October of that year the Winchester firm itself placed ads in the *Omaha Republican* and the *Leavenworth Times & Conservative*, complete with illustrations of the carbine. An early and famous carbine that went West was the special-order arm acquired by Gen. Grenville Dodge, chief engineer for the Union Pacific railroad. This gun (se-

First camp of the John Wesley Powell expedition to explore and map the present state of Utah. A M1866 Winchester rifle leans against a clump of willows to the left of the tripod. During the 1860s and 1870s photographers such as William H. Jackson, Timothy O'Sullivan, and E. O. Beaman (who took this photo in 1871) created lasting images of the West and its inhabitants, despite the difficulties posed by their primitive equipment and techniques. (U.S. Geological Survey photo, courtesy National Archives)

rial no. 14,998) has a sporting-rifle buttplate and fancy wood; the left side of its frame is engraved: "Genl G. M. Dodge/U.P.R.R."[44]

Distribution of the 1866 Winchester grew rapidly during and after 1868. William E. Webb, who traveled across the plains in that year, wrote that:

> I became very fond of a carbine combining the Henry and King patents. It weighed but seven and one-half pounds, and could be fired rapidly twelve times without replenishing the magazine. Hung by a strap to the shoulder, this weapon can be dropped across the saddle in front, and held there very firmly by a slight pressure of the body . . . and with a little practice, the magazine of the gun may be refilled without checking the horse. So light is this Henry and King weapon that I have often held it out with one hand like a pistol, and fired.

Charles Nessiter's party, which left Fort Belknap for Denver in 1868, took along "nine Winchester repeating rifles," four English double rifles, and a double-barreled, eight-bore duck gun (which when loaded with about two ounces of shot in each barrel "would be grand at close quarters"); two Caddo scouts who accompanied the party had Spencer carbines. During a three-day on-and-off fight with Comanches, the Winchesters proved to be the most effective arms.[45]

Traveling across the frontier a year or two later, J. S. Campion and his men found that "our rifles especially interested the Indians, being of a pattern they had never seen before, for they were a then lately invented arm—Winchester's improved Henry's . . . Ours were carbine size, having, when loaded, fourteen shots in them." Winchesters also constituted the principal armament for the two parties that explored the Colorado River in 1869 and 1871.[46]

The popularity of the 1866 Winchester on the frontier continued to increase even after the company brought out an improved model in 1873. But a good many westerners would have nothing to do with the early Winchesters or other repeaters, for reasons they considered very sound, and not until the 1880s did the repeating rifle assert its dominance over the single-shot breechloader.

John F. Steward, photographed in Glen Canyon of the Colorado
River in 1871. In addition to the geologist's hammer in his belt,
he carries a Winchester M1866 rifle. (Courtesy National Archives)

Frank Wesson .44 single-shot carbine used by Gen. Phillip de Trobriand at Ft. Stevenson, Dakota Territory, in 1867–69. The forward trigger releases the barrel for loading. (Courtesy State Historical Society of North Dakota)

SINGLE-SHOT RIFLES: THE BALLARD, THE SPRINGFIELD, AND OTHERS

Single-shot rifles did indeed possess some definite advantages over the early postwar repeaters; as late as 1892 A. C. Gould enumerated them:

less complicated, and less liable to get out of order; will shoot a greater variety of ammunition; will shoot uncrimped ammunition, patched or unpatched bullets; will permit the use of a longer barrel; an explosive bullet can be used; a greater range of rear sights on tang can be used.

The relative importance of these advantages would, of course, depend largely on the individual user, but in the main the factors which best accounted for the single-shot's longevity were simplicity, reliability, and the ability to chamber long, powerful cartridges.[47]

Due to the pressure limitations of rimfire cartridges, however, the early single-shot rifles were chambered for the usual short-case loads adapted to repeaters. For example, Frank Wesson's two-trigger carbine, one of the first single-shot arms to reach the frontier, was designed for the common .32 to .44 rimfire rounds, and there was no significant departure from this practice until the appearance of the .50-70 government cartridge, which prompted the development of various civilian centerfire loads. In April of 1872 Wesson patented a hammer with an adjustable firing pin, which allowed him to chamber his rifle for centerfire as well as rimfire rounds; this gave rise to somewhat more powerful cartridges, such as the Wesson .44 Extra Long Centerfire, loaded with a bullet of about 250 grains and a 48 to 50 grain powder charge.[48]

Although Wesson's rifle had seen limited military use during the war, it was far more popular in civilian circles, where it retained a measure of that popularity for many years after the war. In the late 1860s and early 1870s western dealers such as Carlos Gove of Denver, A. D. McAusland of Omaha, and Liddle and Kaeding of San Francisco handled it, and Wesson himself was still advertising it in the late 1880s.[49]

Another single-shot rifle developed during the Civil War was that patented by James P. Lee in July of 1862. The barrel of Lee's arm was joined to a long frame by means of a vertical pivot, which allowed the barrel breech to swing to the right for loading. Lee set up shop in Milwaukee, and in April of 1865 signed a government contract to supply 1000 of his guns in .44 rimfire. Because of a misunderstanding about chamber dimensions, however, government inspectors rejected the arms, whereupon Lee began manufacturing them for the civilian market. Most commonly Lee sporting rifles had 28 in. octagon barrels, chambered for the .38 Long rimfire cartridge, rather than the 21 1/2 in. round .44 barrels made for the contract arms. By mid-1868 Lee rifles were available from at least two frontier dealers, McAusland of Omaha and the Freund Brothers of Cheyenne, but they never became really popular; Lee's fame was to rest on guns other than his swinging-barrel rifle.[50]

Of the other single-shot rifles used on the postwar frontier—including the Browning, Maynard, Peabody, Phoenix, Stevens, Whitney, Winchester, and a few lesser-known makes—four were to become especially popular: the Sharps, the Springfield, the Remington, and the Ballard.

The first of these to be designed specifically for a self-contained metallic cartridge was the Ballard. As introduced in the spring of 1862, it was available in .32, .38, and .44 rimfire, with some subsequently sold to the military in both .44 and .56-.56 Spencer calibers. By the close of 1864 the Ballard was also available chambered for a new cartridge, the .46 Long rimfire, a load comprising a 300 grain bullet backed by a 35 to 40 grain powder charge. For a Ballard owner without ready access to metallic cartridges, a desirable accessory was the steel chamber insert patented by Merwin and Bray in January of 1864, which permitted the use of loose powder and ball.

Presumably the same range of calibers was still avail-

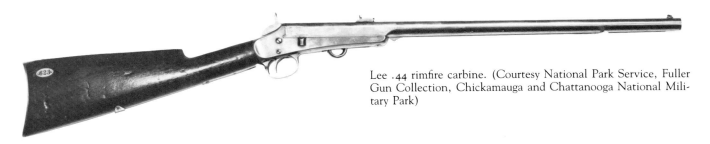

Lee .44 rimfire carbine. (Courtesy National Park Service, Fuller Gun Collection, Chickamauga and Chattanooga National Military Park)

Ballard rifle barrel and frame found near the site of Egan Station in Nevada along the Overland Trail route. To the left is the cylinder and frame of a Colt M1860 revolver, discovered at the site of the Shell Creek stagecoach station in the same state. (Courtesy St. Joseph [Missouri] Museum)

able by the spring of 1865, when the Ballard began arriving on the frontier in quantity. In March of 1866, however, William Hardy of Prescott, Arizona, advertised the Ballard rifle and carbine in only two calibers—.44 and .46 Long rimfire. But a Merwin & Bray ad for the Ballard, placed in the Central City, Colorado, *Miners' Register* three months later, stated that "within the past year we have made immense improvements in the ammunition used in these Rifles, increasing their accuracy and power full twenty per cent., equaling now the best Muzzle-Loaders." (Unfortunately, the ad failed to specify just what these improvements were.)[51]

In July of 1867 Merwin & Simpkins, successors to

Merwin & Bray, advertised the Ballard in the *Rocky Mountain News* with these words:

Ballard Rifles and Carbines, of large calibre, as follows: 44-100, 46-100 and 50-100. This want has long been felt. Now, for the first time, are we prepared to furnish the Large Bores or Calibres. It will be remembered that the Ballard is The only Breech Loader That Can Be Loaded as well with Loose Ammunition as with copper cartridges. Made with long, heavy barrels, from 24 to 30 inch.

Whether the new .50 caliber Ballards were chambered for the .50-70 round or some lesser cartridge is un-

A Ballard single-shot carbine hangs from the pole supporting the tent fly in this scene photographed during the King survey along the Fortieth Parallel. Government treks by cartographers, scien-tists, and photographers in the post–Civil War West helped fill many gaps in existing knowledge of unexplored areas. (U.S. Geo-logical Survey photo, courtesy National Archives)

certain, but at least the distributors for these arms were aware of the demand for single-shot rifles using more powerful loads.[52]

Such loads would become available in considerable variety by the mid-1870s, but evidently some users were satisfied with the medium-power cartridges for which the Ballards of the late 1860s and early 1870s were chambered. In January of 1866 Theo Davis, then in Santa Fe, wrote this letter to an old hunting com-panion:

> You must remember what a determined advocate the old-fashioned muzzle-loader had in me. Its load was certain and the affair was balanced. Many is the loose ball I've dropped from my mouth down the throat of my reliable Lewis rifle. . . . But we are a progressive as well as an aggressive people, [and] I liked the [Ballard] from the first. . . . In a close bush fight it has never failed me. For buffalo hunting it is magnificent. More than one antelope has been brought down at three hundred yards. During our Indian fights it was the treasure of our party. Do you wonder, my dear fellow, that I am an enthusiastic believer in the Ballard rifle?

A group of dignitaries who traveled by rail to the Union Pacific's end of track in the fall of 1866 included Radical Senator Ben Wade of Ohio:

> [he] distinguished himself by making several fine shots with the little Ballard rifle, which had recently done such excellent execution among the elk and antelope of the Rocky Mountains; and he finally became so attached to the rifle, that he would not allow his photograph to be taken without holding it in his hand.

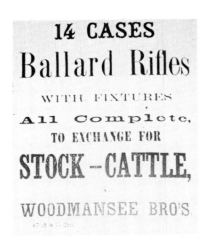

Deseret News (Salt Lake City), September 1867.

IMPORTANT TO
PLAINSMEN AND SPORTSMEN.

WE ARE PREPARED TO FURNISH THE well known

Ballard Rifles and Carbines,

of large calibre, as fo lows: 44-100, 46-100 and 50-100. This want has long been felt. Now, for the first, are we prepared to furnish the

Large Bores or Calibres.

It will be remembered that the Ballard is

The only Breech Loader
THAT CAN BE

Loaded as well with Loose Ammunition
as with copper cartridges. Made with long, heavy barrels, from 24 to 30 inch.
MERWIN & SIMPKINS, Sole Agents,
262 Broadway, New York.
P. S. A full assortment of arms and ammunition, of the most approved kinds, of our own make. Illustrated circulars sent when required.
june26daw3m

Rocky Mountain News (Denver), July 1867.

Luther North recalled that in 1866–67 his sergeant in the Second Nebraska Cavalry, Billy Harvey, "was a crack rifle shot and at that time he carried a Ballard 44 caliber rifle." Harvey gave the rifle to North in 1870, but North lost it shortly afterward while trying to cross a flood-swollen river: "I was very sorry to lose this gun and it was a good many years before I got a gun that I liked as well as that one."[53]

Another incident involving a Ballard took place on the Yellowstone River during the Washburn Expedition of 1870. One Jake Smith openly doubted the revolver-handling skill of the other members of the expedition, and offered to set up his hat at twenty yards as a target; Nathaniel Langford

> could not resist the temptation to drop quietly out of sight behind a clump of bushes, where . . . I sent from my breech-loading Ballard repeating [sic] rifle four bullets in rapid succession, through the hat, badly riddling it. Jack inquired "Whose revolver is it that makes that loud report?" He did not discover the true state of the case. . . .[54]

Hazing beef in Kansas in 1871, Doc Shores rode up beside a sluggish bull and "poked him in the ribs with the muzzle of my Ballard rifle." And about 1872 the redoubtable Clarence King chased down a grizzly "with his pet rifle, a single-shot Ballard, in his hands."[55]

The Ballard was to become even more popular on the plains during the late 1870s, but by that time it had some strong competition in the form of the Sharps, the Remington, and the Springfield. Although designed and made as a military arm, the breech-loading Springfield "needle gun"—so called because of its long, slender firing pin—acquired a rather wide following among frontiersmen during the postwar years. While the trapdoor Springfield action was not particularly strong, it had ample strength for the popular .50-70 and later .45-70 cartridges. It would not jam in the closed position, was fast to reload, easy to clean, and, as service rifles went, it was accurate. A positive feature from the civilian standpoint was that parts and ammunition for it were available almost anywhere on the frontier; and by the early 1870s, civilian users had the option of buying brass rather than copper cartridges, which would seldom bulge or rupture during firing or extraction. For all these reasons frontiersmen generally had a favorable opinion of the trapdoor Springfield.

William Breakenridge obtained a Springfield in northeastern Colorado about 1867:

> The Government had taken the old Springfield rifle and converted it into a breech-loading needle gun of very long range. It would carry a mile or more. I bought one from a soldier when they were first

Springfield M1873 .45 carbine (#9807), identified by a plate in the stock as the one used by Antoine de Vollombrosa, marquis de Mores, in an encounter with outlaws at the Little Missouri River crossing of the Northern Pacific Railroad in North Dakota on June 23, 1883. The specimen illustrates such features of early "Custer era" M1873 carbines as a stacking swivel on the barrel band and the first model of carbine rear sight. Other features of early carbines include a two-notch tumbler, a smooth rather than a grooved trigger surface, no cavity in the butt for a cleaning rod and headless shell extractor, and a high arched cutout in the underside of the breechblock. (Courtesy State Historical Society of North Dakota)

Springfield .45 Type I Officer's Model rifle (with old replaced sights on the barrel), which once belonged to German-born Albert (Al) Sieber. He served as an army scout for about 20 years, participating in the campaigns against the Apaches in the 1870s and 1880s. In 1907, working as a foreman during the construction of Roosevelt Dam, he was crushed to death by rocks as a result of a faulty blasting operation. Manufactured between 1875 and 1877, the Type I Officer's Model rifle lacked the detachable wooden pistol grip found on later Officer's Model .45s. (Courtesy Arizona Historical Society)

Springfield .45 Type II Officer's Model rifle used by scout and buffalo hunter Billy Dixon, who served as chief of scouts under Gen. Nelson Miles. Dixon was one of the participants in the 1874 Battle at Adobe Walls, where a party of buffalo hunters withstood repeated attacks by an overwhelming force of Indians under Quanah Parker. Production of the Type II rifle is estimated at about 250 between April 1, 1877 and the end of 1881. Another .45 Officer's Model, given to Dr. J. N. Blazer by an army officer, figured in the fighting between the warring factions in Lincoln County, New Mexico in 1878. Confronted at Blazer's sawmill by a hostile band that included Billy the Kid, outnumbered "Buckshot" Roberts was mortally wounded in the stomach by Charlie Bowdre. But the plucky little ex-army sergeant wounded two of his attackers before his repeating rifle jammed and he staggered into the room where Blazer's Springfield was located. Roberts then used the .45-70 to kill Dick Brewer at which point the gang withdrew. The Springfield was displayed at the Lincoln County Courthouse Museum until stolen in the 1970s. (Photo by Mr. Roy M. Laing, courtesy Panhandle-Plains Historical Museum)

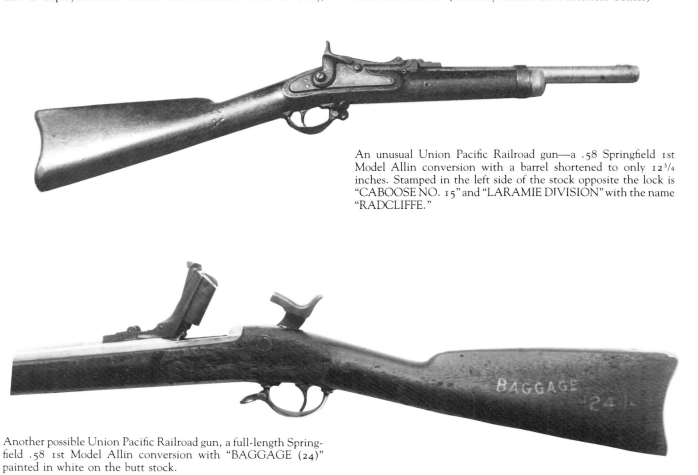

"Lucretia Borgia," the .50 Springfield rifle which Buffalo Bill Cody used while employed as a hunter for the Kansas-Pacific Railroad construction workers. The entire butt has been broken and separated from the rest of the stock, and the gun shows hard use. It now is displayed at the Buffalo Bill Historical Center at Cody, Wyoming, and passed to that museum through the Col. Cody estate. Scientist, hunter, and Indian scholar, George Bird Grinnell observed that when shooting from the ground with a rifle, Cody was a very ordinary shot, "but he was the finest horseback rifle shot ever known." (Courtesy Buffalo Bill Historical Center)

An unusual Union Pacific Railroad gun—a .58 Springfield 1st Model Allin conversion with a barrel shortened to only 12³/4 inches. Stamped in the left side of the stock opposite the lock is "CABOOSE NO. 15" and "LARAMIE DIVISION" with the name "RADCLIFFE."

Another possible Union Pacific Railroad gun, a full-length Springfield .58 1st Model Allin conversion with "BAGGAGE (24)" painted in white on the butt stock.

issued, and by cutting off about four inches of the barrel, I was able to retain it as a condemned piece. I resighted it with peep sights, and it would shoot right where I held it; and I was a good shot.[56]

When William Cody earned the nickname "Buffalo Bill" by hunting buffalo to feed workers on the Kansas Pacific Railroad, the gun he used for the purpose was the 1866 Springfield. An acquaintance described him during one hunt as "mounted on his splendid horse with an improved Springfield rifle in his hands pouring cold lead into the poor buffalo." Cody himself termed the weapon "my celebrated buffalo-killer, 'Lucretia Borgia,'—a newly-improved breech-loading needle gun, which I had obtained from the government." (Appropriately enough, this rifle is now in the Buffalo Bill Museum in Cody, Wyoming.)[57]

In approving the issue of arms to Kansas Pacific crews in 1869, the chief of ordnance noted that "arms and ammunition have heretofore been issued to the

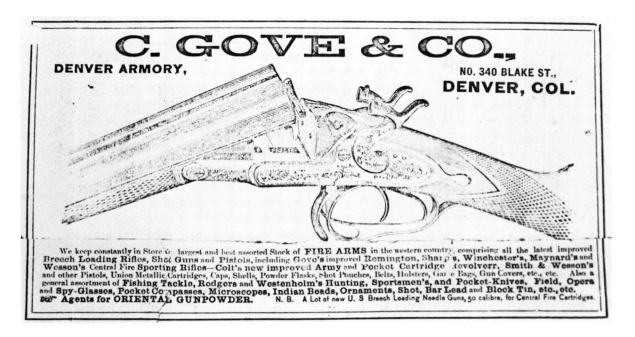

This Carlos Gove ad, from the 1874 Denver City Directory, lists a variety of arms, including "new U.S. Breech Loading Needle Guns, 50 calibre."

'Union Pacific Railway,' and to the 'Western Union Telegraph Company,' under bonds for the return of the same or payment for any that may not be returned." The guns provided to the Union Pacific included a substantial number of Allin-converted Springfields chambered for the .58 rimfire cartridge. One such gun, its barrel cut to 12³/4 in., is stamped on the left side of the stock "Caboose No. 15/Laramie Division." (A large number of fired .58 rimfire cartridge cases, in both the 1³/16 in. and 1⁷/16 in. lengths, have been found along the original U.P. right-of-way in what is now Wyoming.) U.P. engineer W. F. Murphy recalled that when Indians threatened a major attack on the line in August of 1867:

A relief train was sent out from Grand Island, Hank Makely the foreman in charge. I went along with the others. We had all the needle guns we could get and some Spencer Carbines. All classes of employees volunteered [but] Some had only pitch forks and old cavalry sabers.[58]

In 1869 Richard Townshend visited Carlos Gove's gun shop in Denver. Gove had in his workshop:

a Springfield rifle, to which he was putting new

sights . . . every now and then, some discontented U.S. soldier would desert from Ft. Lyon, or one of the other U.S. forts along the frontier, often taking with him his excellent breech-loading Government rifle. . . . This the deserter would promptly trade off to the first ranchman he could strike a bargain with, for a suit of civilian clothes, and go on his way.

A rancher living on the upper Yellowstone in 1870 had two "Army needle guns" which he had supposedly won at faro from soldiers stationed at Fort Ellis. Lt. Gustavus Doane rode out to the ranch to reclaim the guns, but after a long talk with the rancher, Doane conceded that "'a man living in this country needs those guns. Now you keep them but when you come around Fort Ellis you keep them guns scabbarded and well out of sight or I'll have to take them away from you.'"[59]

In his book *Buffalo Land*, published in 1872, William E. Webb claimed that for stalking buffalo, "the most effective weapon is the needle-gun used in the army, having a bore the size of the old Springfield musket and a ball to correspond." He was presumably referring to the .58 rimfire Allin conversions, which were readily available at the time. At Fort Leaven-

Springfield Sporting Breech Loading Rifle.

30 in. Octagon Barrel, Double Trigger, 45-70, 10½ to 11 lbs.	25 00
Springfield Breech Loading Musket, 32 in. Round Barrel, 45-70	17 00
" " " " 32 in. " " 50-70	15 00

Commercially assembled Springfield sporting rifles were advertised
in the 1884 catalogs issued by N. Curry & Bro. of San Francisco
(above) and by the E. C. Meacham Arms Co. of St. Louis.

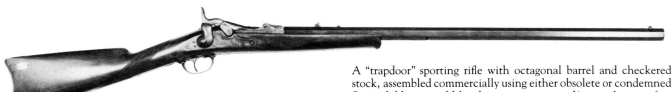

A "trapdoor" sporting rifle with octagonal barrel and checkered
stock, assembled commercially using either obsolete or condemned
Springfield parts sold by the government and/or newly manufactured components. A number of western dealers offered such arms
to civilian buyers in the 1880s and 1890s; most such rifles were
unmarked. The quality and price for such sporters varied considerably, but some compared quite favorably with those produced
by Sharps and other prominent manufacturers. (Courtesy National
Park Service, Fuller Gun Collection, Chickamauga and Chattanooga National Military Park)

worth in June of 1870, in fact, 300 such guns were
sold to the Kansas Pacific railroad. With the military
adoption of a new .45-70 Springfield in 1873, supplies
of the older .50-70s evidently became more accessible
to civilians. War Department General Orders No. 9,
issued in February of 1874, stated that "Department
Commanders may, at exposed frontier settlements in
cases of emergency, direct the sale of arms and ammunition to actual settlers for their protection." Besides "actual settlers," arms dealers in the West also
managed to get up-to-date government guns; early in
1874, for example, Carlos Gove advertised "A Lot of
new U.S. Breech Loading Needle Guns, 50 calibre,
for Central Fire Cartridges."[60]

Presumably most of the Springfields that reached
civilian hands during the late 1860s and early 1870s

retained their basic military configuration, although
in some cases they did acquire minor additions such
as new sights and set triggers. But a trend that was to
become fairly widespread in later years involved much
more than simple modifications. Starting with the
Springfield action, the gunsmith would install a heavy
octagon barrel, sporting-style stock, and fancy fittings,
adding whatever else the customer specified, until the
gun was able to compare favorably with the finest
sporting or target rifle.[61]

Not all the so-called trapdoor or needle rifles used
on the frontier were Springfields, of course. John Cook
left this account of a buffalo hunt in the Texas Panhandle late in 1874:

I was near the wagon; the Enfield was in the front
end of it, and the cartridge-belt around my waist.

Three very good friends, riding mules used in one of Ferdinand Hayden's exploratory expeditions into the Yellowstone country in the early 1870s. Indians in the area still posed a potential threat, as the .50-70 Springfield rifles slung from the saddles indicate.

Hayden's personal lobbying was in large part responsible for the establishment of our first national park, Yellowstone, in 1872, less than a year after Hayden's first view of the area. (U.S. Geological Survey photo, courtesy National Archives)

I hurried for the gun, put in a cartridge, and ran out toward [the buffalo]. . . . I saw the rear of the herd was being followed by one with its right front leg broken and flapping. I aimed and plunked him. . . . Soon Buck came riding out of the coulee and reported that he had killed four buffaloes and broken one's leg that had got away. "Not much he didn't," said his wife; "Mr. Cook killed him with the old needle-gun," which term was used to designate all trap-door breech-blocks. . . .[62]

Exactly which conversion method Cook's Enfield embodied is uncertain, because there were several trapdoor designs adapted to muzzle-loaders and offered to the military. Two of these, the Mont Storm and the Miller, were basically the same as the Springfield: a transverse pivot pin, passing through the upper front corner of the breechblock, allowed the block to swing upward and forward for loading. But two others, the Milbank and the Needham, could also have been considered trapdoor arms; in these designs a vertical pivot, passing through the right front corner of the breechblock, permitted the block to swing outward and forward for loading. A fifth conversion method, designed by Jacob Snider and perhaps best known in connection with the Enfield, was similar to the actions used in the Joslyn and Warner carbines: a longitudinal pivot, passing through the right side of the breechblock, allowed the block to swing upward and to the right to expose the chamber. Conceivably Cook's Enfield could have employed any of these designs, but probabilities are that it was a Mont Storm conversion. Enfields altered to percussion breechloaders by the

An Enfield rifle musket converted to a breechloader using the conversion system designed by Jacob Snider, an American. Although the system was rejected by American officials for military use, it was adopted by England and was used by the Turkish and Serbian armies as well. (Courtesy National Park Service, Fuller Gun Collection, Chickamauga and Chattanooga National Military Park)

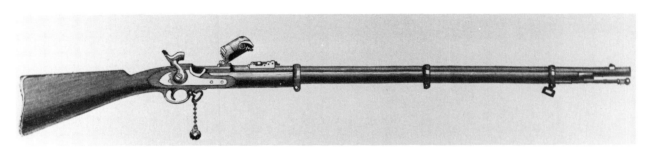

The Mont Storm conversion of the Enfield rifle-musket, from Schuyler, Hartley & Graham's 1864 catalog.

Mont Storm method were marketed by Schuyler, Hartley, and Graham as early as 1864, and by mid-1867 such guns were available in .58 rimfire as well.[63]

On occasion owners of muzzle-loading rifles could find commercial dealers equipped to convert them to breechloaders. An advertisement by James H. Foster & Co. of Chicago, appearing in the Salt Lake City *Telegraph* in April of 1869, included this note: "Muzzle-Loading Shot Guns andRifles altered to Breech-Loaders on the most approved plan." J. P. Gemmer, who took over the Hawken shop after Sam Hawken's retirement, converted a few heavy-barreled plains rifles to .56-.46 breechloaders by the installation of a special trapdoor breechblock, hinged at its upper front corner; the unusual feature of these conversions was that Gemmer cut the chamber into the breechblock itself rather than into the barrel. He also remodeled at least one trapdoor Springfield, fitting the action with Hawken-style barrel and stock, and even adding a modified Hawken hammer to the lock.[64]

San Francisco Mining and Scientific Press, July 1868.

A Sharps carbine is a fitting complement to this scene of hunters skinning a buffalo. (Courtesy Western History Collection, University of Oklahoma Library)

THE SHARPS AND ITS CARTRIDGES

Popular as the Springfield and the Ballard were, frontiersmen also bought two other breechloaders in large numbers—the Remington and the Sharps. Of all the single-shot rifles that came to the postwar West, the Sharps was, in fact, the best known and probably the most widely used. In the early 1880s, after a trip through the Rockies, one writer summed up its popularity by stating that:

A large majority of the frontiersmen I met with—in fact, nearly all of them—used Sharp's rifles. I saw probably a hundred of these in my travels, and only three or four of any other kind. I questioned a great many of the men who use them, as to their effectiveness and adaptation to frontier use, and they all pronounce them the best arm in use, all things considered, for that purpose.[65]

The Sharps Rifle Manufacturing Company had made a few metallic-cartridge arms on an experimental basis during the Civil War, using percussion parts wherever possible, and guns of this type underwent testing in the Ordnance trials of 1865 and 1866. Evidently the first rifle to be designed specifically for a metallic car-

tridge was the "New Model 1866," but it was made in very limited quantity. Far more plentiful were the government-owned percussion carbines converted by Sharps to .50-70 cartridge arms, under a contract signed in November of 1867.[66]

By mid-1868 the company was advertising an "Improved Breech-Loading Metallic Cartridge Rifle And Carbine . . . length of rifle-barrel usually thirty inches; carbine, twenty-four inches; caliber such as may be desired." Whether this rifle was of military or sporting style is uncertain, but by the spring of 1869 the firm was marketing a true half-stock sporting rifle.

Usually made with a 26 in. full-octagon barrel, the Model 1869 was initially chambered for the .50-70 government cartridge, but a few months after its appearance at least three new cartridges were made available for it. All were bottlenecked centerfire rounds; originally called the ".40 Berdan Short," ".44 Berdan Short," and ".44 Berdan Long," they became better known as the .40-50, .44-60, and .44-77 respectively.[67]

In January of 1871 the company brought out a new rifle. External differences between this and the Model 1869 were negligible, but with the new gun came some new cartridges, culminating with high-power loads like

Moses "California Joe" Milner, Custer's chief of scouts during the winter Indian campaigning of 1868. Although armed with a Sharps in this scene, Custer noted that Milner's inseparable companion was a "long Springfield breech-loading rifle." Milner was an in-veterate smoker and was rarely seen without "his stubby, dingy-looking briarwood pipe in full blast. The endurance of his smoking powers was surpassed only by his loquacity." (Courtesy Custer Battlefield Historical and Museum Assn., Inc.)

The classic Sharps "Poison Slinger" or "Big Fifty"—this one with a heavy 30-in. octagon barrel, pewter forestock tip, double set triggers, and a stout rawhide repair at the wrist. (Courtesy Colorado Springs Pioneers' Museum)

the .50-90 and .45-120. After the Sharps firm changed hands in the mid-1870s, the new rifle came to be called the Model 1874, despite the fact that it had made its appearance three years before that. Although preceded by the Model 1869 and followed by the "English" model of 1877 and the hammerless Borchardt model of 1878, the so-called Model 1874 was the real workhorse on the frontier, undoubtedly the most representative of all the single-shot rifles to see service in the postwar West. While professional buffalo hunters sometimes chose the trapdoor Springfield or Remington rolling block, the Sharps probably dropped far more buffalo than either of the others.[68]

When first introduced the Model 1874 sporting rifle was available with round, octagon, or round/octagon barrels from 26 in. to 30 in. long, in weights from about eight to twelve pounds; a purchaser could also select such features as double set triggers, an extralong, extra-heavy barrel, and globe-and-peep sights. A buyer willing to pay for it, in fact, could order a rifle built to any specifications.

During the early and mid-1870s, the company marketed the Model 1874 in a number of distinct versions. Aside from a military-style rifle and carbine, a "Creedmoor" long-range target arm appeared in the spring of 1874; an unadorned, low-priced "Hunter's Rifle" early in 1875; another target rifle, the "Mid Range," early in 1876; and the simple, round-barreled "Business Rifle" in the summer of that year. Even further variations appeared later.[69]

With its vertically sliding breechblock the Sharps had an inherently strong action, and it was a handsomely made rifle; but its popularity did not result from these points alone. What really enhanced the Sharps's popularity among professional buffalo hunters and other frontiersmen was the line of cartridges designed for it, cartridges so ideally suited for the plains that other single-shot manufacturers either copied them directly or devised cartridges which clearly reflected the Sharps influence. In company with Maynard, Sharps was among the first of the large manufacturers to realize that a long slender bullet was ballistically superior to a short fat one of like weight, and demonstrated this by the marketing of .40 caliber loads such as the .40-50 and the .40-70. Any buyer of a Model 1874 who was unwilling to trust his life to these small-caliber rounds could order his rifle chambered for one of the three cartridges available for the Model 1869: the .44-60, the .44-77, or the .50-70.[70]

But during the summer of 1871, when the hide hunters began slaughtering the buffalo in earnest, some Sharps users complained that none of the available loads would drop a buffalo in its tracks, at least not with any consistency. As a result a new Sharps cartridge came out in mid-1872, soon to be famous as the "Poison Slinger" or "Big Fifty"—the .50-90. Essentially a .50-70 case lengthened from 1³/₄ in. to 2¹/₂ in., the .50-90 quickly gained a following among the hide hunters. In mid-1873 the Sharps concern introduced two more cartridges, the .40-90 and the .44-90 "Creedmoor," named after the thousand-yard target range constructed at Creedmoor, Long Island, in 1872. The .44-90, usually loaded with a 520 grain bullet, became a favorite of Kansas and Nebraska hunters, depriving the .50-90 of some of the popularity it would otherwise have had.[71]

Because a hide hunter might fire more than a hundred shots per day, he could seldom justify the expense of factory loaded ammunition; and on the buffalo range during the early 1870s the reloading of cartridge cases by individual shooters really came into its own. In the process a goodly number of hunters devised loads they preferred to the factory standard; in reloading a .44-

Buffaloes slaughtered for their hides (1872). Someone has laid a Sharps rifle against one of the unskinned carcasses. (Courtesy Kansas State Historical Society)

77 cartridge case, for example, a hunter might use only 70 grains of powder, thereby leaving room for a heavier bullet. In like fashion, a .50-90 case could be stuffed with 110 grains of powder, followed by a lighter bullet than the 473 grain standard. As a result of this practice, hunters sometimes referred to the .44-77 as the .44-70 or the .44-75, and called the .50-90 the .50-100 or .50-110.[72]

Because of this variation the only precise way to

The party that discovered gold in the Black Hills of Dakota Territory in 1874—H. N. Ross (1), Dick Stone (2), Harvey Carboot (3), and Jack Cale (4). The latter holds a Winchester M1866 carbine, while Ross poses with a Sharps military rifle and Stone with a Sharps M1874 sporting rifle with full-length scope. (Courtesy State Historical Society of North Dakota)

Reproduction of a tintype view of John A. Williams and hunting companions in west Texas in the 1870s. Williams, at far right, holds a Sharps sporting rifle; another Sharps hangs from the wagon bows. (Courtesy Western History Collections, University of Oklahoma Library)

refer to a standard cartridge was by specifying the caliber and case length, a method preferred by the Sharps company. In fact the company sometimes stamped its rifles "Cal. .40-2^1/$_4$," ".44-2^1/$_4$," or ".50-2^1/$_2$," rather than ".40-70," ".44-77," or ".50-90." The lengths of the more popular Sharps cartridge cases were as follows:

.40-50: 1^{11}/$_{16}$ in.	.44-77: 2^1/$_4$ in.
.40-70: 2^1/$_4$ in.	.44-90: 2^5/$_8$ in.
.40-90: 2^5/$_8$ in.	.50-70: 1^3/$_4$ in.
.44-60: 1^7/$_8$ in.	.50-90: 2^1/$_2$ in.

Except for the .50-70 and .50-90, all these cases were of the bottlenecked type, which permitted the use of relatively large powder charges in cases of comparatively short overall length. But some frontiersmen developed a dislike for necked cartridges, claiming

Johnnie Baker, for a time a marksman with Buffalo Bill Cody's Wild West Show, with an ivory-handled Colt Single Action Army and what appears to be a single trigger, round barrel M1874 Sharps Business rifle. The '74 Sharps was available with various combinations of features. (Courtesy Denver Public Library, Western History Dept.)

Sharps "Business 45" Model 1874 rifle (#161309) shipped to William Coleman & Co. of Deer Lodge, Montana, on June 29, 1878. The wear on the underside of the forestock indicates that the rifle may have traveled many miles across the pommel of a saddle. The original list price for this .45 rifle in 1878 was $35.

that they tended to stick in the chamber after repeated firing. In January of 1875 these complaints were partially stifled by the introduction of the .45-75 Sharps round—simply the .45-70 government case loaded with a little more powder. A straight-cased .40-70 appeared in March of 1876, followed about three months later by the .45-100, characterized by its straight 2⁷/₈ in. case. Still another .45-100, but with a shorter 2⁶/₁₀ in. case, appeared in November of 1876, to be followed by an even shorter .45-90 in June of 1877.[73] Again, however, loads for the new cases often varied: a shooter might fill the .45-2⁷/₈ in. case with as little as 90 grains or as much as 120. Thus the Sharps firm also designated its new straight cases by length:

.40-70: 2¹/₂ in.	.45-100: 2⁶/₁₀ in.
.45-75: 2¹/₁₀ in.	
.45-90: 2⁴/₁₀ in.	.45-100: 2⁷/₈ in.

Consequently a Sharps rifle stamped ".40-2¹/₂" was chambered for the .40-70 straight, while a rifle stamped ".40-2¹/₄" was designed for the older .40-70 necked case.[74]

Whether the cartridge was of .40, .44, .45, or .50 caliber, two types of bullets were available for it. As a rule the lighter bullets for a given caliber were "naked," with two or three grease grooves, while the heavier bullets were "patched and swaged," or compressed to exact shape in a die, with their cylindrical parts covered by a thin paper patch. Paper-patched bullets, which eliminated leading of the bore, usually proved somewhat more accurate than the naked type, but patching a bullet with paper was a tedious job for a hunter in the field. Nevertheless there were some who tried it, and frontier arms dealers occasionally advertised "Patch Paper" among their wares.[75]

As was the case with powder charges, bullet weights often varied widely for a given caliber. For example, bullets for the .44-77, offered at different times by Sharps and other makers, included weights of 297,

312, 280, 395, 400, 405, 422, and 470 grains. The more popular bullet weights for the various Sharps calibers were the following:[76]

.40-50: 265 grains	.44-90: 500–520 grains
.40-70: 330–370 gr.	.45-75: 400–420 gr.
.40-90: 370 gr.	.45-90: 500 gr.
.44-60: 395 gr.	.45-100: 500–550 gr.
.44-77: 395–405 gr.	.50-90: 473 gr.

The muzzle velocities of these cartridges depended upon powder charge, bullet weight, and barrel length. Of the older Sharps loads, the .44-77 would push a 470 grain bullet from the muzzle at about 1250 feet per second. For the .45-70-405 government cartridge, the average muzzle velocity was about 1350 feet per second (when fired in the Springfield rifle barrel); the .45-75-420 Sharps would fall into the same velocity range. The .40-90-370 Sharps bullet could reach 1450 f.p.s.; a .45-90 Sharps, loaded with the company's 293 grain "Express" bullet, could exceed 1500 f.p.s. Some experimenters managed to raise the velocities to even higher levels: in the late 1870s, for example, George B. Grinnell found that a .45-110 load with a special 340 grain bullet would attain the creditable velocity of 1830 f.p.s. Most hunters, however, were satisfied with loads giving velocities of 1400 to 1500 f.p.s.[77]

The gradual improvement in cartridges during the 1870s was accompanied by additional refinements in the rifles that chambered them. In part these refinements resulted from efforts made in connection with an international shooting match held at Creedmoor in September of 1874. The year before, an Irish team had defeated English and Scottish riflemen at Wimbledon, whereupon the victorious Irish challenged American riflemen to a match to decide the world championship in long-range rifle marksmanship. In preparation for this much-publicized event, both Sharps and Remington put together special target rifles chambered for the .44-90 cartridge. Both of these rifles (the

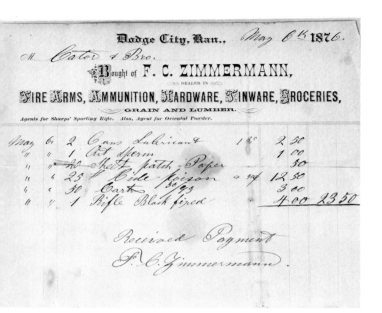

Buffalo hunters' orders invoiced to Robert Cator & Bro. by merchant F. C. Zimmerman of Dodge City, Kansas, agent for Sharps rifles. The purchases included bullet patching paper, .50-95 and .50-110 cartridges, knives, and poison to safeguard hides from insect damage. The $4 entry for "1 Rifle Block fixed" perhaps refers to the repair of a firing pin or cartridge extractor. (Courtesy Panhandle-Plains Historical Museum)

F. C. Zimmerman's gun, hardware, and general store on Front Street in Dodge City, Kansas, in 1875. (Courtesy Kansas State Historical Society)

Ed Schieffelin photographed holding a M1874 Sharps sporting rifle with an unusually heavy barrel; the holstered revolvers appear to be Smith & Wessons. The presence of the miner's pick next to the Sharps puts this image in the category of an occupational view. Schieffelin's Henry rifle is illustrated elsewhere in this chapter. (Courtesy Arizona Historical Society)

Bill Tilghman (right), later a highly regarded lawman, photographed in 1874 with a Sharps sporting rifle. At left is Jim Elder, his hunting partner, with what appears to be a double-barrel shotgun since no rear sight is visible. The image has been reversed, making the Sharps appear to have a left-hand lock. (Courtesy Western History Collection, University of Oklahoma Library)

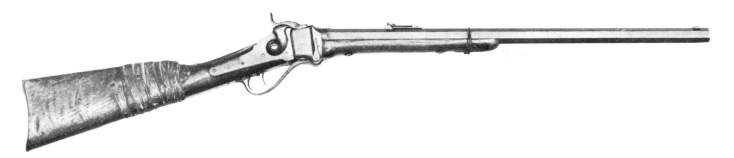

William H. "Bill" Tilghman's Sharps M1874 octagon barrel sporting rifle (#C53858). Factory records show it was first sold to Sharps agent F. C. Zimmerman of Dodge City, Kansas in June of 1874 with a 32-inch .40 caliber barrel, oil-finished stock, and double-set triggers. As a professional hunter, Tilghman reportedly killed some 7,500 buffalo, many of them with this Sharps, including one at a measured distance of one mile while he was camped with a band of Cheyenne Indians. When the rifling became worn, he had the barrel rebored to .50 caliber at the factory. The break in the stock occurred when Tilghman's horse fell. (Courtesy National Cowboy Hall of Fame, Oklahoma City)

Long Range and the Creedmoor) had heavy 32 in. to 34 in. octagon barrels, spirit-level, wind-gauge, globe front sights, finely graduated Vernier peep sights mounted on the tang, and checkered pistol-grip stocks. In short they were the most refined and highly finished rifles of their time.[78]

During the 1874 match the Irish team, using Rigby muzzle-loaders, lost to the Americans by a single point: they lost again in 1875, after a return match in Ireland. Consequently several other makers of single-shot rifles began adding the Creedmoor name to their top-of-the-line guns. In 1875 the Sharps concern offered four different Creedmoor rifles, ranging in price from $65 to $125 and in barrel length from 30 in. to 32 in.; the price depended upon such extras as stock finish and style of sights.[79]

Sharps rifles had been frontier favorites long before the appearance of the Creedmoor models, of course, and dealers all over the West sold them. Even merchants who did not normally handle firearms kept a few on hand. Peter Robidoux, who operated a trading post in Kansas during the late 1860s and early 1870s, wrote later that "I sold everything from a postage stamp to the real old stuff; from a jew's harp to the big Sharps rifle which was used to kill the buffalo and a real menace to the Indians." Despite the many contemporary references to "sixteen pound Sharp's rifles," the average weight of those Sharps shipped west between 1870 and 1876 was eleven and a half pounds, although this increased to fourteen pounds between 1876 and 1878.[80]

Whatever the weight, frontiersmen wanted a Sharps. While Richard Townshend was in Colorado in 1870, he carried a "Sharpe's 50-calibre rifle . . . about the best rifle going in 1870." On one occasion he nailed a "spade-ace" card to a tree and let a Ute warrior named Wolf try the gun; Wolf put three or four shots through it, but Townshend sent a bullet into the nail holding the card: "Wolf fairly fell upon my neck. 'Oh,' he sighed, 'you come with me. Come with me out on the Plains and kill Kiowas.'" Young James Cook, hunting buffalo in the Texas Panhandle in 1874, abandoned his breech-loading Enfield when he was

> fortunate enough to buy of one of [the] hunters a Sharp's 44-caliber rifle, reloading outfit, belt, and 150 shells. The man had used the gun only a short time, and seventy-five of the shells had never been loaded. I got the gun and his interest in the entire buffalo range for thirty-six dollars. . . . It was an elegant, fine-sighted gun, with buckhorn sights.

In late June of that year several hundred Comanche and Cheyenne warriors attacked a buffalo hunters' camp in the Panhandle known as Adobe Walls. But the twenty-eight hunters present, armed largely with Sharps rifles, beat them back with heavy losses. While all the hunters were good marksmen, the best shot of all was made by Billy Dixon, who, using a borrowed .50-90 Sharps, brought down an Indian at a distance later measured at 1538 yards. In Fort Worth at the same time, Frank Collinson bought a "twelve-pound Sharps rifle, forty-four caliber shells, and a reloading outfit." During the civilian-organized Rosebud Expedition, also in 1874, a frontiersman named Jack Bean used a "120-grain long range Sharp's rifle" to shoot an Indian almost a mile away. In Texas the following year John Cook encountered the "dirtiest, greasiest and smokiest looking mortal I had ever seen, as he sat there on a fleet-looking horse, holding in his hands a 44 Sharp's rather carelessly."[81]

Buffalo hunters' camp near Sheridan, Kansas. Seated outside their dugouts, the hunters hold Sharps rifles. (Courtesy Nebraska State Historical Society)

In addition to buffalo hunters and Indian fighters, westerners who used their rifles primarily for target shooting displayed an interest in the Sharps. Early in April of 1875 W. L. Cushing, of Cushing & Moore, Galveston, Texas, wrote the Sharps concern this letter:

If you have any new circulars descriptive of Sharps Creedmoor Rifle I will be pleased to have you forward me same. My intention is to get up a 'long range team' here. We have as fine a range as can be found in the U.S. I am now getting up a Rifle club for shooting range, to be armed with Maynard guns, have already rec'd some of the guns & orders for others. . . . Although Remington's guns seem to have occasioned considerable [?] I must confess to being prejudiced in favor of Sharps though I have seen none of the Creedmoor guns of either make. . . . I am passionately fond of Rifle shooting, have now

a Maynard, Winchester, Spencer, two Ballards, a Wesson & some 3000 rounds of Am. . . .[82]

In Texas, however, the Sharps saw more use as a combat and hunting rifle. A hastily scrawled note from a hunter in Belknap in September of 1875 asked:

What can you send me a gun for—of this patern 44/100 Cal polished stock open sights & double triggers 28 in Half octagon Barrel 70 grain shell (weight 10½ lb) Also What can you send Barrels Already to screw in old Breetches for (30 in) octagon. . . .

An order from Denison, Texas, two months later requested:

one of your long Shell 12 lb Sporting Rifles (or Buffalo Gun) Calliber 50/100 Polished Stock open Sight, Double triggers, 30 inch half round Bbl Reloding outfit for same gun 200 Shells for same gun

Although the parties in this tintype view are unknown today, the arms are a M1866 Winchester rifle at left and a Sharps M1874 sporter. (Courtesy Mr. Herb Peck, Jr.)

100 Sheets patching paper Also one pair Bullet Molds for 50/100 Calliber Short Shell gun (Ring [grooved] Balls). . . .[83]

Months afterward and far to the north, in Wyoming, Edgar Bronson exchanged harsh words with one of his ranch hands, then saw him "throw a cartridge into the great .45-120 Sharps, and cock it." Bronson must have been impressed by the arm, because several years later, during a bloodless engagement with a band of Sioux, he "time and again . . . caught a bead on the chief's breast with my .45-120 Sharps that easily might have sent him into permanent camp on Ghost Creek." For his 1876 exploration of the Snake River, Lt. Gustavus Doane took along a twelve-pound "Sharpes Buffalo Rifle" instead of a standard military arm.[84]

In 1875 a new experimental Sharps had appeared, but it dropped from sight almost immediately. More important was the fact that in that year the Sharps

A Union Pacific Railroad Sharps .45 M1874 sporting rifle with "U.P." burned into the stock and a "J. P. LOWER, DENVER, COLO." dealer stamp on the barrel. (Courtesy Union Pacific Museum)

A street scene in Corinne, Utah, photographed in 1869. Note the sign advertising the establishment of Freund & Bro. (U.S. Geological Survey photo, courtesy National Archives)

operation passed into the hands of new managers, who changed the firm name from the Sharps Rifle Manufacturing Company to the simpler Sharps Rifle Company. Early in 1876 the company moved from Hartford, where it had been since 1851, to a new factory in Bridgeport. The Model 1874s coming out of Bridgeport after April of 1876 had a characteristic "Old Reliable" stamp on their barrels.[85]

Two new Sharps rifles would appear in 1877 and 1878, but improvements came from other sources besides the factory. Among the best known of these unofficial modifications was that patented by Frank Freund of Cheyenne in August of 1876. Freund altered the breechblock and breechblock mortise in the frame to allow the block to tilt backward as it dropped downward for loading; as the block began sliding upward in preparation for firing, the contour of the frame mortise forced the block from the backward-tilted to the vertical position, and the block, in turn, could thereby force a cartridge into a heavily fouled chamber. Besides a modified action, a Freund-Sharps might

have other refinements as well, such as a Freund-made .40-90 barrel and Freund's "More Light" sights. Although he installed his barrels and sights on other rifles, Freund's design efforts were best known in connection with the Sharps, and the Freund-altered Sharps achieved an enviable reputation on the frontier.[86]

Freund's favorite cartridge was the .40-90, a load which remained popular as long as the Sharps rifle itself. During the middle and late 1870s there was a noticeable increase in the use of .40 and .45 caliber cartridges, with a corresponding decrease in the popularity of the older .44 and .50 loads. To be sure, the .44s and .50s stayed in use for many years after the mid-1870s; one of these long-lived rifles was very probably that ordered by Charles Metz ("Dealer In Hides, Furs, Wool and Cotton") of Sherman, Texas, early in 1877: "one gun 44 Calibre. long Shell, to weigh 12#, and reloading outfit. Patched bulls. also 200 Shells."[87]

But John Cook, who by 1877 was still hunting buffalo in the Panhandle, "had bought a Creedmoor 45 Sharp's at Fort Elliot the fall before and most of the

The Freund & Brother gunshop at Laramie, Wyoming Territory, about 1870. Of the four long guns visible in the scene, three are identifiable. The mounted man at far left has a pronghorn antelope across the rear of his saddle and carries a M1866 Winchester rifle.

The man standing on the mound of sand holds a double-key percussion muzzle-loader, while the whiskered individual to his left carries another '66 rifle by Winchester. (Courtesy Union Pacific Museum)

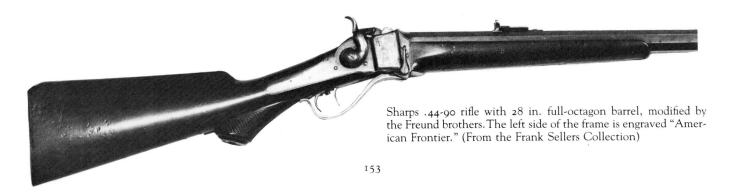

Sharps .44-90 rifle with 28 in. full-octagon barrel, modified by the Freund brothers. The left side of the frame is engraved "American Frontier." (From the Frank Sellers Collection)

153

Field & Farm, September 1888.

old hunters were now using that caliber. They were long-range guns. . . . Sewall had a long-range 45 Creedmoor Sharp's, a nearly new gun, and he was known on the range as a dead shot." In June of 1877 J. C. Short, a Fort Worth arms dealer, wrote the Sharps firm to ask:

> What will an Octagon Bl Cost to Screw in to an old Stock of 44 cal Creedmore Rifle . . . 45 Cal Sighted Ready for use & to weigh heavy enough to make the gun weigh 14 lbs when compleated also the price of Guns of all youre make & the Shortist time you could fill and order of Six or 10 guns and the best terms & c . . . have had calls for youre Guns time & a gain & will have a heavy trade this fall for youre valuable Guns & I want to sell over 100 this fall if I can get them in time for the hunters. . . .

Because of the .45's growing popularity, a factory price list issued in January of 1878 stated that "rifles of 45 calibre having proved to give much better results and

greater satisfaction to our customers, we have discontinued the manufacture of either the 44 or 50 calibre, except on special order."[88]

No less popular than the big .45s were the smaller .40s. Writing from Fort Concho, Texas, in February of 1877, Andrew Roberts asked for:

> the following description of Gun [to be sent] care of *Post-Trader* at Fort Concho . . . Length 28 Inches. Weight 8 lbs. Octagon Barrel. Calibre 40. Globe Sight. double Triggars. 1 11/16 length of Shell. Plain Grip. Oil Stock. With Reloading outfit. Charger for 50 grs. and 200 Shells. . . .

A friendlier, less businesslike letter came from A. B. McDowell, another Texan, at about the same time:

> About twelve months ago I was about to order one of your Rifles when my wife put her Veto on it, as I had then so many on hand, so I then made her a promise that I would not get one of your Rifles until I could kill deer and dress hides enough to pay for it. The fact of the busness is I think she is becoming a little jealous of my fine guns. We have shooting matches in the neighbourhood and I want a gun that I can rely on. The hide I send you is a fair sample of the lot I have, both in size and quality. they are splendid hides, no chemicals used in dressing them. If you can engage them at $2.50 each let me know immdiatly and I will forward the hides while you put me up the Rifle I order. Sporting Rifle. Weight 9 or 10 lbs. Octagon Barrel 32 inch. Caliber 40, Oil finish Stock. Length of shell 2 1/4 inches 70 grains powder Please send Reloading Impliments & c. . . . The Rifle I order is for Target shooting, please have it thoroughly tested particularly where accuracy is concerned . . . I send for a 40 cal. Rifle though if the 44 is a more reliable gun send me one of them. if not, I would prefer the 40. . . . P.S. Please let me know what kind of Pistols you manufacture if any.

And in June of 1878 Isaac Sollers wrote from Fort McKavett, Texas:

> i wish to know the value of your guns of the following Discription Cal. 40 30 inch octagon Barrel weight Between 10. & 12 lbs s single triger Strait Shell 2 1/4 inch Shell 70 grains Powder 1 1/8 inch [330 grain] Patched Ball and Reloading outfitt complete and 200 Shells . . . i have used your gun for Buffalo Hunting and saw them used considerable and consider the 40 cal. the best gun for Hunting as the Buffalo are very wild and Have to be shot while on the run therefore i Beleive the 40 cal. will Penatrate Deeper through the flesh and intrels than any other gun made.[89]

During 1878 James Cook and a hunting partner supplied enough antelope to the hungry residents of Cheyenne to enable Cook to buy "a very fine Sharps 40-90 target rifle, for which I paid $125.00. We loaded all of our cartridge shells and moulded and patched our bullets." In August of the same year Frank Mayer supplemented his income by providing wild meat for the miners in Leadville. He had three rifles, all .40 caliber: a .40-70 Sharps, a .40-90 Ballard, and a .40-70 Maynard with an extra 28-gauge shot barrel. Of the three Mayer liked his Sharps the best. Yet another testimonial for the .40 caliber Sharps came in January of 1879 from T. Holloway, foreman of the San Saba Springs Ranch in central Texas:

> You will do me a favor by sending me the following articles Viz one bullet mold (40 cal) 265 grs " wad cutter (40 cal) "charger 50 grains 100 shells (50 grs—$1^{11}/_{16}$ inch long 40 cal) They are for one of your 40 cal rifles that I bought of J. C. Petmecky Austin Tex last summer, who was to have sent me the above named articles I waited three months & then wrote three times to him & never got an answer, so I thought it best to apply to you direct, as I have only 19 shells & a few bullets & in this part of the country between Indians Mexicans & desperado whites arms have to be your constant companion. & I should like to see more of yours in use here & I believe they would be if there was not so much horse back traveling done when the 'Winchester' is used it being a little handier to carry on the saddle than yours. but I can carry yours without any trouble. but a gun like mine $2^{1}/_{2}$ or 3 in shorter & a couple of lbs lighter would beat a winchester every way. but I am content with my old reliable as it is. at present I am foreman for Messrs Shannon & Black stock men & the fear of the law is not half so great as the fear of a bullet with the characters we have to deal with. . . .

While he was hunting near the Laramie Peaks in September of 1879, John Lord ran into a big silvertip which "stopped quick, with his head as high as he could get it. My rifle was a Sharp's forty caliber, with seventy grains of powder. . . . When the gun cracked the bear went over backwards." During a Montana hunt about two years later, George Bird Grinnell noted that:

> In place of his own rifle, Hofer was carrying one of mine—a .40-90 Sharps business rifle. I had furnished [a] 225-grain hollow-pointed ball. The cartridges were loaded with 100 grains C. & H. [Curtis & Harvey] powder. At short range the effect of this bullet was apparently as killing as my .45 caliber.[90]

Many frontiersmen preferred the .45, especially in

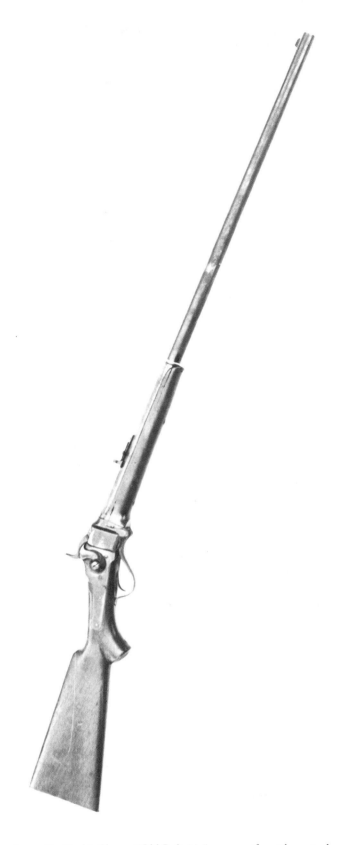

James H. Cook's Sharps "Old Reliable" .40-90 rifle with 34-inch octagonal barrel which he purchased for $125. Carved in the left side of the stock just behind the frame is "Lucy/JHC/1879." (From the James H. Cook Collection, National Park Service)

which weighed over fifteen pounds and cost seventy-five dollars, although I could have gotten a lighter 45-90 No. 13 for the same price.

While traveling through New Mexico in 1879, Richard Townshend, himself a Sharps owner, encountered a band of outlaws: "the biggest of them—the man who filled my eye most—carried not one but two rifles, a sixteen-shot Winchester for quick shooting, and a Sharpe's .45 calibre, the famous 'Buffalo gun' of the plains hunter, for long range work."[91]

After bringing out the .45-90-2⁴/10 in. cartridge in June of 1877 Sharps marketed no new cartridges, concentrating on rifles instead. The "English" model, introduced in the fall of 1877, embodied an action which, although typically Sharps in appearance, was as light as possible, to permit the use of a heavier barrel and still keep the overall weight of the gun within the ten-pound limit required for most formal shooting matches. Production and sale of the Model 1877 in its original target version was limited (although some did reach Nathaniel Curry of San Francisco), and in 1880 the left-over actions were barreled and stocked as sporting rifles and shipped to John P. Lower in Denver.[92]

More widely used than the Model 1877 was a new hammerless Sharps, announced to the arms trade in January of 1878. Based on a patent issued to Hugo Borchardt in December of 1876, the new rifle retained the vertically sliding breechblock, but employed an automatically cocked, longitudinally sliding striker, housed inside the block, to detonate the primer. When the shooter lowered the breechblock, dual camming plates inside the frame forced the striker to full cock, and as the block dropped it automatically engaged the safety; with the block closed, the shooter could disengage the safety by means of a small "safety trigger" behind the main trigger.[93]

Because it did away with the outside hammer and inefficient double-angled firing pin of the Model 1874, the Sharps-Borchardt represented a distinct improvement in the time-honored Sharps action. Although it was available in a number of different styles—Creedmoor-type target rifle, heavy-barreled sporting rifle, full-stocked military rifle, and carbine—conservative frontiersmen did not like its appearance, and early sales in the West were slow. Buyers who preferred a sidehammer Sharps could still purchase a Model 1874 in one of several styles, from the simple round-barreled "Business Rifle," priced at $35, to the octagon-barreled "Mid-Range Rifle" at $65. In September of 1879, more than a year after the Model 1878's appearance, the Beebe brothers, "Gun and Locksmiths" of Denison, Texas, asked the Sharps concern to "please state price of Old model, 40 cal. 12 lb. gun." A year after this

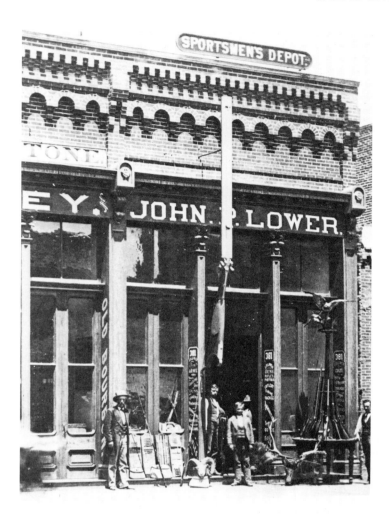

John P. Lower's Sportsmen's Depot in Denver. Among the rifles which can be identified in the rack at right are a Winchester lever action, a Frank Wesson single shot, and a Sharps sporter. Note the overside double rifle or rifle/shotgun (with sights) mounted above the sidewalk for advertising purposes. Another view of the Lower store, perhaps taken at an earlier date, shows an awning above the store front with the wording in large letters "SHARP'S RIFLES AND COLT'S PISTOLS" rather than the double-barrel gun. (Courtesy Denver Public Library, Western History Dept.)

the long 2⁷/8 in. case. Grinnell's favorite hunting rifle during the late 1870s was "a .45-90-450 Sharpe long-range" model. Andrew Garcia, before leaving for the Musselshell in 1878, decided that:

> I had to buy a buffalo gun. Like the Chinaman who took the largest size boot if it was the same price as the smaller size to get more leather for the money, I bought a 45-120 caliber Sharps rifle buffalo gun,

The "hammerless" Borchardt Model 1878 Sharps, represented by this military-style rifle, was one of the strongest and most advanced designs of its era. A Colt M1878 double action revolver worn butt forward completes Arizonan J. L. Redfern's arsenal. (Courtesy Arizona Historical Society)

John P. Lower of Denver and the target he shot offhand at 200 yards (50 shots) with a Sharps M1878 Borchardt rifle on January 2, 1882. Although he had originally advised the Sharps company that their hammerless Borchardt model would not prove popular in the West, he later purchased substantial quantities for resale and used the military model he holds here for much of his own offhand shooting. The Borchardt was produced between 1877 and 1881, in .40, .44, and .45 calibers. Designer of the action, Hugo Borchardt, later became famous for his development of an auto-loading pistol. (Courtesy Denver Public Library, Western History Dept.)

request, a hastily written order came to the company from Overmier and O'Neil of Parker Station, Texas:

Gents we want 1874 Rifle 12#s want the guns by 5 of Nov. or not at all or 10th. We detest so much trouble about the small matter no guns can be sold here after the Hunting season which ends in de-cember we want the guns for Buffaloes and other large Animals & c[94]

Gradually, however, the new Borchardt found its way into western hands. In October of 1879, only a month after requesting prices of the "Old model" Sharps, the Beebe brothers of Denison ordered:

2 Sharps 'Business rifles' Model 1878. 40 cal 28 inch octagon barrell. double triggers 2½ in chambered for straight shell holding 70 gr powder. plain polish American walnut stock. weight 10 lbs or over. 2

A hunting party poses before a photographer's canvas backdrop in the late 1860s. W. N. Byers (standing, right) holds a rolling-block sporting rifle, as does the man seated at left (note the cleaning rod beneath the barrel). Their companions pose with a Spencer carbine (seated, center) and a double-barrel shotgun (seated, right). (Courtesy Denver Public Library, Western History Dept.)

set of reloading impliments for same & 200 shells. 100 sheets of double thickness patch paper.

A year later another Texan, P. H. Fagan of Victoria County, informed the Sharps firm that:

I am very much pleased with the Express Rifle I purchased of you last August Through H. Halfin & Co. I would not exchange it for any Rifle I ever saw I have never lost Deer or other game that I have shot with it . . . at first I did not like it on account of it being Hammerless but now I would not have a gun with a Hammer it is much quicker and Safer I have never had it to snap. The only trouble I have is with the Double Triggers . . . I will do all I can for you in this Section in recommending your Rifles as I think they are the best in the world. . . .[95]

THE REMINGTON ROLLING-BLOCK

The buyer looking for a conventional exposed-hammer rifle had, of course, other choices besides the Sharps. In many areas of the West the Sharps's closest competitor became the Remington rolling-block rifle, the most famous of all Remington cartridge rifles to reach the frontier. Prior to the rolling-block's appearance, however, the Remington concern had offered two single-shot shoulder arms to the civilian purchaser.

The earlier of the two, the split-breech carbine, was based on patents issued to Joseph Rider in December of 1863 and November of 1864. The breechblock in this gun, pivoted near its lower front corner, swung backward and downward for loading. It was locked in place by an L-shaped hammer, whose longitudinal arm

GENERAL PRICE LIST. - - - - - REVISED JANUARY, 1876.

THE BEST BREECH-LOADING RIFLE IN THE WORLD.

E. Remington & Sons,

ILION, N. Y.

The Remington

CREEDMOOR RIFLE.

Shot by Fulton, Bodine, Hepburn, Dakin, Coleman, Canfield, in the great International Contests.

Victorious at Creedmoor, 1874, Dollymount, 1875

Price List of Remingtons' Breech-loading Rifles, Shot Guns, Pistols, Cartridges, &c.

Sporting, Hunting and Target Rifles.

STEEL BARRELS.

Weight of No. 1 Rifle, from 8½ to 15 pounds.
Weight of No. 2 Rifle, from 5½ to 8 pounds.

Length of Barrels	24, 26 in.,	28 in.,	30 in.,	32 in.,	34 in.,
Price	$32.00.	$34 00.	$36.00.	$38.00.	$40.00.

EXTRAS.

Peep and Globe Sights, per set	$5.00	Pistol-Grip Stocks	$10.00
Set Triggers	2.50	Swivel and Sling	2.00
Varnished Stocks, selected	4.00	Re-loading Implements, per set	5.00
Oiled and Polished Stocks, selected	4.00	Rifles of 22-100, extra for calibre	2.00

CREEDMOOR RIFLE, Vernier Peep and Wind Gauge Globe Sight, Pistol Grip ... $100.00
Sole Leather, Trunk Shape, Creedmoor Rifle Case ... 20.00
" " " " " Cartridge Case ... 2.50
Spirit Level for Globe Sight, extra, ... 5.00
Sight Discs for Globe Sight, extra, each ... 1.50
Shells, per 100 ... 2.50
Swedged Bullets, per 100 ... 1.50
Vernier Sights, separate from the gun ... 16.00
Wind Gauge Sights, separate from the gun ... 4.00
Primers, (per box, 250) ... 50
Ball Seater ... 1.25
Primer Extractor ... 1.25

CARTRIDGES FOR SPORTING RIFLES.

Prices per 1000	$8.00.	$13 50.	$18.00.	$24.00	$30.00.	Rim Fire.
Sizes	22 long,	32 long,	38 long,	44 long,	46 long.	
Weight of Ball	29 grs.,	91 grs.,	148 grs.,	222 grs.,	306 grs.	
Weight of Powder	5 grs.,	13 grs.,	18 grs.,	28 grs.,	35 grs.	
Prices per 1000	$35.00.	$37.50.	$45.00.	$33.00.	$37.50.	Centre Fire.
Sizes	40,	44,	44 Creedmoor.	45,	50.	
Weight of Ball	315 grs.,	400 grs.,	550 grs.,	300 grs.,	450 grs.	
Weight of Powder,	50 grs.,	77 grs.,	90 grs.,	45 grs.,	70 grs.	

CASES FOR RIFLES.

Black Walnut, lined, each,	$ 7.00 to $15.00	Bag Leather, flexible, gun shape	$3.00
Mahogany, " "	7.00 to 20 00	Sheepskin " "	2.00
Rosewood, " "	20.00 to 40 00	Canvass, " "	2.50
Russett Leather, stiff, trunk shape	15.00	Cartridge Belts	$2.50 to 5.00
Russett Leather, stiff, gun shape	6.00	Cartridge Box and Belt	1.25

Double-Barreled Breech-Loading Shot-Gun.

Recommended by many of the best American Sportsmen.

WHITMORE'S PATENTS. AUG. 8th, 1871. APRIL 16, 1872.

In order to suit the requirements of our different customers, we make three styles of guns, differing *only in the finish and kind of barrels and stocks*, bore 10 and 12 gauge, weight 8 to 8¾ lbs., which we offer at the follow-ing prices:

Plain Walnut Stock, Decarbonized Steel Barrel ... $45.00
Extra " " Twist Steel Barrel ... 60.00
Extra " " Laminated Barrel, Engraved Lock Plate and Breech Frame ... 75.00
Extra Pairs of Barrels, fitted to same Breech ... $20 to 40.00
Double Gun, one Barrel Rifle and one Shot, Decarbonized Steel Barrels ... 65.00
Length of Barrels, 28, 30 inches.

Breech-Loading Single-Barrel Shot-Gun.

16 bore, 30 in. barrels, w't 6½ lbs. Prices, $22.50, $55, $56, $70, $80, $100, according to style.

BREECH-LOADING SHELLS.

Remington Metal, per doz.	$2.00	Paper Shells, 2d quality, No. 10, ℔ 100,	$2.25
Paper Shells, 1st quality, No. 10, ℔ 100,	2.50	Paper Shells, 2d quality, No. 12, ℔ 100,	1.75
Paper Shells, 1st quality, No. 12, ℔ 100,	2.25	Paper Shells, 3d quality, No. 10, ℔ 100,	1.50
		Paper Shells, 3d quality, No. 12, ℔ 100,	1.25

PRIMERS.

Remington, per box, 250 ... 50 cts. | For Paper Shells, per box, 250 ... 75 cts.

WADS.

Paper, per box ... 25 cts. | Felt, per box ... 35 cts.
Eley's best, per box ... .63 cts.

Breech-Loading Military Fire-Arms.

ABOUT 1,000,000 ARMS OF THIS SYSTEM NOW IN THE HANDS OF TROOPS.

	Without Bayonet.	With Bayonet.
U. S. Model—Cal. 50. Angular Bayonet. Length of Barrel, 32.5 in. Length of Gun, 47.5 in. Weight without Bayonet, 9 lbs. 1 oz. U. S. Cartridge. Weight with Bayonet, 9 lbs, 15 oz.	$16 50	$18 50
Springfield Transformed.—Cal. 58 Angular bayonet. Length of Barrel, 39 in. Length of gun, 54.75 in. Weight without Bayonet, 9 lbs. 11 oz. Weight with Bayonet, 10 lbs. 9 oz.	13 00	15 00
Springfield Transformed.—Cal. 58. (Short Model). Angular Bayonet. Length of barrel, 36 in. Length of Gun, 51.75 in. Weight without Bayonet, 9 lbs. 8 oz. Weight with Bayonet, 10 lbs. 6 oz.	13 00	15 00
Spanish Model.—Cal. .433 in. (or 11mm.) Angular Bayonet. Length of Barrel, 32.2 in. Length of Gun, 50.2 in. Weight without Bayonet, 9 lbs. 4 oz. Spanish or Russian Cartridge Weight with Bayonet, 10 lbs. 2 oz.	16 50	18 50
Civil Guard.—Cal. .433 in. (or 11mm.). Sabre Bayonet. Length of Barrel, 30.35 in. Length of Gun, 45.35 in. Weight without Bayonet, 8 lbs. 10 oz. Spanish or Russian Cartridge. Weight with Sabre Bayonet, 10 lbs. 4 oz.	17 00	20 50
French Model.—Cal .433 in. (or 11mm.) Sabre Bayonet. Length of Barrel, 35.2 in. Length of Gun. 50.2 in. Weight without Bayonet, 9 lbs. 4 oz. Egyptian Cartridge. Weight with Sabre Bayonet, 10 lbs. 14 oz.	17 00	20 50
Carbine.—Cal. .50, or Cal. .433. Length of Barrel, 20.5 in. Weight of Carbine, 7 lbs. Length of Carbine, 35.5 in.	16 00	

Single Shot Navy Pistol.—Cal. .50. New Model of 1870 ... 10 00
Same principle as Remington Breech-Loading Rifle Length of Barrel, 8 in. Weight of Pistol 2 lbs. Using Metallic Cartridge.

Six Shot Army Revolver.—Cal. .44. Remodled ... 12 50
Using Metallic Cartridge, Rim Fire. Length of Barrel, 8 in. Weight, 2 lbs. 14 oz. Using Cartridge .46. Price $2.40 per 100.

Six Shot Navy Revolver—Cal. 36. Remodeled ... 12 00
Using Metallic Cartridge, Rim Fire. .38. Length, 7½ in. Weight 2 lbs. 10 oz. Price $1.70 per 100.

No. 3, ARMY REVOLVER.— ... 15 00
Loaded, and Cartridge ejected, without removing cylinder.
New Model, 1875. Centre Fire Metallic Cartridge. Cal. 44.
(10.000 now being made for a Foreign Government.)

MILITARY CARTRIDGES.

	Weight of Powder.	*Weight of Bullet.*	*Price per Thousand.* *With Patch*		
Egyptian	76 grains.	395 grains.	$39.00	38.00	*Centre Fire.*
Spanish	77 "	400 "			
Russian	77 "	370 "			
.58 Cal. / .50 Cal.	70 "	450 "	35.00		
.50 Cal. Pistols	30 "	320 "	24.00		

For No. 3 Revolvers, .44. Cal. new Centre Fire Cartridge, $18.00.

Remingtons' Celebrated Steel, Iron and Stubs Twisted Rifle and Shot-Gun Barrels, and Gun Mountings.

Standard Remington Pistols.

STYLES.		*Blue.*	*Plated Frame.*	*Full Plate.*	*Eng'vd. Extra.*	*Ivory Stock, Extra.*	*Pearl Stock, Extra.*
Vest Pocket 22, Breech-Loader	Using Metallic Cartridge.	$ 3 25	....	$ 3 75	$ 2 00	$ 4 00	$ 5 00
Vest Pocket 41, Breech-Loader		3 75	$ 4 25	4 75	2 00	4 00	6 00
S. B. Derringer, Breech-Loader, per pair.		7 00	7 75	8 50	4 00	8 00	12 00
Repeater, five shot		8 00	8 50	9 00	4 00	4 00	6 00
Repeater, four shot		8 50	9 00	9 50	4 00	4 00	6 00
Repeater, double-barrel		8 00	8 50	9 00	4 00	4 00	6 00
Pocket, double-action Revolver		8 00	8 50	9 00	4 00	5 00	6 00
New Pocket Revolver, 3½ inch		9 25	9 75	10 50	4 00	5 00	7 50
New Pocket Revolver, 4½ inch		9 50	10 00	10 75	4 00	5 00	7 50
Police Revolver, 3½ and 4½ inch		10 00	10 75	11 50	5 00	5 00	9 00
Police Revolver, 5½ inch		10 50	11 25	12 00	5 00	5 00	9 00
Police Revolver, 6½ inch		11 00	11 75	12 50	5 00	5 00	9 00

New Revolver—Best in the World.

REMINGTONS' NO. 1 POCKET REVOLVER, (Smoot's Patent.)

New Model.—Using No. 30 Metallic Cartridge. Loaded, and cartridge ejected without removing Cylinder. Weight, 10 oz. ALL STEEL—BARREL AND FRAME ONE SOLID PIECE. Price, full plate, $10.00.

Rifle Canes, $10.00. Same, with Ivory Head, $15.00.

Remington price list, January 1876.

turned on a pivot set well in front of the breechblock pivot. As the hammer swung upward to fire, lugs on its longitudinal arm rose into engagement with bearing surfaces on the front face of the breechblock below the breechblock pivot, preventing the block from tilting backward at the moment of discharge. To permit this locking arrangement, a vertical slot was cut through the center of the block; hence the "split-breech" nickname. Made primarily in two calibers, .46 Long rimfire and .56-.50 Spencer, the carbine was first sold to the military; with the end of the war it was also channeled into the commercial market. A Remington price list issued to retail dealers in January of 1866 included the split-breech carbine with 20 in. round barrel, in .46 caliber, at $23. At least one split-breech sporting rifle took shape, but Remington evidently had no serious intention of marketing such a gun.[96]

The other early Remington single-shot, probably introduced in the spring of 1866, was developed by Fordyce Beals exclusively as a civilian arm. Based on three patents granted to Beals between June of 1864 and January of 1866, which dealt primarily with its method of extraction, the Beals was a fairly small, lightweight rifle intended for low-powered rimfire cartridges. With its forward-sliding barrel, which rested in a brass or iron frame, the Beals was mechanically similar to the Sharps & Hankins carbine; the barrel was pushed forward for loading and pulled back for firing by a toggle link connected to an underlever. Made with slender octagon or round/octagon barrels, usually chambered for the .32 and .38 rimfire rounds, the Beals was not really suited for the severe service of the frontier. Nevertheless, Remington advertised it in papers such as the *Dallas Herald* in August of 1867.[97]

Professor A. H. Thompson on "Old Ute" with a rolling-block
sporting rifle beneath Thompson's right leg (c. 1874). (U.S. Geological Survey photo, courtesy National Archives)

"All the officers and the photographer insisted that not only the game but the hunter should appear in the picture. So I sat down, dressed as I was in my buckskins, resting one hand on an antler. . . ." So George Custer described this scene in a letter to his wife in 1873 during the expedition into the Yellowstone country.

He thought highly of Remington rolling-block sporting rifles, as seen here. Although Custer liked to "brag on" some of the fine shots he made, George Bird Grinnell, who accompanied him on the 1874 Black Hills expedition, noted that "Custer did no shooting that was notable." (Courtesy Chicago Historical Society)

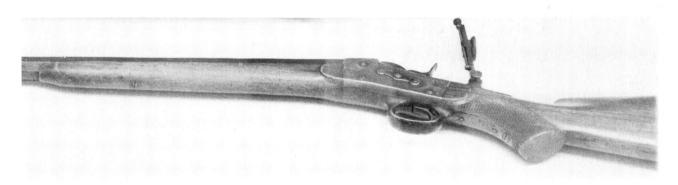

Remington .44 rolling-block sporter once owned by George A. Custer and exhibited at the Monroe County (Michigan) Historical Museum in Monroe.

Remington rifle modified by Carlos Gove to incorporate an underlever to operate the action. The rifle is chambered for the .45-100 Remington cartridge and the 32 in. barrel is marked on top "C. GOVE/DENVER COL." (From the Frank Sellers Collection)

A Freund-modified .44-77 Remington. The 28 in. barrel is marked in script "Freund & Bro. Denver, Colorado. U.S.A." (From the Frank Sellers Collection)

Heavy .45-cal. Remington sporting rifle, its 30 in. octagon barrel marked "C Gove/Denver, Col.," and also stamped "C. H. Utter" four times. "Colorado Charlie" Utter was Wild Bill Hickok's companion during Hickok's last days in Deadwood. (Courtesy Colorado Springs Pioneers' Museum)

A well-known incident involving one of these early Remingtons, very probably the split-breech carbine, occurred in the summer of 1866, when Nelson Story and twenty-odd hands drove a herd of cattle from Texas to Montana. Although attacked by overwhelming numbers of Sioux, Story and his men used their Remingtons with the same telling effect that the .50-70 Springfields were to have at the Hayfield and Wagon Box fights a year later.[98]

Remington's real fame in the West, however, was to rest on its rolling-block rifle. Patented as a side-hammer design by Joseph Rider in January of 1865, the rifle appeared in prototypes in its perfected centerhammer form in mid-1866. Initially Remington officials concentrated on selling the rolling-block to military organizations both here and abroad: Denmark contracted for more than 40,000 in the spring of 1867, and the rifle earned a silver medal at the Paris Exposition later the same year, bringing forth more orders from European powers. At least one early sporting rifle, assembled on the sidehammer rolling-block frame, made its appearance, but the immediate success achieved by the perfected rolling-block in its military version apparently precluded any serious attempt to market a sporting version until 1868.[99]

Cartridges for the early rolling-block sporters were commonly the .32 Long, .38 Long, .44 Long, .46 Long, and .50-70 rimfires, plus a new bottlenecked centerfire .45-45-290, termed the ".45 Sporting" round, and probably the .50-70 centerfire as well. A more powerful rolling-block rifle, however, was the Remington conversion of the Springfield muzzle-loading rifle-musket. Commercially available by 1869 and perhaps earlier, this conversion united the Remington action with a Springfield barrel, forestock, and buttstock; the cartridge this rifle chambered was the .58 Berdan Musket centerfire round, loaded with a 530 to 560 grain bullet and 80 to 85 grains of powder. Labeled the "Springfield Transformed" model, this conversion sold for considerably less than the standard sporting rifle, which by September of 1872, with octagon barrels from 24 in. to 34 in. long and in weights from six and a half to fifteen pounds, retailed at $30 to $40. A company advertisement at that time, which listed the .44-77 among the other caliber choices, noted specifically that "the Remington Sporting Rifle is now the preferred arm for hunting purposes on the Plains; its simplicity and durability especially commending it for frontier use."[100]

Advertisements for the rifle also appeared between February and August of 1872 in such western papers as the *Elko Independent*, San Francisco's *Mining and Scientific Press*, and the *Lincoln County Advertiser*, to be followed by another ad in Denver's *Rocky Mountain News* in March of 1873. Presumably these ads were

for the large-frame "Sporting Rifle No. 1," but in December of 1872 Remington had announced its smaller "Gem" or "new model light rifle"—later termed the "Sporting Rifle No. 2"—designed for .22 to .44 caliber rimfire cartridges, and made in weights ranging from five and a half to eight pounds. Despite its light weight, the No. 2 did see some use on the frontier. Carlos Gove, for example, is known to have converted at least one No. 2 to chamber the .44-40 centerfire cartridge.[101]

Gove, in fact, was among the best known of the western gunsmiths to handle the Remington. Charles B. Norton's *American Breech-Loading Small Arms* of 1872 included a picture of a ten-shot target group of about 15/16 in., fired at 50 yards "by Mr. Gove, of Denver City, Colorado, with a Remington sporting rifle of .44 calibre." By January of 1874 the Denver gunsmith was offering "Gove's Improved Remington," a modification involving the attachment of an underlever to the rolling breechblock to give the shooter greater leverage in extracting a fired case. The Gove-attached underlever could indeed be an asset, because the Remington sometimes did have extraction trouble. Late in April of 1875 John S. Moore of the Galveston house of Cushing & Moore wrote that:

Since I have tried the Remington Creedmoor I am more than ever impressed that I will decidedly prefer the Sharps. I have no fault to find with the shooting of the R. but regard the action as objectionable in several points. Aside from this the gun will do for target practice exclusively but I would never take it into the field for sharpshooting & unless the guns are fit for such service they are of no practical benefit. It is an impossibility nearly (at least without considerable difficulty) to fire a second round with the R.C. without wiping. While we all acknowledge the importance of wiping in target practice occasion may arise elsewhere when the delay would result in the man behind the gun getting "wiped." I believe [the Sharps] Rifle fired twenty five rounds at Creedmoor without cleaning;—its ability to do this I regard as an inestimable advantage;—throwing the shell clear of the gun is another. . . .[102]

Gove was not the only frontier gunsmith to alter and improve the Remington. Frank Freund had listed himself as a Remington agent as early as mid-1868, and the stock of goods in his Denver store late in 1872 included "Winchesters . . . Sharps, [and] Remingtons." Three of Freund's firearms patents, the first issued in July of 1874, covered improvements of the rolling-block action.[103]

Most familiar of the refined rolling-blocks, of course, was the "Long Range Match Rifle, for 'Creedmoor' shooting," introduced in the summer of 1873. With

A Remington was the choice of the man at far left, while the individual third from left holds a double-barrel shotgun. Reclining third from right is the famed frontier photographer William A. Soule. (Courtesy Smithsonian Institution, Bureau of American Ethnology Collection)

this rifle came a new cartridge, the .44-90 Remington, a load very similar to (but not usually interchangeable with) the .44-90 Sharps. The Remington Creedmoor was an expensive item, retailing for $100, but for the less-affluent buyer the company offered its "Deer" rifle; marketed late in 1872, it had a 24 in. round barrel taking the .46 Long rimfire round, weighed only six

and a half pounds, and cost $28. A companion piece for this arm, the "Buffalo" rifle, was on the market by the spring of 1874; it had a 30 in. round barrel chambered for the .50-70 centerfire, weighed only half a pound more than the Deer rifle, and sold for $30. These simple, inexpensive arms may well have inspired the simple, inexpensive Sharps "Hunters'" and

"Business" rifles of 1875–76. However, several of the popular chamberings for the Remington sporting rifle were copied directly from Sharps designs. These included the .40-50, adopted by Remington about 1875, the .40-70, adopted in 1876, and later the .40-90 and .45 Straight. The .40-50 and .40-70 were, in fact, the featured centerfire calibers for Remington's "Short-Range" rifle of 1876. The firm's "Mid-Range" arm took somewhat heavier loads, such as the .44-77, .45-70, and .50-70. The shooter who liked the Remington but who wanted even more power could buy a .50-70 rifle and have it rechambered for yet another Sharps-designed cartridge, the .50-90-2 1/2 in.[104]

Even less expensive than the Deer and Buffalo rifles were the commercially available military rolling-blocks Remington had made since 1867 for foreign governments; an *Army and Navy Journal* article that appeared early in 1872 listed the Egyptian, Spanish, and "Civil Guard" arms, any of which sold for about $17. The special .42 or .43 caliber cartridges for these guns were amply powerful for the West, loaded as they were with 370 to 400 grain bullets and 76 to 77 grains of powder. (Loaded by Remington and other American cartridge manufacturers, these rounds were all noticeably similar to the .44-77.) Carbines in either .43 or .50 caliber sold for $16.[105]

More often than not, however, a Remington fancier living in the West preferred a heavy-barreled sporting rifle to a military-style arm. One observer of plains life, writing in 1876, stated that for experienced buffalo hunters, "one or more of Sharp's or Remington's heaviest sporting rifles, and an unlimited supply of ammunition, is the armament." A government study of the extermination of the buffalo, published in 1887, concluded that the Remington was second only to the Sharps in eliminating the bison:

> The slaughter which began in 1871 was prosecuted with great vigor and enterprise in 1872, and reached its height in 1873. . . . By a coincidence that proved fatal to the bison, it was just at the beginning of the slaughter that breech-loading, long-range rifles attained what was practically perfection. The Sharps 40-90 or 45-120, and the Remington were the favorite weapons of the buffalo hunter. . . .

Frank Mayer, a professional hunter himself, estimated that 80 percent of the buffalo killed by other professionals had died under the muzzles of Sharps or Remington rifles.[106]

A heavy-barreled Remington suitable for buffalo hunting, but which went to the Black Hills instead, took part in an incident in 1877:

> Several small bands of Indians hovered around east of the ranch at the time, [so] I got out my gun. It

Masked in death, this outlaw named Brazelton was charged with robbing four or five stagecoaches in Arizona Territory in the late 1870s before being killed in an arrest attempt. There is no indication whether or not the Remington carbine was his personal gun. (Courtesy Wells Fargo Bank History Room)

was a big Remington with a Hawkins barrel, weighing about sixteen pounds and shot one hundred and twenty grains of powder . . . I took rest on the corner of the house and . . . let go. [A] woman was walking around carrying her baby looking on. She said, 'Why, you killed all three of them." They all dropped, anyhow. The bullets must have gone pretty close.

An elk hunting party out of Denver about 1892. A Remington rifle (center) is flanked by what appear to be two Winchester lever action rifles—a M1892 (left) and a M1873. (Courtesy Denver Public Library, Western History Dept.)

Passing through the same area about 1878, William Allen's party had a brush with Indians whose "unearthly yells pierced our very hearts . . . when the Indians were within seventy yards of us, Thomas Randall, of Chicago, sent the first ball from his Remington rifle 45-105." Brant Street, a mounted mail carrier working in the Black Hills at about the same time, "carried, besides the mail sack tied to his saddle, nothing save a Remington rifle and a bag of cartridges slung accross the pommel." James Cook's hunting partner used a "splendid Remington rifle" to supply antelope to the Cheyenne market in 1878. Rolf Johnson's hunting trip in July of 1879 was less successful: as Johnson confided to his diary, "Ned North and I went hunting on several small lakes about half way between [Hay Creek] and the Belle Fourche. Ned had his Winchester and I had a Remington rifle. We did not have very good luck." A Remington also proved to be an important factor in a murder trial that took place in Mariposa County, California, in the late 1870s. The trial involved an old Scottish rancher named Patterson and a younger

man from Kansas named Clow, who had displayed a strong interest in owning Patterson's ranch. One day Patterson was found dead, shot in the back. As A. P. Vivian, a witness to the trial, recounted the proceedings:

The ball was extracted from the body, and found to be from a Remington rifle. An empty cartridge-case (called here a "shell") found close by, was also of the Remington pattern, and on it was a peculiar mark, as if there had been something wrong with the extractor. Only two men in the county had Remington rifles, Clow and another man. This other individual was proved to have been many miles away that day from the scene of the murder. . . . [Also], the extractor of Clow's rifle on being examined was found to be out of repair, and to mark the cartridge-cases precisely like that picked up . . . even a Californian jury could not ignore such evidence, [and it was] obliged to find Clow guilty of murder of the first degree. . . .[107]

Forest and Stream, April 1876.

Promoting their line of agricultural products as well as firearms, this Remington ad appeared in Loving's *Stock Manual,* published in Ft. Worth, Texas, in 1881. (Courtesy Denver Public Library, Western History Dept.)

A .40-90 Ballard Pacific with heavy 32 in. octagon barrel and a leather sleeve tacked around the stock wrist. The cleaning rod is missing on this example. (Courtesy Colorado Springs Pioneers' Museum)

Carcasses of five elk which fell victim to the military model Sharps (right foreground), and the Ballard slung across the seated hunter's back. (Courtesy Denver Public Library, Western History Dept.)

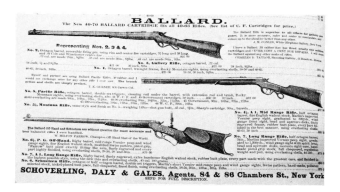

Forest and Stream, March 1883.

MORE SINGLE-SHOT RIFLES

Remington was to bring out a new single-shot rifle in 1880, but it would encounter stiff competition from the Ballard and the Springfield. The Brown Manufacturing Company, makers of the Ballard, went out of business in 1873, but two years later fabrication of the rifle resumed in the hands of Connecticut gunmaker John Marlin, in association with Schoverling & Daly of New York. In April of 1876 *Forest and Stream* announced: "The New Ballard Rifle, With Marlin's Patent Automatic Extractor and Reversible Firing-pin. We are beginning to turn out the new rifles, and will be able to fill orders with reasonable promptness. The workmanship will be found superior to any other in the market. . . ." The reversible firing pin, patented in February of 1875, allowed use of both rim- and centerfire cartridges of like dimensions in the same gun.[108]

Marlin's early Ballards took such popular loads as the .45-70 and .50-70. But in addition to these rounds, a line of new cartridges appeared during the late 1870s, designed specifically for the Ballard: among them were the .38-50, .40-65, .40-90, .44-75, and .44-100. With its neck reamed out to accept a slightly larger bullet, the .44-100 later became the .45-100.[109]

Like other manufacturers of the time, Marlin made the Ballards available in a number of styles, such as the "No. 1 Hunter's Rifle," "No. 2 Sporting Rifle," "No. 4 Perfection Rifle," and "No. 7 Long Range Rifle." These guns differed from one another in barrel length, weight, contour, type of sights, style of underlever, and of course, caliber. At the close of the 1870s and during the early 1880s other variations appeared, such as the "No. 4½ Mid Range Rifle" and the "No. 8 Union Hill Rifle." In the West, however, two popular Ballards were the No. 5 Pacific and a subsequent variation, the No. 5½ Montana. A typical Pacific as made in the late 1870s would have a heavy octagon barrel with a wood cleaning rod below it, a heavy frame, and double set triggers; the barrel length would fall between 28 in. and 32 in., and the weight between nine and twelve pounds.[110]

Distribution of the Marlin Ballards was handled in the main by Schoverling & Daly. Although based in New York, this firm advertised the Ballard even in western papers; for example, their ads in the *Omaha Republican* and the *Colorado Chieftain* in June of 1877 proclaimed the Ballard rifle "Superior to all others. Greater accuracy, greater safety, less recoil. Especially adapted to Far West trade." The ad illustrated the Ballard Pacific, an obvious choice for frontier use.[111]

Noting the armament of his party on the Yellowstone River in the same year, Frank Carpenter wrote that "Mann had a Ballard rifle and a revolver . . . and

Antelope hunters on the plains, probably in the late 1870s. Both the heavy-barreled Ballard at left and the long-barreled Sharps at right are fitted with full-length telescopic sights. (Courtesy Mr. Malcolm Collier)

A hunting party at Magpie Gulch near Helena, Montana, in 1889. Bert Monroe and Wallace Starling, at left, appear to be holding single-shot Ballards, while George Gilpatrick at right has a M1876 Winchester rifle. (Courtesy Montana Historical Society)

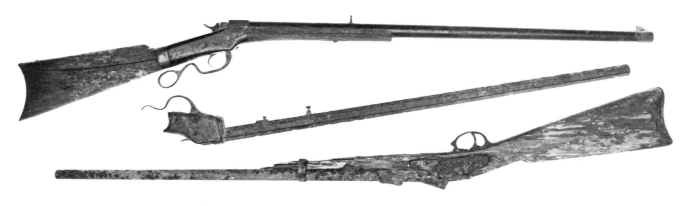

Above, a Marlin-Ballard rifle found near Laramie, Wyoming. Below, the frame and barrel from a single-shot Winchester High-Wall rifle from the gold rush country of California. (Photo by Mr. Ed Prentiss, courtesy Mr. C. V. Hansen)

Colorado Chieftain (Pueblo), June 1877. (Note misspelling of "Ballard.")

Oldham had a Ballard rifle, but with only three rounds of ammunition, and a small revolver." A laudatory editorial notice of the Ballard appeared in a Black Hills Directory of 1878:

Selecting five gunsmiths in five different towns, we aggregated their experience which briefly was that the Winchester rifle is, when handled by inexperienced men, easily got out of order and hard to repair. Owing to the complicated interior works of a Henry rifle, when out of working order, it is next to impossible to be repaired except at the factory where they are made. The Henry rifle when loaded is too much of a solid weight, swung either on the shoulders of a person or on the pommel of a saddle. If not loaded it is not ready for immediate and effective service. Another important feature is that both the Henry and Winchester rifles cost nearly double that of the Ballard, with no corresponding advantages. Experiments have demonstrated the fact that the Ballard can be fired off twenty times in succession, in less time than the same number of shots can be fired from either a Winchester or a Henry. The Ballard Carbine is light, (half ounce cartridge) weighs only six and a half pounds, and can be purchased here by companies, from $20 to $25. The Ballard sporting rifle, with a finer finish and longer barrel can be had here from $30 to $35 according to finish, etc. The Ballard Kentucky rifle is too clumsy to be packed over such a vast range of country. The Ballard carbine is adapted for muzzle or cartridge loading. The Henry rifle can be purchased here at from $30 to $37, according to finish. The Winchester rifles can be purchased here at $45 each.

Three Colorado miners sleeping in their cabin with a Ballard rifle within reach. (Courtesy Mr. Malcolm Collier)

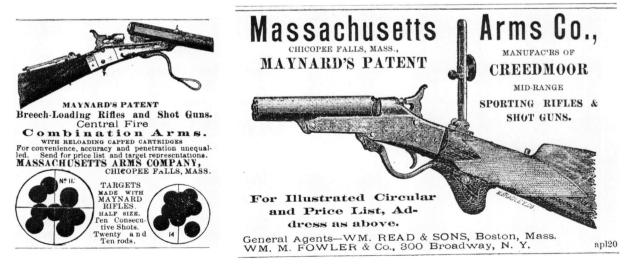

These ads from *Forest and Stream* for 1874 and 1876 show, respectively, the Maynard Model 1873 sporting rifle and the Model 1873 Creedmoor.

Homesteaders in the Laup Valley of Nebraska in 1886. The sturdy youth at right holds a Marlin-made Ballard, probably a No. 5½ Montana rifle, while another Ballard, a No. 5 Pacific, hangs in the wagon. Made in various calibers from .38 to .50, the Pacific Model had a cleaning rod beneath the barrel, as did the less common No. 5½ Montana rifle. The latter was chambered only for the long Sharps 2⅞ in. cartridge and had an extra heavy barrel. (Courtesy Nebraska State Historical Society)

In contrast to this unstinting praise were Frank Mayer's comments. A .40-90 Ballard was among three rifles Mayer had with him in Colorado in 1878, and although Mayer termed the gun "sweet-shooting" and "clean killing," he did complain of extraction trouble. [112]

A rifle more widely noted for extraction problems, at least with copper-cased cartridges, was the trapdoor Springfield. After a buffalo hunt in the late 1870s, Dr. William Allen wrote that "as we came within seventy-five yards of [the buffalo], we lodged balls in two of them . . . I attempted to fire again, but the shell stuck fast, for in my haste I had snatched up an old needle-gun from one of the wagons. . . ."[113]

Apparently, however, this trait had little effect on its popularity with civilians on the frontier; with brass cases, extraction was not usually a problem. Preparing

for a trip to the Black Hills in the spring of 1876, Richard Hughes wrote that "some time previous I had purchased a 'needle gun' as the remodeled Springfield used by the military was generally known, though the term also was applied to some other arms using a similar 'firing pin.'" Although two members of Frank Carpenter's party carried Ballards, Carpenter himself had "a good needle gun with eight rounds of ammunition" while his friend Cowan had "a good needle gun with thirty rounds" for use along the Yellowstone in 1877. At about the same time, Captain George W. Baylor of the Texas Rangers was using "a Winchester rifle, but after the first Indian fight he concluded it was too light"; Baylor then chose

a .45-70 Springfield sporting rifle. He always used what he called rest sticks. . . . In shooting he would squat down, extend the sticks an arm's length out

Travelers in the Yellowstone National Park in 1873, a year after its dedication. The bearded man eighth from right cradles a first model Maynard .35 or .50 carbine, distinguishable from the more common Civil War military model by the patchbox in the stock. (Courtesy Montana Historical Society)

in front of him with the longer ends spread out tripod-fashion on the ground. With his gun resting in the fork he had a perfect rest and could make close shots at long range.[114]

Another Springfield user on the frontier of the late 1870s was the English sportsman J. Mortimer Murphy, who wrote:

Some excellent single-barrel sporting rifles are now made, both in Europe and the United States, which are quite accurate up to four or five hundred yards, and carry powder and ball enough to kill a large animal within that distance. [But] The most effective weapon that I ever used was a fifty-calibre Springfield rifle, which was resighted so that its point-blank range was one hundred and fifty yards. This was almost as accurate at three hundred yards

as it was at half the distance, and I have killed a wolf with it nearly four hundred yards away.[115]

One advantage the Springfield had over the Sharps, Remington, and Ballard was its price. On the frontier $15 would usually be enough to buy a military-style trapdoor, although the remodeled Springfields with octagon barrels and checkered stocks would often bring $10 more.[116]

While Sharps, Remingtons, Springfields, and Ballards dominated the western market for single-shot rifles, they did not hold exclusive rights to it. Among the less popular single-shots to reach the frontier were Maynards, Peabodys, Whitneys, Phoenixes, Stevens, and at least two new Wesson rifles. The Massachusetts Arms Company, maker of the Maynard, was slow to adopt a self-contained metallic cartridge, and the Model

Not often seen in photos of the western frontier is the Model 1873 Maynard rifle, with a wiping stick or perhaps a shooting stick protruding from the muzzle, held by the second Indian from the left in the back row. The revolver in his right hand is a Colt M1860. This group of Utes was photographed in Colorado Springs in 1875. (Courtesy Colorado Historical Society)

1865 Maynard sporting rifle chambered the same broad-rimmed, separately ignited brass cartridges used in previous models. However, it did offer mechanical rather than manual extraction. Massachusetts Arms supplied the Model 1865 in .40 caliber, as well as in the older .35 and .50 calibers. Presumably the "Maynard's Sporting Rifles of improved pattern and superior finish" offered by Isaac Moses & Co. of Galveston early in 1866 included some of the .40 caliber models. Shotgun barrels for the Maynard frame, in both 20 and 28 gauge, continued to be available, and constituted one of the arm's main selling points. In November of 1870, for example, John Day of Central City specifically noted his "choice lot of Maynard rifles with shot barrels for same."[117]

Recognizing the trend toward self-contained centerfire cartridges, Maynard himself patented a modification of his rifle in February of 1873 to allow it to chamber such loads. Curiously, however, the line of cartridges introduced for the Model '73 Maynard had broad, exceptionally thick rims, which prevented their use in other breechloaders and also precluded the use of conventional ammunition in the Maynard. Nevertheless the new Maynard rounds offered sufficient variety for almost any use, including as they did the .35-30, .35-40, .40-40, .40-60, .40-70, .44-60, .44-70, .44-100 Creedmoor, .50-50, .50-70, and .50-100 cartridges. In addition the Maynard 28-gauge shotshell could be loaded with a single bullet, to become the .55-100.[118]

In keeping with its expanded line of cartridges, Massachusetts Arms offered the 1873 Maynard sporter in a wider variety of styles. Round and round/octagon barrels were available not only in the old standard lengths of 20 in. and 26 in., but in 28 in., 30 in., and 32 in. as well. The little .35 caliber "Number 7 Hunter's Rifle" with plain stock, simple sights, and 20 in. round barrel cost about $20; but the "Number 14 Long-Range Creedmoor Rifle," on the market by April of 1876 in the powerful .44-100-520 caliber, with heavy 32 in. round barrel, checkered pistol-grip stock, and elaborate iron sights, cost $70. Besides manufacturing the 1873s, Massachusetts Arms would convert the percussion Model 1865s to centerfire arms for $10. Presumably this conversion method could also be applied to Maynard rifles predating 1865.[119]

It may well have been one of these early Maynards that Granville Stuart carried while passing through Dakota in the spring of 1866. On one occasion Stuart crept up on a band of antelope, which never realized that "death was hovering around, in the guise of my Maynard rifle." In all likelihood the Maynard's popularity increased with the appearance of the Model 1873. When Carlos Gove of Denver began advertising

the Maynard in March of 1873, his stock may have comprised Model 1865s; but his advertisement in January of 1874 for "Sharp's, Wesson's and Maynard's New Model Rifles" very probably referred to the new centerfire arms. John Lower was offering the Maynard by May of 1875, and in that same year John S. Moore of Cushing & Moore, Galveston, wrote that "I have sold quite a number of Rifles here—principally Maynards."[120]

Late in December of 1876 P. C. Bicknell noted that his buffalo-hunting partner in Texas was using

> a Maynard 40 cal—ring ball 70 gr. powder 340 gr lead. He shot a bull last week just to one side below the tail—the ball lodged in the tongue. The bull was 250 yds. distant. Shooting from one side the balls mostly go through & frequently kill two at once. The Maynard seems to do as good work as the 44 cal. Sharps. The only objection my partner has to it is that it ought to shoot a patch ball. Shooting 20 or 30 shots inside of half an hour leads the gun & probably wears it out sooner.

And in February of 1877 A. B. McDowell of Texana, Texas, wrote:

> I am a great man for fine guns, have bought in the last five years two Spencer rifles one Winchester " Ballard two of Rimingtons & one Maynard And a number of shot guns which cost me considerable. Out of the seven Rifles that I have bought not one can be relid on for target shooting over one hundred yds. [but] I find my Maynard the most reliable one. . . .

During a hunt in the Black Hills at about the same time, one deer fell "pierced by a bullet from [John Spaulding's] deadly Maynard rifle." While he was in Colorado in 1878, Frank Mayer had a "Maynard .40-70 with an extra 28 gauge shotgun barrel" among his other guns. Although not fond of the Maynard's break-open design, Mayer did praise its power and accuracy: the rifle "killed three elk almost instantly at 100 yards." Writing from Victoria County, Texas, two years later, P. H. Fagan mentioned that "I have tried Several Diferent makes of Rifles such as Winchester, Ballard, Spencer & Maynard but none is as good as the Sharps. [However,] Maynard is the best of the above list."[121]

Probably less known on the frontier than the Maynard was the single-shot Peabody; yet the Peabody was one of the finest single-shot designs available during the postwar years. Patented by Henry O. Peabody in July of 1862, this action comprised a long breechblock with a transverse hinge pin passing through its rear, a short distance above the bore axis; a downward push on a pivoting trigger guard pulled the front of the

Forest and Stream, May 1877.

block down to expose the chamber for loading. Among the advantages of this action was the fact that the hinge pin absorbed little of the strain of firing. Instead, the convex rear face of the breechblock, resting against a concave recess in the rear face of the frame mortise, took most of the shock of discharge. Because the hinge pin was at the rear of the block, rather than at the front as in the Springfield, it could also be closer to the bore axis, thereby lessening the tendency of the block to swing open during firing. In fact, the tendency of the Peabody breechblock to swing open under pressure was so slight that the friction generated by the cartridge-case head, as it pressed against the front face of the block at the moment of discharge, was more than sufficient to keep the block closed. Another advantage of the design was that as the front of the block swung downward for loading it also swung slightly backward, away from the case head; therefore, jamming of the action due to a bulged or ruptured cartridge was unlikely. In the face of these advantages W. W. Greener, the famous British gunmaker, conceded that "the Peabody we class as one of the best of the American inventions."[122]

Even so, the Peabody met with much greater success abroad than it did in this country. Although it successfully underwent U.S. Ordnance tests in 1862, 1865, 1866, 1870, and 1872–73, it never dislodged the trapdoor Springfield from its favored position with the military. As a sporting rifle the Peabody fared little better. By September of 1865 Rhode Island's Providence Tool Company, maker of the arm, was able to offer only a limited number of military and sporting rifles, the manufacture of which involved a considerable amount of handwork, with much of the material for the guns coming from outside suppliers. Nevertheless, Providence advertised the arms in a San Francisco directory that year, and by the late spring of 1866 the company was set up for full-scale production. Although several .45 caliber rimfire cartridges were developed for the Peabody, none were widely used; the only Peabody rounds to gain any popularity whatever were two .50 rimfire loads: a sporting cartridge loaded with 50 grains of powder, and a military round loaded with 60 grains. As made during the late 1860s, the Peabody sporting rifle had a 20 in., 26 in., or 28 in. barrel, and retailed for $38 to $44. A carbine with a 20 in. barrel cost $30; a full-stocked, two-band military rifle cost $35 without bayonet. All these guns were expensive, and this was probably one reason why the original Peabody never became very popular. By the spring of 1867 the gun was available in a centerfire version, but this apparently did little to help domestic sales. However, Morgan L. Rood of Denver did offer the "Peabody Needle Gun" in November of 1870, and was still advertising it in 1877 as "Improved by M. L. Rood." Presumably the rifles Rood handled were all centerfire models; the earlier types were probably chambered for the .50-70 and a .43-77 military load, while the later ones were available in a special ".45 Sporting" necked cartridge and the .45-70 government round as well. About 1873 Providence abandoned the original Peabody and began manufacturing the hammerless Peabody-Martini instead, so the rifles Rood had in 1877 may have been hammerless models.[123]

A name better known to westerners than Peabody's was that of Eli Whitney. Evidently Whitney's first serious attempt to enter the cartridge-rifle market of the late 1860s was made with the single-shot "Thunderbolt" designed by Charles Howard. Based on three patents issued to Howard between October of 1862 and October of 1865, this rifle had a longitudinally sliding breechbolt, opened and closed by an under-lever-controlled toggle link, and a concealed striker powered by a coil spring. The loading and ejecting aperture was in the underside of the tubular frame; and since the frame and barrel were the same diameter, the Howard resembled nothing more than a simple

Howard .44 single-shot carbine. (Courtesy National Park Service, Fuller Gun Collection, Chickamauga and Chattanooga National Military Park)

Whitney .45 rolling-block military-style rifle. (Courtesy National Park Service, Fuller Gun Collection, Chickamauga and Chattanooga National Military Park)

tube attached to a buttstock. Although entered in the Ordnance trials of 1865 the rifle did not do well, and had only slightly more success on the commercial market. As made in .44 caliber, the gun would chamber almost any .44 rimfire cartridge regardless of length, including a special .44 Extra Long round designed specifically for it. It was also made as a shotgun.[124]

John C. Anderson carried a Howard with him when in 1866 he traveled from St. Louis to Virginia City, Montana, and back. In his journal he noted that his Spencer repeater would "shoot hard—but not straight. I got out my 'Howard' and tried the relative merits of each for distance. I beat the 'Spencer' very badly— and then mine will shoot with some accuracy." In April of 1869 James H. Foster & Company of Chicago, advertising in the Salt Lake City *Telegraph,* offered "the celebrated 'Whitney Gun,' 'Howard' Breech-Loading Shot Gun and Rifle, and all the manufactures of the Whitney Arms Co." Whether any Utah residents were prompted to order a Howard from Foster's establishment is uncertain, but apparently Whitney himself was already considering the manufacture of another type of rifle.[125]

In May of 1866 Col. T. T. S. Laidley and C. A. Emery had patented a breech-loading rifle very similar to the Remington rolling-block, except that in Laidley's design the hammer and locking block were sep-

arate components rather than integral. A prototype of this arm entered in the 1865 trials had blown apart during the overload tests, but the gun did much better in the 1866 trials. Using the Laidley arms as a basis, Whitney patented four modifications of the design between March of 1871 and July of 1872, and by mid-1872 he was marketing a military rifle under his own name; a sporting rifle appeared at about the same time. These sporters, usually available with round or octagon barrels from 24 in. to 30 in. long, were chambered for almost every popular cartridge of the time. In addition the Whitney rolling-block action served as the foundation for a Creedmoor-style target rifle and for a military-style carbine. One such carbine (now in the Wyoming State Museum in Cheyenne) was owned by Thomas Sturgis, an early Wyoming settler, and other Whitneys very probably crossed the plains as well.[126]

Although Whitney's rolling-block was a soundly designed, well-made arm, his son, Eli Whitney, III, designed another single-shot and patented it in May of 1874. Termed the "Phoenix" in company catalogs, this rifle was mechanically similar to the 1861 Joslyn, the Warner, and the Snider: a longitudinal hinge pin, passing through the right side of the breechblock, allowed the block to rotate upward and to the right for loading. Unlike the Warner, however, the Phoenix had a mechanical rather than a manual extractor.

Officers and ladies near Ft. Laramie, Wyoming, in the 1880s. One officer holds a rolling-block sporting rifle, either a Remington or a Whitney. (Courtesy Ft. Laramie Historical Assn.)

Whitney offered it in the usual military, sporting, and target versions, and chambered it for most of the better cartridges of the day, but the Phoenix never really became popular. At least one Phoenix—originally a saddle-ring carbine, but subsequently fitted with a 28 in. Freund-made .45-70 barrel—did reach the West, and there may have been others.[127]

Like his competitors, Frank Wesson was not content to market only one type of breechloader. His two-trigger break-open rifle sold briskly during the late 1860s and early 1870s, but he also saw fit to introduce a "pocket rifle" and two Creedmoor-style target arms. The brass-framed pocket rifle, patented in May of 1870, involved a rather short, fairly heavy octagon barrel,

which rested on a longitudinal pin projecting from the standing breech; pressing a catch on the underside of the frame permitted the barrel to rotate to one side and downward for loading. A detachable skeleton stock allowed the arm to be used either as a rifle or a pistol. It was commonly available in .22 or .32 rimfire, and in barrel lengths from 10 in. to 20 in.; while a large-frame version in .38 and .44 rimfire also appeared, the .32 caliber model with 10 in. barrel was apparently the most popular. None of the pocket rifle's calibers really qualified it for all-around use on the frontier, but in spite of that fact, Carlos Gove advertised the "Wesson pocket Target Rifles" in March of 1873.[128]

A maker of pocket rifles that were perhaps better

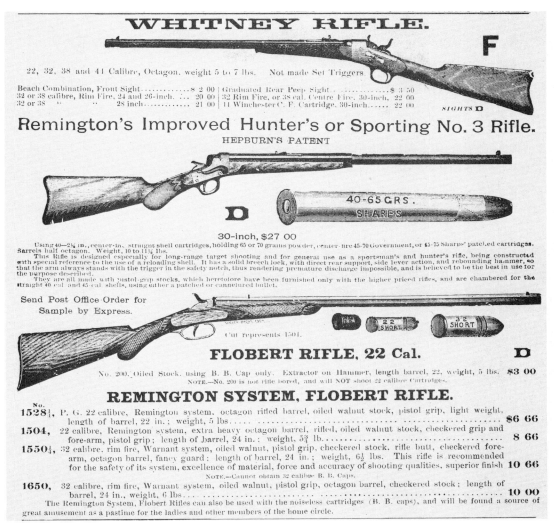

From the 1884 catalog of the E. C. Meacham Arms Co., St. Louis.

known than those of Wesson was Joshua Stevens. He had worked for the Massachusetts Arms Company in the 1850s, but in 1864 he set up shop for himself and began manufacturing small break-open pocket pistols. Then, about 1869, he started making pocket rifles, which were simply long-barreled versions of his pistols, equipped with adjustable sights and detachable skeleton shoulder stocks. These were principally lightweight .22 caliber arms, but by September of 1871 Stevens's firm had introduced a heavier "New Model" pocket rifle, as well as a conventional wood-stocked break-open sporting rifle. At that time Charles Folsom of New York, advertising in the San Antonio *Daily Express,* offered the new model pocket rifle in .22 and

.32 caliber, with barrels from 10 in. to 18 in. long, and also Stevens's "Breech Loading Globe Sighted Cartridge Rifle, 22, 32, or 38 calibre," with barrels from 26 in. to 30 in.[129]

During the 1870s, however, Stevens offered nothing in the line of a Creedmoor rifle, while Wesson did. In 1875 Gove's former partner, John P. Lower, went into business for himself, and a year later he was offering "Wesson's Creedmoor Rifles" among his wares. Two Wesson rifles, both made in very limited quantities, could have qualified for this title. Both had vertically sliding breechblocks, external hammers, long octagon barrels, and fancy sights. However, the "No. 1 Long Range Rifle, National Regulation," bore a

Stevens' Combined Central Fire Rifle and Shot Gun.

Rifle Barrel, 38 and 44 C. F. Extra Long Cartridges.

SHOT BARREL TO FIT IN SAME STOCK.

Plain Shot Gun with 26 inch Rifle Barrel, Blued finish $27 50; with Nickel Mountings.................................. 29 50

N. Curry & Bro., San Francisco (1884).

striking resemblance to a British single-shot rifle patented by Alexander Henry in 1865 and 1866; Wesson's "No. 2 Long and Mid-Range and Hunting Rifle," on the other hand, was more Wesson-like in appearance, and had a brass frame, an unusual feature in a long-range rifle. Just which of these two models Lower offered is uncertain; he may have handled both.[130]

While other single-shot rifles, such as the Stevens, saw occasional use in the West, a number of breech-loading double-barreled rifles also played a part on the frontier. Like their muzzle-loading predecessors, these breech-loading doubles were less than ideal for conditions on the plains, and were usually much more costly than a single-shot or a repeater. As A. C. Gould put it:

> It calls for the very highest skill of the gunmaker to build a double rifle. There are but few gunmakers who can successfully accomplish it, and the cost is excessive . . . the makers of double rifles, with a world-wide reputation, are obliged to use the greatest care in putting the barrels together; to often shoot, take apart and rearrange them, in order to regulate the arm so as to have both barrels shoot on the same line of elevation, as well as to keep the shots from crossing or shooting out . . . no double rifle can have anything like the accuracy of a single shot, and [I] believe the double rifles do not possess accuracy enough for hunting certain game found in America.[131]

In spite of these arguments some plains travelers preferred doubles, and even Gould conceded that

> there is no rifle in the world equal to a fine double English express for shooting dangerous game at short range, when quick shooting is essential. . . . [Moreover,] some of the experts who test double rifles are so familiar with their idiosyncrasies, they can make allowance for the spread of the shots, or shoot-

ing outward; and, by aiming differently for right and left barrel, place the shots well together.

The majority of breech-loading doubles used in the West after the war were of British manufacture and, regardless of maker, shared certain characteristics. They were invariably break-open arms, and usually employed the "double grip" action, which first became popular in the early 1860s; this design comprised a vertically pivoted, T-shaped locking bolt, the head of which rotated into or out of engagement with a T-shaped cutout in the barrel underlug. As a rule, the doubles of the late 1860s and the 1870s were large, ranging from .450 to 8-bore (.835 caliber), and from ten to twelve pounds in weight, with barrels about 25 in. long.[132]

In addition to a Purdey shotgun and a Spencer carbine, F. Trench Townshend carried a "breech-loading 12-bore double-barreled rifle by Westley Richards" while traveling through the West in 1868. The extralarge bores remained popular with many users in later years, but during the late 1870s and 1880s, in keeping with the general trend, the calibers decreased somewhat. After a hunt near the Judith Mountains in 1878, George Bird Grinnell noted that:

> I was shooting a 450-grain solid ball with 90 grains of powder, and this penetrated the willow brush admirably. On the other hand, Messiter's rifle was a double-barreled Long rifle, carrying a 160-grain express bullet, with 120 grains of powder. This bullet was too light to penetrate far.[133]

A double rifle more unusual than Messiter's, but with enough power to handle most situations, was assembled by the Freund brothers, presumably in the late 1870s. Built on a scroll-engraved English double-grip action, this rifle had side-by-side 30 in. octagon barrels, chambered for the .45-2⁴/10 in. Sharps cartridge, and came complete with a set of 10-gauge shot barrels fitted to the same action.[134]

Noncommissioned officers of the Third Infantry at Ft. Stanton, New Mexico Territory, about 1885. Although the cartridges in the uniformed soldier's belt are probably .45-70s for a Springfield rifle, he holds a Stevens single-shot tip-up sporting rifle. Similar Stevens were produced from the early 1870s to about 1895, in a variety of calibers from .22 to .44. (Courtesy Museum of New Mexico)

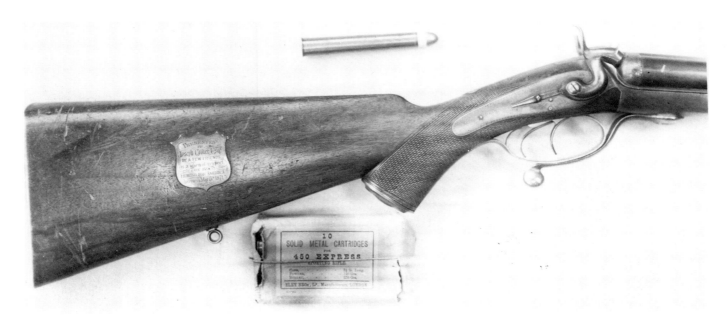

.450 Express double rifle with double-grip action made by Alex R. Henry of Edinburgh, Scotland. The inscribed plaque in the stock states "Presented to Joseph Collier Esq. by a few friends as a token of respect on his leaving for America Inverness May 13th 1871." Collier founded the First Federal Savings of Denver in 1885, still a leading Colorado financial institution today. The label on the box of Eley cartridges indicates a loading of 120 grains of powder behind a 270-grain bullet. (Photo by and courtesy Mr. Gerald Kelver)

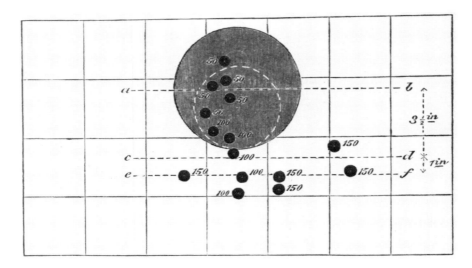

Fifteen shots from a .500 Express double rifle at ranges of 50, 100, and 150 yards. The squares are three inches in size. (From Walsh's *The Modern Sportsman's Gun and Rifle*, 1884)

An 1882 hunting scene at Hugo, Colorado. Joseph E. Collier is seated in the center, holding his Alex Henry .450 Express double rifle. The double-barrel shotgun in the scene is unidentified. At far right, with a Ballard Pacific rifle fitted with a full-length Mal-

colm scope, is thought to be Winfield Scott Stratton, who became a millionaire mine owner in Victor, Colorado. (Courtesy Mr. Malcolm Collier via Mr. Gerald Kelver)

NEW REPEATING RIFLES: THE WINCHESTER, MARLIN, AND OTHERS

Double rifles would be more in evidence on the frontier during the 1880s, but even then they would be rare compared to the number of repeating arms in use at that time. For it was during the 1880s that the repeater came into its own. The man largely responsible for this was Oliver Winchester.

Doubtless Winchester realized that his brass-frame model of 1866, with its little .44-28 rimfire cartridge, suffered in a comparison of power with some of the single-shots, and he lost little time before trying to correct this situation. Various experimental "muskets" took shape at his New Haven factory, one of which underwent testing during the Ordnance trials of 1872–73. Far more important, however, was the fact that the company began delivery of a new civilian-style rifle in the fall of 1873, a rifle later to be famous as the "Winchester '73." Designed to remedy some of the 1866 model's shortcomings, the new gun retained the toggle-link action, but housed it in an iron receiver, which was both stronger and lighter than brass. In lieu of the old rimfire round, the 1873 chambered a

new .44-40-200 centerfire cartridge, a big improvement. It was more powerful than the rimfire load, and had the additional advantage of being reloadable. A so-called .38-40 (actually .40 caliber) cartridge came out in 1879, and a .32-20 in 1882, but for the 1873s sold in the West, the .44-40 remained the caliber of choice.[135]

For the rifle a 24 in. round or octagon barrel was standard, with a 20 in. round barrel standard for the carbine. The rifle magazine would hold fifteen rounds, the carbine magazine twelve. Winchester also offered a musket with a 30 in. round barrel, protected by a full-length forestock; because of the long barrel, the musket's magazine capacity was seventeen rounds. All sorts of optional features were available for these arms— extralong or extrashort barrels, fancy stocks, special sights, plating and engraving, and the like. A highly desirable variation of the Winchester 1873 was announced in the company's 1875 catalog:

All of those barrels that are found to make targets of extra merit will be made up into guns with set triggers and extra finish, and marked as a designating name "one of a thousand" and sold at $100.

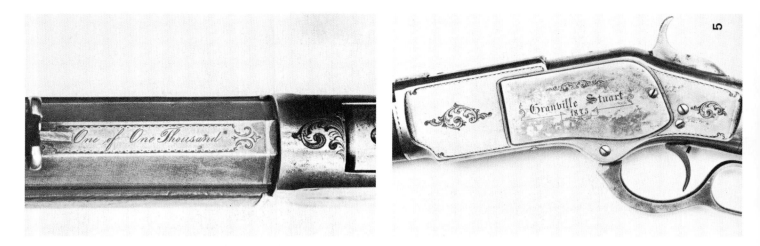

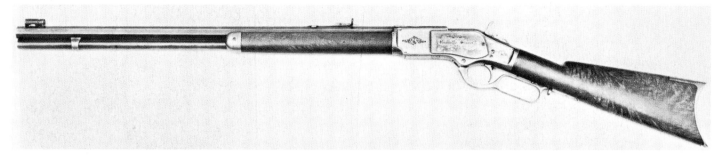

A factory-engraved Winchester M1873 .44 "One of One Thousand" rifle (#7282). The receiver is engraved with the name "Granville Stuart 1875." Stuart, who first settled in Montana in 1856, later became a prominent cattle rancher and president of the Montana Stock Growers Assn. As a Montana vigilante, he was also "credited" with being instrumental in hanging some 30 alleged cattle rustlers and other criminals. (Courtesy Amon Carter Museum of Western Art, Ft. Worth, Texas)

The next grade of barrels, not quite so fine, will be marked "one of a hundred," and set up to order in any style at $20 advance over the list price. . . .

Ironically, more than a hundred barrels qualified for the "1 of 1000" mark, but only eight for the "1 of 100" stamp.[136]

Although the factory shipped out very few 1873s during the fall of the model year, more than 2500 left the warehouse in 1874. John Cook was in New Mexico that year, and with him was "a 44 center-fire Winchester, the first magazine gun I had owned. I had practiced with it until it had gained my confidence completely as *the* gun." Making entries in his journal in September of 1878, Frank Mayer noted that four years previously a Denver dealer had lavished such praise on the new Winchester that he had bought one. Mayer was nevertheless skeptical about its usefulness for plains game until, on the Dismal Fork of the Loup River, he ran into seven buffalo: his 1873 dropped all seven, only three requiring a second bullet. He acquired a new respect for the rifle on the spot.[137]

The dealer Mayer referred to may well have been Carlos Gove, who was advertising "Winchester New Model Rifles" by May of 1874. Throughout 1874 and 1875 shipments of the new arms continued to go to frontier dealers, some of whom were in Texas. Dissatisfied with the .50 caliber Sharps carbine issued by the state, Texas Ranger James Gillett went to Austin in December of 1875 to get something else:

The new center-fire 1873-model Winchester had just appeared on the market and sold at $50 for the rifle and $40 for the carbine . . . ten men in Company D, myself included, were willing to pay the price to have a superior arm. I got carbine number 13401, and for the next six years of my ranger career I never used any other weapon.

Another ranger, N. A. Jennings, said that "the state supplied carbines and ammunition, but the men could choose any style of arms they preferred. Winchesters or Sharp's carbines were the favorite guns. . . ."[138]

Besides the Texas Rangers, other well-known frontier organizations, such as express companies, pur-

James H. Cook, cowboy and author of *Fifty Years on the Frontier*, in buckskins with a deluxe M1873 Winchester rifle with engraved frame and checkered pistol grip and forestock. (Courtesy Nebraska State Historical Society)

The significant feature of this view, taken in a photographer's studio in Sherman, Texas, is what may be a genuine Winchester M1873 "baby carbine," with a barrel about five inches shorter than the standard 20-inch carbine length. Any factory-original '73 rifle or carbine with a shorter-than-standard barrel length is rare. One curious feature of the M1873 in this photo is the disproportionately long wooden forestock, which normally is a little shorter than normal on such special order guns. (Courtesy Mr. Herb Peck, Jr.)

chased 1873s, issuing them not only to stagecoach guards but also, on occasion, to employees for meritorious service. One such rifle (now in the Shasta County, California, Historical Museum) is engraved "WF [Wells Fargo] & Co. to Indian Charley for Capture of Highway Robber July 21 1877." Ami Frank Mulford penned this account of a Black Hills stagecoach of 1877:

Considerable excitement was created . . . by the first appearance of one of the new Black Hills stages,

or gunboats as we call them. They consist of a very heavy and large stage with a 2-pound Mountain Howitzer mounted on top. They also have twelve Winchester repeating rifles inside, with plenty of ammunition in little pockets near the windows, or rather port-holes. These stages are run [from] Bismarck to the Black Hills, and despite all their arms and caution, are very frequently held up, by white as well as red devils. . . .

While working as an Indian trader in 1878, Manuel

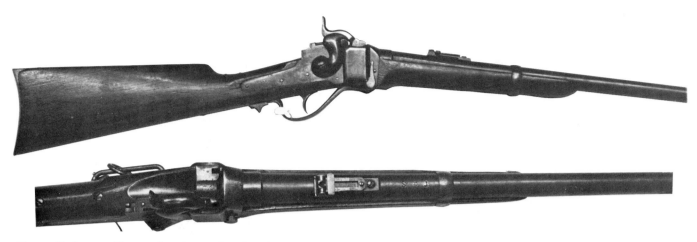

George Durham, a Georgia farm boy, enlisted in Capt. Leander McNelly's company of Texas Rangers in the spring of 1875. He later recalled that McNelly obtained 36 .50 Sharps carbines from Corpus Christi merchant Sol Lichtenstein for ranger use. The Sharps performed well, but in April of 1876, a wagon delivered 30 new .44-40 Winchester (M1873) carbines to the camp and McNelly told his men to turn in their Sharps if they'd rather have repeaters. "Most of us did," Durban remembered. The "T·S" barrel marking on this Sharps M1863 carbine (#C,4593) converted to .50-70 identifies this as one of the Texas Ranger Sharps. (Courtesy Mr. Tom Keilman)

Garcia took a "73-model Winchester carbine" into the Musselshell country, but had difficulty holding onto it. As he described it:

I had a forty-four Winchester carbine which I carried on my saddle. A young warrior saw it and wanted to trade for it, but I would not give it to him to look at. It was loaded and all ready for action. He got mad as the devil and offered me five horses for the gun and belt full of cartridges. I told him "no." Then he offered me ten head of horses [But] I told Beaver Tom to tell him that I could not trade it. . . .

James W. Schultz took special note of another 1873, used in the Blackfoot country in 1881:

[Three deer] came on in single file, and as each one leaped into the open of the trail, Eli fired at it with his '73 model Winchester repeater. He fired three shots about as fast as I could count them, with the result of three dead bucks lying within a yard or two of one another. Some shooting!

A more dramatic incident involving an 1873 occurred the same year, when Texas Rangers ran into a sharp fight with Indians. One ranger, George Lloyd:

unfortunately slipped a .45 Colt's pistol cartridge into the magazine of his .44 Winchester and in attempting to throw a cartridge into his gun it jammed, catching him in a serious predicament.

However, taking his knife from his pocket the fearless ranger coolly removed the screw that held the side plates of his Winchester together, took off the plates, removed the offending cartridge, replaced the plates, tightened up the screw, reloaded his gun, and began firing. It takes a man with iron nerve to do a thing like that, and you meet such a one but once in a lifetime.[139]

Not all plainsmen, of course, were enthusiastic about the Winchester. Although the .44-40 represented a real advance over the .44 Henry rimfire, it still could not match a cartridge like the .45-70. In December of 1876 P. C. Bicknell, discussing the preferences of professional buffalo hunters, noted that "the Winchester is the laughing stock among these men—they would not take one as a gift if they had to use it." And J. Mortimer Murphy added:

I have found the Winchester magazine or repeating rifle very convenient for general shooting; but that also had its faults, not the least of which was that the bullet would sometimes tilt as soon as it reached the breech from the magazine, at seemingly the most critical moment; and ere it could be extricated and placed in its proper position, the game would probably be out of sight. I was compelled to leave a buffalo hunt on two occasions on account of this. . . . Another fault that it possessed for shoot-

The posse that captured Henry Brown and other robbers who held up the Medicine Lodge Bank in Kansas in 1884. Winchester M1873 carbines plus one Sharps carbine (far right) were the posse members' choices as saddle guns. (Courtesy Kansas State Historical Society)

Colorado elk hunters with their "bag" as well as their array of hunting rifles, which include two Sharps and two M1873 Winchesters. (Courtesy Denver Public Library, Western History Dept.)

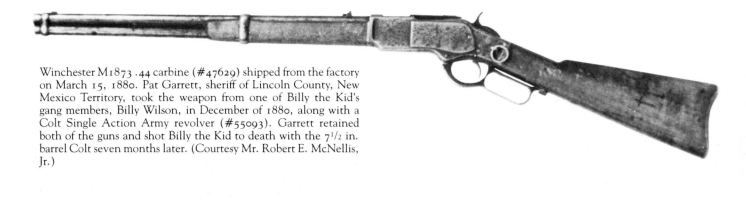

Winchester M1873 .44 carbine (#47629) shipped from the factory on March 15, 1880. Pat Garrett, sheriff of Lincoln County, New Mexico Territory, took the weapon from one of Billy the Kid's gang members, Billy Wilson, in December of 1880, along with a Colt Single Action Army revolver (#55093). Garrett retained both of the guns and shot Billy the Kid to death with the 7½ in. barrel Colt seven months later. (Courtesy Mr. Robert E. McNellis, Jr.)

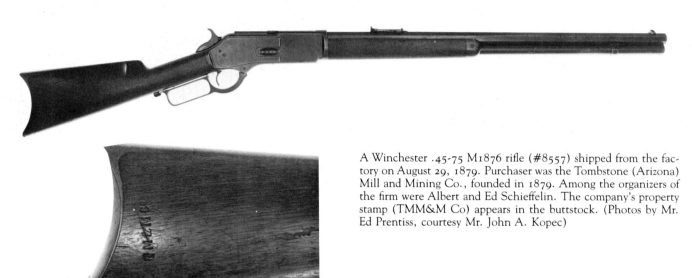

A Winchester .45-75 M1876 rifle (#8557) shipped from the factory on August 29, 1879. Purchaser was the Tombstone (Arizona) Mill and Mining Co., founded in 1879. Among the organizers of the firm were Albert and Ed Schieffelin. The company's property stamp (TMM&M Co) appears in the buttstock. (Photos by Mr. Ed Prentiss, courtesy Mr. John A. Kopec)

ing heavy game was that the charge of powder it carried was too small . . . but it atoned in some respect for this by the rapidity with which it could be fired. . . .[140]

By 1877, however, the claim that the Winchester was underpowered was about to lose its validity. At Philadelphia's Centennial Exposition of 1876 Winchester displayed a new lever-action. At first glance it might have passed for a Model 1873, and, in fact, was mechanically the same as that arm. But the Centennial Model of 1876 had a receiver about 1½ in. longer, and correspondingly heavier, to enable it to handle a new and powerful Winchester cartridge, the .45-75-350. This was a bottlenecked cartridge with a case length of 1⅞ in. and an overall length of about

2¼ in., longer by far than any previous Winchester-designed load.[141]

Deliveries of the Model 1876 began early in 1877. The standard sporting rifle had a 28 in. round, round/octagon, or octagon barrel, with a magazine capacity of twelve rounds. The carbine had a 22 in. barrel and a nine-shot magazine, plus the unusual feature of a full-length forestock. Buyers who objected to this feature, however, could purchase a "short rifle," with 22 in. or 24 in. barrel and conventional half-length forestock. There was also a musket with a 32 in. barrel and thirteen-round magazine, but sales of this arm were limited. Two new cartridges for the 1876 appeared in 1879, the .45-60 and .50-95 Express; a third new round came out in 1884, the .40-60.[142]

The two coyotes, their carcasses hanging from the rear of one of
the freight wagons, may have fallen victim to the Winchester
M1876 rifles in the scene. The setting is desert country in Idaho.
(Courtesy Oregon Historical Society)

Besides securing a market for its new rifle, Winchester had to deal with the inevitable competition, but the firm had no serious rivals until the 1880s. One early competitor was the Robinson repeater, first patented in May of 1870. Robinson's design comprised a tubular magazine under the barrel, and a longitudinally sliding breechbolt with a pivoting locking block on its underside; a backward pull on two knurled wings projecting from the rear of the bolt first swung the rear of the locking block upward, out of engagement with its bearing surface in the receiver, then drew the bolt straight back for loading. Although this was basically a sound design, Robinson took out another patent in April of 1872 to cover a different action. The new design involved a long locking block, positioned directly behind the bolt and transversely pivoted at its rear; an upward and backward pull on the block automatically drew back the bolt by means of a link which connected the two.[143]

A small company in Plattsburgh, New York, undertook manufacture of the Robinson in both its early and later versions. Although production of both versions was limited and did not constitute much of a threat to the Winchester line, Winchester nevertheless took advantage of an opportunity to buy out the company in 1874. As early as March of 1873, however, Morgan L. Rood of Denver had listed himself as "agent for the Robinson Repeating Rifle; can use any length cartridge, that is 44 calibre." By June of 1873 LeRoux & Cosgrove of San Antonio were also handling the arm. Presumably most or all of the Robinsons sold by Rood and LeRoux & Cosgrove were of the later type; but whatever they were, Rood continued advertising them through May of 1876.[144]

More widely distributed than the Robinson was an unusual lever-action repeater patented by Warren R. Evans in September of 1871, and made in a small factory in Mechanic Falls, Maine. The Evans was manufactured as a sporting rifle, military rifle, and carbine; regardless of the form it took, its outstanding feature was its huge tubular magazine, about $1\frac{1}{2}$ in. in diameter, which extended from the rear of the receiver to the buttplate. Designed on the principle of the Archimedean screw, this magazine assembly con-

Al Wishand, one of John Slaughter's cowboys, posed for a photographer with a M1876 Winchester carbine and a Colt Single Action. (Courtesy Arizona Historical Society)

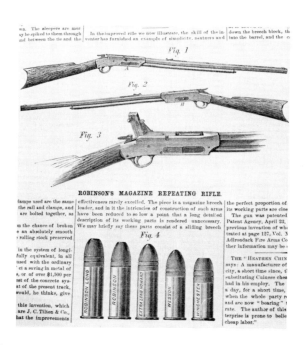

The first-model Robinson repeating rifle, from the *Scientific American*, August 1871.

The second-model Robinson rifle, from the *Scientific American*, August 1872.

Charlie, a buffalo hunter photographed about 1883 with a Winchester M1876 rifle across his shoulder plus a sheath knife and unidentified Smith & Wesson revolver at his waist. The location may be in the Dakotas. (Courtesy Mr. Wade R. Lucas)

tained a long four-fluted carrier, with a train of cartridges resting in each flute; this carrier revolved one-quarter turn with each throw of the lever, to feed a cartridge into the action by means of a fixed screw thread coiled around the inside wall of the magazine tube. In other respects the Evans action, despite its concealed hammer, was somewhat similar to the Spencer's: the breechblock was loosely hinged near its lower front corner, with its rear face resting against a shoulder at the rear of the receiver; the usual downward and forward push on the lever forced the block to rotate backward and downward to extract a fired case and chamber a fresh round. When fully loaded the

rifle, because of its oversize magazine, would hold thirty-four special .44 centerfire cartridges, each carrying a 220 grain bullet and about 30 grains of powder.[145]

In an attempt to interest the military in his design, Evans entered a carbine in the Ordnance trials of 1872–73, only to see it rejected when sand effectively jammed the action. It was probably shortly after these trials that Merwin & Hulbert, distributors of the arm, tried to develop a commercial market for it. They succeeded with a number of dealers in the East, and at least two in the West: in 1876 both Carlos Gove and Nathaniel Curry advertised "Winchester and Evans Rifles." Even though dealers of this stature handled

Evans lever-action repeating carbine. (Courtesy National Park Service, Fuller Gun Collection, Chickamauga and Chattanooga National Military Park)

Army and Navy Journal, January 1879.

it, the Evans never became very popular, even after the introduction of the more powerful "New Model 1877." Evans officials presented one of these to Buffalo Bill Cody in May of 1877, but this did little to help sales; the company went out of business about 1880.[146]

Notably more popular than either the Robinson or the Evans was a repeater designed by Andrew Burgess and manufactured by Eli Whitney. Based primarily on patents issued to Burgess in January of 1873 and Oc-

tober of 1875, this was still another lever-action with a tubular magazine under the barrel. It was a simple, strong design, with fewer parts than most other rifles of its type. Concealed inside the receiver was an integral extension of the lever; the longitudinal arm of this lever extension was pivoted to the rear of a short, longitudinally sliding bolt, with the vertical arm resting against the rear face of its mortise in the receiver to take up the shock of firing.[147]

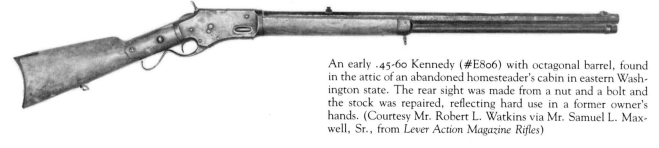

An early .45-60 Kennedy (#E806) with octagonal barrel, found in the attic of an abandoned homesteader's cabin in eastern Washington state. The rear sight was made from a nut and a bolt and the stock was repaired, reflecting hard use in a former owner's hands. (Courtesy Mr. Robert L. Watkins via Mr. Samuel L. Maxwell, Sr., from *Lever Action Magazine Rifles*)

A chuck wagon scene in the 1890s, perhaps in New Mexico Territory. The rifle leaned against the wagon is a Whitney-Kennedy, and the several revolvers appear to be Colt Single Actions. (Courtesy Museum of New Mexico)

Using a small workshop in Owego, New York, Burgess assembled a few lever-actions and a few long arms of different type to display at the Philadelphia Centennial Exposition in 1876. There they caught the eye of Eli Whitney, who subsequently contracted with Burgess to undertake their manufacture. The real desideratum for a maker of breech-loading rifles, of course, was the marketing of a lever-action repeater chambered for the .45-70 cartridge; Whitney, well aware of this fact, entered two Burgess rifles in the Ordnance trials of 1878, both chambered for the government round. During the supplementary rust test of one Burgess a heavy load blew off the bolt cover, "binding and wedging the piece" and rendering it unserviceable. But the gun still showed promise, and by January of 1879 Whitney was advertising it in the *Army and Navy*

Journal. Some months later Whitney also marketed it in a version designed for short-cased cartridges such as the .44-40. As made by Whitney, however, the new rifle had a carrier patented by Samuel V. Kennedy in May of 1879, and bore a stamp which included Kennedy's name. Thus the arm came to be known as the Whitney-Kennedy, or simply as the Kennedy, even though Burgess was primarily responsible for the design.[148]

The so-called Whitney-Kennedy was available in two basic sizes. The smaller of the two, chambered for cartridges like the .44-40 and (on rare occasions) .38-40, was made as a sporting rifle with a 24 in. round or octagon barrel, and as a carbine with a 20 in. round barrel. The larger, usually chambered for the .45-60 and later the .40-60 Winchester loads, had a 28 in.

Jno. P. Lower,

Sportsmen's Depot,

381 Blake St,, - Denver

Prospectors will find the largest stock and best assortment in Colorado of

Sharp's, Kennedy's, Burgess', Winchester's

And Other

RIFLES.

Colt's Pistols and Breech-Loading Double Guns. Ammunition, Fishing Tackle, Cutlery, Magnifying Glasses, Orange Gunpowder, Chicago Shot, Bar Lead, Eley's Caps, Wads, Cartridges, Field and Spy Glasses, Pocket Compasses, Indian Beads and Curiosities, Buffalo Robes, Bear Skins, Elk, Deer, Mountain Sheep and Antelope Heads, Canadian Web Snow Shoes, etc.,

A John P. Lower ad promoting the Kennedy and Burgess arms in addition to more common makes.

A quartet of Californians pose in a studio in Marysville, California. Their lever-action rifles include, from left: Whitney-Kennedy with folding tang sight, two M1873 Winchesters, and a Ballard No. 5 Pacific single shot. (Courtesy Mr. Herb Peck, Jr.)

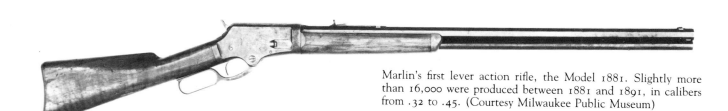

Marlin's first lever action rifle, the Model 1881. Slightly more than 16,000 were produced between 1881 and 1891, in calibers from .32 to .45. (Courtesy Milwaukee Public Museum)

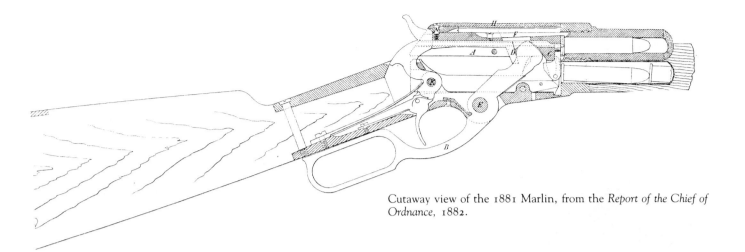

Cutaway view of the 1881 Marlin, from the *Report of the Chief of Ordnance,* 1882.

round or octagon barrel, or, in a shorter version, a 22 in. round barrel. At extra cost a purchaser could have double set triggers or an extralong barrel.[149]

An advertisement by Charles Kiessig of Leadville, Colorado, in June of 1880 included this note: "Just received, the latest improved Kennedy Repeating Rifle." John Lower, however, outdid Kiessig by marketing both the Kennedy and the Burgess. By 1882 Nathaniel Curry and C. D. Ladd, both of San Francisco, offered the Kennedy, but Matt Parrott of Reno listed the Burgess instead. Montana photographer L. A. Huffman owned a .44 caliber Kennedy which proved less than adequate for the game he encountered. After an unsuccessful elk hunt, Huffman

> raved and danced like an escaped lunatic; he tore his hair, slung his hat and trampled our grub and cooking utensils into the ground with his big boots as he waltzed around the camp-fire. He pronounced all the maledictions he could think of on that condemned little Kennedy pea-slinger of his. He wished he had a car load of them to dam the Yellowstone river with . . . Sawyer said he would like to have been there with his Winchester Express; Mike and Allen would have liked to have been there with their .45-75 Winchesters; and I whispered in Huffman's ear that I might have wounded another one or two if I had been there with my old 40-75 Sharps.[150]

The Whitney-Kennedy was not Andrew Burgess's only contribution to the field of lever-action arms. About 1880 John Marlin, maker of the single-shot Ballard, decided to bring out a repeater of his own, and asked Burgess's help in designing it. Burgess already had two patents he thought suitable, both issued in November of 1878, so with these as a basis, he and Marlin patented an improved carrier in December of

1881. Mechanically the Model 1881 Marlin was as simple as Burgess's earlier designs. An integral extension of the lever, straight instead of angled as in the Whitney-Kennedy, projected diagonally upward and forward through the receiver to bear against a recess just behind the head of a longitudinally sliding breechbolt. The shock of discharge was absorbed by the lever pivot pin, but this was nearly half an inch in diameter and well suited to take the strain. Aside from the mechanics of the arm, its important feature was that it chambered the .45-70 cartridge; it was the first .45-70 lever-action repeater to achieve anything like commercial success. With the standard 28 in. and 30 in. octagon barrels, the underbarrel tubular magazine held ten rounds; the shorter magazine used with the 24 in. barrel held eight. Initially the Marlin was offered only in .45-70 and a special .40-60 Marlin load, but by 1885 it was adapted to two Ballard cartridges, the .32-40 and .38-55. Extraheavy barrels, double set triggers, engraving, and fancy stocks were available at extra cost.[151]

Evidently the new rifle was ready for the market well before Marlin and Burgess received their joint patent on the carrier. Schoverling, Daly & Gales advertised it in the East as early as March of 1881; in late October of that year Broadwater, Hubbell & Co. of Miles City, Montana, announced that they were "Agents For the Improved Ballard Rifles And also the New Marlin Rifles—a case of each are already sold to Hunters and these guns promise to be very popular and take preference over all others." Again in March of 1882 Broadwater, Hubbell & Co. advertised the Marlin, calling it "the New Buffalo Gun. A large Stock on hand, of various weights, from 8 to 16 lbs., from which to make selection. These are THE Buffalo Gun." By 1882 other dealers in the West were also handling

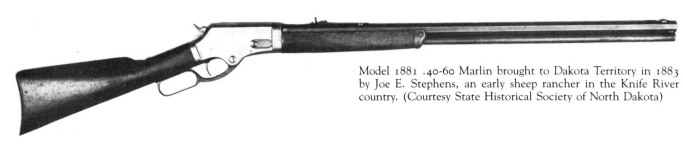

Model 1881 .40-60 Marlin brought to Dakota Territory in 1883 by Joe E. Stephens, an early sheep rancher in the Knife River country. (Courtesy State Historical Society of North Dakota)

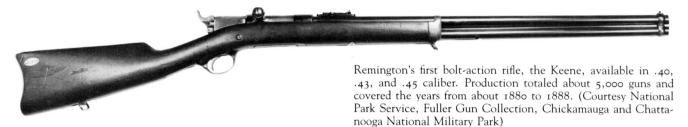

Remington's first bolt-action rifle, the Keene, available in .40, .43, and .45 caliber. Production totaled about 5,000 guns and covered the years from about 1880 to 1888. (Courtesy National Park Service, Fuller Gun Collection, Chickamauga and Chattanooga National Military Park)

A Brown-Merrill .58 centerfire single-shot bolt action (built on a B.S.A. Enfield rifle-musket), owned by a Colorado settler in the 1870s. At the rear of the bolt are two large locking lugs. The .58 centerfire cartridge this gun chambered was a potent round, loaded with 80 to 85 grains of powder and a 530- to 560-grain bullet. (Courtesy Colorado Springs Pioneers' Museum)

Rocky Mountain News (Denver), July 1885.

Leadville, Colorado, city directory advertisement (1882).

the Marlin, including W. H. Bradt of Leadville and C. D. Ladd of San Francisco. Marlin himself had enough faith in his repeater to submit it to the Ordnance Department in December of 1881 for formal testing during the trials of 1881–82. Although three bolt actions took the prize, Marlin's lever-action performed surprisingly well, thereby demonstrating its suitability for the rigorous service of the frontier.[152]

The Marlin was one of the few repeaters to take part in the slaughter of the northern buffalo herd, a slaughter which began in 1880 and lasted well into 1884. Another lever-action that would have served the needs of the professional hide hunter at that time was the 1876 Winchester in .45-75 or .50-95; but Winchester, advertising in the *Yellowstone Journal* in 1881, illustrated not the 1876 but the 1873 and a Hotchkiss bolt-action sporting rifle instead. Bolt-action rifles, of course, had crossed the plains in civilian hands well before the Hotchkiss made its appearance—besides the Palmer carbines sold in Texas, a single-shot Brown-Merrill bolt action came to the Pike's Peak area in the early 1870s. But despite the bolt action's simplicity and reliability, it attained only a modicum of popularity among frontiersmen. The Hotchkiss sporter was ready for the commercial market by the summer of 1879, and remained on that market for about twenty years, but its sales lagged well behind those of Winchester's lever-action arms. The same could be said of the Hotchkiss's closest competitor, the Remington-Keene. Although bought by the U.S. Indian Department, advertised repeatedly in the *Army and Navy Journal,* and handled by big gun houses such as Curry's in San Francisco during the 1880s, the Keene made few inroads among westerners.[153]

Aside from the Keene and what revolving rifles may have remained on hand, Remington had no repeating long arms with which to tempt an undecided buyer until the firm introduced the Lee in the mid-1880s; but this was still another bolt action. For the bulk of its long-arm sales, therefore, Remington had to rely on its single-shot rifles. Even Smith & Wesson tried to market a repeating shoulder arm. In 1880 the firm introduced a special .320 caliber revolving rifle, based on the New Model No. 3 revolver frame. While a few were sold in the West—Curry retailed some in the early 1880s—a lack of buyer interest, especially because of gas leakage between barrel and cylinder, resulted in the production of fewer than 1000 guns. Winchester, on the other hand, had no such problems: throughout the 1880s its lever-actions continued to dominate the repeating-rifle market, especially in the West. Early in 1879 Richard Townshend, then in New Mexico, bought a "new-model .45 Winchester, an improvement over the old .44," and a few months later encountered a band of outlaws. "Besides their revolv-

A winter hunter in South Dakota with a Remington-Keene carbine. (Courtesy Kansas State Historical Society)

ers, they carried Winchesters of the very newest and latest model, and they wore two belts apiece stuffed full of cartridges." In 1882, for a hunt on the Yellowstone, one of Doc Allen's companions "flourished a .45-75 Winchester, and from his use of this weapon, convinced us he 'had been there before.'" Allen himself concluded that "to hunt bears one needs a 45-60 Winchester, or something as good, if it can be found, and a sharp bowieknife." Another incident involving an 1876 Winchester occurred in 1882: the notorious John Ringo ran into a fatal bullet in Arizona. Lying near his corpse were a Colt single-action and "1 winchester rifle—octagon barrel, Cal. .45, Model 1876, No. 21896, containing a cartridge in the breech end and 10 in the magazine. . . ." After traveling through Yellowstone Park in the early 1880s, George Wingate noted that "outside the Park both a rifle and shotgun are needed. I carried a .45-75 Winchester . . . and I wish for no better weapon." Daniel Barringer mentioned using "an extra long-barreled .45-60 Winchester" near the park in 1883.[154]

Black Coyote, an Arapahoe Indian policeman, stands before a photographer's cloth or canvas backdrop. His arms, a Remington-Keene rifle and probably a Remington M1875 revolver, are models quite often seen in the hands of Indian police in nineteenth-century photos. The 1883 Remington catalog, in fact, promoted the Keene as the "Model Furnished Interior Dept. for Indian Police." (Courtesy Amon Carter Museum of Western Art, Ft. Worth, Texas)

A Wyoming cowboy, probably photographed in the 1880s. His saddle gun is a Remington-Keene bolt action. (Courtesy Wyoming State Archives and Historical Dept.)

In spite of the fact that Winchester, Remington, Whitney, and Marlin were firmly established in the repeating-rifle business, officials at Colt decided to bring out a lever-action repeater of their own. Announced in an 1883 pamphlet as "Colt's New Magazine Rifle," the arm was based primarily on a patent issued to Andrew Burgess in April of 1879, and embodied a modified toggle-link action. Chambered only for the .44-40, it was made as a rifle with a 25½ in. round, octagon, or round/octagon barrel, or as a carbine with a 20 in. round barrel. The Colt-Burgess was a direct competitor of the 1873 Winchester; at the same time, Winchester officials ordered the assembly of some experimental revolvers. Whether this was actually a subtle threat is uncertain, but late in 1884 Colt discontinued production of its lever-action, with some 6400 already completed. Despite the short production span, some of the guns did reach the West. John P. Lower, for example, advertised them in the *Rocky Mountain News* in May of 1883. He had mixed

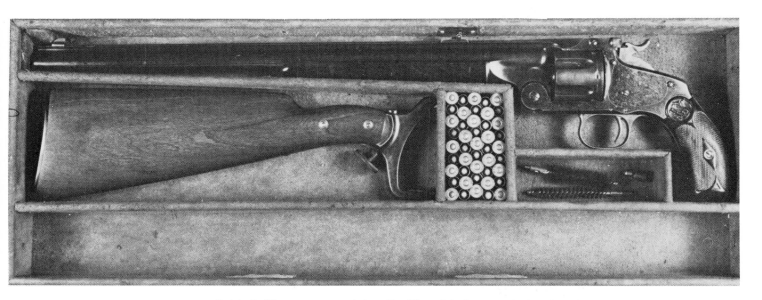

Smith & Wesson .320 revolving rifle. The 16-, 18-, or 20-inch barrel with which these revolvers were fitted was manufactured in two sections which were joined together several inches in front of the breech. (Courtesy Mr. Robert B. Berryman)

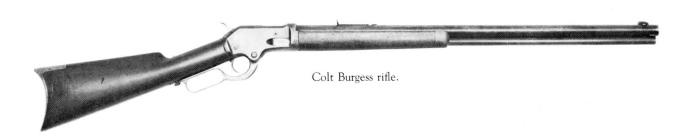

Colt Burgess rifle.

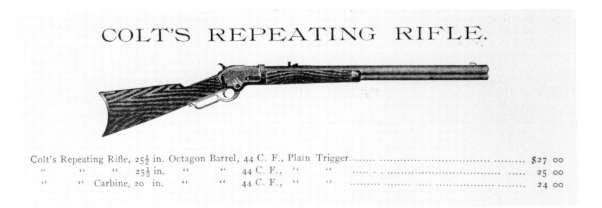

COLT'S REPEATING RIFLE.

Colt's Repeating Rifle, 25½ in. Octagon Barrel, 44 C. F., Plain Trigger... $27 00
    "   "   " 25½ in.   "   " 44 C. F., "   "   25 00
    "   " Carbine, 20 in.   "   " 44 C. F., "   "   24 00

The 1883 catalog issued by N. Curry & Bro. of San Francisco contained this ad for the short-lived line of Colt Burgess lever-action rifles and carbines.

Illustrative of the market competition between the Colt Burgess and the Winchester M1873 is this view of Company "D" of the Texas Rangers at Realitas, Texas, in 1887. With few exceptions, the choice of shoulder arms was the standard M1873 Winchester, but Ranger Ernest E. Rogers (standing sixth from left) appears to have selected a Colt Burgess carbine. Other nonconformists are Walter Durbin (seated fourth from left) with a pistol-grip stocked M1876 Winchester rifle, and Jim Robinson (seated fifth from left) holding a short-barrel Winchester M1873 "baby carbine." On September 5, 1881, Winchester shipped a group of M1873 carbines in the 68101 to 68300 serial number range to Texas for ranger use, and some of those guns probably appear in this scene. Walter Jones (standing far right) has a Colt M1877 double-action revolver in his belt, in addition to the Colt Single Actions which some of his compatriots carry. (Courtesy Western History Collections, University of Oklahoma Library)

feelings about the gun, however, expressed in a letter to Colt at that time:

> The Repeating Rifle I like very much, and have no doubt it will make its own reputation if there is any demand for such . . . as I have already advertised them in about 6 or 8 newspapers I may stir up at least some enquiries about them—but business is exceedingly dull hereabouts . . . and if you take into consideration the fact of the easy procuring of Government 45/70 Ctgs. and the desire for long range shooting, you would do better to make [a gun] to compete with the Burgess, Marlin & Kennedys. . . .

Nevertheless, the 1884 Curry catalog offered the carbine for $24 and the rifle for $25 to $27. Far more expensive was the heavily engraved octagon-barreled model presented by the Colt company to Buffalo Bill in July of 1883, presumably as a promotional measure.[155]

IMPROVED SINGLE-SHOT AND DOUBLE-BARRELED RIFLES

The proliferation of repeaters on the frontier during the 1880s had no real effect on the popularity of the single-shot rifle until the close of the decade. And even at this time the Sharps reigned supreme. In 1882 young James McNaney and his older brother decided to become professional buffalo hunters; the equipment they purchased in Miles City included the following items:

> Two wagons, 2 four-horse teams, 2 saddle-horses, 2 wall-tents, 1 cook-stove with pipe, 1 40-90 Sharp's rifle (breech-loading), 1 45-70 Sharps rifle (breech-loading), 1 45-120 Sharps rifle (breech-loading), 50 pounds gunpowder, 550 pounds lead, 4,500 primers,

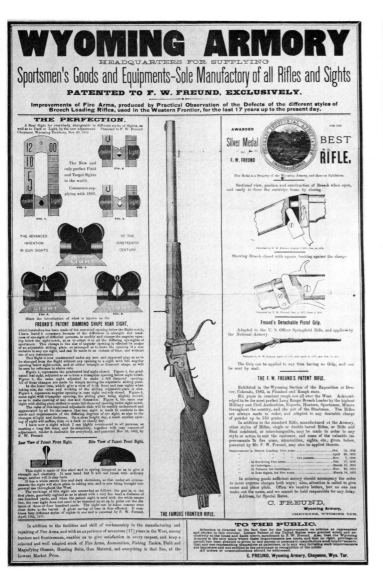

Both sides of an advertising poster for the Freund Wyoming Armory at Cheyenne, Wyoming Territory (c. 1883). It illustrates the variety of Freund sights offered, as well as the patented Freund rifle. (Courtesy Mr. Norm Flayderman)

600 brass shells, 4 sheets patch-paper, [and] 60 Wilson skinning knives . . . The entire cost of the outfit was about $1,400.

During a buffalo hunt late the same year, a correspondent of *Forest and Stream* used "a Sharps .45-cal. hammerless . . . loaded with 120 grains of Dupont FG powder, and the U.S. Government 405-grain grooved bullet." In alluding to his companion's gun, he noted "that sharp, wicked crack I knew came from Price's .40-90. No other guns talks like a .40-caliber Sharps

with 90 grains of Dupont." Three years later, during an Apache scare in New Mexico, James Cook "opened fire on the Indians with a 40-90 Sharps rifle at a range of about one thousand yards. This checked them, and they ran to cover in the rocks and brush." Writing in 1883, George Shields mentioned that "nearly all [Sharps rifles] now in use are of the new hammerless model, forty-five caliber." Reginald Aldridge, an Englishman spending some time on a ranch that year, acquired "a Sharp's hammerless carbine, .400 cal., which I can carry in a leather scabbard attached to my saddle, and

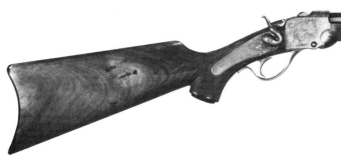

An F. W. Freund "Wyoming Saddle Gun," as the model was advertised. Made almost entirely by hand, it is one of the seven or eight such rifles produced by the famed frontier gunmaker. This .40 single-shot breechloader features deluxe grained wood, fancy checkering, and intricate engraving, including a panel of a fox stalking game. The gun was made for Clarence King, famed western surveyor and explorer, and bears his initials "CK" inlaid in gold in the left side of the frame. (Courtesy Mr. Norm Flayderman)

Remington-Hepburn .45 sporting rifle used by Catch-the-Bear during the struggle to arrest Sitting Bull in December of 1890, which resulted in the latter's death. (Courtesy State Historical Society of North Dakota)

Remington-Hepburn No. 3 military-style match rifle with full-length musket-type stock. (Courtesy National Park Service, Fuller Gun Collection, Chickamauga and Chattanooga National Military Park)

passing under the right leg." Frank Collinson "killed the last wild buffalo I ever saw with my Sharps hammerless forty-caliber gun in the spring of 1885." While hunting in Montana in the late 1880s, Dr. William Allen had this exchange with his companion:

Hiram Steward had looked at my Winchester with contempt, calling it an old popgun. His weapon was an old Sharp's rifle, of the first issue . . . "why don't you get a Sharps?" said he. "Simply because I prefer the Winchester." "Have you ever been on the buffalo range?" he queried. "No." "Wal, I thought so; when you tackle them ar bar, you will larn more." . . . [Steward] slid down from his jackass, pulled his old Sharp's from the sling and inserted a .44-75.[156]

For the Sharps Rifle Company Hiram Steward's defense of their product came a little late. Well aware of the increasing demand for repeaters, Sharps officials had entered a bolt-action Vetterli in the 1878 Ordnance trials; about a year afterwards they assembled a few Lee bolt-action box-magazine sporting rifles, using octagon barrels with the characteristic "Old Reliable" stamp. But no Sharps repeating rifle ever progressed beyond the experimental stage. Apparently the redoubtable Phineas T. Barnum, president of the firm, misappropriated company funds for use in his other projects; as a result of this and other factors the mighty Sharps concern shut down completely in 1881. New Sharps rifles, however, did continue to be available from dealers' stocks for several years afterwards.[157]

In the mid-1870s Frank Freund had attempted to persuade Sharps to produce an action incorporating his improvements, but company officials did not consider them very important, and simply let the matter drop. Freund then continued modifying Sharps rifles on an individual basis at his Cheyenne shop until the

A Colorado prospector of the 1880s with a Remington-Hepburn sporting rifle. (Courtesy Mr. Malcolm Collier)

company failed. Shortly afterward he began building in its entirety a highly finished rifle which embodied most of his improvements. Called the "Wyoming Saddle Gun" in his 1883 price list, the rifle retained the basic Freund-modified vertically sliding breechblock, but the action was about two-thirds the size of a Sharps action, with a line-engraved flat-sided frame. The octagon barrel was usually short, 20 in. or so, and was usually chambered for the .40-90 Sharps load. The slender back-action lock was engraved "Freund's Pat./ Wyoming Armory/Cheyenne, Wyo." Although the arm was elegant in appearance and handsomely finished, it was also prohibitively expensive, selling for $200 or more, and production was understandably limited.[158]

Remington officials undoubtedly shed few tears at Sharps's passing. In an effort to gain a greater share of the single-shot-rifle market, the company introduced a new single-shot about 1880. Patented by Lewis Hepburn in October of 1879, this arm employed a vertically sliding breechblock, controlled by a thumb lever mounted on the right side of the frame. The Remington-Hepburn, termed the "No. 3 Sporting & Target Rifle," was made as a hunting, match, and military rifle, and was chambered for nearly every popular caliber of the day. During the early 1880s Nathaniel Curry offered the sporting rifle with 28 in. or 30 in. octagon or round/octagon barrels, chambered for the .38-40-1 3/4 in., the .40-50 and .40-70 Sharps, the .45-70, .50-70, and .50-110. Despite the introduction of the new rifle, sales of the No. 1 and No. 2 rolling-block sporters remained brisk.[159]

Presumably sales of the Ballard also continued unabated, at least during the early 1880s. Broadwater, Hubbell & Co. of Miles City offered it at that time, as did C. D. Ladd of San Francisco and Matt Parrott of Reno. Marlin himself still advertised the Ballard in his 1888 catalog, but the rifle was by that time more widely associated with the target ranges of New En-

Office shared by Wild Bill, bronco buster, and a real estate agent and the Deltis, Oklahoma, post office. Wild Bill, if it be he, carries a Colt M1878 double-action revolver, while the seated individual holds an unidentified double-barrel shotgun. At far left is what appears to be a Hopkins & Allen .22 or one of the Stevens "Favorite" series of single-shot rifles made in .22, .25, and .32 calibers. Stevens was one of this country's most prolific makers of single-shot light rifles, particularly well suited for youthful shooters. (Courtesy Western History Collections, University of Oklahoma Library)

Forest and Stream, July 1885.

gland than with the plains and mountains of the West. Nevertheless some of the finest of the target Ballards were those with barrels made by George Schoyen of Denver, who succeeded Carlos Gove in 1884. Whether barreled by Schoyen or at the factory, Ballards proved especially accurate when chambered for one of two cartridges—the .32-40 and the .38-55. A. C. Gould commented that either of these rounds would put nearly all of its shots into a six-inch circle at 200 yards, even when fired from a rifle less accurate than a finely finished target arm.[160]

Another candidate for rebarreling was the trapdoor Springfield. In his book *Rustlings in the Rockies*, published in 1883, George Shields commented that the Springfield was "well adapted to both military and sporting purposes," and evidently many westerners agreed with him. A notable Springfield user of the

1880s was Tom Horn, who (before turning to other things) served as a civilian scout against the Apaches. Horn evidently liked the gun but did complain that "a hundred rounds of 45-70 cartridges weighs eleven pounds when you first put them on, and at the end of twenty days, they weigh about as much as a small sized locomotive." One reason for the rifle's continuing popularity was that in its unaltered military version it sold for about $15. However, the handsome half-stocked, octagon-barreled Springfield sporting arms, sold by Meacham of St. Louis and Curry of San Francisco during the 1880s, brought about $25. These sporters were available not only in .45-70 but also in calibers such as .40-65 and .40-70.[161]

Less popular in the West than Sharps, Remingtons, Springfields, and Ballards were the break-open single-shots such as the Maynard. In 1882 the Massachusetts Arms Company finally abandoned the Model 1873 Maynard, with its peculiar thick-rimmed cartridges, and introduced a modified arm designed for conventional ammunition. The new Maynard cases, however, held many of the old loadings: .35-40, .38-50, .40-40, .40-60, .40-70, .44-70, and .44-100. The 1882 Maynard was also chambered for the .45-70 government round.[162]

Presumably it was an 1882 Maynard that A. C. Gould was referring to when he wrote that:

I was hunting in Dakota several years ago, and made for a small river. [As] I crept through the cottonwood growth which fringed the banks . . . a deer plunged wildly up the bank. I had a Maynard rifle in my hands, and shot and missed the deer. . . . It was very cold, and I was heavily clad with a thick reefer, which was buttoned snugly about me, had on buckskin gloves, and my cartridges were in my outside pocket. Before I could reload my rifle the deer had disappeared, and I was muttering, "If I only had a repeater."

Obviously Gould could have had a similar problem with any single-shot rifle; and by the late 1880s many westerners shared his wish for a repeater.[163]

Another break-open single-shot rifle that made an occasional appearance in the West was the Stevens. Initially made without a forestock, the Stevens sporting rifle (as opposed to the firm's pocket rifle) came with an octagon or round/octagon barrel from 24 in. to 36 in. long, and a nickel-plated frame of distinctive configuration. The first rifles were chambered for such cartridges as the .32, .38, and .44 Long rimfire loads, but in mid-1875 the company announced a more powerful version, which took the .38 and .44 Extra Long Wesson and Ballard centerfire rounds.[164]

While simple in the extreme, the Stevens was not

Successful pronghorn antelope hunters. The youth in the center holds a Stevens "tip-up" single-shot rifle while the adults employ M1876 Winchesters and a M1873 Winchester at far left, and a Sharps Borchardt (second from left). The keen-eyed, fleet American pronghorn antelope is not a true antelope at all and has no close relatives.

particularly strong. The only component that kept barrel and frame together at the moment of discharge was the transverse barrel pivot screw at the front of the frame; the Stevens barrel, unlike those of the Maynard and the Wesson, had no underlugs to relieve the pivot screw from the strain of firing. But this did allow a minimum of machining and fitting, and still proved amply strong for the cartridges normally used in the gun. Moreover the rifle earned praise from many quarters, both for its accurate barrel and its light, crisp trigger pull.

Apparently Stevens made few efforts to market his rifle in the West until the 1870s had passed. In 1880 and 1882, however, large Stevens advertisements appeared in the Omaha Republican, and by 1884 Curry of San Francisco was handling both the light .22 caliber gallery rifles and the centerfire sporting rifles with interchangeable shot barrels.[165]

The simple break-open action appealed to other makers besides Wesson, Maynard, and Stevens. At least two San Francisco gun houses, those of Slotterbek and Liddle & Kaeding, offered break-open rifles of their own design; Slotterbek, in fact, patented his design in October of 1880. A third proprietary break-

Members of the Central City (Colorado) rifle team, which won the sixth annual Colorado Rifle Assn. tournament on September 2–3, 1901. From left: Dr. A. O. Asquith with a Stevens No. 52-44 rifle equipped with a false muzzle; D. H. Allen, P. R. Alsdorf, and J. H. Hopper with Winchester Schuetzen-type rifles; W. S. Green with a Winchester single-shot High Wall; and Fred Alsdorf with a Model No. 45-44 Stevens. (Courtesy Mr. John Dutcher)

open arm was marketed by Powell of Cincinnati, Ohio, who occasionally advertised in western newspapers, such as the Hays, Kansas, *Sentinel* and New Mexico's *Grant County Herald*, during the late 1870s and early 1880s. Once in a while an isolated frontier gunsmith attempted to build a single-shot rifle as well. Emil Topperwein, the father of the famous Winchester exhibition shooter Ad Topperwein, was a talented gunsmith of Boerne, Texas, and demonstrated it by building a fine .38-55 single-shot target rifle with round/octagon barrel, pistol-grip stock, and double set triggers; mechanically the arm was similar to the Whitney-Phoenix, but Topperwein made the action in its entirety.[166]

Destined to become far better known than the elder Topperwein was young John Moses Browning of Ogden, Utah. The son of Jonathan Browning, maker of percussion harmonica and revolving rifles which saw service on the frontier before the Civil War, John patented a single-shot design in October of 1879, when he was twenty-four years old. In Browning's action the hammer was pivoted inside the vertically sliding breechblock; as the shooter swung the underlever downward and forward to lower the block, the sear caught the hammer, and brought it to full-cock automatically as the shooter raised the block to fire. In essence it was a compact and refined Sharps. It was as fast to reload as the Borchardt, because it required

D. Meek's sod house south of Broken Bow, Nebraska, in 1890. The man second from right has a Belgian or French-made single-shot Flobert-type rolling-block rifle. Large numbers of such rifles were sold in the U.S. as inexpensive, light hunting arms, particularly in .22 caliber. (Courtesy Nebraska State Historical Society)

no separate effort to cock, but also offered the advantage of an exposed hammer for the shooter who preferred the option of manual cocking.[167]

Using heavy octagon-barrel blanks made by Remington and other companies, Browning and his brothers assembled about 550 rifles between 1880 and 1883. Evidently the most popular chambering was for the .45-70 government round, but a goodly number of guns took the .40-70 Sharps straight, with a lesser quantity chambered for such little-known cartridges as the .32-40 Remington.[168]

The reason for the short production life of this rifle was that in 1883 Andrew McAusland, one of the better-known arms dealers on the frontier and an agent for Winchester products, happened onto one of the Brownings. McAusland, whose father had sold guns in Omaha before the Civil War, was thoroughly familiar with firearms; after studying the Browning, he

sent it to Winchester. The firm's vice-president and general manager, Thomas G. Bennett (who was also a mechanical engineer) liked the gun so well he personally traveled from New Haven to Ogden to buy the rights to it. With only minor modifications the weapon appeared on the market in 1885 as the "Winchester Single Shot Rifle." As the company phrased it: "It can be furnished with or without set trigger, with barrels of all ordinary lengths and weights, and for all standard cartridges; also with rifle and shot-gun butt, plain or fancy wood, or with pistol grip." Round, octagon, or round/octagon barrels were available, in a standard 30 in. length for the larger calibers, but at extra cost a shooter could have a barrel as long as 36 in. and in one of five different weights. Within a few years of its appearance the rifle was chambered (or rechambered by independent gunsmiths) for practically every conceivable cartridge of the period. Among

General George Crook's personal hunting rifles. At top is his Sharps M1874 .45 (#159139) with Freund rear sight. The receiver is engraved on the right side with an elk and on the left with the initials "GC." At bottom is his .40-90 Winchester High Wall single shot (#10062) with a scope made by the William Maldolm Co. of Syracuse, New York. These guns passed to Crook's godson and frequent companion on western hunting trips, Webb C. Hayes, son of President Rutherford B. Hayes. The middle rifle, a Marlin .45-70 M1881 (#4254), was one of Hayes's favorites and may have belonged to Crook as well. (Courtesy Rutherford B. Hayes Presidential Center, Fremont, Ohio)

Forest and Stream, December 1885.

the more interesting of these cartridges were three so-called Sharps loads: the .40-90, .45-120, and .50-140, all of which had straight cases 3¼ in. long. Made by U.M.C. and Winchester especially for shooters who disliked necked cases, these extralong straight rounds did not appear until about 1884, well after the Sharps firm had closed its doors. Local gunsmiths, however, did rechamber some Sharps rifles for these loads.[169]

Although many dealers in the West sold it, the single-shot Winchester was a latecomer to the frontier. On occasion it did elicit comment, as in Oklahoma about 1893, when Marquis James took note of "Mr. Howell's .40-70 single-shot Winchester, his bear gun." But Theodore Roosevelt, writing near the close of the frontier era, better summarized those single-shots that were really popular in the West when he stated that:

> One of my friends invariably uses an old Government Springfield, a 45-caliber, with an ounce bullet. Another cares for nothing but the 40-90 Sharp's, a weapon for which I myself have much partiality. Another uses always the old 45-caliber Sharp's, and yet another the 45-caliber Remington.

He also mentioned a .38 caliber Ballard he had given to his brother.[170]

For the plainsmen who wanted to use cartridges longer and more powerful than the .45-70, and who also wanted more than one shot without reloading, there were the double-barreled rifles. While they were expensive and not well suited for game of different sizes at widely varying distances, the doubles nevertheless had their advocates in the West. James Cook, guiding a bear-hunting party of five Englishmen in

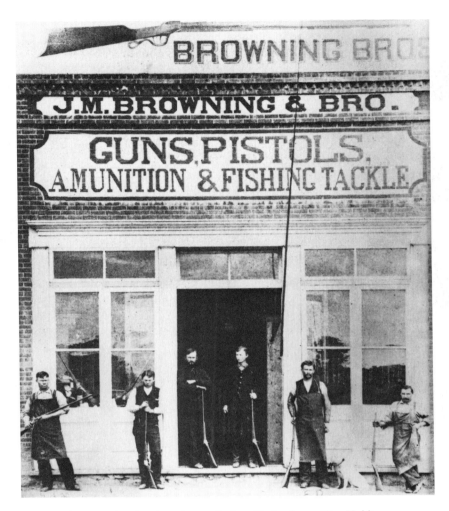

Browning brothers' gunshop at Ogden, Utah, about 1882. Holding
Browning single-shot rifles are, from left: Sam, George, John M.,
Matthew S., and Ed Browning, with Frank Rushton at far right.
(Courtesy Mr. Jan Schrader)

1880, noted that they all carried "double-barreled express rifles of heavy bore." But British sportsmen were
not the sole users of doubles; Theodore Roosevelt, for
example, told the following story:

In 1882, one of the buffalo-hunters on the Little
Missouri obtained from some Englishman a double-
barrelled 10-bore rifle of the kind used against rhi-
noceros, buffalo, and elephant in the Old World;
but it proved very inferior to the 40 and 45 caliber
Sharp's buffalo guns when used under the conditions
of American buffalo-hunting, the tremendous shock
given by the bullet not compensating for the gun's
great relative deficiency in range and accuracy, while
even the penetration was inferior at ordinary dis-

tances. It is largely also a matter of individual taste.
At one time I possessed a very expensive double-
barrelled 500 Express, by one of the crack English
makers; but I never liked the gun, and could not
do as well with it as with my repeater, which cost
barely a sixth as much. So one day I handed it to
a Scotch friend, who was manifestly ill at ease with
a Winchester exactly like my own. He took to the
double-barrel as naturally as I did to the repeater,
and did excellent work with it.[171]

Officials at Colt thought there might be a market
for an American-made double, and in the early 1880s
made up some samples based on the company's Model
1878 shotgun action. In May of 1883 John P. Lower,

Unidentified settlers, one of whom (right) holds a Winchester Hi-Wall sporting rifle. (Courtesy Mr. Malcolm Collier)

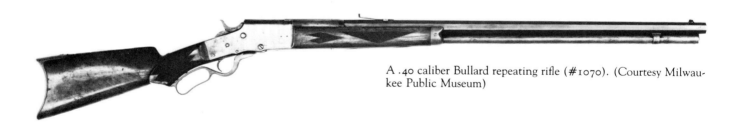

A .40 caliber Bullard repeating rifle (#1070). (Courtesy Milwaukee Public Museum)

after receiving one of the guns, wrote to Colt's Hugh Harbison: "The Double Express Rifle . . . came to hand this morning, and I must congratulate your folks on having [made] what I think is *the Express Dbl Rifle of the Age.*" But few others were as impressed with the rifle as was Lower, and Colt assembled only about 40 such guns before turning to other matters.[172]

Another American with a high opinion of the double was Daniel Barringer, who used one in Montana during the 1880s. He described it as "a splendid En-glish Holland & Holland double express hammer rifle, .450 caliber, the shells being loaded with something like 120 grains of Curtis & Harvey black powder and heavy solid lead bullets, containing about 1-20 tin." In a letter to *Shooting and Fishing* magazine in the early 1890s, a Californian who owned two doubles gave his opinion of their advantages:

Double shots from the double rifle can be fired quicker than with the repeaters; besides, it has the advantage of equal, if not superior, accuracy up to its range—200 to 250 yards; has a flatter trajectory and greater smashing power than has the repeater of the same calibre, besides being about 1½ lbs. lighter in weight, which is quite an item in climbing around the mountains in a long day's tramp.

A rifle's weight, of course, was always an important factor in mountain hunting. An 1884 correspondent of *Forest and Stream,* one "D. M. B.," disregarded the point, and later bemoaned his oversight:

> Before going to the Rockies on a prolonged trip I had Lefevre make me a double-barreled 13½-pound rifle, chambered to shoot six or seven drams of powder and an ounce and a half of lead . . . [but] it kicked tremendously [and] seemed to weigh a ton after a hard day's tramp in search of elk or sheep. . . .[173]

Use of doubles in the mountains sometimes revealed an unusual effect of high altitude. In February of 1884 Henry Holland, the noted English gunmaker, wrote:

> I have had complaints from correspondents who have been shooting with Expresses in the . . . Rocky Mountains in America, that their rifles shoot low. . . . This morning I received an order for an Express from America. The writer of this order particularly mentions that the barrels must be extra long, and sighted rather high, as he is shooting some 9000 feet or more above sea level. . . .

Such peculiarities still did not deter the fanciers of doubles. The Californian who wrote to *Shooting and Fishing* owned not one but two double rifles; he described one as "a hammerless, self-ejecting, double express, made by the prince of double-express rifle makers. Length of barrels, 26 in.; [and] calibre, .400 (.40-100-300 3¼ inch shell)." The other was a .25-20, also hammerless, which weighed less than six pounds. J. H. Walsh described the typical British double of the mid-1880s in the following way:

> The [barrel] length of double-barrelled Expresses is on the average 27 inches. . . . The total weight for .400 bores is usually about from 7 lb. to 8 lb. . . . and .577, 10 lb. to 12 lb. . . . nearly every kind of breech action described [elsewhere] may be used, [but] as a rule, for some considerable time, riflemakers have almost unanimously preferred the kind of action known as the "double-grip" . . . together with those almost invariable features in such weapons as the "pistol grip" and "cheek piece."

The popular double-rifle calibers during the 1880s were .400, .450, .500, and .577, with the .450 caliber rifles representing a good compromise for the American West.

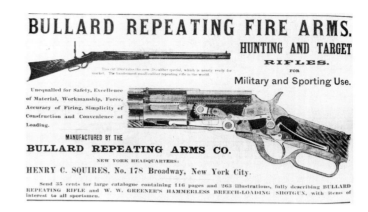

Forest and Stream, July 1884.

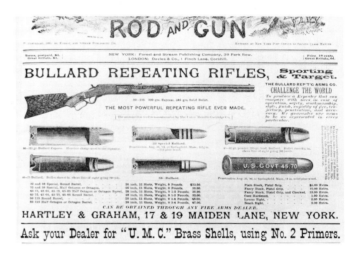

Forest and Stream, February 1885.

James Schultz, who guided a hunting party of three English bankers through the West around 1889, noted that "the weapons of all three of them were double-barreled Purdy express rifles of .45 caliber."[174]

THE 1886 WINCHESTER AND THE ASCENDANCY OF THE REPEATER

During the course of the 1880s new repeating rifles appeared on the market which were nearly as powerful as the big doubles—and far less expensive. One such repeater, the Bullard, had reached the Texas and California markets by 1884. Patented in August of 1881 by James H. Bullard, this lever-action was characterized by its glass-smooth action; it was undoubtedly one of the smoothest-operating rifles of its type ever made.

Bear hunters with traps and guns at Paul Bretesche's ranch in Carbon County, Montana, in the late 1880s. The hunters' handguns are a Colt Single Action (left) and what resembles a second or third model Smith & Wesson .44 Russian with its characteristic hump in the backstrap. The man at right holds a large-frame Colt Lightning slide-action magazine rifle, while at left may be a single-shot English sporting rifle. (Courtesy Montana Historical Society)

As a Bullard circular of the period phrased it: "It is possible to fire the Bullard with greater rapidity than any other repeating rifle, as it works easier and smoother . . . [it] has been fired twelve shots in five seconds, the best record of any other gun being eleven shots in seven seconds, using U.S. cartridges." In achieving this fast and smooth operation, however, Bullard resorted to a somewhat complex design. The longitudinally sliding breechbolt was withdrawn and advanced by compound levers, acting through a rack-and-pinion assembly, and was locked at the rear by what amounted to a separate rolling-block action.[175]

As commercially produced the Bullard usually had a 28 in., octagon or round/octagon barrel, with full- or half-length magazine. The 1884 Curry catalog offered it in .45-70, plus two special Bullard calibers, .40-75 and .40-90. Within a year the arm was available chambered for additional Bullard cartridges, among which were the .32-40, .38-45, and .50-115 Express. These Bullard loads were somewhat advanced for their time—the .50-115, for instance, had a semirimmed, solid-head case—but none were interchangeable with other cartridges of similar designations; as a result none became very popular.[176]

Despite its mechanical complexity the Bullard repeater did see some use in the West. One enthusiastic owner was Doc Allen, formerly a stout Winchester advocate. Preparing for a Wyoming hunt in 1886, Allen "grasped my faithful old friend, threw down the lever, and surveyed the inside which gleamed like a mirror. It was my Bullard rifle, 45 calibre, eighty-five grains of powder, ten pounds weight and ten shots." Some of Allen's associates liked the rifle also: during another Wyoming hunt four years later, Allen "had just crossed [a] little stream when Chappell's old Bullard rifle awoke the neighborhood with a piercing sound." Relfecting later upon his frontier adventures, Allen wrote that "death had stared me in the face many times . . . in many different forms, and the old Bullard had never been found wanting." Another Bullard user was Theodore Roosevelt, who owned a six-shot model chambered for the .50-115 Express cartridge.[177]

For a repeater, however, the Bullard was expensive, retailing for about $35 in the West in its unadorned version. Less costly, and correspondingly more popular, was a new Colt repeater introduced in the spring of 1885. Patented by the famous William Elliot in May and September of 1883, the new Colt was a slide-action or pump-action rifle, in which a short, longitudinally sliding forestock opened and closed the action. The action itself comprised a longitudinally sliding breechbolt, on the underside of which was a pivoting locking block. The design, in fact, was similar to that of the Robinson repeater patented in 1870, with the idea of a moveable forestock presumably borrowed from the Spencer repeating shotgun of 1882. Whatever its genesis, the new gun, styled the "Lightning Magazine Rifle," was mechanically sound and easy to operate.[178]

Colt initially made the Lightning as a sporting rifle, with 26 in. round or octagon barrel, and as a carbine with 20 in. round barrel. When fully loaded the sporting rifle would hold fifteen .32-20, .38-40, or .44-40 cartridges, the carbine twelve. Besides the standard carbine, Colt offered a "Baby carbine" weighing less than six pounds. Other variations appeared subsequently, but of these the most important was the scaled-up "Express Rifle" introduced in 1888. Made with a 26 in. or 28 in. round or octagon barrel, the Express version was chambered for such cartridges as the .40-60, .45-60, 45-85, and .50-95. In part this rifle, especially in .40-60 caliber, may have been developed because of suggestions made by E. C. Meacham of St. Louis. Writing to the Colt concern in June of 1885, Meacham had noted that:

> If your line covers the 22, 32, 38, 44 [W.C.F.] & 40-60 and you can furnish them as fast as the trade demands we think our New Haven friend [Winchester] will find a great falling off in his rifle business. . . . In our opinion [these calibers] will cover the wants of the trade. Particularly because there is so much of this kind of ammunition in the market. A party does not wish to buy a rifle and feel that it is necessary for him to take his entire quantity of ammunition with the rifle. . . . Any party now purchasing a 40-60 caliber or any other caliber named by us is sure of having the ammunition for the rifle in any section of the country he proposes visiting.

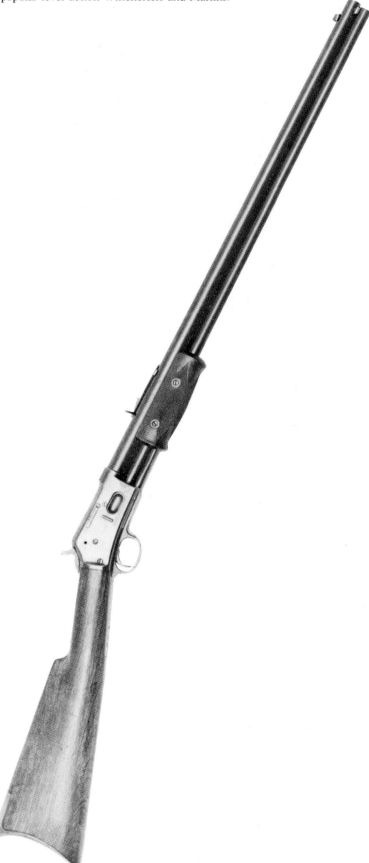

A Colt .32 Lightning magazine rifle. Produced from 1884 to 1904 and offered in calibers from .22 to .50-95 Express, the Lightning series of Colt rifles never provided significant competition to the popular lever-action Winchesters and Marlins.

A penciled notation on the reverse of this studio cabinet card view indicates it was taken in northern Mexico. Identifiable guns are a Colt Lightning rifle, a holstered large frame Merwin & Hulbert (center), and probably a Colt Single Action (left). (Courtesy Mr. Herb Peck, Jr.)

His M1886 Winchester rifle across his kill, a western hunter refreshes himself. (Courtesy Western History Collections, University of Oklahoma Library)

We understand the Winchester 40-60 does better shooting in the Indian country than any of the Winchester large caliber guns. . . .

During the first several months of the Lightning's production, Colt had a few mechanical problems with it; and before they could be corrected the company received some unhappy letters. One letter, written in December of 1885 to J. P. Lower & Sons by E. H. Bonnett of Nunda, Colorado, and forwarded by Lower to Colt, stated that:

I have a Colt's 44 magazine rifle which does not eject the shells. While apparently nothing looks wrong in any way, have taken it apart twice to see if I could find out the reason of it, but I cannot find anything missing or broken. Do you know of any other . . . that has acted the same?

In forwarding this letter, Lower added that:

We have only to say that this is but one of several similar letters we have received lately and our own experience with the new Lightning Rifle goes to prove that these complaints are well-founded. Not *one* of the rifles we have in stock except the model you made for us will work correctly. . . . Now what are we to do?

Colt soon corrected the ejection problem, and in 1889 George H. Sickels, a professional exhibition shooter, wrote the company to say that:

I understand you have made an Improvement on your 44 Cal Carbine—does it eject the shell perfectly in doing rapid shooting I do shooting at *Glass Balls* and *Marbles* I understand that a person can do more rapid shooting with your Carbine Improved than I can with a *Winchester*. . . .[179]

Regarding the Lightning's speed of operation, Colt advertisements pointed out that "by holding the trigger back, and using the reciprocating motion with the left hand, the rifle can be fired with great rapidity and without further use of the trigger."[180]

In addition to John Lower, most of the Colt dealers in the West sold Lightning rifles; even the San Francisco Police Department bought a quantity in .44-40.[181]

One competitor that undoubtedly hurt the Lightning's sales, and sales of the Bullard as well, was a new lever-action Winchester, brought out in the late summer of 1886. And if any one repeater was responsible for putting the single-shot rifle out of business, that repeater was the 1886 Winchester. As an experienced rifleman from California put it: "the Winchester 1886 model repeater . . . is the only large bore repeating rifle that I have ever seen that I would use

An awed youngster peers through a crack at the corpses of those Dalton gang members killed in their dual bank robbery attempt at Coffeyville, Kansas, in 1892. The M1886 Winchester in the scene may have belonged to one of the deceased. (Courtesy Kansas State Historical Society)

in preference to the best single-shot rifle." Developed by the talented John Browning, who patented it in October of 1884, the new Winchester could handle the .45-70 and even longer cartridges, and did it with a fairly short and compact receiver. In the "'86" the lever was pivoted on the longitudinally sliding breech-bolt instead of on the receiver, and locking was accomplished not by the time-honored toggle link, but by twin vertically sliding locking blocks on either side of the bolt. The action was far smoother than that of any previous Winchester, and far stronger than necessary for any cartridge of the period.

At long last the Winchester concern had what it wanted: a lever-action repeater capable of chambering the .45-70 and other lengthy loads. Initially the rifle was chambered for the government cartridge and two new rounds, the .40-82 and .45-90 (any of which, according to A. C. Gould, would put most of its shots into an eight-inch circle at 200 yards); but other loads, developed especially for the 1886, followed shortly: among these were the .38-56, the .40-65, and the .50-110 Express. In its standard form the sporting rifle had a 26 in. round, round/octagon, or octagon barrel; the carbine, which appeared in 1887, had a 22 in. round barrel. Nine .45-70 cartridges could be loaded into the sporting rifle with full-length magazine. The arm was also available with half-magazine, fancy stocks, and many other variations in barrel length, overall weight, triggers, sights, and finish.[182]

Dealers all over the West sold the "'86," and the arm earned unstinting praise from the frontiersmen who used it. Frank Canton, for example, declared that

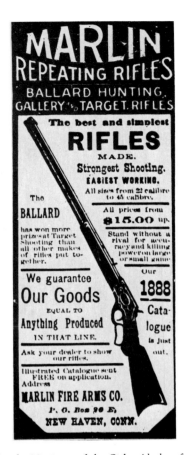

Ad from an April 1889 issue of the Sitka *Alaskan* for a pistol-grip Marlin Model 1881. Within a year the paper was carrying similar ads for Marlin's new "Safety Model 1889."

"the best rifle we had in [the 1890s] was the .45-70 Winchester, the .40-82 and the .38-56 magazine gun." Canton was in a position to know. He was one of the fifty-odd "invaders" hired by Wyoming cattlemen in 1892 to drive the homesteaders out of Johnson County. But the homesteaders banded together, surprised the invaders, and forced them to take shelter in a large barn. Three troops of the Sixth Cavalry arrived at the scene in time to prevent serious bloodshed, but then confiscated the invaders' arms. Of 44 rifles surrendered there were (aside from two Sharps) fully 38 Winchesters; of these, at least 15 were "'86s," including a .38-56 turned in by Canton himself. James Herron's rifle was a ".40-82 Winchester, a good gun at that time." John Rollinson owned an "'86" in .45-70 and liked it, but he found the barrel too long and shortened it by eight inches with a meat saw.[183]

Fittingly enough John Browning's gun shop in Ogden became one of the many retail outlets for the 1886. Despite the gun's overwhelming commercial successs, however, Browning himself did not rest on his well-earned laurels. After introducing a Browning-designed repeating shotgun in 1887 and a slide-action .22 rifle in 1890, Winchester marketed a new lever-action rifle in 1892, this one with a scaled-down and simplified Model 1886 action designed to handle the .32-20, .38-40, and .44-40 rounds, plus a .25-20 load made later specifically for this rifle. In its turn the Model 1892 Winchester was to become even more popular than the 1886. Available in the same basic styles as the Winchester 1873—24 in. round or octagon barrel for the sporting rifle, and 20 in. round barrel for the carbine—the 1892 was presumably to serve as a replacement for its famous predecessor. But the 1873 and its companion, the 1876, remained in production through the 1890s; the 1873, in fact, endured well into the twentieth century.[184]

As was the case with the 1886, Winchester offered the 1892 with many variations, including a take-down version introduced in 1893. At that time John Browning was busily working on still other designs, including a lever-action that would help bring about radical changes in the sporting-arms industry. So successful were the Browning-designed repeaters that by the early 1890s Winchester had only one serious competitor in the lever-action field: John Marlin. The Spencer, Robinson, Evans, and Colt-Burgess had all fallen by the wayside. Possible competition from Whitney disappeared when, in December of 1887, Winchester's directors voted to buy out that firm, completing the deal within two months. The bolt-action Remington-Keene and Lee sporting rifles were no threat to the lever-action's popularity. The Bullard was complicated and expensive, and the Colt Lightning, while refined into a reliable arm and competitively priced, could not oust the lever-action from its favored position in the West.[185]

During the late 1880s, with the big 1881 Marlin selling well, John Marlin brought out a smaller lever-action designed for cartridges of the .44-40 class. Patented by Lewis Hepburn (previously with Remington) in December of 1886 and October of 1887, the Model 1888 Marlin was mechanically somewhat similar to the Winchester 1886, in that it employed a vertically sliding locking block to keep the breechbolt closed during discharge. About a year after its appearance, however, the Model 1888 gave way to a successor, the Model 1889, which set the pattern for most of the lever-action Marlins to follow. Mechanically the Model 1889 was about the same as the 1888, with one important difference: in the new gun the ejection of fired cases took place through the upper

Log cabin on the Gray Bull River in Montana at the turn of the century. Both rifles appear to be Marlins, that on the left either a M1893 or M1895. (Courtesy Kansas State Historical Society)

Hunters near Springville, Utah. Each man carries a lever-action rifle, that on the far right being a Marlin, probably a M1893 rather than the similar appearing but scarcer M1895. (Courtesy State Historical Society of Colorado)

Armed for a manhunt—Deputy Sheriff C. H. Farnsworth (left) with a Marlin rifle and Arizona Ranger W. K. Foster armed with a M1895 Winchester. (Courtesy Arizona Historical Society)

right side of the receiver instead of through the top. Marlin catalogs claimed several advantages for the solid-top side-ejection receiver, among which was the fact that a telescopic sight could be mounted directly over the action, close to the bore axis.[186]

Advertised as far afield as Nevada and Alaska, the rifle version of the Model 1889, with 24 in. barrel, became quite popular, even though its production life lasted only about ten years. A model 1889 may have been involved in a fray in western Colorado in December of 1891; after the action Doc Shores noticed "some abandoned guns lying in the snow below us. They had obviously been dropped there by some of our ambushers. . . . One of them was a new Marlin rifle." But because it chambered short-cased cartridges such as the .44-40, the Model 1889 did not really qualify as an all-around rifle for remote areas like Alaska.

However, Marlin himself evidently felt no immediate need to bring out a mechanically comparable arm of more power; his models of 1891 and 1892 were small-bore rifles which, except for their side-ejection receivers, were essentially scaled-down renditions of the Model 1881. Things changed in August of 1893, when Lewis Hepburn patented a modification of the Model 1889, designed to handle long cartridges such as the .32-40 and .38-55. Characterized by its fast, smooth action and ease of disassembly, the Model 1893 was marketed in a wide range of styles and barrel lengths, with 20 in. the standard length for the carbine and 26 in. standard for the rifle.[187]

Marlin followed this gun with the Model 1894— simply the 1893 action shortened to take the .25-20, .32-20, .38-40, and .44-40 loads. Whether made as a rifle with a 24 in. barrel, or as a carbine with a 15

David Hughes with a Colt Bisley Model Single Action revolver and a M1894 Winchester carbine, the first lever-action Winchester produced for smokeless powder ammunition. (Courtesy Arizona Historical Society)

Nat Love with the tools of his trade—lariat, stock saddle, and a Winchester M1894 carbine. The double-action revolver thrust in his belt, perhaps an Iver Johnson, may be a photographer's prop. Love was one of the many blacks who rode the range herding cattle in the last three decades of the nineteenth century. Love was better known by his nickname of "Deadwood Dick." (Courtesy Denver Public Library, Western History Dept.)

Army scout and interpreter, miner, and lawman, but finally hanged as a paid killer, Tom Horn gave this Model 1894 Winchester .30-30 rifle (#82667) to Wyoming rancher C. B. Irwin shortly before Horn's execution on November 20, 1903. The gun was originally shipped from Winchester on June 19, 1900, with an uncommon in existing factory records. The Frontier Museum in Temecula, California displays Horn's Colt .41 Single Action revolver, an ejectorless short-barrel "Sheriff's Model." (Courtesy National Cowboy Hall of Fame, Oklahoma City)

A pair of unidentified but well-armed express company guards. In addition to double-barrel shotguns, they carry Winchester M1894 rifles and Colt Single Action revolvers. (Courtesy Wells Fargo Bank History Room)

in. or 20 in. barrel, the Model 1894, like the Model 1893, became widely popular and eventually replaced the Model 1889 which had sired it.[188]

While Marlin and Hepburn had been working on their models of 1893 and 1894, the Winchester-Browning team had also kept busy. The result of their labors, announced in the fall of 1894, was the lever-action Winchester Model 1894. A direct competitor of the 1893 Marlin, the new Winchester was initially chambered for the .32-40 and .38-55 rounds; a major change came about in the spring of 1895, when the

arm was adapted for two newly developed cartridges, the .25-35 and the .30-30. The important aspect of these rounds was that they were loaded not with black but with smokeless powder, which drove their bullets from the muzzle at velocities in excess of 2000 feet per second. These comparatively high velocities imparted the requisite power to the relatively light, small-caliber bullets, which, in fact, were merely the logical outcome of the trend begun by the .40-caliber Sharps and Maynard loads in the 1860s and 1870s. The price for the higher velocity was, of course, higher chamber

Bear hunters with M1895 Winchester rifles, following a successful hunt near Browning, Montana, in the 1890s. (Courtesy Montana Historical Society)

Members of a posse that chased the elusive "Wild Bunch," which included such outlaws as Butch Cassidy and Harvey "Kid Curry" Logan at the turn of the century. Identifiable weapons in this railroad car scene are M1895 Winchester rifles. (Courtesy Union Pacific Museum)

Colorado hunters about 1900. Their arms appear to include a M1894 Winchester (far left) and a pair of M1895 or M1899 Savage lever-action rifles. (Courtesy Denver Public Library, Western History Dept.)

pressure; the pressure generated by the new powder—some 35,000 pounds per square inch in the .30-30—was about 10,000 pounds per square inch higher than that generated by the heaviest black-powder load. But the 1894 Winchester, with a heavy vertically sliding locking block mortised into the rear of the receiver, and a barrel made of special nickel steel, proved itself easily capable of containing such pressures.[189]

Coupled with the new cartridges the Winchester Model 1894 became such a resounding success that it is still in extensive use. Although offered in standard form as a rifle with 26 in. octagon barrel, and a carbine with 20 in. round barrel, the 1894 soon became the subject of numerous special orders, and as a result the company furnished it with numerous barrel lengths, weights, stock styles, sights, and ornamentation.[190]

The 1894 heralded a new era for sporting arms. A second smokeless-powder Winchester, the Browning-designed lever-action box-magazine Model 1895, quickly followed. Aside from its box magazine, the 1895 took even more powerful cartridges than the .30-30, such as the .30-40 Krag. Winchester, however,

enjoyed only a short monopoly on smokeless-powder sporting rifles. In 1896 a new hammerless lever-action repeater designed by Arthur Savage appeared, taking a special .303 Savage smokeless round. Given detailed coverage in the *Army and Navy Journal*, the *Scientific American*, and other periodicals, this rifle, refined into the Savage Model 1899, became a strong rival of the 1894 Winchester. Watching these developments, John Marlin adapted his Model 1893 to the .30-30 and the .25-36, a variant of Winchester's .25-35, but also brought out his own Model 1895, a heavier version of the 1893 designed for cartridges of the .45-90 class. As the 1890s drew to a close other rifles chambered for smokeless-powder loads came into evidence in the West, including foreign-made bolt-actions. Between 1899 and 1900, in fact, Frank A. Ellis of Denver advertised not only Stevens target rifles but, in addition, rifles by Winchester, Marlin, Mannlicher, Mauser, and Savage. Nevertheless, whether in the form of the venerable 1873 or the new 1894, the Winchester remained the westerner's favorite well into the twentieth century.[191]

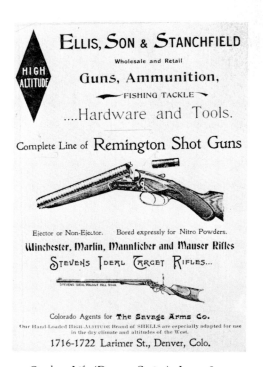

Outdoor Life (Denver Series), Jan. 1899.

·4·

SHOTGUNS

MUZZLE-LOADERS

PLAINS TRAVELERS OF THE postwar period found big-bore shotguns as useful as did their prewar counterparts. In 1867 Regis de Trobriand mentioned that:

I brought from Berthold a double-barreled shotgun for hunting this fall, and hunting paraphernalia, powder flask, and bullet sack that I found for sale at Gustave's. The weapon seemed to be a good one, although it didn't cost very much . . . and I suspect that this is an English weapon which paid no duty at the frontier.

Taking note of the lawlessness in Cheyenne early in 1868, James Chisholm wrote:

The condition of the town is very unsettled, the Vigilantes are abroad, and there may soon be a necessity of putting the city under martial law. I am rooming with the U.S. Marshal of the territory . . . and we have each to keep a double barreled shot gun at the head of our couch besides revolvers.

When Richard Townshend came to Colorado a year later, he bought:

a settler's double gun by W. W. Greener of Birmingham; this was a muzzle-loading smoothbore, with 30-inch barrels and a weight of about 9 lb., and it was made to shoot round bullets twelve to the pound for big game as well as small shot and buckshot; though a trifle heavy, it served its purpose well.

Later, involved in conversation with a talkative frontier dweller, Townshend described his gun:

"Very good thing to have too sometimes," [the frontiersman] said, with the air of a wise judge. "But a shotgun's not very handy at close quarters, unless it's a sawed-off. For fighting in a bar-room, let me tell you, or on top of a stage-coach, they like to cut the barrels off a foot in front of the hammers, so the gun handles more like a pistol."

Wild Bill Hickok owned such a gun while he was in Abilene in 1871. An associate described the weapon as "a sawed off shot Gun (Double Barreled) with a strap on it so he could swing it over his shoulder and Carry it under his Coat out of sight   I dont think the Barrell was More than 1½ feet long. . . ."[1]

Aside from their use by law-abiding westerners, shotguns continued to be a favorite tool of hold-up men. As Granville Stuart noted uncomfortably early in 1866: "a party of passengers crowded into a coach have no chance against a few 'Road Agents' armed with double barreled shot-guns." While Sidford Hamp was traveling from Montana to Utah in October of 1872, his coach suddenly lurched to a halt: "Then I knew in an instant that the coach was stopped by *highwaymen* . . . the first thing I saw was a man with a double barrelled shotgun fullcocked pointed at the driver, & another behind the coach with 2 six barrelled pistols in his hands." John Wesley Hardin had a shotgun in 1874 when he and James Taylor attempted to elude a band of Texas Rangers under Captain William Waller:

Capt. Waller apparently conceived the idea of running on us and turned his horse loose after us for that purpose. I told Jim to hold up as I wanted to kill him. I wheeled, stopped my horse, and cocked my shotgun. I had a handkerchief over the tubes to keep the caps dry, and just as I pulled the trigger, the wind blew it back and the hammer fell on the handkerchief. That saved his life. Waller checked up his horse and broke back to his men.[2]

Shotguns were such salable items on the postwar frontier that even business establishments ordinarily having nothing to do with firearms sold them. In November of 1869, for example, Finch's Saloon of Gold Hill, Nevada, advertised "Wines, Liquors . . . Shotguns, Powder Flasks, Powder, Shot, [and] Caps."[3]

For many years after the war, even when cartridge arms had almost completely displaced muzzle-loading rifles and pistols, the muzzle-loading shotgun remained

Cradling a double-barrel shotgun, Wells Fargo armed messenger Ely Fisher shares the driver's seat in front of the National Hotel in Jackson, California. (Courtesy Wells Fargo Bank History Room) Roger D. McGrath's *Gunfighters, Highwaymen & Vigilantes* offers a stagecoach driver's quote that appeared in the Bodie (Calif.) *Standard* for July 20, 1881. "I have had a six-shooter pulled on me across a faro table; I have proved that the hilt of a dirk can't go between two of my ribs; . . . but I was never really surprised until I looked down the muzzle of a double-barreled shotgun in the hands of a road agent. Why, my friend, the mouth of the Sutro tunnel is like a nailhole in the Palace Hotel compared to a shotgun."

Gold Hill (Nevada) *Daily News*, November 1869.

in common use. As late as 1884 Nathaniel Curry of San Francisco, who at that time listed no muzzle-loading pistols whatever and only a few old muzzle-loading military long arms, offered a varied assortment of single- and double-barrel English and German muzzle-loading shotguns, ranging in price from $9.50 to $27.00. During the late 1860s and early 1870s, the buyer of a muzzle-loading shotgun had an especially wide variety of guns from which to choose. He could, for instance, purchase one of the "fine English Stub and Twist Shot Guns," advertised by such dealers as C. B. Johns of Elko, Nevada. For considerably less money—say $3.00—he could buy one of the many muzzle-loading military long arms, altered to sporting smoothbores by the thousands after the war. In the case of a smoothbore musket, such an alteration might comprise only a shortened forestock and the addition of a bead front sight; the barrel of a military rifle would also be reamed out smooth, or "draw bored," to better handle a shot charge.[4]

ENGLISH MUZZLE-LOADING DOUBLE GUNS.

BAR LOCKS.

Bores. 11 to 14 ; Length 32 to 34 inches.

D

No. 1941, English Fine Twist, Patent Breech, Bar Locks, Oiled Walnut Stocks, Ebony Rod, Checkered Hand, **$ 11 33**
No. 1942, English Laminated Steel, Full Checkered, otherwise as No. 1941......................... **13 33**
No. 1943, English Laminated Steel Barrels, Fine Bar Locks, Patent Breech, Percussion Fence,
    Fine English Walnut Oiled Stock, Checkered Grip and Fore-End, Ebony Rod, Solid Head Tip, 10, 11,
    12, 13, 14 and 15 Bores, 30, 32, 34 and 36 inch Barrels, Weight from 7 to 8½ lbs................. **12 66**
No. 1943T, Same as 1943, but **heavier for Texas Trade,** 11 Bore, 34 to 36 inch, Weight 9 to 10 lbs. **14 00**
No 1943, Heavy, same as 1943, but heavy for Western Trade, 10, 11 and 12 Bore, 30 to 34
    inch Barrels, Weight 10 to 12 lbs.......................... .... **14 66**

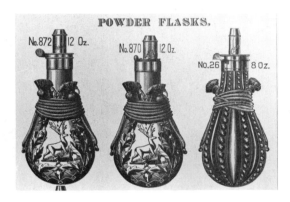

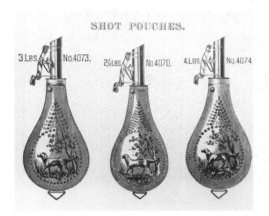

These illustrations from the E. C. Meacham and Nathaniel Curry catalogs of 1884 show that, even at that time, the muzzle-loading shotgun and its accessories were popular sellers.

Gen. Regis de Trobriand's Belgian-made 14-gauge pinfire double-barrel shotgun. He served as commander at Ft. Stevenson, Dakota Territory, from 1867 until 1869. (Courtesy State Historical Society of North Dakota)

Railroad commission members at Ft. Sanders, Wyoming Territory, in the late 1860s. Two of the youths hold Winchester M1866 rifles, while the third (far right) has a double-barrel percussion shotgun with a powder flask and shot pouch suspended from his shoulder. (Courtesy Union Pacific Museum)

L. L. Paulson's Handbook and Directory of Yolo, Solano, Napa, Lake, Sonoma and Marin Counties (California), 1874. (Courtesy Bancroft Library, University of California)

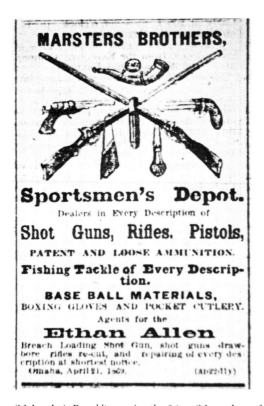

Omaha (Nebraska) *Republican*, April 1869. (Note the reference to baseball equipment in the ad.)

Two guns which figured prominently in the infamous career of "Billy the Kid" Bonney (or McCarty). Above is the 10-gauge Whitney shotgun (#903) owned by Deputy Sheriff Bob Ollinger and which the Kid used to kill him during the outlaw's escape from the Lincoln County, New Mexico, jail in 1881. The stock, possibly broken at the time of the shooting, was repaired with wire wrapped about the wrist. Below is Billy the Kid's M1873 Winchester carbine (#20181). Both guns were authenticated by Sheriff Pat Garrett in 1883, two years after he killed the outlaw. (Courtesy Mr. Robert E. McNellis, Jr.)

EARLY BREECHLOADERS AND REPEATERS

Until the close of the 1860s breech-loading shotguns had little effect on the muzzle-loader's popularity and, in fact, were not even very well known. A reporter for the *Missouri Republican*, describing T. J. Albright's display at the St. Louis Fair in the fall of 1868, wrote: "A breech-loading shot gun, which is a curiosity here, and which is valued at $300, awakens general comment." At the time this article appeared, at least four American manufacturers—Ethan Allen, Daniel Wesson, Eli Whitney, and the Parker Brothers—were working diligently to build a market for breech-loading shotguns of their own. Of these four, only one would be really successful.[5]

The most unusual of all the shotguns fabricated by these makers was the double-barreled arm produced by Allen. Based primarily on a patent issued in August of 1865, the Allen did not employ the common pivoting-barrel or break-open design, but instead used fixed barrels, closed at the rear by a double-width breechblock. A longitudinal hinge pin, passing through the left side of the block, allowed it to swing upward and to the left for loading, just as in the Warner carbine and British Snider rifle. A downward and forward push on the trigger guard extracted the fired cases; made of steel, they were designed to be reloaded almost indefinitely.

Allen's breechloader was on the market in the East by mid-1868; by March of 1869 the Folsom brothers of St. Louis and New Orleans were offering it at prices ranging from $100 to $150, depending on the amount of engraving. But the Allen had other distributors farther west: in May of 1869 the Marsters Brothers of Omaha listed themselves as dealers in shotguns, rifles, pistols, "Patent & loose ammunition, [and] Agents for the Ethan Allen Breach Loading Shot Gun." Allen's gun was obviously expensive, and this factor alone prevented it from becoming popular.[6]

Two other shotguns that proved little more popular than the Allen were the Wesson and the Whitney. Patented in December of 1867 and June of 1868, Daniel Wesson's shotgun was a break-open centerfire breechloader in which a transversely pivoted thumb lever, positioned on top of the standing breech, engaged a rib extension projecting rearward from the barrel breeches to hold the barrels down during discharge. As early as the spring of 1867 Wesson had formed his own company to manufacture this arm, but evidently none of them reached the market before the fall of 1868. Commonly made in 12 gauge with 30 in. barrels, the Wesson shotgun was very well constructed and highly finished; but it was also expensive, and only a few hundred guns appeared before the company folded.[7]

Made in greater numbers was the Whitney. In November of 1867 Eli Whitney Jr., had patented a double-barreled pinfire shotgun with forward-sliding barrels, but apparently this arm, if made at all, was short-lived. In July of 1869, however, Whitney, in association with Charles Gerner and Frank Tiesing (who was the copatentee for Whitney's rolling-block rifle action) patented a break-open centerfire double with

Republican Daily Journal (Lawrence, Kansas), October 1869.

sold most of the guns still on hand to William Read & Sons of Boston, who retailed them at $35 to $40.[11]

Although manufactured by well-established arms-making firms, none of the above-mentioned guns even remotely approached in popularity a shotgun fabricated by a general manufacturing firm in West Meriden, Connecticut—Parker Brothers. After entering the manufacturing business in the 1830s, Charles Parker, in association with various partners, made coffee mills, vises, and similar hardware, not taking his first big step into the firearms field until 1863. In September of that year, however, his firm, Parker, Snow & Co., accepted a government contract for 15,000 Springfield rifle-muskets. Apparently the successful completion of this contract gave Parker a taste for the gun business in general, for as president of the Merdian Manufacturing Company, he manufactured both the Triplett & Scott repeating carbine and William Miller's single-shot cartridge conversion of the Springfield muzzle-loader. Neither of these arms became overly successful, but in November of 1866 Miller patented a design for a double-barreled breech-loading shotgun which would form the real basis for Parker's renown.[12]

Based on the common pivoting-barrel or break-open system, in which the barrel breeches swung upward for loading, Miller's design involved a long locking bar, pivoted at the top of the standing breech, which extended forward to engage a recess in the rib between the barrels. A vertically sliding "lifter" projected from the underside of the frame just ahead of the trigger guard; an upward push on this lifter raised the front of the locking bar from its recess in the rib and allowed the barrels to open.

While this design was not especially noteworthy, the gun itself was very well made. Equally important was the fact that it was chambered for reloadable centerfire ammunition and, compared with other centerfire shotguns, sold for low prices: $50 in its plain version, $75 when better finished. Under the superintendency of Charles Parker and his brother John, the first few guns were ready for the market by the close of 1867; by the summer of 1868 they were becoming fairly well known. Offered with barrels as short as 24 in. or as long as 32 in., the early Parkers were made as 10-, 11-, or 12-gauge arms.[13]

Presumably the brothers made a bid for frontier sales shortly after introducing their guns. The Folsom brothers had them by mid-1869, and in October of that year the Parkers themselves began an advertising campaign in western papers, starting with the *Republican Journal* of Lawrence, Kansas. Parker ads subsequently appeared in the *Colorado Miner* in 1870, the Council Bluffs *Nonpareil* in 1871, the Elko (Nevada) *Independent* in 1872, and the Fort Worth *Democrat* in 1873. While some frontier residents probably ordered Par-

a trigger-like latch, positioned in front of the firing triggers; when it was pulled it allowed the barrel breeches to swing upward for loading. Although the first examples of this gun had no guard to protect the barrel-release trigger, later examples did incorporate such a feature.[8]

Presumably this centerfire Whitney was on the market even before its designers received their patent for it. The Folsom price list for March of 1869 included the arm in 10 and 12 gauge at $60 to $70, noting that it used the "brass composition, or Eley Central Fire Shell." In April of 1869 James H. Foster and Company of Chicago, advertising in the Salt Lake City *Telegraph,* termed themselves "Sole Agents for the celebrated 'Whitney Gun,' . . . and all the manufactures of the Whitney Arms Co." Mention of the Whitney breechloader also appeared in an ad by Schuyler, Hartley & Graham printed in the *Galveston News* a month later.[9]

(This Schuyler, Hartley & Graham ad also listed a little-known breech-loading shotgun, the Boyd. Patented by Francis Boyd and P. S. Tyler in January of 1868 and April of 1869, this gun was mechanically unusual: its barrels rested on a longitudinal pivot projecting forward from the frame, and rotated to one side and downward for loading. Although made in 10 and 12 gauge and chambered for "Patent Combination Central Fire Metallic Shells," the Boyd offered the Whitney very little competition.)[10]

While Whitney's gun cost less than the Allen or the Wesson, and was somewhat more popular, it never became a solid commercial success; the factory discontinued it about 1874. Shortly afterward Whitney

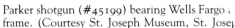

Parker shotgun (#45199) bearing Wells Fargo
frame. (Courtesy St. Joseph Museum, St. Jose[

kers from these ads, others undoubtedly got them through the efforts of James Bown & Son of Pittsburgh, whose Enterprise Gun Works had been shipping guns to the West since the 1850s. By 1875, and perhaps earlier, Bown had become one of the major suppliers of the Parker, and was prepared "to supply the western and southern trade."[14]

Although the Parker could retail for $50 in its unadorned version, it could cost $200 or more in its "superior finish" style. A buyer willing to spend that much for a shotgun often disregarded American-made guns entirely and instead bought a high-quality British breechloader. Within two years after the war, major American dealers in the East were importing such guns in quantity. By December of 1866, for example, Schuyler, Hartley & Graham were able to offer "Breech Loading Sporting Guns, Of all the best English Manufacturers, with Ammunition To Suit. Greener's, Dougall's, Lancaster's, Matthews', Needham's, LeFaucheux, [and] Westley Richards." In March of 1867 William Read & Sons listed "All the best Breech Loaders, Westley Richards, Greener's, Daw's, Dougall's, W. Richards of Liverpool, Reilly's, Matthews', The Lancaster Central Fire, Ellis', and others." Most of these guns were expensive—from $75 to $300—but some of them nevertheless found buyers in the West: in July of 1867, for instance, Nathaniel Curry of San Francisco described himself as an importer of "Breech

and muzzle loading Shot Guns, of the best English makers." Curry's stock of breechloaders undoubtedly included some of the same makes handled by Schuyler, Hartley & Graham, and William Read. And still other British makers sent their wares to American shores: by August of 1868 Merwin, Simpkins, & Taylor were acting as agents for William R. Pape of Newcastle; at about the same time D. R. Richardson, agent for Alexander Thomson & Son of Edinburgh, inserted notices regarding Thomson's breechloaders in such papers as the New Orleans *Picayune* and Galveston *News*. Additional British breechloaders were available from American dealers by the spring of 1869, among them guns by James Purdey and W. & C. Scott.[15]

So lucrative was the market for British shotguns in this country that a number of British makers—specifically Greener, Pape, and Dougall—advertised their own guns in American sporting papers during the late 1860s; other makers adopted the practice in the 1870s. A major reason for the American demand for such guns was that the leading British manufacturers were generally acknowledged to be unsurpassed in their craft. Although established in the days of the flintlock muzzle-loader, this reputation also extended to early break-open breechloaders, and pertained not only to the fit and finish of these guns, but to their design as well. As early as the fall of 1858, with an early form of the "double grip" system coming into use, Westley Rich-

Drawing of the action of a Westley-Richards centerfire shotgun built in 1868. (From Walsh's *Modern Sportsman's Gun and Rifle,* 1882)

Purdey shotgun action. (From Walsh's *Modern Sportsman's Gun and Rifle,* 1882)

Advertisement by Carlos Gove of Denver, featuring an English-made shotgun by James Purdey. (Courtesy Denver Public Library, Western History Dept.)

ards patented both the "top lever" and a hook-shaped rib extension which, dropping into a recess in the top of the standing breech as the barrels were closed, held the barrels tightly against the breech during discharge. With another patent issued in September of 1862, Richards added a cylindrical "doll's head" to his rib extension, which served the same purpose as the hook. Four months earlier, in May of 1862, George H. Daw of London had patented both a practical centerfire shotshell and a break-open shotgun whose action was adjustable to compensate for wear. In May of 1863 James Purdey patented a spring-loaded, longitudinally sliding underbolt which engaged notches in double underlugs, one behind the other, to lock the barrels against the frame. And in 1865 W. W. Greener designed his "Wedge-Fast" locking system, in which a cylindrical, transversely sliding bolt, concealed in the top of the standing breech, passed through a hole in the rib extension to hold down the barrels. All these designs—the Westley Richards top lever and doll's head, the Purdey underbolt engaging double underlugs, and the Greener cross-bolt—were to see extensive use in all types of breech-loading shotguns, regardless of country of origin. Daw's centerfire shotshell was little used through the mid-1860s, since most British breechloaders continued to chamber the pinfire shotshell popularized by the French maker Le-Faucheux. But by mid-1868 Westley Richards was adapting his guns for centerfire loads; and thereafter the use of centerfires increased rapidly.[16]

Whether pinfire or centerfire, some British breechloaders traveled to the frontier in the hands of individual users. F. Trench Townshend carried a 12-gauge double-barreled Purdey breechloader among his other guns when he crossed the plains in 1868. And a Greener breechloader accompanied Thomas P. Roberts down the Upper Missouri in 1872. In all probability, however, many more British doubles reached the West through the efforts of established dealers. Some dealers advertised these guns only in general terms: the Freund brothers, for example, noted in 1869 that they carried "Breech-Loading Double Barreled Shot Guns Of the latest improved American and English manufacture," while in 1872 Warren & Company of Topeka labeled themselves "Importers Of And Dealers In English And American Muzzle And Breech-Loading Guns." However, an item in the *Rocky Mountain News* in December of 1872 specifically stated that Freund was handling the Greener, and in May of 1873 Carlos Gove noted that he carried shotguns by "W. R. Pape, W. & C. Scott & Son, [and] W. W. Greener."[17]

Although probably not one of the more popular imports, an English centerfire double by George Gibbs of Bristol (now in the Beeson Museum in Dodge City)

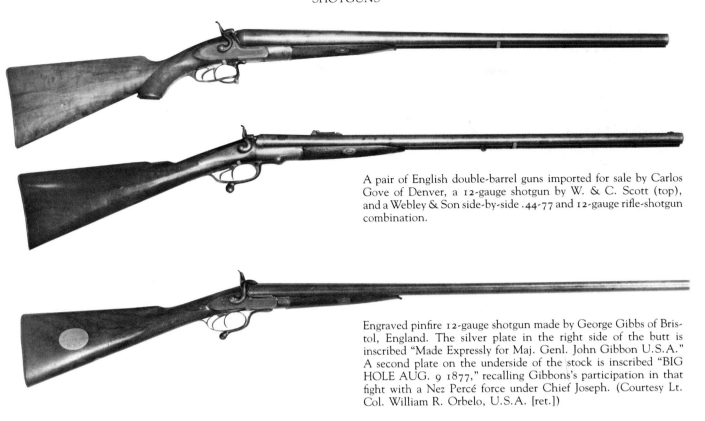

A pair of English double-barrel guns imported for sale by Carlos Gove of Denver, a 12-gauge shotgun by W. & C. Scott (top), and a Webley & Son side-by-side .44-77 and 12-gauge rifle-shotgun combination.

Engraved pinfire 12-gauge shotgun made by George Gibbs of Bristol, England. The silver plate in the right side of the butt is inscribed "Made Expressly for Maj. Genl. John Gibbon U.S.A." A second plate on the underside of the stock is inscribed "BIG HOLE AUG. 9 1877," recalling Gibbons's participation in that fight with a Nez Percé force under Chief Joseph. (Courtesy Lt. Col. William R. Orbelo, U.S.A. [ret.])

was once the property of Texas cattleman Ben Thompson. It may have been this gun, in the hands of Thompson's brother Bill, that fatally shot Sheriff C. B. Whitney in Ellsworth, Kansas, in August of 1873. Once safely back in Texas, Thompson testified that the shooting had been accidental, a point disputed by other witnesses:

when I left Jake New's Saloon I met my brother Wm. Thompson, who was very drunk and had his double barrel shot gun in his hand with both barrells cocked. I then advised & entreated him to go in the house & put up his gun as he was too drunk to do anything and that he would kill some of his best friends if he was not careful how he handled his gun. I had no sooner told him this, than one barrel of his gun went off accidentally and struck in the lower part of the side-walk in front of New's Saloon very near the feet of two of our friends to wit: Maj. Seth Mabry and Capt. Millett—I then got the gun away from him and tried to remove the cartridges but they were brass and so much swollen that I could not get them out. [I then] went out on the railroad in the middle of the street. A moment or so after I got there my brother came out where I was with

his gun. . . . When [I] asked Billy to let down the hammers of his gun he made no reply & failed to let them down, but said he would leave the gun when he got to the saloon . . . my brother at this time was very drunk, so much so that he staggered a great deal. He had his gun in his hands at the time both barrells being Cocked, and just as he was coming out of the [saloon] door the gun went off accidentally and struck Whitney. . . .[18]

Whether fabricated by the better English or American makers, the centerfire breechloaders of the early 1870s were expensive enough to force the parsimonious buyer to look for another type of gun. Considerably cheaper than the double-barreled breechloader was the single-barreled variety, especially when offered by a maker of single-shot rifles. With a factory already tooled up for the manufacture of single-shot rifle actions, it was a simple matter to substitute a smoothbore tube for a rifled barrel. Sharps and Maynard had offered shot barrels for their rifles before the war; while Sharps largely abandoned the practice with the advent of the metallic cartridge, the Maynard models of 1865 and 1873 both came with readily interchangeable 20- or 28-gauge shot barrels, in lengths from 20 in. to 32 in., when the buyer so desired. During the late 1860s Eli Whitney, possibly taking a leaf from Maynard's book, occasionally installed 20-gauge barrels on the frame of the little Howard single-shot rifle, and in the mid-1870s he began mounting 10- to 20-gauge tubes on his Phoenix action as well.[19]

Two other makers who installed shot barrels on their rifle actions were Remington and Stevens. About 1870 Remington started offering its famous rolling-block action with 16- or 20-gauge barrels 30 in. or 32 in. long, and by mid-1872 Steven was marketing a break-open 14-gauge arm with the same style of frame used for his pistols and pocket rifles. Barrels of 28 in. and 32 in. were added to the 30 in. standard shortly after the gun made its appearance; within five years 12- and 16-gauge barrels were also available.[20]

Yet another single-barreled shotgun built on a rifle frame was on the market by mid-1872. Based on patents issued between January of 1867 and March of 1871, this gun was made by Dexter Smith of Springfield, Massachusetts, who had earlier been involved in the manufacture of the Daniel Wesson double gun. The Dexter Smith employed a breechblock hinged at its lower front corner, and in that respect was similar to the Remington rolling-block. But the Smith differed in its method of locking: instead of using the base of the hammer to lock the breechblock, the gun utilized the sear tip of the trigger. The Smith was comparatively costly, retailing for about $28 in 1872, whereas the prices of the other single-barrels usually fell between $16 and $24.[21]

Both the Dexter Smith and the Stevens would chamber the Draper reloadable shotshell, the first such shell to attain real popularity. Patented in November of 1864 by William Wills and made by F. Draper & Company, this shell comprised an all-brass body and a screw-off, knurled-rim head with integral small-diameter nipple. Draper shells were expensive, costing $3 or more per dozen, but they were strong and easily reloaded, using standard percussion caps. Because of this they remained in use through the 1880s, and probably inspired a number of similar cartridges, such as the steel cases designed for the early Allen and Parker breechloaders.[22]

Well-known as it was, the Draper was only one of many shotshells patented in the 1860s and 1870s. Some of these were pinfire, but more—including those by Allen, Berdan, Sturtevant, Williams, Wesson, Orcutt, Kenney, and Buffington—were centerfire. Aside from Draper's, however, the only patented shells to acquire a widespread following were those by Berdan, Sturtevant, and Orcutt. Although not as popular as these, one shotshell especially adapted to the requirements of the frontier was John P. Lower's "Transparent Wad Shot Cartridge." Since many frontiersmen could not read, Lower did not stamp the number of the shot size on the body of this cartridge, as was common practice. Instead, the top wad that held the shot in the case was made of a clear, somewhat flexible "glass" (quite similar to modern plastic), so that the illiterate shooter could tell at a glance what size shot he was buying.[23]

Whatever the merits of the various shells, most of them were fired in shotguns limited to only one or two shots before reloading. Although repeating shotguns capable of delivering four or five shots were available in the late 1860s, some twenty years would pass before such guns attained widespread acceptance. Probably the best-known repeater of the early postwar years was the five-shot Colt solid-frame revolving percussion shotgun. While it was offered in 12 and 20 gauge and with several barrel lengths, it never became popular. By mid-1867, however, there was another repeater on the market; patented by Sylvester Roper in April of 1866, the new gun was designed to take four reloadable steel shells. The shells themselves were nothing new, but in other respects the Roper was unusual. It embodied a longitudinally sliding breechbolt, linked to and locked by a heavy hammer, and a rotating carrier, housed within a steel sleeve; this carrier was similar to a revolver cylinder with the outer walls of its chambers cut away. With the gun loaded and the hammer cocked, a pull on the trigger allowed the hammer to snap forward; in falling, the hammer forced the bolt forward, which in turn pushed a shell from the carrier into the chamber, which was in the rear of the bore; just before the hammer struck the firing pin, an inclined surface on its head came into bearing with a corresponding surface on the rear of the bolt and locked the bolt in place. As the shooter cocked the hammer for the next shot, the hammer drew the bolt back and simultaneously compressed a strong V-spring bearing against a tooth on the carrier; as the hammer neared the full-cock position, the bolt moved rearward far enough to free the carrier and permit the compressed spring to revolve it, thereby bringing the next shell into line with the chamber.

Aside from its unusual action, the Roper offered another innovation in its detachable choke. This was a steel ring threaded onto the muzzle, whose inner walls tapered to a smaller diameter than that of the bore. The taper served to constrict the shot charge as it left the muzzle, and kept the pellets together, in a tight pattern, over a longer distance.[24]

Although assembled in small numbers as a rifle, the Roper was more commonly made as a 12- or 16-gauge shotgun, with 24 in. to 28 in. barrel. Its makers were advertising it in the *Army and Navy Journal* by May

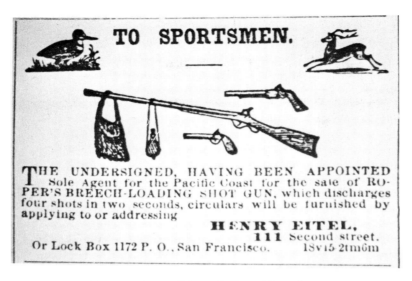

San Francisco Mining & Scientific Press, November 1867.

of 1867, and in November of that year Henry Eitel of San Francisco began calling himself "Sole Agent for the Pacific Coast for the sale of Roper's Breech-Loading Shot Gun, which discharges four shots in two seconds."[25]

IMPROVED BREECHLOADERS

While it was manufactured well into the 1870s, the Roper never threatened the popularity of the breechloading double guns. But such guns were expensive; in a strong effort to bring their price within the reach of most buyers, Remington announced, in October of 1873, that "Our Double Barrel Breech Loading Gun Is Now Ready . . . Top Snap action, half-cocked, breech opened and shells extracted by one motion." Based primarily on a patent issued to Andrew Whitmore in April of 1872, the new Remington incorporated Purdey-style double underlugs, engaged by a longitudinally sliding underbolt controlled by a top lever. In the Remington-Whitmore, however, the top lever was transversely pivoted; instead of pushing it to one side, the shooter had to push the tail of the lever upward to unlock the barrels. This upward push on the lever automatically brought the hammers to half-cock as well. The gun further employed a lockout, which prevented drawing the hammers to full-cock unless the barrels were firmly locked against the frame. Besides the usual 10- and 12-gauge barrels in the common 28 in. and 30 in. lengths, the gun would come on special order with combination barrels—one rifled, the other smooth—or, by 1877, as a double rifle. Prices ranged from $45 to $75.[26]

Within a few months of its appearance the Remington-Whitmore was available on the frontier: in May of 1874, for example, LeRoux & Cosgrove of San Antonio offered "Remington Breech Loading Shot Guns" among their other arms, and during the summer of that year the new guns found their way to other Remington dealers in the West, including A. J. Plate of San Francisco, and shortly afterward Carlos Gove of Denver.[27]

As the Remington made its first inroads into the market, it almost certainly cut into the sales of its most closely priced competitor, the Parker. Although the Parker had proven itself a strong and salable item even in its earliest mechanical form, the ungainly locking bar at the top of the standing breech was one of the gun's less desirable features, and in March of 1875 Wilbur Parker patented an improved design. He retained the vertically sliding lifter, the gun's most noticeable characteristic, but dispensed with the top-mounted locking bar; now an upward push on the lifter cammed back a longitudinally sliding underbolt, which in locking posture engaged the notch in the upper rear of the barrel underlug. The bearing surfaces were slightly angled, to take up wear automatically.[28]

The improved design could not help but increase Parker sales. One of the new dealers for the gun was John P. Lower of Denver, who in July of 1875 advertised himself as "Agent for Parker's Breech Loading Double Gun." By 1877 Lower was handling other breech-loading shotguns, including English, Belgian, and American doubles and the Dexter Smith single-barrel; but the Parker seemed to be his special favorite.

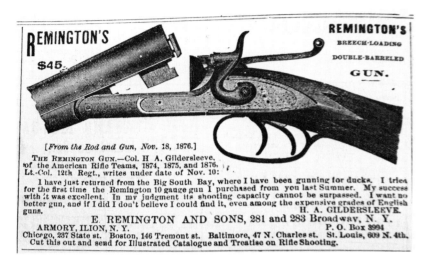

Forest and Stream, 1877.

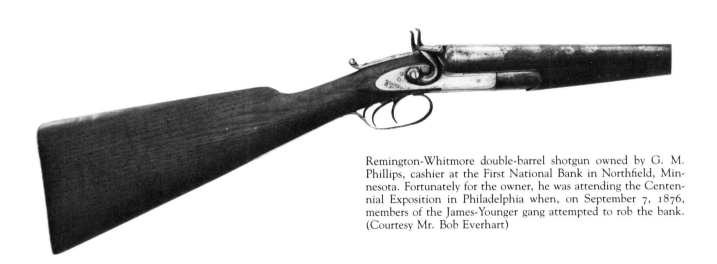

Remington-Whitmore double-barrel shotgun owned by G. M. Phillips, cashier at the First National Bank in Northfield, Minnesota. Fortunately for the owner, he was attending the Centennial Exposition in Philadelphia when, on September 7, 1876, members of the James-Younger gang attempted to rob the bank. (Courtesy Mr. Bob Everhart)

Lower, of course, was far from the only western outlet for the gun. Early in 1878 this notice appeared in the *Daily Herald* of Denison, Texas: "1 Shot Gun—Parker Bro's make. A Double Barrel Breech Loading Shot Gun, together with 3 doz. Shells, One Thousand Caps and one Capper. Cost $100.00; is entirely new and warranted and will be sold for $75.00."[29]

By this time, however, the Parker and the Remington were in competition with yet another double-barreled breechloader in the same price range—the Fox. Proclaimed in the summer of 1876 as "the best $50 gun yet offered," this gun had been patented in January of 1870 by George H. Fox, of Boston's American Arms Company. From a design standpoint, the Fox was a departure from most other shotguns: instead

of swinging upward for loading, its barrel breeches swung outward to the right, on an imaginary vertical pivot just to the left of the frame. This vertically pivoted barrel design was in common use for cartridge derringers—the Allen, the Southerner, the Colt No. 3, and others employed it—but was seldom used for long arms.[30]

American Arms probably started making the Fox within a year or two of the inventor's patent for it, but such factors as the Boston fire of 1872 and the financial panic of 1873 evidently precluded manufacture or promotion on a commercial scale until 1876. Nevertheless at least one of the guns reached the West before that. Henry W. Henshaw, who from 1872 to 1875 was involved in Lt. George Wheeler's explora-

THE FOX GUN.

This gun is acknowledged by our best sportsmen to be the finest made. It is wonderfully simple and wonderfully strong, easy to handle, easy to clean; not liable to get out of order or become shaky. It has no HINGE to get loose, as the BARRELS SLIDE ONE SIDE. For pattern and penetration they cannot be surpassed.

PRICE FROM $45 TO $150.
Send stamp for catalogue and reduced price list.

AMERICAN ARMS CO.,
No. 103 Milk Street, Boston, Mass.

Forest and Stream, August 1881.

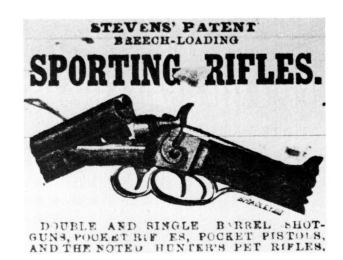

STEVENS' PATENT BREECH-LOADING **SPORTING RIFLES.**

DOUBLE AND SINGLE BARREL SHOT-GUNS, POCKET RIFLES, POCKET PISTOLS, AND THE NOTED HUNTER'S PET RIFLES.

Omaha (Nebraska) *Republican*, July 1880.

tions west of the hundredth meridian, wrote later that during hard service in Arizona his Fox shotgun had served him well. By 1878 Carlos Gove & Sons were styling themselves "Agents for the Celebrated Fox Gun," and continued handling the arm for several years afterward. In November of 1877 Fox patented a modification of his gun which presumably helped its sales. Instead of resting directly on the frame, the barrels now rested on a guide plate bolted to the frame; after a period of severe use, the guide-plate-and-barrel assembly could be moved rearward, against the standing breech, to compensate for wear.[31]

Even before Fox applied for this patent, he found that his company had still another rival shotgun with which to contend. Early in 1877 the Stevens concern brought out a reasonably priced breech-loading double of its own, and by the fall of 1878 was advertising it in such western papers as the *Omaha Republican*. As in earlier guns, the Stevens embodied a trigger-like lever in front of the firing triggers, which drew back an underbolt and allowed the barrels to swing open for loading. Made in 10 and 12 gauge, with barrels from 24 in. to 32 in. long, the gun ranged in price from $40 to $60. For $65, it was available as a combination rifle-shotgun.[32]

Yet another reasonably priced double reached the market in 1878; this one was a formidable competitor because it carried the magic name—Colt. Mechan-ically it was no different from many other doubles of the time: it employed Purdey-type double underlugs, engaged by an underbolt activated by a top lever. But the gun was very well made and highly finished, and became deservedly popular. Although the actions were made in Colt's Hartford factory, the 10- and 12-gauge barrels, ranging from 28 in. to 32 in. long, were imported from England, and Colt made no secret of that fact. In its unadorned version the gun sold for $50, but fancy twist barrels and extra ornamentation could boost the price to $125.[33]

One of the Colt's early enthusiasts was John P. Lower, who wrote the factory in June of 1878 concerning "your new B.L. Dbl Gun":

I am pleased to know you have put up such and hope it will prove as good as the Double Action Pistols . . . If your new ShotGun is adapted to the ordinary Central Fire Shells of the UMC Co's make— I would like you to send me one at once *"10 gauge"* preferred from 8 to 9 lb 30 to 32 in. . . .

More restrained in his enthusiasm was J. W. Morton of the Simmons Hardware Company of St. Louis, who wrote in December of 1878:

The B/L Guns [came] to hand & have examined them carefully & while we are pleased to acknowledge their general excellence, we at your suggestion

Shotgun- and revolver-armed Wells Fargo guard with bars made from silver extracted from the Silver King Mine. (Courtesy Arizona Historical Society)

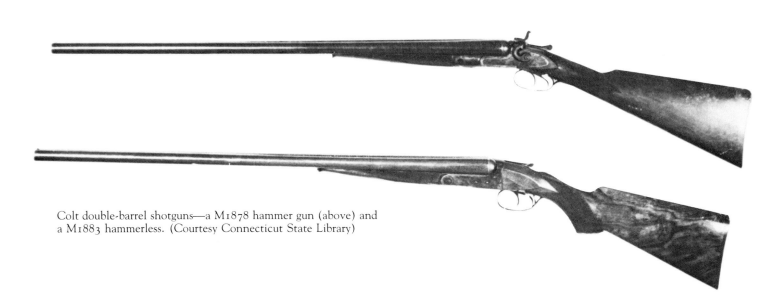

Colt double-barrel shotguns—a M1878 hammer gun (above) and a M1883 hammerless. (Courtesy Connecticut State Library)

Express messengers at the Wells Fargo office in Reno, Nev. Guard guns include a Winchester M1873 rifle and a pair of double-barrel shotguns. On top of the strongbox is what appears to be a pair of obsolescent percussion .31 Colt M1849 revolvers. (Courtesy Wells Fargo Bank History Room)

notice the following objections:—the breech is not heavy enough for our trade & the barrels not sufficiently tapering, the hammers stand up too high as you will notice by comparing with the Fox gun & the striking pin we think is rather too small in diameter; also the price is high in comparison with English makers. The chief objection made by jobbers to American Guns, is that owing to the plan of lists & discounts, they cannot make a paying profit on them. . . .

Morton's objections notwithstanding, Simmons soon became one of the major distributors of this arm; one order to Colt in October of 1880 called for 70 shotguns, in both 10 and 12 gauge, with 30 in. to 32 in. barrels.[34]

Colt was hardly alone in using imported components for its shotguns. In 1876 Carlos Gove had advertised that "we manufacture fine breech loading shot guns," but Gove's "manufactured" guns were actually a combination of Gove-made barrels and English-made actions. The Freund brothers adopted the same policy, joining their own shot barrels to English frames.[35]

In its 1878 catalog the Sharps Rifle Company announced that owing to repeated requests it would market a double gun equal in quality to the famous Sharps rifle. As early as the spring of 1875, in fact, Sharps officials had made serious inquiries regarding the purchase of George Fox's shotgun and the machinery to make it, but these inquiries came to nothing. Company officials then investigated other alternatives; by the summer of 1879 they were able to offer a limited number of doubles with the well-known "Old Reliable" marking on the barrel rib. Most of these guns were actually made for the firm in England by Philip Webley & Son. Only about 200 Sharps-marked shotguns appeared before the company, claiming that its rifle business required all its attention, abandoned the project.[36]

Sharp's choice of an overseas manufacturer to fur-

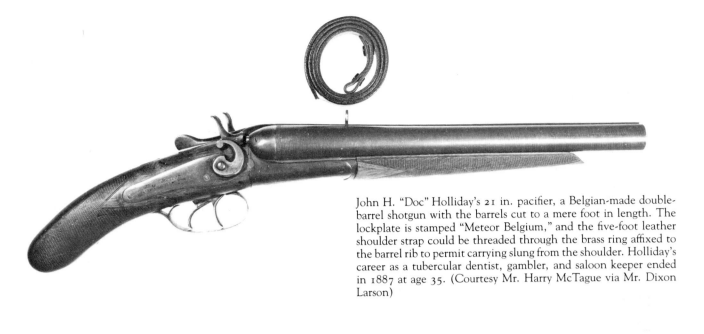

John H. "Doc" Holliday's 21 in. pacifier, a Belgian-made double-barrel shotgun with the barrels cut to a mere foot in length. The lockplate is stamped "Meteor Belgium," and the five-foot leather shoulder strap could be threaded through the brass ring affixed to the barrel rib to permit carrying slung from the shoulder. Holliday's career as a tubercular dentist, gambler, and saloon keeper ended in 1887 at age 35. (Courtesy Mr. Harry McTague via Mr. Dixon Larson)

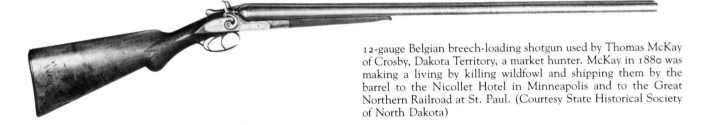

12-gauge Belgian breech-loading shotgun used by Thomas McKay of Crosby, Dakota Territory, a market hunter. McKay in 1880 was making a living by killing wildfowl and shipping them by the barrel to the Nicollet Hotel in Minneapolis and to the Great Northern Railroad at St. Paul. (Courtesy State Historical Society of North Dakota)

nish its shotguns may have resulted in part from the great number of British and other foreign gunmakers who displayed their products at the 1876 Philadelphia Exhibition. After this event the variety of foreign-made smoothbores carried by American dealers seems to have increased. In August of 1876 Nathaniel Curry offered the W. & C. Scott and the Greener "treble wedge-fast" guns (Greener's treble wedge-fast system was a combination of his crossbolt with Purdey's double underlugs and underbolt); by 1878 Carlos Gove was advertising "Greener's Treble Wedge Fast [and] Webley Single and Double Bolt B.L. Double Guns" in addition to his stock of American-made doubles. Within two years he had added W. & C. Scott guns to his line. Advertising in a Leadville paper in 1880, John Lower, Gove's former partner, listed "Colt's, Parker's, Scott's, Greener's, and other English Breech Loading Double and Single Guns."[37]

Understandably the wider availability of both foreign and domestic breechloaders resulted in an increase in their use by frontiersmen. Describing his service with the Texas Rangers in the mid-1870s, N. A. Jennings wrote that "two or three of the men had fine breech-loading shotguns—very effective weapons at close quarters with nine buckshot to the barrel." During the travels of Frank Carpenter and his party along the Yellowstone in 1877, the threat of Indian trouble caused them to look to their armament; besides rifles and handguns, the group had "a double-barrel shotgun [but] with only three shells loaded with fine birdshot." While Rolf Johnson was at French Creek in the summer of 1879, "the Black Hills Treasure Coach came along. . . . This coach carries no passengers—nothing but gold dust, money, and valuables. With the coach were nine guards or Shot-gun messengers as they are called . . . well armed with six-shooters,

Hunters at the mouth of Boulder Canyon, Colorado, about 1880. The man at far right holds a Ballard rifle, the one second from right a Winchester. Three others, however, have double-barrel shotguns. Note the very short barrels of the shotgun held by the man reclining in the center. (Courtesy Mr. Malcolm Collier)

Winchester rifles and breechloading shot-guns." J. T. Morley, a stagecoach driver for Wells Fargo in California in the late 1870s and early 1880s, said later that:

> We stage drivers were furnished with .45 calibre Colt revolvers and sawed off shotguns especially made in the east for the company. The shot gun barrels were charged with 7½ grams of powder and loaded with 16 buck shots in four layers with four shot to the layer, or as we said, four layers of four shot to chamber in shell. One of the strict rules of the company to all drivers was as follows. "Whenever you leave your stage, extract the shells from your guns and revolvers." If a driver left either his shotgun or revolver in the stage, as was frequently necessary, and returned to find either pointed at him by a bandit, the driver knew that the gun or revolver was not loaded.[38]

As Morley's account suggests, Wells Fargo was among the better-known users of sawed-off shotguns. Fred

Dodge, a detective for the firm, referred on occasion to the utility of his "Short Wells Fargo Double barrell Shot Gun." During the late 1870s the company purchased a number of lifter-action-and-underbolt Parkers, stamping them "W.F. & Co." inside the frame, and probably bought some Remington-Whitmores as well.[39]

Railroaders also found shotguns desirable weapons. Once, in the early 1880s, James Kyner was faced with the dangerous prospect of taking a payroll to workers on an Idaho short-line railroad, and asked an old acquaintance to accompany him: "'Sure, I'll go,' he agreed, and it was not necessary to discuss it much. He had done such things before, and had a sawed-off shotgun that he carried on such errands, its walnut stock tucked up under his right arm."[40]

Throughout the 1880s the variety of foreign shotguns imported by American dealers continued to broaden. In 1882, for example, C. D. Ladd of San Francisco and C. J. Chapin of St. Louis offered high-quality doubles stamped "Charles Daly." Despite its

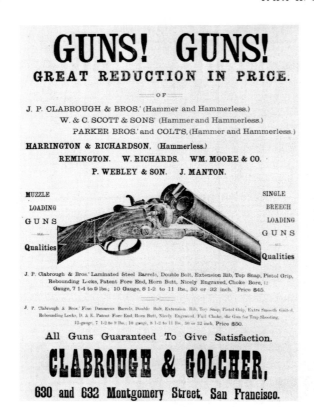

Forest and Stream, March 1883.

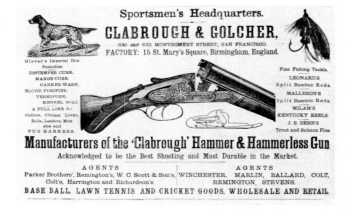

Advertisements by Clabrough & Golcher, San Francisco. (Courtesy California State Library)

English-sounding name the Daly was actually made in Suhl, Germany, largely for export to the United States. In October of 1882 C. J. Chapin began handling the Belgian-made Pieper double, a practice taken up in 1883 by A. B. Meacham and in 1885 by Schoverling, Daly & Gales, distributors of the Marlin and Ballard rifles, who advertised it in such papers as Tucson's *Arizona Citizen*.[41]

For those who could afford it, however, English-made shotguns remained the smoothbores of choice. Besides guns carrying the well-known names—Greener, Scott, Webley, Pape, and others—less-famous names became more familiar in the 1880s, among them J. P. Clabrough and Christopher Bonehill. Although based in London, the Clabrough brothers had their own retail outlet in San Francisco, through which they funneled many of their shotguns to other parts of the West; they had, in fact, followed this practice since the early 1870s. By 1884 shotguns made by Christopher Bonehill of Birmingham were available from Nathaniel Curry, A. B. Meacham, and C. J. Chapin, although such guns had first reached eastern dealers some five years earlier.[42]

Aside from the Bonehill, Curry offered Greener

240

hammerless doubles at $160 and up. While shotguns with exposed hammers remained widely popular through the 1890s, concealed-hammer or "hammerless" doubles, cocked automatically by the opening of the barrels, had been energetically promoted by leading British makers such as Westley Richards since the late 1870s. By the early 1880s these guns were making an impression on the American market; and in 1883 Colt brought out its own hammerless double. In addition to concealed hammers, the gun incorporated double underlugs and underbolt, plus a doll's head rib extension. Made in 10 and 12 gauge with 28 in. to 32 in. barrels, the new Colt was a high-quality item, but its prices started at a fairly reasonable $80.[43]

There was another hammerless double on the market by 1883, this one made by the Massachusetts firm of Harrington & Richardson. The design for this gun was the work of William Anson and John Deeley, English gunmakers who had patented a hammerless shotgun in Britain as early as 1875. Advertised in the *Omaha Republican* in February of 1884 as the "Automatic Hammerless Gun," the Harrington & Richardson sold for even more than the Colt—$85.[44]

Other American manufacturers were not quite so quick to offer hammerless guns. The Remington Model 1882 had a conventional side-swinging top lever for opening the barrels instead of Whitmore's upward-swinging type, and had a doll's head rib extension beside its double underlugs; but the gun retained its outside hammers. Like the Remington, a new Parker marketed in 1882 offered top lever and doll's head, but again kept its external hammers. However, the old-style lifter-action Parker was so popular that it continued to be available through the 1890s.[45]

As was the case with imported guns, shotguns by some of the lesser-known American makers also came to the attention of westerners during the 1880s. Advertising in *Loving's Stock Manual*, pubished in Fort Worth in 1881, A. J. Anderson listed himself as "Agent For The Baker Breech Loading Shot-Guns." Both A. B. Meacham and C. J. Chapin of St. Louis were handling the Baker by the fall of 1883, Newton & Andrews of El Paso were selling it by 1884, and by 1885 Schoyen & Butt of Denver, successors to Carlos Gove, were also offering it. Forerunner of such guns as the Ithaca and the L. C. Smith, this arm was first patented by William H. Baker of Lisle, New York, in August of 1875; it was on the market in the East as early as the spring of 1876. Its unusual feature was its front trigger: pulling the trigger in the normal manner dropped the hammer for firing, but a forward push on the trigger withdrew the locking bolt and allowed the barrels to open. The Baker's external appearance was characteristic, therefore, in the absence of a top-, side-, or underlever. The gun was made not only as a conven-

A nineteenth-century redwood figure of a hunter with a percussion double-barrel shotgun. It is thought to have been carved by a German immigrant who had failed to "strike it rich" in the gold fields and who sold it to earn passage home. It reputedly advertised a gunshop in San Jose, California, and later stood in front of a cigar store in Alameda, California. It is exhibited at the Smithsonian Institution's National Museum of American History.

Forest and Stream, August 1881.

Forest and Stream, March 1883.

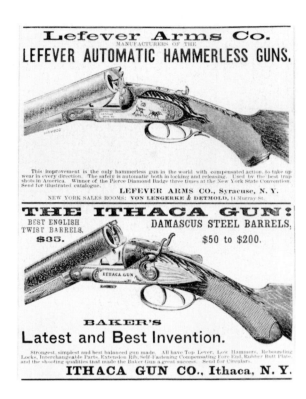

Forest and Stream, January 1885.

tional double, but also as a three-barrel "drilling," with a rifle barrel mounted between and below two side-by-side shot barrels.[46]

Another New York gunmaker whose shotguns were in the West by the 1880s was Daniel LeFever. LeFever, who had been involved in arms manufacture since the 1850s, started making breech-loading shotguns on a commercial scale in the early 1870s. Between that time and about 1880 he was associated with at least three partnerships, including the firm of Nichols & LeFever. One result of this unstable business situation

was that the production of LeFever shotguns during those years was limited. The inventor nevertheless made constant attempts to improve his guns; in June of 1878 and again in June of 1880 he patented methods of compensating for wear in break-open guns, and finally, in September of 1882, patented his "ball joint," soon to become the best-known feature of LeFever shotguns. Designed to replace the conventional hinge pin, this ball joint was simply a short, large-diameter screw, positioned longitudinally at the front of the frame. The inner end of the screw was hemispherical

This frontier veteran poses in front of a Colorado cabin with a Hopkins & Allen single-barrel shotgun. (Courtesy Mr. Malcolm Collier)

Springfield Breech Loading Single Barrel Shot Gun.

30 inch Barrel, taking 16 B Brass Shell or 20 Gauge Paper Shell. $12 00

In 1884 N. Curry & Bro. of San Francisco advertised breech-loading single-shot shotguns in 16- or 20-gauge, assembled using obsolete or condemned Springfield parts. Although similar to the army's M1881 Springfield shotgun, the government arm had a 26 in. barrel and was manufactured only in 20 gauge.

243

Breech-loading shotgun used by Texas gambler and gunfighter Ben Thompson. He was involved in a dozen or so gunfights in Texas and Kansas prior to his death in a "shoot out" in 1884. (Courtesy Kansas State Historical Society)

and, resting in a hemispherical recess in the front of the barrel underlug, served as the pivot on which the barrels swung open for loading. More importantly, if looseness developed between barrels and breech, the shooter had only to screw the ball joint in until it forced the rear face of the barrels snugly against the standing breech.[47]

Two express company guards photographed in Astoria, Oregon, with the tools of their trade—double-barrel breech-loading shotguns. (Courtesy Mr. Emory A. Cantney, Jr.)

The first LeFever shotgun to incorporate the ball joint was a "semihammerless" double, in which the concealed hammers were cocked by a thumb lever on the side of the action. By January of 1885, however, this gun had been replaced by a true hammerless, cocked automatically by the opening of the barrels. Made in the usual 10- and 12-bore sizes, and also on occasion as a double rifle, this new "sidelock" LeFever was a handsome and graceful arm. Its distribution in the West was handled largely by H. A. Penrose, a traveling representative for the company. Early in 1887, in partnership with J. J. Hardin, Penrose opened a large gun shop in Omaha and continued handling LeFever's products.[48]

While doubles doubtless commanded more attention, the 1880s also saw an increase in the number of available single-barreled shotguns. In the late 1860s and the 1870s most such guns had been based on single-shot rifle actions, but by mid-1880 this situation was changing, with at least three single-barreled shotguns specifically designed as such making their appearance in the East. These guns, all of break-open type, included Hyde & Shattuck's "American," the "Champion" made by John P. Lovell of Boston, and the sidehammer Forehand & Wadsworth. Other singles which followed shortly were George Fox's thumb-lever-cocked "Semi-Hammerless," made by the American Arms Company, and the "Richards," which resembled the Champion. Still others followed: besides the Champion, John Lower's 1888 catalog offered the Dickerman and the Rupertus. Nathaniel Curry had sold Champion, Forehand & Wadsworth, American Arms Semi-Hammerless, and the Richards guns since 1884, and possibly even before that.[49]

Two single-barreled shotguns widely available in the 1880s that were based on military rifle actions were the Springfield and the Zulu. A number of gun houses fitted 16- or 20-gauge barrels to surplus trapdoor Springfield actions, added simple stocks, and sold the result for about $12. The "Zulu" gun was made in the same manner: its Snider-type action, in which the breechblock opened on a longitudinal hinge pin on the right side of the frame, had originally been made

Two gentlemen ready to hold down their town lot in Guthrie, Oklahoma Territory, by force if necessary, with double-barrel shotgun, revolver, or M1886 Winchester rifle (left) in 1889. (Courtesy Western History Collections, University of Oklahoma Library)

in France to convert .71-caliber muzzle-loading rifled muskets to Boxer-cartridge breechloaders. Called the "Tabatiere" by the French, this action lent itself nicely to the making of cheap 12-gauge shotguns, which retailed for a lowly $4 or so. Dealers sometimes assembled cheap double-barreled guns by reversing this principle; they joined together a pair of bored-out military rifle or musket barrels, then mounted them on a cast-iron, double-grip action. A third single-barreled shotgun, designed and made strictly as a commercial venture, appeared at the close of the 1880s. Manufactured by Hopkins & Allen, this gun was basically the same as the Sharps; it had a vertically sliding breechblock, lowered for loading by a hinged trigger guard. Although sometimes fitted with rifle barrels chambered for low- or moderately powered cartridges, the arm was probably more popular as a 12- or 16-gauge shotgun.[50]

Regardless of type or quality, shotguns continued to play an important role in the West of the 1880s. An incident of notable irony connected with a shot-

gun occurred in Ogallala, Nebraska, in 1882, and involved Bill Thompson, who had killed Sheriff Whitney with a shotgun in Ellsworth in 1873. One day in early July Thompson had harsh words with James Tucker, proprietor of the Cowboy's Rest Saloon; by nightfall Thompson had decided to shoot Tucker, who was then overseeing a dance in his establishment. Edgar Beecher Bronson was also in attendance, and later reported what happened:

Bill suddenly stepped within the door of the saloon and took a quick snapshot at Tucker, who was directly across the bar from us and in the act of passing Fant a glass of whisky with his left hand. The ball cut off three of Tucker's fingers and the tip of the fourth, and, the bar being narrow, spattered us with his blood. Tucker fell, momentarily, from the shock. Supposing from Tucker's quick drop he had made an instant kill, Bill stuck his pistol in his waistband and started leisurely out of the door and down the street. But no sooner was he out of the house than

The result of a single day's hunt by these shotgunners in Oklahoma's Cherokee Strip in the 1890s. (Courtesy Kansas State Historical Society)

Jim sprang up, seized a sawed-off ten-gauge shotgun, ran to the door, levelled the gun across the stump of his maimed left hand, and emptied into Bill's back, at about six paces, a trifle more No. 4 duckshot than his system could assimilate. Perhaps altogether ten minutes were wasted on this incident and the time taken to tourniquet and tie up Jim's wound and to pack Bill inside and stow him in a corner behind the faro lookout's chair, and then Jim's understudy called, "Pardners fo' th' next dance!" . . .[51]

About a year later Reginald Aldridge rendered his opinion of the shotgun bore size most practical for the West:

In the way of firearms, a 10-bore shot gun is perhaps the most useful size for all-round work. I had originally a 12-bore, but, though a very good gun for prairie-chicken and quail, it is too light for ducks and turkey. Last winter I had a 10-bore built for me to take Kynoch's "Perfect" cases, and weighing 9¾ lbs., which I find an excellent weapon . . . Kynoch's cases can be obtained in the United States at about double the price paid in England for them.[52]

After traveling through Yellowstone Park and its surroundings by horseback in the mid-1880s, George Wingate wrote that, outside the park boundaries:

both a rifle and shotgun are needed. . . . In the wagon I carried a twelve-bore shot-gun. This had an auxiliary rifle barrel, carrying a Winchester 44-50 [?] cartridge. This is a short rifle barrel made to fit one of the shot barrels, and which slips into the latter like a cartridge and has an extractor which is actuated by the extractor of the gun itself. A little practice is required to learn how to shoot with it. If used in the right barrel, the aim should be from the right edge of the rib to the fore sight. If in the left, the aim must be over the left edge of the rib, as the shot barrels incline inward; when the proper method to use it was learned, we could break a bottle with it at sixty yards every time. I carried shells for my twelve-bore loaded with No. 6, 4 and 2 shot and a few with buckshot.[53]

James Cook found a more serious use for his shotguns in 1885, during an Apache scare in New Mexico. Cook and a companion "stood guard all night, he at the corrals and I at the main ranch house. I took my

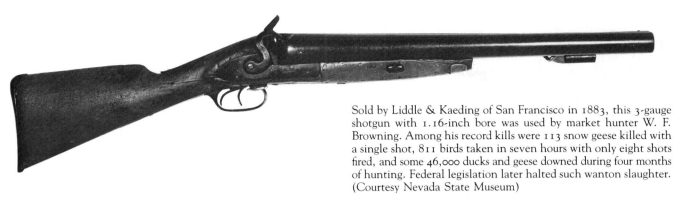

Sold by Liddle & Kaeding of San Francisco in 1883, this 3-gauge shotgun with 1.16-inch bore was used by market hunter W. F. Browning. Among his record kills were 113 snow geese killed with a single shot, 811 birds taken in seven hours with only eight shots fired, and some 46,000 ducks and geese downed during four months of hunting. Federal legislation later halted such wanton slaughter. (Courtesy Nevada State Museum)

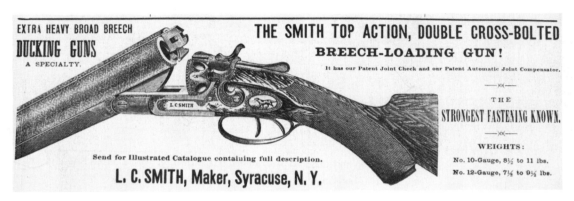

Forest and Stream, May 1884.

pistols and two double-barreled shotguns loaded with buckshot, and stayed outside within the shadow of the buildings." During a coroner's inquest involving Texas John Slaughter's killing of a bandit in Arizona's Whetstone Mountains in 1888, this exchange took place: "Q. Did you have a rifle? A. No! I had a breech loading shotgun."[54]

Describing the armament on hand at his North Dakota ranch in the 1880s, the indomitable Theodore Roosevelt wrote:

I have two double-barreled shotguns: a No. 10 chokebore for ducks and geese made by Thomas of Chicago; and a No. 16 hammerless built for me by Kennedy of St. Paul, for grouse and plover. On regular hunting trips I always carry the Winchester rifle, but in riding round near home, where a man may see a deer and is sure to come across ducks and grouse, it is best to take the little ranch gun, a double-barrel No. 16, with a 40-70 rifle underneath the shotgun barrels.[55]

Breech-loading doubles continued to be the dominant type of shotgun in the West until well after the turn of the century, with new models appearing con-

stantly. Two new doubles that would reach the West by the late 1880s were the Ithaca and the L. C. Smith, both direct offshoots of the trigger-action Baker. Based on patents issued in May and June of 1880, the Ithaca was originally manufactured by William Baker himself. In fact the arm was advertised in January of 1885 as "The Ithaca Gun ! . . . Baker's Latest and Best Invention." Explaining the difference between his earliest shotgun and the new Ithaca, Baker wrote in May of 1885: "The 'Ithaca Gun' Has The Top Lever, Instead Of The Trigger Action, An Entirely New Arrangement Of Locks, And Construction, Making It More Desirable In Every Respect."[56]

Initially patented in March of 1883 and announced in the spring of 1884, the L. C. Smith double was the namesake of Lyman C. Smith, one of Baker's business associates and himself an arms manufacturer. The Smith's principal feature was a rotary locking bolt housed in the standing breech, engaging a prominent rib extension. The bearing surfaces of bolt and rib extension were contoured to take up wear automatically. A note in John Lower's 1888 catalog specifically mentioned the Smith, and some other doubles as well: "L. C. Smith, Parker, Webley, Clabrough, Greener,

Army officers and family members combine a hunting excursion and a picnic luncheon near Ft. Thomas, Arizona Territory, in February 1886. Second from left is Lt. Col. Anson Mills, then serving with the Tenth Cavalry. The shotguns leaning against a giant saguaro cactus are a double-hammer gun on the left and a Spencer pump-action repeater. (Courtesy National Archives)

E. A. Meacham Arms Co., St. Louis, 1884 ad featuring Spencer repeating shotguns.

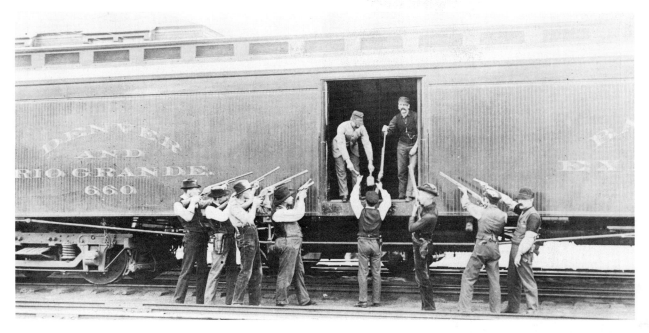

A simulated holdup of the Denver & Rio Grande railroad. Except for a Winchester M1873 rifle at right, all other shoulder arms are M1887 Winchester lever-action shotguns. The man at far right points a Smith & Wesson New Model No. 3 revolver. The man second from right has a hammerless Smith & Wesson in his back pocket. (Courtesy Denver Public Library, Western History Dept.)

Chas. Daly and other B.L. Double Guns not kept in stock, [but] will be furnished to order promptly at 25 per cent. off List Prices." Though the Ithaca was not on Lower's list, it was later purchased by Wells Fargo.[57]

Neither George Fox's vertically pivoted barrel double nor the Harrington & Richardson hammerless survived the 1880s; the Colt shotgun did not outlast the mid-1890s. But in one form or another Parker, Remington, Stevens, Baker, LeFever, Ithaca, and L. C. Smith shotguns all remained in production well past 1900. By the 1890s the quality of the better American-made doubles was high indeed. As an observer at Chicago's 1893 Columbian Exposition remarked:

[British shotguns] differ from the American guns in that, with the exception of a little machine work on the breech frame and the barrels, they are wholly hand made, and consequently are expensive, whereas the American guns are made almost entirely by machinery, which enables them to be sold much cheaper and in much larger quantities. The idea so long prevalent that close-fitting joints can not be made by machinery was demonstrated to be an error by many if not all of the American exhibits in firearms. To show how finely fitted the joints of the working parts were, a pencil mark was made on some of the parts, and so close was the fit that a single movement of the barrels completely removed it; and this was a gun taken from the regular stock, and not one specially prepared for exhibition.[58]

ADVANCED REPEATERS

By the mid-1880s repeating shotguns were again diverting attention from the time-honored doubles. While Sylvester Roper's four-shot revolving-carrier repeater had not been overwhelmingly successful, its inventor nevertheless regarded the market for repeating shotguns as promising; and in April of 1882 he and the famous Christopher Spencer patented a new repeater. Based on an idea which Spencer alone had patented as early as May of 1863, the Spencer-Roper shotgun was of the slide-action or "pump" type, in which the shooter pulled back and pushed forward a short, longitudinally sliding forestock to operate the mechanism.

The gun's action was unusual. The breechblock and the carrier were cut from a single piece of steel, with the carrier positioned just below the block proper. This breechblock-carrier unit swung up and down on a transverse hinge pin at the rear which intersected the bore axis. With the action at rest, the breechblock supported the shell in the chamber, while the carrier below it was aligned with a tubular magazine under the barrel. Once the gun was fired, a rearward pull on the forestock first cammed the front of the breechblock

Montana hunters ready for any kind of game with (left) a M1887
Winchester shotgun and a Winchester M1876 rifle. (Courtesy
Denver Public Library, Western History Dept.)

down, below the level of the chamber, and allowed
extraction of the fired case; near the end of the rearward stroke, the breechblock suddenly sprang upward,
bringing the carrier, which held a fresh shell, into line
with the bore. A forward push on the forestock first
pulled the shell off the carrier into the chamber, then
cammed the front of the breechblock-carrier unit down,
until the block proper was in position to support the
shell head for firing. What appeared to be a reversed
front trigger was actually a cocking spur for the concealed hammer, to be used in case of a misfire. Cocking
of the hammer was otherwise automatic, during the
rearward stroke of the forestock.[59]

Although somewhat unusual in operation and appearance, the Spencer was mechanically a very sound
design. The Ordnance Department tested it in a rifle
version during the trials of 1881–82 and, with even
more plaudits, tested it again in shotgun form in 1886.
Very few rifles of this type were made, however, and
it was as a shotgun that the design proved most successful. Made principally as a 12-gauge six-shot arm
with 30 in. or 32 in. barrel, the Spencer passed through
models of 1882, 1890, and 1896. A special version

was displayed at the 1893 Columbian Exposition by
the Simmons Hardware Co. of St. Louis; this gun had
a "2-foot barrel and a sling, as a defense for travelers."[60]

But the Spencer had been on the market less than
a year when, in mid-1885, the highly talented John
Browning applied for a patent on a repeating shotgun
of his own. A lever-action design with an underbarrel
tubular magazine, Browning's gun was mechanically
similar to the earlier Spencer repeating carbine and
the Evans repeating rifle. A downward and forward
push on the lever first pulled the breechblock down,
dropping an integral locking shoulder at its rear below
a corresponding shoulder in the receiver, then rotated
the block through a backward and downward arc, extracting the fired case, cocking the hammer, and read-
ying a fresh shell for chambering; the backward and
upward pull on the lever chambered the cartridge and
locked the breechblock behind it.[61]

Marketed by Winchester in the summer of 1887,
the Model 1887 was available in both 10 and 12 gauge,
with barrels of 30 in. and 32 in. John P. Lower and
other dealers in the West were offering the gun by the
spring of 1888, and it was soon a pronounced success.

A well-guarded Wells Fargo express wagon near Deadwood, South Dakota, about 1890. The two shotgun-armed guards at far left carry repeating M1887 Winchesters; the other two guards are armed with breech-loading double-barrel "scatterguns." (Courtesy Library of Congress)

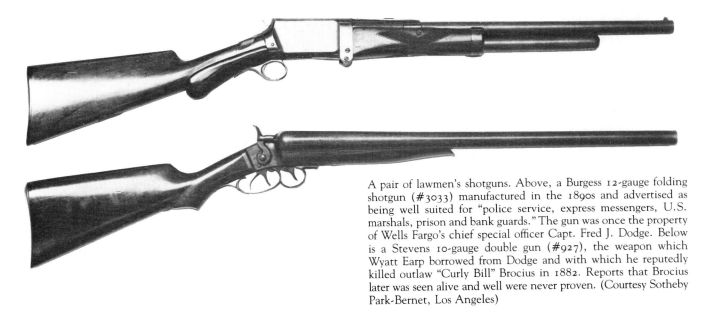

A pair of lawmen's shotguns. Above, a Burgess 12-gauge folding shotgun (#3033) manufactured in the 1890s and advertised as being well suited for "police service, express messengers, U.S. marshals, prison and bank guards." The gun was once the property of Wells Fargo's chief special officer Capt. Fred J. Dodge. Below is a Stevens 10-gauge double gun (#927), the weapon which Wyatt Earp borrowed from Dodge and with which he reputedly killed outlaw "Curly Bill" Brocius in 1882. Reports that Brocius later was seen alive and well were never proven. (Courtesy Sotheby Park-Bernet, Los Angeles)

On February 15, 1900, five members of the Stilles-Alvord gang attempted to hold up the Southern Pacific railroad near Fairbanks, Arizona Territory. During the attempt, noted lawman Jefferson (Jeff) Davis Milton, then working as a Wells Fargo express guard, killed Three Fingered Jack Dunlop with a load of buckshot from this Winchester M1887 10-gauge lever-action shotgun (#36549). Milton was wounded in the affair, but the four surviving robbers were taken into custody. Another owner of an M1887 shotgun was George Scarborough, who shot "old" John Selman in El Paso in 1896. (Courtesy Arizona Historical Society)

It would deliver its six shots somewhat faster than the Spencer, and had the more familiar underlever action. Among its major purchasers was the Denver & Rio Grande Railroad, which used the gun to arm its messengers.[62]

Both the Spencer and the 1887 Winchester established the repeating shotgun as a practical proposition. Surprisingly, the Browning-designed slide-action Winchester Model 1893 which followed had mechanical problems. Also, it faced a new competitor: a repeating shotgun designed by Andrew Burgess, and, like the Winchester, displayed at Chicago's 1893 Columbian Exposition. The Burgess was another slide-action arm,

but instead of a moveable forestock, Burgess's "slide" was a moveable pistol grip. Although the gun was briefly popular, Winchester's new Model 1897, a perfected version of its Model 1893, became one of the most widely sold repeating shotguns ever produced, and had nearly the same effect on the dominance of the double-barreled gun as the Model 1886 Winchester repeater had on the single-shot rifle. But whether single-barrel, double-barrel, or repeater, the shotgun continued to be an important part of the westerner's armament until long after the frontier era had drawn to a close.[63]

Lady shotgunners, Mrs. Henry Houghton and Mrs. Jerome Marble of Worchester, Mass. photographed in 1876 in Dakota Territory. Presumably they are participants in one of the hunting excursions which western railroads frequently offered. (From Haynes Foundation Collection, Courtesy Montana Historical Society)

· 5 ·

HANDGUNS

PERCUSSION PISTOLS AND REVOLVERS

IN JAMES COOK'S VIEW, handguns were highly important weapons for many a postwar plainsman:

> Everyone [on cattle drives] went armed with a heavy revolver and a knife. But few carried rifles. One reason for this was that the added weight on one side of a horse, on those long, hard trips, was a great cause of saddle galls—something to be strictly guarded against on an eighteen-hundred-mile drive. . . . A revolver and a sheath knife were very necessary parts of a cowboy's equipment. Both these weapons had to be carried in the most get-at-able manner, [since] Sudden and expert work with both pistol and knife was quite likely to be required at times in the work with the cattle. . . . Constant practice with both knife and pistol made some of the boys very expert with these weapons.[1]

Philippe Regis de Trobriand's description of Omaha in 1867 included this note: "In the streets one constantly meets hardy, sun-tanned men with long hair and beards who carry unconcealed in their belts the hunting knife and revolver, inseparable companions of the plainsman." And in describing a typical Missouri River steamboat, de Trobriand added: "We carry two howitzers forward, and in the salon there is a gun rack loaded with rifles and carbines, not to mention the revolver that every male passenger carries as a matter of course for his own protection."[2]

By and large the revolvers used in the West in the years immediately following the war were percussion arms. Smith & Wesson, zealously guarding the Rollin White patent on the bored-through chamber, prevented the widespread distribution of competing arms using metallic cartridges until 1869, when the patent expired. Besides Smith & Wesson's own products, small numbers of Plant, Moore, and LeFaucheux revolvers, with their special ammunition, saw service in the West, but all such guns were in the minority until the 1870s.[3]

Undoubtedly the officials at Colt were less than happy with the patent situation. But even in the face of the advantages offered by the metallic cartridge, Colt percussion revolvers continued to enjoy vast popularity and active sales. On the frontier this popularity was partly due to the ready availability of loose ammunition, but it also stemmed from the well-established Colt reputation, which assumed near-legendary proportions after the Civil War.

Even at this time the old Colt Dragoon, a veteran of the late 1840s, sometimes made an appearance. On the buffalo range, in fact, there was a strong demand for this gun. Theodore Davis, who toured the plains in 1868, wrote:

> Of the revolvers in use [for buffalo hunting] the old style dragoon pistol of the Colt pattern seems the favorite, though the bullet that it shoots is no heavier than that used in the present style known as Colt's army revolver. The pistol itself is heavier and more steady to shoot, and the cylinder is chambered for more powder. I am not aware that this arm is any longer manufactured. The Plains men who possess a pair hold them in great esteem.

While Richard Townshend was in Colorado about 1870, he noticed one man carrying "an enormous revolver, one of the old dragoon Colt's, with a barrel about a foot long."[4]

More widely used during the late 1860s than the Dragoon, however, were the six-shot .36 caliber Navy models of 1851 and 1861, and the six-shot .44 caliber Army model of 1860. Another popular Colt was the .31 caliber pocket model of 1849, which was still going strong in the 1860s. Less in demand were the five-shot fluted-cylinder .36 caliber Police revolver of 1861 (now often called the Model 1862) and the five-shot "Pocket Navy" sold alongside it. Lagging well behind in sales to the West was the small solid-frame side-hammer "Root model," first marketed in 1856. The Colt revolvers brought back to various states and territories west of the Missouri River by returning Civil War veterans—over 1600, according to official figures,

Colt .44 M1860 carried by Capt. P. D. Watson, a former Civil War Union artillery officer, who was conductor in charge of a Union Pacific material train engaged in the original construction of the line. He also was the conductor on the train pulled by UP engine #119, which was used at completion ceremonies at Promontory, Utah, on May 19, 1869. (Courtesy Union Pacific Museum)

Engraved and fitted with carved ivory grips, this magnificent Colt M1860 was the property of John S. "Jack" Casement, boss of the Union Pacific track laying crews. (Courtesy Union Pacific Museum)

Colt .44 Third Model Dragoon, #13856, presented to Maj. Gen. John C. Frémont, western explorer, by his father-in-law, Senator Thomas Hart Benton, Jr. (Courtesy Arizona Historical Society)

as opposed to some 900 Remingtons, 90 Starrs, and 60 Whitneys—accounted for only a small part of the Colt's widespread acceptance. Such was the market for the arm that it was sometimes available from unusual outlets. Early in 1868, for instance, this notice appeared in the Brownsville *Ranchero:* "N. Chano, Wholesale And Retail Grocer . . . Also, Colt's Fire Arms, For Sale As Low Or Lower Than The Lowest." Another example of the demand for these weapons is that in June of 1869 William Rotton of Nebraska City, himself an arms dealer, inserted this notice in the *Nebraska City News:* "Wanted. 1,000 Colt's Pistols, For which I will pay the highest price in the market. Wanted Immediately!"[5]

For the majority of handgun buyers, then, the problem was not whether to choose a Colt, but which Colt to choose. On occasion, even an experienced plainsman might select a .31 caliber pocket model because of its light weight, but in general the .36 caliber Navy or the .44 caliber Army was the weapon of choice.

Although the .44 was the more effective arm, it was slightly heavier and somewhat bulkier than the .36. Describing a westerner he met in Cheyenne in 1869, Richard Townshend wrote:

> He wore his belt slack, so that it hung rather low on his right side; the butt of the pistol just showed at the top of the holster, and I noticed, too, that the lower end of the holster was provided with two long pieces of buckskin string, by which it was securely bound round his thigh.

When Townshend asked about the buckskin string, the westerner replied that it was "to keep [the gun] from joggling about too much when I'm riding at a lope. A gun travels better so; and if you ever want to pull it, it pulls better so. Let me tell you that a .44-calibre Colt is a heavyish thing to tote around." Possibly because of this last remark, Townshend went to Carlos Gove's Denver gunshop a month or so later and bought a handier gun, "a navy Colt, a .36-calibre muzzle-loading six-shooter."[6]

James Cook also had a "muzzle-loading Colt" while working as a cowhand in Texas in the early 1870s. Besides the gun, he owned

a copper flask made especially for use with the revolver. This flask would contain six charges of powder, and had a shut-off measuring gauge to regulate the amount of powder, as well as a compartment that held six bullets (we made our own bullets). It was small enough to be carried in my trousers pocket, and so became a handy device to help me load my six-shooter more quickly and accurately. It was the only powder flask of the kind I ever saw.[7]

Colt percussion revolvers remained in use well into the days of metallic-cartridge arms. When Richard Hughes left for the Black Hills in 1876, "a friend contributed an old style Colt's cap and ball revolver." In addition, one of Hughes's companions on the journey carried "two old-fashioned Colt revolvers, which used loose ammunition." John Wesley Hardin's own account of his capture by Texas Rangers in 1877 included this note:

[Jack Duncan] said he was from Texas and was only feeling good over the capture of the notorious John Wesley Hardin. He said to Armstrong and others standing by, "Have you taken his pistol?" They replied no, that I had no gun. Jack Duncan said, "That's too thin," and ran his hand between my over and undershirt, pulling out a .44 Colt's cap-and-ball six-shooter, remarking to the others, "What did I tell you?"

During the Cheyenne scare in Kansas in 1878, one settler and his wife "forted up" in their cabin: when the Indians got too close "we opened fire on them. My wife with a one-shot gun and I with a cap and ball, Colt's Navy revolver, fired through loopholes . . . in the wall. They immediately left us."[8]

All the Colt percussion revolvers made in the 1860s and early 1870s were single-action arms. On the other hand, Remington, whose revolvers were close behind the Colts in popularity, marketed not only single-action but also double-action guns. As offered by Albert E. Crane, Remington's San Francisco agent, in 1867, the company's percussion handgun line comprised the New Model Army, Navy, and Belt revolvers, a navy-caliber Police revolver, a "New Pocket Revolver (with loading lever)," and the "Pocket Revolver (Self Cocking)." There were actually two versions of the New Model Belt revolver: both were six-shot .36-caliber guns with 6 in. barrels, but one was a single-action arm, while the other employed double-action lockwork. Evidently the newest revolver in this series was

George W. Nichols, writing in the February 1867 issue of *Harpers* magazine, described his 1865 meeting with Wild Bill Hickok in Springfield, Missouri, in this manner: "His waist was girthed by a belt which held two Colt's Navy revolvers." The same description seems appropriate for this Hickok image. (Courtesy Kansas State Historical Society)

255

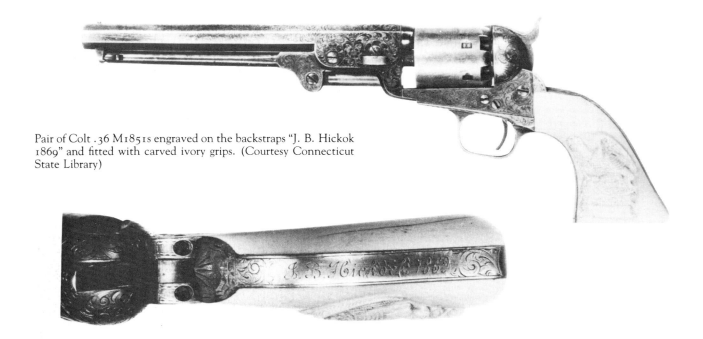

Pair of Colt .36 M1851s engraved on the backstraps "J. B. Hickok 1869" and fitted with carved ivory grips. (Courtesy Connecticut State Library)

the five-shot Police revolver, few of which appeared before 1866. Advertising it in September of that year, Albert Crane had termed it "a new model, navy size ball, 4½ to 6 inch barrel," although a 6½ in. barrel was also available.[9]

Besides the Remington agencies in St. Louis, New Orleans, and San Francisco, individual dealers all over the West sold the firm's products, and together with Colts, Remington percussion revolvers were among the most prevalent of such guns on the postwar frontier. Other manufacturers were also represented in the West, among them the Manhattan Firearms Company of New Jersey. By 1866 Manhattan was offering only

one type of percussion revolver, a five-shot .36 caliber "Navy" which, except for ten bolt notches in the cylinder, resembled the Colt M1851. In mid-1867, after making more than 60,000 of these guns, the company started manufacture of a new six-shot Navy with twelve bolt notches in the cylinder, but it completed only about 9000 before production stopped, presumably in the fall of 1868. While not rivaling the Colts or Remingtons in quantity, the Manhattan .36s nevertheless sold fairly well during the late 1860s; their western dealers at that time included Trumpler & Dabbs of Little Rock, John Biringer of Leavenworth, and William Beck of Portland. Barrel lengths for the six-shot

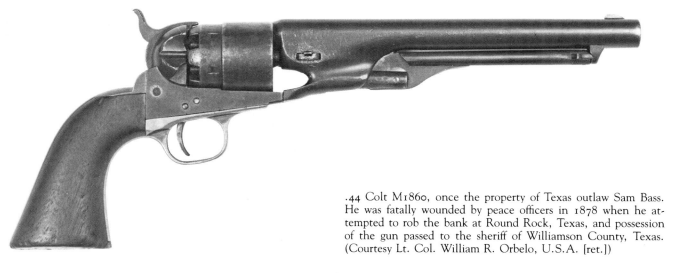

.44 Colt M1860, once the property of Texas outlaw Sam Bass. He was fatally wounded by peace officers in 1878 when he attempted to rob the bank at Round Rock, Texas, and possession of the gun passed to the sheriff of Williamson County, Texas. (Courtesy Lt. Col. William R. Orbelo, U.S.A. [ret.])

Unidentified black cowboys, perhaps with studio prop guns. At left, a Colt M1860 and at right, a large-frame Remington, perhaps a New Model 1863 .44. (Courtesy Kansas State Historical Society)

Although made before the Civil War, this scroll-engraved five-shot Colt Model 1849, with ivory grips and ivory front sight, was brought to Colorado by John G. Smalley in 1871. (Courtesy Colorado Springs Pioneers' Museum)

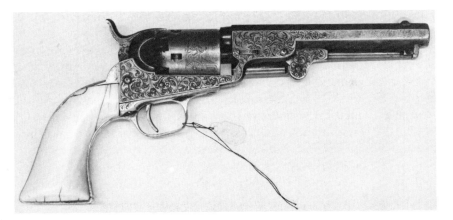

Colt M1860 .44 (#168475), its barrel shortened to a more convenient length, carried by itinerant frontier merchant A. B. Franklin. (Courtesy Arizona Historical Society)

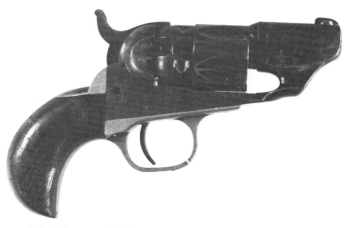

Colt Police .36 skillfully reduced in weight and bulk to serve as an easily concealed "belly gun." The loading lever has been removed, the barrel shortened, and the butt reshaped. Examples of similarly modified Police Colts can be found in several museum collections in the West. (Courtesy History Department, Los Angeles County Museum of Natural History)

San Francisco Mining and Scientific Press, September 1866.

.36 ranged between 4 in. and 6½ in.; on the frontier, the 6½ in. size was apparently the best seller.

Less numerous than the Manhattans were the double-action percussion revolvers made by James M. Cooper of Pennsylvania. Cooper, who had been in the gun business since the early 1840s, started making revolvers in Pittsburgh about 1860. His early models, most or all of which were five-shot .31 caliber arms, relied heavily on features patented by Josiah Ells during the 1850s, although most also embodied design elements patented by Cooper himself in September of 1860. In 1864, after the fabrication of about 1000 of these early revolvers, Cooper moved from Pittsburgh to Philadelphia, where he began offering five-shot .36 caliber arms in addition to the smaller .31s. Most of the guns made in Philadelphia incorporated features of two patents issued in September of 1863, one to Cooper and the other to C. W. Harris. Of a total of some 15,000 .31 and .36 revolvers produced there, each size displayed various modifications: early examples of the .36, for example, had cylinders of uniform diameter, but later examples employed rebated cylinders; the early .31s had five-shot cylinders, but the cylinders of the later .31s had a six-shot capacity.

Though well designed and well made, Cooper's revolvers were not particularly long-lived. Cooper himself closed up shop in May of 1869, but by that time some of his guns had already reached the West: an advertisement by Trumpler & Dabbs of Little Rock late in 1868 stated that "the Cooper pistol is a No. 1: can be used as self-cocking or thumb-cocking." William Beck of Portland was handling the Cooper by mid-1869, and Benjamin Kittredge of Cincinnati was still advertising it in 1876.[11]

Aside from American-made guns, a few foreign percussion revolvers saw service in the postwar West. (The products of such English makers as Robert Adams and William Tranter had, in fact, reached the frontier even before the war.) In 1868 William Pinkerton and another detective were escorting a prisoner named Taylor from Galveston to Cheyenne; as their steamboat pushed off from Galveston, Taylor jumped overboard and tried desperately to swim to safety. Pinkerton

began firing with considerable rapidity, so as to strike the water within a few feet of the man who was so unsuccessfully struggling against the tide. . . . He was provided with two magnificent English Trenter revolvers, which will carry a half-ounce ball a fourth of a mile with absolute accuracy; and as he could use [them] with great precision he could easily have killed the man in the water . . . as Taylor held up his hand and yelled—"I surrender!" the balls were cutting into the water all about him savagely, and the captain shouted, "For God's sake, don't kill the man!"[12]

While they were less in evidence on the postwar frontier than percussion revolvers, percussion single-

Remingtons' New Patterns of Fire Arms. Ilion, N. Y.

ARMY AND NAVY REVOLVER.

Six Chamber Cylinder. Army Size, 8 inch Barrel; Caliber, 44-100ths of an inch; carrying 33 Elongated, or 48 Round Balls to the pound. Price, $12.50; Silver-Plated Frame, $14.50.
Navy Size, 7½ inch Barrel; Caliber, 36-100ths of an inch; carrying 50 Elongated, or 86 Round Balls to the pound. Price, $11.50; Silver-Plated Frame, $13.25.

SINGLE SHOT, BREECH-LOADING
ARMY AND NAVY PISTOL.

New Model. Pattern adopted for the U. S. Navy. Caliber, or size of bore, 50-100ths of an inch, using Metallic Cartridge. 8 inch Barrel. Weight, 2 lbs. Price, $12.

BELT REVOLVER.

Double Action, or Self Cocking. Also Single Action, same size.

Six Chamber Cylinder; 6 inch Barrel; Caliber, 36-100ths of an inch; Carrying 50 Elongated, or 86 Round Balls to the pound. Price, Double Action, $11; Silver-Plated Frame, $12.50. Single Action, $11; Silver-Plated Frame, 12.50. With cylinder using metallic cartridge, $11.50.

POLICE REVOLVER.

Five Chamber Cylinder; Caliber, 36-100ths of an inch; carrying 50 Elongated, or 86 Round Balls to the pound. Belt Size, 6½ inch Barrel; price, $9.50; silver-plated frame, $10.75. Pocket or Belt Size, 5½ inch Barrel; price, $9.25; silver-plated frame, $10.50. Pocket size, 4½ inch Barrel, price, $9; silver-plated frame, $10.25. With cylinder using metallic cartridge, $10, $10.50, and $11.

NEW POCKET REVOLVER.

Five Chamber Cylinder; 3½ and 4½ inch Barrels; Caliber, 31-100 inch; carrying 92 elongated or 140 round balls to the pound. Price, 3½ inch, $8.25; silver-plated frame, $9.25. 4½ inch, $8.50; silver-plated frame, $9.50. With cylinder using metallic cartridge, $9.25, $9.50.

DOUBLE ACTION.
OR
Self-Cocking Revolver.
POCKET SIZE.
3 inch Barrel; carrying 140 Round Balls to the pound; Five Shots. Price, $7.00; Silver-Plated Frame, $7.75.

BREECH-LOADING RIFLE. Beal's Pat.
One Shot. 24, 26 and 28 inch Barrel; using Metallic Catridge; No. 32 & 38; weight 6½ lbs. Price, 24 inch, $23.00—26 inch, $24.00—28 inch, $25. With plated mountings, $2 extra.

RIFLE CANE 2 Sizes, using Met. Ctgs. Nos. 22, 32. Price, $10.

REVOLVING BREECH RIFLE.
Six shots; 24, 26, and 28 inch steel barrel; caliber, 36-100 inch; carries 44 elongated or 86 round balls to the pound. Also, 44-100 inch bore, carries 30 elongated or 48 round balls to the pound. Weight, 6 lbs. Price, $25, $26, $27; with plated mountings, adjustable sights, and extra finished stock, extra, $5.

REMINGTON'S SPORTING RIFLE—Breech-Loading
Using Metallic Cartridges Nos. 38 and 46. Caliber, 36-100 and 44-100 of an inch; weight, from 9 to 14 lbs. Price, 30-inch steel barrel, $36.00—32-inch, $38.00—34-inch, $40.00.

In these days of House breaking and Robbery, every Dwelling, Store, Office and Bank should have one of the Remington Fire Arms.

From a Remington broadside, c. 1870.

Cased .44 New Model percussion Remington (#40451) presented by financier Jay Gould to Gen. G. M. Dodge, who in 1866 became chief engineer for the Union Pacific construction project. (Courtesy Sotheby Park-Bernet, Los Angeles)

REVOLVERS,

Army, Navy and Belt, single and double action.

RIFLES,

Breech Loading, Revolving and U. S. Muskets.

GUN CANES, REPEATERS,

Single Barrel Vest Pocket Pistols, (New Models.) All the different patterns and styles of finish.

Gun Barrels and Material.

UPWARDS of two hundred thousand furnished the United States Government since 1861.

Army Revolver, 44 100 in Caliber.
Navy Revolver, 36-100 in. Caliber.
Belt Revolver (Self Cocking), Navy Caliber.
Belt Revolver, Navy Size Caliber.
Police Revolver, Navy size Caliber.
New Pocket Revolver (with loading lever).
Pocket Revolver (Self Cocking).
Repeating Pistol (Elliot pt.). No. 32 Cartridge.
Repeating Pistol (Elliot pt.) No. 22 Cartridge.
Vest Pocket Pistol No. 22, 30 and 32 Cartridge.
Gun Cane, using No 32 Cartridge.
Single Barrel Shot Gun.
Revolving Rifle, 36 and 45-100 in Caliber.
Breech Loading Carbine, No 46 Cartridge.
U. S. Rifle (Steel Barrel), with Sabre Bayonet.
U. S. Rifle Musket, Springfield pattern.
Our Breech Loading Arms have just been approved and adopted for Military service in Europe
E. REMINGTON & SONS, Ilion, N. Y.
ALBERT E. CRANE.
April 27, 1867.   25:tf

Olympia, *Washington Standard*, May 1867.

Union Pacific railroad construction train at Granite Canyon in Wyoming Territory in 1868. The view is one of those taken by A. J. Russell, who recorded the transcontinental railroad con-struction effort on glass-plate negatives. The man seated on a wagon seat holds aloft what appears to be a percussion Remington. (Courtesy Union Pacific Museum)

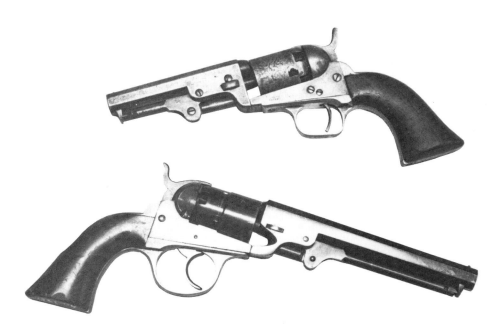

A Colt .31 M1849 pocket model (above) and a .36 Cooper, the latter easily distinguished by its double-action mechanism.

Gold Hill (Nevada) *Daily News*, July 1866.

About 1868 Manhattan brought out a single-shot sheath-trigger percussion pocket pistol stamped "Hero." Made with a brass frame and a .34 caliber turn-off smoothbore barrel normally two or three inches long, this pistol was manufactured not only by Manhattan but also by its successor, the American Standard Tool Company, which operated from the close of 1868 to the spring of 1873. The fact that the two firms turned out some 30,000 pistols of this kind indicates that a market for them still existed.[15]

Even at low prices, however, percussion pistols were hard pressed to offer much competition to single-shot metallic-cartridge handguns, the manufacture of which was not hampered by the Rollin White patent. Nor, for that matter, did White's patent restrict the manufacture of multibarreled cartridge pistols. As a result both types were easily available, and both found ready sales on the postwar frontier.

MULTI-SHOT POCKET PISTOLS FOR METALLIC CARTRIDGES

Several multibarreled, metallic-cartridge pocket pistols had been marketed prior to 1866: the Sharps, the Remington-Elliot, the Bacon, the Rupertus, and the Starr. These pistols, later classified as pepperboxes but compact enough to be called "derringers" by their original owners, had small .22 to .32 caliber bores, for which they compensated by providing more than one or two ready shots.

The unquestioned leader among these makes was the four-barreled Sharps, which had reached the frontier as early as 1859. Both the first and the second models, designed for the .22 and .30 rimfire loads respectively, had brass frames; by mid-1862, however, Sharps and his new partner, William Hankins, were ready to offer a bigger .32-Long-rimfire model with an iron frame. When the Sharps & Hankins partnership broke up in 1867, the four-barreled pistol carrying that name disappeared also; but about 1868 Sharps brought out a somewhat smaller iron-frame .32, with a $2^1/2$ in. or 3 in. barrel group and a parrot-beak butt. Evidently this gun, along with the older brass-frame .22s and .30s, remained in production until Sharps's death in 1874. The brass-frame guns constituted the really big sellers: Sharps's Philadelphia establishment turned out some 90,000 .22s and more than 35,000 .30s, as opposed to about 16,000 Sharps & Hankins and 15,000 parrot-beak .32s. The four-barreled Starr .32 could offer no significant advantage over the Sharps and, simply overwhelmed by its rival, did not last more than two or three years after its introduction in 1864.[16]

Not far behind the Sharps in sales were the Remington ring-trigger .22s and .32s designed by William Elliot. The Remington-Elliot "Zig-Zag" .22 of 1861,

and double-barreled pistols held onto some of their former popularity well into the 1870s. The big .54 caliber U.S. military pistols sold for low prices after the war, making them attractive for buyers who planned to do little shooting. More common, however, were percussion pistols of the pocket variety; of these the best known were the products of Henry Deringer and his imitators. Despite the increasing competition from metallic-cartridge arms, Deringer continued making his typical pocket pistols until his death in February of 1868, and his workmen assembled additional pairs even after that time. C. F. Scholl of Virginia City was still advertising himself as an "Exclusive Agent for Derringer's Pistols" in 1868, as was Nathaniel Curry of San Francisco in 1871. Other dealers marketed imitations, such as those made by Deringer's old rival, Slotter & Co., which persisted in manufacturing look-alike pistols through 1868. And as late as 1875, Tryon of Philadelphia continued to offer close copies of the Deringer original.[13]

Less costly than the Deringer or its copies were the small .31 to .36 caliber iron-frame centerhammer pistols of the type popularized by Ethan Allen. Described by dealers as "Powder And Ball Pistols," or simply as "Common pistols," these guns sold in the late 1860s and early 1870s for less than $2.50 a pair. Double-barreled pistols of similar style and size might bring $3.00 or so. More sophisticated than these guns were the bar-hammer self-cocking single-shot pistols made by Allen and others. Although their manufacture may not have extended past the mid-1860s, the fact that these pistols were capable of being drawn and fired so rapidly, with no hammer spur to snag in the pocket, probably kept them in active use into the 1870s.[14]

One of a pair of genuine .41-caliber Henry Deringer, Jr., percussion pocket pistols.

A Slotter & Co. copy of the Deringer with 2 in. barrel. The lockplate marking of this example, "J. Deringer," dates its manufacture between 1866 and 1868.

with its rotating cluster of six barrels, was replaced in 1863 by two new models, a five-shot .22 and a four-shot .32, both of which (like the Sharps) had fixed barrel groups and rotating firing pins. Yet some of the older guns remained in use. Early in April of 1866 the following notice appeared in the *Galveston News:* "Five Dollars Reward Will be paid, and no questions asked, for the delivery at this office of an Elliott's Patent Pocket Six-Shooter, lost about one week ago." Although not made in Sharps-like quantities, the Remington-Elliots of 1863 sold well enough to remain on factory price lists through 1876.[17]

Far less popular than the Sharps or the Remington were three newer multishot pocket pistols. The first of them was a three-barreled arm originally patented in May of 1857 by William W. Marston. The barrel arrangement—one atop the other—was unusual, and required a special striker design which formed the real basis for Marston's patent. Although initially conceived as a percussion arm, Marston's pistol, usually stamped "Improved 1864," appeared in *Army and Navy Journal* advertisements in mid-1866 as a metallic-cartridge gun. Production centered principally on a .32 rimfire arm with a 3 in. or 4 in. barrel group, but a .22 caliber version also appeared, sometimes with a sliding dagger mounted alongside the barrels.[18]

Two other pocket pistols, both capable of delivering more shots than the Marston, were the Reid and the Continental Arms. Patented by James Reid in December of 1865, the arm called "My Friend" was a cartridge pepperbox with a solid frame, because of which it resembled a conventional revolver with its barrel missing. However, the overall contour of Reid's

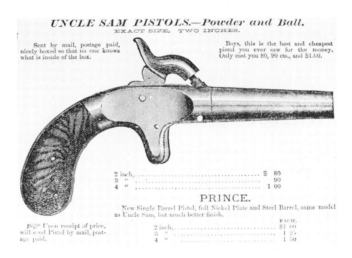

Enterprise Gun Works catalog, 1876. Sheath-trigger pocket pistols of this type were widely sold from the early 1860s through the mid-1870s.

Inexpensive sheath trigger percussion pocket pistol found during excavation work in Pueblo, Colo.

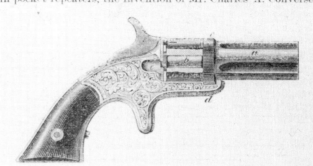

Continental Arms "Ladies' Companion" from the *Scientific American*, February 1867.

Army and Navy Journal, August 1876.

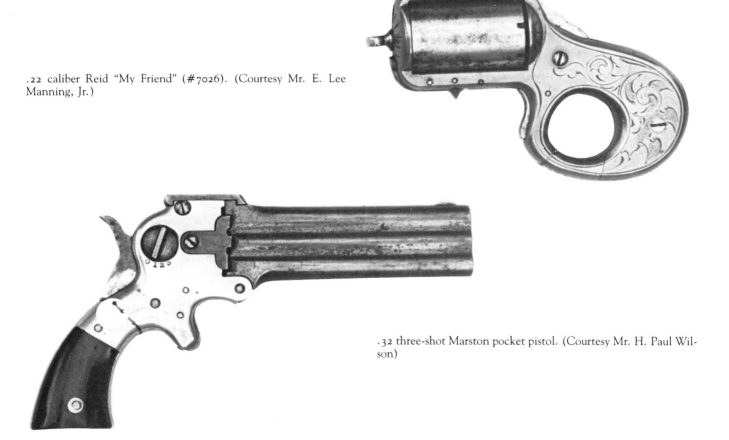

.22 caliber Reid "My Friend" (#7026). (Courtesy Mr. E. Lee Manning, Jr.)

.32 three-shot Marston pocket pistol. (Courtesy Mr. H. Paul Wilson)

Colt No. 1 .41 deringer. Another Colt No. 1, displayed at the Fort Smith (Arkansas) National Historic Site, is one that was carried by a guard at the former federal courthouse and jail during Judge Isaac Parker's reign there as "the hanging judge." (Courtesy Mr. H. Paul Wilson) Yet another, at the Mammoth Hot Springs museum in Yellowstone Park, belonged to Nathaniel P. Langford.

Colt No. 2 .41 derringer. (Courtesy Mr. H. Paul Wilson)

The brass frame of this Colt .41 No. 2 derringer was scarcely marred by the years it lay unnoticed along the bank of the Arkansas River near Salida, Colorado. But the wooden grips have weathered away and its iron parts are badly corroded. No attempt should be made to polish or restore such relics, for their appeal lies in their untouched state.

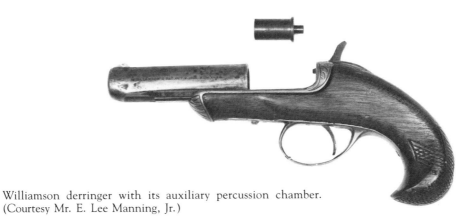

Williamson derringer with its auxiliary percussion chamber. (Courtesy Mr. E. Lee Manning, Jr.)

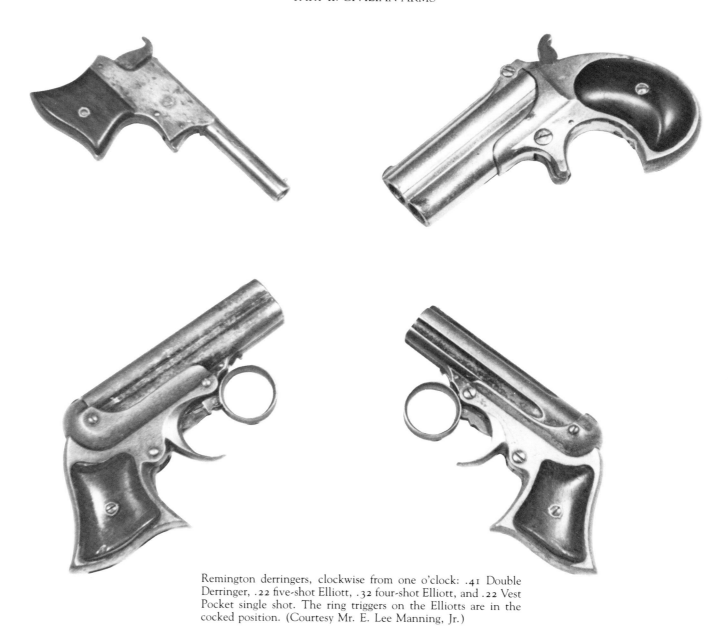

Remington derringers, clockwise from one o'clock: .41 Double Derringer, .22 five-shot Elliott, .32 four-shot Elliott, and .22 Vest Pocket single shot. The ring triggers on the Elliotts are in the cocked position. (Courtesy Mr. E. Lee Manning, Jr.)

pistol, designed to fit nicely into the fist for use as a "knuckler," comprised its real selling point. Most numerous of the Reids were the brass-frame seven-shot .22s and the brass-frame five-shot .32s, production of which extended to some 10,000 and 3000 arms respectively. A few .22s and .32s were made with iron frames, but more interesting was the brass-frame five-shot .41 rimfire model, stamped "J. Reid's Derringer" on the topstrap, of which only a few hundred were made.

Also manufactured in small quantities was a five-shot .22 pepperbox patented by Charles Converse and Samuel Hopkins in August of 1866. Trade-named the "Ladies' Companion," this gun was brought to public attention by the *Scientific American* in February of 1867. Despite such coverage the little pistols never became overly popular, and the Continental Arms Company of Norwich, Connecticut, put together only about 1000 of them. The limited production, however, did not prevent some of the guns from reaching the West.[19]

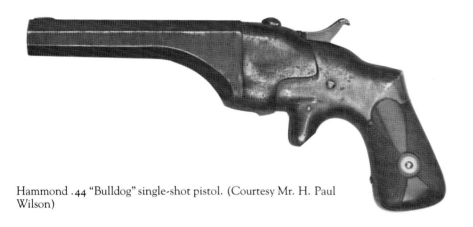

.41 caliber iron-frame Southerner derringer, similar to one carried by Neal Caldwell, a Texas Ranger from 1874 until 1883. (Courtesy Mr. Edward Higginbotham)

Hammond .44 "Bulldog" single-shot pistol. (Courtesy Mr. H. Paul Wilson)

A price list put out in March of 1869 by the Folsom Brothers of St. Louis and New Orleans offered the four-barreled Sharps in all three calibers (.22, .30, and .32), plus the Remington-Elliot four-shot .32s and five-shot .22s. Shortly afterward William Beck of Portland advertised the Sharps, the three-barreled Marston, Reid's "My Friend," and the "Ladies' Companion."[20]

BREECH-LOADING DERRINGERS

Longer lived than multishot pocket arms, and more widely used on the frontier, were small single-shot cartridge pistols of large bore—true derringers of .38 to .44 caliber. So popular did these guns become that two of them remained in production well into the twentieth century.

By 1866 any number of single-barreled .22 or .32 rimfire pistols were available, including those by Allen, Bacon, Remington, Stevens, Wesson, and other makers. But because pistols with bigger bores—notably the Moore-National, the single-shot Starr, and

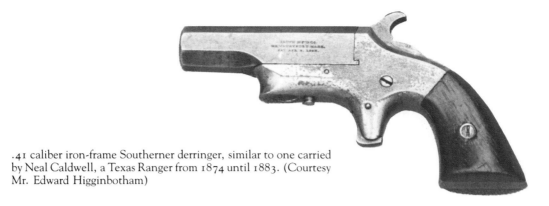

Portland *Oregonian*, June 1869.

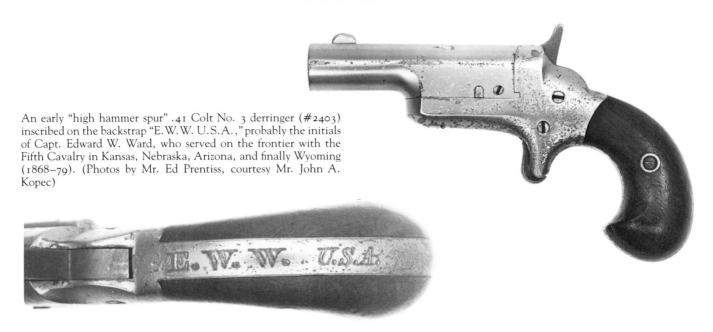

An early "high hammer spur" .41 Colt No. 3 derringer (#2403) inscribed on the backstrap "E.W.W. U.S.A.," probably the initials of Capt. Edward W. Ward, who served on the frontier with the Fifth Cavalry in Kansas, Nebraska, Arizona, and finally Wyoming (1868–79). (Photos by Mr. Ed Prentiss, courtesy Mr. John A. Kopec)

the .41 Allen—had already reached the market, westerners gradually laid the smaller guns aside. To help match the multishot pistol's firepower, single-barreled derringers were commonly priced and sold in pairs.

Although it was the earliest of the .41 rimfire derringers, the Moore, whether under that name or that of the National Arms Co., remained a highly popular item for nearly twenty years after its appearance in 1861. Even after Colt took over the National firm about 1870, the new owner continued marketing both the all-metal No. 1 and the wood-gripped No. 2 without material change. An auction by H. B. Chamberlain at the Fort Smith post office in November of 1866 included not only Colt, Smith & Wesson, and Manhattan revolvers, but also "One pr. National Derringers." John Biringer of Leavenworth sold Nationals at the same time; and after Colt bought out the National concern, the distribution of the derringers bearing that name probably increased, due to the number of dealers on the frontier who handled Colt arms.[21]

Well behind the Moore-National in popularity was the Allen, patented in March of 1865. While a round/

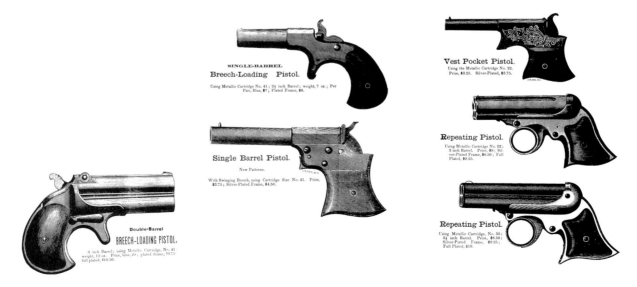

From a Remington broadside, c. 1870.

Swivel-barrel two-shot .41 American Arms, made from about 1866 to 1878. Similar models were offered in .32 and .38, and one incorporated a block chambered for a .22 and a .32 cartridge. (Courtesy Mr. E. Lee Manning, Jr.)

octagon barrel later replaced the full-octagon barrel of the early Allens, the arm remained otherwise unchanged until Forehand & Wadsworth took over its manufacture after Allen's death in 1871. Forehand & Wadsworth's version employed a thicker frame, but in other respects—the sheath trigger, 2½ in. barrel, and .41 rimfire chambering, all representative of single-barreled cartridge derringers—it survived unaltered.[22]

The popularity of cartridge derringers was to endure for many years after the war, and there were enough early indications of this fact to lead a number of new manufacturers into the field. Aside from the well-known Colts and Remingtons, derringers bearing the names Williamson, Southerner, and Ballard reached the market, and all of them found their way west.

Describing the prostitutes in Julesburg in 1867, Henry M. Stanley wrote:

These women are expensive articles, and come in for a large share of the money wasted. In broad daylight they may be seen gliding through the sandy streets in Black Crook dresses, carrying fancy derringers slung to their waists, with which tools they are dangerously expert.

Frontier women of many persuasions liked the little pistols because of their small size and light weight. In her narrative of life at an army post, Elizabeth Custer remarked:

It would be expected that army women would know a great deal about firearms: I knew but few who did. I never even went into the corner of my husband's library where he kept his stand of unloaded arms, if I could help it. . . . One of our ladies, however, had a little of the Molly Pitcher spirit. She had shot at a mark, and she promised to teach us to put in the cartridges and discharge the piece. We were filled with envy because she produced a tiny Rem-

ington pistol that heretofore she had carried in her pocket when traveling in the States. It was not much larger than a lead pencil, and we could not help doubting its power to damage. She did not insist that it would kill, but . . . we had to laugh at the vehement manner in which she declared that she could disable the leg of an enemy.[18]

As Libby Custer implied, Remington's tiny Vest Pocket .22 was just too small to constitute much of a weapon, but by mid-1866 the firm had corrected this situation by marketing a larger pistol. While also called a "Vest Pocket Pistol," the new arm employed the "split-breech" action patented by Joseph Rider in December of 1863 and November of 1864. Initially the gun was chambered for the .30 and .32 rimfire cartridges, but by the spring of 1867, as stocked by Remington's Texas agents, such as Miller & Co. of Galveston and Wexell & DeGress of Brownsville, it was also available in .41 rimfire with a 4 in. barrel.[23]

In this version the split-breech pistol was similar in size to another single-shot arm, the Hammond "Bulldog." The Bulldog's breechblock, resting on a stout longitudinal pivot that joined barrel to stock, swung leftward and downward for loading. Patented in October of 1864 by Henry Hammond and made by the Connecticut Arms & Manufacturing Co., this pistol had one big advantage over the Remington: it chambered the .44 Short rimfire cartridge. (A few samples were even adapted for a .50 rimfire load!) Remington, however, soon had other pocket pistols to offer. By the close of 1868 the firm had introduced at least one and possibly two other .41 rimfire derringers, both somewhat more compact than the Hammond or the split-breech pistol. One of these, a single-barreled arm with parrot-beak butt, patented by the prolific William Elliot in August of 1867, was simplicity itself. The hammer, pivoted at its rear just below the bore axis, also served as the breechblock, while the trigger dou-

Colorado Miner (Georgetown), October 1869.

bled as the extractor. While the little Remington-Elliot never became very popular, the other Remington entry in the cartridge-derringer field, the "Double Repeating Deringer Pistol," became such an overwhelming success that its manufacture continued into the 1930s. The subject of yet another Elliot patent, issued in December of 1865, the Double Deringer had two 3 in. over-under barrels, pivoted at their upper rear to the top of the standing breech; rotating a latch in the frame just below the barrels allowed them to swing upward and backward for loading. This system was hardly novel, and the basis of Elliot's patent was not the barrel arrangement but the firing mechanism. Every time the shooter cocked the hammer, a ratchet wheel raised or lowered the firing pin to discharge the upper or lower barrel alternately, without conscious effort on the shooter's part. When first introduced, presumably in 1868, the Double Deringer had no extractor, but the company soon added a manually operated one; and except for periodic changes in the rifling, the arm underwent no important modifications thereafter. Two other double-barreled derringers contemporary with the Remington, the American Arms

and the Frank Wesson, were both turn-over or swivel-barrel arms, requiring manual rotation of the barrels to fire the second shot; partly because of the extra motions necessary for functioning, neither ever approached the Remington in popularity.[24]

An 1868 advertisement in the Brownsville *Ranchero* by J. Rouede of Matamoros offered "Deringers of the latest paterns," a listing which presumably included the products of such leading manufacturers as Remington, National, and Sharps. Rouede's ad, however, may also have referred to the Williamson, an arm which (like the Southerner and Ballard to follow) could boast distinctive features. Patented in October of 1866, the Williamson had a forward-sliding barrel couched in a wood frame, which gave the gun a strong resemblance to the original percussion Deringer. Appearances aside, however, an eminently practical aspect of this pistol was its steel chamber insert, similar to that used with the early Ballard rifles. When .41 caliber copper cartridges were in short supply, a Williamson equipped with the chamber insert would function as a percussion breechloader.[25]

Made in greater numbers than the Williamson was the Southerner, patented by Charles H. Ballard in April of 1867. First assembled by the Merrimack Arms and Manufacturing Co., and later produced by the Brown Manufacturing Co. (both of which also made the Ballard rifle), the Southerner had a 2½ in. vertically pivoted octagon barrel whose breech end swung to the left for loading. (Other derringers with vertically pivoted barrels, such as the Allen and a new Marlin patented in April of 1870, were designed to open to the right.) Furnished with either a brass or an iron frame, the Southerner proved popular enough to justify a total production of more than 10,000 arms. Like most other cartridge derringers, it was available either plain and unadorned, or embellished with engraving, ivory grips, and the like.[26]

The 1869 Folsom Brothers price list offered the Southerner, the Williamson, and the National in both the all-metal and wood-gripped versions; moreover, the firm handled Allen pocket pistols with 2 in. to 4 in. barrels and Remington vest-pocket pistols. Nearly as varied was the selection advertised in June of that year by William Beck of Portland: Nationals, Southerners, Remingtons, and Allens. On the other hand Alford, Farr & Clapp, advertising in Georgetown's *Colorado Miner* in October of 1869, offered only one make: "'Southerner' Pistols, (Breech-Loading Derringer,) Half Ounce Ball Larger Than Navy."[27]

While Charles Ballard had patented the Southerner, his name did not appear on it, but did appear on another derringer, actually patented by Louis Fairbanks in June of 1869. Made with either a brass or an iron frame, the Ballard was characterized by a 2¹³/₁₆ in. round/octagon barrel, whose breech end swung upward for loading, and by its rack-and-pinion extractor. Despite the fact that Fairbanks had patented it, the Ballard derived its name from the "C. H. Ballard & Co." often stamped on its barrel. At least one Ballard, engraved "M. J. R. Treat/Hays, Kansas," reached the frontier; there were probably others as well. [28]

With several makes of cartridge derringers already on the market and selling well, Colt finally decided to enter the field and in 1870 introduced a bronze-frame model patented by Alexander Thuer in July of that year. Although it had a vertically pivoted barrel, the Colt differed in a number of points from the Allen, Southerner, and Marlin. Its lightweight round barrel was locked in place by the hammer nose instead of by a separate spring-backed catch, and in lieu of a simple mechanical extractor, the Colt offered a strong spring-loaded ejector which threw the fired case clear of the gun. Available in a variety of finishes, the Colt sold so briskly that, like the Remington Double Deringer, it remained in production well past 1900. Colt termed this pistol the "No. 3" to distinguish it from the National No. 1 and No. 2, which Colt continued to offer after taking over the National concern. [29]

Thus by May of 1871, when Nathaniel Curry advertised "every description of breech-loading Derringer Pistols," his stock could have included the Colt-National, Colt No. 3, Ballard, Southerner, Williamson, Allen, Sharps, the single-, double-, and multi-barreled Remingtons, and a few lesser makes. In May of 1874 Leroux & Cosgrove of San Antonio listed "Colts' and a variety of Pocket Deringers," and at about the same time James Bown's Enterprise Gun Works offered Colt, National, and Williamson derringers, plus the Reid "My Friend" pepperbox. Remington's pocket pistols, advertised repeatedly in western newspapers and in the *Army and Navy Journal* during the late 1860s and early 1870s, likewise enjoyed wide distribution. [30]

Getting his first look at the West in 1869, Richard Townshend met a Colorado man who "produced several pistols ranging from a Colt .44 calibre to a derringer, and he showed me how to handle each of them individually." In Texas later the same year, two men tried to arrest John Wesley Hardin:

> When they came, I covered them with a double-barreled shotgun and told them their lives depended on their actions, and unless they obeyed my orders to the letter, I would shoot first one and then the other . . . I made both men . . . lay down their arms. One had a double-barreled gun and two six-shooters; the other had a rifle and two derringers. They complied with my request under the potent

persuasion of my gun levelled first on one and then the other.

Another incident involving a derringer occurred during a fun-filled day in Abilene in June of 1871. According to the Abilene *Chronicle*:

> A shooting affray occurred this morning on First Street, between two men . . . one drew his revolver, and No. 2 remarked 'you know you have the advantage of me.' No. 1 then put back his weapon, whereupon No. 2 drew a Derringer and fired at No. 1, who also managed to draw his six-shooter. Each fired two shots; one was hit in the wrist and the other in the shoulder. . . . Each party violated the law by carrying weapons while in town.

John Wesley Hardin was carrying a derringer when he had a disagreement with a Texas State Policeman in mid-1872: "Spites started to draw a pistol. I pulled a derringer with my left and my six-shooter with my right and instantly fired with my derringer. The dauntless policeman ran to the courthouse. . . ." During a misunderstanding in northeastern Nebraska in the same year, C. W. "Doc" Shores

> pulled a small derringer out of my pocket. I had left my big six-shooter back at camp. [Shortly afterward] two hostile looking men confronted me with long needle rifles . . . realizing that my little derringer was no match for their rifles . . . I rode back to my camp along the Missouri and got my big .45 caliber Sharps rifle, which would help even up the odds.

A reporter for the *Rocky Mountain News*, describing the merchandise in the Freund Brothers' Denver store late in 1872, noted that "the showcases are filled with pistols,—revolvers, single-barrel, Derringers and others." [31]

One of the most dramatic incidents involving derringers occurred in April of 1873, during a peace conference between General E. R. S. Canby and Captain Jack, a Modoc chief. Just before the conference former Indian agent A. B. Meacham (writing of himself in the third person) received a life-saving gift:

> A man passes close to Meacham and drops something in a side pocket of his coat. His hand grasps it, and his face indicates hesitation. The other says, in a low tone, "It's sure fire;—it's all right." 'Tis a small Derringer pistol, and it is not thrown out of the pocket. [Leroy S.] Dyar caught sight of this little manoeuvre, and he goes into his tent and quickly slips a Derringer into *his* pocket.

At the conference Meacham felt uneasy, a feeling that proved justified when Captain Jack suddenly jerked out a revolver and shot General Canby through the head. Meacham vividly described what followed: "Two

Missouri Democrat (St. Louis), May 1865.

men are running. The foremost one is Dyar, and following him is Hooker Jim, who fires repeatedly at Dyar, who turns, and pointing his pistol, [causes] Jim [to drop] to avoid the shot." Schonchin, the Modoc opposite Meacham, whipped out a concealed revolver:

> Meacham draws his derringer, and pushing the muzzle squarely against the heart of Schonchin, pulls the trigger, but, alas! it does not fire . . . it is but *half-cocked* . . . the ball from Schonchin's pistol tears through the collar of [Meacham's] coat, vest, and shirt . . . [Schonchin] continues the attack, but dare not close on the Derringer still in the hands of Meacham . . . Meacham now fires at Schonchin, who leaps up and falls on the rocks, wounded.[32]

EVADING THE SMITH & WESSON DESIGN: FRONT- AND SIDE-LOADING CARTRIDGE REVOLVERS

As Meacham's account showed, a derringer could be a handy tool under certain circumstances. Obviously, however, it was not suitable for all-around use; a well-made .41 cartridge derringer could prove reasonably accurate against a man-size target up to 15 yards or so, but its little rimfire load, containing only 10 to 13 grains of powder, had little power at that range. On the other hand, a well-made .38 or .44 revolver might shoot accurately at 50 yards or more, and demonstrate ample power at that distance. But because of Rollin White's patent, there were comparatively few large-caliber metallic-cartridge revolvers available in the West until after 1869. Those that

did reach the frontier before that included the .38 rimfire Bacons and Prescotts sold in St. Louis during the war, foreign-made revolvers, such as the Le-Faucheux, that had survived the war, and perhaps most prominent, examples of a commercially successful evasion of White's patent: the .42 caliber Plant. Evidently this revolver and its small .28 caliber counterpart (their barrels stamped either "Plant's Mfg. Co." or "Eagle Arms Co.") were fairly common in the West during the late 1860s. The larger model offered the advantage of an interchangeable percussion cylinder, for use when the special front-loading cup-primer cartridges were unavailable.[33]

Curiously, William F. Hardy of Prescott, Arizona, did not mention this feature when he advertised the Plants in March of 1866. Nor did J. Miller & Co. of Galveston, who offered the guns at about the same time. Merwin and Bray, however, were more careful; their advertisement for these guns in the Central City *Miners' Register* in June of 1866 noted that "the Eagle Pistols, now so well known, are an indispensable accompaniment to all travelers, tourists, and sportsmen. Both the Ballard Rifle and Eagle Pistol, *belt size*, can be loaded with *loose ammunition*, if desirable." Merwin & Simpkins, successors to Merwin & Bray, were still advertising "Eagle Arms Co.'s front-loading cartridge Pistols—Navy and Pocket Sizes" in March of 1867, but thereafter they apparently devoted more attention to the pocket-size arm. William Beck of Portland advertised the Eagle in 1869, the year White's patent expired.[34]

Beck's advertisement also mentioned the National, another front-loading metallic-cartridge revolver which, although marketed almost exclusively as a pocket-size .32 caliber arm, rivaled the Plant-Eagles in popularity. Shortly before it sold out to Colt, National made a handful of solid-frame .45 caliber revolvers which took the same type of teat-fire cartridge as the smaller guns; when Schuyler, Hartley & Graham offered "National Revolvers" in the *Galveston News* in May of 1869, they may have been referring to the big .45s as well as the little .32s. As was the case with the pocket-size Plants, the National .32s remained in use well after the expiration of the White patent, and the major arms suppliers continued offering the cup-primer and teat-fire cartridges for these guns well into the 1880s. Evidently the cup-primer loads for the large-frame Plant were more scarce, but a skillful gunsmith could, without much trouble, bore through the chambers of a Plant cylinder and adapt them to the common .41 rimfire round.[35]

Another revolver occasionally converted to handle standard rimfire ammunition was the Allen lipfire. Small quantities of discharged lipfire cartridge cases found at isolated points in the West indicate that the

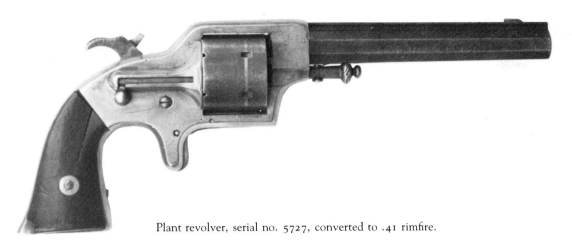

Plant revolver, serial no. 5727, converted to .41 rimfire.

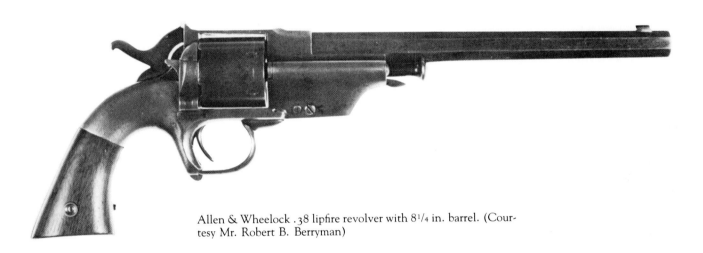

Allen & Wheelock .38 lipfire revolver with 8¼ in. barrel. (Courtesy Mr. Robert B. Berryman)

"Slocum's [sic] Patent Side-Loading revolver," as T. J. Albright advertised it in the *Missouri Democrat* in January of 1865, "can be loaded in the dark, and quicker than any other pistol." (Courtesy Mr. E. Lee Manning, Jr.)

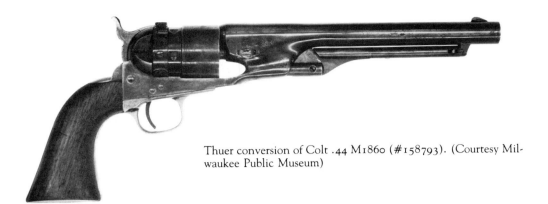

Thuer conversion of Colt .44 M1860 (#158793). (Courtesy Milwaukee Public Museum)

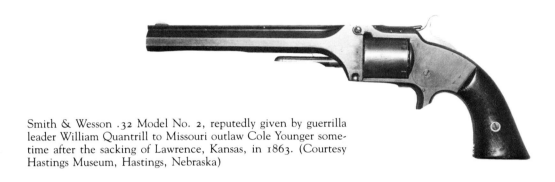

Smith & Wesson .32 Model No. 2, reputedly given by guerrilla leader William Quantrill to Missouri outlaw Cole Younger sometime after the sacking of Lawrence, Kansas, in 1863. (Courtesy Hastings Museum, Hastings, Nebraska)

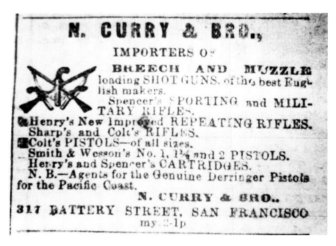

Alta California (San Francisco), July 1867.

guns saw some use on the frontier in their original state; but at least one example, converted from .38 lipfire to .38 rimfire, was carried by Colorado lawman James Clark until his death in Telluride in the 1890s.[36]

An evasion of the Rollin White patent that needed no alteration was the Slocum sliding-sleeve revolver, designed to take standard .32 rimfire cartridges. The Folsom concern still carried "Slocomb" revolvers in 1869, and, presumably, so did T. J. Albright, who had advertised them in 1865. Because it took readily available ammunition, the Slocum probably stayed in active service even longer than the Plant and the National.[37]

Much shorter lived and far less popular than these three guns was a fourth attempt to evade White's patent, the Colt Thuer revolver. Late in 1866 Alexander Thuer began working on a method to convert the ordinary percussion Colt to a front-loading cartridge arm, and after numerous experiments he finally patented his design in September of 1868. Thuer's alteration comprised two new components—a short cylinder and, mounted behind it on the cylinder pin, a rotating conversion ring which carried the firing pin and a crescent-shaped two-piece ejector lever. After slipping the slightly tapered metallic cartridges into

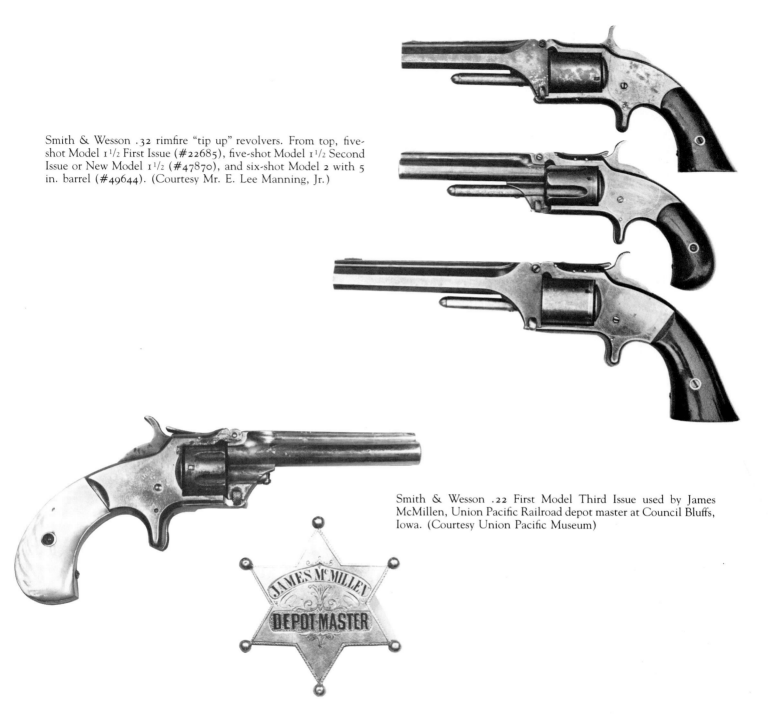

Smith & Wesson .32 rimfire "tip up" revolvers. From top, five-shot Model 1½ First Issue (#22685), five-shot Model 1½ Second Issue or New Model 1½ (#47870), and six-shot Model 2 with 5 in. barrel (#49644). (Courtesy Mr. E. Lee Manning, Jr.)

Smith & Wesson .22 First Model Third Issue used by James McMillen, Union Pacific Railroad depot master at Council Bluffs, Iowa. (Courtesy Union Pacific Museum)

the cylinder from the front, the shooter seated them firmly in the chambers with the help of the loading lever. Once all six rounds were fired, the shooter half-cocked the arm and rotated the conversion ring from right to left, thereby bringing one end of the ejector lever opposite the hammer nose; cocking and snapping the hammer then forcibly ejected each fired case to the front, as its chamber came into position to the right of the barrel. The cartridge cases were reloadable by means of special tools, but if the Thuer cartridges were unavailable, the shooter could readily remove the cylinder and conversion ring and substitute "an interchangeable nipple cylinder . . . which can then

be loaded with loose powder and ball, a matter of so much importance in countries where made-up ammunition is not easily procurable."[38]

Thuer's system was cleverly worked out, and probably could have given a good account of itself commercially except for the fact that it reached the market only a few months before White's patent expired. Partly because of this and partly because of the special cartridges required, very few Thuer Colts were sold. Those that did reach the market were based principally on the 1851 and 1861 Navy and the 1860 Army models. In spite of the limited quantity, however, a few Thuers may have gone west; Schuyler, Hartley & Graham's advertisement in the *Galveston News* in May of 1869 specifically listed "Colt's Revolving Pistols and Rifles; also, Colt's Metallic Cartridge Revolvers." In view of the date these were almost certainly Thuer Colts. Although Schuyler, Hartley & Graham was based in New York, the frontiersman's high regard for Colts and the obvious advantages of the metallic cartridge may well have prompted Texas dealers to order a few samples as a result of this ad.[39]

Besides the legally marketed Thuer Colts there were a few Colt conversions available prior to 1869 which chambered conventional ammunition. Writing of the Colt percussion revolver in 1868, a cavalry colonel added that "there is a modification of this pistol, which is loaded by taking the cylinder out and dropping the six cartridges from the rear into the chambers, and then the cylinder is returned to its place and fastened in." This rear-loaded alteration was obviously illegal, and very few examples of it materialized.[40]

In all probability Horace Smith and Daniel Wesson viewed these occasional, piecemeal conversions with little concern. What really concerned them was the prospect of large-scale production of revolvers with bored-through chambers; because of this the partners tried vigorously, but unsuccessfully, to get an extension of the White patent. Even without the extension, however, they remained dominant in the cartridge-revolver field for several years after the patent lapsed. The second version of the little brass-frame seven-shot .22 caliber "No. 1," introduced in 1860, and the bigger iron-frame six-shot .32-caliber "No. 2" of 1861, stayed in production until 1868 and 1871 respectively, and both enjoyed widespread distribution in the West. When William Dixon and a companion were in Leavenworth in 1866, they were

> but slightly armed with Colts, since we have all along been dreaming that if any fighting is to be done, it will be the work of our gallant escort, riding by our sides in defence of the Imperial Mail . . . [however,] we are the only passengers booked for the trip [to Salt Lake]; so that the number of revolvers coming into play, in case of a scrimmage with the Cheyennes and Comanches, in aid of the military escort, seems to be reduced to two. All our acquaintance[s] in this city urge us to get more and better arms; a suggestion in which the mail-agents cordially agree. The new arm of the west, called a Smith-and-Weston, is a pretty tool; as neat a machine for throwing slugs into a man's flesh as an artist in murder could desire to see. . . . [So] we buy a couple of these Smith-and-Westons, and then pay our fare of five hundred dollars to Salt Lake.

In the Rockies later that year Andrew Fisk traded a "large sized Wesson revolver" to his brother Van for a small "seven shooter" of the same make. Unlike the Nos. 1 and 2, the small five-shot .32 caliber "No. 1½," with cylinder bolt in the bottomstrap, brought out in 1865, did not prove very popular. Late in 1868 the company replaced it with a "New Model 1½," which had a round instead of an octagon barrel, a fluted instead of a plain cylinder, and a parrot-beak instead of a square butt. In addition, the cylinder bolt was relocated in the topstrap. (Near the start of production Smith & Wesson found that it had some octagon barrels left over from the manufacture of the old model 1½; the company consequently installed these barrels and old-style unfluted cylinders on New Model 1½ frames, to form a "transition model 1½." Only a few were made and it is questionable whether any reached the West.) With the New Model 1½ came a new look-alike seven-shot .22, distinguished by the same round barrel, fluted cylinder, and parrot-beak butt.[41]

Despite its small caliber this gun, as well as the Model 1½ in both its old and new versions, reached the frontier in some quantity. Advertisements by some dealers were specific; from 1867 through 1870, for example, Nathaniel Curry of San Francisco offered "Smith & Wesson's No. 1, 1½, and 2 Pistols." Other dealers—and there were many of them—listed only "Smith & Wesson" arms, but probably sold all the standard versions available. While he was on the Kansas plains in 1872, Henry Raymond "traded my two pistols [to] Joe for his Smith & Wesson No. 2, and $4.00 to boot." The following year, during a stagecoach trip from Fairplay to Denver, Major J. B. Thompson carried "a 32 Smith & Wesson pistol, with which I could, at that time, hit the size of a dollar every time at forty feet."[42]

LARGE-FRAME RIMFIRE AND CENTERFIRE REVOLVERS: SMITH & WESSON, REMINGTON, AND COLT

The new Nos. 1 and 1½ sold briskly, as did the older No. 2, but until 1870 all the production arms offered by Smith & Wesson were either in .22 or .32 caliber. (An experimental four-shot .41 rimfire revolver assembled in 1867 never went into production.) On the plains, of course, a large-caliber handgun could be a definite asset. Smith and Wesson were well aware of this, but before they were ready to market such a gun, they licensed one of their major competitors, Remington, to do so. In February of 1868 the two firms concluded an agreement whereby Remington would convert some 4500 of its .44 percussion revolvers to rimfire arms by the installation of new five-shot cylinders, chambered for a short .46 caliber cartridge. Most of the conversion work took place between September of 1868 and April of 1869, with

Remington New Model Army, fitted with a five-shot cylinder chambered for .46 rimfire cartridges. The cylinder bears the Rollin White patent date for the patent on bored-through chambers.

the bulk of the altered revolvers going to Benjamin Kittredge of Cincinnati. At least one, however, went to Wexell and DeGress, who had an office in Brownsville, Texas, and some of those which Kittredge acquired may have found their way farther west.[43]

Remington made much wider use of an alternate conversion method, one which evidently did not require the payment of royalties to Smith & Wesson. Using its .31 and .36 caliber percussion revolvers as a base, Remington began manufacturing new cylinders with bored-through chambers for them; the rear face of the new cylinder, however, was covered by a readily detachable steel cap which carried the ratchet teeth. To load, the shooter had to remove the cylinder from the gun, slip off the cap, insert the requisite number of .32 or .38 rimfire cartridges, replace the cap, and again install the cylinder in the gun; but this process could be carried out almost as quickly as loading a Smith & Wesson. Moreover, the Remington revolver had the advantage of a solid instead of a hinged frame.

Apparently Frank D. Bliss of New Haven had first devised this detachable-cap idea, using it on the tiny .25 rimfire revolvers he made in the early 1860s. The year Remington initially marketed handguns employ-

Remington factory conversion of a .36 New Model Police revolver to fire .38 metallic ammunition. The gun was once the property of the U.S. Express Company and is so marked on the frame. (Courtesy Mr. E. Lee Manning, Jr.)

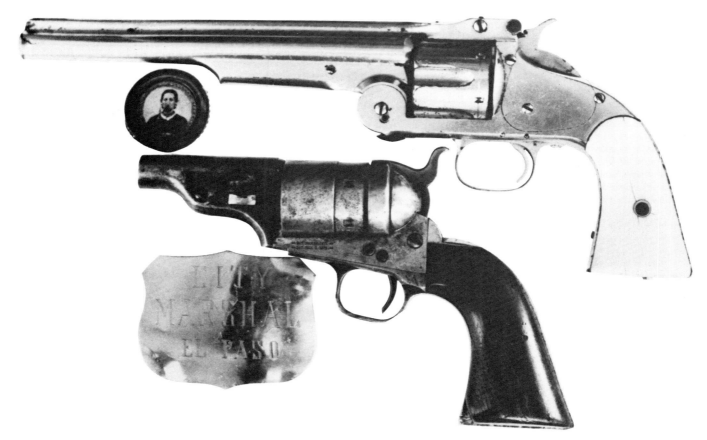

Dallas Stoudenmire's city marshal badge, Smith & Wesson .44 American (#7056) at top, Colt M1860 .44 converted to fire metallic cartridges by the Richards-Mason system, and a picture he had in his pocket at the time he was fatally shot in 1882 in El Paso, Texas. The rare Richards-Mason conversion of the Colt

M1860 utilized a new barrel and a redesigned ejector housing. In addition, the separate firing pin used in the standard Richards conversion was replaced by a pin mounted in the hammer nose. (Courtesy Mr. Robert E. McNellis, Jr.)

ing this design is uncertain, but it may have been as early as 1868. A big advantage of this system was that a revolver thus modified would still accept an inter-changeable percussion cylinder. It may have been one of the .38 caliber models that Henry Ailman acquired in Colorado in March of 1871, in preparation for a mining expedition into New Mexico: "After paying my fee, I was furnished with a Winchester rifle, a Remington revolver, a cartridge belt and ammunition, a long Bowie knife, and a knife and pistol holster."[44]

Smith & Wesson offered no interchangeable per-cussion cylinders, but in the fall of 1870 (at about the same time that powerful single-shot rifles were rising to prominence in the West), the firm began marketing a new .44 caliber centerfire cartridge revolver that would soon become a frontier favorite. Approved by the St. Louis Ordnance board in June of 1870, the new .44, officially termed the "No. 3" but later called the "American," offered significant advantages over

Smith & Wesson's earlier guns. Aside from caliber, the major differences were a hinged-frame design far sturdier than that used for previous arms, and an au-tomatic extractor, which threw out all the fired cases simultaneously when the shooter broke the gun open for reloading. The single-action lockwork was similar to that in earlier guns, except for the hammer-acti-vated cylinder bolt housed within the frame.[45]

Before production stopped in 1874, the American underwent several modifications. After the manufac-ture of about 6500 arms, a notched hammer which interlocked with the barrel catch was added; after the completion of about 19,000 guns, the cylinder bolt was changed from a hammer-activated to a trigger-activated type. Other features, such as the 8 in. barrel and the fluted six-shot cylinder, remained standard. On special order, however, the revolver was available with shorter barrels, butt swivels, and later, detachable shoulder stocks. A few were also ordered chambered

John King Fisher (left) and John H. Culp pose for their tintype portrait in 1873. The former's revolver is indistinct, but Culp carries a Smith & Wesson .44 No. 3 or first-model Russian. (Courtesy Western History Collections, University of Oklahoma Library)

Alford Day, a Texas cowboy, from an old tintype. One revolver is a Smith & Wesson .44 No. 3 or a first-model Russian, while the other appears to be a Colt Single Action. (Courtesy Western History Collections, University of Oklahoma Library)

A Smith & Wesson No. 3, with serial number in the 5300 range, which belonged to Gen. William J. Palmer, builder of the Denver and Rio Grande Railroad. The gun is nickel-plated with sports checkered ivory grips. Wyatt Earp reportedly used an engraved Smith & Wesson .44 No. 3 during the famed gunfight outside the O.K. Corral in 1881. It was a gift from Tombstone *Epitaph* editor John Clum. (Courtesy Colorado Springs Pioneers' Museum)

Moose Camp in Teton Canon, Wyoming, in 1872. The man seated at the base of the tree has an S&W American or a first-model Russian revolver holstered beside him, while his companion lean-ing against the tree holds a .50-70 Springfield rifle. A Frank Wesson single-shot rifle rests against the tree in front of the tent at right. (U.S. Geological Survey photo, courtesy National Archives)

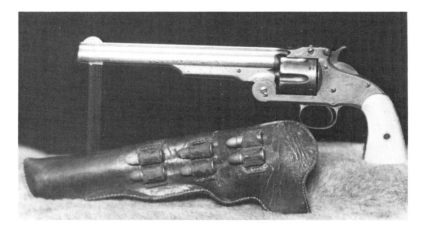

Ivory-gripped S&W first-model or "Old Old Model" Russian .44 (#25274). The gun is one used by John Wesley Hardin to kill Deputy Sheriff Charley Webb in 1874 in Comanche, Texas. The "slim Jim" style of contoured holster is fitted with loops for six extra .44 cartridges. (Courtesy Mr. John Wilson)

The popularity of the S&W .44 No. 3 size revolvers in the West in the early 1870s is reflected by the frequency with which these arms can be seen, as in this view taken by William H. Jackson. The shoulder arms include three Springfield M1873 rifles and a Sharps carbine across the subject's lap. (U.S. Geological Survey photo, courtesy National Archives)

for the .44 rimfire cartridge instead of the centerfire American load.[46]

A major variation of the American model appeared in May of 1871, when the Russian government contracted for 20,000 to be chambered for a new centerfire cartridge, the .44 Russian, which had a slightly longer case and a somewhat heavier bullet than the American load. When Grand Duke Alexis visited the Smith & Wesson factory in December of 1871 to witness the production of revolvers there for his government, the company presented him with a handsomely engraved and cased No. 3 which had cost $400 to produce. The Grand Duke later used this gun on a western buffalo hunt organized for his benefit, a hunt which included Buffalo Bill Cody among the participants.[47]

Only the new cartridge and the barrel markings distinguished the first "Russian model" from the American model. But the cartridge was an excellent one, and after the company completed the Russian contract in the fall of 1872, it put some of the Russian models on the commercial market, where they found a ready

acceptance. As on the American, an 8 in. barrel was standard; however, the Russian was also available with handier barrels of 6 in. and 7 in.[48]

From the time it first reached the market the No. 3 sold well. Smith & Wesson had completed only a few hundred by the close of 1870, but more than 6500 left the factory the following year. By mid-May of 1871 Nathaniel Curry of San Francisco was advertising "Smith & Wesson's No. 1, 1½, 2 and 3 Pistols," and other western dealers, such as Carlos Gove of Denver, took delivery of the No. 3 at about the same time. One American made in 1871, plated and with checkered ivory grips, went to General William J. Palmer, builder of the Denver and Rio Grande Railroad. Two other nickel-plated samples found their way to Nathaniel P. Langford, first superintendent of Yellowstone National Park, and to western artist Thomas Moran. Another became the property of Texas Jack Omohundro, who had his name engraved in the sideplate. A fifth American was presented in April of 1873 to George Chittenden, a member of the U.S. Geological Survey party.[49]

N. CURRY & BRO.,

No. 118 Sansome St., between Pine and Bush.

IMPORTERS OF BREECH and muzzle-loading SHOT GUNS, of every description; Spencer's SPORTING AND MILITARY RIFLES; Winchester and Remington's new improved REPEATING RIFLES; Sharp's REPEATING RIFLES; Colt's PISTOL'S—of all sizes; every description of breech-loading DERRINGER PISTOLS; Smith & Wesson's No. 1, 1½, 2 and 3 PISTOLS; METALLIC CARTRIDGES of every description.

N. B.—Sole Agents for the Genuine Derringer Pistols for the Pacific Coast.   my14-1p

Alta California (San Francisco), May 1871.

Sales continued to be brisk. In March of 1873 Nathaniel Curry ordered "100 S&W #3 Army Pistols Wood Blued" and another 25 "wood and plated" if he could get the plated guns for less than $17 each. A. J. Plate, Curry's local competitor, wrote the factory a month later to request the lowest possible prices on Smith & Wessons, noting that he had "succeeded somewhat in establishing them as the leading pistol on this coast so that my sales now reach some 300 per month, mostly #3, and the principal market Mexico on account of the political disturbances there." In July of 1873 George Wilson, a bank president in Lexington, Missouri, wrote the factory to order

one of your Army Revolvers (No. 3). The pistol you sent me was *nickel plated* cost $17.00 and can't be excelled: it had the notch in the hammer to hold down the latch. . . . Please send at once, one of my sons will start for the Rocky Mountains in a few days and wants one of your revolvers. Another son has been there several years, an Army Contractor, and [is] now getting out timber for Union Pacific R.R. he is a first rate hunter. They think there are no pistols equal to yours, to use where they find deer and bear every day.

A Colt .44 1st Model Richards conversion of the M1860, its barrel shortened from 8 inches to 5 inches. The gun and holster were found beneath the mattress following the death of an elderly New Mexico rancher. He had served as a peace officer in the 1890s near Socorro, New Mexico. The so-called Mexican loop style holster in its various forms was popular throughout the West in the 1880s and after, although this example with its short skirt is not typical. (Photo by Mr. Richard K. Halter, courtesy Mr. Willis E. Neuwirth)

Described in the caption accompanying an old print as New Mexico cattle rustlers in the late 1870s, this trio is armed with a Winchester M1873 carbine and a pair of Richards conversions of the Colt M1860 .44. (Courtesy Museum of New Mexico)

In a letter to the company written at about the same time, a Colorado resident commented:

> I have one of your 32s that uses a Rim fire. Please let me know what a Revolver will cost (no. 44) that will use a 44 Rim Fire Winchester Cartridge. As I use a Rim fire Winchester Rifle I would like to have one of your 44 Pistols that would fire the same cartridge as carrying two sizes of or Kinds of cartridges in this Indian country is a nonsense.[50]

Despite its limited availability, the Russian version of the #3 also became fairly popular because of the more potent round it chambered. Russell & Swink, merchants of Rocky Ford, Colorado, ordered a quantity in February of 1873, and five months later one J. W. Carroll wrote the factory from Green River, Wyoming Territory, to order "one pair of your Revolvers .44 cal. Russian Model together with accoutrements complete—500 cartridges and 2000 caps." In October of 1873 an army officer at Fort Bridger requested a Russian with 6 in. barrel, because his 8 in. revolver punched his horse in the back when he was in the saddle with the gun in his belt.[51]

Neither Colt nor Remington could offer their customers anything as mechanically advanced as Smith & Wesson's #3. But by the fall of 1871 Colt could at least market a metallic-cartridge revolver of like caliber, by converting its large-frame guns to chamber conventional centerfire loads. The method used for conversion was developed by C. B. Richards and applied to several different models, but probably became best known as applied to the 1860 Army. Colt successfully offered the .44 Richards conversion to the

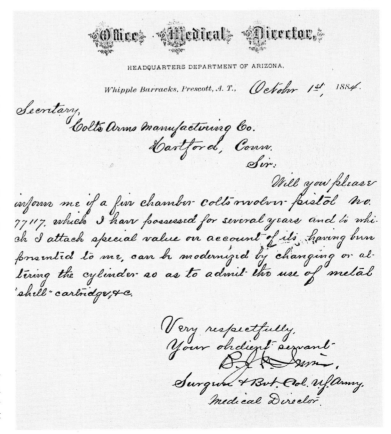

As late as 1884, army surgeon B. J. Irwin wrote to the Colt factory from Arizona Territory inquiring about converting his percussion Colt to fire metallic ammunition. The serial number of his five-shot revolver indicates it was a percussion .31 M1849 Pocket Model. (Courtesy Connecticut State Library)

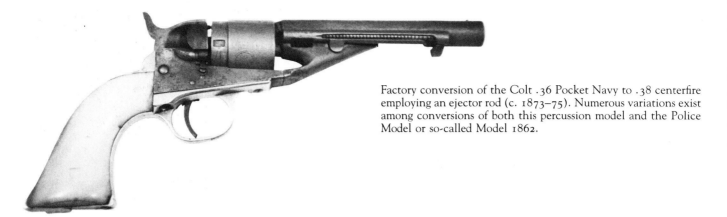

Factory conversion of the Colt .36 Pocket Navy to .38 centerfire employing an ejector rod (c. 1873–75). Numerous variations exist among conversions of both this percussion model and the Police Model or so-called Model 1862.

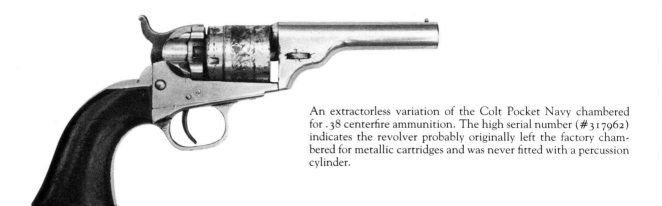

An extractorless variation of the Colt Pocket Navy chambered for .38 centerfire ammunition. The high serial number (#317962) indicates the revolver probably originally left the factory chambered for metallic cartridges and was never fitted with a percussion cylinder.

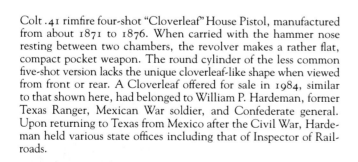

Colt .41 rimfire four-shot "Cloverleaf" House Pistol, manufactured from about 1871 to 1876. When carried with the hammer nose resting between two chambers, the revolver makes a rather flat, compact pocket weapon. The round cylinder of the less common five-shot version lacks the unique cloverleaf-like shape when viewed from front or rear. A Cloverleaf offered for sale in 1984, similar to that shown here, had belonged to William P. Hardeman, former Texas Ranger, Mexican War soldier, and Confederate general. Upon returning to Texas from Mexico after the Civil War, Hardeman held various state offices including that of Inspector of Railroads.

Ordnance Department in January of 1871, and months later started selling it commercially. With its simple loading gate and rod ejector, the Colt conversion was notably slower to reload than the Smith & Wesson, but it was also several dollars cheaper. In 1872, for example, Colt advertised the .44 Richards for $16, and a Richards alteration of the .36 Navy Colt to .38 rimfire for $15. The Smith & Wesson No. 3, on the other hand, could cost from $18 to $20.[52]

Besides converting the 1860 Army and the 1851 and 1861 Navy revolvers, the factory also altered its Police and .36 caliber pocket models to .38 cartridge arms. On an individual basis other models—including at least one Paterson—were converted, either by the factory or by local gunsmiths. But Colt did not depend on conversions alone for continued sales. In 1871 the company introduced a newly designed cartridge revolver, the .41 rimfire "House Pistol"; in cross section, its deeply fluted four-shot cylinder resembled a clover-leaf. C. B. Richards patented this arm in September of 1871, but it was probably on the market several months before that. Its sheath trigger, parrot-beak butt, and solid frame of brass were hardly noteworthy, but the gun did incorporate some desirable mechanical features. Its pawl had two bearing surfaces (as did the pawl used in the Richards conversions), and there was a bushing between cylinder and cylinder pin to ensure easy rotation. Although later offered with a round five-shot cylinder and a barrel as short as 1½ in., the Cloverleaf Colt never became overly popular.[53]

Appearing at about the same time as the Cloverleaf, but made in greater numbers, was a seven-shot .22 with open-top frame and readily detachable barrel. Like all Colt products the little .22 went to dealers on the frontier, but because of the availability of large-caliber cartridge revolvers, westerners were developing a prejudice against handguns as small as .22 caliber. Far better suited for the West was Colt's big .44 rimfire "open-top Army" revolver, assembled late in 1872. While its major components were newly manufactured, this arm was constructed like the company's earlier percussion revolvers: its frame had no topstrap, and the barrel was held to the elongated cylinder pin by a wedge. In appearance the gun strongly resembled the standard Richards conversion.[54]

Prior to 1873 all of Colt's big-bore revolvers were characterized by their open-top frames, a fact made much of by Remington. Evidently the simple Remington conversions, employing new cylinders with detachable caps at the rear, sold well, even though they required removal of the cylinder for loading. But about

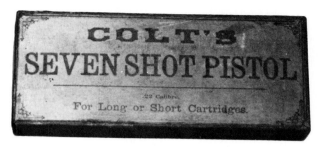

Colt Open Top Pocket Model .22, identified on the original box label as "Colt's Seven Shot Pistol." (Courtesy Mr. E. Lee Manning, Jr.)

1872 the firm introduced its "Improved Army" and "Improved Navy" revolvers. These were also conversions, with the added advantage of a loading gate behind the cylinder and a rod ejector ahead of it, which allowed loading and reloading without removing the cylinder. Undoubtedly referring by implication

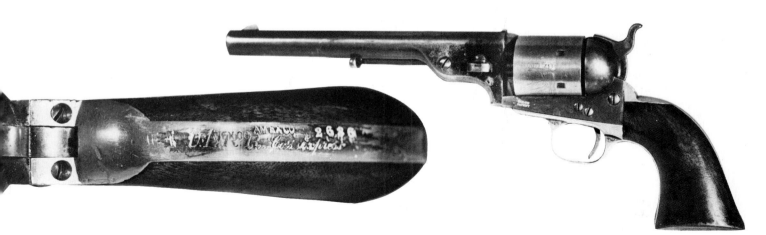

Colt .44 Model 1872 "Open Top," immediate predecessor of the solid-frame Single Action or "Model P." The original Union Pacific Railroad Company's Express marking on the backstrap was later overstamped with American Express Company stampings, indicating usage by both firms. (Courtesy Mr. Willis E. Neuwirth)

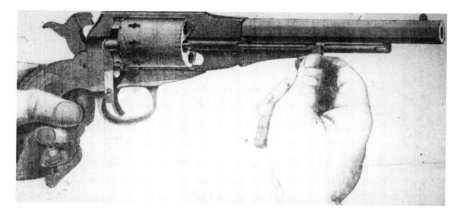

Cut from an ad in the *Army and Navy Journal* for January 25, 1873, illustrating a Remington New Model Navy fitted with a one-piece cylinder bored through to accept metallic cartridges. Many such Remingtons sold in the 1870s were not actual conversions from percussion, but originally left the factory as metallic-cartridge arms, either with or without an ejector.

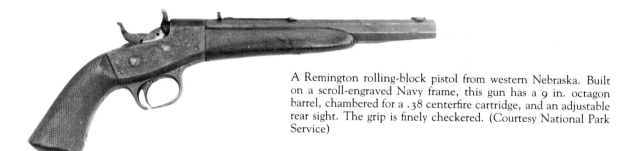

A Remington rolling-block pistol from western Nebraska. Built on a scroll-engraved Navy frame, this gun has a 9 in. octagon barrel, chambered for a .38 centerfire cartridge, and an adjustable rear sight. The grip is finely checkered. (Courtesy National Park Service)

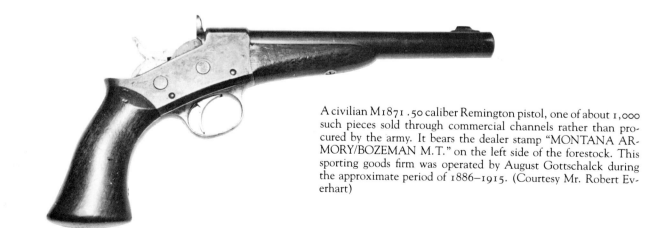

A civilian M1871 .50 caliber Remington pistol, one of about 1,000 such pieces sold through commercial channels rather than procured by the army. It bears the dealer stamp "MONTANA ARMORY/BOZEMAN M.T." on the left side of the forestock. This sporting goods firm was operated by August Gottschalck during the approximate period of 1886–1915. (Courtesy Mr. Robert Everhart)

to both the Colt and the Smith & Wesson, a Remington advertisement for the Improved Navy in the *Army and Navy Journal* in January of 1873 noted pointedly that:

> The Remington Navy Revolver in its design is perhaps the strongest weapon of its type, having no hinges, as its frame is constituted of a single piece of metal. The present improvement, it is worth noting, has been secured without deviating from the original strength or simplicity of the arm. . . .

Remington also offered another rugged metallic-cartridge handgun at this time, one with a genuinely big bore: the .50 caliber single-shot rolling-block pistol. The firm supplied this arm to the civilian market in two slightly different versions, the Navy Model of 1870 and the saw-handled Army Model of 1871. Either version boasted the same advantages as a good single-shot rifle: simplicity, reliability, and the use of a powerful cartridge. In this instance the cartridge was a .50 caliber centerfire load with a 320-grain bullet, backed by a 30-grain powder charge.[55]

Even as advertisements for these pistols appeared, however, the Colt factory was beginning to tool up for the production of the most famous of all handguns in the postwar West—the Single Action Army revolver. Official Ordnance Department approval of this weapon in December of 1872, and the resultant army order for 8000 in July of 1873, precluded widespread commercial distribution until the spring of 1874. (A few hundred civilian models did leave the factory late in 1873, but most of these went to Schuyler, Hartley & Graham in New York.) With its solid frame, mechanical refinements, and good handling qualities, the new single-action was in demand from the moment it reached the market. Because of the army orders, the gun was initially available chambered only for the .45 Colt centerfire cartridge, and only with a 7½ in. barrel, but this did not deter eager purchasers.[56]

Despite the immediate popularity, some time passed before the new Colt displaced the .44 Richards conversions and open-top models of 1872; both the older guns continued to be available from the factory through the mid-1870s. In fact, manufacture of the open-top 1872 persisted until 1876. Carlos Gove's advertisement in February of 1874 for "Colt's New Cartridge Revolvers, [Colt's] Winchester Army Pistols, [Colt's] Central Fire Army Pistols, and [Colt's] Pocket, House, and Police [Pistols]" undoubtedly referred to both the Richards and the open-top 1872, and may even have included the new Single Action Army. Other western dealers such as Freund sold the 1872, and the Union Pacific Railroad procured an undetermined quantity to arm its employees.[57]

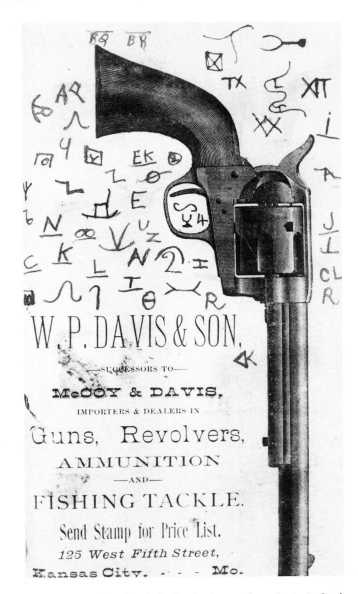

Advertisement for the Colt Single Action from *Loving's Stock Manual*, published in Ft. Worth, Texas, in 1881. The cattle brands were penciled in by the manual's original owner. (Courtesy Western History Department, Denver Public Library)

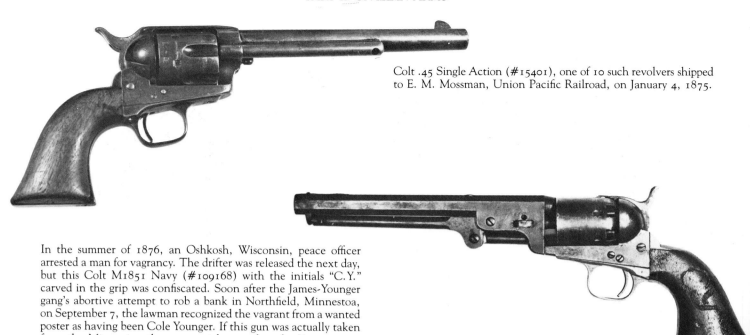

Colt .45 Single Action (#15401), one of 10 such revolvers shipped to E. M. Mossman, Union Pacific Railroad, on January 4, 1875.

In the summer of 1876, an Oshkosh, Wisconsin, peace officer arrested a man for vagrancy. The drifter was released the next day, but this Colt M1851 Navy (#109168) with the initials "C.Y." carved in the grip was confiscated. Soon after the James-Younger gang's abortive attempt to rob a bank in Northfield, Minnestoa, on September 7, the lawman recognized the vagrant from a wanted poster as having been Cole Younger. If this gun was actually taken from the Missouri outlaw, one might wonder why Younger was armed with an obsolescent percussion revolver at the time, rather than a Colt Single Action he was known to own. (Courtesy Oshkosh Public Museum)

Colt Single Action with 16 in. barrel and detachable shoulder stock, the so-called Buntline Special. Single Actions with barrels longer than 7½ inches were available on special order, and some were bought by western dealers. But the often-repeated tale of dime novelist E. Z. C. "Ned Buntline" Judson's presentation of six such revolvers to Wyatt Earp and other Dodge City lawmen appears to have no basis in fact. Colt factory records fail to substantiate such a tale, and the only source is the highly questionable Earp biography written by Stuart N. Lake. (Courtesy Mr. Harry C. Knode)

A unique photo showing a Colt Single Action with detachable shoulder stock and possibly a 16 in. barrel. Unfortunately nothing is known about the individuals pictured or where the photo was taken. (Courtesy Mr. Richard M. Heuer)

One of the unsung heroes of frontier history, the beast of burden, surrounded by Arizona prospectors armed with Colt Single Actions. (Courtesy Southern Pacific Transportation Co.)

Chow time at the chuckwagon. The cowboy at right may be eating a piece of dried apple pie, a perennial favorite with trail hands. He wears his ivory-handled Colt Single Action butt forward. (Courtesy Montana Historical Society)

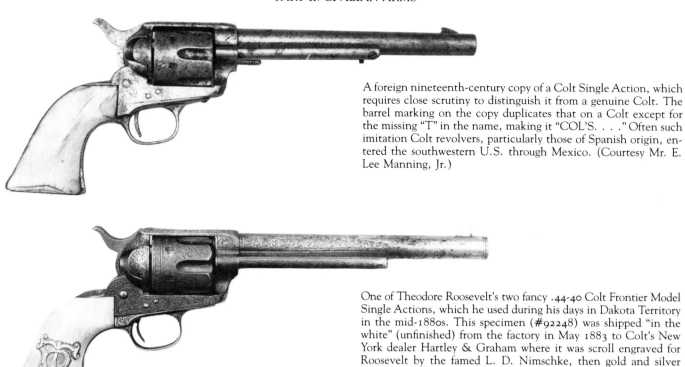

A foreign nineteenth-century copy of a Colt Single Action, which requires close scrutiny to distinguish it from a genuine Colt. The barrel marking on the copy duplicates that on a Colt except for the missing "T" in the name, making it "COL'S. . . ." Often such imitation Colt revolvers, particularly those of Spanish origin, entered the southwestern U.S. through Mexico. (Courtesy Mr. E. Lee Manning, Jr.)

One of Theodore Roosevelt's two fancy .44-40 Colt Frontier Model Single Actions, which he used during his days in Dakota Territory in the mid-1880s. This specimen (#92248) was shipped "in the white" (unfinished) from the factory in May 1883 to Colt's New York dealer Hartley & Graham where it was scroll engraved for Roosevelt by the famed L. D. Nimschke, then gold and silver plated, and the carved ivory grip fitted. One side of the grip has the "TR" monogram and the other a bison head. His other .44 (#92267) was shipped to Hartley & Graham in June 1883 where it was engraved but fitted with pearl grips with the future president's name in script on the right grip. (From Theodore Roosevelt Collection, courtesy Harvard College Library)

Colt Single Action .44-40 (frame #42870) modified for fast close range shooting by fanning the hammer. The original backstrap and trigger guard were replaced with those from a Colt M1872 .44 "Open Top," and the cylinder is held in place by a special base pin secured with a thumb screw. The trigger has been removed and the trigger slot welded closed with most of the guard discarded. The barrel has been cut to only 3 inches. The weapon was given in lieu of cash to the undertaker who buried ex-Texas Ranger Bass Outlaw, who was shot to death in El Paso by constable John Selman in 1894. (Courtesy El Paso Historical Society via Mr. Robert E. McNellis, Jr.)

After 1873, however, the Single Action Army—termed the "Model P" by the factory and the "Peacemaker" by Benjamin Kittredge—commanded the most attention. About a year after its introduction Colt made the gun available with a 5¹/₂ in. barrel, and by the spring of 1877 had added still another barrel length, 4³/₄ in. These three barrel lengths—4³/₄ in., 5¹/₂ in., and 7¹/₂ in.—represented the factory standards, but on special order a purchaser could also order a barrel as short as 2¹/₂ in. or as long as 16 in.; orders for 10 in., 12 in., or 16 in. barrels were often accompanied by requests for detachable shoulder stocks. In 1875 the company began chambering the Peacemaker for the widely popular .44 rimfire, and by February of 1878 it had broadened the gun's appeal by adapting it for the .44-40 centerfire, labeling it the "Frontier" when so chambered. Colt subsequently offered the arm in every popular caliber of the day. Besides a choice of

The night hawk in his nest. His horse tethered nearby and his Colt Single Action near his hand, a cowboy sleeps after his turn at night watch. Popular as the Colt Single Action was, it occasionally presented the owner with a problem. Hot-headed Ike Stockton, a spectator at a trial in Arriba County, New Mexico, in 1879, would have shot the constable who tried to disarm him had not the cylinder pin of his revolver, probably a Colt SA, fallen out, preventing cylinder alignment and rotation. Ike's companion, George W. Coe, defused the situation when he got the drop on the lawman and also halted Stockman from going for his Winchester on his saddle. The parties agreed to call the affair a draw and separate peaceably. (Courtesy Amon Carter Museum of Western Art, Ft. Worth, Texas)

caliber and barrel length, the buyer could select from a variety of finishes, grip materials, and engraving styles.[58]

Nearly every notable frontier character of the 1870s, 1880s, and 1890s owned at least one Peacemaker, but it was not just the gun's use by the famous or infamous that made it so important; rather, it was that so many anonymous westerners—cowboys, farmers, hunters, freighters, expressmen—found it so well suited to their needs. It was strong and simple, functioned reliably, and was easily repaired; the tail of the cylinder bolt and the sear tip of the trigger might break, but even so the arm could still be made to work.

When compared with the Smith & Wesson, one of the Colt's most apparent advantages involved its "handling qualities," the combination of a noticeably comfortable grip, a long, low hammer spur for easy cocking, and good balance. In any handgun designed for self-

All collectors dream of finding a "sleeper," and this nickel-plated Colt .45 Single Action (#109319) is proof that such opportunities occasionally do arise. Purchased merely as a sound example of a used Single Action, the nickel finish and higher-than-normal front sight eventually prompted the owner to contact the Colt factory, which confirmed its original sale on October 19, 1885 to a W. B. Masterson, almost certainly the "Bat" Masterson of western fame.

Letter from William B. "Bat" Masterson ordering a nickel-plated .45 Single Action Colt. His stated preference for a modified front sight appears in other similar letters in which he ordered Colt Single Actions. (Courtesy Connecticut State Library)

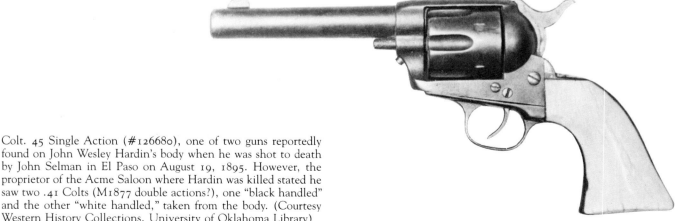

Colt. 45 Single Action (#126680), one of two guns reportedly found on John Wesley Hardin's body when he was shot to death by John Selman in El Paso on August 19, 1895. However, the proprietor of the Acme Saloon where Hardin was killed stated he saw two .41 Colts (M1877 double actions?), one "black handled" and the other "white handled," taken from the body. (Courtesy Western History Collections, University of Oklahoma Library)

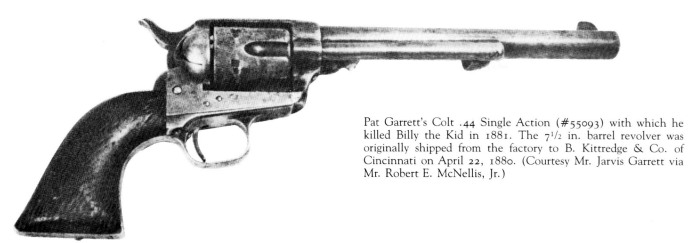

Pat Garrett's Colt .44 Single Action (#55093) with which he killed Billy the Kid in 1881. The 7½ in. barrel revolver was originally shipped from the factory to B. Kittredge & Co. of Cincinnati on April 22, 1880. (Courtesy Mr. Jarvis Garrett via Mr. Robert E. McNellis, Jr.)

defense, handling qualities could assume special importance. Gradually the "fast draw," which had reached full bloom in the Montana mining camps during the early 1860s, was coupled with other quick-shooting techniques, such as the "road agent's spin." On one occasion John Wesley Hardin found himself staring into the muzzle of a peace officer's revolver and had to surrender his guns. Hardin "handed him the pistols, handle foremost. One of the pistols turned a somerset in my hand and went off." Tricks of this kind, however, were used effectively only by highly skilled pistoleers facing do-or-die situations. As A. C. Gould wrote:

> I have seen a great many cowboys shoot revolvers, and I have seen some splendid shots among them, but they never did any good shooting by twirling the revolver around, snapping it in a careless manner, shooting it upside down, or any other of the absurd ways which stage shots sometimes attempt. I have seen several narrow escapes from death by attempts to handle a revolver in such a ridiculous manner, and have known of several deaths from such cause.

But when the necessity for such shooting did arise, the Colt single action proved to be very well adapted for it.

Either wearing newly purchased clothes or ones borrowed from the photographer, three cigar-smoking cowboys pose with Colt Single Actions in Dodge City, Kansas, in 1885. (Courtesy Kansas State Historical Society)

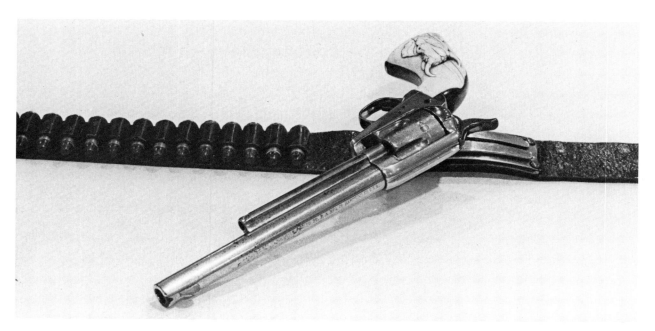

Colt .44 Single Action (#83150) in a so-called Bridgeport rig. Patented in 1882, this "Pistol and Carbine Carrier" consisted of a spring steel two-pronged belt clip designed by Louis S. Flatau. The revolver was suspended from the carrier by a special button-head screw which replaced the hammer screw, thus eliminating the need for a holster. In addition to civilian sales, 500 such devices were ordered for army trials by the Sixteenth and Nineteenth Infantry and by the Eighth and Tenth Cavalry in Texas. But an 1883 report from Ft. Davis, Texas, indicated the rig was inferior to a holster since it did not hold the revolver securely, failed to protect the gun from rain and sand, and exposed the hammer to snagging. Although unsatisfactory for army use, the rig could have had limited appeal to lawmen and others for hip shooting. Original specimens are quite rare, although fakes and reproductions are sometimes encountered. (Photo by Mr. Charles E. Workman, Jr., courtesy Mr. Hume Parks)

Wyatt Earp's .45 Colt Single Action (#69562), its barrel shortened to five inches. The gun was manufactured in 1881, the same year in which Earp figured in the highly publicized gun fight at the O. K. Corral in Tombstone, Arizona. Hard rubber eagle grips like those on this specimen were available from the factory between 1882 and 1896. Presumably Earp was more careful with this gun than he was with an earlier revolver, which, when he was in a Wichita saloon in January of 1876, "slipped from its holster and in falling to the floor the hammer which was resting on the cap, is supposed to have struck the chair, causing the discharge of one of the barrels [sic]. The ball passed through his coat, struck the north wall then glanced off and passed out through the ceiling. It was a narrow escape. . . ." (Courtesy Sotheby Park-Bernet, Los Angeles)

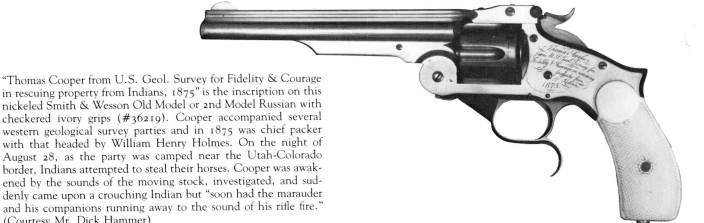

"Thomas Cooper from U.S. Geol. Survey for Fidelity & Courage in rescuing property from Indians, 1875" is the inscription on this nickeled Smith & Wesson Old Model or 2nd Model Russian with checkered ivory grips (#36219). Cooper accompanied several western geological survey parties and in 1875 was chief packer with that headed by William Henry Holmes. On the night of August 28, as the party was camped near the Utah-Colorado border, Indians attempted to steal their horses. Cooper was awakened by the sounds of the moving stock, investigated, and suddenly came upon a crouching Indian but "soon had the marauder and his companions running away to the sound of his rifle fire." (Courtesy Mr. Dick Hammer)

In another rare photo, Deputy Sheriff W. I. Smith of Las Animas County, Colorado carries a pearl- or ivory-gripped Smith & Wesson Model 1903 .32 Hand Ejector suspended from a "Bridgeport rig." (Courtesy Mr. Alex Gibson)

Facing page:
Undoubtedly one of the few existing views showing a "Bridgeport rig" in use. San Diego detective Tom Burns (far right) carries his 7½ in. barrel Colt Single Action on his right hip in such a rig as he stands with local ranchers and other law officers around the mortally wounded outlaw John Sontag in 1904. The Harry Morse Detective Agency of San Francisco later presented Burns with a New Winchester rifle after the "shootout" in which Sontag was captured. (Courtesy Mr. William B. Secrest)

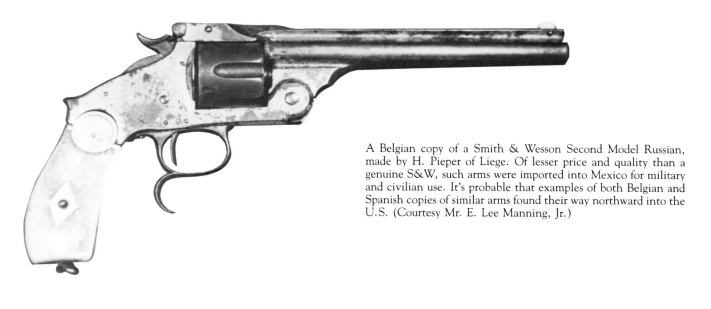

A Belgian copy of a Smith & Wesson Second Model Russian, made by H. Pieper of Liege. Of lesser price and quality than a genuine S&W, such arms were imported into Mexico for military and civilian use. It's probable that examples of both Belgian and Spanish copies of similar arms found their way northward into the U.S. (Courtesy Mr. E. Lee Manning, Jr.)

Smith & Wesson .44 Third Model (or New Model) Russian (#40369) taken from the body of Charlie Pitts, one of the James-Younger gang killed at Northfield, Minnesota. (Courtesy Schilling Museum)

Smith & Wesson .44 Third Model Russian (#30197), inscribed on the backstrap "Col. John K. Rankin, Lawrence, Kansas." Lt. Rankin was present in Lawrence on August 21, 1863, and engaged in a revolver duel with several of the Quantrill raiders who attacked the town that day. During the 1870s and 1880s, Rankin held various offices in Lawrence, including those of mayor and postmaster, and was also a special Indian agent and trader. The grips are pearl, the right carved with a horse's head with simulated rubies inlaid for eyes.

Crow Agency, Montana Territory, 1877. Guns are, from left: Sharps military-style rifle, S&W 2nd or 3rd Model Russian revolver, a holstered Colt M1877 double action, and a Winchester M1866 carbine. (Courtesy Montana Historical Society)

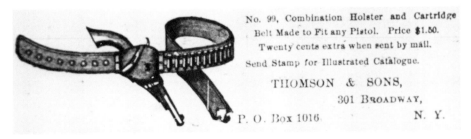

No. 99, Combination Holster and Cartridge Belt Made to Fit any Pistol. Price $1.50. Twenty cents extra when sent by mail. Send Stamp for Illustrated Catalogue.

THOMSON & SONS,
301 BROADWAY,
P. O. Box 1016. N. Y.

Army and Navy Journal, May 1878.

Remington price list, January 1876.

As but one of hundreds of examples of the Peacemaker's use, young Edgar Bronson left this account of his first trip to Cheyenne about 1875:

Before leaving the train, I had prudently strapped to my waist a new (how distressingly new) .45 Colt's six-shooter, that looked and felt a yard long. The one possession larger than this pistol that left the train with me was my desire to learn to use it . . . [shortly afterward] the pistol had to be stripped of its flap holster and rehabited in the then new decollete Olive scabbard.[59]

The arm was no less popular with companies than it was with individuals. The Union Pacific (which had begun ordering it by January of 1875), Wells Fargo, and other express companies bought it, as did mining concerns, law-enforcement agencies, and foreign governments, such as that of Mexico.[60]

Early in 1874, with the Peacemaker making its first appearances in the West, Smith & Wesson began advertising a new version of its Russian revolver. In 1873 the Russian captain who was inspecting the guns made for his government had requested certain changes in the design, and because the Russian contracts were important to Smith & Wesson, the firm acquiesced. The most apparent changes in the arm were a hump or prawl at the top of the backstrap and a finger spur on the trigger guard. In addition, the barrel was short-

Remington M1875 .44 used by "Redtop" Callihan, who reportedly killed six men. He was shot to death in Bodie, California, in 1892 by the partner of one of his victims. The holster is an example of a typical double loop Mexican-style rig. While U.S. military holsters of the period had a flap to protect the revolver, flaps are seldom found on civilian belt holsters. (Photo by Mr. Ed Prentiss, courtesy Mr. John A. Kopec)

ened to 7 in. and the heel of the butt was more rounded. Since it was impractical to make two different frame shapes, Smith & Wesson used the new Russian frame for all its .44s, even those sold commercially. While the majority of these "second-model Russians" were chambered for the .44 Russian centerfire load, some were adapted to the .44 rimfire, a cartridge of continuing popularity in the West.[61]

A modified version of the second-model Russian, the "third-model Russian," appeared commercially early in 1875. Its barrel was shortened to 6 1/2 in., it had a shorter extractor housing, and it incorporated a thumbscrew in the topstrap to release the cylinder for cleaning. Otherwise the arm was the same as its predecessor and could easily pass for it. The fact that it and the second model were both available with detachable shoulder stocks and other special-order items helped sales somewhat, but the Russian or "saw handle" precluded widespread popularity in the West. Although a prawl on the backstrap was often desirable on a double-action revolver, it could hamper the fast cocking of a single-action. As one of Smith & Wesson's distributors wrote: "The Texas people will not buy the Russian handle. They do not like it and therefore buy a good many Colt Army when they would prefer the No. 3, if with the old stock. The objection is, that they cannot cock the arm as they pull it from the holster." Residents of the Southwest who did buy second- or third-model Russians often cut off the finger spur on the trigger guard; other westerners, who refused to have anything to do with the Russian model, continued calling for the old-style "square handle." Late in 1876, to help satisfy this demand, Smith & Wesson began making its .45 caliber Schofield available on a commercial basis.[62]

Smith & Wesson's troubles in selling the Russian

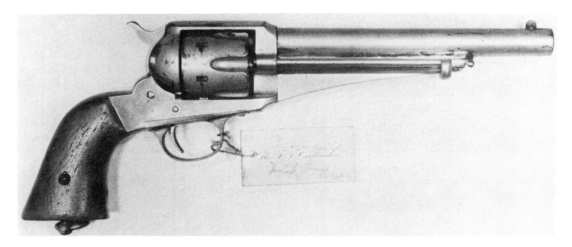

Outlaw Frank James's .44 Model 1875 Remington (#15116).

models at home undoubtedly worked in Remington's favor when, in the fall of 1875, the New York concern announced a new military-size revolver of its own. Remington's "New Model 1875" was a single-action solid-frame six-shooter which, except for the distinctive metal web under the barrel, bore a marked similarity to the Colt Peacemaker. Remington initially marketed this gun only with a 7½ in. barrel and chambered only for a special .44 centerfire cartridge; but within a few years it was offered in .44-40 and .45 Colt as well.[63]

One of the better-known incidents involving a Remington took place in a Dodge City saloon in April of 1879. As City Marshal Charles Bassett testified afterward:

> When I first heard the firing I was at Beatty & Kelley's saloon. Ran up to the Long Branch as fast as I could. Saw Frank Loving, Levi Richardson and Duffey. Richardson was dodging and running around the billiard table. Loving was also running and dodging around the table. I got as far as the stove when the shooting had about ended. I caught Loving's pistol. Think there was two shots fired after I

Uniformed Dakota Indian policemen Red Tomahawk (left) and Eagle Man. Their guns are Remington M1875 revolvers, a Winchester M1873 carbine (left), and one of the small-frame Whitney-Kennedy carbines, probably a .44-40. Each man wears an "Indian Police" badge while Red Tomahawk's round buckle encircled by a wreath bears the word *Police* in the center. (Courtesy Western History Collection, Denver Public Library)

got into the room, am positive there was one . . . I examined the pistol which was shown me as the one Richardson had. It contained five empty shells . . . Richardson fell immediately after the shot I heard. . . . There was a considerable smoke in the room. Loving's pistol was a Remington, No. 44 and was empty after the shooting.

When John Lord was in a Colorado mountain town a year later,

[he] found in the bookkeeper's desk a little old pepperbox pistol. If anybody had shot me with it and I had ever found it out I would have been real mad at them. I found in one of the drawers of Mr. Huff's desk a good forty five Remington. I took both pistols out and loaded them.

The infamous Frank James carried not one but two Remingtons, chambered for the .44-40 cartridge. In October of 1882, when he surrendered to Missouri Governor T. T. Crittenden, Crittenden's secretary asked him why he preferred the Remington to the Colt or Smith & Wesson. James answered:

Because the Remington is the hardest and the surest shooting pistol made, and because it carries exactly the same cartridge that a Winchester rifle does. My armament was two Remingtons and a Winchester rifle. The cartridges of one filled the chambers of the other. You can now see why I prefer the Remington. There is no confusion of ammunition here. When a man gets into a close, hot fight, with a dozen men shooting at him all at once, he must have his ammunition all of the same kind.[64]

Remington's introduction of its Model 1875 meant that all the major American handgun manufacturers of the postwar period could now offer up-to-date big-bore metallic-cartridge revolvers. In part because such guns could be reloaded comparatively quickly, the old practice of carrying two or even more large-caliber revolvers, widely prevalent during the percussion era, began to disappear. N. Howard Thorp said:

I have heard of a blacksmith's son in Jackson County, Texas, who could fire two powder-and-ball Colt's pistols (one after the other) and do great execution. He once won a bet of two hundred and fifty dollars that he could kill six quails out of a flock sitting on the ground before they could get away. Some he killed on the wing after they had raised to fly. But the two-gun man, so-called, was a rare specimen. . . .

And E. C. "Teddy Blue" Abbott added that:

I punched cows from '71 on, and I never yet saw a cowboy with two guns. I mean two six-shooters.

Along with revolvers by S&W, Colt, and others, readers of the 1884 N. Curry & Bro. catalog could choose from such inexpensive "suicide specials" as a .38 Smoker for $3, or a better XL No. 5 .38 for $6.50.

Wild Bill carried two guns and so did some of those other city marshals, like Bat Masterson, but they were professional gunmen themselves, not cowpunchers. . . .[65]

MORE COLTS AND SMITH & WESSONS, AND NEW POCKET REVOLVERS

Because big-bore revolvers tended to be large and heavy, the major American makers continued to supply the market with pocket-size revolvers. In that field they had plenty of competition. Since the expiration of Rollin White's patent, the demand for small cartridge revolvers had attracted a host of manufacturers, most of them little known. Pocket revolvers by makers such as Whitney, Deringer-Clark, Marlin, and Wesson & Harrington were well above average in quality, but the arms by little-known fabricators were often low-grade items—so low, in fact, that instead of makers' names and addresses, the guns were stamped only with trade names: "Defender," "Dictator," "Ranger," "Victor," and the like. As a class these guns were later referred to as "Suicide Specials," presumably because

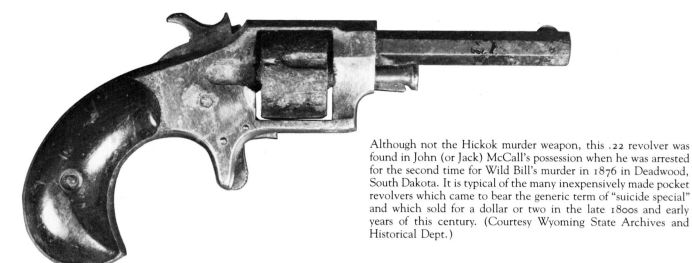

Although not the Hickok murder weapon, this .22 revolver was found in John (or Jack) McCall's possession when he was arrested for the second time for Wild Bill's murder in 1876 in Deadwood, South Dakota. It is typical of the many inexpensively made pocket revolvers which came to bear the generic term of "suicide special" and which sold for a dollar or two in the late 1800s and early years of this century. (Courtesy Wyoming State Archives and Historical Dept.)

Engraved .41 Forehand & Wadsworth "Swamp Angel" (#4318) presented to Sheriff Pat Garrett, probably in honor of his killing Billy the Kid in 1881. The revolver features ivory grips, silver plating, and a gold-plated cylinder. Garret's name is inscribed on the backstrap. (Courtesy Mr. Calvin Moerbe)

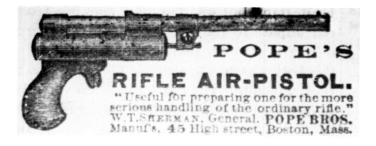

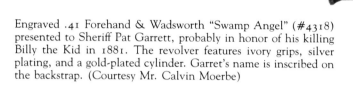

North Platte (Nebraska) *Republican*, May 1875.

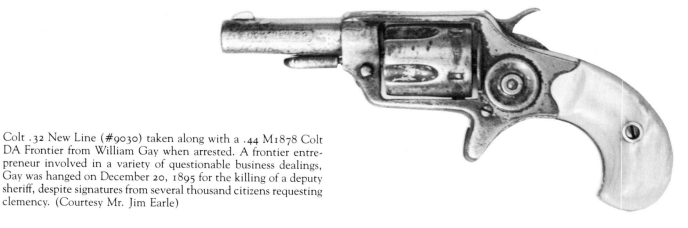

Colt .32 New Line (#9030) taken along with a .44 M1878 Colt DA Frontier from William Gay when arrested. A frontier entrepreneur involved in a variety of questionable business dealings, Gay was hanged on December 20, 1895 for the killing of a deputy sheriff, despite signatures from several thousand citizens requesting clemency. (Courtesy Mr. Jim Earle)

302

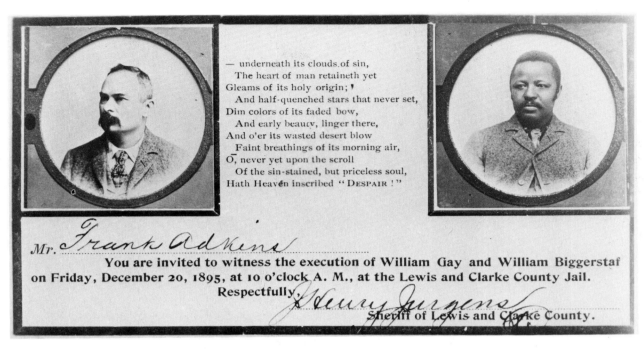

— underneath its clouds of sin,
The heart of man retaineth yet
Gleams of its holy origin;
And half-quenched stars that never set,
Dim colors of its faded bow,
And early beauty, linger there,
And o'er its wasted desert blow
Faint breathings of its morning air,
O, never yet upon the scroll
Of the sin-stained, but priceless soul,
Hath Heaven inscribed "DESPAIR!"

Mr. *Frank Adkins*

You are invited to witness the execution of William Gay and William Biggerstaf on Friday, December 20, 1895, at 10 o'clock A. M., at the Lewis and Clarke County Jail.

Respectfully, *Henry Jurgens*

Sheriff of Lewis and Clarke County.

Invitation to Gay's hanging. (Courtesy Montana Historical Society)

some were used for that purpose during the financial panic of 1873. Typically they were short-barreled, sheath-trigger, nickel-plated arms with hard-rubber grips. On occasion dealers did advertise these items in western papers. During the 1870s, for example, the Western Gun Works of Chicago offered its "Buffalo Bill" and its "New Model Long Range Revolver, 'Tramps Terror,'" in the Hays City *Sentinel*, the *Colorado Chieftain*, and the *Dodge City Times*, but it is highly unlikely that experienced plains dwellers wasted their money on such things. While the guns were cheap, retailing for two or three dollars, the prices were also indicative of the quality involved.[66]

There were, however, a few higher-quality revolvers with colorful trade names—those by Forehand & Wadsworth, Hopkins & Allen, Rupertus, and one or two others—that were well designed and made of good materials. While they were not as highly finished as a Colt, Smith & Wesson, or Remington, they could prove as serviceable as the higher-priced arms. The Forehand & Wadsworth .32, .38, and .41 rimfire products, termed the "Terror," "Bull Dog," and "Swamp Angel," respectively, and the Hopkins & Allen "XL" series—all of which appeared between 1871 and 1874—were handled by dealers such as John Lower of Denver and Nathaniel Curry of San Francisco. Because the

Swamp Angel was advertised in the *Army and Navy Journal* early in 1873, a few military men may have purchased it also.[67]

William A. Rogers probably had a Forehand & Wadsworth Bulldog when he was in southern Colorado in 1879. At that time this locale was the scene of frequent brawls between the employees of two rival railroads, the Denver & Rio Grande and the Kansas Pacific. Anticipating trouble, Rogers "went to the gun shop in Colorado Springs and bought a box of cartridges. The shopkeeper also loaded my revolver at the same time." During a misunderstanding shortly afterwards Rogers came close to using his gun, but the affair ended bloodlessly. A day later he traveled to a ranch on the Huerfano River, south of Pueblo:

Several of the cowboys were out in a ruined part of the old Spanish house and had put up a target against the thick walls of masonry. They were all shooting away at it, and as one or two of them were indifferent shots I felt myself quite a good enough marksman to compete with them. I stood up with my "bulldog" .38, aimed, and pulled the trigger. The gun missed fire. I felt a cold sweat ooze out on my forehead as I reflected what that might have meant the morning before. I examined the cartridge which had been placed in my revolver by the Colorado

Marshal Paden Tolbert's posse, photographed in 1892 beside the steam-driven saw mill which Ned Christie used to construct his log fort. A Cherokee youth who turned to horse stealing and robbery, Christie withstood a day-long siege before his fort was finally breached with dynamite. In addition to double-barrel shot-guns, Springfield "trapdoor" rifles, and a lever-action rifle with a half-length magazine, the Oklahoma Territory posse members display a variety of pocket revolvers—a double action of unknown origin (possibly a Hopkins & Allen, Harrington & Richardson, or Iver Johnson) second from left, a Colt New Line third from left, and possibly a Smith & Wesson .32 Model 1½ thrust into the seated youth's belt. The man at far right carries a Colt M1878 Double Action Frontier. (Courtesy Mr. C. H. McKennon)

A studio cabinet card by photographer D. A. Frederick of Ashland, Kansas. Subjects' guns are, from left, a Colt Single Action and a Colt New Line; a Winchester M1873 rifle, percussion Colt M1860 .44, and probably a Colt Single Action; and a Smith & Wesson double action and what appears to be another Colt New Line. The holstered revolvers are all pushed forward for an added air of bravado, but may all be studio prop guns. (Courtesy Mr. Emory A. Cantney, Jr.)

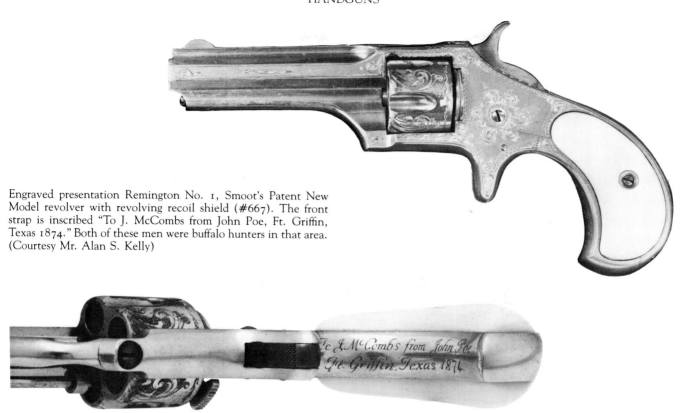

Engraved presentation Remington No. 1, Smoot's Patent New Model revolver with revolving recoil shield (#667). The front strap is inscribed "To J. McCombs from John Poe, Ft. Griffin, Texas 1874." Both of these men were buffalo hunters in that area. (Courtesy Mr. Alan S. Kelly)

Springs gunsmith. My revolver was of the "rim fire" variety, the cartridge "center fire." I returned to the house and buried that gun down in the bottom of my gripsack, never to be carried again.[68]

By January of 1874 Colt had begun to market a newly designed group of pocket revolvers, its "New Line" series. These solid-frame sheath-trigger guns offered nothing really new, but they were nicely finished, and they did have the allure of the Colt name. At about the same time Remington introduced the first of its "Smoot's Patent" revolvers, so called because of William Smoot's 1873 patent on a technique for making frame and barrel in one piece. As was the case with the New Line Colts, Remington's Smoot was fabricated in different frame sizes to suit different calibers. The .30, .32, and .38 rimfire models all had simple rod ejectors alongside their barrels, but the large .41 rimfire size (also available in .38 caliber) lacked this feature. The .38 was marketed in two different frame shapes: one had a simple recurved frame-backstrap contour, while the others had a "saw handle" and square butt.[69]

Until 1870, of course, Smith & Wesson's specialty had been pocket revolvers, and despite the success of its .44 caliber No. 3, the firm continued working diligently on smaller-caliber arms. In 1871 the company discontinued the long-popular No. 2, and dropped the New Model 1½ in 1875, but early in 1876 a newly designed five-shot .38, largely the handiwork of Daniel Wesson himself, reached the market. The new centerfire cartridge, called (appropriately enough) the .38 Smith & Wesson, was loaded with a 145 grain bullet and a 16 grain powder charge, and was to become one of the most popular and widely used handgun loads ever devised. The gun that chambered this cartridge had come about as a result of demands for a revolver of reasonable power without the weight and bulk that characterized the company's .44s. Essentially it was a scaled-down Russian, with the same type of hinged frame and automatic extractor, but the prawl was less obtrusive, as was its sheath trigger. Although more properly termed the "New Model .38 Single Action," the gun's later nickname, "Baby Russian," aptly described it. By October of 1876 M. W. Robinson, Smith & Wesson's general sales agent, was advertising the

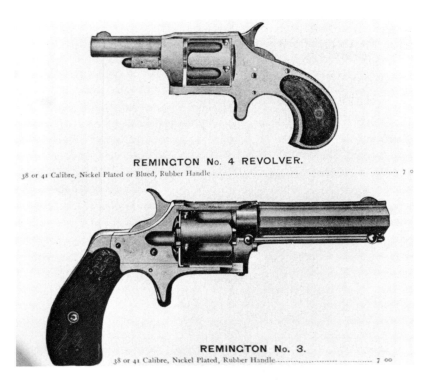

N. Curry & Bro. 1884 catalog.

Above, a Smith & Wesson .38 First Model Single Action or "Baby Russian" (#22220) and a Second Model .38 (#81377). (Courtesy Mr. E. Lee Manning, Jr.)

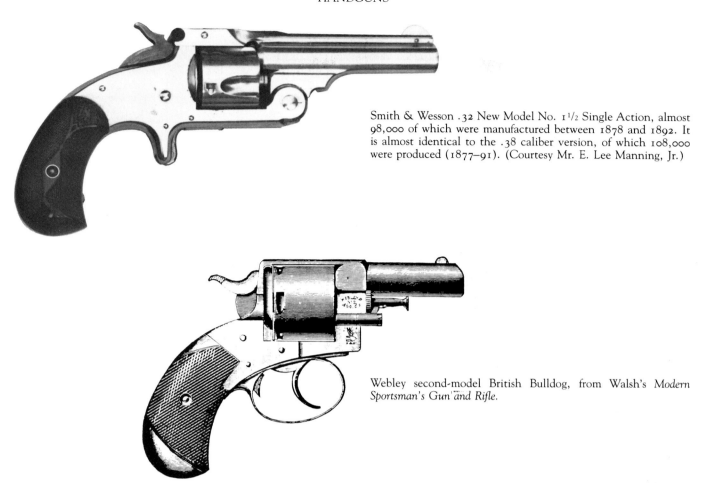

Smith & Wesson .32 New Model No. 1½ Single Action, almost 98,000 of which were manufactured between 1878 and 1892. It is almost identical to the .38 caliber version, of which 108,000 were produced (1877–91). (Courtesy Mr. E. Lee Manning, Jr.)

Webley second-model British Bulldog, from Walsh's *Modern Sportsman's Gun and Rifle.*

new gun in papers such as the *Dallas Herald* and the *Rocky Mountain News,* but the first shipments may have gone west before that.[70]

Initially the new .38 was available only with barrels of 3¼ in. and 4 in., but in 1877, when an improved version with a more compact extractor mechanism appeared, barrels of 5 in. and 6 in. (and later 8 in. and 10 in.) became available also. Whatever the barrel length, the light but powerful Baby Russian greatly bolstered Smith & Wesson's already active sales, and the firm turned out a total of more than 130,000 before production stopped in 1891.[71]

When the first shipments of single-action .38s reached the West Coast, however, they ran into unexpected competition in the form of an even more powerful pocket revolver—the "British Bulldog." Made by P. Webley & Son, the Bulldog was a solid-frame, double-action, five-shot arm with 2½ in. barrel. Although widely copied both here and abroad, the genuine Webley product, on the market by 1874 and perhaps earlier, had (in its earlier versions) an unfluted cylinder, a simple recurved frame-backstrap contour

"Seven shots in 5 seconds" proclaimed the ad for the Forehand & Wadsworth "Improved British Bull-Dog" double action revolver in the December 25, 1884, catalog issued by the E. C. Meacham Arms Co. of St. Louis. Identical revolvers were sold by Nathaniel Curry of San Francisco.

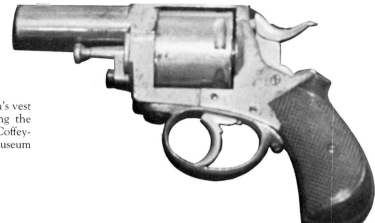

.38 caliber "British Bulldog," taken from outlaw Bob Dalton's vest pocket by Condon Bank bookkeeper Tom Babb following the Dalton gang's abortive attempt to hold up two banks in Coffeyville, Kansas. (The revolver is displayed in the Dalton Museum in Coffeyville.)

An imported Bulldog-type double action five-shot revolver of about .45 caliber. The gun is unmarked except for the name "LIDDLE & KAEDING/SAN FRANCISCO" in two lines on the barrel. The firm was in operation under that name from 1866 until 1889. One of their 1876 ads in *The Pacific Life* listed handguns by "Colt's, Smith & Wesson, Swamp Angel, Wesson & Harrington, National, La Faucheauz [sic], XL, Hopkins & Allen, Whitney, and all other makes, including the famous and much celebrated Double Action Self-Cocking Bull Dog Pistol."

Another Bulldog-type revolver, marked "SHREVE & WOLF/SAN FRANCISCO" on the barrel.

without prawl, and a parrot-beak butt. In spite of its compact size this was a big-bore arm, chambered first for the .442 Webley centerfire load, and later for such rounds as the .44 short rimfire and .450 centerfire. Both Winchester and U.M.C. could supply this ammunition.[72]

Evidently the Bulldogs were coming to the West Coast in quantity by late 1875, because in February of 1876 a resident of Cerro Gordo, California, wrote Smith & Wesson to ask:

Why do you not put something in the market to

compete with "Webly's British Bulldog" of .44 or .45 calibre. This pocket pistol-revolver has an immense sale on this coast and men do not hesitate to pay $25.00 and $30.00 for them either. While it is admitted that the S&W Russian Model is the best belt revolver in the world, "Webly's British Bulldog" is hard to beat for the pocket, the only objection to the B.D. being the material and finish is very poor. The general tendency on the Pacific slope is to increase the size of the bore of both belt and pocket revolvers. Five years ago a 38-100 for the pocket was considered large, now one cannot be hardly given away if a 44-100 or 45-100 can be bought. . . .

Nathaniel Curry's advertisement in August of 1876 for "Webley's double action revolvers" undoubtedly referred to the Bulldog, but may have included other models also. John Henry Tunstall, the English-born rancher whose death helped touch off New Mexico's Lincoln County War, also owned a Bulldog. In June of 1877 he noted in his diary: "I saddled up the mule Nancy . . . & started for Lincoln . . . I left my carbine with Rob . . . so all I had was my 'British Bulldog five shooter' I am however, so used to travelling about now that I never bother my head about danger or no danger."[73] Newspapers in the mining town of Bodie, Calif. in the late 1870s and early 1880s carried various accounts in which British Bulldog revolvers were cited by name. A miner claimed he had been robbed of $15 and his British Bulldog at Spanish Dora's brothel. Office clerk W. A. Irwin was awakened by the attempted forcible entry into a storeroom at the mill where he slept, but a shot through the door from his "bulldog" caused the two men outside to depart hastily. And on Oct. 2, 1879 the Bodie *Morning News* reported that a mine employee the night before had placed a British Bulldog to his head and taken his own life.

The popularity of the Bulldog contributed to the spreading popularity of double-action revolvers in general. Anticipating the demand for such guns, the Colt concern brought out its "New, Double Action, Self Cocking, Central Fire, Six Shot Revolver" early in 1877. A solid-frame arm with parrot-beak butt, the revolver weighed only about 1½ pounds, but (except for a few in .32 caliber) chambered the relatively powerful .38 and .41 Long Colt cartridges. In the longer 4½ in. to 6 in. barrel lengths the gun usually carried the side-rod ejector, but in the shorter 2½ in. and 3½ in. lengths it had none. Known soon after its introduction in .38 caliber as the "Lightning," a trade name conferred upon it by Benjamin Kittredge of Cincinnati, the new Colt was noticeably light and handy. (Kittredge called the .41 caliber version the "Thunderer," but only the Lightning nickname stuck.) How-

A Bulldog up a tree. A "British Bulldog" found imbedded in a tree near Placerville (formerly Hangtown), California. The revolver may have been used by one of Charley Jack's outlaw "gang," which preyed on travelers. After one attempted holdup, it was found that his gang consisted of coats cleverly placed on tree branches and arranged to resemble concealed individuals holding revolvers. (Courtesy Harrah's Automobile Collection, Reno, Nevada)

ever, it was hampered by its inefficient lockwork; the cylinder bolt, which engaged notches in the rear face of the cylinder instead of the side, was frail, easily broken, and difficult to replace. But largely because it was stamped with the Colt name, the Lightning sold well in the West.[74]

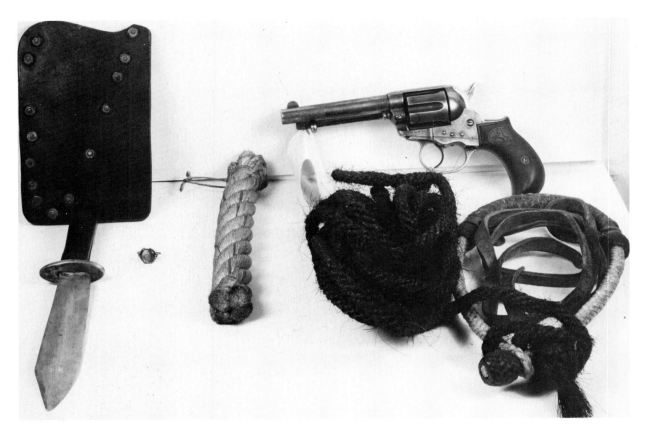

Colt M1877 double-action revolver, knife, ring, quirt, and halter used by scout and manhunter Tom Horn. (Courtesy Union Pacific Museum)

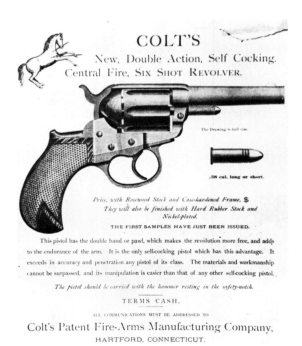

One of the earliest advertisements (January 1877) for Colt's Model 1877 double action, initially offered only in .38 caliber. (Courtesy Connecticut State Library)

Army and Navy Journal, August 1878.

Female bandit Pearl Hart with a Colt M1877 in her belt, a holstered Colt Single Action, and a M1873 Winchester rifle. The
photo was probably taken following her release from the Yuma
(Arizona) Territorial Prison. (Courtesy Arizona Historical Society)

Colt. .44 M1878 Double Action (#38960) with Wells Fargo stamping on the backstrap and "Yuma, AT" scratched inside one of the hard rubber grips.

Jennie Metcalf, female Oklahoma outlaw, with a 5½ in. Colt M1878. (Courtesy Western History Collections, University of Oklahoma Library)

Although the model of Winchester carbine in this view can't be determined with certainty, the length of the cartridges in the belt make it likely that it is a M1894, although the trap in the buttplate is not a common feature. The revolver is readily distinguishable as a nickel-plated Colt M1878 Double Action Frontier with pearl or ivory grips. (Courtesy Wyoming State Archives and Historical Dept.)

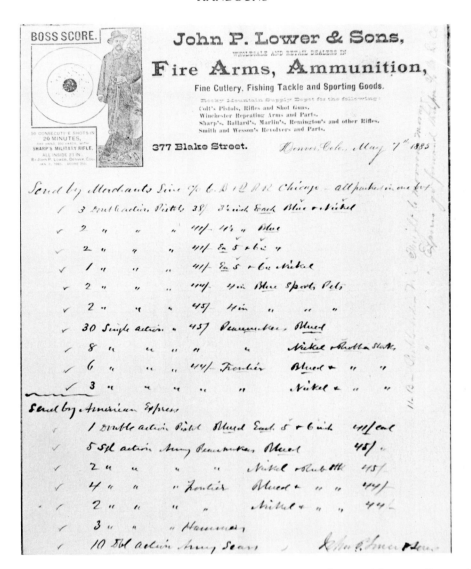

An 1885 order from John P. Lower & Sons of Denver for a variety of Colt revolvers, including both M1877 and M1878 double actions. But the greatest number of handguns ordered were Single Actions. Note the use of the terms *Peacemaker* and *Frontier* when referring to the .45 and .44 caliber Single Actions, respectively. (Courtesy Connecticut State Library)

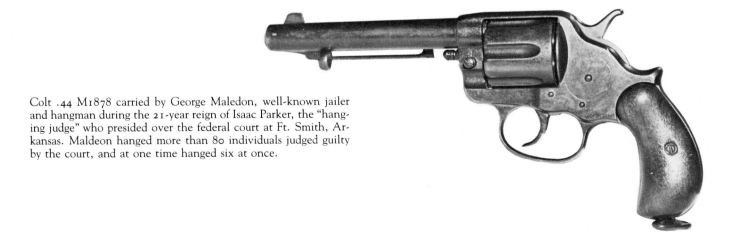

Colt .44 M1878 carried by George Maledon, well-known jailer and hangman during the 21-year reign of Isaac Parker, the "hanging judge" who presided over the federal court at Ft. Smith, Arkansas. Maledon hanged more than 80 individuals judged guilty by the court, and at one time hanged six at once.

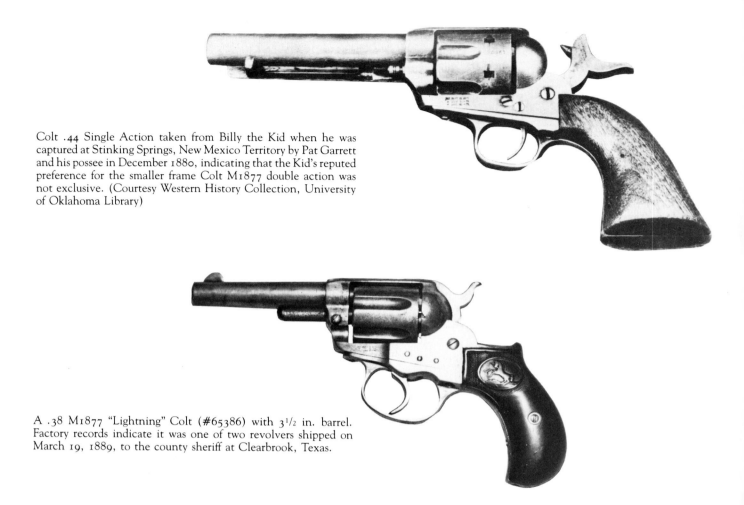

Colt .44 Single Action taken from Billy the Kid when he was captured at Stinking Springs, New Mexico Territory by Pat Garrett and his possee in December 1880, indicating that the Kid's reputed preference for the smaller frame Colt M1877 double action was not exclusive. (Courtesy Western History Collection, University of Oklahoma Library)

A .38 M1877 "Lightning" Colt (#65386) with 3½ in. barrel. Factory records indicate it was one of two revolvers shipped on March 19, 1889, to the county sheriff at Clearbrook, Texas.

More suitable for the frontier than the Lightning was a second double-action Colt, marketed in mid-1878. Termed by Kittredge the "Omnipotent," but better known as the "Double Action Army" or "Double Action Frontier," this gun was built on a large, newly designed one-piece frame, and was chambered for the same cartridges available for the Single Action Army—the .45 Colt, .44-40, and subsequently other rounds, such as the .38-40. While far from the epitome of double-action design, its lockwork was considerably better than the Lightning's. One notable feature was that the pawl served not only to rotate the cylinder, but also to bolt it in firing alignment. Offered with the same barrel lengths as the Single Action, Colt's Double Action Army rapidly became one of the most popular double-action revolvers in the West.[75]

But the Lightning had reached the market first, and it found more than its share of buyers. During Sam Bass's fatal encounter with Texas Rangers at Round Rock in July of 1878, Ranger Commander John B. Jones, "returning from the telegraph office, ran into the fight. He was armed with only a small Colt's double-action pistol, but threw himself into the fray."[76]

A better-known owner of a Lightning Colt was Billy the Kid. Frank Collinson, who encountered the famous outlaw in 1878, left this impression:

He was supposed to be about eighteen, but looked older when you saw him closely. He was sunburned and not much to look at. . . . There were scores just like him all up and down the Pecos. Everything he had on would not have sold for five dollars—an old black slouch hat; worn-out pants and boots, spurs, shirt, and vest; a black cotton handkerchief tied loosely around his neck, the ever-ready Colt double-action .41 pistol around him and in easy reach; [and] an old style .44 rim-fire brass-jawed Winchester. . . . He had a pair of gray-blue eyes that never stopped looking around.[77]

Lightnings were perhaps more popular with lawmen than with outlaws. In May of 1878 C. C. Stevens of California's Placer County Sheriff's Office ordered from

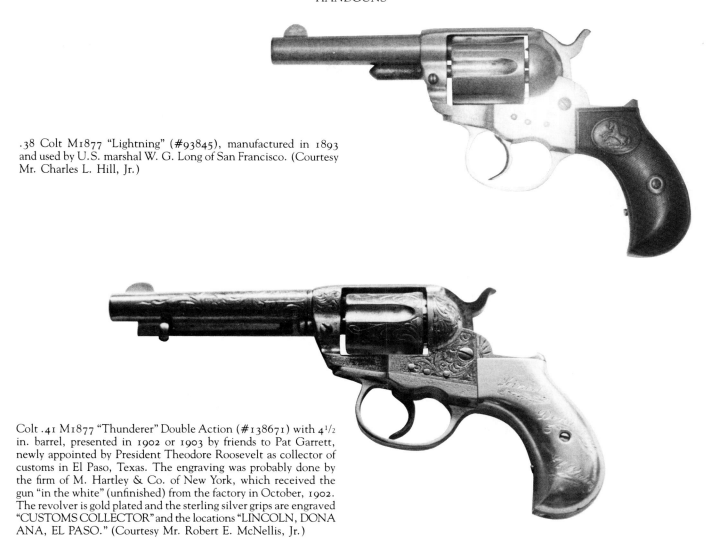

.38 Colt M1877 "Lightning" (#93845), manufactured in 1893 and used by U.S. marshal W. G. Long of San Francisco. (Courtesy Mr. Charles L. Hill, Jr.)

Colt .41 M1877 "Thunderer" Double Action (#138671) with 4½ in. barrel, presented in 1902 or 1903 by friends to Pat Garrett, newly appointed by President Theodore Roosevelt as collector of customs in El Paso, Texas. The engraving was probably done by the firm of M. Hartley & Co. of New York, which received the gun "in the white" (unfinished) from the factory in October, 1902. The revolver is gold plated and the sterling silver grips are engraved "CUSTOMS COLLECTOR" and the locations "LINCOLN, DONA ANA, EL PASO." (Courtesy Mr. Robert E. McNellis, Jr.)

the Colt firm "1 D.A. 41 Cal. 5 inch [barrel] with ejector [and] 1 [D.A.] 38 " 4½ " without [ejector]." Besides the guns, Stevens ordered:

1 Set loading tools for each pistol. 200 caps for each pistol's cartridges . . . to have the package come C.O.D. would make it more expensive and I desire to get off as cheaply as possible in the matter of express charges which are high enough. Please advise me of cost of an extra cartridge cylinder for the 38 cal. Should these pistols give good satisfaction of which I have no doubt I shall take pleasure in recommending them.

Writing to Colt in June of 1878, John Lower of Denver stated that:

the Double Action Pistols . . . are ahead of all others now—[send] 6—41/Cal Dbl action Pistols Nickel & Rubber assorted from *Shortest* to 3½ inch barrels—2 ditto with Plain Ivory Stocks . . . send by *Express at once*—as I am putting up a circular cat-

alogue & price list and would like to include [them] if possible. . . .

A Lower-retailed Lightning may have been involved in the shooting of Thomas Bennett by John Hoover in Fairplay, Colorado, in April of 1879: one witness testified that Hoover's gun was "a double action 38 caliber six chambered Colt's revolver."[78]

Watching the popularity of double-action arms spread, William C. Dodge informed Daniel Wesson in June of 1878 that:

My son spent the winter at Hot Springs, and he says that they won't buy any pistol there, that is not *self-cocking*. Every man and boy carries one. Colt's self-cocker 38 sells readily there for $25 while your 38 won't sell for $15 . . . [but] Colt's and F & W's [double-action locks] are exceedingly complicated, and the former is very delicate.[79]

At the time he received this letter Wesson was already working on a double-action mechanism, but

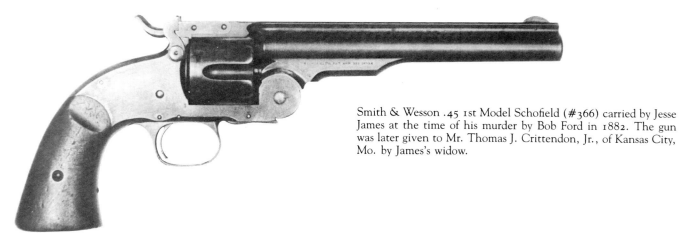

Smith & Wesson .45 1st Model Schofield (#366) carried by Jesse James at the time of his murder by Bob Ford in 1882. The gun was later given to Mr. Thomas J. Crittendon, Jr., of Kansas City, Mo. by James's widow.

Schofield Model .45 Smith & Wesson revolvers are rarely seen in nineteenth-century photos of frontier life, although one is evident here. Far more common is the M1866 Winchester carbine in the scene. (Courtesy Mr. Herb Peck, Jr.)

Handsomely garbed Buckskin Jim (left) and Pawnee Bill of Pawnee Bill's Wild West Show. While the former's revolver is identifiable as a Schofield .45 S&W, the latter's rifle could be a single-shot Winchester Low or High Wall, or a Ballard Hunter's or Sporting Rifle. (Courtesy Western History Collections, University of Oklahoma Library)

316

Militia officers and men of the Rocky Mountain Rifles at Leadville, Colorado, in 1887. The youth at far left is armed with a Smith & Wesson Russian revolver, as perhaps is the man at far left, while their companions carry Colt Single Actions in a variety of holster styles. (Courtesy Denver Public Library, Western History Collection)

he had not neglected his single actions. Sales of the more than 600 .45 caliber Schofields sent to civilian markets in 1876–77 had not been especially brisk (partly because of the special cartridge the gun required); yet the arm did elicit some interest in the West. In February of 1876 James Brock of Fort Griffin, Texas, wrote the company that he had seen the Schofield and decided to adopt it for all his "cattle herders that I may have a uniform pistol and cartridges etc." Another Schofield found its way to the infamous Jesse James.[80]

A better-selling arm than the Schofield, particularly in the East, was the .38 centerfire Baby Russian. To help western sales, Wesson displayed six highly finished Baby Russians at the San Francisco Fair of 1877. Because of the increasing demand for guns chambering reloadable centerfire cartridges, he also introduced a new .32 centerfire single-action revolver in the spring of 1878. Like the Baby Russian and the earlier .44s, this new five-shot .32 had its barrel hinged at the front of the bottom strap, and when it was broken open for reloading, it ejected all the fired cases simultaneously. A new feature of this gun was its "rebounding hammer," which could not reach the primer unless the shooter deliberately pulled the trigger.[81]

Much more powerful than the little .32 was another single-action brought out in mid-1878, the large-frame "New Model No. 3," which except for its conventional trigger and guard bore a very close resemblance to the Baby Russian. While the new gun embodied no major internal changes from its immediate predecessors, Wesson had simplified a number of its components,

The setting is Dakota Territory, probably in the 1880s. The revolver is either a .32 or .38 Smith & Wesson single-action top break. Because of their relative ease of concealment, such revolvers were usually carried in a pocket and so seldom appear in contemporary photos despite their popularity. (Courtesy Mr. R. L. Ainsley)

Wells Fargo–marked revolvers. Above is a Smith & Wesson New Model No. 3 .44 (#189) marked "W.F. & CO. EXP. NO. 721" and a Colt .45 M1878 (#4325) stamped on the backstrap "W.F. & CO. NO. 978." (Photo by Mr. Richard K. Halter, courtesy Mr. Willis E. Neuwirth)

Studio portrait of a cowboy in leather chaps wearing what by butt shape is probably a Smith & Wesson No. 3 New Model single action. (Courtesy Denver Public Library, Western History Dept.)

Virgil Earp's Smith & Wesson .44 New Model No. 3 (#14289) with a 6½ in. barrel, ivory grips, and traces of original nickel finish. Like his famous brother Wyatt, Virgil served as a lawman in Dodge City and Tombstone before being crippled by buckshot in an assassination attempt in the latter town in December of 1881. (Courtesy National Cowboy Hall of Fame, Oklahoma City)

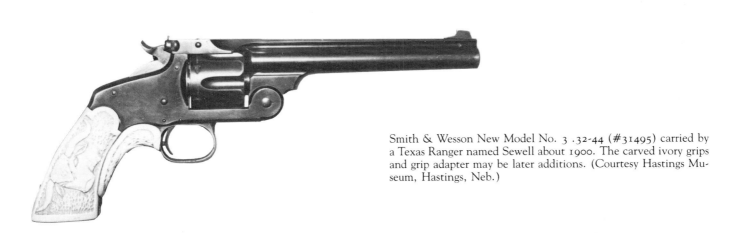

Smith & Wesson New Model No. 3 .32-44 (#31495) carried by a Texas Ranger named Sewell about 1900. The carved ivory grips and grip adapter may be later additions. (Courtesy Hastings Museum, Hastings, Neb.)

and the arm was consequently somewhat more reliable. Although chambered primarily for the .44 Russian cartridge and commonly fitted with a 6½ in. barrel, it was eventually available in several other calibers and with barrels as short as 3½ in. or as long as 8 in. When equipped with adjustable sights the New Model proved quite accurate, and became a popular target arm. Texas Jack Omohundro bought a pair of the new .44s in the fall of 1878, and a year later Buffalo Bill Cody ordered a gold-and-silver-plated example for stage shooting. Subsequent purchasers included "Little Sure Shot" herself, Annie Oakley. It was a New Model No. 3 in the hands of Bob Ford that killed Jesse James, himself a Smith & Wesson owner, in 1882.[82]

As good as it was, however, the New Model No. 3 could not satisfy the shooter who wanted a double-action revolver. Wesson dealt with this problem by

marketing two revolvers of this type in 1880—a .38 in the spring and a .32 in the summer. Like the single-actions, the new guns were hinged-frame, simultaneous-extraction arms, but their double-action lockwork was notably superior to that in either of the double-action Colts. Although the Smith & Wessons incorporated features of two U.S. patents, issued in December of 1879 and May of 1880, their lockwork basically copied a rugged and durable European design sometimes called the Chamelot-Delvigne. Because of the double or "rocker type" cylinder bolt on the trigger, the cylinders of the new arms required a series of circumferential grooves which lent them an unusual appearance. The detachable sideplates originally used in these revolvers necessitated the removal of too much metal from the frame; and within a year of their introduction the guns acquired smaller sideplates and correspondingly stiffer frames.[83]

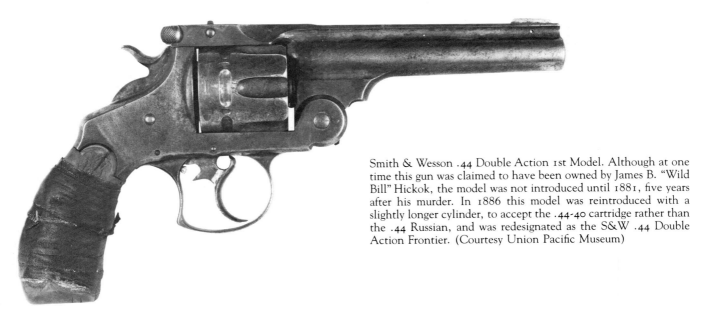

Smith & Wesson .44 Double Action 1st Model. Although at one time this gun was claimed to have been owned by James B. "Wild Bill" Hickok, the model was not introduced until 1881, five years after his murder. In 1886 this model was reintroduced with a slightly longer cylinder, to accept the .44-40 cartridge rather than the .44 Russian, and was redesignated as the S&W .44 Double Action Frontier. (Courtesy Union Pacific Museum)

Cow punchers, as they may well have been, in a studio cabinet card view taken in Glendive, Montana. The clothing, like the revolver, may have been loaned by the photographer if his customers had nothing appropriate for the occasion. The revolver, apparently an S&W large-frame double action, dates the scene as being no earlier than about 1882. (Courtesy Mr. Emory A. Cantney, Jr.)

By June of 1880 Carlos Gove of Denver was able to offer "a full line of Colt's and Smith & Wesson New Double Action Pistols," while competitor John Lower advertised "Colt, Smith & Wesson and other Double Action Pistols." These double-action Smith & Wessons were undoubtedly .38s; and although both dealers very probably handled the .32s once they were on the market, westerners by 1880 generally avoided anything smaller than .38 caliber for defense purposes. Better adapted for such buyers was the big six-shot double-action .44—simply a scaled-up version of the .38—that Daniel Wesson introduced in the summer of 1881. Initially chambered for the Russian cartridge, the double-action .44 was available with a barrel from 4 in. to 6½ in. long. While it did not sell as well as his double-action .38, Wesson's new .44 nevertheless became reasonably successful.[84]

One Smith & Wesson earned a fair amount of newspaper publicity as the result of a nearly fatal accident. In May of 1882 an unnamed "public officer" came into O. H. Viergutz's gun shop in Pueblo, Colorado, and asked Mr. Ed. T. Smith, who was behind the counter, to show him a double action Smith & Wesson revolver. Mr. Smith handed him one of the weapons asked for, which the man examined minutely and declared himself well satisfied with its working and finish, stating that he had a very similar one, at the same time drawing the weapon from his overcoat pocket. As he drew the weapon he pointed it directly across the counter about one degree to the left of Mr. Smith's position, and pulled the trigger to show how it worked. The bullet struck the counter, shattered two pocket knives into kindling wood,

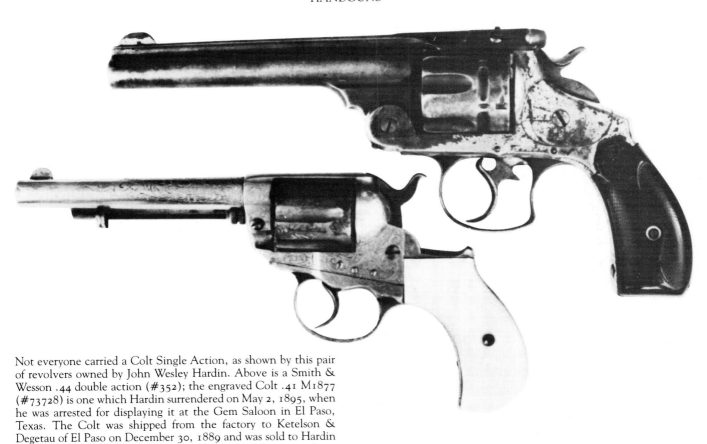

Not everyone carried a Colt Single Action, as shown by this pair of revolvers owned by John Wesley Hardin. Above is a Smith & Wesson .44 double action (#352); the engraved Colt .41 M1877 (#73728) is one which Hardin surrendered on May 2, 1895, when he was arrested for displaying it at the Gem Saloon in El Paso, Texas. The Colt was shipped from the factory to Ketelson & Degetau of El Paso on December 30, 1889 and was sold to Hardin in April 1895. (S&W from the Ron Peterson Collection, photo courtesy Mr. Robert E. McNellis, Jr.)

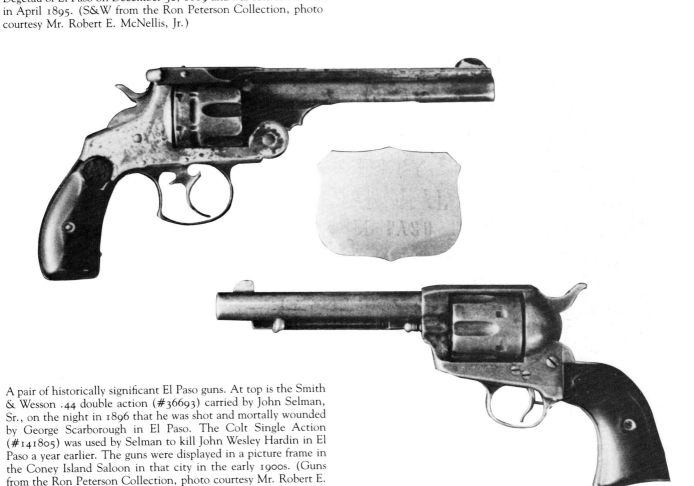

A pair of historically significant El Paso guns. At top is the Smith & Wesson .44 double action (#36693) carried by John Selman, Sr., on the night in 1896 that he was shot and mortally wounded by George Scarborough in El Paso. The Colt Single Action (#141805) was used by Selman to kill John Wesley Hardin in El Paso a year earlier. The guns were displayed in a picture frame in the Coney Island Saloon in that city in the early 1900s. (Guns from the Ron Peterson Collection, photo courtesy Mr. Robert E. McNellis, Jr.)

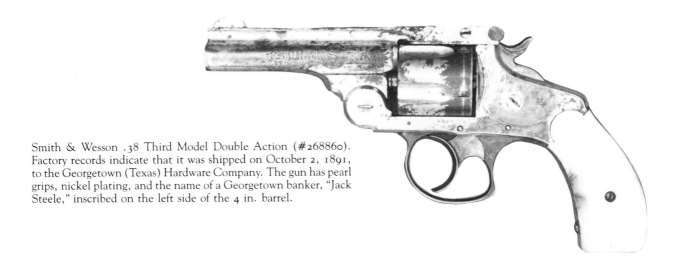

Smith & Wesson .38 Third Model Double Action (#268860). Factory records indicate that it was shipped on October 2, 1891, to the Georgetown (Texas) Hardware Company. The gun has pearl grips, nickel plating, and the name of a Georgetown banker, "Jack Steele," inscribed on the left side of the 4 in. barrel.

A Missouri Pacific Railroad–marked brass padlock and .45 Colt Single Action (#149875), the latter produced about 1893. The revolver is stamped "MO. PAC. RY." on the bottom of the butt.

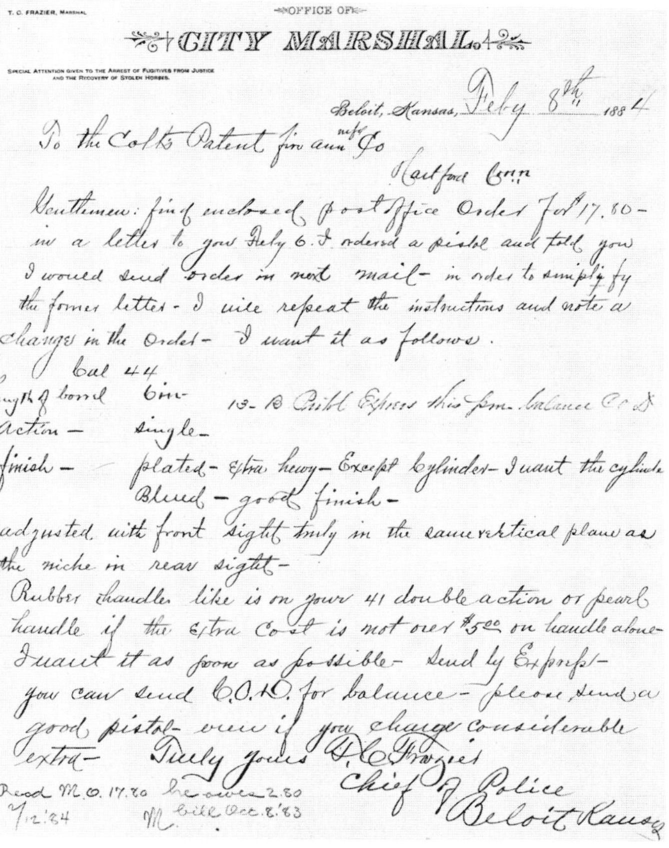

A letter from the city marshal of Beloit, Kansas, in 1884 ordering a .44 Colt Single Action with combination of nickel plate and blued finish. (Courtesy Connecticut State Library)

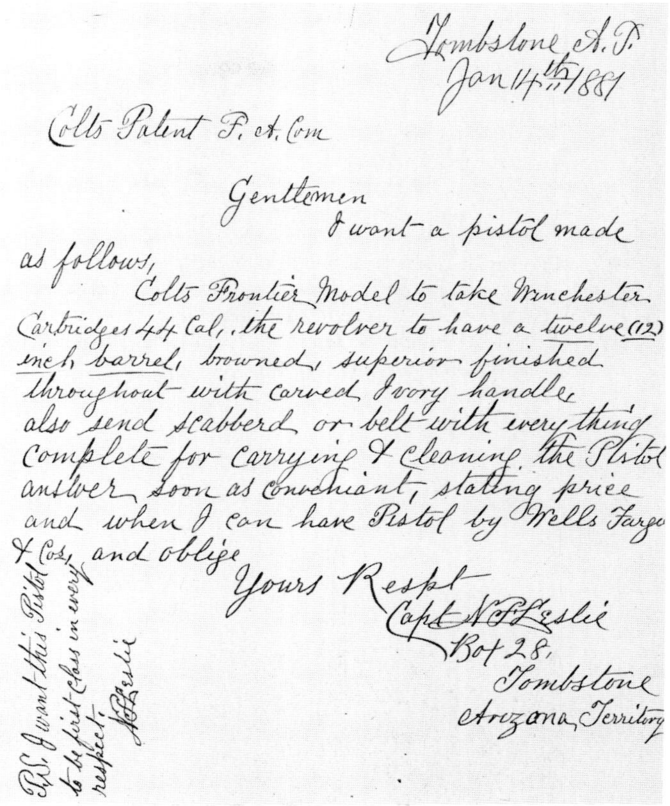

Capt. N. "Buckskin" Frank Leslie's order from Tombstone, Arizona, for a 12 in. barrel .44-40 Single Action Colt with browned finish. The colorful Leslie spent much of his time in Tombstone dispensing drinks at the Oriental Saloon. (Courtesy Connecticut State Library)

and glancing, passed through a box filled with table knives, coming out in three pieces. . . . With the announcement that he "did not know it was loaded," the officer planked down the cash for the pistol he had been examining, and pocketing both weapons departed as quickly as possible.

This article was subtitled "Another Case of Careless Handling of Fire Arms" because yet another accidental discharge had occurred near Pueblo just a few weeks earlier, in a railroad express car. The individual involved was Samuel Robinson, the local Adams Express Company agent:

The train was bowling along at a lively rate about half way between Canon City and Florence, and Mr. Robinson having everything in tip top style stooped down and unlocked his safe and placed

therein some valuable packages. As he was in the act of arising to a standing position again, a forty-four calibre Colt's revolver, which was lying upon the edge of the coal box near which the safe was standing, and which had not been noticed by Mr. Robinson, was jolted from its position, and falling on the floor of the car almost directly in front of him, exploded, the ball passing through the left lapel of his coat, thence through his vest and shirt, striking the collar bone and glancing. . . .[85]

As this account suggests, the Colt's widespread popularity, in both single- and double-action versions, continued unabated. Some buyers, unwilling to settle for standard models, special-ordered their guns directly from the factory, explaining in detail just what they wanted. In January of 1881, for example, W. R.

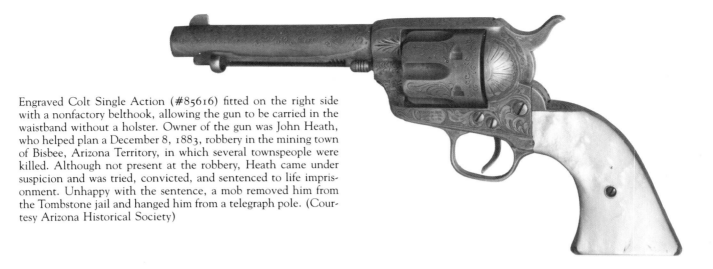

Engraved Colt Single Action (#85616) fitted on the right side with a nonfactory belthook, allowing the gun to be carried in the waistband without a holster. Owner of the gun was John Heath, who helped plan a December 8, 1883, robbery in the mining town of Bisbee, Arizona Territory, in which several townspeople were killed. Although not present at the robbery, Heath came under suspicion and was tried, convicted, and sentenced to life imprisonment. Unhappy with the sentence, a mob removed him from the Tombstone jail and hanged him from a telegraph pole. (Courtesy Arizona Historical Society)

McFarland of the U.S. Marshal's Office in Austin, Texas, ordered from the Colt concern:

> A single action pistol, 41. cal. but the same size & c, as the 45 cal. With ejector. Barrell 5 inches. Hind sight finer than that commonly made. Plated in the very heaviest manner possible, even if it costs extra. I want you to have blued, a stripe across the frame of the pistol about 1/2 an inch wide, including the rear sight, and extending behind and below it. You made a double action pistol for me about 2 years [ago], which you blued in the manner I wish, and it was very satisfactory. Best Pearl handle. . . . And do not forget to fix the price as low as you consisten[t]ly can, in consideration of my many orders to you, as well as my official possition under the U.S.

A few days later the company received a letter from another southwesterner. Writing from Tombstone, Arizona Territory, Captain N. F. Leslie ordered:

> [a] Colts Frontier Model to take Winchester Cartridges 44 Cal, the revolver to have a *twelve (12) inch barrel,* browned, superior finished throughout with carved ivory handle, also send scabberd or belt with everything complete for carrying & cleaning the Pistol. . . . P.S. I want this Pistol to be first class in every respect.[86]

Reflecting the enduring appeal of the Colt single-action was a letter from John Lower, written in the fall of 1881. In addition to an order for nine .38 and

.41 Lightnings with 2 1/2 in. and 3 1/2 in. barrels, Lower asked for "6—Frontier Army Sgl Action" and noted that:

> as I have only 22 Peacemakers on hand and it takes a month to get Freight goods through here—I would suggest the sending of another *Case* of Peacemakers by Freight on same terms as heretofore—Would prefer 10 or 15 of the case to be *Nickel Plated* if admissable.

At least two of the six-shooters used in the famous gunfight at Tombstone's OK Corral in 1881 were Colt single action .44s. One of them (serial no. 46,338) belonged to slain outlaw Frank McLowery, the other (serial no. 52,196) to his equally unfortunate comrade, young Billy Clanton.[87]

An interesting series of letters came to the Colt firm from City Marshal T. C. Frazier of Beloit, Kansas. (The marshal's letterhead stated: "Special Attention given to the Arrest of Fugitives from Justice and the Recovery of Stolen Horses.") In September of 1882 Frazier bought "one of your Colt's .41 Cal. 5 inch D. A. Pistols No 31783." In a shooting match, however, the marshal was badly beaten by a "Smith & Weston pistol," and found that the front sight of his .41 was incorrectly aligned. He asked the factory for a new gun in exchange, because

> at 100 yds I am unable to hit a target 5 ft square. I have owned your Peacemaker 45 cal and your Police 38 and with both these in the month of March last, I put 12 consecutive shots into a 12

Merwin & Hulbert .44 "open top" and holster, found in a house in Lincoln County, New Mexico, with an arrest warrant signed by Sheriff Pat Garrett. The barrel was long ago cut to 4¹/₂ in. and the original sight replaced, possibly for carrying in a shoulder holster, partially suspended by the high sight. (Courtesy Mr. E. Lee Manning, Jr.)

inch target at 100 yds distant firing at the Call of one two three—

In April of 1883 Frazier wrote again:

about the 1st of Nov. 1882 you Exchanged Pistols with me—you sent me a plated D.A. 6 in 41 cal. with a request to let you know how I liked [it]—I have used every Pistol that is made in America and some of European manufacture. I consider the Pistol you sent me the best of all—it is more easily carried than your 44 or 45 cal.—has with 41 cartridges (long) a greater penetration I think, than your 45— I have shot through a 5 inch cedar post at 100 yards—for Police Marshals, or Sheriffs in the West where every second or third man that is arrested resists, it is the best gun an officer can carry. . . . The self cocking apparatus works well but I do not use it—I consider it the best Pistol made I will wager money & big money on hiting a Man at 200 yards for 24 consecutive shots (I mean the size of a man). . . .

But the marshal encountered an unexpected problem with the .41, and penned yet another letter to Colt in February of 1884:

I want a 44 calibre single action pistol—what is called in the West "The Frontier"—I want it made or finished as follows: cal. 44 single action 6 in barrel, instead of 7¹/₂ in—I don't want a wooden handle—I want a rubber or pearl handle . . . I want it extra heavily Nickel plated [Except Cylinder—I want the cylinder Blued]—not too hard on triger— Centre fire . . . send me a good one and a nice one, so that I can still preach Colts pistols to the boys . . . I sold my 41 to our New Sheriff—it was and is the finest arm ever turned out of a shop—the reason I sold it was, 2 months since while traveling in pursuit of a man I ran out of Colts 41 cartridges and could hardly find any of them in any of the country towns while every village and hamlet would offer 44 cartridges—I can find 44 cartridges anywhere—not so with the 41. . . .[88]

NEW COMPETITORS: THE MERWIN & HULBERT, AND OTHERS

The fact that both Colt and Smith & Wesson were offering buyers double-action as well as single-action arms undoubtedly influenced other domestic manufacturers to add double-actions to their lines. During the 1880s Harrington & Richardson, Marlin, American Arms, Iver Johnson, and others, all of whom had earlier made sheath-trigger pocket revolvers, began turning out new double-action pistols. Illustrating this trend was the progression of Merwin & Hulbert revolvers made by Hopkins & Allen, with their unusual rotating and sliding barrel-cylinder assemblies. From its formal introduction in 1876 until well into 1879, the Merwin & Hulbert was evidently available only as an open-top single-action with 7 in. barrel, chambered for a .44 centerfire cartridge. Although the army's interest in this gun was fleeting, the State of Kansas bought some of them, stamping the frames

A probable Union Pacific Railroad Company Merwin & Hulbert
.44 (#941). The backstrap bears the letters "UPRR CO."

Army and Navy Journal, October 1880.

Mine guard E. H. "Wild Ben" Raymond holding a .44 Merwin &
Hulbert "open top" and wearing what is probably a holstered S&W
No. 3 New Model. The guns, knife, and holster rig are probably
studio props, since they duplicate those appearing in the photo
of another mine guard named Anderson. Both photos were taken
in the studio of a photographer named Needles in Leadville, Colorado, about 1879. (Courtesy Mr. William B. Secrest)

326

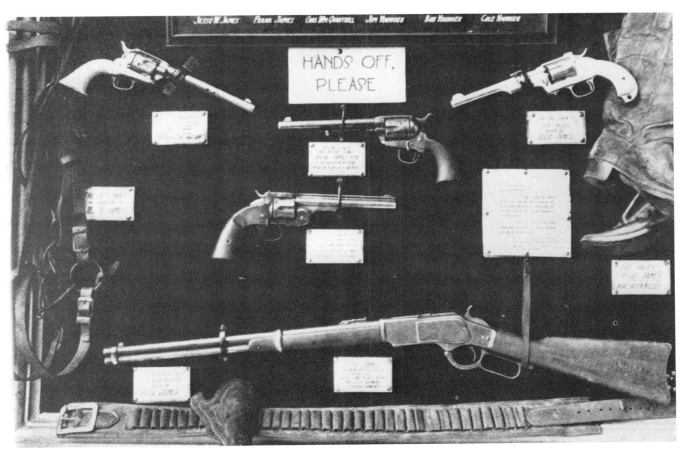

A display of Jesse James's guns, authenticated by his son, including a pair of Colt Single Actions, a .45 Smith & Wesson Schofield (bottom center), a .44 Merwin & Hulbert (upper right), and a Winchester M1873 carbine.

"Property Of The State Of Kansas" on one side and "Not Transferable" on the other.[89]

Ostensibly the reason for omitting the topstrap was that without it, less of the gas and powder fouling escaping from the barrel-cylinder gap was deflected downward into the mechanism. By 1880, however, Merwin & Hulbert had brought out another model, a five-shot single-action sheath-trigger .38 centerfire arm, complete with topstrap over the cylinder. About 1881 the firm introduced its "Pocket Army," which except for the 3⁵/16 in. barrel and parrot-beak butt, was the same as the long-barreled open-top .44. A Merwin & Hulbert advertisement in September of 1882 for "38 & 44 Cal. Pocket [and] 44 Cal Belt" revolvers noted that the "Pocket Sizes [are] Also Made With Extra Barrels, Belt Size, Interchangeable"; thus the purchaser of a short-barreled pocket model could, for a few extra dollars, have a longer barrel for his gun, which he could install in a few moments.[90]

The revolver shown in this 1882 ad was a .44 single-action with topstrap over the cylinder, an improvement which was incorporated in all the Merwin & Hulberts made thereafter. And if double-action Merwin & Hulberts were not available in the fall of 1882, they were available soon afterward. A double-action .38 was on the market by the fall of 1883, and by mid-1884 the firm's offerings included .38s and .44s in both single- and double-action versions. The .44s were chambered not only for the special Merwin & Hulbert cartridge, but also for the more desirable .44-40 Winchester load. As late as 1889 the .44, and possibly the .38, were still on hand in single-action form, but after the mid-1880s the company put much more emphasis on its double-actions, especially the double-action .38, and marketed it not ony with interchangeable barrels, but also with such novelties as folding hammer spurs.[91]

Although a Merwin & Hulbert ad of 1880 stated that its revolvers "can be procured through any Hardware or Fire Arms Dealer in the United States," there

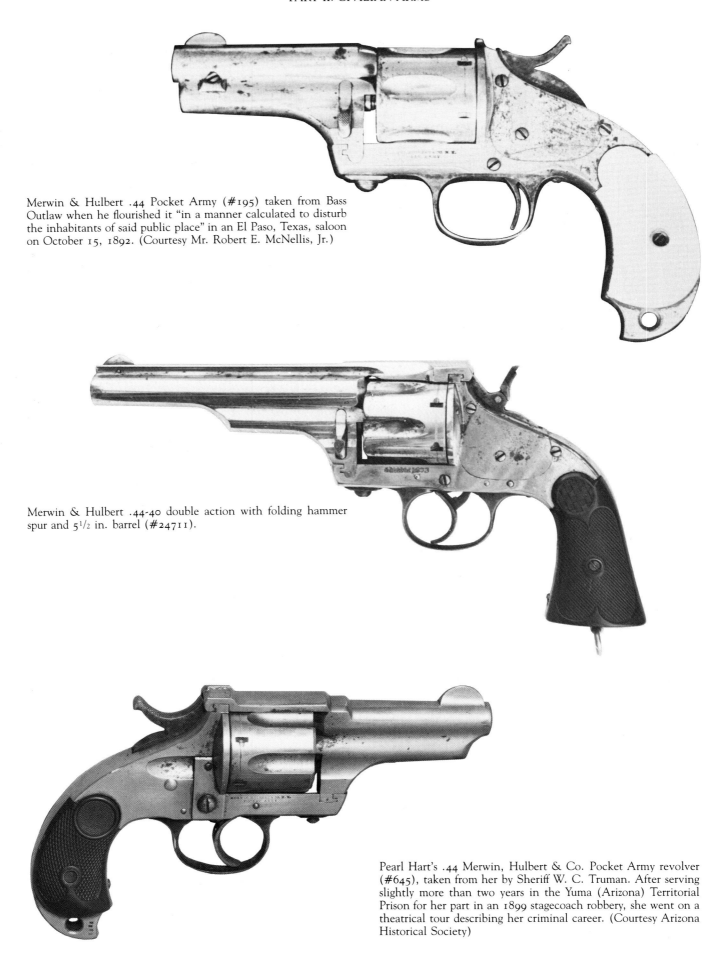

Merwin & Hulbert .44 Pocket Army (#195) taken from Bass Outlaw when he flourished it "in a manner calculated to disturb the inhabitants of said public place" in an El Paso, Texas, saloon on October 15, 1892. (Courtesy Mr. Robert E. McNellis, Jr.)

Merwin & Hulbert .44-40 double action with folding hammer spur and 5½ in. barrel (#24711).

Pearl Hart's .44 Merwin, Hulbert & Co. Pocket Army revolver (#645), taken from her by Sheriff W. C. Truman. After serving slightly more than two years in the Yuma (Arizona) Territorial Prison for her part in an 1899 stagecoach robbery, she went on a theatrical tour describing her criminal career. (Courtesy Arizona Historical Society)

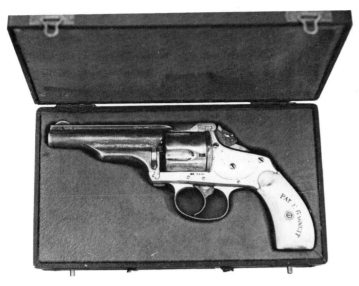

Cased .38 Merwin & Hulbert (#16648), one of several revolvers presented to Sheriff Pat Garrett of Lincoln County, New Mexico, probably in recognition of his ridding the territory of the outlaw Billy the Kid. Garrett's name appears in gold letters on the top of the case and in black enamel on the ivory grips. A Hopkins & Allen .32 Model XL (#3164) with Garrett's name inscribed on the barrel was inventoried with his other possessions after his murder in 1908. (Courtesy Mr. Calvin Moerbe)

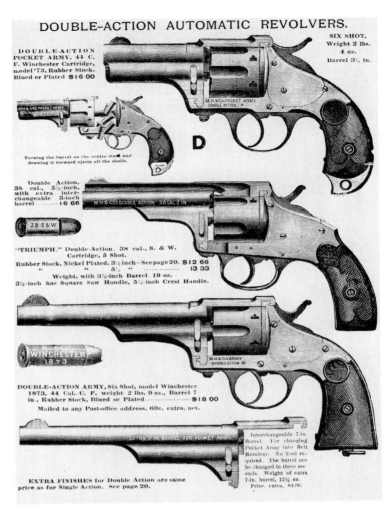

From the 1884 E. C. Meacham Arms Co. (St. Louis) catalog, illustrating the variety of Merwin & Hulbert revolvers available.

was evidently no surplus of the guns in the West until later. One reason for this may have been that sizable quantities were exported to Mexico under the auspices of Wexel & DeGress. In the spring of 1888, however, John Lower of Denver listed the guns in all three calibers, and other western dealers were very probably handling them at about the same time.[92]

Because they were beautifully made and finished, the Merwin & Hulberts were highly creditable to their manufacturer, Hopkins & Allen. Under its own name Hopkins & Allen made less beautifully finished and less-sophisticated revolvers, which nevertheless enjoyed a rather widespread distribution in the West. These guns, the "XL" series of sheath-trigger pocket arms introduced in the early 1870s, sold briskly through the mid-1880s. While they were somewhat roughly finished, they were well designed and fabricated of good material; these factors, combined with a slightly lower price than that for a similar pocket-model Colt, helped prolong their popularity. During the late 1870s Hopkins & Allen did market two highly finished solid-frame single-actions, the "XL Navy" and the "XL #8," in .38 and .44 rimfire respectively, but the firm evidently found the medium-price field more to its liking,

and made these large-frame XLs only in limited quantities. More plentiful were the "XL Double Action" revolvers which the company began marketing in the mid-1880s. Made with octagon barrels from 2 1/2 in. to 6 in. long, these solid-frame arms were again in the medium-price bracket, but were nonetheless serviceable. As A. C. Gould described one of the .32 centerfire models after testing it: "the parts [bore] no comparison with the workmanship of a Smith & Wesson or a Colt revolver, and it was not a smooth-working revolver. It was poorly sighted. . . . But with the above faults, it shot quite well and regularly." Also available in .38 centerfire, the XL Double Action was distributed by a number of dealers in the West, including John Lower of Denver and Nathaniel Curry and Liddle & Kaeding, both of San Francisco.[93]

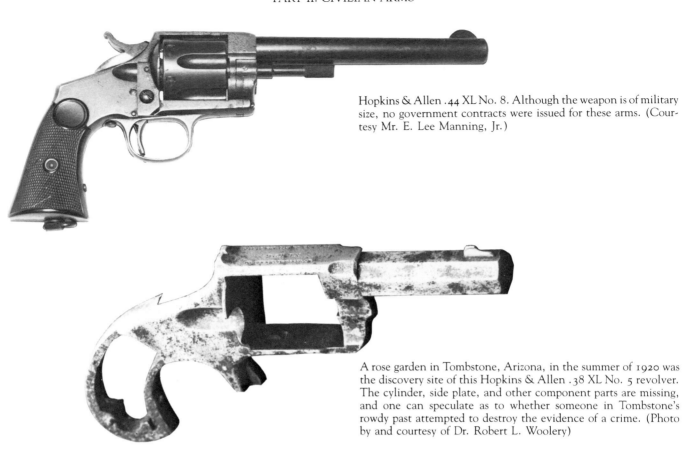

Hopkins & Allen .44 XL No. 8. Although the weapon is of military size, no government contracts were issued for these arms. (Courtesy Mr. E. Lee Manning, Jr.)

A rose garden in Tombstone, Arizona, in the summer of 1920 was the discovery site of this Hopkins & Allen .38 XL No. 5 revolver. The cylinder, side plate, and other component parts are missing, and one can speculate as to whether someone in Tombstone's rowdy past attempted to destroy the evidence of a crime. (Photo by and courtesy of Dr. Robert L. Woolery)

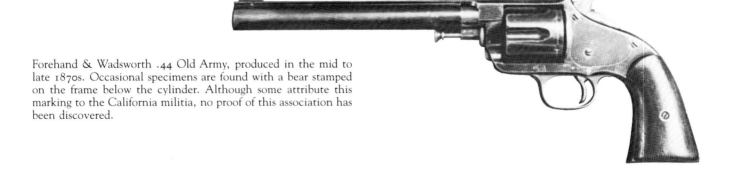

Forehand & Wadsworth .44 Old Army, produced in the mid to late 1870s. Occasional specimens are found with a bear stamped on the frame below the cylinder. Although some attribute this marking to the California militia, no proof of this association has been discovered.

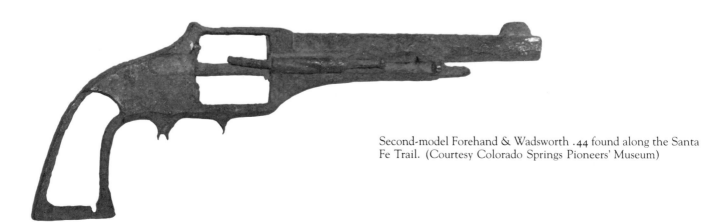

Second-model Forehand & Wadsworth .44 found along the Santa Fe Trail. (Courtesy Colorado Springs Pioneers' Museum)

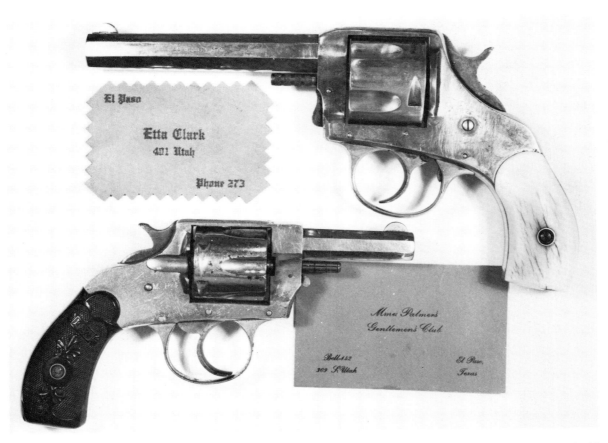

A pair of El Paso prostitutes' guns. Above, a Harrington & Richardson "American Bulldog" in .44 Webley caliber used in an 1886
shooting affair between Alice Abbott and Etta Clark, madams
whose business establishments were across the street from each
other. Alice was shot in the "public arch" with this revolver, but
survived. Below is a Forehand & Wadsworth .32 double action
(#144884) owned by May Palmer, who moved to El Paso in 1889
and opened her own house in 1898. The revolver is marked "M.P."
on the right side of the frame. (Courtesy Mr. Robert E. McNellis,
Jr.)

Hopkins & Allen's closest competitor was Forehand
& Wadsworth, a firm which recognized the trend toward double-action revolvers sooner than most other
American manufacturers. Although the .44 caliber
single-action arm they submitted to the army for testing in December of 1874 was unsuccessful, Forehand
& Wadsworth had a modification of it ready for the
market within two years. Unlike the older gun, whose
ejector was housed inside a hollow cylinder pin, the
new .44 had a more conventional side-rod ejector, as
well as a Remington-like metal web under the barrel.
A John Lower advertisement in the 1877 Denver Directory specifically mentioned "Forehand & Wadsworth's New Army Pistols, just out, using same cartridge
as Winchester Central Fire Rifle, 44 cal." By May of
1877 the firm was chambering this revolver for the
.45 Colt round as well as for the .44-40. Despite the
fact that it was a high-quality arm, the gun became
no more successful than the Hopkins & Allen XL Navy
or XL #8.[94]

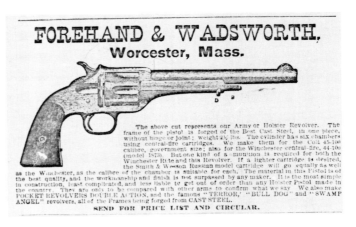

Forest and Stream, May 1877.

Arthur L. Walker, one of the many nineteenth-century black cowboys. The bulldog-type revolver is undoubtedly a studio prop, for the holster is much better suited to carry a larger frame Colt Single Action. (Courtesy Denver Public Library, Western History Dept.)

As early as 1876, however, Forehand & Wadsworth had brought out a pocket-size solid-frame double-action chambered for the .32, .38, and .41 Long rimfire cartridges. In somewhat modified form this gun was listed by Nathaniel Curry in the early 1880s. Curry also handled another Forehand & Wadsworth in the early 1880s, the company's "British Bull Dog," which except for its fluted cylinder and "saw handle" was a fairly close copy of the original Webley Bulldog. Offered in .32, .38, and .44 caliber, the F & W Bulldog was, in Curry's words, "decidedly the best and cheapest of the low grades of American self-cocking revolvers. . . . Parts are interchangeable, and quality is far superior to the imported."[95] A .38 double action Forehand & Wadsworth was the weapon used in the murder of a woman's husband by her suspected lover in January of 1881. The murderer was removed from jail by a vigilante committee and was hanged from a blacksmith's hoisting frame on the site of the killing in Bodie, California.

Presumably, the F & W Bulldog cut into the sales of Webley's Bulldog, but that model was not the only Webley to reach the West. For that matter, other English handguns besides Webleys were also in use there. In the 1881 edition of *The Gun and Its Development*, W. W. Greener wrote:

> The large double horse-pistols used for buffalo-shooting in America are of .577 bore, and usually have [the] double-grip action. . . . They are sometimes, however, made with side-lever action . . . they take the Snider case and spherical bullet; the barrels are about six inches long. These pistols are generally made in pairs for the saddle-holsters, and weigh about 3½ lbs. each; they are clumsy but very effective weapons. . . .[96]

By the 1880s, however, revolvers were more in evidence than big double-barreled pistols. Writing to a British sporting paper, *The Field*, early in 1884, an English sportsman who styled himself "Disarmed" told of his experience on the American frontier in 1883. Before embarking, "Disarmed" bought "a Webley revolver of the latest pattern, [which] shot with great precision, and before leaving England I was thoroughly satisfied with it." Upon reaching the frontier, however, Disarmed found that although the .45 caliber cartridges made by Eley had fit his revolver, those made by Winchester would not. With questionable logic, he concluded that "the only thing to be done, therefore, was to file away the back of the breech. This I did, and then was able to shoot my pistol as well as look at it." Shortly afterward the gun began to malfunction, and Disarmed ended up with a Colt single-action .44. Another of the *Field*'s correspondents, referring to Disarmed's filing away of the breech, wrote caustically:

> Applying the most ordinary rules of reasoning, "Disarmed" might have seen that the cartridges were at fault, not the revolver. . . . Has [he] read, in "Alice in Wonderland," how the March hare lubricated the hatter's watch with butter, put in with the bread knife, and how the watch stopped because some bread crumbs had got in, although the butter was the very best?[97]

Other British revolvers that came to the West in the 1870s and 1880s ranged in quality from superb to miserable. It may have been one of the latter that yet another *Field* correspondent, "E.S.B.," was describing when he wrote in 1884:

> Some time ago, when travelling in the Western States, I carried an English [revolver]. My American friends did not fancy it, and said it was sure to get out of order. One day I had occasion to use it, luckily not in self-defence. I attempted to fire at a large badger; the pistol would not go off. The shaking caused by constant galloping had disarranged the lock. Since then I have invariably used an American single action. It has always answered perfectly; indeed, I have never heard of one getting out of order. A Western man cocks and fires his single action Colt almost as quickly, and shoots straighter with it, than most Europeans with their double-action revolvers.[98]

In spite of E.S.B.'s enthusiasm for American single-actions, British double-actions, especially Webleys, were fairly popular items among American arms dealers during the late 1870s and early 1880s, particularly in the East. In 1880, for example, Homer Fisher of New York offered a selection of "Webley's Double Action Holster Size, for Frontier Use," in .38 and .44 calibers. A bigger New York house, H. & D. Folsom, had advertised Webley Bulldog and "Pug" revolvers in 1878, and

Three friends "cut up" with revolver, knife, and club as they pose for a tintype, a popular form of photographic image during the post–Civil War era. Owing to prohibitions against carrying concealed weapons in many western towns and cities, the bulldog-type revolver is probably a prop. The scene may have been taken somewhere in the Southwest, judging from the sombrero. (Courtesy Mr. Emory A. Cantney, Jr.)

An engraved .44 Webley "Bulldog" revolver with pearl grips, owned by nineteenth-century Tucson Mayor Charles Strauss. (Courtesy Arizona Historical Society)

333

Detective William A. Pinkerton (seated) with an English Webley–
style revolver in his belt. Pat Connell (left), Southern Express
Co. special agent, has a Colt New Line–type revolver thrust in
his pocket. Both Pinkerton and Sam Finley, Southern Express Co.
assistant special agent, hold Winchester M1873 carbines.

A miners' court in session in Cripple Creek, Colorado, probably in the 1890s. A variety of revolvers decorate the temporary courtroom, most significant of which is an English-made double action, possibly a Webley, in the center. Webley made such a revolver in various forms and in many popular English and American calibers from .32 to .476. (Courtesy Denver Public Library, Western History Dept.)

Belgian or German six-shot 9 mm pinfire revolver found along the old Pike's Peak Trail. (Courtesy Colorado Springs Pioneers' Museum)

in August of 1882 listed still another model in the *Army and Navy Journal:* "Webley's New Army Double Action Revolver, adapted to our .45 cal. Government Cartridges." This was probably the Webley "New Model Army Express," a heavy-barreled, solid-frame arm with side-rod ejector whose cylinder would accept .455 British service or .45 Colt cartridges interchangeably. The frame, in fact, was stamped "455 CF & 45 Long." Whether Folsom shipped any of the Webley "Army"

revolvers to the West is uncertain, but they would have been well suited for frontier service.[99]

Regardless of which Webley models reached the West, the Bulldog was unquestionably the most popular. During a pursuit of outlaws across Colorado's western slope in 1887, Doc Shores noted that "in our hurry to get started . . . Allison forgot his customary plug of tobacco and the cartridges to his Winchester. Fortunately, he did remember to load the little British

An example of early firearms regulatory legislation, the sign in the center of Front Street in Dodge City, Kansas, in the 1880s warns that "The Carrying of Firearms [Is] Strictly Prohibited." (Courtesy Kansas State Historical Society)

Bull Dog pistol, which he carried in a holster at his hip." Again, the Bulldog's appeal lay in the fact that it was small and readily concealed, yet chambered a potent cartridge. The westerner's contempt for small-bore, low-powered handguns had reached full bloom by the 1880s, as illustrated by an incident that occurred in Flagstaff, Arizona, in 1886. After enduring the taunts of a dusty cowboy, a well-dressed easterner displayed a little .22 caliber pistol, whereupon the cowboy pulled his big .45 and scoffed, "Here, bring that damn thing over and let it suck."[100]

Besides its power the Bulldog's compact size was often a desirable asset in locales which frowned upon the open carrying of handguns; by the 1880s, especially in settled areas, there was growing disapproval of the wearing of handguns in belt or holster. A decade earlier the Abilene *Chronicle* had editorialized approvingly:

The Chief of Police [Wild Bill Hickok] has posted up printed notices, informing all persons that the ordinance against carrying fire arms or other weapons in Abilene, will be enforced. That's right. There's no bravery in carrying revolvers in a civilized community. Such a practice is well enough and perhaps necessary when among Indians or other barbarians, but among white people it ought to be discountenanced.[101]

Most frontiersmen, however, were used to carrying sidearms, and continued to carry them whenever possible. Recounting the story of an 1879 cattle drive, Baylis Fletcher mentioned that:

Since Montague was a border county, we were told that we could wear side arms without fear of arrest, so every cowpuncher who had a six-shooter buckled it on just to enjoy the privelege of carrying a weapon. [But] I had brought no pistol, my only weapon being a Winchester carbine, which hung in a leather scabbard from my saddle horn.

Even cowboys working cattle far from any settlement might fall afoul of regulations concerning handguns. In 1882 the Wyoming Stock Growers Association decreed that:

the custom of carrying fire arms by those engaged in the round-up and in working the cattle ranges is productive of great evil and frequently results in the damage of persons and property. Be it therefore Resolved, That the custom of carrying fire arms, except in the immediate vicinity of Indian reservations, should be discontinued. . . .

One of the rules of the XIT Ranch, formulated about three years later, stated that "Sixshooters or other small fire-arms will not be permitted to be carried on the ranch. If there were no other reasons, it is forbidden by statute in the State of Texas."[102]

In many quarters the prohibitions against handguns undoubtedly boosted the sales of concealable weapons. To a majority of plains dwellers, however, the carrying of concealed or "belly" guns was even more objectionable than the wearing of handguns in plain view. An ordinance adopted by the tiny rail crossing of Green River, Dakota Territory, as early as 1868 declared that "it shall be unlawful for any person to carry concealed weapons of any kind within the corporate limits." And in a cleverly worded editorial, the Tombstone *Nugget* stated in 1881:

The people who are anxious to assert their constitutional right to bear arms ought to do it openly. The revolutionary fathers, who put this into the bill of rights, did not go around with little pistols concealed in their hip pockets; they carried their rifles or muskets over their shoulders like men. If this be thought inconvenient in these undegenerate modern days, there is nothing to prevent the adop-

tion of the old Texan plan of carrying a brace of pistols and a knife or two in the belt. Or a neat modern breech-loading carbine might be worn gracefully slung over the shoulder by an embroidered strap, thus combining the ornamental and the useful. There are numerous ways of carrying arms that are much more picturesque than the hip-pocket plan. . . .[103]

Nevertheless, the practice continued to be widespread through the 1880s, and accounted largely for the protracted popularity of the most concealable of all big-bore pistols—the derringer. Railroad builder James Kyner

had learned in Idaho that the most effective way of covering a man without showing a gun was with a pair of Derringers in one's side pockets. Everyone knew, of course, that a man with his hands in the side pockets of a double-breasted coat had a Derringer in each hand.

Kyner's knowledge came in handy during the early 1880s, when he faced down a would-be assailant in Buena Vista, Colorado, "my hands still on those Derringers in my pockets." The derringers most in demand at this time were the Colt-Nationals, Colt No. 3, and the Remington over-under. Even though the National design was some twenty years old by the early 1880s, it still found its share of buyers. As late as July of 1887, in fact, the Simmons Hardware Company of St. Louis, a major firearms jobber which often supplied guns to dealers farther west, ordered from the Colt concern a quantity of revolvers and "5 prs Natl Derringers #1 full plated [and] 5 [prs] . . . #2 [full plated]."[104]

Frank Canton owned a Colt derringer in the early 1890s, while he was working as a lawman in Oklahoma: "I had a heavy pocket derringer that I usually carried in my hip pocket when in town. It was a forty-one-caliber Colt. I thought it was a good one, but had never tried it out." Canton's opinion of the gun changed abruptly in 1894, when a prisoner in his custody suddenly jumped him:

[Canton] pushed him away from me, and at the same time drew my derringer and fired at his head. The bullet struck him in the forehead just over the left eye. He fell on his back, and I supposed from the appearance of the wound that he was shot square through the head. [But] when the doctor examined the wound . . . he found that the bullet had not penetrated his head, but had glanced around the skull under the skin, and come out at the back of his head. He was unconscious for twelve hours, then commenced to improve . . . I threw away this derringer that I had, and have never carried one since.[105]

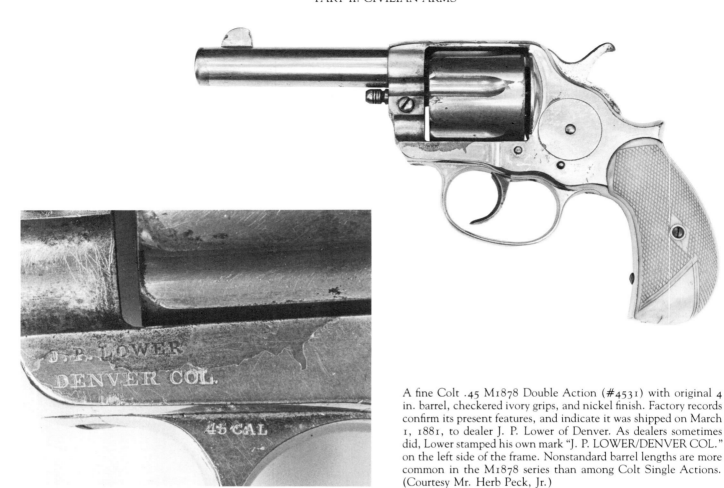

A fine Colt .45 M1878 Double Action (#4531) with original 4 in. barrel, checkered ivory grips, and nickel finish. Factory records confirm its present features, and indicate it was shipped on March 1, 1881, to dealer J. P. Lower of Denver. As dealers sometimes did, Lower stamped his own mark "J. P. LOWER/DENVER COL." on the left side of the frame. Nonstandard barrel lengths are more common in the M1878 series than among Colt Single Actions. (Courtesy Mr. Herb Peck, Jr.)

Remington's over-under derringer was proving to be one of the most popular firearms the company had ever made. As far as larger handguns were concerned, however, Remington had nothing up-to-date to offer. The firm's single-action Model 1875 was moderately successful, and the Smoot series of .32, .38, and .41 rimfire pocket and belt revolvers remained in wide distribution through the 1880s. But the company's line of handguns included no modern double-actions. The Remington-Rider double-action pocket and belt revolvers, converted to .32 and .38 rimfire respectively, were still available during the 1880s, but the guns had first appeared in the early 1860s, and they were not really competitive with the newer Colt and Smith & Wesson double-actions.[106]

THE PREDOMINANCE OF THE COLT AND THE SMITH & WESSON

Orders from all parts of the West continued to flood the Colt factory. One order from the Simmons Hard-ware Company in May of 1884 called for 148 Lightnings in .38 and .41 calibers, 65 Double-Action Armies in .44 and .45, and fully 200 Single-Action Armies, also in .44 and .45. Besides the standard blue and nickel finishes, Simmons ordered some of the Lightnings and Double-Action Armies "Plated And Eng[raved]." A year later John Lower sent for 4 Double-Action Armies, 10 Lightnings, and no fewer than 60 Single-Actions.[107]

Together with large orders from major dealers came orders from individuals for single guns. In January of 1887, for example, Gordon Blanding of Wells Fargo's San Francisco Office asked for a "*special* pistol":

I want a .44 calibre double-action 'frontier six-shooter' made with a barrel two and a half (2½) inches long. Then, instead of chambering the cylinder and barrel to shoot the Winchester model '73 cartridge which the 'frontier six-shooter' takes, I want both cylinder and barrel chambered to shoot the .41 calibre center-fire cartridge. . . .

Blanding's short-barreled double-action revolver had a good deal in common with the Colts ordered by Simmons and other dealers. Of the 148 Lightnings the Simmons concern purchased in 1884, 73 had 2¹/₂ in. and 3¹/₂ in. barrels; of the 65 Double-Action Armies bought at the same time, 15 had shorter than standard 4 in. barrels. A Simmons order of 1887 which included 39 Lightnings required that 35 of them have 3¹/₂ in. barrels.[108] There was obviously no lack of demand for revolvers with short, easily concealed barrels. During his stay in the Southwest, Major Frederick R. Burnham owned both a Winchester and a "sawed-off Colt to be carried under my arm or boot-leg." Thomas E. Crawford, alias the "Texas Kid," noted that while he was in Jackson's Hole at the close of the 1880s:

I found it necessary to wear at least one six-shooter where it could not be seen; for while it sometimes seemed to me to be a bit cowardly to do so, self-preservation is the first law of nature. I packed a sawed-off .45 in a light scabbard, inside my shirt in front at the belt-buckle location. The shirt was split down the front to give easy and quick access to the gun, and the scabbard was sewed to my underwear. It was quite common among gunmen and sheriffs at that time to carry one pistol upside down in a scabbard under the arm, with the gun hanging by the front sight. There was no drawing to it. You simply reached under your coat, flipped out your pistol, and fired from your stomach. It was all very quickly done. I seldom wore a coat; hence, the split shirt.

And N. Howard Thorp wrote:

Sometimes a bad man had a special leather pocket sewed inside his *chaparejos*. He would have it sewed with buckskin, using the same stitching as for the outside pockets, so it didn't show. He would carry a small gun in this hidden holster, and if he were expecting trouble, he could stand with his hands inside the chaps, looking innocent, but actually with his hand on his gun. One of the tricks I sometimes used when out alone was to sleep with my gun in my hand between my doubled-up knees. Another trick was to hold the gun in the crook under the knee when hunkered down cooking supper; it was handy there in case somebody suddenly spoke up out of the dark. . . .[109]

Whether long- or short-barreled, the Colt remained the weapon of choice. After his experience as a rancher in North Dakota, Theodore Roosevelt wrote: "Of course every ranchman carries a revolver, a long 45 Colt or Smith & Wesson, by preference the former." To help counter this situation, Daniel Wesson brought out his

The characteristic butt shape identifies a Colt M1878 Double Action revolver in the shoulder holster worn by Bertrand Sinclair (seated, right). He and his cowboy companions had their photo taken in the 1890s at Big Sandy, Montana. The shotgun in the scene may be a Frank Wesson double barrel. (Courtesy Montana Historical Society)

five-shot .38 caliber "Safety Hammerless" revolver in 1887. Like earlier Smith & Wessons, this was a hinged-frame, automatic-extraction design, but was distinctive because of its concealed hammer and grip safety. Although the field tests of this arm by the U.S. Cavalry in 1890–91 failed to result in government orders, the gun was almost immediately successful in the civilian market, and insired copies by Hopkins & Allen, the American Arms Company, Harrington & Richardson, Iver Johnson, and other makers. Before the close of the 1890s the barrel catch of the new Smith

The interior of a saloon in Albany County, Wyoming. The Iver Johnson or similar small-frame revolver stuck muzzle down in the glass at the bartender's left adds an element of humorous intrigue to the furnishings. (Courtesy Wyoming State Archives and Historical Dept.)

& Wesson underwent modification three times, with the frame contour altered accordingly; a second-model .38 replaced the first model in 1888, and in 1890 the second model gave way to a third model, which endured until displaced by a fourth in 1898. In contrast, the barrel catch of a little .32 caliber hammerless introduced in 1888 remained unchanged until after the turn of the century. The standard barrel lengths for the first two .38 caliber models were 3¼ in., 4 in., and 5 in., but a 6 in. barrel was available for the third model; the .32 came with a barrel of 3 in. or 3½ in. Besides their concealed hammers and grip safeties, the .32 and .38 had another feature in common—a "hesitation" trigger pull, which allowed their owners to shoot them almost as accurately as they could fire a single-action arm. A. C. Gould, who wrote one laudatory remark after another about the hammerless Smith & Wesson, stated:

> it has been found by actual experiment that, in the hands of those who only occasionally use a revolver, some of whom were cowboys of Colorado, a number would do more accurate work with one of these revolvers than with the target revolver,—due, no doubt, to the fact that the necessary [long trigger] pull rather steadied than disturbed the untrained nerves.

The guns used by the "cowboys of Colorado" may have come from John Lower, who was handling them by the spring of 1888 and perhaps earlier. Advertisements

Oklahoma State Capitol (Guthrie), July 1891.

Smith & Wesson .32 Safety (or Safety Hammerless or "Lemon Squeezer"). Popular as an easily concealed pocket revolver, the series was produced in .32 and .38 caliber from the late 1880s until shortly before World War II. (Courtesy Mr. E. Lee Manning, Jr.)

Wells Fargo–marked Colt Single Action (#147497), manufactured in 1892. Apparently, local Wells Fargo agents purchased many of the firm's guns prior to the centralization of purchasing by William Ashton of New York City about 1900. (Courtesy Mr. Willis E. Neuwirth)

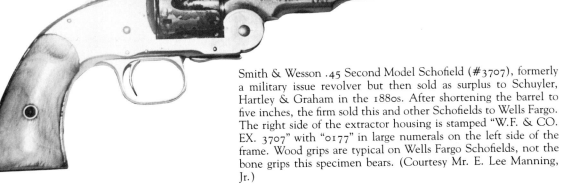

Smith & Wesson .45 Second Model Schofield (#3707), formerly a military issue revolver but then sold as surplus to Schuyler, Hartley & Graham in the 1880s. After shortening the barrel to five inches, the firm sold this and other Schofields to Wells Fargo. The right side of the extractor housing is stamped "W.F. & CO. EX. 3707" with "0177" in large numerals on the left side of the frame. Wood grips are typical on Wells Fargo Schofields, not the bone grips this specimen bears. (Courtesy Mr. E. Lee Manning, Jr.)

Waiting in Cowley County, Kansas, in 1893 to enter the Cherokee Strip, former Indian country. While the settler in the middle holds what appears to be a Sharps rifle, his companions' holstered re- volvers reflect the trend away from big handguns popular in earlier years to more compact .38 or .44 pocket-size weapons. (Courtesy Kansas State Historical Society)

for the hammerless were carried by a number of west- ern newspapers, such as the *Oklahoma State Capitol* and Colorado's *Buena Vista Herald*. Besides cowboys, railroad men and express messengers also used this gun. The U.S. Express Company bought some of the third-model .38s, stamping them with the company name and a code number.[110]

Where express companies were concerned, how- ever, the hammerless found itself in competition with an earlier Smith & Wesson, the single-action Scho- field. In the early 1880s Schuyler, Hartley & Graham had purchased a quantity of used Schofields from the federal government, and subsequently sold them to Wells Fargo. These guns, their barrels cut to a handy 5 in., were stamped "W. F. & Co. Ex." on the right side of the extractor housing.[111]

In site of the widespread sales of their solid-frame rod-ejecting revolvers, Colt executives realized that a handgun with faster loading and extraction charac- teristics (similar to those offered by the Smith & Wes- son) would be a highly desirable addition to their line.

During the early 1880s their designers had patented several simultaneous-extraction systems, various fea- tures of which went into the company's double-action "New Navy" revolver, adopted by the navy in 1888. Introduced commercially in the fall of 1889, the New Navy was characterized by its solid frame, crane- mounted "swing-out" cylinder, "push-button" extrac- tor, and rebounding hammer.[112]

Initially furnished in .38 and .41 Long Colt, with barrels of 3 in., 4½ in., and 6 in., the commercial version of the New Navy caused a good deal of interest among shooters. Mechanically, however, it was far from the ideal revolver, and was superseded by the "New Army" models of 1892 and 1894, with their more positive and durable cylinder-bolting system. But due to the multiplicity of parts, hard double-action trigger pull, and other drawbacks, the New Army revolvers were actually little better than their predecessor. In the entire New Navy/New Army series, the cylinder rotated to the left (or counterclockwise) and also swung outward to the left for loading. This meant that the

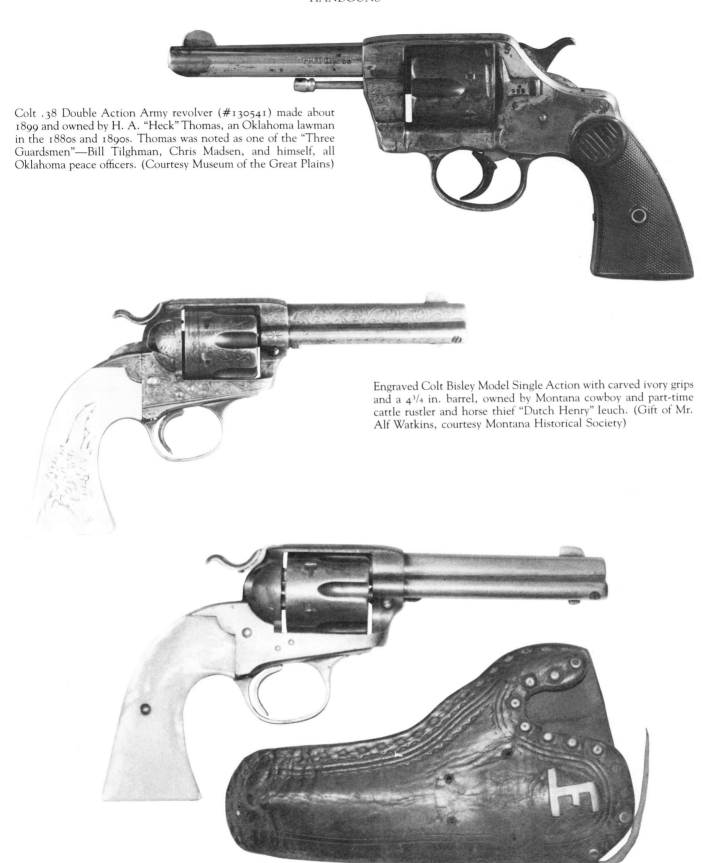

Colt .38 Double Action Army revolver (#130541) made about 1899 and owned by H. A. "Heck" Thomas, an Oklahoma lawman in the 1880s and 1890s. Thomas was noted as one of the "Three Guardsmen"—Bill Tilghman, Chris Madsen, and himself, all Oklahoma peace officers. (Courtesy Museum of the Great Plains)

Engraved Colt Bisley Model Single Action with carved ivory grips and a 4³/₄ in. barrel, owned by Montana cowboy and part-time cattle rustler and horse thief "Dutch Henry" Ieuch. (Gift of Mr. Alf Watkins, courtesy Montana Historical Society)

Colt .41 Bisley Model (#294017) made in 1907 and carried by Warren A. "Chip" Miles, a cowboy employed by the South Springs Ranch & Cattle Co. of Roswell, New Mexico, John Chisum's home ranch. The holster bears the Chisum brand. Miles started as a wrangler in 1887 at age nine and worked for other prominent cattlemen such as Charles Goodnight and Shanghai Pierce. (Courtesy Mr. Robert Bell)

343

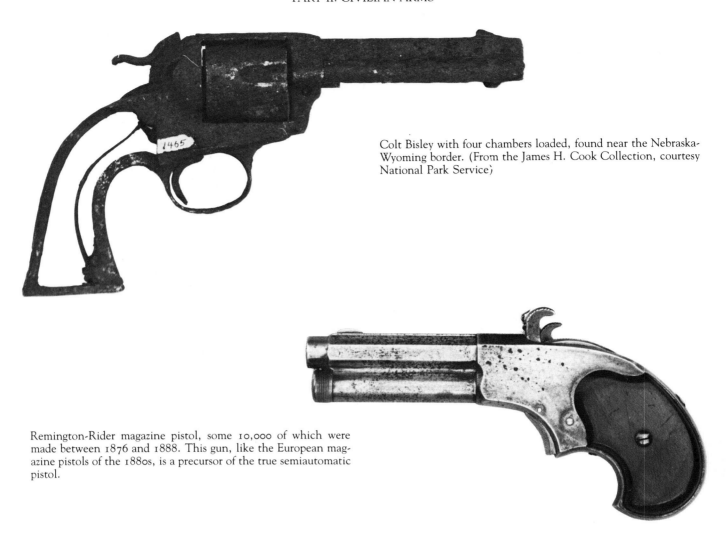

Colt Bisley with four chambers loaded, found near the Nebraska-Wyoming border. (From the James H. Cook Collection, courtesy National Park Service)

Remington-Rider magazine pistol, some 10,000 of which were made between 1876 and 1888. This gun, like the European magazine pistols of the 1880s, is a precursor of the true semiautomatic pistol.

pawl, thrusting upward against the ratchet teeth to the right of the cylinder axis, not only rotated the cylinder but tended to push it to the left, toward its open position, and thus put more wear on the latch that held the cylinder-crane assembly in place.[113]

To correct this shortcoming yet another double-action Colt with swing-out cylinder had materialized by 1894, the "New Pocket." At first glance this gun appeared to be merely a scaled-down version of the New Army, but in reality it embodied important mechanical improvements: the lockwork was simplified considerably and the cylinder, although still swinging out to the left for loading, now rotated to the right. From a mechanical standpoint, in fact, the New Pocket set the pattern for the hundreds of thousands of Colt revolvers to follow. A "New Police" came out in 1896, and a big "New Service" two years later. While the New Pocket and New Police were .32 caliber arms,

the New Service chambered much more powerful loads, including the .38-40, .44-40, .44 Russian, and .45 Colt.[114]

During the 1890s, of course, Colt's emphasis was on double-action arms, but in 1895 the company introduced still another large-frame single-action, the "Bisley Model." The Bisley was basically a single-action Army modified especially for target shooting: its backstrap formed one sharp curve from frame to butt, eliminating the intermediate hump just behind the recoil shield characteristic of the earlier single-action; in addition, its hammer spur was lower and wider and its trigger wider and more curved.[115]

Although it was designed as a target arm, the Bisley also rode in the holsters of working cowboys and other westrners. N. Howard Thorp noted that:

Guns were as natural a part of a cowhand's equipment as, say, a jackknife is of a boy's pocket kit,

Texas Rangers of Company A in 1902. The characteristic butt shape of a Colt Bisley protrudes from Tom Franks's holster (at right) while others carry standard model Colt Single Actions. Their Winchester rifles are all M1895s except for the M1886 in the center. (Courtesy Mr. Charles Schreiner, III)

Sheriff of Anadarko County, Oklahoma, and his deputies about 1901. Partially visible at the top of the stack of Winchester rifles is a German Mauser autoloading pistol with a detachable wooden holster/shoulder stock attached. Also in the stack of rifles is a Savage lever-action Model 1895 or 1899. (Courtesy Western History Collections, University of Oklahoma Library)

Members of Company A of the Texas Rangers photographed about 1902 at Brownsville, Texas. Captain J. A. Brooks (seated, third from left) holds a Mauser autoloading pistol with detachable stock, in contrast to his companions' Colt Single Actions and M1895 Winchester rifles. (Courtesy Mr. Charles Schreiner, III)

and only a few didn't carry them. A favorite kind was a Bisley Colt's .45 short, on which the barrel was no longer than the extractor. Many had a .38 built on a .45 frame; a gun like this didn't have as much kick as a .45, but was very heavy for the reason that there was so much more steel in it than in a regular .38.

John K. Rollinson, who joined the M-Bar Ranch in Wyoming in the 1890s, wrote later that:

We all carried guns. I remember that each of the six men had guns almost exactly alike. We all preferred the Colt single-action six-shooter. Some liked the Bisley model, others the Frontier model. Some were of different caliber, but all were built on a .45-caliber frame. I noticed that these men carried their guns with one empty shell in the cylinder, and five loaded cartridges. This was for safety's sake. The gun was carried with the hammer on the empty shell. . . .

Rollinson himself owned a ".45 single-action Bisley model Colt" and commented that it was exactly like that of Steve Clark, an associate.[116]

By 1900 new handguns of advanced design were making their appearance on the market almost continuously. Smith & Wesson had brought out a double-action .32 with swing-out cylinder in 1896, and a somewhat similar .38 in 1899. Far more sophisticated than these guns was the "new Colt automatic pistol, Browning's patent," which Frank A. Ellis & Son of Denver were selling by June of 1900, and the "new Luger Automatic Pistol" offered in December of 1901 by Ellis and other Denver dealers. Even at this late date, however, the Colt single-action revolver, in one form or another, was the most representative handgun in the West.

'MAUSER'

Self-Loading

Pistols or Carbines

are rapidly taking the place of the larger revolvers and less modern automatic or self-loading pistols all over the world. It has been adopted by many military governments, and as an offensive or defensive weapon for the Military, Sheriffs, Prospectors, Surveyors, Cowboys, and Frontiersmen, it has no equal. It is sighted up to 1000 yards. It will shoot a mile. It will penetrate 17 inches of pine. It can be fired six shots within one second, and holds six or ten cartridges, smokeless powder soft nose or full mantled bullets. It can be reloaded in a couple of seconds, and it is fully guaranteed. No other weapon will command the same WHOLESOME RESPECT among the awless, and as a BURGLARY, VIOLENCE, or RIOT PREVENTER there is nothing like it. It has killed bear, deer, and nearly all big game and little game to be found on this continent, and ts small size and light weight make it a most desirable auxiliary.

Price, Six Shot, Skeleton Stock, New Small Model......................$22.65
Ten Shot, Wooden Holster and Stock combined.........................25.00
Cartridges, either Soft Nose or Full Mantled, per 1,000.................25.00

Mauser, Latest Model, 7 mm. and 8 mm. SPORTING RIFLES, $45.00, with Double Set Trigger, $50.00.

Address your dealer or the U. S. Agents,

VON LENGERKE & DETMOLD,
318 Broadway,   New York.

Shooting & Fishing, January 1902.

Outdoor Life (Denver series), April 1902.

· PART III ·

INDIAN ARMS

THE IMMEDIATE POSTWAR YEARS saw renewed attempts to resolve the Indian problem, but the situation was muddled by disagreement regarding the proper policy to follow. On one point, however, there was general accord: that the Indians would have to relocate on reservations, away from areas of white settlement, and there learn to subsist for themselves by adopting the ways of the whites. But how best to get them there—and how to keep them there—was a matter of dispute. In the fall of 1865, for example, peace commissioners had signed treaties with the Sioux at Fort Sully and with the Cheyennes, Comanches, Kiowas, and Arapahos on the Little Arkansas; the treaties stipulated that if the Indians kept away from emigrant travel routes, the government would provide them with annuity payments. General John Pope, commanding the Department of the Missouri, took issue with annuity payments to Indians, calling them little more than bribes. He proposed instead a simple treaty stating that the army would keep the peace only so long as the Indians kept it, but as soon as the Indians displayed hostility the army would react overwhelmingly. In pushing this idea, however, Pope reflected the strong differences between the army and government civilians about how to deal with Indians. Since 1849 Indian affairs had been the responsibility of the Interior Department rather than the War Department; but once hostilities had become apparent, the responsibility for quelling them had shifted to the army. This situation had given rise to considerable friction during the 1850s, friction that increased during the 1860s and 1870s. As General Sherman himself said: "The Indian Bureau keeps feeding and clothing the Indians, regardless of their behavior, till they get fat and saucy, and then [only are we] notified that the Indians are troublesome, and are going to war, after it is too late to provide a remedy." Army officers were especially at odds with the Interior Department's Indian Bureau, which by the late 1860s was earning itself a black reputation for dishonesty and patronage politics.

But whether part of the Indian Bureau or another agency, civilians were nevertheless shaping the government's Indian policy. By 1866 there was growing sentiment in Congress for dealing with the tribes in a peaceful and conciliatory fashion, with the assumption that they would respond in kind. This feeling and the resultant idea of a "peace policy" were strengthened early in 1867 by publication of the findings of the Doolittle Committee. In 1865 Senator James R. Doolittle of Wisconsin and his colleagues had toured the frontier to determine the nature of the Indian problem; they returned to Washington convinced that most of the recent Indian wars had been the consequence of white transgression. Following General Hancock's excessive use of force against the Cheyennes in 1867 another peace commission, among which was former Tennessee Congressman Nathaniel Taylor, took the field. In October of 1867, on Medicine Lodge Creek south of Fort Larned, the commission negotiated treaties with the Kiowas and Comanches, and soon after with the disgruntled Cheyennes, promising them annual presents for thirty years and two large reservations in Indian Territory, where they would learn to farm. Traveling to the north, the commission also tried negotiating a similar treaty with the Sioux, but due to Red Cloud's implacable opposition to the army's presence on the Bozeman Trail, no prominent Sioux signed until the summer of 1868, when the military abandoned the Bozeman Trail posts. Only after that event did Red Cloud come to Fort Laramie and add his name to the treaty. The Laramie treaty gave the Sioux and other northern tribes the usual presents and a great reservation north of Nebraska and west of the Missouri River, with hunting rights outside that area as well.

The Taylor Commisson's report of 1868 laid the foundation for a formal peace policy toward the Indians. "Conquest by kindness" would henceforth guide relations with the tribes. The policy assumed broader dimensions when Ulysses S. Grant entered the White House in 1869; to the army's surprise, Grant proved amenable to a nonviolent approach to the Indian problem. But in addition to nonviolence, the policy also embodied other provisions. Despite the army's agitation for transfer of the Indian Bureau back to the War Department, civilians continued to control it. Moreover, due to the widespread corruption in the bureau, church groups would nominate new Indian agents. Initially all the agents were Quakers, but they later came from other faiths as well. A board of Indian commissioners made up of philanthropists, "ten good men," would watch over the disbursement of funds. Because the tribes were now to be regarded as wards of the government rather than separate nations, the long-lived treaty system was abandoned, although promises made in earlier treaties would be strictly honored. The one point on which most parties had agreed earlier remained prominent: the Indians were to settle on reservations, there to take up agriculture and Christianity. The army would be responsible for all Indians off the reservations, but those Indians on the reservation would be under control of the agent or superintendent, and military men would be barred from the reservation unless specifically invited thereon by the agent. Implicit throughout the policy was the point that force would be used only as a last resort.

Although admirable in concept, the peace policy displayed certain failings in practice. A major obstacle to the agricultural reservation idea was the traditional view of many tribes that farming was woman's work, degrading to a male. Furthermore, some of the areas set aside for the promotion of Indian agriculture were totally unsuited for the type of farming practiced in the East. As many Indians found, the reservations encouraged indolence; the annuities promised by the Medicine Lodge and Fort Laramie treaties were poor substitutes for the free, nomadic lives the people had previously enjoyed. As the Sioux chief Sitting Bull said later to a group of reservation Indians: "Look at me—see if I am poor, or my people either. . . . You are fools to make yourselves slaves to a piece of fat bacon, some hard-tack, and a little sugar and coffee."

Sitting Bull was no fool, nor were most of the Kiowas and Comanches who shared his philosophy. They soon realized that they could steal away from their reservation near Fort Sill, continue their raids on Texas settlements, and then, because troops could not enter reservations, slip back to the reservation and safety. Even the agent at Sill conceded the fact, and on one occasion in 1871 called in troopers of the Tenth Cavalry to arrest Kiowas who had openly admitted such depredations.

A real crack in the peace policy's foundation occurred in April of 1873. During a conference under a flag of truce with some warring Modoc chiefs, General E. R. S. Canby and Peace Commissioner Eleasar Thomas were treacherously shot and killed. Most westerners viewed the killings as solid evidence that Indians would not respond to "conquest by kindness." Other cracks in the foundation came between the fall of 1873 and the summer of 1874. During the winter of 1873/74 large numbers of hostile Sioux from the north edged onto the Indian agencies in northwestern Nebraska, threatening and abusing the agents and their employees and even killing several whites, including an army officer. Desperate, the agents finally called for the military. In March of 1874 a strong infantry-cavalry expedition from Fort Laramie frightened the troublemakers back to the north, putting a temporary end to the violence. By that time, however, Kiowa and Comanche raiders from the Fort Sill reservation were beginning to strike all across the Texas frontier. General Sherman repeatedly demanded permission for troops to pursue the raiders across reservation boundaries, and in July the secretary of the interior and the commissioner of Indian affairs gave in. No longer safe at the agency, the Indians had to flee or fight; military pressure kept on them during the Red River War forced most of them back to the reservation early in 1875.

The military solution to the Kiowa-Comanche raids gave the army more voice in shaping Indian affairs. Those chiefs judged responsible for the Red River hostilities were punished in a way they could hardly have anticipated: in the spring of 1875 the military shipped them all the way to Fort Marion, Florida, and kept them there for three years. A similar fate was to overtake the entire Chiricahua Apache tribe in 1886.

What remained of the peace policy's foundation crumbled altogether during the Sioux War of 1876-77, a war caused primarily by white violation of the Fort Laramie treaty. The annihilation of five troops of the Seventh Cavalry by Sioux and Cheyenne warriors on the Little Bighorn stunned the country and resulted in a stiffening of the general attitude toward the Indians. For the rest of the 1870s, and well into the 1880s, the measures taken against hostile tribes were sharper and more decisive. Besides active pursuit of hostiles—between the summer of 1876 and the summer of 1877 U.S. troops pushed repeatedly into Mexico with little regard for Mexican sovereignty—the army also guarded the Indians on their reservations.

Although most parties had agreed upon the necessity for them, the reservations themselves continued to give rise to numerous problems. Sincere as many of the religiously oriented agents were, they proved unable to cope with the task before them. In some instances they saw Indian religious and tribal customs as obstructions to civilization and tried to outlaw or obliterate them. Agent Nathan Meeker's attempts in this area were a direct cause of the bloody Ute uprising of 1879. In trying to pry the Indians away from their traditional ways of life a number of agents with Meeker's viewpoint used Indian police and Indian courts as tools, or threatened to withhold rations or to use military force when necessary. As in earlier cases, a large number of the newer reservations were laid out on harsh, inferior land, for which whites had no use. More trouble developed when tribes which had been traditional enemies were located on the same land. Nevertheless, by the mid-1880s there were more than 180 reservations in existence, covering some 180,000 square miles, on which lived about 240,000 Indians.

To combat the evils of the reservation system, President Chester Arthur had in 1881 recommended the allotment of land to individual Indians rather than to entire tribes, a recommendation which became law with the passage of the Dawes Act in 1887. As far as the Indians were concerned, however, the Dawes Act had major shortcomings, among which was the fact that after each of them had selected a 160-acre plot, whatever land was left on the reservation would revert to public domain. Moreover, these allotments often proved too small for successful crop production in the West. For years the Indians, especially the Five Civilized Tribes, fought this plan; but now, with rare exception, they fought it in the courts instead of on the battlefield.

Two Ute Indians, one counting while the other holds a heavily tack-studded full-stock muzzle-loading rifle. The photo was taken by John K. Hillers in the Uintah Valley of Utah early in the 1870s. (Courtesy Smithsonian Institution)

·6·

POSTWAR
INDIAN GUNS

PERCUSSION ARMS

URING THE LATE 1860s and early 1870s the most common firearms in the hands of Indians on the frontier were muzzle-loading rifles and smoothbores. Though Indians sometimes purchased such guns with horses, furs, or buffalo robes, the arms also reached them as partial payment from the federal government for cession of lands or for promises to keep the peace. Presents given at Fort Laramie in 1867 and 1868 to Indians who came to participate in treaty negotiations included 62 "Indian Rifles," bought at $22.50 each, and another 36 at $25.00 each, together with 17 kegs of powder, 1225 pounds of bar lead, and thousands of percussion caps. Besides these items, all purchased at the post trader's store at Laramie, the commissioners may have furnished the Indians with a quantity of surplus Civil War materials. (Existing ledgers documenting purchases by the commissioners reveal such other diverse commodities as needles, kettles, blankets, cloth, three pounds of brass tacks, one umbrella, and even three pairs of "eye-goggles.") On the strength of the Arapahos' promises that the weapons would be used only for hunting, Agent Edward Wyncoop delivered to them near Fort Larned, Kansas, 100 "pistols" and 80 muzzle-loading Lancaster rifles, plus the requisite powder, lead, and caps. The Apaches received only 40 pistols and 20 rifles.[1]

Indian rifles sometimes included those by the best-known makers. While traveling through Colorado in the late 1860s, J. S. Campion took special note of a band of Utes, "nearly every man having his Hawkins' rifle, Colt's revolver, knife, tomahawk, bow and arrows, and lasso." Often listed in official reports and invoices were the muzzle-loading rifles made by Henry Leman. Typically plain but very serviceable fullstock percussion arms of about .50 caliber, the Lemans had been popular with both Indians and whites on the frontier for many years. From the Spotted-Tail Sioux agency in Nebraska, Agent Washburn wrote to the commissioner of Indian affairs in October of 1871 for approval to buy, among other items, "one hundred Leman Rifles, short barrel, full stock, half inch bore

with single trigger, the cost not to exceed $12 each at Manufactory." In the winter of 1871/72 Colonel J. J. Reynolds reported that Spotted Tail and his band had appeared at Fort McPherson on the Platte to request "200 Leman guns" and 30 ponies so they could hunt buffalo. (As late as 1877 John P. Lower of Denver was still advertising these rifles, in "full and half stock" styles, at $12 to $15 each.)[2]

Although Indian traders mentioned percussion double-barrel shotguns only infrequently, some of these arms did reach Indian hands, along with muzzle-loading rifles and handguns, through the agents and peace commissioners. In September of 1866 Indian Agent J. R. Hanson wrote from Dakota's Crow Agency: "The government has furnished many of these Indians with double barrel shotguns. This spring I distributed eighteen, and the commission almost as many more. These went into the hands of Indians who always have been friendly to the government." Invoices for the 1867–68 period indicate that the commissioners bought for the Sioux 36 double guns at $18 each from Robert Campbell & Company of St. Louis, a similar number of "Double Barrel Guns twist brl., patent breech" at $20 each from Hunt & Co. of New York, and other shotguns from several additional sources.[3]

Nearly as popular among plains warriors as the muzzle-loading long arm was the percussion revolver. Its advantages—handiness, light weight, and multishot capacity—were just as apparent to the Indians as to their white adversaries. As a result, a number of them made concerted efforts to get such guns. Sergeant F. M. Fessenden of the Eighteenth Infantry, who served at Fort Phil Kearny in 1866, recalled that: "One buck offered me five ponies for my Colt revolver." Writing to the War Department from Fort Dodge in January of 1867, a Third Infantry major graphically illustrated the popularity of six-shooters among the plains tribes:

Between the authorized issue of agents and the sales of the traders, the Indians were never better armed than at the present time. Several hundred Indians

Shee-zah-nan-tan, a Jicarilla Apache, with a half-stock muzzle-loading rifle. The rawhide wrapping at the breech probably repaired a broken stock. (U.S. Geological Survey photo, courtesy National Archives)

have visited this post, all of whom had revolvers in their possession. A large majority had two revolvers, and many of them three. The Indians openly boast that they have plenty of arms and ammunition in case of trouble in the spring. The Interior Department does not seem to appreciate the danger of thus arming those Indians. The evil of presenting a revolver to each of the chiefs of bands would hardly be appreciable but when the whole rank and file are thus armed, it not only gives them greater courage to murder and plunder, but renders them formidable enemies. . . . For a revolver the Indian will give ten, even twenty times its value, in horses and furs. . . .[4]

The Medicine Lodge treaty, concluded in October of 1867 with tribes on the southern plains, was climaxed by the distribution of percussion revolvers manufactured by the Union Arms Company. But when the first warrior tested his new prize, it blew up in his hands. He seemed more disturbed about the loss of the gun than about his bleeding hand, however, and the issuance of a few Colt revolvers prompted the Indians to forget the episode.[5]

Some tribes found handguns more convenient for buffalo hunting than shoulder arms, and in October of 1873 an agent for the Blackfeet requested approval for the sale of revolvers for just that purpose. At about the same time, trader Henry Kennerly wrote Washington for permission to sell the Piegans "40 Dragoon Revolvers of Remington and Colts Manufacture." Among the items which Thomas Bogy wanted to sell Indians at Fort Clagett in October of 1873 were 12 Remington revolvers, plus 5 .44 caliber Henry carbines, 5 Spencer carbines, 10,000 Berdan cartridges, 20,000 Henry cartridges, 6000 Spencer rounds, 10 kegs of rifle powder, and 1000 pounds of trade balls and lead. Requisitions for firearms parts for the Red Cloud Agency for the third quarter of 1874 substantiated the popularity of Colt and Remington handguns by calling for:

25 Remington Army & Navy Main Springs
25 do   Hands
10 do   Sear Springs
50 Colts Army Main Springs
25 do   do   Hands
50 do   do   Sear Springs
 4 do   do   O. M. Levers & Rammers
 4 do   do   M.H. Levers & Rammers
500 do   do   & Navy screws asstd.
 3 Winchester finger levers[6]

The steady flow of arms to Indian camps under the auspices of agents and traders caused understandable concern for commanders of frontier garrisons, and some commanders did everything they could to prevent it.

Ute Indians breaking camp in the Uintah Valley of Utah in the early 1870s. The man seated at the right holds a Leman-style full-stock muzzle-loading rifle. (Courtesy Smithsonian Institution, Bureau of American Ethnology Collection)

In July of 1866 Brigadier General Philip St. George Cooke, commanding the Department of the Platte, issued General Order No. 10, forbidding Indian agents to deal in firearms and instructing all post commanders to "take vigilant and decisive measures for the prevention of all sale, barter, or gift of arms or ammunition to Indians within reach of their power." Under instructions from General W. T. Sherman, General Winfield Scott Hancock took much the same action in January of 1867. As Sherman reported to Ulysses S. Grant, the sale of arms by government-licensed traders was "the most delicate operation conceivable." Indian agents and commissioners to the Comanches, Kiowas, Arapahos, and Cheyennes appeared to have given almost unlimited authority to licensed traders to sell guns to any Indians then at peace with, and receiving annuities from, the government. Moreover, Sherman warned: "Those Indians are only nominally friendly, and for buffalo robes can buy the best carbines, revolvers, and guns of all kinds with the ammunition to match. . . . Commissioned agents . . . have surrendered all control of the matter to the licensed traders." Grant in turn appealed to the secretary of war, urging the abolition of civil Indian agents and licensed traders. But agents and traders were within the purview of the Department of the Interior, and in a dispute between the departments of War and the Interior, only Congress could be the arbitrator.[7]

Colt M1860 (#187277/E) showing a rare form of Colt factory scroll engraving, unusual because of its similarity to the heavy leaf style. The hammer bears the image of a wolf's head, the most common of the animal motifs which sometimes appear on engraved nineteenth-century Colts. The letter "E" accompanying the serial number was the factory's means from 1861 to the early 1870s of identifying a revolver intended for engraving. Assembled about 1870, the gun remained unsold until April 10, 1877, when with 69 other Colts it was shipped (already engraved) to Schuyler, Hartley & Graham of New York. Its history for the next 25 years is unknown, but in 1902 it was found in a cave in Arizona's Dragoon Mountains wrapped in a blanket along with the remains of an Indian. Although the two prospectors intended to return later to the cave for the rifle, saddle, and other artifacts which they had found there, they never were able to locate the exact site. (Photo by and courtesy Dr. Robert L. Woolery)

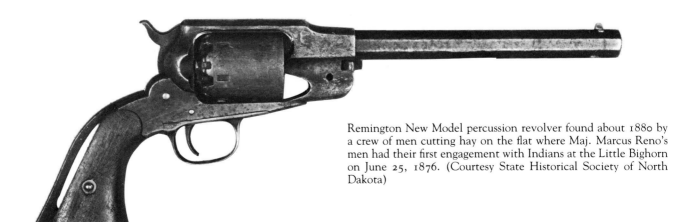

Remington New Model percussion revolver found about 1880 by a crew of men cutting hay on the flat where Maj. Marcus Reno's men had their first engagement with Indians at the Little Bighorn on June 25, 1876. (Courtesy State Historical Society of North Dakota)

358

A street scene in Salt Lake City in 1869. The several uncased Indian rifles that can be seen are all muzzle-loaders. (Courtesy Kansas State Historical Society)

Photographed at Ft. Laramie during 1868 treaty negotiations, this Indian holds a civilian half-stock muzzle-loading rifle but is garbed in army overcoat, trousers, and hat. (Courtesy Ft. Laramie Historical Assn.)

A Paiute near St. George, Utah, in the early 1870s demonstrates the use of a wiping stick (ramrod) as a rest. The stock of his muzzle-loading rifle apparently was broken near the breech and has been securely repaired with wet rawhide sewn about the break and allowed to dry. (Courtesy Smithsonian Institution, Bureau of American Ethnology Collection)

360

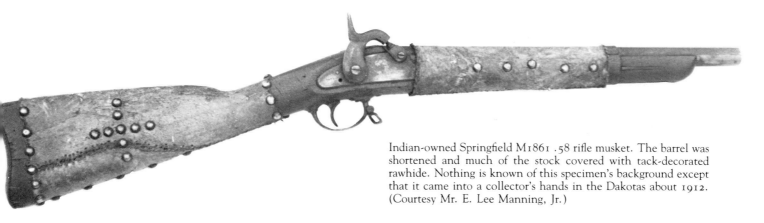

Indian-owned Springfield M1861 .58 rifle musket. The barrel was shortened and much of the stock covered with tack-decorated rawhide. Nothing is known of this specimen's background except that it came into a collector's hands in the Dakotas about 1912. (Courtesy Mr. E. Lee Manning, Jr.)

Certain other individuals, both military and civilian, supported the Indians' demand for guns for hunting to supplement agency rations. In January of 1867 Lewis V. Bogy, commissioner of Indian affairs, explained to the secretary of the interior that:

the Indian has to depend upon the chase for his subsistence and that of his wife and children. Arms and ammunition are of absolute necessity; he will therefore, if possible, and no matter at what cost, procure them. Then, again, it is perfectly idle to say that he will accumulate them to make war on the whites. No Indian will buy two guns; one he will and ought to have; nor will he lay up any large quantity of powder, for he has no means of keeping it. He needs one gun and a little powder, and this is his only means of subsistence.

On the assumption that agency-issued rations would be supplemented by hunting, the Medicine Lodge and Fort Laramie treaties of 1867–68 authorized a mere $3 per month per reservation Indian as an individual food allowance. For many tribes, however, the increasing slaughter of the buffalo and other game by professional hunters was severely reducing hunting opportunities, a situation which added to the undercurrent of resentment and unrest. Recognizing this, General C. C. Auger, who followed Cooke as commander of the Department of the Platte, urged in 1870 that the Indians be given small quantities of guns and ammunition, since game was becoming harder to approach and kill with bow and arrow. The open distribution of guns for hunting purposes, he felt, would preclude the Indians' attempts to obtain them by smuggling or raiding.[8]

Still other individuals concurred with Auger. But there was justifiable concern over the Indian acquisition of modern breechloaders and repeaters. As General Hancock argued with obvious logic in 1872, any guns given to Indians as annuity payments or sold to them by licensed traders should be of a design suitable only for hunting. Such a policy, in fact, was in effect in Canada at the time. During the same year Special Indian Agent A. J. Simmons, then at the Milk River Agency in Montana Territory, advised Indian traders under his jurisdiction that:

you will not be permitted to dispose of . . . any breechloading fire arms, cartridges or fixed ammunition . . . to any Sioux Indians. . . . The ordinary muzzle loading Indian trade rifle and ammunition for that character of arms may be sold during the ensuring year in quantities sufficient for hunting purposes, viz., rifles not exceeding twenty-four for the time above specified, powder twenty five and lead seventy five pounds per month at any one trading post, to Indians belonging to this agency and receiving subsistence herefrom but in no case to any others.

Failure of any trader to abide by these instructions meant forfeiture of his license and forcible removal beyond the limits of the Indian country.[9]

In areas under Interior Department control, of course, traders had to be licensed to do business. But some traders, unconcerned with the formalities of getting a license, carried on their business illegally, in remote regions, where there was little opportunity for government supervision of their operations. During 1870, for example, Kiowas and Comanches in New Mexico secured substantial numbers of guns from Mexican traders, in exchange for horses stolen in Texas. Two years later, Red River half-bloods on the Canadian side of the border were reported to be supplying the Sioux with many of their arms. According to one source, Indian-owned breechloaders were seldom in evidence at this time: the commission to the Teton Sioux near Fort Peck, Montana, stated that of almost

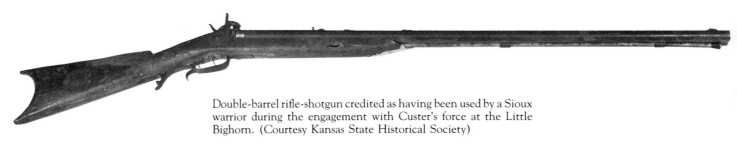

Double-barrel rifle-shotgun credited as having been used by a Sioux warrior during the engagement with Custer's force at the Little Bighorn. (Courtesy Kansas State Historical Society)

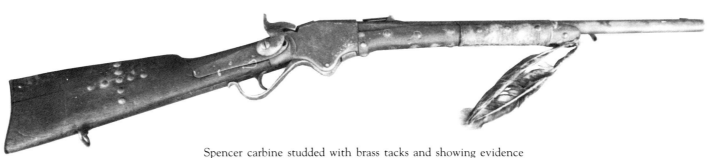

Spencer carbine studded with brass tacks and showing evidence of hard use, probably by an Indian. The forearm has been repaired with rawhide and decorated with an eagle feather.

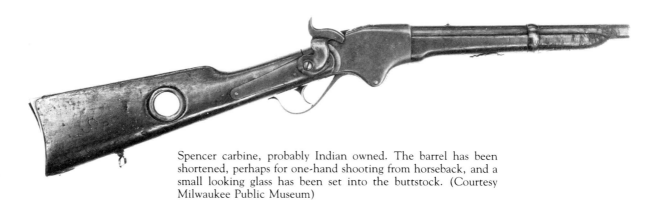

Spencer carbine, probably Indian owned. The barrel has been shortened, perhaps for one-hand shooting from horseback, and a small looking glass has been set into the buttstock. (Courtesy Milwaukee Public Museum)

3000 Indians observed, most carried bows and arrows and some "old-pattern muzzle-loading guns and pistols"; there were probably no more than a dozen breechloaders among them, which were almost useless due to shortages of ammunition.[10]

METALLIC-CARTRIDGE ARMS

In other parts of the West breechloaders were much more evident. As early as 1867, in fact, journalist Henry M. Stanley, then in Kansas, had noted that:

The Indians . . . are armed with Spencer rifles, and their first attempts to use them appear to have resulted in several of them getting their hands injured by the explosion of the metallic cartridges, while they attempted to force them into the muzzle by pounding, not being posted in the breech-loading business.[11]

The Indians learned quickly, however—not only about Spencers but about other breechloaders as well. In June of 1873, for instance, officials of Nelson Story & Company reported to Agent Daniels that since the first of the year they had sold the habitually friendly Crows 15 "needle guns," 15,380 "needle cartridges" for trapdoor Springfields, 2000 .44 rimfire rounds for Henry and 1866 Winchester rifles, and over 2000 Spencer cartridges. Vouchers for hardware procured as

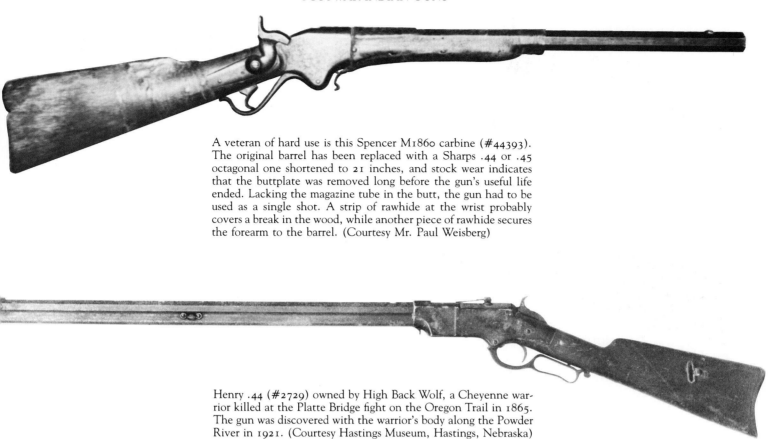

A veteran of hard use is this Spencer M1860 carbine (#44393). The original barrel has been replaced with a Sharps .44 or .45 octagonal one shortened to 21 inches, and stock wear indicates that the buttplate was removed long before the gun's useful life ended. Lacking the magazine tube in the butt, the gun had to be used as a single shot. A strip of rawhide at the wrist probably covers a break in the wood, while another piece of rawhide secures the forearm to the barrel. (Courtesy Mr. Paul Weisberg)

Henry .44 (#2729) owned by High Back Wolf, a Cheyenne warrior killed at the Platte Bridge fight on the Oregon Trail in 1865. The gun was discovered with the warrior's body along the Powder River in 1921. (Courtesy Hastings Museum, Hastings, Nebraska)

government gifts for the Mountain and River Crows in August of 1873 listed four Smith & Wesson revolvers at $30 each, more than 20,000 rimfire and centerfire cartridges, 500 paper cartridges, and varying quantities of powder, lead, and caps. A sergeant who served in Texas between 1870 and 1876 later wrote:

> There is a belief common among people of this day and time that the Indians fought solely with bow and arrow, but in all my Indian fighting, which amounted to seven pitched battles, besides several skirmishes, I have always found them well equipped with good guns and plenty of ammunition.

Richard B. Hughes, who traveled to the Black Hills in 1876, mentioned that at one campsite

> a party of Ogalallas had visited us. . . . The adult men were splendidly armed—indeed much better than the average man of our party—their guns being mostly Sharps' or Winchester rifles of late pattern. . . . One of the men, armed with a Sharps' forty-five—as fine a rifle as was in use at that time—gave us an exhibition of his skill.

Another traveler, who passed through the Rockies shortly afterward, wrote later that the Utes he encountered were "all well-armed with Sharp's and Ballard rifles and the latest improved Winchester carbines. They have plenty of cartridges, too, and always wear revolvers." Captain Charles King undoubtedly spoke for many of his fellow officers on the frontier when he said:

> No end of silk-hatted functionaries have hurried out from Washington, shaken hands and smoked a pipe with a score of big Indians; there has been a vast amount of cheap oratory and buncombe talk about the Great Father and the guileless red men, at the end of which we are told to go back to camp and bury our dead, and our late antagonists, laughing in their sleeves, link arms with their aldermanic friends, are "dead-headed" off to Washington, where they are lionized at the White House, and sent the rounds of the great cities, and finally return to their reservations laden down with new and improved rifles and ammunition. . . .[12]

Henry .44 repeating rifle presented to Sitting Bull of the Sioux by President U. S. Grant. The inscription on the sideplate reads: "Sitting Bull from the President For Bravery & True Friendship." (Courtesy Museum of the American Indian, Heye Foundation, and Western History Collections, University of Oklahoma)

Tzi-kal-tza, reportedly the son of Capt. William Clark who accompanied Capt. Merriwether Lewis to the Pacific, photographed holding a .44 Henry repeater about 1871 by William H. Jackson. (Courtesy Montana Historical Society)

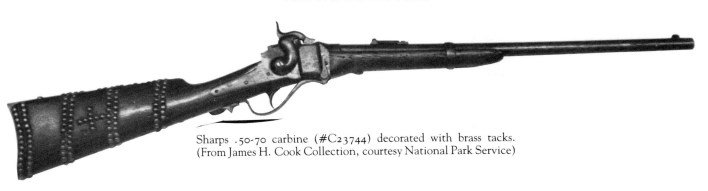

Sharps .50-70 carbine (#C23744) decorated with brass tacks.
(From James H. Cook Collection, courtesy National Park Service)

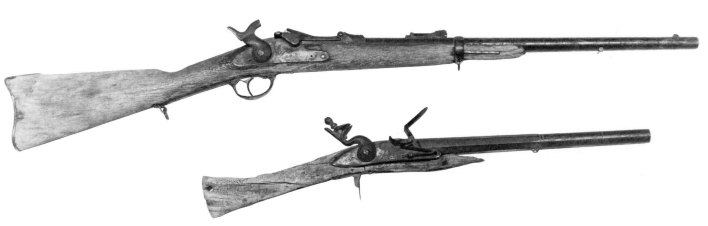

Above, Springfield M1873 .45 carbine (#15004) owned by Ogalala Sioux chief Young-Man-Afraid-of-His-Horses. A grand nephew
claimed the chief captured the weapon from soldiers in 1876, but
the chief was not involved in the major engagements with the
army in that year. Below is a trade gun made by Henry Leman of

Lancaster, Pa., and found in the Colorado mountains. The buttstock and barrel may have been shortened for use on horseback
or to permit continued use of the gun after the barrel had been
damaged. (Courtesy Museum of the Fur Trade)

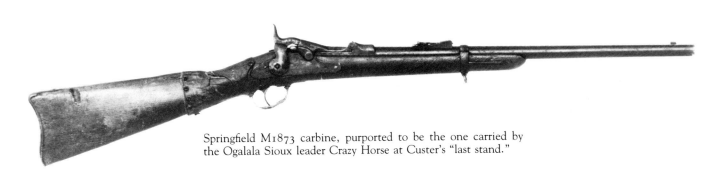

Springfield M1873 carbine, purported to be the one carried by
the Ogalala Sioux leader Crazy Horse at Custer's "last stand."

During the mid- and late 1870s, with more and more Indians acquiring up-to-date weapons, it was not uncommon to hear the charge that hostile warriors were often better armed than the soldiers sent to pacify them. The one event which really brought the quality of Plains Indian armament under scrutiny, however, was the defeat of Custer's Seventh Cavalry in June of 1876. At the Reno court of inquiry Lt. Charles Varnum testified that during the retreat by Reno's companies across the river into the hills, "there were a great many Indians riding along the column with Winchester rifles across saddles, firing into the column." In his official report Reno himself remarked that "every [Indian] rifle was handled by an expert and skilled marksman, and with a range that exceeded our carbine." Exhibiting greater concern for the truth, Lt. Varnum pointed out that the range of the Winchester was less than that of the .45 Springfield carbine used by the troopers. (Sergeant Windolph of the Seventh Cavalry called the Springfield carbine an "accurate and deadly weapon up to 600 yards.") Also contrasting with Reno's official remark was the statement of a soldier who after the battle deduced that the sharp-shooter who had wounded him, split the stock of his carbine, and killed a comrade must have been either a renegade white man or a half-blood: "He could shoot too well to have been a full-blood Indian."[13]

Sergeant Windolph estimated that "fully half of all the warriors carried only bows and arrows and lances, and . . . possibly half of the remainder carried odds and ends of old muzzle-loaders and single-shot rifles of various vintages. Probably not more than 25 or 30 percent of the warriors carried modern repeating rifles." Evidently, however, there were enough repeaters in evidence to bring about a biting editorial in the *Army and Navy Journal*:

We advised the Winchester Arms Company to act upon the suggestion offered them by Capt. Nickerson, of Gen. Crook's staff, and prosecute the Indians for infringement of their patent. The captain testifies, with others, that Winchester rifles are plenty among them; the agency people and the traders solemnly affirm that they don't furnish them; so it can only be inferred that the Indians manufacture them themselves. If Gov. Winchester could get out a preliminary injunction, restraining the Indians from the use of his rifle, it might be of signal service to our troops in the next engagement.[14]

Years afterward Wooden Leg, a Cheyenne warrior who had been present at the Custer battle, recalled that:

Of the Cheyennes, Two Moons and White Wolf each had a repeating rifle. Some others had single-shot breech-loading rifles. But there was not much ammunition for the good guns. The muzzle-loaders usually were preferred, because for these we could mold the bullets and put in whatever powder was desired, or according to the quantity on hand. I believe the Sioux had, in proportion to their numbers, about the same supply of firearms material that we had.[15]

As a result of the Custer fight the Indians captured an estimated 592 Springfields and Colts, as well as metallic cartridges for them. But as Wooden Leg's account indicates, some Indians made no effort to procure metallic-cartridge arms because of the difficulty of obtaining the proper ammunition. Even when such ammunition was available, it was often prohibitively expensive. In 1870 an observer at Fort Berthold, Dakota, had seen one Indian vainly attempting to trade three ponies for a box of about fifty cartridges. About five years later Colonel Richard Irving Dodge observed a man offering a well-tanned buffalo robe for only three cartridges![16]

In August of 1876, only weeks after Custer's defeat, Congress passed a joint resolution authorizing the president "to take such measures . . . to prevent such special metallic ammunition being conveyed to such hostile Indians, and . . . to declare the same contraband of war in such district of the country as he may designate during the continuance of hostilities." In November of 1876 President Grant signed an executive order prohibiting the sale of fixed ammunition, or metallic cartridges, in "country occupied by Indians, or subject to their visits, lying within the Territories of Montana, Dakota, and Wyoming and the states of Nebraska and Colorado." But for some Indians such restrictions posed few problems. As Colonel Dodge explained:

Every male Indian who can buy, beg, borrow, or steal them, has now firearms of some kind. . . . The trade in arms is entirely illicit. The trader slips into the Indian country, now here, now there, and not knowing beforehand the caliber of the ammunition required, takes that which is most commonly in use. Some guns of a band were almost always out of use on this account, but necessity . . . has so stimulated the ordinarily uninventive brain of the Indian, that if he can only procure the moulds for a bullet that will fit his rifle, he manages the rest by an ingenious method of reloading his old shells peculiar to himself. He buys from the trader a box of the smallest percussion caps, [and] forces the cap in[to the shell] until it is flush. Powder and lead can always be obtained from the traders; or, in default of these, cartridges of other calibers are broken

Ute Indians photographed in 1874 at an encampment at Los Pinos in Colorado by famed western photographer William H. Jackson. If the three Winchester rifles belong to the Indians, the brave at left must have obtained one of the first M1873s to reach the frontier. The Winchester in the center is a M1866, while the third specimen could be of either model. (Courtesy Smithsonian Institution, Bureau of American Ethnology Collection)

Comanches with Frank Waltby (right), interpreter, about 1875. The array of guns includes (from left) a .44 Henry repeater, a Remington or Whitney rolling block, and a Sharps carbine. (Courtesy Smithsonian Institution)

up, and the materials used in reloading his shells. Indians say that the shells thus reloaded are nearly as good as the original cartridges, and that the shells are frequently reloaded 40 or 50 times.[17]

Moreover, there were always traders ready to sell metallic cartridges, regardless of the legalities of the situation. In 1878 Manuel Garcia traded the Blackfeet

two needle guns for sixteen fine robes; they left five robes for five boxes of fifty-caliber cartridges for the needle guns, which cost me one-fifty per box by the case in Bozeman. . . . [The next morning] two Pend d'Oreilles came and I robbed one of them of seven buffalo robes for a second-hand needle gun and for two buffalo robes I gave him three boxes of fifty-

caliber cartridges, and I got two robes from the other buck for three boxes of Henry cartridges.[18]

Many Indians refused to pay exorbitant prices for metallic-cartridge guns and their ammunition, and instead got them through other means. In June of 1878 a band of warriors ambushed and looted a stagecoach near Owyhee Crossing, Nevada; as a lieutenant of the Twelfth Infantry reported afterward:

The stage was found at this point completely demolished, it having been burned together with such of the United States mail and express matter they did not carry off with them. Some Winchester arms and ammunition had been on this stage, which, to judge from the empty boxes that had contained the arms, there must have been about 12 rifles.[19]

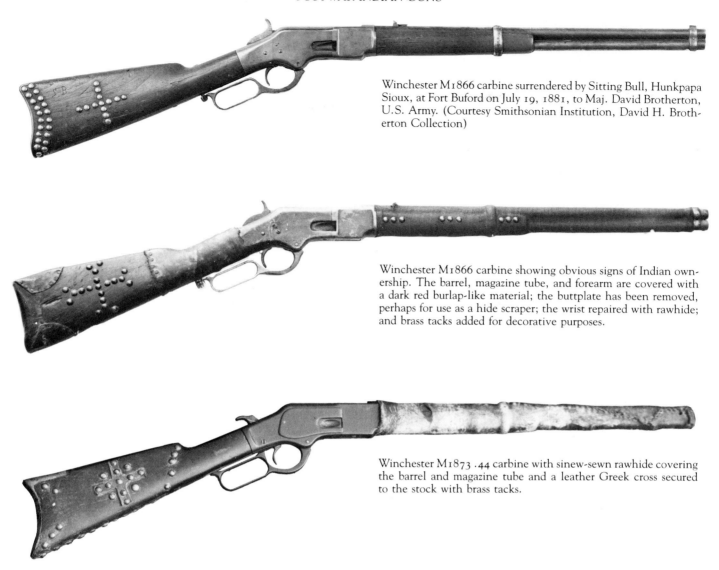

Winchester M1866 carbine surrendered by Sitting Bull, Hunkpapa Sioux, at Fort Buford on July 19, 1881, to Maj. David Brotherton, U.S. Army. (Courtesy Smithsonian Institution, David H. Brotherton Collection)

Winchester M1866 carbine showing obvious signs of Indian ownership. The barrel, magazine tube, and forearm are covered with a dark red burlap-like material; the buttplate has been removed, perhaps for use as a hide scraper; the wrist repaired with rawhide; and brass tacks added for decorative purposes.

Winchester M1873 .44 carbine with sinew-sewn rawhide covering the barrel and magazine tube and a leather Greek cross secured to the stock with brass tacks.

THE USE OF OLDER ARMS ALONGSIDE THE NEWER

By the late 1870s, various officials were raising questions concerning the quality of Indian armament—especially as opposed to the quality of arms carried by U.S. troops—and the Ordnance Department consequently made a determined effort to supply answers. The results of this effort, published in the 1879 Ordnance report, showed that the Indians were not as well armed as some of their adversaries seemed to think. Writing from the ordnance depot at Tongue River, Montana Territory, in November of 1878, Lt. J. W. Pope of the Fifth Infantry reported that

I conceive that many ideas of the superiority of Indian arms are acquired in action, uncorrected by accurate facts, a time when to the best of men an arm that has whizzed a bullet close to the ear seems an excellent weapon; and I feel convinced, from a considerable knowledge of arms carried by friendly Indians and surrendered by the hostiles, that such investigation would prove conclusively that any tribe fully armed with even the old caliber .50 Springfield carbine would be more formidable than with their present arms. That the Sioux and Cheyennes have had some fine breech-loaders, giving color to the opinion that they are better armed than the cavalry, is undoubtedly true. The principal of these, the Sharp's rifle, with its 120-grain cartridge, has tremendous range and penetration, and drifted into the hands of those Indians in considerable number, either directly or indirectly, through the buffalo

A shortened flintlock Northwest trade gun which Maj. James H. Bell said was a gun turned in to authorities by Sitting Bull when he surrendered. (Courtesy Western History Collections, University of Oklahoma Library)

hunters (with whom it was a favorite). . . . But these and like arms are comparatively few, while a very considerable number of muzzle-loaders greatly reduce the average of Indian armament below that of the troops.[20]

As Pope noted, some of the plains warriors carried eminently serviceable breechloaders. In October of 1878 troopers of the Third Cavalry had taken from Cheyennes at Chadron Creek, Nebraska:

One Winchester rifle.
One Sharp's carbine, caliber .50.
One Spencer carbine.
One shot-gun, double-barreled.
Nine muzzle-loading rifles, various patterns.
One Schofield-Smith & Wesson revolver.
One Colt's revolver, old pattern.
One Remington revolver, old pattern.
One horse-pistol, and
Fifteen or twenty sets of bows and arrows.

At about the same time Dull Knife's band of Cheyennes surrendered to a cavalry patrol near Camp Robinson, Nebraska. After supposedly searching the Indians thoroughly for concealed weapons, the soldiers interned them at the camp. But in January of 1879, after a desperate but unsuccessful attempt to escape, the Cheyennes gave up:

Seven Springfield breech-loading rifles, caliber .50.
One Springfield carbine, caliber .45.
Three Sharp's carbines, caliber .50.
One Sharp's rifle (old reliable).
One Colt's revolver, caliber .36.
One Colt's revolver, Navy, old pattern.
One Remington revolver, Army, old pattern.

(The Cheyennes were able to conceal these guns primarily because the soldiers failed to search the women and children. The enterprising Indians had disassembled the arms and scattered various parts among their clothing or wore them as ornaments. Children, for instance, might wear a hammer, trigger, spring, or other inconspicuous part in their hair or around the neck or waist.)[21]

In March of 1879, when Little Wolf's Northern Cheyennes surrendered to Second Cavalrymen in southeastern Montana, they turned over:

Four Springfield carbines, caliber .45.
Three Springfield rifles, caliber .50.
Four Sharp's rifles, caliber .45.
One Sharp's rifle, caliber .50.
Four Sharp's carbines, caliber .50.
One muzzle-loading rifle (old).
Three Winchester and Henry repeating rifles.
Two Colt's revolvers, caliber .45.
Two Smith & Wesson revolvers, caliber .44.
Five Colt's revolvers, calibers .44 and .31.
One Remington revolver, caliber .44.

The Sharps .45 rifles may have been the ones Little Wolf's braves captured from a party of buffalo hunters near the Arkansas River in 1878. When the hunters agreed to surrender their rifles, ammunition, and reloading tools, the Indians left them unharmed.[22]

As Pope mentioned, some of these guns did indeed qualify as "fine breech-loaders"; but as he also noted, "these and like arms are comparatively few," and the 1879 Ordnance report supported his statement. The report listed a total of 284 shoulder arms seized from or surrendered by hostile plains Indians (primarily Sioux and Cheyenne), and of this total 160, or more than half, loaded from the muzzle. Of these 160 muzzle-loaders 94 had been made by Henry Leman, 10 by J. P. Lower of Philadelphia, 6 by Samuel Hawken, 6 by J. Henry & Son, and 4 by Henry Folsom & Co. of St. Louis, with lesser-known makers accounting for

Model 1876 Winchester .45-60 rifle owned by Hunkpapa Sioux chief Gall. (Courtesy State Historical Society of North Dakota)

Tribal leaders at a Blackfoot Indian agency. One holds a M1876 Winchester carbine. (Courtesy Montana Historical Society)

the balance. (Only 2 of these muzzle-loaders could be identified as Northwest trade guns, and both were of English manufacture. One was made by W. Chance & Son, the other by Parker, Field, & Co.)[23]

In contrast to the high proportion of muzzle-loading rifles, the report included only 49 Springfields of post–Civil War vintage, 23 Spencers, 13 Sharps, 12 .44 Winchesters, and 4 .44 Henry repeating rifles, plus an assortment of single-shot arms by Warner, Joslyn, Wesson, Ballard, Remington, Starr, Gallagher, Merrill, and Smith. Whether breechloaders or muzzle-loaders, a goodly number of these guns would have been classified as unserviceable at an arsenal, "though many of them could be used by so enterprising an

enemy as the American Indian." In numerous instances stocks were broken or badly worn, lock mechanisms were inoperative or faulty, and original sights were loose, missing entirely, or crudely replaced.[24]

Aside from long arms, the report listed a total of 125 revolvers and single-shot pistols recovered from various tribes. But with the exception of one Colt converted to fire metallic cartridges, and one Remington .50-caliber single-shot pistol, all the other arms were percussion. Of 121 percussion revolvers 72 were Colts, 37 were Remingtons, 5 were Whitneys, 4 were Starrs, 1 was a Manhattan, 1 a Pettengill, and 1 a Savage.[25]

This scene illustrates the folly of attributing extensive use of Wesson carbines to various western Indian tribes. It's possibly the same Wesson that was used as a studio prop in many such posed scenes in the National Archives' and Smithsonian Institution's photo collections. Such photos probably were the products of a late-nineteenth-century government ethnological study. Identifiable revolvers are a Colt M1877 double action (left) and a .32 Smith & Wesson No. 1½ or No. 2 in the far right Indian's belt. (Courtesy National Archives)

Skin lodges on the Yellowstone River in Montana in 1871. The Nez Percé warrior holds a Colt M1860 .44 revolver, its grip decorated with tacks or other circular inlays. Chokeberries are spread on the hides in front of the lodge. (Courtesy Smithsonian Institution, Bureau of American Ethnology Collection)

Feathered Wolf, a Cheyenne, photographed in 1875 holding a Winchester M1866 brass-frame carbine. (Courtesy Smithsonian Institution, Bureau of American Ethnology Collection)

Cheyenne warrior in full war regalia, armed with a Colt Single Action. (Courtesy W. H. Over Museum, University of South Dakota)

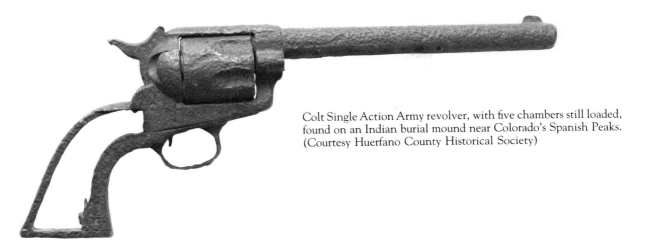

Colt Single Action Army revolver, with five chambers still loaded, found on an Indian burial mound near Colorado's Spanish Peaks. (Courtesy Huerfano County Historical Society)

Commenting generally on the range and power of the most commonly encountered Indian guns, Captain O. E. Michaelis wrote that:

During my tour of service in this department [Dakota] I have never met an officer, either in the field, or at posts, and of course as an ordnance officer I took especial pains to inform myself, who claimed that the Indians, as a class, had longer-ranging guns than our own troops. . . . As General Miles states of the Nez Perces, the use of fine sights and measurement of distances is the result of civilization. The typical Indian is a point-blank marksman. The use of bright muzzle and buckhorn sights proves this. He steals upon his quarry and fires at it. Hence they prefer arms with long dangerous spaces [flat trajectories], an attribute that overcomes the difficulty attending fine sighting and the accurate estimation of distances.

To support his contention, Michaelis singled out 2 Sharps .44 sporting rifles from a group of 8 weapons seized from the Bannocks, pointing out that: "The fine sights of these guns, upon which their shooting at long range is supposed to depend, have been removed; very coarse front sights, and old model carbine rear sights, altered to buckhorn, have been substituted in an unworkmanlike manner."[26]

As one phase of the 1879 study of Indian armament, firing tests at Springfield Armory pitted representative Indian guns against the Springfield to determine relative rapidity, penetration, and accuracy. Surprisingly, when the Springfield .45 carbine and an 1866 Winchester repeating rifle were fired over an extended period of time, their firing rates were not too dissimilar. Beginning with the magazine loaded with seventeen cartridges, the Winchester discharged thirty-three shots in two minutes, while the Springfield managed twenty-nine shots in the same period. In situations in which a high volume of rapid fire was needed, the repeater provided it, but the time required to reload the magazine reduced its extended firing rate. Penetration tests at 200 yards showed that on the average the Springfield carbine bullet punched almost 11 in. into white pine boards, while the '66 Winchester's .44 slug averaged only 5 in. For accuracy at 300 and 600 yards, the Springfield again proved to be superior to the Winchester.[27]

Comments made by Ordnance Captain J. W. Reilly, serving in the Division of the Missouri, generally confirmed the analysis made by his comrades:

As is well known to all acquainted with arms, the Henry and Winchester are vastly inferior in range and accuracy to the Springfield carbine, though these seem to be preferred by the Indians on account of their rapidity of fire to the extent of the contents of the magazines, in this respect offering some advantages in a moment of emergency to a horseman. . . . Our Springfield carbine, caliber .45, has a greater effective range . . . than any carbine made, and much greater than the Winchester and Henry repeating rifles. But the Indians do possess a rifle here and there, possibly one in ten of their armament, that exceeds it in range and accuracy at long range. To overcome this advantage the method in use in the Fifth Cavalry, giving to each company five Springfield rifles [instead of carbines] for se-

Indian scout with a Winchester M1866 rifle. (Courtesy National Archives)

From 1893, this M1866 Winchester carbine remained in the fork of a tree near Independence, North Dakota, where it had been placed by Red Bear, an Arikara Indian, as an offering to the spirits of the sun. It was recovered in 1932, after the tree had grown around it. (Courtesy State Historical Society of North Dakota)

lected marksmen, and in the Seventh Cavalry, giving ten rifles per company for the same purpose, seems to answer.[28]

Since the heavy Sharps sporting rifles had the potential for being the most accurate and powerful of the captured Indian arms, two .44 caliber specimens surrendered by the hostiles underwent testing at Springfield Armory. Except for thoroughly cleaned bores and the use of fresh ammunition, the guns were in "as-captured" condition. The results showed that:

> The long-barrel Sharp's is a more powerful arm than the Springfield rifle, its barrel alone weighing more than the Springfield complete. It is not, however, a practicable service arm on account of its great weight, 13 pounds, and that of its ammunition. While this one gun is undoubtedly capable of firing at longer range than the Springfield, this very quality has been ignored by the Indians, as may be seen by examining its sight and those of other arms received at this armory from the Indian agencies. Both the Sharp's have had peep-sights, and the longer one probably a telescopic sight, judging from the slots in the barrel. All of these have been removed. Evidently the Indians did not desire to waste their ammunition (which they probably obtained with more or less difficulty) at long ranges. In nearly all the other arms referred to, the sights are adapted to short range. . . .[29]

Even in the 1880s the muzzle-loading rifle remained a significant element in the Indian arsenal, but the breechloader came increasingly into evidence. During a visit to Fort Defiance in 1881 Lt. John G. Bourke noticed that "the Navahos who were present at the agency were poorly provided with warlike weapons, the most dangerous being the old-time Yager rifle. Bows and arrows and lances are still retained in use, but shields have been discarded." A year later, however, the situation had changed, at least on the northern borders of the reservation. Col. George P. Buell, commanding Fort Lewis, Colorado, found that Navahos of the San Luis Valley were being armed by local settlers: "Where one would see one Indian with an old cap lock muzzle-loading rifle three years ago, he will see today a half-dozen armed with the Winchester and plenty of ammunition."[30]

Observing a band of Apaches in Arizona early in 1883, Lt. Britton Davis noted specifically that:

> This party was armed, as in fact were nearly all the hostiles in Mexico, with the latest models of Winchester magazine rifles, a better arm than the single-shot Springfield with which our soldiers and scouts were armed. The Indians obtained their arms from settlers and travelers they killed, or purchased them

Jim, an Apache scout who served under Lt. Charles B. Gatewood in the 1880s. Gatewood's personal notes indicated that the percussion three-barrel rifle-shotgun was Jim's own gun. The revolver is a Colt M1878 double action. (Courtesy Arizona Historical Society)

Lt. Col. George Custer's trunk and a M1866 Winchester, the latter surrendered by Apache warrior Geronimo's son to Lt. Charles B. Gatewood. It is thought that Geronimo himself captured the weapon during a raid on a wagon train in October 1881. Both artifacts are in the West Point Museum collection.

from white scoundrels who made a business of selling arms, ammunition, and whiskey to Indians.

Two years later Commissioner of Indian Affairs J. D. C. Atkins wrote:

The licensed traders on the various reservations are strictly prohibited from dealing in [firearms] without special permit, but the ready access that Indians have to military and other trading posts, located off but near the reservations, make it an easy matter for them to secure an abundant supply, and the consequence is that the worst and most troublesome Indians are armed with the best breech loaders that can be found in the market.

During the Apache campaign of 1886 Captain John Bourke, then on General Crook's staff, described the scene at a conference between Crook and Geronimo: "Twenty-four warriors listened to the conference or loitered within earshot; they were loaded down with metallic ammunition, some of it reloading and some not. Every man and boy in the band wore two cartridge belts."[31]

The "best breech loaders," including Winchester repeaters, remained in evidence through the 1880s, and were prominent in Indian hands at the battle of Wounded Knee in 1890. However, even when armed with repeating rifles, Indians had small chance of victory in the face of the advanced technology—symbolized at Wounded Knee by the Hotchkiss mountain cannon—and the numerical superiority of the whites.

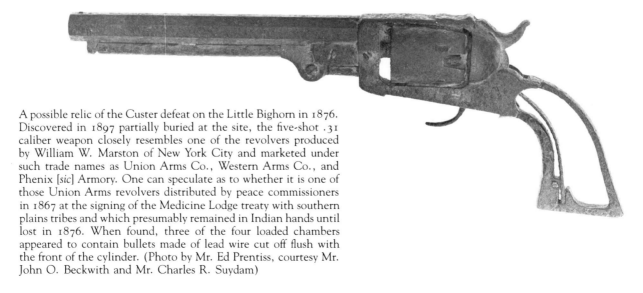

A possible relic of the Custer defeat on the Little Bighorn in 1876. Discovered in 1897 partially buried at the site, the five-shot .31 caliber weapon closely resembles one of the revolvers produced by William W. Marston of New York City and marketed under such trade names as Union Arms Co., Western Arms Co., and Phenix [sic] Armory. One can speculate as to whether it is one of those Union Arms revolvers distributed by peace commissioners in 1867 at the signing of the Medicine Lodge treaty with southern plains tribes and which presumably remained in Indian hands until lost in 1876. When found, three of the four loaded chambers appeared to contain bullets made of lead wire cut off flush with the front of the cylinder. (Photo by Mr. Ed Prentiss, courtesy Mr. John O. Beckwith and Mr. Charles R. Suydam)

Geronimo's Springfield .50-70 M1868 rifle (#28988). The stock has been studded with tacks, the buttplate removed, and the butt thinned to perhaps half its original thickness. The barrel and forestock have been shortened, a crude brass front sight replaces the original iron blade sight, and a single barrel band secures the barrel to forestock rather than the original two. Historical society acquisition records indicate the weapon came from descendents of John P. Clum, an agent to the Apaches who obtained the rifle from Geronimo in 1877. (Courtesy Arizona Historical Society)

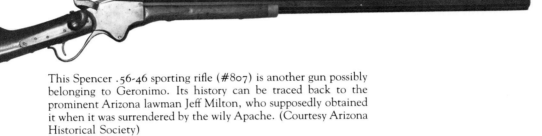

This Spencer .56-46 sporting rifle (#807) is another gun possibly belonging to Geronimo. Its history can be traced back to the prominent Arizona lawman Jeff Milton, who supposedly obtained it when it was surrendered by the wily Apache. (Courtesy Arizona Historical Society)

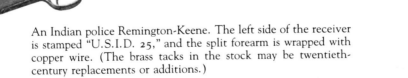

An Indian police Remington-Keene. The left side of the receiver is stamped "U.S.I.D. 25," and the split forearm is wrapped with copper wire. (The brass tacks in the stock may be twentieth-century replacements or additions.)

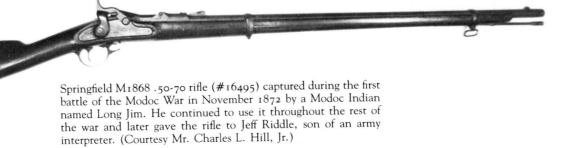

Springfield M1868 .50-70 rifle (#16495) captured during the first battle of the Modoc War in November 1872 by a Modoc Indian named Long Jim. He continued to use it throughout the rest of the war and later gave the rifle to Jeff Riddle, son of an army interpreter. (Courtesy Mr. Charles L. Hill, Jr.)

NOTES

CHAPTER 1

1. Report of the Secretary of the Navy, 1864, House Ex. Doc. 1, 38th Cong., 2nd Sess., Series No. 1221.

2. *Army and Navy Journal*, 24 Dec. 1864 (cited hereafter as *ANJ*).

3. War Department Contracts, 1858 (cited hereafter as WDC), House Ex. Doc. 50, 35th Cong., 2nd Sess., Serial No. 1006. Mont Storm's U.S. pat. 15,307 of 8 July 1856; this inventor's name was actually William Montgomery Storm, but official records often list it as "Mont Storm." Morse's U.S. pats. 15,995 of 28 Oct. 1856, and 20,503 of 8 June 1858. The *Scientific American*, 14 Aug. 1858. National Armories Expenditures Statements, 1859, 27, 36th Cong., 1st Sess., Serial No. 1048; 1860, House Ex. Doc. 35, 36th Cong., 2nd Sess., Serial No. 1097. Report of the Chief of Ordnance, 1860 (cited hereafter as *RCO*), and Report of the Secretary of War, 1860 (cited hereafter as *RSW*), both in Senate Ex. Doc. 1, 36th Cong., 2nd Sess., Serial No. 1079.

4. *RCO*, 1864, in *The War of the Rebellion: A Compilation of the Official Records of the Union and Confederate Armies* (Washington, D.C., 1880–1900), Series III, vol. 4, 802.

Andrew F. Lustyik, *Civil War Carbines* (Aledo, Ill., 1962), 38–41, 44–47.

6. U.S. pat. 49,959 of 19 Sept. 1865. *RCO*, 1865; specific locations for the annual reports of the chief of ordnance from 1865 to 1907 are given in the bibliography.

7. House Misc. Doc. 20, Pt. 1, 47th Cong., 2nd Sess., Serial No. 2119.

8. *ANJ*, 9 June 1866. *RCO*, 1866. *Description and Rules for the Management of the Springfield Breech-Loading Rifle Musket, Model 1866* (Springfield, Mass., 1867), 1. Quotation in Claud E. Fuller, *The Breech-Loader in the Service, 1816–1917* (1933; reprint ed., New Milford, Conn., 1965), 293–94.

9. Senate Report 173, 40th Cong., 2nd Sess., Serial No. 1320. Although concerned principally with artillery, this report contains a good deal of testimony about the Allin conversions. *Springfield Rifle Musket, Model 1866*, 1–2.

10. U.S. pat. 45,126 of 15 Nov. 1864. *RCO*, 1866. *Springfield Rifle Musket, Model 1866*, 2.

11. *RCO*, 1866. U.S. pat. 52,925 of 27 Feb. 1866. The *American Artisan*, 5 Sept. 1866. Charles B. Norton, *American Breech-Loading Small Arms* (New York, 1872), 166–68.

12. *RCO*, 1866–67. House Ex. Doc. 309, 42nd Cong., 2nd Sess., Serial No. 1520.

13. Fuller, *Breech-Loader in the Service*, 294. *Description and Rules for the Management of the Springfield Breech-Loading Rifle Musket, Model 1868* (Springfield, Mass., 1869), 16–18. Herschel C. Logan, *Cartridges* (Harrisburg, Pa., 1959), 76–81, 97–98. House Misc. Doc. 20, Serial No. 2119.

14. *Springfield Rifle Musket, Model 1866*, 7. Brig. Gen. Anson Mills, *My Story*, ed. C. H. Claudy (Washington, D.C., 1918), 111–12. *ANJ*, 12 April 1884.

15. House Misc. Doc. 152, 40th Cong., 2nd Sess., Serial No. 1350. "Summary Statement of Ordnance and Ordnance Stores on hand in the Infantry Regiments in the Service of the United States during the second quarter ending June 30, 1866" (cited hereafter as *SSOI*), Entry 111, Record Group 156 (Records of the Office of the Chief of Ordnance), National Archives, Washington, D.C. (cited hereafter as RG 156, NA). Senate Ex. Doc. 33, 50th Cong., 1st Sess., Serial No. 2504. Senate Ex. Doc. 16, 39th Cong., 2nd Sess., Serial No. 1277. J. W. Vaughn, *Indian Fights: New Facts on Seven Encounters* (Norman, Okla., 1966), 14–90 passim.

16. *SSOI*, 30 June 1867. John E. Parsons, *The First Winchester* (New York, 1955), xxxi. Philippe Regis de Trobriand, *Military Life in Dakota*, trans. and ed. Lucille M. Kane (St. Paul, Minn., 1951), 125–26. A number of .58 rimfire cartridge cases have been excavated at Ft. Larned, Kansas, and are now displayed there.

17. *RCO*, 1867. Vaughn, *Indian Fights*, 109–10. Robert A. Murray, *Military Posts in the Powder River Country of Wyoming, 1865–1894* (Lincoln, Neb., 1968), 67–70. Letter to the authors from Robert A. Murray, 25 April 1970.

18. Grace Raymond Hebard and E. A. Brininstool, *The Bozeman Trail* (Cleveland, Ohio, 1922), 2: 53–54, 74, 77, 84.

19. *RSW*, 1867. House Ex. Doc. 1, 40th Cong., 2nd Sess., Serial No. 1324. Senate Rpt. 183, 42nd Cong., 2nd Sess., Serial No. 1497. *RCO*, 1869.

20. House Ex. Doc. 309, Serial No. 1520. *Springfield Rifle Musket, Model 1868*. Fuller, *Breech-Loader in the Service*, 299.

21. *Springfield Rifle Musket, Model 1868*. House Ex. Doc. 309, Serial No. 1520. Springfield Armory Expenditures Statement, 1868 (cited hereafter as *SAES*). Specific loca-

tions for most of the annual Springfield Armory expenditures statements from 1866 to 1904 are given in the bibliography. U.S. pats. 37,501 of 27 Jan. 1863; 40,887 of 8 Dec. 1863; 45,123 of 15 Nov. 1864; and 45,797 of 3 Jan. 1865. RCO, 1866. The 1869 SAES lists the manufacture of another 498 Remingtons, but these are labeled "cadet" arms; see also the summary of operations at Springfield in the 1869 RCO.

22. ANJ, 20 Oct. 1866 and 1 Jan. 1870. American Artisan, 24 Oct. 1866. House Ex. Doc. 1, Pt. 3, 41st Cong., 3rd Sess., Serial No. 1448. Norton, Breech-Loading Small Arms, 20–81 passim.

23. ANJ, 23 and 30 July 1870; also in House Ex. Doc. 152, 43rd Cong., 2nd Sess., Serial No. 1648.

24. House Ex. Doc. 309, Serial No. 1520. SAES, 1871.

25. RCO, 1870 and 1873. For an explanation of the Model 1868's long receiver, see House Misc. Doc. 20, Serial No. 2119.

26. RCO, 1873. Norton, Breech-Loading Small Arms, 170.

27. Norton, Breech-Loading Small Arms, 166–71. ANJ, 9 Feb. 1867. RCO, 1873. An earlier trapdoor design that employed this technique was the Westley Richards "monkey-tail" rifle of 1858 (Br. pat. 633 of 25 March 1858; U.S. pat. 39,246 of 14 July 1863). It was sold in this country by Tomes Son and Melvain (later Tomes, Melvain & Co.) of New York City; see Spirit of the Times, 27 Aug. 1859, and ANJ, 5 Dec. 1863.

28. The "positive cam" Springfield of 1888 was designed to overcome this problem; see the RCO, 1888 and 1890. See also Edward S. Farrow, American Small Arms (New York, 1904), 296.

29. SSOI, 31 Dec. 1870 to 31 Dec. 1871. Dyer to Chief Ordnance Officers, Departments of the Platte and the Missouri, 7 March 1871; Dyer to Benecia and San Antonio Arsenals, 27 March 1871, vol. 37, Entry 7, RG 156, NA. Summary of field trials, in RCO, 1873.

30. RCO, 1873.

31. House Ex. Doc. 309, Serial No. 1520. SAES, 1872. Norm Flayderman, Flayderman's Guide to Antique American Firearms, 2nd ed. (Northfield, Ill., 1980), 506.

32. U.S. pats. 26,475 of 20 Dec. 1859 and 81,059 of 11 Aug. 1868. Description and Rules for the Management of the Ward-Burton Rifle Musket, Model 1871 (Springfield, Mass., 1872). Norton, Breech-Loading Small Arms, 119–44.

33. SAES, 1872. RCO, 1872–73. SSOI, 31 March 1872; in 1872 this heading was changed to "Summary of Ordnance and Ordnance Stores in the hands of Troops . . . ," but for the sake of simplicity we have continued to use the initials of the older heading.

34. RCO, 1873. SAES, 1873. Senate Ex. Doc. 16, 45th Cong., 1st Sess., Serial No. 1828. Flayderman, Antique American Firearms, 467.

35. "Summary Statement of Ordnance and Ordnance Stores on hand in the Cavalry Regiments in the service of the United States during the Second Quarter ending June 30, 1866 [and] June 30, 1867," Entry 110, RG 156, NA (cited hereafter as SSOC). RCO, 1866. House Ex. Doc. 99, 40th Cong., 2nd Sess., Serial No. 1338.

36. House Ex. Doc. 99, Serial No. 1338. WDC, 1867–

68; specific locations for most of the annual summaries of contracts made by the War Department from 1866 to 1894 are given in the bibliography. RCO, 1869. Frank M. Sellers, Sharps Firearms (N. Hollywood, Calif., 1978), 176–80.

37. Card 00190, Arrott Collection, Fort Union National Monument, Watrous, N.M.

38. House Ex. Doc. 99, Serial No. 1338. House Ex. Doc. 53, 39th Cong., 2nd Sess., Serial No. 1290. Spencer 1866 catalog, in L. D. Satterlee, comp., Ten Old Gun Catalogs for the Collector (1940; reprint ed., Chicago, 1962). Stabler's U.S. pat. 46,828 of 14 March 1865. Schuyler, Hartley & Graham 1864 catalog.

39. Donald F. Danker, ed., Man of the Plains: The Recollections of Luther North, 1856–1882 (Lincoln, Neb., 1961), 53.

40. Gen. George A. Forsyth, Thrilling Days of Army Life.

41. David L. Spotts, Campaigning with Custer and the Nineteenth Kansas Volunteer Cavalry (Los Angeles, 1928), 44–45. General George A. Custer, My Life on the Plains, ed. Milo M. Quaife (Chicago, 1952), 264–68.

42. Elizabeth B. Custer, Following the Guidon (Norman, Okla., 1966), 40. See also the sources cited in Robert M. Utley, Frontier Regulars (New York, 1973), 161–62.

43. RCO, 1869.

44. ANJ, 23 and 30 July 1870.

45. SAES, 1870–72. RCO, 1872–73. Dyer to Springfield Armory, 2 May 1871, vol. 37, Entry 6, RG 156, NA. SSOC, 30 June 1871 to 30 June 1872.

46. Dyer to Springfield Armory, 18 Nov. 1871, vol. 38, Entry 7, RG 156, NA. Summary of field trials, in RCO, 1873. Cos. F and K, 7th Cav., received the experimental Springfields, Sharps, and Remingtons in 1871, but were still stationed east of the Mississippi at that time; SSOC, 30 June–31 Dec. 1871.

47. SSOC, 30 June 1866. "Ledgers and Journals of Ordnance and Ordnance Stores Issued to the Militia, 1816–1904," Entry 118, RG 156, NA (cited hereafter as LJOM).

48. Quotation in Don Rickey, Jr., Forty Miles a Day on Beans and Hay (Norman, Okla., 1963), 291–92.

49. SSOC, 30 Sept. 1873 to 30 Sept. 1874. Parsons, The First Winchester, 148. H. H. McConnell, Five Years a Cavalryman (Jacksboro, Tex., 1889), 114.

50. RCO, 1873.

51. RCO, 1873.

52. RCO, 1873.

53. RCO, 1873. Advertisements for Ward-Burton sporting rifles appear in Forest and Stream, 11 Dec. 1873 and subsequently.

54. Capt. S. C. Lyford to Springfield Armory, 8 July 1873, Entry 13, RG 156, NA.

55. Description and Rules for the Management of the Springfield Rifle, Carbine, and Army Revolvers, Calibre .45 (Springfield, Mass., 1874), 20–21, 30. RCO, 1879–80. Rickey, Forty Miles a Day, 211–12.

56. ANJ, 26 Feb. and 23 July 1870. Dyer to Capt. John R. McGinniss, 15 May 1871, vol. 37, Entry 6, RG 156, NA.

57. SAES, 1874–75. RCO, 1874–75. SSOI and SSOC, 31 Dec. 1873 to 30 June 1874. San Antonio Arsenal to

the Chief of Ordnance, 31 Dec. 1873, Entry 1346, RG 156, NA. An account of the 1871–72 field trials of the trowel bayonet is in House Ex. Doc. 60, 42nd Cong., 2nd Sess., Serial No. 1515. See also *ANJ*, 10 April and 15 May 1875; and Albert N. Hardin, Jr., *The American Bayonet, 1776–1964* (Philadelphia, 1964), 195–214.

58. *SAES*, 1874. Senate Ex. Doc. 16, Serial No. 1828. Capt. Clifton Comley (sp?), San Antonio Arsenal, to the chief of ordnance, 23 Feb. 1874, Entry 1346, RG 156, NA. See also M. D. "Bud" Waite and B. D. Ernst, *Trapdoor Springfield* (N. Hollywood, Calif., 1980), 133–45.

59. *LJOM*, 1870–74. *SSOI*, 30 June 1875 to 31 March 1876. House Misc. Doc. 20, Serial No. 2119.

60. *RCO*, 1875. *SSOC*, 30 June 1874 to 30 June 1875. Donald Jackson, *Custer's Gold* (New Haven, Conn., 1966), 23, 33–34.

61. *SAES*, 1875. Senate Ex. Doc. 16, Serial No. 1828. Archer L. Jackson, "Rare Trapdoor Springfields," *American Society of Arms Collectors Bulletin* No. 16, Fall 1967, n.p.

62. *ANJ*, 8 Nov. 1873. DuMont, *Custer Battle Guns*, 67–68.

63. Jackson, "Rare Trapdoor Springfields." Parsons, *The First Winchester*, 146.

64. Jackson, "Rare Trapdoor Springfields." *Description and Rules for the Management of the Springfield Rifle, Carbine, and Army Revolvers, Caliber .45* (Washington, D.C., 1898), 30–31. Waite and Ernst, *Trapdoor Springfield*, 31–46.

65. Jackson, "Rare Trapdoor Springfields." J. W. Vaughn, *With Crook at the Rosebud* (Harrisburg, Pa., 1956), 32.

66. *Springfield Rifle Musket, Model 1866*, 5. *Springfield Rifle, Carbine, and Army Revolvers* (1874), 23.

67. Senate Ex. Doc. 16, Serial No. 1828. *SAES*, 1876. *Springfield Rifle, Carbine, and Army Revolvers* (1898), 27–28.

68. *ANJ*, 19 Aug. 1876.

69. E. A. Brininstool, *Troopers with Custer* (Harrisburg, Pa., 1952), 55. *ANJ*, 30 Sept. and 14 Oct. 1876. See also John F. Finerty, *War-Path and Bivouac* (Norman, Okla., 1961), 138.

70. *ANJ*, 26 Aug. 1876.

71. Ibid.

72. *ANJ*, 7 and 14 Oct. 1876.

73. Henry to Chief of Ordnance, 6 Aug. 1876, Letter no. 4350, Correspondence received by the Office of the Chief of Ordnance, 1876, RG 156, NA. Gibbon's testimony is in House Misc. Doc. 56, Pt. 2, 45th Cong., 2nd Sess., Serial No. 1818. *ANJ*, 18 Jan. 1877.

74. San Antonio Arsenal to the chief of ordnance, 7 Feb. 1874, Entry 1346; and Miscellaneous Letters Sent from San Antonio Arsenal, 21 June 1875–31 Dec. 1879, Entry 1344, RG 156, NA.

75. Senate Ex. Doc. 16, Serial No. 1828. *SAES*, 1881. Information on the changes in the trapdoor Springfield during its service life is in Waite and Ernst, *The Trapdoor Springfield*, 53–68.

76. *RCO*, 1877. The Belgian Albini-Braendlin trapdoor rifle, familiar to U.S. ordnance officers by 1868, had dual extractors; see the *RCO*, 1877, and House Misc. Docs. (no number), 40th Cong., 2nd Sess., Serial No. 1355.

77. *Springfield Rifle, Carbine, and Army Revolvers* (1898), 3–5. See also Waite and Ernst, *The Trapdoor Springfield*.

78. *RCO*, 1879. Rickey, *Forty Miles a Day*, 99–100, 103.

79. Oliver Knight, *Following the Indian Wars* (Norman, Okla., 1960), 19. *RCO*, 1881.

80. Jackson, *Custer's Gold*, 17. House Misc. Doc. 56, Pt. 2, Serial No. 1818.

81. *ANJ*, 13 April 1878.

82. *ANJ*, 13 April 1878. *RCO*, 1883. Jackson, "Rare Trapdoor Springfields." Leonard C. Weston and Dorrel Garrison, "Incidents in the Development of the Army's Marksmanship Program," *Gun Report*, May 1966, 23–24. *RCO*, 1880–81. *SAES*, 1881.

83. *RCO*, 1878–83; the 1883 *RCO* terms the new cartridge the "Model 1882." F. W. Hackley, W. H. Woodin, and E. L. Scranton, *History of Modern U.S. Military Small Arms Ammunition, 1880–1939* (New York, 1967), 204–7. Rickey, *Forty Miles a Day*, 98–99. A. E. Neidner and John J. Barsotti, "Hardtack and Black Powder," *American Rifleman*, Nov. 1950, 28.

84. Rickey, *Forty Miles a Day*, 103–4, 236–37. Trobriand, Military Life in Dakota, 62–63. Neidner and Barsotti, "Hardtack and Black Powder," 30. *RCO*, 1879.

85. *RCO*, 1873. *ANJ*, 13 April 1878.

86. *RCO*, 1878.

87. *RCO*, 1878. U.S. pats. 93,822 of 17 Aug. 1869 and 99,898 of 15 Feb. 1870. Two Hotchkiss rifles were displayed at the Philadelphia Exposition, a single-shot and a repeater; House Misc. Doc. 20, Serial No. 2119.

88. *RCO*, 1879. Flayderman, *Antique American Firearms*, 279–80. Jackson, "Rare Trapdoor Springfields."

89. *RCO*, 1879–81. Misc. letters sent from San Antonio Arsenal, 21 June 1875–31 Dec. 1879, Entry 1344; and San Antonio Arsenal to Ft. Concho, 3 Jan. 1881, Entry 1346, RG 156, NA.

90. *RCO*, 1878–82. *SAES*, 1881.

91. Jackson, "Rare Trapdoor Springfields." *RCO*, 1882. *SAES*, 1882.

92. *RCO*, 1874–82. *SAES*, 1874. San Antonio Arsenal to the chief of ordnance, 7 March 1879, Entry 1346, RG 156, NA.

93. Capt. Frank Phipps, San Antonio Arsenal, to H. L. Noble, 5 May 1882, Entry 1346, RG 156, NA.

94. T. A. Falvey to Sharps, 15 Oct. 1879, Sharps Rifle Co. correspondence, Texas Tech University Library, Lubbock, Texas. *ANJ*, 23 Nov. 1878. Taylor to Colt, 24 Sept. 1879; Hearn to Colt, 2 Oct. 1882; Loring to Colt, 13 March 1882; Colt Pat. F. A. Mfg. Co. correspondence, Connecticut State Library, Hartford, Conn. (cited hereafter as Colt letters). Lawrence P. Shelton, "A U.S. Army Officer's Shotgun," *Gun Report*, Feb. 1979, 56–59.

95. Murray to Colt, 29 Jan. 1887, Colt letters.

96. *RCO*, 1882–85. *SAES*, 1882–85. Fuller, *Breech-Loader in the Service*, 304–5.

97. Charles E. Hanson, Jr., and Archer L. Jackson, "The 1881 Springfield Shotgun," *American Rifleman*, June 1965, 52. Fuller, *Breech-Loader in the Service*, 305.

98. Hanson and Jackson, "Springfield Shotgun," 53.

99. *RCO*, 1882. *SAES*, 1882. Hardin, *The American*

Bayonet, 71. Fuller, *Breech-Loader in the Service*, 306. As early as 1877 Asst. Inspector-General Baird had recommended adoption of a cavalry arm with 26-in. or 28-in. barrel; *RCO*, 1877. Waite and Ernst, *Trapdoor Springfield*, 106.

100. *RCO*, 1882.

101. House Ex. Doc. 53, Serial No. 1290. *RCO*, 1873–75. *SAES*, 1875. Senate Ex. Doc. 16, Serial No. 1828.

102. *RCO*, 1873, 1875, 1878, and 1882. *ANJ*, 9 Aug. 1879.

103. U.S. pat. 221,328 of 4 Nov. 1879.

104. *RCO*, 1882.

105. *RCO*, 1882–85. Sellers, *Sharps Firearms*, 289–98.

106. Summary of field trials, in *RCO*, 1886.

107. Joseph Hamblen Sears, *The Career of Leonard Wood* (New York, 1920), 44–45.

108. *Springfield Rifle, Carbine, and Army Revolvers* (1898), 4, 14–15. A. C. Gould, *Modern American Rifles* (1892; reprint ed., Plantersville, S.C., 1946), 64. Quotations in Richard Upton, ed., *Fort Custer on the Big Horn, 1877–1898* (Glendale, Calif., 1973), 85.

109. Upton, *Fort Custer*, 88–89.

110. This rifle was formerly in the collection of Tom Lewis.

111. *RCO*, 1884–86. *SAES*, 1886. Asst. Adj. Gen., Dept. of Texas, to San Antonio Arsenal, 9 Aug. 1886, Entry 1348, RG 156, NA.

112. *RCO*, 1888–90, and 1892. *SAES*, 1890, 1892–93.

113. *RCO*, 1888–93. *SAES*, 1888, 1891–93. *Springfield Rifle, Carbine, and Army Revolvers* (1898), 31. Hardin, *The American Bayonet*, 73–74.

114. *Springfield Rifle, Carbine, and Army Revolvers* (1898). *RCO*, 1889–90. *SAES*, 1889–90.

115. "Monthly Statements of Ordnance Stores on hand at Ordnance Depots, Jan.–June 1890," Entry 105, RG 156, NA. *ANJ*, 13 March 1886, and 25 Jan. 1896. *Scientific American Supplement*, 27 March 1886. *RCO*, 1886–93.

116. *RCO*, 1887 and 1889. Hackley, Woodin, and Scranton, *Small Arms Ammunition*, 208–10.

117. *RCO*, 1888. *Scientific American*, 27 Oct. 1888.

118. *RCO*, 1888. Col. Joseph P. Farley, "Notes on Small-Arms and Ammunition," *Journal of the Military Service Institution*, Jan., 1899, 43–44. Farrow, *American Small Arms*, 296.

119. *RCO*, 1888, 1890, 1892. *SAES*, 1888, 1890.

120. *RCO*, 1892.

121. "Monthly Statements of Ordnance Stores on hand at Arsenals, June, 1897–Feb., 1902," Entry 106, RG 156, NA.

122. Stan Nelson, "An Ode to the Trapdoor Springfield," *Gun Report*, March 1962, 34.

123. *RCO*, 1892. *Scientific American*, 31 Dec. 1892.

124. *RCO*, 1892.

125. *Description and Rules for the Management of the U.S. Magazine Rifle and Carbine, Calibre .30* (Washington, D.C., 1898), 31.

126. *U.S. Magazine Rifle and Carbine*, 49, 54. Information on the development of this cartridge is in Hackley, Woodin, and Scranton, *Small Arms Ammunition*, 72–76.

127. *RCO*, 1893–94. *Scientific American*, 15 April 1893.

128. *U.S. Magazine Rifle and Carbine*, 21–22, 62. *RCO*, 1893–95. *SAES*, 1894–95. *ANJ*, 12 Jan. 1895. See also the *Scientific American Supplement*, 20 Oct. 1894.

129. *RCO*, 1895, 1900–1903. *SAES*, 1903–1904.

CHAPTER 2

1. Undated Ordnance return (c. 1865), Entry 101, Record Group 156 (Records of the Chief of Ordnance), National Archives (cited hereafter as RG 156, NA). House Misc. Doc. 152, 40th Cong., 2nd Sess., Serial No. 1350. John D. Billings, *Hardtack and Coffee*, ed. Richard Hartwell (1887; reprint ed., Chicago, 1960), 302–3.

2. Quotation in John E. Parsons, *The Peacemaker and Its Rivals* (New York, 1950), 152.

3. House Misc. Doc. 152, Serial No. 1350. "Summary Statement of Ordnance and Ordnance Stores on Hand in the Cavalry Regiments in the Service of the United States during the Second Quarter ending June 30, 1866 [and] June 30, 1867," Entry 110, RG 156, NA. Dyer to Secretary of War, 12 July 1870, vol. 16, Entry 5, RG 156, NA. Chris Emmett, *Fort Union and the Winning of the Southwest* (Norman, Okla., 1965), 324. William Murphy, "The Forgotten Battalion," *Annals of Wyoming*, Oct. 1930, 389.

4. Robert A. Murray, *Military Posts in the Powder River Country of Wyoming, 1865–1894* (Lincoln, Neb., 1968), 68. John S. DuMont, *Custer Battle Guns* (Ft. Collins, Colo., 1974), 75, 78–79, 82, 84. Alson B. Ostrander, *An Army Boy of the Sixties* (New York, 1924), 87–88, 102–4, 193. Frances C. Carrington, *My Army Life and the Fort Phil Kearney Massacre* (Philadelphia, 1910), 78.

5. *Army and Navy Journal*, 6 March 1867 (cited hereafter as *ANJ*).

6. [Frank M. Sellers], *The William M. Locke Collection* (East Point, Ga., 1973), 257. Parsons, *The Peacemaker*, 152–54.

7. Roy G. Jinks and Robert J. Neal, *Smith and Wesson, 1857–1945*, rev. ed. (New York, 1975), 260. Capt. Albert Barnitz, *Life in Custer's Cavalry*, ed. Robert M. Utley (New Haven, Conn., 1977), 205. *ANJ*, 25 Sept. 1869.

8. Murray, *Military Posts*, 68. DuMont, *Custer Battle Guns*, 70–77, 80–81. W. W. Greener, *Modern Breech-Loaders: Sporting and Military*, 2nd ed. (1874?; reprint ed., Pueblo, Colo., n.d.), 158–59. A. W. F. Taylerson, *The Revolver, 1865–1888* (New York, 1966), 82–84.

9. Springfield Armory Expenditures Statement, 1870 (cited hereafter as *SAES*). Specific locations for most of the annual Springfield Armory expenditures statements from 1866 to 1904 are given in the bibliography. John E. Parsons, *Smith & Wesson Revolvers* (New York, 1957), 66–71.

10. *ANJ*, 23 and 30 July 1870; also in House Ex. Doc. 152, 43rd Cong., 2nd Sess., Serial No. 1648.

11. *ANJ*, 23 July 1870.

12. Charles B. Norton, *American Breech-Loading Small Arms* (New York, 1872), 76–80, 176–82. Parsons, *Smith & Wesson*, 66–71.

13. War Department Contracts, 1870 (cited hereafter as

WDC). Specific locations for most of the annual summaries of War Department contracts from 1866 to 1894 are given in the bibliography. Parsons, *Smith & Wesson*, 75. Dyer to Springfield Armory, 27 March 1871, vol. 37, Entry 7, Record Group 156 (Records of the Office of the Chief of Ordnance), National Archives, Washington, D.C. (cited hereafter as RG 156, NA).

14. Jinks and Neal, *Smith & Wesson*, 160–62. Parsons, *Smith & Wesson*, 72.

15. Dyer to Leavenworth and Benecia Arsenals and to Omaha Depot, 9 May 1871, vol. 37, Entry 6, RG 156, NA. "Summary Statement of Ordnance and Ordnance Stores on Hand in the Cavalry Regiments in the Service of the United States during the Second Quarter Ending June 30, 1871 [and] Oct. 30, 1871," Entry 110, RG 156, NA (cited hereafter as SSOC). Parsons, *Smith & Wesson*, 74–75.

16. "Journal of Accounts for Arms Sold at Ordnance Depots and Arsenals," 1871–74 (cited hereafter as ASDA), Entry 125, RG 156, NA. Parsons, *Smith & Wesson*, 72.

17. SSOC, 31 Dec. 1871. U.S. pat. 117,461 of 25 July 1871. Charles R. Suydam, *U.S. Cartridges and Their Handguns, 1795–1975* (N. Hollywood, Calif., 1977), 204–5.

18. James E. Serven, *Colt Firearms from 1836* (Harrisburg, Pa., 1979), 179. SAES, 1871. WDC, 1872.

19. SSOC, 31 Dec. 1871; 31 March and 30 Oct. 1872. San Antonio Arsenal to the chief of ordnance, 2 April 1872, Entry 1346, RG 156, NA.

20. Sgt. James Hill to Colt, 14 Jan. 1873, Colt. Pat. F. A. Mfg. Co. correspondence, Connecticut State Library, Hartford, Conn. (cited hereafter as Colt letters).

21. Senate Report 183, 42nd Cong., 2nd Sess., Serial No. 1497. SSOC, 31 March to 31 Dec. 1872. Dyer to arsenals and depots, 29 March 1871, vol. 37, Entry 6, RG 156, NA.

22. SSOC, 30 June 1873.

23. Ordnance Notes V, in *ANJ*, 20 May 1876; also in Charles T. Haven and Frank A. Belden, *The History of the Colt Revolver* (New York, 1940), 395–96. John Kopec, Ron Graham, and C. K. Moore, *A Study of the Colt Single Action Army Revolver* (La Puente, Calif., 1976).

24. Ordnance Notes V.

25. Parsons, *Smith & Wesson*, 87–89, 178. U.S. pats. 116,225 of 20 June 1871, and 138,047 of 22 April 1873.

26. Ordnance Notes V.

27. WDC, 1873. Report of the Chief of Ordnance, 1874 (cited hereafter as RCO). Specific locations for the annual reports of the Chief of Ordnance from 1865 to 1907 are given in the bibliography. Parsons, *The Peacemaker*, following p. ix. SSOC, 31 Dec. 1873 to 31 March 1874.

28. RCO, 1873. House Misc. Doc. 20, Pt. 1, 47th Cong., 2nd Sess., Serial No. 2119. *Description and Rules for the Management of the Springfield Rifle, Carbine, and Army Revolvers, Calibre .45* (Springfield, Mass., 1874), 36–39. Ordnance Notes V.

29. SSOC, 30 June 1874 to 31 March 1876.

30. Ordnance Notes LIV, in *ANJ*, 10 Feb. 1877; also in Haven and Belden, *The Colt Revolver*, 397–98. Parsons, *Smith & Wesson*, 78–79.

31. Ordnance Notes LIV.

32. WDC, 1874–75. RCO, 1875. Parsons, *Smith & Wesson*, 91.

33. Parsons, *The Peacemaker*, 64–67.

34. SSOC, 31 March 1875 to 30 Sept. 1875. RCO, 1875. Parsons, *Smith & Wesson*, 91–92. ASDA, 1875–79.

35. F. W. Hackley, W. H. Woodin, and E. L. Scranton, *History of Modern U.S. Military Small Arms Ammunition, 1880–1939* (New York, 1967), 10–11. *Springfield Rifle, Carbine, and Army Revolvers*, 45. Capt. Charles King, *Trials of a Staff-Officer* (Philadelphia, 1891), 55–57.

36. ANJ, 4 Dec. 1875.

37. Ordnance Notes LIV. Parsons, *The Peacemaker*, 36–41.

38. Parsons, *Smith & Wesson*, 94–95. Jinks and Neal, *Smith & Wesson*, 212–14. Letter from Karl F. Moldenhauer to James Roller, 6 Oct. 1972, courtesy Remington Arms Museum.

39. ANJ, 6 May 1876 and 21 April 1877.

40. Quotation in Parsons, *The Peacemaker*, 33. Miscellaneous Letters Sent from San Antonio Arsenal, 21 June 1876–31 Dec. 1879, Entry 1344, RG 156, NA.

41. Gen. George A. Custer, *My Life on the Plains*, ed. Milo M. Quaife (Chicago, 1952), 479–80. Sgt. James Hill to Colt, 14 Jan. 1873, Colt letters. Lt. Col. Richard Irving Dodge, *The Plains of the Great West and Their Inhabitants* (New York, 1877), xlix. Custer's National No. 1 is mentioned in DuMont, *Custer Battle Guns*, 85.

42. John E. Parsons and John S. DuMont, *Firearms in the Custer Battle* (Harrisburg, Pa., 1953), 17–18. "Birmingham Industries," *Iron* (London), 7 Nov. 1874. William Chipchase Dowell, *The Webley Story* (Kirkgate, Leeds, 1962), 62; pls. 2 and 28. J. H. Walsh, *The Modern Sportsman's Gun and Rifle* (London, 1882–84), 2: 418. See also note 73, chapter 5. Parsons and DuMont speculate that Custer carried a pair of Webley R.I.C. revolvers instead of Bulldogs, and he may well have done so. It is fair to note, however, that other British double-action cartridge revolvers besides Webleys were available prior to 1876, including the Adams, Tranter, Galand & Sommerville, Thomas, and a few lesser lights; see Greener, *Modern Breech-Loaders*, 151–60, and Taylerson, *The Revolver*, 1865–1888, Ch. 4.

43. Parsons, *The Peacemaker*, 34, 73–75. *ANJ*, 17 Aug. 1878. Michaelis to Colt, 1 Aug. 1877; Moran to Colt, 19 Sept. 1879; Kendall to Colt, 2 Dec. 1879; Smith to Colt, 12 Feb. 1884, Colt letters.

44. U.S. pats. 157,860 of 15 Dec. 1874; 187,975 and 187,980 of 6 March 1877.

45. House Misc. Doc. 20, Serial No. 2119. Parsons, *The Peacemaker*, 67–72. *ANJ*, 9 Oct. 1880 and 2 Sept. 1882.

46. John F. Finerty, *War-Path and Bivouac* (Norman, Okla., 1961), 76–77.

47. ANJ, 18 May 1878.

48. Ami Frank Mulford, *Fighting Indians in the 7th United States Cavalry* (1878; reprint ed., Bellevue, Neb., 1970), 91–92. RCO, 1879; summarized in Parsons, *The Peacemaker*, 56–63.

49. RCO, 1879.

50. ANJ, 26 July and 9 Aug. 1879. RCO, 1879.

51. Parsons, *The Peacemaker*, 75. Parsons, *Smith & Wes-*

son, 97. Kopec, Graham, and Moore, *Single Action Army Revolver.*

52. *RCO,* 1889; also in A. C. Gould, *Modern American Pistols and Revolvers* (1894; reprint ed., Plantersville, S.C., 1946), 81–96. Report of the Secretary of the Navy, 1888, House Ex. Doc. 1, Pt. 3, 50th Cong., 2nd Sess., Serial No. 2634.

53. Parsons, *The Peacemaker,* 73–75.

54. A. W. F. Taylerson, *The Revolver, 1889–1914* (New York, 1971), 32–35. Gould, *Pistols and Revolvers,* 44–49.

55. Gould, *Pistols and Revolvers,* 62–65. Jinks and Neal, *Smith & Wesson,* 122–24, 379–81. Taylerson, *The Revolver, 1889–1914,* 71–72.

56. *RCO,* 1889. Gould, *Pistols and Revolvers,* 81–96, 200–203.

57. *ANJ,* 5 April 1890.

58. *RCO,* 1891–92.

59. *RCO,* 1892–93.

60. *RCO,* 1893.

61. *RCO,* 1893–94.

62. *RCO,* 1895. Taylerson, *The Revolver, 1889–1914,* 35–36.

63. *RCO,* 1893 and 1895.

64. *RCO,* 1907.

65. Gould, *Pistols and Revolvers,* 48–50. Taylerson, *The Revolver, 1889–1914,* 39–41. Haven and Belden, *The Colt Revolver,* 427, 430, 433. *RCO,* 1891–1902. See also *ANJ,* 20 April 1901.

CHAPTER 3

1. San Francisco *Alta California,* 2 July 1865. St. Louis *Missouri Democrat,* 28 Feb. and 19 May 1865. Denver *Rocky Mountain News,* 10 May 1865. Omaha *Republican,* 10 Oct., 3 Nov., and 4 Dec. 1865. Atchison (Kansas) *Champion,* 6 Oct. 1865. Boise *Idaho Statesman,* 15 June and 27 July 1865. Gold Hill (Nev.) *Daily News,* 1 July 1865.

2. St. Louis *Missouri Republican,* 21 April 1850. *Alta California,* 6 Feb. 1854. *Missouri Democrat,* 8 May 1854 and 28 March 1859. Tubac *Arizonian,* 2 June 1859. Senate Rpt. 183, 42nd Cong., 2nd Sess., Serial No. 1497.

3. Union Metallic Cartridge Co. price list, 1869 (reprinted by Ray Riling, Philadelphia, 1960). Winchester Repeating Arms Co. 1878 catalog. Glen Barrett, ed., *Mackinaws Down the Missouri . . .* (Logan, Utah, 1972), 77.

4. Capt. Eugene F. Ware, *The Indian War of 1864,* ed. Clyde C. Walton (New York, 1960), 315, 369–70.

5. Senate Rpt. 183, Serial No. 1497.

6. Quotation in A. C. Gould, *Modern American Rifles* (1892; reprint ed., Plantersville, S.C., 1946), 82.

7. *Rocky Mountain News,* 5 Sept. 1865 and 25 April 1866.

8. J. W. Vaughn, *Indian Fights: New Facts on Seven Encounters* (Norman, Okla., 1966), 98, 102.

9. Senate Rpt. 183, Serial No. 1497.

10. Irving Howbert, *Memories of a Lifetime in the Pike's Peak Region* (New York and London, 1925), 210–11.

11. John R. Cook, *The Border and the Buffalo,* ed. Milo M. Quaife (Chicago, 1938), 53.

12. Richard Townshend, *A Tenderfoot in Colorado* (New York, 1923), 5, 108. Frank Collinson, *Life in the Saddle,* ed. Mary W. Clarke (Norman, Okla., 1963), 12.

13. Letter to the authors from Pauline Louviere, Houston Public Library, 7 Sept. 1974, citing the Houston city directories of 1866–73. Jackson Arms (Dallas, Tex.) Catalog Supplement 21A, item 697, and Catalog 24, item 400A.

14. Ad in Wallihan & Co.'s *Rocky Mountain Directory and Colorado Gazetteer,* 1871.

15. This rifle, and another Rudolph rifle very similar to it, are now in the Municipal Museum in Canon City, Colorado.

16. Charles E. Hanson, Jr., *The Hawken Rifle: Its Place in History* (Chadron, Neb., 1979), 44–46. Margaret J. Carrington, *Ab-sa-ra-ka, Home of the Crows* (Philadelphia, 1868), 189. Briggs & Lowry's *Omaha Directory,* 1872–73.

17. A. M. Strope, "A Buffalo Hunt in 1874," *Outdoor Life* (Denver Series), Feb. 1901, n.p.

18. "Carlos Gove," *The Colorado Gun Collectors 1974 Annual. Rocky Mountain News,* 26 April 1876. Corbett, Hoye & Co.'s *Denver City Directories,* 1876 and 1877. *The Westerner's Brand Book* (Denver Posse), 1963, 143 (cited hereafter as *WBB*).

19. Senate Rpt. 183, Serial No. 1497. House Ex. Doc. 99, 40th Cong., 2nd Sess., Serial No. 1338. *Army and Navy Journal,* 29 Aug. 1863 (cited hereafter as *ANJ*). Robert A. Murray, *Fort Laramie: Visions of a Grand Old Post* (Ft. Collins, Co., 1974), 44–45. "Journal of Accounts for Arms Sold at Ordnance Depots and Arsenals," 1866–68 (cited hereafter as *ASDA*), Entry 125, Record Group 156, National Archives (cited hereafter as RG 156, NA).

20. *WBB,* 1954, 9. Virginia City *Montana Post,* 24 Nov. 1866.

21. San Antonio *Express,* 29 July 1867. House Ex. Doc. 53, 39th Cong., 2nd Sess., Serial No. 1290. House Ex. Doc. 99, Serial No. 1338. U.S. pat. 41,017 of 22 Dec. 1863. Andrew F. Lustyik, *Civil War Carbines* (Aledo, Ill., 1962), 52. Nearly as vigorous in salesmanship as Miller was another Texas merchant, H. Brainard of Brownsville, who early in 1868 advertised Springfield muzzle-loaders plus "Breech Loading Maynard, Spencer, Sharp's, and Henry Rifles"; Brownsville *Ranchero,* 15 Feb. 1868.

22. U.S. pats. 38,935 of 23 June 1863, and 43,827 of 16 Aug. 1864. *Ball's Patent Repeating and Single-Loading Fire-Arms . . .* (Claremont, N.H., 1866). Lustyik, *Civil War Carbines,* 45.

23. James Chisholm, *South Pass, 1868* (Lincoln, Neb., 1960), 173. Cook, *Border and the Buffalo,* 54. C. W. Shores, *Memoirs of a Lawman,* ed. Wilson Rockwell (Denver, 1962), 99.

24. U.S. pats. 41,732 of 23 Feb., and 45,660 of 27 Dec. 1864. Lustyik, *Civil War Carbines,* 62–63. House Ex. Doc. 99, Serial No. 1338. Maj. John H. Nankivell, *History of the Military Organizations of the State of Colorado, 1860–1935* (Denver, 1935), 43. Townshend, *Tenderfoot in Colorado,* 217.

25. Lustyik, *Civil War Carbines,* 54. Richard B. Hughes, *Pioneer Years in the Black Hills,* ed. Agnes Wright Spring (Glendale, Calif., 1957), 83.

26. *Alta California*, 18 July 1869. Prescott, *Arizona Miner*, 9 Jan. 1867. James E. Serven, *Colt Firearms from 1836* (Harrisburg, Pa., 1979), 198. Howbert, *Memories of a Lifetime*, 201. Cook, *Border and the Buffalo*, 424.

27. John E. Parsons, *Smith & Wesson Revolvers* (New York, 1957), 60, 62. E. Remington & Sons Price List, 1 Jan. 1866 (reprinted by Ray Riling, Philadelphia, 1960). William E. Florence and Karl F. Moldenhauer, "The Firearms of Remington," in James E. Serven, ed., *The Collecting of Guns* (Harrisburg, Pa., 1964), 148–49. Leavenworth (Kansas) *Times*, 20 Jan. 1866. *Arizona Miner*, 13 June 1866. Olympia (Washington) *Standard*, 4 May 1867. Dallas *Herald*, 31 Aug. 1867. Elko (Nev.) *Independent*, 30 July and 8 Oct. 1870. Frank M. Sellers and Samuel E. Smith, *American Percussion Revolvers* (Ottawa, Ontario, 1971), 148–49. *Rocky Mountain News*, 22 May 1863 and 26 April 1876.

28. See, for example, the *Alta California*, 1 Jan. 1866 and 1 July 1867; the Gold Hill (Nev.) *News*, 2 July and 13 Aug. 1866; the Brownsville (Tex.) *Ranchero*, 20 Aug. 1868; and the *Arizona Miner*, 9 Jan. 1869. John E. Parsons, *The First Winchester* (New York, 1955), 36, 47. Edward Ordway, "Reminiscences," *Annals of Wyoming*, June 1929, 149–50. William M. Breakenridge, *Helldorado* (Glorieta, N.M., 1970), 50.

29. William A. Bell, *New Tracks in North America* (London and New York, 1869), 1: 66.

30. Wagon Train Report, June–July 1868, Post H.Q. Records, Ft. Phil Kearny, Wyo., Provost Record Book, Record Group 393, NA.

31. John B. Armor, "Pioneer Experiences in Colorado," *Colorado Magazine*, July 1932, 148.

32. WBB, 1961, 441.

33. Ordway, "Reminiscences," 153–55. Another account of what may be the same incident is in Robert McReynolds, *Thirty Years on the Frontier* (Colorado Springs, Colo., 1906), 210–11.

34. Nathaniel P. Langford, *Vigilante Days and Ways* (Chicago, 1912), 504–7.

35. Parsons, *The First Winchester*, 64. David, *Finn Burnett*, 170, 173–74.

36. Helen McCann White, ed., *Ho! For the Gold Fields* (St. Paul, Minn., 1966), 251. Philippe Regis de Trobriand, *Military Life in Dakota*, trans. and ed. Lucille M. Kane (St. Paul, Minn., 1951), 79. Henry M. Stanley, *My Early Travels and Adventures in America and Asia* (New York, 1895), 141. Luther S. Kelly, *Yellowstone Kelly . . .*, ed. Milo M. Quaife (New Haven, Conn., 1926), 32. Orrin H. and Lorraine Bonney, *Battle Drums and Geysers* (Chicago, 1970), 222.

37. Frank M. Canton, *Frontier Trails* (Norman, Okla., 1966), 7.

38. James H. Cook, *Fifty Years on the Old Frontier* (New Haven, Conn., 1923), 10–11, 25–26. James H. Cook, *Longhorn Cowboy*, ed. Howard R. Driggs (New York, 1942), 20.

39. Spencer Repeating Rifle Co. 1866 catalog, in L. D. Satterlee, comp., *Ten Old Gun Catalogs for the Collector* (1940; reprint ed., Chicago, 1962). *Alta California*, 1 July 1867 and 14 May 1871. ANJ, 24 Nov. 1866.

40. ANJ, 27 Nov. 1869. *Scientific American*, 11 Dec. 1869.

41. U.S. pat. 55,012 of 22 May 1866. Parsons, *The First Winchester*, 52–53.

42. Parsons, *The First Winchester*, 50, 52, 94–97. San Francisco *Mining and Scientific Press*, 23 March 1872.

43. Parsons, *The First Winchester*, 58–59. David, *Finn Burnett*, 144. The Dodge Winchester is in the Historic General Dodge House, Council Bluffs, Iowa.

44. Galveston *News*, 19 Feb. 1868. Brownsville *Ranchero*, 23 Feb. 1868. Cheyenne *Leader*, 5 March 1868. Ft. Sanders (Wyo.) *Frontier Index*, 24 March 1868. Collins's Omaha City Directory, 1868. San Antonio *Express*, 7 July 1868. Leavenworth's *Times and Conservative*, 7 Oct. 1868.

45. William E. Webb, *Buffalo Land* (Cincinnati and Chicago, 1872), 454. Charles A. Nessiter, *Sport and Adventure Among the North-American Indians* (London, 1890), 215, 225.

46. J. S. Campion, *On the Frontier* (London, 1878), 318. Frederick S. Dellenbaugh, *A Canyon Voyage . . .* (New York, 1908), 12, 205. Parsons, *The First Winchester*, 179.

47. Gould, *Modern American Rifles*, 117.

48. Edward C. Barber, *The Crack Shot* (New York, 1868), 154–57. U.S. pat. 125,640 of 9 April 1872. Winchester Repeating Arms Co. 1878 catalog.

49. Collins's Omaha City Directory, 1868. Briggs & Lowry's Omaha City Directory, 1872–73. *Rocky Mountain News*, 26 March 1873. Photostat in Parsons, *The First Winchester*, 47. Photostat in James J. Grant, *Single Shot Rifles*, 238–39.

50. U.S. pat. 35,941 of 22 July 1862. House Ex. Doc. 53, Serial No. 1290. *Scientific American*, 19 Aug. 1865. Norm Flayderman, *Flayderman's Guide to Antique American Firearms*, 2nd ed. (Northfield, Ill., 1980), 564. Collins's Omaha City Directory, 1868. Cheyenne *Leader*, 30 May 1868.

51. *Frank Leslie's Illustrated Newspaper*, 29 March 1862. House Ex. Doc. 99, Serial No. 1338. Schuyler, Hartley & Graham 1864 catalog. U.S. pat. 41,166 of 5 Jan. 1864. *Missouri Republican*, 8 Feb. 1865. *Arizona Miner*, 14 March 1866. Central City *Miners' Register*, 11 June 1866. Frank DeHaas, *Single Shot Rifles and Actions*, ed. John T. Amber (Chicago, 1969), 9–12.

52. *Rocky Mountain News*, 24 July 1867.

53. Barber, *The Crack Shot*, 121–24. Silas Seymour, *Incidents of a Trip Through the Great Platte Valley . . .* (New York, 1867), 101. Donald F. Danker, ed., *Man of the Plains: The Recollections of Luther North, 1856–1882* (Lincoln, Neb., 1961), 54, 136.

54. Nathaniel Pitt Langford, *The Discovery of Yellowstone Park, 1870 . . .*, 2nd ed. (St. Paul, Minn., 1923), 65–66.

55. Shores, *Memoirs of a Lawman*, 97. Edgar Beecher Bronson, *Reminiscences of a Ranchman* (Lincoln, Neb., 1962), 352.

56. Breakenridge, *Helldorado*, 41.

57. Luke Cahill, "An Indian Campaign and Buffalo Hunting with 'Buffalo Bill,'" *Colorado Magazine*, Aug. 1927, 132. Col. William F. Cody, *Life and Adventures of "Buffalo Bill"* (Chicago, 1917), 108, 122.

58. Dyer to Secretary of War, 16 June 1869, vol. 16, Entry 5, RG 156, NA. Letter to the authors from William

Barnhart of Cheyenne, Wyoming, n.d. William Lee Parke, *Pioneer Pathways to the Pacific* (New York, 1935), 81–84.

59. Townshend, *A Tenderfoot in Colorado*, 51. Bonney, *Battle Drums and Geysers*, 227–29.

60. Webb, *Buffalo Land*, 457. ASDA, June–July 1870. U.S. War Dept. Gen. Order No. 9, 5 Feb. 1874. Pueblo *Colorado Chieftain*, 19 Feb. 1874. Corbett & Hoye's *Denver City Directory*, 1874. See also the *Annals of Wyoming*, Apr. 1931, 472.

61. See, for example, *ANJ*, 30 June 1883; the N. Curry & Bro. 1884 catalog; and the E. C. Meacham 1884 catalog, in Joseph J. Schroeder, comp., *Rare Selections from Old Gun Catalogs, 1880–1920* (Northfield, Ill., 1977).

62. Cook, *Border and the Buffalo*, 126.

63. Claud E. Fuller, *The Breech-Loader in the Service, 1816–1917* (1933; reprint ed., New Milford, Conn., 1965), 258–59, 266, 269–75. Flayderman, *Antique American Firearms*, 454–55. *ANJ*, 14 Sept. 1867. Schuyler, Hartley & Graham 1864 catalog.

64. Salt Lake City *Telegraph*, 9 April 1869. A Gemmer breechloader is in the collection of the Missouri Historical Society, St. Louis.

65. G. O. Shields, *Rustlings in the Rockies* (Chicago, 1883), 151–52.

66. Frank M. Sellers, *Sharps Firearms* (N. Hollywood, Calif., 1978), 176, 206. Lustyik, *Civil War Carbines*, 34–41. Report of the Chief of Ordnance, 1866. House Ex. Doc. 1, 39th Cong., 2nd Sess., Serial No. 1285. War Department Contracts, 1867, House Ex. Doc. 145, 40th Cong., 2nd Sess., Serial No. 1337.

67. Advertisement in Barber, *The Crack Shot*. Sellers, *Sharps Firearms*, 195, 205, 209, 338–39.

68. Sellers, *Sharps Firearms*, 195–97, 211, 218. Council Bluffs *Nonpareil*, 31 March 1871.

69. *ANJ*, 13 March 1875. Sellers, *Sharps Firearms*, 218, 225, 230, 234–37.

70. Sellers, *Sharps Firearms*, 218, 338–41. *Forest and Stream*, 11 June 1874.

71. Sellers, *Sharps Firearms*, 305, 339–41. Cook, *Border and the Buffalo*, 120. Winchester 1878 catalog, 57.

72. James Bown & Son 1876 catalog, in Satterlee, *Ten Old Gun Catalogs*. W. A. Allen, *Adventures with Indians and Game* (Chicago, 1903), 156. George Bird Grinnell, ed., *Hunting at High Altitudes* (New York, 1913), 93–94.

73. Sellers, *Sharps Firearms*, 217, 338–41. Sharps Rifle Co. 1875 and 1878 catalogs, in L. D. Satterlee, comp., *Fourteen Old Gun Catalogs* (1941; reprint ed., Chicago, 1962); also in Martin Rywell, *The Gun That Shaped American Destiny* (Harriman, Tenn., 1957).

74. Sharps 1878 catalog, in Satterlee, *Fourteen Old Gun Catalogs*.

75. Sharps 1875 and 1878 catalogs in Satterlee, *Fourteen Old Gun Catalogs*. Sellers, *Sharps Firearms*, 311. Miles City, Montana, *Yellowstone Journal*, 21 Oct. 1881. Gould, *Modern American Rifles*, 289–95.

76. Sharps Rifle Co. 1877, 1878, and 1879 catalogs, in Satterlee, *Fourteen Old Gun Catalogs*. Winchester 1878 catalog, 45, 48–49, 51.

77. Report of the Chief of Ordnance, 1879, House Ex. Doc. 1, Pt. 2, 46th Cong., 2nd Sess., Serial No. 1907; and Report of the Chief of Ordnance, 1880, House Ex. Doc. 1, Pt. 2, 46th Cong., 3rd Sess., Serial No. 1956. Grinnell, *Hunting at High Altitudes*, 93–97.

78. *ANJ*, 16 Aug. 1873 and 3 Oct. 1874. Sellers, *Sharps Firearms*, 321–24.

79. *ANJ*, 3 Oct. 1874 and 3 July 1875. Sellers, *Sharps Firearms*, 225. Sharps 1875 catalog, in Satterlee, *Fourteen Old Gun Catalogs*.

80. Sellers, *Sharps Firearms*, 304–5.

81. Townshend, *A Tenderfoot in Colorado*, 151. Cook, *Border and the Buffalo*, 139, 184. Paul I. Wellman, "Some Famous Kansas Frontier Scouts," *Kansas Historical Quarterly*, Nov. 1931, 31. Collinson, *Life in the Saddle*, 44. E. S. Topping, *Chronicles of the Yellowstone* (Minneapolis, 1968), 120.

82. Cushing to Sharps, 3 April 1875, Sharps Rifle Co. correspondence, Texas Tech University Library, Lubbock, Texas (cited hereafter as Sharps letters).

83. Yount to Sharps, 26 Sept. 1875, and Lobenstein(?) to Sharps, 22 Nov. 1875, Sharps letters.

84. Bronson, *Reminiscences of a Ranchman*, 91, 218. Bonney, *Battle Drums and Geysers*, 454.

85. Sellers, *Sharps Firearms*, 196–97, 199–200, 217. Rywell, *American Destiny*, 79.

86. U.S pat. 180,567 of 1 Aug. 1876. Sellers, *Sharps Firearms*, 187–91.

87. Sellers, *Sharps Firearms*, 305. Metz to Sharps, 8 Feb. 1877, Sharps letters.

88. Cook, *Border and the Buffalo*, 280, 292. Short to Sharps, 19 June 1877, Sharps letters. Sharps 1878 catalog. See also *WBB*, 1961, 366.

89. Roberts to Sharps, 1 Feb. 1877; McDowell to Sharps, 25 Feb. 1877; and Sellers to Sharps, 31 June [*sic*] 1878; Sharps letters.

90. Cook, *Fifty Years*, 126. *WBB*, 1961, 331. Holloway to Sharps, 23 Jan. 1879, Sharps letters. John Lord, *Frontier Dust*, ed. Natalie Shipman (Hartford, Conn., 1926), 141. Grinnell, *Hunting at High Altitudes*, 187.

91. Grinnell, *Hunting at High Altitudes*, 63, 85. Andrew Garcia, *Tough Trip Through Paradise, 1878–1879* (Boston, 1967), 7. Richard B. Townshend, *A Tenderfoot in New Mexico* (London, 1923), 232.

92. Sellers, *Sharps Firearms*, 246–50, 253. *ANJ*, 13 Oct. 1877.

93. Sellers, *Sharps Firearms*, 263–84. U.S. pat. 185,721 of 26 Dec. 1876.

94. Sharps 1878 catalog. Beebe Brothers to Sharps, 27 Sept. 1879, and Overmeier & O'Neil to Sharps, 30 Oct. 1880, Sharps letters.

95. Beebe Bros. to Sharps, 23 Oct. 1879, and Fagan to Sharps, 24 Dec. 1880, Sharps letters.

96. U.S. pats. 40,887 of 8 Dec. 1863 and 45,123 of 15 Nov. 1864. Remington Price List, 1 Jan. 1866. James J. Grant, *More Single Shot Rifles* (New York, 1959), 262–63.

97. U.S. pats. 43,284 of 28 June 1864; 46,207 of 7 Feb. 1865; and 52,258 of 30 Jan. 1866. DeHaas, *Single Shot Rifles*, 43–46. Dallas *Herald*, 31 Aug. 1867. See also the Brownsville *Ranchero*, 11 May 1867, the San Antonio *Ex-*

press, 8 Oct. 1867, and *ANJ*, 2 March 1872.

98. Grace Raymond Hebard and E. A. Brininstool, *The Bozeman Trail* (Cleveland, Ohio, 1922), 1; 229–31. Dorothy M. Johnson, *The Bloody Bozeman* (New York, 1971), 239–41.

99. U.S. pat. 45,797 of 3 Jan. 1865. *ANJ*, 20 Oct. 1866. *American Artisan*, 24 Oct. 1866. House Misc. Doc . (no number), 40th Cong., 2nd Sess., Serial No. 1355. Charles B. Norton, *American Breech-Loading Small Arms* (New York, 1872), 20–74 passim. Grant, *More Single Shot Rifles*, 91.

100. Union Metallic Cartridge Co. Price List, 1869. Great Western Gun Works 1871 catalog, in Satterlee, *Ten Old Gun Catalogs*. *ANJ*, 13 Jan., 3 Feb., 2 March, and 7 Sept. 1872.

101. Elko (Nevada) *Independent*, 24 Feb. 1872. San Francisco *Mining and Scientific Press*, 1 July 1872. North Platte (Nebraska) *Lincoln County Advertiser*, 14 Aug. 1872. *ANJ*, 28 Dec. 1872. "Carlos Gove."

102. Norton, *Breech-Loading Small Arms*, 72. *Rocky Mountain News*, 28 Jan. 1874. Moore to Sharps, 28 April 1875, Sharps letters.

103. Salt Lake City *Telegraph*, 25 July 1868. *Rocky Mountain News*, 12 Dec. 1872. U.S. pats. 153,432 of 28 July 1874; 160,762 of 16 March 1875; 162,224 of 20 April 1875.

104. *ANJ*, 23 Aug. 1873; 28 Dec. 1872; 2 May and 30 May 1874; 20 Nov. 1875; 30 Sept. and 30 Dec. 1876.

105. *ANJ*, 3 Feb. 1872 and 20 Nov. 1875. E. Remington & Sons 1877 catalog, 7, 42.

106. Lt. Col. Richard Irving Dodge, *The Plains of the Great West and Their Inhabitants* (New York, 1877), 135. Frank H. Mayer and Charles B. Roth, *The Buffalo Harvest* (Denver, 1958), 40.

107. Frank Hebert, *Forty Years Prospecting and Mining in the Black Hills of South Dakota* (Rapid City, S.D., 1921), 63. Allen, *Adventures with Indians*, 36. Richard B. Hughes, *Pioneer Years in the Black Hills*, ed. Agnes Wright Spring (Glendale, Calif., 1957), 165. Cook, *Fifty Years*. *WBB*, 1954, 262. A. P. Vivian, *Wandering in the Western Land* (London, 1879), 360–61.

108. Col. Robert E. Gardner, *Small Arms Makers* (New York, 1963), 26. *Forest and Stream*, 27 April 1876. U.S. pat. 159,592 of 9 Feb. 1875.

109. *Forest and Stream*, 27 April 1876. Homer Fisher 1880 catalog, in Satterlee, *Ten Old Gun Catalogs*. Grant, *Single Shot Rifles*, 1–49 passim. Grant, *More Single Shot Rifles*, 1–21 passim.

110. Homer Fisher 1880 catalog, in Satterlee, *Ten Old Gun Catalogs*. *Forest and Stream*, 27 April 1876; 27 Feb. 1879; 12 April 1883; 11 Sept. 1884.

111. Omaha *Republican*, 9 June 1877. Colorado Springs *Gazette*, 2 June 1877. Pueblo *Colorado Chieftain*, 14 June 1877.

112. Frank D. Carpenter, *Adventures in Geyser Land* (Caldwell, Idaho, 1935), 96. Charles Collins, *History and Directory of the Black Hills* (Central City, D.T., 1878), 12. *WBB*, 1961, 366ff. See also Mayer and Roth, *The Buffalo Harvest*, 40.

113. Allen, *Adventures with Indians*, 130.

114. Hughes, *Pioneer Years*, 20. Carpenter, *Adventures in Geyser Land*, 96. James B. Gillett, *Six Years with the Texas Rangers, 1875–1881* (New Haven, Conn., 1925), 144.

115. J. Mortimer Murphy, *Sporting Adventures in the Far West* (New York, 1880), 33.

116. *WBB*, 1955, 176. N. Curry & Bro. 1884 catalog.

117. Massachusetts Arms Co. 1880 catalog, 4, 22–24. U.S. pat. 48,966 of 25 July 1865. Galveston *News*, 14 Feb. 1866. Central City, Colo., *Register*, 15 Nov. 1870. See also *Scientific American*, 14 July 1866; 15 Sept. 1866; and 26 June 1869.

118. U.S. pat. 135,928 of 18 Feb. 1873. *Forest and Stream*, 26 Feb. 1874. Mass. Arms Co. 1880 catalog, 9, 13, 20, 23–24.

119. Mass. Arms Co. 1880 catalog, 7–17, *Forest and Stream*, 20 April 1876.

120. Granville Stuart, *Diary and Sketchbook of a Journey . . . 1866* (Los Angeles, 1963), 22. *Rocky Mountain News*, 26 March 1873; 28 Jan. 1874; and 26 May 1875. Cushing to Sharps, 20 Nov. 1875, Sharps letters.

121. Quotation in Sellers, *Sharps Firearms*, 308–9. McDowell to Sharps, 25 Feb. 1877, and Fagan to Sharps, 24 Dec. 1880, Sharps letters. Hughes, *Pioneer Years*, 101. *WBB*, 1961, 368–69.

122. U.S. pat. 35,947 of 22 July 1862. Report of the Chief of Ordnance, 1873, House Ex. Doc. 1, Pt. 2, 43rd Cong., 1st Sess., Serial No. 1599. DeHaas, *Single Shot Rifles*, 29–34. W. W. Greener, *Modern Breech-Loaders: Sporting and Military*, 2nd ed. (1874?; reprint ed., Pueblo, Colo., n.d.), 198.

123. Providence Tool Co. 1865 and 1866 catalogs, in Satterlee, *Ten Old Gun Catalogs*. Report of the Chief of Ordnance, 1866, House Ex. Doc. 1, 39th Cong., 2nd Sess., Serial No. 1285. Langley's San Francisco Directory, 1865. *ANJ*, 15 Sept. 1866. *American Artisan*, 17 Oct. 1866. Union Metallic Cartridge Co. Price List, 1869. Norton, *Breech-Loading Small Arms*, 82–115 passim. *Rocky Mountain News*, 22 Nov. 1870. Corbett, Hoye, & Co.'s Denver City Directory, 1877. *Forest and Stream*, 3 May 1877. John E. Parsons, *Smith & Wesson Revolvers* (New York, 1957), back endpapers.

124. U.S. pats. 36,779 of 28 Oct. 1862; 50,125 of 26 Sept. 1865; and 50,358 of 10 Oct. 1865. *Spirit of the Times*, 24 Oct. 1868. Lustyik, *Civil War Carbines*, 45, 48. Union Metallic Cartridge Co. Price List, 1869. Flayderman, *Antique American Firearms*, 251–52.

125. Barrett, *Mackinaws Down the Missouri*, 71–72. Salt Lake City *Telegraph*, 9 April 1869. In January of 1867 the federal government sold the Overland Stage Co. 40 "Whitney Rifles" at $15 each. These were probably breechloaders of the Cochran or "Excelsior" type but at this point have not been positively identified; see House Ex. Doc. 89, Serial No. 1511.

126. U.S. pat. 54,743 of 15 May 1866. Lustyik, *Civil War Carbines*, 45–46. House Ex. Doc. 1, Serial No. 1285. U.S. pats. 112,997 of 21 March 1871, and 129,637 of 16 July 1872. *ANJ*, 12 Aug. 1871. *Forest and Stream*, 25 March 1875. DeHaas, *Single Shot Rifles*, 157–61. Flayderman, *Antique American Firearms*, 253–54. Norton, *Breech-Loading Small Arms*, 185–91.

127. U.S. pat. 151,458 of 26 May 1874. Flayderman, *Antique American Firearms*, 252–53. DeHaas, *Single Shot Rifles*, 167–70. Jackson Arms (Dallas, Tex.) catalog supplement 22A, item 1047. *Forest and Stream*, 27 Feb. 1879.

128. U.S. pat. 103,694 of 31 May 1870. Flayderman, *Antique American Firearms*, 233–35. *Rocky Mountain News*, 26 March 1873. Photostat in Grant, *Single Shot Rifles*, 239.

129. U.S. pat. 44,123 of 6 Sept. 1864. *Harper's Weekly*, 7 Aug. 1869. J. Stevens & Co. catalog, 1 July 1875, 2–4. San Antonio *Express*, 1 Sept. 1871. Gould, *Modern American Rifles*, 127, 144–52.

130. *Rocky Mountain News*, 26 May 1875. Corbett, Hoye & Co.'s Denver City Directory, 1876. *Forest and Stream*, 3 May 1877. Flayderman, *Antique American Firearms*, 230–31. Photostat in Grant, *Single Shot Rifles*, 238.

131. Gould, *Modern American Rifles*, 115–16.

132. Gould, *Modern American Rifles*, 116. Greener, *Modern Breech-Loaders*, 106–17, 130–31. G. E. Lewis ad in *ANJ*, 22 Aug. 1874.

133. F. Trench Townshend, *Ten Thousand Miles of Travel, Sport, and Adventure* (London, 1869), 93. Grinnell, *Hunting at High Altitudes*, 85. See also Murphy, *Sporting Adventures*, 31–32.

134. The Freund double rifle is presently in the Frank Sellers collection in Denver, Colo.

135. Parsons, *The First Winchester*, 108–10, 112, 114–16. House Ex. Doc. 1, Pt. 2, Serial No. 1599.

136. Parsons, *The First Winchester*, 114–15, 125–26.

137. Parsons, *The First Winchester*, 16. Cook, *Border and the Buffalo*, 74. WBB, 1961, 376.

138. *Rocky Mountain News*, 6 May 1874. Gillett, *Texas Rangers*, 56–57. N. A. Jennings, *A Texas Ranger* (New York, 1899), 111–12.

139. Ami Frank Mulford, *Fighting Indians in the 7th United States Cavalry* (1878; reprint ed., Bellevue, Neb., 1970), 66. Garcia, *Tough Trip Through Paradise*, 84. James W. Schultz, *Blackfeet and Buffalo . . .* (Norman, Okla., 1962), 51. Gillett, *Texas Rangers*, 224.

140. Quotation in Sellers, *Sharps Firearms*, 309. Murphy, *Sporting Adventures*, 32.

141. Parsons, *The First Winchester*, 121.

142. Parsons, *The First Winchester*, 121–24. *Forest and Stream*, 16 May 1878.

143. U.S. pats. 103,504 of 24 May 1870 and 125,988 of 23 April 1872. *Scientific American*, 26 Aug. 1871 and 17 Aug. 1872.

144. Harold F. Williamson, *Winchester, the Gun That Won the West* (Washington, D.C., 1952), 75, 445–46. *Rocky Mountain News*, 12 March 1873. San Antonio *Express*, 3 June 1873. See also Flayderman, *Antique American Firearms*, 557.

145. U.S. pat. 119,020 of 19 Sept. 1871. Dwight B. DeMerritt, Jr., *Maine Made Guns and Their Makers* (Hallowell, Me., 1973), 92–95. Flayderman, *Antique American Firearms*, 555–57. See also the *Journal of the Royal United Service Institution*, 11 June 1880.

146. House Ex. Doc. 1, Pt. 2, Serial No. 1599. House Misc. Doc. 20, Serial No. 2119. Corbett, Hoye & Co.'s Denver City Directory, 1876. *Alta California*, 12 Aug. 1876. *ANJ*, 25 Sept. 1880. Jackson Arms Catalog 24, item 438A.

147. U.S. pats. 134,589 of Jan. 1873 and 168,966 of 19 Oct. 1875. House Misc. Doc . 20, Serial No. 2119.

148. House Misc. Doc. 20, Serial No. 2119. Report of the Chief of Ordnance, 1878, House Ex. Doc. 1, Pt. 2, 45th Cong., 3rd Sess., Serial No. 1847. *ANJ*, 11 Jan. 1879. *Forest and Stream*, 27 Feb. 1879. U.S. pats. 215,227 of 13 May 1879 and 218,462 of 12 Aug. 1879.

149. S. L. Maxwell, *Lever Action Magazine Rifles* (Bellevue, Wash., 1976). Flayderman, *Antique American Firearms*, 256. *ANJ*, 10 Feb. 1883. N. Curry & Bro. 1884 catalog.

150. Leadville *Democrat*, 27 June 1880. *Rocky Mountain Health Resorts* (Boston, 1880), Denver *Inter-Ocean*, 6 June 1880. John S. Hittell, *The Commerce and Industries of the Pacific Coast* (San Francisco, 1882), 671–72. McKenney's *Business Directiry of California, Nevada, Utah, Wyoming, Colorado, and Nebraska*, 1882, 118, 657. Shields, *Rustlings in the Rockies*, 31.

151. U.S. pats. 210,091 of 19 Nov. 1878; 210,181 of 26 Nov. 1878; and 250,825 of 13 Dec. 1881. Flayderman, *Antique American Firearms*, 123. Marlin-Ballard 1888 catalog, in Satterlee, *Fourteen Old Gun Catalogs. Forest and Stream*, 4 Aug. 1881; 23 Aug. 1883; and 12 March 1885. *ANJ*, 6 Aug. 1881.

152. *ANJ*, 26 March 1881. *Forest and Stream*, 31 March 1881. *Yellowstone Journal*, 29 Oct. 1881 and 4 March 1882. Leadville City Directory, 1882. McKenney's *Business Directory of California, Nevada, Utah . . .* 1882, 118. N. Curry & Bro. 1884 catalog. Report of the Chief of Ordnance, 1882, House Ex. Doc. 1, Pt. 2, 47th Cong., 2nd Sess., Serial No. 2095.

153. *Yellowstone Journal*, 11 June 1881. *ANJ*, 15 Nov. 1879; 28 Aug. 1880; 19 Aug. 1882; 23 May 1885. *Forest and Stream*, 16 Sept. 1880. Curry 1884 catalog. E. Remington & Sons 1885 catalog.

154. Gould, *Modern American Rifles*, 137–38. Parsons, *Smith & Wesson*, 156–64. Curry 1884 catalog, 13. Townshend, *Tenderfoot in New Mexico*, 182–232. Allen, *Adventures with Indians*, 83, 247. Allen A. Erwin, *The Southwest of John H. Slaughter, 1841–1922* (Glendale, Calif., 1965), 204. George W. Wingate, *Through the Yellowstone Park on Horseback* (New York, 1886), 39. Grinnell, *Hunting at High Altitudes*, 304.

155. Photostat in Charles T. Haven and Frank A. Belden, *A History of the Colt Revolver* (New York, 1940), 402. U.S. pat. 213,865 of 1 April 1879. *ANJ*, 17 Nov. 1883. Curry 1884 catalog, 12. Flayderman, *Antique American Firearms*, 111. *Rocky Mountain News*, 24 May 1883. Lower to Colt, 31 May 1883, Colt Pat. F. A. Mfg. Co. correspondence, Connecticut State Library, Hartford, Conn. (cited hereafter as Colt letters). Jackson Arms Catalog 16, item 529.

156. *Extermination of the American Bison*, 467. *Forest and Stream*, 16 July 1885. Shields, *Rustlings in the Rockies*, 152. Reginald Aldridge, *Life on a Ranch* (1884; reprint ed., New York, 1966), 223. Collinson, *Life in the Saddle*, 70. Allen, *Adventures with Indians*, 134, 136, 156. Cook, *Fifty Years*, 167.

157. Sellers, *Sharps Firearms*, 258–61, 286–95. Photostat in Behn, *.45-70 Rifles*, 139.

158. Sellers, *Sharps Firearms*, 187–93. N. Flayderman & Co. (New Milford, Conn.) Catalog 89, item 875.

159. U.S. pat. 220,285 of 7 Oct. 1879. Curry 1884 catalog, 8. Remington 1885 catalog, 19–23.

160. *Yellowstone Journal*, 29 Oct. 1881 and 4 March 1882. *McKenney's Business Directory of California, Nevada, Utah . . . 1882*, 118, 657. Marlin-Ballard 1888 catalog, in Satterlee, *Fourteen Old Gun Catalogs*. Corbett & Ballenger's Denver City Directory, 1885. John Dutcher, "Geo. C. Schoyen, Gun Maker," *The Colorado Gun Collectors 1973 Annual*. Gould, *Modern American Rifles*, 190. See also the ad in *Outdoor Life* (Denver series), Sept. 1900, n.p.

161. Shields, *Rustlings in the Rockies*, 152. Tom Horn, *Life of Tom Horn . . . Written by Himself* (Denver, 1904), 169, 217. Curry 1884 catalog, 13. Meacham 1884 catalog, in Schroeder, *Old Gun Catalogs*.

162. Massachusetts Arms Co. 1885 catalog, in Satterlee, *Fourteen Old Gun Catalogs*.

163. Gould, *Modern American Rifles*, 120–21.

164. San Antonio *Express*, 1 Sept. 1871. Stevens 1875 catalogs, 5–7. ANJ, 11 Sept. 1880.

165. DeHaas, *Single Shot Rifles*, 95–98. Omaha, *Republican*, 13 July 1880 and 1 June 1882. Curry 1884 catalog.

166. Grant, *More Single Shot Rifles*, 166–67, 169–70. U.S. pat. 233,034 of 5 Oct. 1880. Jackson Arms catalog 23, item 786. Hays *Sentinel*, 22 Dec. 1876. Grant County (N.M.) *Herald*, 10 Nov. 1883. Jackson Arms catalog 16, item 549B. Parsons, *Smith & Wesson*, back endpaper.

167. John Browning and Curt Gentry, *John M. Browning, American Gunmaker* (Garden City, N.Y., 1964), 58–62, 227–28. U.S. pat. 220,271 of 7 Oct. 1879.

168. Louis E. Yearout, "John Browning's First Rifle," Montana Arms Collectors Assn. bulletin, n.d.

169. Browning and Gentry, *John M. Browning*, 97–102. *Forest and Stream*, 31 Dec. 1885. Winchester Repeating Arms Co. 1891 catalog, 20–25. Sellers, *Sharps Firearms*, 337.

170. Marquis James, *The Cherokee Strip* (New York, 1945), 6. Theodore Roosevelt, *The Wilderness Hunter; Outdoor Pastimes of an American Hunter* (New York, 1926), 187, 370–71.

171. Cook, *Fifty Years*, 138. Roosevelt, *Wilderness Hunter*, 371–72.

172. Serven, *Colt Firearms*, 372–73. Lower to Colt, 31 May 1883, Colt letters.

173. Grinnell, *Hunting at High Altitudes*, 297. Gould, *Modern American Rifles*, 87. *Forest and Stream*, 13 March 1884.

174. J. H. Walsh, *The Modern Sportsman's Gun and Rifle* (London, 1882–84), 2: 123, 259–61. Gould, *Modern American Rifles*, 83. Schultz, *Blackfeet and Buffalo*, 111.

175. U.S. pat. 245,700 of 16 Aug. 1881. Quotation in Jack Behn, *.45-70 Rifles* (Harrisburg, Pa., 1956), 59.

176. *Forest and Stream*, 28 Feb. 1884. Curry 1884 catalog, 52. Hartley & Graham 1885 catalog, 11, 30–31, 33.

177. Allen, *Adventures with Indians*, 54, 107, 239, 256, 269, 274, 288. Roosevelt, Theodore, *Hunting Trips of a Ranchman; Ranch Life and the Hunting Trail* (New York, 1927), 27.

178. *Forest and Stream*, 23 April 1885. U.S. pats. 278,324 of 29 May 1883, and 285,020 of 18 Sept. 1883.

179. Serven, *Colt Firearms from 1836*, 361–67. ANJ, 16 Jan. 1886. Haven and Belden, *The Colt Revolver*, 408–10, 414. Meacham to Colt, 5 and 11 June 1885; Bonnett to Lower, 10 Dec. 1885; Lower to Colt, 12 Dec. 1885; Sickels to Colt, 30 Dec. 1889; Colt letters.

180. Photostat in Haven and Belden, *The Colt Revolver*, 408.

181. Serven, *Colt Firearms*, 361.

182. Gould, *Modern American Rifles*, 87, 190. U.S. pat. 306,577 of 14 Oct. 1884. Watrous, *Winchester Firearms*, 32–35. Winchester Repeating Arms Co. catalog, March, 1891.

183. Canton, *Frontier Trails*, 96. Robert A. Murray, "The Arms of Wyoming's Cattle War," *Shooting Times*, July 1967, 42. Jim Herron, *Fifty Years on the Owl Hoot Trail*, ed. H. E. Chrisman (Denver, 1962), 42, 160. John K. Rollinson, *Pony Trails in Wyoming*, ed. E. A. Brininstool (Caldwell, Idaho, 1944), 394.

184. Winchester 1891 catalog. Browning and Gentry, *John M. Browning*, 108–9, 127–29. Watrous, *Winchester Firearms*, 39–41.

185. Flayderman, *Antique American Firearms*, 242, 257. Williamson, *Winchester*, 112–13.

186. U.S. pats. 354,059 of 7 Dec. 1886, and 371,455 of 11 Oct. 1887. Marlin-Ballard 1888 catalog, in Satterlee, *Fourteen Old Gun Catalogs*. House Doc. 510, 57th Cong., 1st Sess., Serial No. 4374.

187. Sitka *Alaskan*, 27 April 1889 and 8 March 1890. Battle Mountain *Central Nevadan*, 15 Oct. 1891. Shores, *Memoirs of a Lawman*, 241. U.S. pat. 502,489 of 1 Aug. 1893. Flayderman, *Antique American Firearms*, 125–26.

188. Hartley & Graham 1895 catalog, in Bill West, comp., *Hartley & Graham Catalogs, 1895–1899* (Santa Fe Springs, Calif., 1972). Flayderman, *Antique American Firearms*, 126.

189. Browning and Gentry, *John M. Browning*, 129–31. U.S. pat. 524,702 of 21 Aug. 1894. Watrous, *Winchester Firearms*, 43–46.

190. Watrous, *Winchester Firearms*, 43–46. Flayderman, *Antique American Firearms*, 274–75.

191. Watrous, *Winchester Firearms*, 46–49. RCO, 1892, House Ex. Doc. 1, Pt. 2, 52nd Cong., 2nd Sess., Serial No. 3083. U.S. pats. 491,138 of 7 Feb. 1893, and 502,018 of 25 July 1893. ANJ, 18 July and 3 Oct. 1896. *Scientific American*, 5 Sept. 1896. Hartley & Graham 1899 catalog, in West, *Hartley & Graham Catalogs*. Flayderman, *Antique American Firearms*, 125–27, 557–58. *Outdoor Life* (Denver Series), Dec. 1898; Jan. 1899, and June 1900, n.p.

CHAPTER 4

1. Philippe Regis de Trobriand, *Military Life in Dakota*, trans. and ed. Lucille M. Kane (St. Paul, Minn., 1951), 119. James Chisholm, *South Pass, 1898* (Lincoln, Neb., 1960), 31. Richard B. Townshend, *A Tenderfoot in Colorado*

(New York, 1923), 5. Joseph G. Rosa, *They Called Him Wild Bill,* 2nd ed. (Norman, Okla., 1974), 191.

2. Granville Stuart, *Diary and Sketchbook of a Journey . . . 1866* (Los Angeles, 1963), 6. *Westerner's Brand Book* (Denver Posse), *1948,* 262 (cited hereafter as *WBB*). John Wesley Hardin, *The Life of John Wesley Hardin as Written by Himself* (Norman, Okla., 1961), 99–100.

3. Gold Hill, Nev., *Daily News,* 24 Nov. 1869.

4. N. Curry & Bro. 1884 catalog (reprinted by Paradox Press, Berkeley, Calif., 1965). Elko, Nev., *Independent,* 8 Oct. 1870. Great Western Gun Works 1871 catalog, in L. D. Satterlee, comp., *Ten Old Gun Catalogs for the Collector* (1940; reprint ed., Chicago, 1962). See also Parker Gillmore, *Gun, Rod, and Saddle* (New York, 1869), 74.

5. St. Louis *Missouri Republican,* 6 Oct. 1868.

6. U.S. pats. 49,491 of 22 Aug. 1865 and 84,929 of 15 Dec. 1868. *American Artisan,* 23 Jan. 1867. Ad in Edward C. Barber, *The Crack Shot* (New York, 1868). *Spirit of the Times,* 22 Feb. 1868. Harold R. Mouillesseaux, *Ethan Allen, Gunmaker* (Ottawa, 1973), 148–50. Omaha *Republican,* 30 May 1869.

7. U.S. pats. 72,434 of 17 Dec. 1867 and 78,847 of 9 June 1868. Roy G. Jinks and Robert J. Neal, *Smith & Wesson, 1857–1945,* rev. ed. (New York, 1975), 253–58.

8. U.S. pats. 71,349 of 26 Nov. 1867 and 93,149 of 27 July 1869. *Spirit of the Times,* 24 Oct. 1868. William Read & Sons Whitney circular, c. 1874 (reprinted by Ray Riling, Philadelphia, 1960).

9. Folsom Bros. & Co. 1869 catalog, in Satterlee, *Ten Old Gun Catalogs.* Salt Lake City *Telegraph,* 9 April 1869. Galveston *News,* 31 May 1869.

10. U.S. pats. 73,494 of 21 Jan. 1868 and 88,540 of 6 April 1869. Galveston *News,* 31 May 1869. *Turf, Field, and Farm,* 14 Oct. 1870.

11. William Read & Sons Whitney circular, c. 1874.

12. Col. Robert E. Gardner, *Small Arms Makers* (New York, 1963), 130, 146. House Ex. Doc. 99, 40th Cong., 2nd Sess., Serial No. 1338. Norm Flayderman, *Flayderman's Guide to Antique American Firearms,* 2nd ed. (Northfield, Ill., 1980), 454, 507. U.S. pat. 59,723 of 13 Nov. 1866.

13. Parker Bros. 1869 catalog (reprint ed., n.p., n.d.). *Spirit of the Times,* 27 June 1868.

14. Folsom Bros. & Co. 1869 catalog, in Satterlee, *Ten Old Gun Catalogs.* Lawrence, Kansas, *Republican Journal,* 15 Oct. 1869. Georgetown *Colorado Miner,* 8 Sept. 1870. Council Bluffs *Nonpareil,* 22 Sept. 1871. Elko *Independent,* 20 July 1872. Fort Worth, Tex., *Democrat,* 20 Sept. 1873. Enterprise Gun Works 1876 catalog, in Satterlee, *Ten Old Gun Catalogs.*

15. Parker Bros. 1869 catalog. *Turf, Field, and Farm,* 22 Dec. 1866 and 23 March 1867. *Army and Navy Journal,* 23 March 1867 (cited hereafter as *ANJ*). San Francisco *Alta California,* 1 July 1867. *Spirit of the Times,* 15 Aug. 1868; 27 Feb. and 13 March 1869. Galveston *News,* 19 May 1868. New Orleans *Picayune,* 25 Oct. 1868.

16. *Spirit of the Times,* 21 March and 16 May 1868; 25 Sept. 1869. *Forest and Stream,* 29 April 1875 and 20 April 1876. See also the *Chicago Field,* various issues, 1876. [John

Deane], *Deane's Manual of the History and Science of Fire-Arms* (1858; reprint ed., Huntington, W. Va., n.d.) Br. pats. 2,149 of 24 Sept. 1858; 1,594 of 27 May 1862; 2,506 of 11 Sept. 1862; and 1,104 of 2 May 1863. W. W. Greener, *The Gun and Its Development,* 9th ed. (1910; reprint ed., New York, n.d.), 152. J. H. Walsh, *The Modern Sportsman's Gun and Rifle* (London, 1882–84), 1: 144, 148–49, 156–61.

17. F. Trench Townshend, *Ten Thousand Miles of Travel, Sport, and Adventure* (London, 1869), 93. John E. Parsons, *The First Winchester* (New York, 1955), 75. Sloan's *Salt Lake City Directory,* 1869. *Topeka City Directory,* 1872–73. *Rocky Mountain News,* 12 Dec. 1872. Pueblo *Colorado Chieftain,* 22 May 1873.

18. Joseph G. Rosa, *The Gunfighter: Man or Myth?* (Norman, Okla., 1963), 101. Nyle H. Miller and Joseph W. Snell, *Great Gunfighters of the Kansas Cowtowns, 1867–1886* (Lincoln, Neb., 1963), 447–48.

19. Massachusetts Arms Co. 1880 catalog (reprint ed., n.p., n.d.). Salt Lake City *Telegraph,* 9 April 1869. Enterprise Gun Works 1876 catalog, in Satterlee, *Ten Old Gun Catalogs.* Flayderman, *Antique American Firearms,* 252.

20. *ANJ,* 16 Nov. 1872. Great Western Gun Works 1873 catalog (published 1872; reprinted by American Reprints, St. Louis, 1969). J. Stevens & Co. 1875 and 1877 catalogs.

21. Great Western Gun Works 1873 catalog. U.S. pats. 60,998 of 8 Jan. 1867 and 112,505 of 7 March 1871. Frank DeHaas, *Single Shot Rifles and Actions,* ed. John T. Amber (Chicago, 1969), 227–30.

22. U.S. pat. 45,292 of 29 Nov. 1864. Great Western Gun Works 1873 catalog. Homer Fisher 1880 catalog, in Satterlee, *Ten Old Gun Catalogs.*

23. J. Stevens & Co. 1877 catalog. Enterprise Gun Works 1876 catalog, and Homer Fisher 1880 catalog, in Satterlee, *Ten Old Gun Catalogs.* N. Curry & Bro. 1884 catalog. John P. Lower trade card, undated, in the Western History Dept., Denver Public Library.

24. James E. Serven, *Colt Firearms from 1836* (Harrisburg, Pa., 1979), 350–51. U.S. pat. 53,881 of 10 April 1866. The *American Artisan,* 5 Dec. 1866. Flayderman, *Antique American Firearms,* 577–78.

25. *ANJ,* 4 May and 1 June 1867. San Francisco *Mining and Scientific Press,* 2 Nov. 1867.

26. *Forest and Stream,* 2 Oct. 1873 and 16 April 1874. U.S. pat. 125,775 of 16 April 1872. E. Remington & Sons 1877 catalog (reprinted by Pioneer Press, Harriman, Tenn., n.d.).

27. San Antonio *Herald,* 6 May 1874. Lawrence P. Shelton, *California Gunsmiths, 1846–1900* (Fair Oaks, Calif., 1977), 182. *Rocky Mountain News,* 26 April 1876.

28. U.S. pat. 161,267 of 23 March 1875.

29. *Rocky Mountain News,* 14 July 1875. Corbett, Hoye & Co.'s *Denver City Directory,* 1877. Denison *Herald,* 20 Feb. 1878.

30. *Forest and Stream,* 10 Aug. 1876. U.S. pat. 98,579 of 4 Jan. 1870.

31. Elliott L. Minor, "Imaginative Firearms by a Little-Known Company," *American Rifleman,* April 1970, 20–24.

Ad in Edward S. Farrow, *Mountain Scouting* (New York, 1881). Blake's *Colorado State Business Directory*, 1878. U.S. pat. 196,748 of 6 Nov. 1877.

32. J. Stevens & Co. 1877 catalog. *Forest and Stream*, 2 Aug. 1877. Omaha *Republican*, 3 Oct. 1878.

33. *ANJ*, 23 Nov. 1878. *Forest and Stream*, 6 Nov. 1879. Serven, *Colt Firearms*, 370. Charles T. Haven and Frank A. Belden, *The History of the Colt Revolver*, (New York, 1940), 412.

34. Lower to Colt, 1 June 1878; Morton to Colt, 10 Dec. 1878; and Simmons to Colt, 29 Oct. 1880, Colt Pat. F. A. Mfg. Co. correspondence, Connecticut State Library, Hartford, Conn.

35. *Rocky Mountain News*, 26 April 1876. Gove and Freund guns of this type are in the Frank Sellers collection, Denver, Colo.

36. Sharps Rifle Co. 1878 catalog, in L. D. Satterlee, comp., *Fourteen Old Gun Catalogs* (1941; reprint ed., Chicago, 1953). Frank M. Sellers, *Sharps Firearms* (N. Hollywood, Calif., 1978), 299–302.

37. *Forest and Stream*, 10 Aug. 1876. *Alta California*, 12 Aug. 1876. Ads in Blake's *Colorado State Business Directory*, 1878, and Charles Denison, *Rocky Mountain Health Resorts* (Boston, 1880). Leadville *Democrat*, 27 June 1880. *Rocky Mountain News*, 18 June 1880.

38. N. A. Jennings, *A Texas Ranger* (New York, 1899), 111–12. Frank D. Carpenter, *Adventures in Geyser Land* (Caldwell, Idaho, 1935), 96, 254. *WBB*, 1954, 267. The Morley statement is filed in the Wells Fargo Bank History Room, San Francisco.

39. Fred Dodge, *Undercover for Wells Fargo*, ed. Carolyn Lake (Boston, 1969), 17, 60, 73, 98, 128, 169, 254. A Wells Fargo Parker is in the St. Joseph Museum, St. Joseph, Mo. A later Wells Fargo Remington is in Jackson Arms (Dallas, Tex.) Catalog Supplement 22A, item 1051.

40. James H. Kyner, *End of Track* (Lincoln, Neb., 1960), 157, 208.

41. *McKenney's Business Directory of California, Arizona, New Mexico, Colorado, and Kansas, 1882–83*. Gardner, *Small Arms Makers*, 176, 285. Tucson *Arizona Citizen*, 6 June 1885.

42. Langley's *San Francisco Directory*, 1873. N. Curry & Bro. 1884 catalog. Homer Fisher 1880 catalog, in Satterlee, *Ten Old Gun Catalogs*.

43. N. Curry & Bro. 1884 catalog. Walsh, *Gun and Rifle*, 183–84. Haven and Belden, *The Colt Revolver*, 411. Serven, *Colt Firearms*, 371.

44. *Forest and Stream*, 8 March 1883. Greener, *The Gun*, 166–68. Flayderman, *Antique American Firearms*, 238. Omaha *Republican*, 28 Feb. 1884.

45. E. C. Meacham 1884 catalog, in Joseph J. Schroeder, comp., *Rare Selections from Old Gun Catalogs, 1880–1920* (Northfield, Ill., 1977). E. Remington & Sons 1885 catalog (reprinted by the Wyoming Armory, Inc., Cheyenne, Wyo., n.d.). *ANJ*, 19 Aug. 1882. *Forest and Stream*, 8 March 1883. Parker catalog, c. 1899, in John T. Amber, comp., *Ten Rare Gun Catalogs, 1860–1899* (New York, 1952).

46. *Loving's Stock Manual* (Fort Worth, Tex., 1881). El Paso *Lone Star*, 17 Jan. 1884. Corbett & Ballenger's *Denver City Directory*, 1885. U.S. pat. 167,293 of 31 Aug. 1875. *Forest and Stream*, 30 March and 27 April 1876. Kenneth H. Shanks, "W. H. Baker: Gunmaker of Distinction," *American Rifleman*, June 1968, 54–60.

47. Gardner, *Small Arms Makers*, 114–15. *Forest and Stream*, 27 April 1876. U.S. pats. 205,193 of 25 June 1878; 229,429 of 29 June 1880; and 264,173 of 12 Sept. 1882.

48. *Forest and Stream*, 2 Oct. 1884; 22 Jan. 1885; 1 Oct. 1885; 5 Nov. 1885. *The Industries of Omaha* (Omaha, 1887), 157.

49. *ANJ*, 8 Sept. 1877. Homer Fisher 1880 catalog, in Satterlee, *Ten Old Gun Catalogs*. John P. Lower 1888 catalog. N. Curry & Bro. 1884 catalog. See also Edward S. Farrow, *American Small Arms* (New York, 1904).

50. N. Curry & Bro. 1884 catalog. E. C. Meacham 1884 catalog, in Schroeder, *Old Gun Catalogs*. Hartley & Graham 1885 catalog. Great Western Gun Works 1888–89 catalog, in John T. Amber, ed., The 1966 *Gun Digest* (Chicago, 1966). Hopkins & Allen 1889 price list. DeHass, *Single Shot Rifles*, 212–13.

51. Edgar Beecher Bronson, *Reminiscences of a Ranchman* (Lincoln, Neb., 1962), 272.

52. Reginald Aldridge, *Life on a Ranch* (1884; reprint ed., New York, 1966), 222.

53. George W. Wingate, *Through the Yellowstone Park on Horseback* (New York, 1886), 43.

54. James H. Cook, *Fifty Years on the Old Frontier* (New Haven, 1923), 167.

55. Theodore Roosevelt, *Hunting Trips of a Ranchman* (New York, 1927), 27–28.

56. U.S. pats. 228,020 of 25 May 1880, and 228,165 of 1 June 1880. Shanks, "W. H. Baker," 55–56. *Forest and Stream*, 15 Jan. 1885.

57. U.S. pat. 274,435 of 20 March 1883. *Forest and Stream*, 3 April 1884. John P. Lower 1888 catalog.

58. House Doc. 510, 57th Cong., 1st Sess., Serial No. 4374.

59. U.S. pat. 255,894 of 4 April 1882. See also U.S. pat. 38,702 of 26 May 1863.

60. *RCO*, 1882, House Ex. Doc. 1, Pt. 2, 47th Cong., 2nd Sess., Serial No. 2095. *Scientific American Supplement*, 27 March 1886. *Forest and Stream*, 26 Feb. 1885. Hartley & Graham 1885 catalog. Hartley & Graham 1895 and 1899 catalogs, in Bill West, comp., *Hartley & Graham Catalogs, 1895–1899* (Santa Fe Springs, Calif., 1972). House Doc. 510, Serial No. 4374.

61. John Browning and Curt Gentry, *John M. Browning, American Gunmaker* (Garden City, N.Y., 1964), 109–10, 255–56. U.S. pat. 336,287 of 16 Feb. 1886. George R. Watrous, *The History of Winchester Firearms, 1866–1966*, ed. Thomas E. Hall and Pete Kuhlhoff, 3rd ed. (New Haven, Conn., 1966), 36–37. Winchester Repeating Arms Co. catalog, March 1891.

62. John P. Lower catalog, May 1888. See photo, p. 249.

63. Browning and Gentry, *John M. Browning*, 126–28, 256–57. Watrous, *Winchester Firearms*, 41–43, 50–52. House Doc. 510, Serial No. 4374.

CHAPTER 5

1. James H. Cook, *Fifty Years on the Old Frontier* (New Haven, Conn., 1923), 98, 110–11.

2. Philippe Regis de Trobriand, *Military Life in Dakota*, trans. and ed. Lucille M. Kane (St. Paul, Minn., 1951), 17, 34.

3. Testimony regarding the Rollin White/Smith & Wesson patent is in Senate Ex. Doc. 23, 41st Cong., 2nd Sess., Serial No. 1405.

4. Theodore R. Davis, "The Buffalo Range," *Harper's New Monthly Magazine*, Jan. 1869, 155. Richard B. Townshend, *A Tenderfoot in Colorado* (New York, 1923), 115. Townshend's "Dragoon" may actually have been a Walker Colt with 9 in. barrel.

5. Senate Rpt. 183, 42nd Cong., 2nd Sess., Serial No. 1497. Brownsville (Texas) *Ranchero*, 23 Feb. 1868. Nebraska City *News*, 30 June 1869.

6. Townshend, *A Tenderfoot in Colorado*, 11, 51.

7. James H. Cook, *Longhorn Cowboy*, ed. Howard R. Driggs (New York, 1942), 79–80.

8. Richard B. Hughes, *Pioneer Years in the Black Hills*, ed. Agnes Wright Spring (Glendale, Calif., 1957), 20, 50. John Wesley Hardin, *the Life of John Wesley Hardin, as Written by Himself* (Norman, Okla., 1961), 118–20. *Westerner's Brand Book* (Denver Posse), 1963, 145 (cited hereafter as WBB).

9. E. Remington & Sons price list, 1 Jan. 1866 (reprinted by Ray Riling, Philadelphia, 1960). Olympia *Washington Standard*, 4 May 1867. San Francisco *Mining and Scientific Press*, 7 July and 22 Sept. 1866.

10. Waldo E. Nutter, *Manhattan Firearms* (Harrisburg, Pa., 1958), 167–80. Little Rock *Arkansas Gazette*, 25 Dec. 1868. John Biringer Daybooks, 1866–67, Kansas State Historical Society, Topeka, Kansas. Portland *Oregonian*, 12 June 1869.

11. Frank M. Sellers and Samuel E. Smith, *American Percussion Revolvers* (Ottawa, Ontario, 1971), 47–51. U.S. pats. 29,864 of 4 Sept. 1860; 39,771 of 1 Sept. 1863; and 40,021 of 22 Sept. 1863. *Scientific American*, 29 May 1869. *Arkansas Gazette*, 1 Sept. and 25 Dec. 1868. Portland *Oregonian*, 12 June 1869. *Army and Navy Journal*, 19 Aug. 1876 (cited hereafter as *ANJ*).

12. Allen Pinkerton, *The Spy of the Rebellion . . .* (New York, 1886), 685–86.

13. Great Western Gun Works 1871 catalog, in L. D. Satterlee, comp., *Ten Old Gun Catalogs for the Collector* (1940; reprint ed., Chicago, 1962). John E. Parsons, *Henry Deringer's Pocket Pistol* (New York, 1952), 23–24, 77, 86–87, 95, 180–81. Brownsville *Ranchero*, 7 Oct. 1869. San Francisco *Alta California*, 15 May 1871. Nonspecific ads for "derringers" are also in the Santa Fe *New Mexican*, 9 Feb. 1866; Galveston *News*, 26 Jan. and 14 Feb. 1866; *Rocky Mountain News*, 25 April 1866; Gold Hill, Nev., *News*, 2 July 1866; *Arkansas Gazette*, 24 Dec. 1867; Silver City, Idaho, *Owyhee Avalanche*, 30 May 1868; and the Idaho City *Idaho World*, 2 Feb. 1871.

14. Folsom Bros. 1869 catalog; Great Western Gun Works 1871 catalog; and Enterprise Gun Works 1876 catalog, in Satterlee, *Ten Old Gun Catalogs*. See also the illustration from the Tryon catalog in James E. Serven, "Tryon Gunmaking Firm Grew with the Nation," *American Rifleman*, Dec. 1970, 41.

15. Nutter, *Manhattan Firearms*, 185, 188, 191, 193. Norm Flayderman, *Flayderman's Guide to Antique American Firearms*, 2nd ed. (Northfield, Ill., 1980), 117. A Manhattan "Hero" with 3 in. barrel, and a very similar iron-frame pistol with 4 in. barrel (accession no. 2797), are now in the Sutter's Fort collection, Sacramento.

16. Lord George C. G. Berkeley, *The English Sportsman in the Western Prairies* (London, 1861), 370. *Alta California*, 25 Aug. 1860. Schuyler, Hartley & Graham 1864 catalog, 138, 144. Frank M. Sellers, *Sharps Firearms* (N. Hollywood, Calif., 1978), 125–60 passim. *ANJ*, 22 July and 23 Sept. 1876. Parsons, *Deringer's Pocket Pistol*, 121, 123. Flayderman, *Antique American Firearms*, 401.

17. *Leslie's Weekly*, 14 Sept. 1861 and 29 Aug. 1863. *Harper's Weekly*, 14 Dec. 1861 and 17 Oct. 1863. Schuyler, Hartley & Graham 1864 catalog, 139, 143. Galveston *News*, 6 April 1866. *ANJ*, 20 Nov. 1875. E. Remington & Sons price list, Jan. 1876. Flayderman, *Antique American Firearms*, 146.

18. U.S. pat. 17,386 of 26 May 1857. *ANJ*, 23 June 1866. Flayderman, *Antique American Firearms*, 339–40, 382–83.

19. Reid's U.S. pat. 51,752 of 26 Dec. 1865. Flayderman, *Antique American Firearms*, 374, 394–96. Jack Dunlap, *American, British, & Continental Pepperbox Firearms* (Palo Alto, Calif., 1967), 190–94, 200–202. Converse & Hopkins's U.S. pat. 57,622 of 28 Aug. 1866. *Scientific American*, 9 Feb. 1867.

20. Folsom Bros. 1869 catalog, in Satterlee, *Ten Old Gun Catalogs*. Portland *Oregonian*, 12 June 1869.

21. Parsons, *Deringer's Pocket Pistol*, 104–5, 115–16, 135, 208–11. Ft. Smith, Ark., *Herald*, 22 Nov. 1866. Biringer daybooks, 1866–67. Charles T. Haven and Frank A. Belden, *A History of the Colt Revolver* (New York, 1940), 649. James E. Serven, *Colt Firearms from 1836* (Harrisburg, Pa., 1979), 201–3.

22. Parsons, *Deringer's Pocket Pistol*, 121, 123–24, 212–15.

23. Henry M. Stanley, *My Early Travels and Adventures in America and Asia* (New York, 1895), 166. Elizabeth B. Custer, *Boots and Saddles* (New York, 1885), 163. See also the *Annals of Wyoming*, Jan. 1932, 584. Elliot's U.S. pat. 33,382 of 1 Oct. 1861 (on the Vest Pocket .22). Rider's U.S. pats. 40,887 of 8 Dec. 1863 and 45,123 of 15 Nov. 1864. See also British pat. 3,253 of 23 Dec. 1864. Olympia *Washington Standard*, 4 May 1867. Brownsville *Ranchero*, 11 May 1867. Dallas *Herald*, 31 Aug. 1867. San Antonio *Express*, 8 Oct. 1867.

24. Hammond's U.S. pat. 44,798 of 25 Oct. 1864. Flayderman, *Antique American Firearms*, 378. See also the *American Artisan*, 12 June 1867. Elliot's U.S. pats. 51,440 of 12 Dec. 1865, and 68,292 of 27 Aug. 1867. Parsons, *Deringer's Pocket Pistol*, 122–27, 137, 158, 218–23. *ANJ*, 13 Jan. and 2 March 1872. Most previous writers claim that the Double Deringer was introduced in 1866; however, no known Rem-

ington advertisement or price list of 1866 or 1867 mentions this arm. See, for example, the Remington ads in the newspapers cited in note 23 above.

25. Brownsville *Ranchero*, 20 Aug. 1868. U.S. pat. 58,525 of 2 Oct. 1866. Parsons, *Deringer's Pocket Pistol*, 103, 220–21. Flayderman, *Antique American Firearms*, 404–5.

26. U.S. pat. 63,605 of 9 April 1867. Parsons, *Deringer's Pocket Pistol*, 121, 124, 212–15. ANJ, 13 May 1871. A few Southerners were made with 4 in. barrels and longer grips; see Flayderman, *Antique American Firearms*, 372–73. Marlin's U.S. pat. 101,637 of 5 April 1870.

27. Folsom Bros. 1869 catalog, in Satterlee, *Ten Old Gun Catalogs*. Portland *Oregonian*, 12 June 1869. Georgetown *Colorado Miner*, 21 Oct. 1869.

28. U.S. pat. 91,616 of 22 June 1869. Parsons, *Deringer's Pocket Pistol*, 124, 216–17. Letter to the authors from Herschel C. Logan, 13 Dec. 1968.

29. Parsons, *Deringer's Pocket Pistol*, 105–16, 134. U.S. pat. 105,388 of 12 July 1870. Serven, *Colt Firearms*, 199, 200–201, 204–5.

30. *Alta California*, 14 May 1871. San Antonio *Herald*, 6 May 1874. Enterprise Gun Works 1876 catalog, in Satterlee, *Ten Old Gun Catalogs*.

31. Townshend, *A Tenderfoot in Colorado*, 32. Hardin, *John Wesley Hardin*, 22–23, 67. Nyle H. Miller and Joseph W. Snell, *Great Gunfighters of the Kansas Cowtowns, 1867–1886* (Lincoln, Neb., 1963), 130. C. W. (Doc) Shores, *Memoirs of a Lawman*, ed. Wilson Rockwell (Denver, 1962), 130. *Rocky Mountain News*, 12 Dec. 1872.

32. A. B. Meacham, *Wigwam and War-Path* (Boston, 1875), 476, 492, 496.

33. Louis A. Garavaglia, "In Defense of Cartridge Derringers," *American Rifleman*, Feb. 1969, 18–19. St. Louis *Missouri Democrat*, 25 April and 31 Aug. 1863. Sellers and Smith, *American Percussion Revolvers*, 131.

34. Prescott *Arizona Miner*, 14 March 1866. Richardson & Co.'s *Galveston City Directory, 1866–67*. Central City, Colo., *Miner's Register*, 22 June 1866. Flayderman, *Antique American Firearms*, 389–90. *Harper's Weekly*, 23 March 1867. Portland *Oregonian*, 12 June 1869.

35. Flayderman, *Antique American Firearms*, 386–87. ANJ, 30 March 1867. Galveston *News*, 31 May 1869. Hartley & Graham 1885 catalog, 29. [Frank M. Sellers], *The William M. Locke Collection* (East Point, Ga., 1973), 380–81.

36. G. Hubert Smith, "Like-a-Fishhook Village and Fort Berthold, Garrison Reservoir, North Dakota," *National Park Service Anthropological Papers 2* (Washington, D.C., 1972), 165. Shores, *Memoirs of a Lawman*, 203. Philip F. Van Cleave, "Rebuttal to an Unusual Allen & Wheelock," *Gun Report*, May 1960.

37. Folsom Bros. 1869 catalog, in Satterlee, *Ten Old Gun Catalogs*. *Missouri Democrat*, 21 Jan. 1865. See also *Harper's Weekly*, 23 March 1867.

38. John E. Parsons, *The Peacemaker and Its Rivals* (New York, 1950), 141–58. U.S. pat. 82,258 of 15 Sept. 1868. Serven, *Colt Firearms*, 174–77.

39. Flayderman, *Antique American Firearms*, 88–89. Galveston *News*, 31 May 1869.

40. Quotation in Parsons, *The Peacemaker*, 170.

41. Senate Ex. Doc. 23, Serial No. 1405. Senate Rpt. 84, 42nd Cong., 3rd Sess., Serial No. 1576. Roy G. Jinks and Robert J. Neal, *Smith & Wesson, 1857–1945*, rev. ed. (New York, 1975), 25–29, 54–59, 62–65. John E. Parsons, *Smith & Wesson Revolvers* (New York, 1957), 25–40. William Hepworth Dixon, *New America*, 7th ed. (London, 1867), 1: 28, 34. Helen McCann White, ed., *Ho! For the Gold Fields . . .* (St. Paul, Minn., 1966), 216.

42. *Alta California*, 1 July 1867 and 1 July 1869. Brownsville *Ranchero*, 20 Aug. 1868. Portland *Oregonian*, 30 Oct. 1867 and 12 June 1869. Joseph W. Snell, ed., "Diary of a Dodge City Buffalo Hunter," *Kansas Historical Quarterly*, Winter 1965, 376. Maj. J. B. Thompson, "A Shot at a Murderer," *The Trail*, July 1907, 15.

43. Jinks and Neal, *Smith & Wesson*, 260. Parsons, *Smith & Wesson*, 62–63.

44. Flayderman, *Antique American Firearms*, 145–46, 371–72. See also A. W. F. Taylerson, *The Revolver, 1865–1888* (New York, 1966), 40–41, 247–48. Sellers, *The Locke Collection*, 300–306, 309. ANJ, 31 May 1873. Helen J. Lundwall, ed., *Pioneering in Territorial Silver City* (Albuquerque, 1983), 12.

45. Parsons, *Smith & Wesson*, 66–71. Jinks and Neal, *Smith & Wesson*, 160–61.

46. Jinks and Neal, *Smith & Wesson*, 166–69. Parsons, *Smith & Wesson*, 83–84, 123–24.

47. Parsons, *Smith & Wesson*, 99–109. ANJ, 13 May 1871.

48. Jinks and Neal, *Smith & Wesson*, 169, 171.

49. Parsons, *Smith & Wesson*, 71–74. *Alta California*, 14 May 1871. The Palmer S&W (serial no. in the 5000 range) is now in the Pioneer Museum in Colorado Springs. The Langford and Moran guns are in the museum at Mammoth Hot Springs, Yellowstone National Park. The Crittenden S&W (serial no. 17,643) is with the Colorado State Historical Society in Denver. The society also owns a Russian model (serial no. 49,358) engraved "Hayt/Colorado," and a Model 1½ Second Issue .32 found in La Veta Pass (formerly Sangre de Christo Pass), Colorado.

50. Curry to Smith & Wesson, 3 March 1873; Plate to Smith & Wesson, 10 April 1873; Wilson to Smith & Wesson, 14 July 1873; George D. Merriam to Smith & Wesson, 9 June 1873; Smith & Wesson Archives, Smith & Wesson, Springfield, Mass. (cited hereafter as Smith & Wesson letters).

51. Parsons, *Smith & Wesson*, 109. Carroll to Smith & Wesson, 28 July 1873; Capt. Robert Young to Smith & Wesson, 13 Oct. 1873, Smith & Wesson letters.

52. Parsons, *The Peacemaker*, 112. Serven, *Colt Firearms*, 179–83, 196. R. L. Wilson, *The Colt Heritage* (New York, n.d.), 163.

53. Serven, *Colt Firearms*, 192–95, 197, 206–9. William B. Edwards, *The Story of Colt's Revolver* (Harrisburg, Pa., 1953), 136. U.S. pat. 119,048 of 19 Sept. 1871. Wilson, *Colt Heritage*, 163, 170.

54. Serven, *Colt Firearms*, 186–88, 197, 210–11. Parsons, *The Peacemaker*, 18–20, 112–13. Wilson, *Colt Heritage*, 165, 170.

55. ANJ, 3 Feb. and 4 May 1872; 25 Jan. and 14 June

1873. See also Paul S. Lederer, "Remington Navy Pistols," *American Rifleman*, Jan. 1966, 68–71.

56. Parsons, *The Peacemaker*, 18–24, 86, 113. John Kopec, Ron Graham, and C. K. Moore, *A Study of the Colt Single Action Army Revolver* (La Puente, Calif., 1976).

57. Parsons, *The Peacemaker*, 112–13. Pueblo *Colorado Chieftain*, 19 Feb. 1874. A Colt M1872 in the Wyoming State Museum in Cheyenne is stamped "Freund & Bro." on the barrel.

58. Parsons, *The Peacemaker*, 84–100, 102. ANJ, 13 May 1876. Kopec, Graham, and Moore, *Single Action Army Revolver*, 37. A. C. Gould, *Modern American Pistols and Revolvers* (1894; reprint ed., Plantersville, S.C., 1946), 38–42.

59. Berkeley, *The English Sportsman*, 370. Prof. Thomas Dimsdale, *The Vigilantes of Montana* (Norman, Okla., 1953), 25, 138–39. Nathaniel Pitt Langford, *Vigilante Days and Ways* (Chicago, 1912), 161. See also Helen Fitzgerald Sanders, ed., *X. Beidler, Vigilante* (Norman, Okla., 1957), 145–46, 158, 160. Hardin, *John Wesley Hardin*, 62. Gould, *Pistols and Revolvers*, 199. Edgar Beecher Bronson, *Reminiscences of a Ranchman* (Lincoln, Neb., 1962), 24.

60. Letter to Arnold Chernoff from Colt, 21 Jan. 1976, re: Colt Single Action .45, serial no. 15,401; this revolver and nine others like it were shipped to E. M. Mossman of the U.P. on 4 Jan. 1875. Parsons, *The Peacemaker*, 95.

61. Parsons, *Smith & Wesson*, 106, 111–13. Jinks and Neal, *Smith & Wesson*, 171–75.

62. Parsons, *Smith & Wesson*, 94–95, 97, 113–19. Jinks and Neal, *Smith & Wesson*, 176–79, 213. Only 35 first-model Schofields were sold commercially; see Jinks and Neal, 211.

63. ANJ, 20 Nov. 1875. E. Remington & Sons 1877 and 1885 catalogs. Parsons, *The Peacemaker*, 36–44. Flayderman, *Antique American Firearms*, 149–50.

64. Miller and Snell, *Great Gunfighters*, 29–30. John Lord, *Frontier Dust*, ed. Natalie Shipman (Hartford, Conn., 1926), 101. H. H. Crittenden, comp., *The Crittenden Memoirs* (New York, 1936), 269–70.

65. N. Howard Thorp, *Pardner of the Wind*, with Neil M. Clark (Caldwell, Idaho, 1945), 277. E. C. Abbott and Helena Huntington Smith, *We Pointed Them North* (New York, 1939), 28–29.

66. Donald B. Webster, Jr., *Suicide Specials* (Harrisburg, Pa., 1958). Hays City, Kansas, *Sentinel* supplement, 26 July 1876. *Colorado Chieftain*, 7 June 1877. Dodge City *Times*, 24 March 1877.

67. Webster, *Suicide Specials*, 20–21, 24–25, 27–28, 55, 71–72, 122–23, 133–37. Enterprise Gun Works catalog, July 1874. Corbett, Hoye & Co.'s *Denver City Directory*, 1877. *Forest and Stream*, 3 May 1877. N. Curry & Bro. 1884 catalog. J. P. Lower catalog, May, 1888. ANJ, 25 Jan. 1873. See also Parsons, *Deringer's Pocket Pistol*, 238–39.

68. W. A. Rogers, *A World Worth While* (New York and London, 1922), 188–96. Forehand & Wadsworth applied the "Bulldog" stamp to both single-action and double-action .38 rimfire revolvers; see Homer Fisher's 1880 catalog, in Satterlee, *Ten Old Gun Catalogs*, and Flayderman, *Antique American Firearms*, 379.

69. Wilson, *Colt Heritage*, 170, 172–73. Serven, *Colt Firearms*, 212–17. ANJ, 20 Nov. 1875. Remington 1877 catalog. Flayderman, *Antique American Firearms*, 148–49. Curry 1884 catalog.

70. Jinks and Neal, *Smith & Wesson*, 56, 59, 65, 106–10. Parsons, *Smith & Wesson*, 133–38. Dallas *Herald*, 7 Oct. 1876. *Rocky Mountain News*, 25 Oct. 1876.

71. Jinks and Neal, *Smith & Wesson*, 110–11. Parsons, *Smith & Wesson*, 139–40.

72. "Birmingham Industries," *Iron* (London), 7 Nov. 1874. William Chipchase Dowell, *The Webley Story* (Kirkgate, Leeds, 1962), 68–70. Dowell claims that the Bulldog was first marketed in 1878, but this is obviously an error; see the issue of *Iron* cited above and note 73 below. J. H. Walsh, *The Modern Sportsman's Gun and Rifle* (London, 1882–84), 2: 418.

73. William Crasro (sp?) to Smith & Wesson, 13 Feb. 1876, Smith & Wesson letters. In an earlier letter, dated 17 Jan. 1876, Crasro asked the firm for a double action revolver "on the same principal as 'Webly's British Bull Dog.'" *Alta California*, 12 Aug. 1876. Lawrence P. Shelton, *California Gunsmiths, 1846–1900* (Fair Oaks, Calif., 1977), 79. H. R. Ficken, "Frontier Five-Shooters," *Gun Report*, June 1974, 64–65. Frederick W. Nolan, *The Life and Death of John Henry Tunstall* (Albuquerque, 1965), 223.

74. ANJ, 20 Jan. 1877. Wilson, *Colt Heritage*, 199–201.

75. ANJ, 17 Aug. 1878. Parsons, *The Peacemaker*, 73–75. Wilson, *Colt Heritage*, 201–3. A. W. F. Taylerson, *The Revolver, 1889–1914* (New York, 1971), 27–29.

76. James B. Gillett, *Six Years with the Texas Rangers* (New Haven, Conn., 1925), 124.

77. Frank Collinson, *Life in the Saddle*, ed. Mary W. Clarke (Norman, Okla., 1963), 118.

78. C. C. Stevens to Colt, 1 May 1878; Lower to Colt, 1 June 1878, Colt Pat. F. A. Mfg. Co. correspondence, Connecticut State Library, Hartford, Conn. (cited hereafter as Colt letters). WBB, 1966, 267.

79. Parsons, *Smith & Wesson*, 164–65.

80. Parsons, *Smith & Wesson*, 97, 211–12. Jinks and Neal, *Smith & Wesson*, 213. Brock to Smith & Wesson, 26 Feb. 1876, Smith & Wesson letters. The *Texas Gun Collector*, Oct., 1954, 10–12. See also WBB, 1956, 335.

81. Parsons, *Smith & Wesson*, 140–42. Jinks and Neal, *Smith & Wesson*, 59–62.

82. Jinks and Neal, *Smith & Wesson*, 180–90. Parsons, *Smith & Wesson*, 145–55. Gould, *Pistols and Revolvers*, 54, 56–62. Carl W. Breihan, *The Escapades of Frank and Jesse James* (New York, 1974), n.p. Carl W. Breihan, *The Complete and Authentic Life of Jesse James* (New York, 1953), 183.

83. Parsons, *Smith & Wesson*, 164–66. Jinks and Neal, *Smith & Wesson*, 65–67, 116–18. U.S. pats. 222,168 of Dec. 1879 and 228,009 of 25 May 1880. Taylerson, *The Revolver, 1889–1914*, 72–73, 96–98.

84. *Rocky Mountain News*, 18 June 1880. Denver *Inter-Ocean*, 6 June 1880. Parsons, *Smith & Wesson*, 166. Jinks and Neal, *Smith & Wesson*, 195–98.

85. Pueblo *Colorado Chieftain*, 30 March and 11 May 1882.

86. W. R. McFarland to Colt, 4 Jan. 1881, and N. F. Leslie to Colt, 14 Jan. 1881, Colt letters.

87. Lower to Colt, 7 Oct. 1881, Colt letters. Alfred E. Turner, ed., *The O.K. Corral Inquest* (College Station, Tex., 1981), 135. One story says that Wyatt Earp used a Smith & Wesson American at the O.K. Corral fight, but we could find no verification of this in available primary sources.

88. T. C. Frazier to Colt, 23 Sept. 1882; 27 April 1883; 6 and 8 Feb. 1884, Colt letters.

89. House Misc. Doc. 20, Pt. 1, 47th Cong., 2nd Sess., Serial No. 2119. Parsons, *The Peacemaker*, 67–72. The Kansas-marked Merwin & Hulbert is in the collection of M. C. Forester, Pueblo, Colo. Another Merwin & Hulbert of the same style is stamped "UPRR CO." on the backstrap and "U110" on the butt.

90. Edward S. Farrow, *American Small Arms* (New York, 1904), 175–76. *ANJ*, 9 Oct. 1880 and 2 Sept. 1882. Charles B. Norton, *American Inventions and Improvements in Breech-Loading Small Arms* (Springfield, Mass., 1880), 100.

91. Gould, *Pistols and Revolvers*, 75–80. Hartley & Graham 1885 catalog. Hopkins & Allen 1889 price sheet (reprinted by Ray Riling, Philadelphia, 1960). E. C. Meacham 1884 catalog, in Joseph J. Schroeder, comp., *Rare Selections from Old Gun Catalogs, 1880–1920* (Northfield, Ill., 1977).

92. *ANJ*, 9 Oct. 1880. John Lower catalog, May 1888.

93. Curry 1884 catalog. Flayderman, *Antique American Firearms*, 380. Taylerson, *The Revolver, 1889–1914*, 55–56. Gould, *Pistols and Revolvers*, 114, 120, 124.

94. Parsons, *The Peacemaker*, 64–67. Corbett, Hoye & Co.'s *Denver City Directory*, 1877. *Forest and Stream*, 3 May 1877. Flayderman, *Antique American Firearms*, 378.

95. Enterprise Gun Works 1876 catalog, in Satterlee, *Ten Old Gun Catalogs*, Curry 1884 catalog. See also Parsons, *Smith & Wesson*, 164, 166. The Kittredge ad in *ANJ*, 19 Aug. 1882, offers "a variety of British Bull-Dog and kindred English Pistols" but disparages the quality of Webley's Bulldog.

96. W. W. Greener, *The Gun and Its Development* (London, 1881), 376–77. Laudatory comments on these pistols are also in Greener's earlier work, *Modern Breech-Loaders*, 152, 160–61. Both Greener and Lancaster displayed big-bore two-barreled and four-barreled pistols at Chicago's 1893 Columbian Exposition; see House Doc. 510, 57th Cong., 1st Sess., Serial No. 4374.

97. *The Field* (London), 12 and 19 Jan. 1884.

98. *The Field*, 19 Jan. 1884.

99. Homer Fisher 1880 catalog, in Satterlee, *Ten Old Gun Catalogs. Forest and Stream*, 26 Sept. 1878. *ANJ*, 19 Aug. 1882. Meacham 1884 catlog, in Schroeder, *Old Gun Catalogs*. Dowell, *The Webley Story*, 72–73 and pl. 35.

100. Shores, *Memoirs of a Lawman*, 157. George H. Tinker, *A Land of Sunshine: Flagstaff and Its Surroundings* (Glendale, Calif., 1969), introduction.

101. Miller and Snell, *Great Gunfighters*, 130.

102. Baylis John Fletcher, *Up the Trail in '79* (Norman, Okla., 1968), 27, 32. Parsons, *The Peacemaker*, 140, 171.

103. Photostat in Keith Wheeler, ed., *The Townsmen* (The Old West Series, Time-Life Books, New York, 1975),

136. Odie B. Faulk, *Tombstone: Myth and Reality* (New York, 1972), 131.

104. James H. Kyner, *End of Track* (Lincoln, Neb., 1960), 180–81. Simmons to Colt, 23 July 1887, Colt letters.

105. Frank M. Canton, *Frontier Trails* (Norman, Okla., 1966), 117.

106. *The Texas Gun Collector*, Oct. 1954, 10–12. Remington 1885 catalog. Curry 1884 catalog.

107. Simmons to Colt, 5 May 1884, and Lower to Colt, 7 May 1885, Colt letters.

108. Blanding to Colt, 3 Jan. 1887; Simmons to Colt, 5 May and 23 July 1884, Colt letters.

109. Frederick R. Burnham, *Scouting on Two Continents*, ed. Mary Nixon Everett (Garden City, N.Y., 1926), 43. Thomas Edgar Crawford, *The West of the Texas Kid, 1881–1910*, ed. Jeff C. Dykes (Norman, Okla., 1962), 54–55. Thorp, *Pardner of the Wind*, 276–77.

110. Theodore Roosevelt, *Hunting Trips of a Ranchman* (New York, 1927), 27. Jinks and Neal, *Smith & Wesson*, 70–73, 122–25. Taylerson, *The Revolver, 1889–1914*, 25, 52–53, 55–57, 59–60. Gould, *Pistols and Revolvers*, 62–73. John Lower catalog, May 1888. Buena Vista, Colo., *Herald*, 16 Jan. 1891. Guthrie *Oklahoma State Capitol*, 25 July 1891. Jackson Arms (Dallas, Tex.) Catalog 19, item 258.

111. Jinks and Neal, *Smith & Wesson*, 210–12. Parsons, *Smith & Wesson*, 92.

112. Taylerson, *The Revolver, 1889–1914*, 32–34. Wilson, *Colt Heritage*, 204–7. Haven and Belden, *The Colt Revolver*, 415–21. Gould, *Pistols and Revolvers*, 44, 46–49.

113. Haven and Belden, *The Colt Revolver*, 420, 434. Taylerson, *The Revolver, 1889–1914*, 34–39. Gould, *Pistols and Revolvers*, 45–46.

114. Gould, *Pistols and Revolvers*, 48–50. Wilson, *Colt Heritage*, 211–12, 215–16. Haven and Belden, *The Colt Revolver*, 427–30, 433, 435–36.

115. Parsons, *The Peacemaker*, 103–8. Haven and Belden, *The Colt Revolver*, 429, 431, 438.

116. Thorp, *Pardner of the Wind*, 276. John K. Rollinson, *Pony Trails in Wyoming*, ed. E. A. Brininstool (Caldwell, Idaho, 1944), 270, 287.

117. Jinks and Neal, *Smith & Wesson*, 74–75, 128–30. Haven and Belden, *The Colt Revolver*, 440–43. *Outdoor Life* (Denver series), June 1900, back cover; Dec. 1901, n.p. Parsons, *The Peacemaker*, 86, 88, 116, 118–19.

CHAPTER 6

1. Robert A. Murray, "Treaty Presents at Fort Laramie, 1867–68," *Museum of the Fur Trade Quarterly*, Fall 1977, 2–5. George A. Custer, *My Life on the Plains* (New York, 1874), 153. Philip H. Sheridan, *Personal Memoirs of Philip H. Sheridan* (New York, 1888), 2: 288–90.

2. J. S. Campion, *On the Frontier* (London, 1878), 81, 228. Charles E. Hanson, Jr., "The Post-War Indian Gun Trade," *Museum of the Fur Trade Quarterly*, Fall 1968, 3.

3. Senate Ex. Doc. 16, 39th Cong., 2nd Sess., Serial No. 1277. Hanson, "Indian Gun Trade," 9.

4. Grace Raymond Hebard and E. A. Brininstool, *The*

Bozeman Trail (Cleveland, Ohio, 1922), 2: 92. House Misc. Doc. 41, 39th Cong., 2nd Sess., Serial No. 1302.

5. Douglas C. Jones, *The Treaty of Medicine Lodge* (Norman, Okla., 1966), 136–37.

6. Hanson, "Indian Gun Trade," 6–8.

7. Otis E. Young, *The West of Philip St. George Cooke* (Glendale, Calif., 1955), 348–49. Carl Coke Rister, *The Southwestern Frontier, 1865–1881* (Cleveland, Ohio, 1928), 78–81.

8. Senate Ex. Doc. 16, Serial No. 1277. National Park Service, *Soldier and Brave* (New York and London, 1963), 46.

9. Report of the Secretary of War, 1872, House Ex. Doc. 1, Pt. 2, 42nd Cong., 3rd Sess., Serial No. 1558 (cited hereafter as *RSW*). Hanson, "Indian Gun Trade," 7.

10. Report of the Commissioner of Indian Affairs, 1870, House Ex. Doc. 1, Pt. 4, 41st Cong., 3rd Sess., Serial No. 1449 (cited hereafter as *RCIA*). *RCIA*, 1872, House Ex. Doc. 1, Pt. 5, 42nd Cong., 3rd Sess., Serial No. 1560.

11. Henry M. Stanley, *My Early Travels and Adventures in America and Asia* (New York, 1895), 115.

12. Hanson, "Indian Gun Trade," 6–7. Capt. Robert G. Carter, *The Old Sergeant's Story* (Chicago, 1926), 131. Richard B. Hughes, *Pioneer Years in the Black Hills*, ed. Agnes Wright Spring (Glendale, Calif., 1957), 41. Ernest Ingersoll, *Knocking Round the Rockies* (New York, 1883), 97. See also George Bird Grinnell, ed., *Hunting at High Altitudes* (New York, 1913), 19. Capt. Charles King, *Campaigning with Crook* (New York, 1890), 144.

13. Col. W. A. Graham, ed., *Abstract of the Official Record of the Proceedings of the Reno Court of Inquiry* (Harrisburg, Pa., 1954), 51. Letter to C. G. Worman from Don Rickey, Jr., 26 June 1957. *RSW*, 1876, House Ex. Doc. 1, Pt. 2, 44th Cong., 2nd Sess., Serial No. 1742. Frazier and Robert Hunt, *I Fought with Custer: The Story of Sergeant Windolph* (New York, 1947), 92, 104.

14. Hunt and Hunt, *I Fought with Custer*, 92. *Army and Navy Journal*, 22 July 1876.

15. Quotation in John E. Parsons and John S. DuMont, *Firearms in the Custer Battle* (Harrisburg, Pa., 1953), 26.

16. Parsons and DuMont, *Custer Battle*, 42. O. E. Byrne, *Soldiers of the Plains* (New York, 1926), 203. Col. Richard Irving Dodge, *Our Wild Indians . . .* (Hartford, Conn., 1883), 493.

17. *RCIA*, 1877, House Ex. Doc. 1, Pt. 5, 45th Cong., 2nd Sess., Serial No. 1800. Hanson, "Indian Gun Trade," 9. Dodge, *Our Wild Indians*, 422.

18. Andrew Garcia, *Tough Trip Through Paradise, 1878–1879*, ed. Bennett H. Stein (Boston, 1967), 151, 153.

19. *RSW*, 1878, House Ex. Doc. 1, Pt. 2, 45th Cong., 3rd Sess., Serial No. 1843.

20. App. V, Report of the Chief of Ordnance, 1879, House Ex. Doc. 1, Pt. 2, 46th Cong., 2nd Sess., Serial No. 1907 (cited hereafter as *RCO*).

21. App. V, *RCO*, 1879. George B. Grinnell, *The Fighting Cheyennes* (Norman, Okla., 1956), 415.

22. App. V, *RCO*, 1879. Grinnell, *Fighting Cheyennes*, 408. See also Francis Haines, ed., "Letters of an Army Captain on the Sioux Campaign of 1879–1880," *Pacific Northwest Quarterly*, Jan. 1948, 58–59.

23. App. V, *RCO*, 1879.

24. App. V, *RCO*, 1879.

25. App. V, *RCO*, 1879.

26. App. V, *RCO*, 1879.

27. App. V, *RCO*, 1879.

28. App. V, *RCO*, 1879.

29. App. V, *RCO*, 1879.

30. Frank McNitt, *The Indian Traders* (Norman, Okla., 1962), 48.

31. Britton Davis, *The Truth About Geromino*, ed. M. M. Quaife (New Haven, Conn., 1929), 59. McNitt, *The Indian Traders*, 50. Odie B. Faulk, *The Geronimo Campaign* (New York, 1969), 87.

BIBLIOGRAPHY

MANUSCRIPTS

Record Group 156 (Records of the Office of the Chief of Ordnance), National Archives, Washington, D.C.

Colt Patent Fire Arms Mfg. Co. correspondence, Connecticut State Library, Hartford, Conn.

Sharps Rifle Co. correspondence, Texas Tech University Library, Lubbock, Texas.

Smith & Wesson correspondence, Smith & Wesson, Springfield, Mass.

GOVERNMENT DOCUMENTS

The most valuable published sources of information on military arms are the dozens of pertinent volumes in the U.S. Congressional Serial Set, available at the Government Documents section in some of the larger municipal and college libraries.

ANNUAL REPORTS OF THE CHIEF OF ORDNANCE

1865: House Ex. Doc. 1, 39th Cong., 1st Sess., Serial No. 1250.

1866: House Ex. Doc. 1, 39th Cong., 2nd Sess., Serial No. 1285.

1867: House Ex. Doc. 1, 40th Cong., 2nd Sess., Serial No. 1324.

1868: House Ex. Doc. 1, 40th Cong., 3rd Sess., Serial No. 1367.

1869: House Ex. Doc. 1, Pt. 2, 41st Cong., 2nd Sess., Serial No. 1412.

1870: House Ex. Doc. 1, Pt. 2, 41st Cong., 3rd Sess., Serial No. 1446.

1871: House Ex. Doc. 1, Pt. 2, 42nd Cong., 2nd Sess., Serial No. 1503.

1872: House Ex. Doc. 1, Pt. 2, 42nd Cong., 3rd Sess., Serial No. 1558.

1873: House Ex. Doc. 1, Pt. 2, 43rd Cong., 1st Sess., Serial No. 1599.

1874: House Ex. Doc. 1, Pt. 2, 43rd Cong., 2nd Sess., Serial No. 1635.

1875: House Ex. Doc. 1, Pt. 2, 44th Cong., 1st Sess., Serial No. 1677.

1876: House Ex. Doc. 1, Pt. 2, 44th Cong., 2nd Sess., Serial No. 1746.

1877: House Ex. Doc. 1, Pt. 2, 45th Cong., 2nd Sess., Serial No. 1797.

1878: House Ex. Doc. 1, Pt. 2, 45th Cong., 3rd Sess., Serial No. 1847.

1879: House Ex. Doc. 1, Pt. 2, 46th Cong., 2nd Sess., Serial No. 1907.

1880: House Ex. Doc. 1, Pt. 2, 46th Cong., 3rd Sess., Serial No. 1956.

1881: House Ex. Doc. 1, Pt. 2, 47th Cong., 1st Sess., Serial No. 2014.

1882: House Ex. Doc. 1, Pt. 2, 47th Cong., 2nd Sess., Serial No. 2095.

1883: House Ex. Doc. 1, Pt. 2, 48th Cong., 1st Sess., Serial No. 2186.

1884: House Ex. Doc. 1, Pt. 2, 48th Cong., 2nd Sess., Serial No. 2282.

1885: House Ex. Doc. 1, Pt. 2, 49th Cong., 1st Sess., Serial No. 2374.

1886: House Ex. Doc. 1, Pt. 2, 49th Cong., 2nd Sess., Serial No. 2465.

1887: House Ex. Doc. 1, Pt. 2, 50th Cong., 1st Sess., Serial No. 2538.

1888: House Ex. Doc. 1, Pt. 2, 50th Cong., 2nd Sess., Serial No. 2633.

1889: House Ex. Doc. 1, Pt. 2, 51st Cong., 1st Sess., Serial No. 2720.

1890: House Ex. Doc. 1, Pt. 2, 51st Cong., 2nd Sess., Serial No. 2836.

1891: House Ex. Doc. 1, Pt. 2, 52nd Cong., 1st Sess., Serial No. 2928.

1892: House Ex. Doc. 1, Pt. 2, 52nd Cong., 2nd Sess., Serial No. 3083.

1893: House Ex. Doc. 1, Pt. 2, 53rd Cong., 2nd Sess., Serial No. 3205.

1894: House Ex. Doc. 1, Pt. 2, 53rd Cong., 3rd Sess., Serial No. 3302.

1895: House Doc. 2, 54th Cong., 1st Sess., Serial No. 3378.

1896: House Doc. 2, 54th Cong., 2nd Sess., Serial No. 3485.

1897: House Doc. 2, 55th Cong., 2nd Sess., Serial No. 3637.

1898: House Doc. 2, 55th Cong., 3rd Sess., Serial No. 3752.

1899: House Doc. 2, 56th Cong., 1st Sess., Serial No. 3911.

1900: House Doc. 2, 56th Cong., 2nd Sess., Serial No. 4097.

1901: House Doc. 2, 57th Cong., 1st Sess., Serial No. 4285.

1902: House Doc. 2, 57th Cong., 2nd Sess., Serial No. 4449.

1903: House Doc. 2, 58th Cong., 2nd Sess., Serial No. 4641.

1904: House Doc. 2, 58th Cong., 3rd Sess., Serial No. 4790.

1905: House Doc. 2, 59th Cong., 1st Sess., Serial No. 4950.

1906: House Doc. 2, 59th Cong., 2nd Sess., Serial No. 5110.

1907: House Doc. 2, 60th Cong., 1st Sess., Serial No. 5276.

ANNUAL SPRINGFIELD ARMORY EXPENDITURES STATEMENTS

1866: House Ex. Doc. 47, 39th Cong., 2nd Sess., Serial No. 1289.

1867: House Ex. Doc. 83, 40th Cong., 2nd Sess., Serial No. 1332.

1868: House Ex. Doc. 80, 40th Cong., 3rd Sess., Serial No. 1374.

1869: House Ex. Doc. 32, 41st Cong., 2nd Sess., Serial No. 1416.

1870: House Ex. Doc. 45, 41st Cong., 3rd Sess., Serial No. 1453.

1871: Senate Ex. Doc. 49, 42nd Cong., 2nd Sess., Serial No. 1479.

1872: Senate Ex. Doc. 22, 42nd Cong., 3rd Sess., Serial No. 1545.

1873: Senate Ex. Doc. 15, 43rd Cong., 1st Sess., Serial No. 1580.

1874: Senate Ex. Doc. 10, 43rd Cong., 2nd Sess., Serial No. 1629.

1875: Senate Ex. Doc. 14, 44th Cong., 1st Sess., Serial No. 1664.

1876: Senate Ex. Doc. 12, 44th Cong., 2nd Sess., Serial No. 1718.

1877: Senate Ex. Doc. 1, 45th Cong., 2nd Sess., Serial No. 1780.

1878–80: The expenditures statements for 1878–80 were not published in the Serial Set.

1881: Senate Ex. Doc. 43, 47th Cong., 1st Sess., Serial No. 1987.

1882: Senate Ex. Doc. 50, 47th Cong., 2nd Sess., Serial No. 2076.

1883: Senate Ex. Doc. 8, 48th Cong., 1st Sess., Serial No. 2162.

1884: Senate Ex. Doc. 8, 48th Cong., 2nd Sess., Serial No. 2261.

1885: Senate Ex. Doc. 3, 49th Cong., 1st Sess., Serial No. 2333.

1886: House Ex. Doc. 35, 49th Cong., 2nd Sess., Serial No. 2479.

1887: Senate Ex. Doc. 12, 50th Cong., 1st Sess., Serial No. 2504.

1888: Senate Ex. Doc. 2, 50th Cong., 2nd Sess., Serial No. 2610.

1889: Senate Ex. Doc. 5, 51st Cong., 1st Sess., Serial No. 2678.

1890: House Ex. Doc. 77, 51st Cong., 2nd Sess., Serial No. 2858.

1891: Senate Ex. Doc. 2, 52nd Cong., 1st Sess., Serial No. 2892.

1892: Senate Ex. Doc. 3, 52nd Cong., 2nd Sess., Serial No. 3055.

1893: Senate Ex. Doc. 2, 53rd Cong., 2nd Sess., Serial No. 3160.

1894: House Ex. Doc. 12, 53rd Cong., 3rd Sess., Serial No. 3319.

1895: Senate Doc. 20, 54th Cong, 1st Sess., Serial No. 3347.

1896: Senate Doc. 3, 54th Cong., 2nd Sess., Serial No. 3467.

1897: Senate Doc. 11, 55th Cong., 2nd Sess., Serial No. 3590.

1898: Senate Doc. 19, 55th Cong., 3rd Sess., Serial No. 3725.

1899: House Doc. 26, 56th Cong., 1st Sess., Serial No. 3954.

1900: Senate Doc. 26, 56th Cong., 2nd Sess., Serial No. 4029.

1901: Senate Doc. 16, 57th Cong., 1st Sess., Serial No. 4220.

1902: House Doc. 57, 57th Cong., 2nd Sess., Serial No. 4489.

1903: House Doc. 51, 58th Cong., 2nd Sess., Serial No. 4670.

1904: House Doc. 29, 58th Cong., 3rd Sess., Serial No. 4829.

WAR DEPARTMENT CONTRACTS

With one exception (1871), the War Department contract list was published annually in the Serial Set from 1866 to 1875; thereafter, however, publication became sporadic.

1866: House Ex. Doc. 27, 39th Cong., 2nd Sess., Serial No. 1289.

1867: House Ex. Doc. 145, 40th Cong., 2nd Sess., Serial No. 1337.

1868: Senate Ex. Doc. 29, 40th Cong., 3rd Sess., Serial No. 1360.

1869: Senate Ex. Doc. 17, 41st Cong., 2nd Sess., Serial No. 1405.

1870: Senate Ex. Doc. 23, 41st Cong., 3rd Sess., Serial No. 1440.

1872: House Ex. Doc. 158, 42nd Cong., 3rd Sess., Serial No. 1567.

1873: House Ex. Doc. 159, 43rd Cong., 1st Sess., Serial No. 1610.

1874: House Ex. Doc. 111, 43rd Cong., 2nd Sess., Serial No. 1648.

1875: House Ex. Doc. 95, 44th Cong., 1st Sess., Serial No. 1689.

1878: Senate Ex. Doc. 40, 45th Cong., 3rd Sess., Serial No. 1828.

1879: Senate Ex. Doc. 56, 46th Cong., 2nd Sess., Serial No. 1884.

1881: Senate Ex. Doc. 51, 47th Cong., 1st Sess., Serial No. 1987.

1883: Senate Ex. Doc. 83, 48th Cong., 1st Sess., Serial No. 2165.

1884: Senate Ex. Doc. 53, 48th Cong., 2nd Sess., Serial No. 2263.

1885: Senate Ex. Doc. 42, 49th Cong., 1st Sess., Serial No. 2333.

1886: House Ex. Doc. 64, 49th Cong., 1st Sess., Serial No. 2479.

1887: House Ex. Doc. 99, 50th Cong., 1st Sess., Serial No. 2558.

1890: House Ex. Doc. 91, 51st Cong., 2nd Sess., Serial No. 2858.

1893: House Ex. Doc. 39, 53rd Cong., 2nd Sess., Serial No. 3223.

1894: House Ex. Doc. 99, 53rd Cong., 3rd Sess., Serial No. 3319.

MISCELLANEOUS DOCUMENTS

House Ex. Doc. 53, 39th Cong., 2nd Sess., Serial No. 1290. (Ordnance contracts, 1864–65.)

Senate Rpt. 173, 40th Cong., 2nd Sess., Serial No. 1320. (Although it deals principally with artillery, this report contains a good deal of testimony concerning the Allin conversions.)

House Ex. Doc. 99, 40th Cong., 2nd Sess., Serial No. 1338. (Ordnance contracts and purchases, 1861–66.)

House Misc. Doc. 152, 40th Cong., 2nd Sess., Serial No. 1350. (Arms owned by the U.S., c. 1867.)

House Misc. Docs. (no number), 40th Cong., 2nd Sess., Serial No. 1355. (Arms displayed at the Paris Exposition, 1867.)

Senate Ex. Doc. 23, 41st Cong., 2nd Sess., Serial No. 1405. (Testimony regarding the Rollin White patent.)

Senate Rpt. 183, 42nd Cong., 2nd Sess., Serial No. 1497. (Arms sold by the U.S., 1867–71.)

House Ex. Doc. 89, 42 Cong., 2nd Sess., Serial No. 1511. (Arms sold by the U.S., 1865–71.)

House Ex. Doc. 60, 42nd Cong., 2nd Sess., Serial No. 1515. (Field trials of the trowel bayonet, 1871–72.)

House Ex. Doc. 309, 42nd Cong., 2nd Sess., Serial No. 1520. (Operations at Springfield Armory, 1867–71; also in Senate Ex. Doc. 72, 42nd Cong., 2nd Sess., Serial No. 1479.)

House Ex. Doc. 152, 43rd Cong., 2nd Sess., Serial No. 1648. (Proceedings of the St. Louis Ordnance Board, 1870.)

Senate Ex. Doc. 16, 45th Cong., 1st Sess., Serial No. 1828. (Operations at Springfield Armory, 1872–77.)

Senate Ex. Doc. 17, 45th Cong., 1st Sess., Serial No. 1828. (Arms for the Army.)

House Misc. Doc. 20, Pt. 1, 47th Cong., 2nd Sess., Serial No. 2119. (Arms displayed at the Philadelphia Exposition, 1876.)

House Doc. 510, 57th Cong., 1st Sess., Serial No. 4374. (Arms displayed at Chicago's Columbian Exposition, 1893.)

ANNUAL COMMISSIONER OF PATENTS REPORTS

1866: House Ex. Doc. 109, 39th Cong., 2nd Sess., Serial Nos. 1298–1300.

1867: House Ex. Doc. 96, 40th Cong., 2nd Sess., Serial Nos. 1333–36.

1868: House Ex. Doc. 52, 40th Cong., 3rd Sess., Serial Nos. 1375–78.

1869: House Ex. Doc. 102, 41st Cong., 2nd Sess., Serial Nos. 1420–22.

1870: House Ex. Doc. 89, 41st Cong., 3rd Sess., Serial No. 1455.

1871: House Ex. Doc. 86, 42nd Cong., 2nd Sess., Serial No. 1511.

1872: House Ex. Doc. 190, 42nd Cong, 3rd Sess., Serial No. 1564.

1873: Senate Ex. Doc. 58, 43rd Cong., 1st Sess., Serial No. 1583.

1874: House Ex. Doc. 150, 43rd Cong., 2nd Sess., Serial No. 1643.

1875: House Ex. Doc. 107, 44th Cong., 1st Sess., Serial No. 1685.

1876: House Ex. Doc. 36, 44th Cong., 2nd Sess., Serial No. 1754.

1877: House Ex. Doc. 61, 45th Cong., 2nd Sess., Serial No. 1805.

1878: House Ex. Doc. 48, 45th Cong., 3rd Sess., Serial No. 1855.

1879: House Ex. Doc. 33, 46th Cong., 2nd Sess., Serial No. 1916.

1880: House Ex. Doc. 67, 46th Cong., 3rd Sess., Serial No. 1965.

1881: House Ex. Doc. 62, 47th Cong, 1st Sess., Serial No. 2024.

1882: House Ex. Doc. 71, 47th Cong, 2nd Sess., Serial No. 2109.

1883: House Ex. Doc. 73, 48th Cong., 1st Sess., Serial No. 2202.

1884: House Misc. Doc. 18, 48th Cong., 2nd Sess., Serial No. 2313.

1885: Senate Misc. Doc. 71, 49th Cong., 1st Sess., Serial No. 2344.

1886: House Misc. Doc. 135, 49th Cong., 2nd Sess., Serial No. 2492.

1887: House Misc. Doc. 164, 50th Cong., 1st Sess., Serial No. 2569.

1888: House Misc. Doc. 109, 50th Cong., 2nd Sess., Serial No. 2658.

1889: Senate Misc. Doc. 78, 51st Cong., 2nd Sess., Serial No. 2699.

1890: Senate Misc. Doc. 58, 51st Cong., 2nd Sess., Serial No. 2822.

1891: Senate Misc. Doc. 68, 52nd Cong., 1st Sess., Serial No. 2906.

1892: Senate Misc. Doc. 53, 52nd Cong., 2nd Sess., Serial No. 3066.

1893: Senate Misc. Doc. 127, 53rd Cong., 2nd Sess., Serial No. 3173.
1894: House Misc. Doc. 70, 53rd Cong., 3rd Sess., Serial No. 3334.
1895: Senate Doc. 242, 54th Cong., 1st Sess., Serial No. 3356.
1896: Senate Doc. 183, 54th Cong., 2nd Sess., Serial No. 3472.
1897: Senate Doc. 185, 55th Cong., 2nd Sess., Serial No. 3609.
1898: Senate Doc. 104, 55th Cong., 3rd Sess., Serial No. 3733.
1899: Senate Doc. 185, 56th Cong., 1st Sess., Serial No. 3855.
1900: Senate Doc. 138, 56th Cong., 2nd Sess., Serial No. 4041.

CITY DIRECTORIES

Cheyenne, Wyo., 1876.
Colorado Springs, Colo., 1879–80; 1882; 1888.
Council Bluffs, Iowa, 1866; 1868–74; 1876.
Denver, 1866; 1876–86.
Ft. Scott, Kan., 1865–66; 1869–70; 1871–72; 1875.
Kansas City, 1865–66; 1867–71; 1873–75.
Laramie, Wyo., 1875.
Leadville, Colo., 1880–86.
Leavenworth, Kan., 1865–75.
Lincoln, Neb., 1880–81.
Nebraska City, Neb., 1870; 1881.
Omaha, Neb., 1866; 1868–69; 1870; 1872–79.
St. Joseph, Mo., 1869–70; 1872–73.
Salt Lake City, 1867; 1869; 1874; 1879–80.
San Francisco, 1867; 1873.
Topeka, Kan., 1868–73; 1879.
Wichita, Kan., 1878.

STATE AND REGIONAL DIRECTORIES

Black Hills, 1878.
California, Arizona, New Mexico, Colorado, and Kansas, 1882–83.
California, Nevada, Utah, Wyoming, Colorado, and Nebraska, 1882.
Colorado, 1871; 1875–76; 1878; 1881.
Colorado, New Mexico, Utah, Nevada, Wyoming, and Arizona, 1884–85.
Kansas, 1870; 1878.
Kansas-Nebraska, 1866–67.
New Mexico, 1882.
Upper California, 1866.
Utah, 1874.
Utah, Idaho, Montana, Wyoming, Colorado, Kansas, Nebraska, and Dakota, 1879–80.

RAILWAY GUIDES

Atchison, Topeka, & Santa Fe, and Wichita & Southwestern, 1872.
Hannibal & St. Joseph, 1873.
Missouri Pacific/Kansas Pacific, 1867–68; 1870.
Nebraska, 1872.

NEWSPAPERS

Abilene, Kan., *Chronicle*, 1867; 1870–71.
Austin, Tex., *State Gazette*, 1866–69.
Atchison, Kan., *Champion*, 1865–69.
Black Hills *Pioneer*, 1876–77.
Boise, Idaho, *Statesman*, 1865–66; 1868–69; 1877.
Brownsville, Tex., *Ranchero*, 1867–69.
Buena Vista, Colo., *Herald*, 1891.
Central City, Colo., *Miner's Register*, 1866–70.
Cheyenne, Wyo., *Leader*, 1867–79.
Colorado Springs, Colo., *Gazette*, 1877–78.
Council Bluffs, Iowa, *Nonpareil*, 1868–71.
Dallas *Herald*, 1866–76.
Denver *Rocky Mountain News*, 1865–85.
Dodge City, Kansas, *Times*, 1876–82.
Elko, Nev., *Independent*, 1869–73.
Ely, Nev., *White Pines News*, 1869–70.
Ft. Scott, Kan., *Monitor*, 1867–69.
Frontier Index (Julesburg, Colo.; Ft. Sanders, Wyo.; and Green River, Wyo.), 1867–68.
Ft. Smith, Ark., *Herald*, 1866–67; 1870.
Ft. Worth, Tex., *Democrat*, 1873.
Galveston, Tex., *News*, 1866–70.
Georgetown, Colo., *Colorado Miner*, 1868–70.
Gold Hill, Nev., *News*, 1865–70.
Guthrie, Okla., *State Capitol*, 1891–92.
Hays City, Kan., *Sentinel*, 1876–77.
Lawrence, Kan., *State Journal* and *Republican Journal*, 1868–69.
Lawrence, Kan., *Tribune*, 1867–69.
Leadville, Colo., *Democrat*, 1880.
Leavenworth, Kan., *Times* and *Times & Conservative*, 1865–70.
Lewiston, Idaho, *Northerner*, 1876.
Liberty, Mo., *Tribune*, 1866–69.
Little Rock *Arkansas Gazette*, 1868–70.
London *Field*, 1884.
Manhattan, Kan., *Standard*, 1868–70.
Medora, N.D., *Bad Lands Cow Boy*, 1884–86.
Miles City Mont., *Yellowstone Journal*, 1879–83.
Nebraska City, Neb., *News*, 1866–69.
New Orleans *Picayune*, 1866–69.
New York *Spirit of the Times*, 1868–69.
New York *Turf, Field, and Farm*, 1865–70.
North Platte, Neb., *Lincoln County Advertiser*, 1872.
North Platte, *Enterprise*, 1873–74.
North Platte, *Republican*, 1875.
Olympia, *Washington Standard*, 1865–70.
Omaha, Neb., *Republican*, 1865–85.
Portland, *Oregonian*, 1867–69; 1874.
Prescott, *Arizona Miner*, 1865–70; 1880–88.
Pueblo, *Colorado Chieftain*, 1868–82.
Pueblo *Courier*, 1898–1900.
St. Louis *Globe-Democrat*, 1882.
St. Louis *Missouri Democrat*, 1865–69.
St. Louis *Missouri Republican*, 1865–68.
Salt Lake City *Deseret News*, 1865–67.
Salt Lake City *Telegraph*, 1867–69.
San Antonio, Tex., *Express*, 1867–73.

San Antonio, *Herald*, 1867–74.
San Francisco *Alta California*, 1865–76.
San Francisco *Mining & Scientific Press*, 1865–72.
Santa Fe *New Mexican*, 1865–67; 1873–74.
Silver City, Idaho, *Owyhee Avalanche*, 1868–69.
Silver City, N.M., *Grant County Herald*, 1876–84.
Sitka *Alaskan*, 1888–92.
South Pass., Wyo., *Sweetwater Mines*, 1868–69.
Tombstone, Ariz., *Epitaph*, 1880–81.
Tucson, *Arizona Citizen*, 1870–75; 1884–86.
Virginia City, Mont., *Montana Post*, 1865–69.
Wichita, Kan., *Eagle*, 1872–74.
Yankton, S.D., *Dakotian* and *Union & Dakotian*, 1865–74.

CATALOGS AND PRICE LISTS

Ball Patent Firearms Price List, 1866. Reprinted by the Ordnance Chest, Madison, Conn., n.d.
N. Curry & Bro. Catalog, 1884. Reprinted by the Paradox Press, Berkeley, Cal., 1965.
Enterprise Gun Works Catalog, July 1874.
Great Western Gun Works Catalog, 1873. Reprinted by American Reprints, St. Louis, 1969.
Great Western Gun Works Catalog, 1888–89. Reprinted by the Gun Digest, Chicago, 1966.
Hartley & Graham Catalog, 1885. Reprinted by the Ordnance Chest, Madison, Conn., n.d.
Hopkins & Allen Price List, 1889. Reprinted by Ray Riling, Philadelphia, 1960.
J. P. Lower Catalog, May 1888.
Massachusetts Arms Co. Catalog, 1880.
Parker Bros. Catalog, 1869.
William Read & Sons Whitney Circular, c. 1874. Reprinted by Ray Riling, Philadelphia, 1960.
E. Remington & Sons Price List, 1 Jan. 1866. Reprinted by Ray Riling, Philadelphia, 1960.
E. Remington & Sons Price List, Jan. 1876, Reprinted by Ray Riling, Philadelphia, 1960.
E. Remington & Sons Catalog, 1877. Reprinted by the Pioneer Press, Harriman, Tenn., n.d.
E. Remington & Sons Catalog, 1885. Reprinted by the Wyoming Armory, Cheyenne, Wyo., n.d.
Remington-U.M.C. Catalog, 1910. Reprinted by Jayco, Newhall, Cal., 1962.
Schuyler, Hartley & Graham Catalog, 1864. Reprinted by Norm Flayderman, Greenwich, Conn., 1961.
Union Metallic Cartridge Co. Price List, 1869. Reprinted by Ray Riling, Philadelphia, 1960.
United States Cartridge Co. Price List, 1881.
Winchester Repeating Arrms Co. Catalog, 1878. Reprinted by Charles G. Worman, Dayton, Ohio, n.d.
Winchester Repeating Arms Co. Catalog, March 1891. Reprinted by W. A. O'Hara, New Preston, Conn., n.d.

PERIODICALS

1865–1900

American Artisan, 1865–68.
Army and Navy Journal, 1865–1901.
Forest and Stream, 1873–85.
Harper's Weekly, 1865–70.
Iron (London), 1874.
Journal of the Royal United Service Institution, 1865–96.
Outdoor Life (Denver Series), 1891–1900.
Scientific American, 1865–1900.
Scientific American Supplement, 1876–1900.

CURRENT AND RECENT HISTORICAL

American Rifleman.
Annals of Wyoming.
Arms Gazette.
Colorado Magazine.
Gun Report.
Kansas Historical Quarterly.
Nebraska History.
Man at Arms.
Pacific Northwest Quarterly.
Texas Gun Collector.
The Trail.

BOOKS

PRIMARY SOURCES

Abbott, E. C., and Smith, Helena Huntington. *We Pointed Them North.* New York, 1939.
Aldridge, Reginald. *Life on a Ranch.* 1884. Reprint ed., New York, 1966.
Allen, W. A. *Adventures with Indians and Game.* Chicago, 1903.
Amber, John T., comp. *Ten Rare Gun Catalogs, 1860–1899* New York, 1952.
Barber, Edward C. *The Crack Shot.* New York, 1868.
Barnitz, Capt. Albert. *Life in Custer's Cavalry.* Edited by Robert M. Utley. New Haven, Conn., 1977.
Barrett, Glen, ed. *Mackinaws Down the Missouri: John C. Anderson's Journal . . . 1866.* Logan, Utah, 1972.
Bell, William A. *New Tracks in North America.* London and New York, 1869.
Bourke, Capt. John G. *On the Border with Crook.* New York, 1891.
Breakenridge, William M. *Helldorado.* 1928. Reprint ed., Glorieta, N.M., 1970.
Bronson, Edgar Beecher. *Reminiscences of a Ranchman.* Lincoln, Neb., 1962.
Burnham, Frederick R. *Scouting on Two Continents.* Edited by Mary Nixon Everett. Garden City, N.Y., 1926.
Campion, J. S. *On the Frontier,* London, 1878.
Canton, Frank M. *Frontier Trails.* Norman, Okla., 1966.
Carpenter, Frank D. *Adventures in Geyser Land.* Caldwell, Idaho, 1935.
Carrington, Frances C. *My Army Life and the Fort Phil Kearney Massacre.* Philadelphia, 1910.
Carrington, Margaret J. *Ab-sa-ra-ka, Home of the Crows.* Philadelphia, 1868.
Carter, Capt. Robert G. *The Old Sergeant's Story.* Chicago, 1926.
Chase, C. M. *The Editor's Run in New Mexico and Colorado.* 1882. Reprint ed., Ft. Davis, Tex., 1968.

Chisholm, James. *South Pass, 1868.* Lincoln, Neb., 1960.

Cleveland, H. W. S. *Hints to Riflemen.* New York, 1864.

Cody, Col. William F. *Life and Adventures of "Buffalo Bill."* Chicago, 1917.

Collinson, Frank. *Life in the Saddle.* Edited by Mary W. Clarke. Norman, Okla., 1963.

Cook, James H. *Fifty Years on the Old Frontier.* New Haven, Conn., 1923.

———. *Longhorn Cowboy.* Edited by Howard R. Driggs. New York, 1942.

Cook, John R. *The Border and the Buffalo.* Edited by Milo M. Quaife. Chicago, 1938.

Crawford, Thomas Edgar. *The West of the Texas Kid, 1881–1910.* Edited by Jeff C. Dykes. Norman, Okla., 1962.

Crittenden, H. H., comp. *The Crittenden Memoirs.* New York, 1936.

Crook, George. *General George Crook, His Autobiography.* Edited by Martin F. Schmitt. Norman, Okla., 1946.

Custer, Elizabeth B. *Boots and Saddles.* New York, 1885.

———. *Following the Guidon.* Norman, Okla., 1966.

Custer, Gen. George A. *My Life on the Plains.* Edited by Milo M. Quaife. Chicago, 1952.

Danker, Donald F., ed. *Man of the Plains: The Recollections of Luther North, 1856–1882.* Lincoln, Neb., 1961.

Davis, Britton. *The Truth About Geronimo.* Edited by Milo M. Quaife. New Haven, Conn., 1929.

Description and Rules for the Management of the Springfield Breech-Loading Rifle Musket, Model 1866. Springfield, Mass., 1867.

Description and Rules for the Management of the Springfield Breech-Loading Rifle Musket, Model 1868. Springfield, Mass. 1869.

Description and Rules for the Management of the Springfield Rifle, Carbine, and Army Revolvers, Calibre .45. Springfield, Mass., 1874.

Description and Rules for the Management of the Springfield Rifle, Carbine, and Army Revolvers, Caliber .45. Washington, D.C., 1898.

Description and Rules for the Management of the U. S. Magazine Rifle and Carbine, Calibre .30. Washington, D.C., 1898.

Description and Rules for the Management of the Ward-Burton Rifle Musket, Model 1871. Springfield, Mass., 1872.

Dixon, William H. *New America.* 7th ed. London, 1867.

Dodge, Fred. *Undercover for Wells Fargo.* Edited by Carolyn Lake. Boston, 1969.

Dodge, Lt. Col. Richard Irving. *The Plains of the Great West and Their Inhabitants.* New York, 1877.

———. *Our Wild Indians. . . .* Hartford, Conn., 1883.

Farrow, Edward S. *American Small Arms.* New York, 1904.

———. *Farrow's Military Encyclopedia.* New York, 1885.

———. *Mountain Scouting.* New York, 1881.

Finerty, John F. *War-Path and Bivouac.* Norman, Okla., 1961.

Fletcher, Baylis F. *Up the Trail in '79.* Norman, Okla., 1968.

Flory, J. S. *Thrilling Echoes from the Wild Frontier.* Chicago, 1893.

Forsyth, Gen. George A. *Thrilling Days in Army Life.* New York, 1902.

Frost, Lawrence A., ed. *With Custer in '74.* Provo, Utah, 1979.

Garcia, Andrew. *Tough Trip Through Paradise.* Edited by Bennett H. Stein. Boston, 1967.

Gillett, James B. *Six Years with the Texas Rangers, 1875–1881.* New Haven, Conn., 1925.

Gillmore, Parker. *Gun, Rod, and Saddle.* New York, 1869.

Gould, A. C. *Modern American Pistols and Revolvers.* 1894. Reprint ed., Plantersville, S.C., 1946.

———. *Modern American Rifles.* 1892. Reprint ed., Plantersville, S.C., 1946.

Graham, Col. W. A., ed. *Abstract of the Official Record of the Reno Court of Inquiry.* Harrisburg, Pa., 1954.

Greener, W. W. *The Gun and Its Development.* London, 1881.

———. *The Gun and Its Development.* 9th ed., 1910. Reprint ed., New York, n.d.

———. *Modern Breech-Loaders: Sporting and Military.* 2nd ed., 1874? Reprint ed., Pueblo, Colo., n.d.

Grinnell, George Bird, ed. *Hunting at High Altitudes.* New York, 1913.

Hardin, John Wesley. *The Life of John Wesley Hardin, as Written by Himself.* Norman, Okla., 1961.

Hebert, Frank. *Forty Years Prospecting and Mining in the Black Hills of South Dakota.* Rapid City, S.D., 1921.

Hittell, John S. *The Commerce and Industries of the Pacific Coast.* San Francisco, 1882.

Horn, Tom. *Life of Tom Horn . . . Written by Himself.* Denver, 1904.

Hornaday, William T. *The Extermination of the American Bison.* Washington, D.C., 1889.

Howbert, Irving. *Memories of a Lifetime in the Pike's Peak Region.* New York and London, 1925.

Hughes, Richard B. *Pioneer Years in the Black Hills.* Edited by Agnes Wright Spring. Glendale, Cal., 1957.

Hunt, Frazier and Robert, eds. *I Fought with Custer: The Story of Sergeant Windolph.* New York, 1947.

Ingersoll, Ernest. *Knocking Round the Rockies.* New York, 1883.

The Industries of Omaha, Nebraska. Omaha, 1887.

James, Marquis. *The Cherokee Strip.* New York, 1945.

Jennings, N. A. *A Texas Ranger.* New York, 1899.

Kelley, Luther S., *"Yellowstone Kelly": The Memoirs of Luther S. Kelly.* Edited by Milo M. Quaife. New Haven, Conn., 1926.

King, Capt. Charles A. *Campaigning with Crook.* New York, 1890.

———. *Trials of a Staff-Officer.* Philadelphia, 1891.

Kyner, James H. *End of Track.* Lincoln, Neb., 1960.

Langford, Nathaniel P. *The Discovery of Yellowstone Park, 1870.* 2nd ed. St. Paul, Minn., 1923.

———. *Vigilante Days and Ways.* Chicago, 1912.

Lord, John. *Frontier Dust.* Edited by Natalie Shipman. Hartford, Conn., 1926.

Lundwall, Helen J., ed. *Pioneering in Territorial Silver City.* Albuquerque, 1983.

Mandat-Grancey, Edmond. *Cow-Boys and Colonels.* 1887. Reprint ed., Philadelphia and New York, 1963.

Mayer, Frank H., and Charles B. Roth. *The Buffalo Harvest.* Denver, 1958.

McConnell, H. H. *Five Years a Cavalryman.* Jacksboro, Tex., 1889.

McReynolds, Robert. *Thirty Years on the Frontier.* Colorado Springs, Colo., 1906.

Meacham, A. B. *Wigwam and War-Path.* Boston, 1875.

Mills, Anson. *My Story.* Edited by C. H. Claudy. Washington, D.C., 1918.

Mulford, Ami Frank. *Fighting Indians in the 7th United States Cavalry.* 1878. Reprint ed., Bellevue, Neb., 1970.

Murphy, J. Mortimer. *Sporting Adventures in the Far West.* New York, 1880.

Nessiter, Charles Alston. *Sport and Adventure Among the North-American Indians.* London, 1890.

Norton, Charles B. *American Breech-Loading Small Arms.* New York, 1872.

————. *American Inventions and Improvements in Breech-Loading Small Arms.* Springfield, Mass., 1880.

Patents for Inventions. Abridgements of Specifications. Class 119, Small-Arms, 1855–1866. London, 1905.

Pinkerton, Allan. *The Spy of the Rebellion. . . .* New York, 1886.

Rogers, W. A. *A World Worth While.* New York and London, 1922.

Rollinson, John K. *Pony Trails in Wyoming.* Edited by E. A. Brininstool. Caldwell, Idaho, 1944.

Roosevelt, Theodore. *Hunting Trips of a Ranchman: Ranch Life and the Hunting Trail.* New York, 1927.

————. *Wilderness Hunter: Outdoor Pastimes of an American Hunter.* New York, 1926.

Satterlee, L. D., comp. *Fourteen Old Gun Catalogs for the Collector.* 1941. Reprint ed., Chicago, 1962.

————. *Ten Old Gun Catalogs for the Collector.* 1940. Reprint ed., Chicago, 1962.

Schroeder, Joseph J., comp. *Rare Selections from Old Gun Catalogs, 1880–1920.* Northfield, Ill., 1977.

Schultz, James W. *Blackfeet and Buffalo: Memories of Life Among the Indians.* Norman, Okla., 1962.

Seymour, Silas. *Incidents of a Trip Through the Great Platte Valley. . . .* New York, 1867.

Sheridan, Gen. Philip H. *Personal Memoirs of Philip H. Sheridan.* New York, 1888.

Shields, G. O. *Rustlings in the Rockies.* Chicago, 1883.

Shores, C. W. *Memoirs of a Lawman.* Edited by Wilson Rockwell. Denver, 1962.

Siringo, Charles A. *Riata and Spurs.* Boston, 1927.

Stanley, Henry M. *My Early Travels and Adventures in America and Asia.* New York, 1895.

Stockbridge, V. D. *Digest of Patents Relating to Breech-Loading and Magazine Small Arms . . . 1836–1873.* 1874. Reprint ed., Greenwich, Conn., 1963.

Stuart, Granville. *Diary and Sketchbook of a Journey to "America," 1866.* Los Angeles, 1963.

————. *Forty Years on the Frontier.* Edited by Paul C. Phillips. Glendale, Cal., 1957.

Thorp, N. Howard. *Pardner of the Wind.* With Neil M. Clark. Caldwell, Idaho, 1945.

Townshend, F. Trench. *Ten Thousand Miles of Travel, Sport, and Adventure.* London, 1869.

Townshend, Richard B. *A Tenderfoot in Colorado.* New York, 1923.

————. *A Tenderfoot in New Mexico.* London, 1923.

Trobriand, Philippe Regis de. *Military Life in Dakota: The Journal of Philippe Regis de Trobriand.* Translated and edited by Lucille M. Kane. St. Paul, Minn., 1951.

Turner, Alfred E., ed. *The O.K. Corral Inquest.* College Station, Tex., 1981.

Vivian, A. P. *Wanderings in the Western Land.* London, 1879.

Walsh, J. H. *The Modern Sportsman's Gun and Rifle.* London, 1882–84.

Ware Eugene F. *The Indian War of 1864.* Edited by Clyde C. Walton. New York, 1960.

Webb, William E. *Buffalo Land.* Cincinnati and Chicago, 1872.

West, Bill, comp. *Hartley & Graham Catalogs, 1895–1899.* Santa Fe Springs, Cal., 1972.

————. *J. Stevens Arms Catalogs, 1876–1899.* Whittier, Cal., 1970.

White, Helen McCann, ed. *Ho! For the Gold Fields. . . .* St. Paul, Minn., 1966.

Wingate, George W. *Through the Yellowstone Park on Horseback.* New York, 1886.

SECONDARY SOURCES

Barnes, Frank C. *Cartridges of the World.* 2nd rev. ed. Edited by John T. Amber. Chicago, 1969.

Behn, Jack. *.45-70 Rifles.* Harrisburg, Pa., 1956.

Bonney, Orrin H. and Lorraine. *Battle Drums and Geysers.* Chicago, 1970.

Brininstool, E. A. *Troopers with Custer.* Harrisburg, Pa., 1952.

Browning, John, and Curt Gentry. *John M. Browning, American Gunmaker.* Garden City, N.Y., 1964.

Byrne, O. E. *Soldiers of the Plains.* New York, 1926.

David, Robert B. *Finn Burnett, Frontiersman.* Glendale, Cal., 1937.

DeHaas, Frank. *Single Shot Rifles and Actions.* Edited by John T. Amber. Chicago, 1969.

DeMerritt, Dwight B. *Maine Made Guns and Their Makers.* Hallowell, Maine, 1973.

Dowell, William Chipchase. *The Webley Story.* Kirkgate, Leeds, 1962.

DuMont, John S. *Custer Battle Guns.* Ft. Collins, Colo., 1974.

Dunlap, Jack. *American, British, and Continental Pepperbox Firearms.* Palo Alto, Cal., 1967.

Erwin, Allen A. *The Southwest of John H. Slaughter, 1841–1922.* Glendale, Cal., 1965.

Faulk, Odie B. *The Geronimo Campaign.* New York, 1969.

————. *Tombstone: Myth and Reality.* New York, 1972.

Flayderman, Norm. *Flayderman's Guide to Antique American Firearms and Their Values.* 2nd ed. Northfield, Ill., 1980.

Fuller, Claud E. *The Breech-Loader in the Service, 1816–1917.* 1933. Reprint ed., New Milford, Conn., 1965.

Gardner, Col. Robert E. *Small Arms Makers.* New York, 1963.

Grant, James J. *Single Shot Rifles.* New York, 1947.

———. *More Single Shot Rifles.* New York, 1959.

Grinnell, George Bird. *The Fighting Cheyennes.* Norman, Okla., 1956.

Hackley, F. W., W. H. Woodin, and E. L. Scranton. *History of Modern U.S. Military Small Arms Ammunition, 1880–1939.* New York, 1967.

Hanson, Charles E., Jr. *The Hawken Rifle: Its Place in History.* Chadron, Neb., 1979.

———. *The Plains Rifle* Harrisburg, Pa., 1960.

Hardin, Albert N., Jr. *The American Bayonet, 1776–1954.* Philadelphia, 1964.

Haven, Charles T., and Frank A. Belden. *The History of the Colt Revolver.* New York, 1940.

Hebard, Grace Raymond, and E. A. Brininstool. *The Bozeman Trail.* Cleveland, Ohio, 1922.

Herron, Jim. *Fifty Years on the Owl Hoot Trail.* Edited by H. E. Chrisman. Denver, 1962.

Jackson, Donald. *Custer's Gold.* New Haven, Conn., 1966.

Jinks, Roy G., and Robert J. Neal. *Smith & Wesson, 1857–1945.* Rev. ed. New York, 1975.

Johnson, Dorothy M. *The Bloody Bozeman.* New York, 1971.

Jones, Douglas C. *The Treaty of Medicine Lodge. . . .* Norman, Okla., 1966.

Kopec, John, Ron Graham, and C. Kenneth Moore. *A Study of the Colt Single Action Army Revolver.* La Puente, Cal., 1976.

Lustyik, Andrew F. *Civil War Carbines.* Aledo, Ill., 1962.

Martin, Douglas D. *Tombstone's Epitaph.* Albuquerque, 1951.

Maxwell, S. L. *Lever Action Magazine Rifles.* Bellevue, Wash., 1976.

McNitt, Frank. *The Indian Traders.* Norman, Okla., 1962.

Miller, Nyle H., and Joseph W. Snell. *Great Gunfighters of the Kansas Cowtowns, 1867–1886.* Lincoln, Neb., 1963.

Mouillesseaux, Harold R. *Ethan Allen, Gunmaker: His Partners, Patents, and Firearms.* Ottawa, 1973.

Murray, Robert A. *Military Posts in the Powder River Country of Wyoming, 1865–1894.* Lincoln, Neb., 1968.

Nankivell, Maj. John H. *History of the Military Organizations of the State of Colorado, 1860–1935.* Denver, 1935.

National Park Service. *Soldier and Brave.* New York and London, 1963.

Nolan, Frederick W. *The Life and Death of John Henry Tunstall.* Albuquerque, 1965.

Parke, William Lee. *Pioneer Pathways to the Pacific.* New York, 1935.

Parsons, John E. *The First Winchester.* New York, 1955.

———. *Henry Deringer's Pocket Pistol.* New York, 1952.

———. *The Peacemaker and Its Rival.* New York, 1950.

———. *Smith & Wesson Revolvers.* New York, 1957.

Parsons, John E., and John S. DuMont. *Firearms in the Custer Battle.* Harrisburg, Pa., 1953.

Rister, Carl Coke. *The Southwestern Frontier, 1865–1881.* Cleveland, Ohio, 1928.

Rosa, Joseph G. *The Gunfighter: Man or Myth?* Norman, Okla., 19—.

———. *They Called Him Wild Bill.* 2nd ed. Norman, Okla., 1974.

Rywell, Martin. *The Gun That Shaped American Destiny.* Harriman, Tenn., 1957.

Sellers, Frank M. *Sharps Firearms.* N. Hollywood, Cal., 1978.

———. *The William M. Locke Collection.* East Point, Ga., 1973.

Sellers, Frank M., and Samuel E. Smith. *American Percussion Revolvers.* Ottawa, 1971.

Serven, James E., ed. *The Collecting of Guns.* Harrisburg, Pa., 1964.

———. *Colt Firearms from 1836.* Harrisburg, Pa., 1979.

Shelton, Lawrence P. *California Gunsmiths, 1846–1900.* Fair Oaks, Cal., 1977.

Spotts, David L., and E. A. Brininstool. *Campaigning with Custer and the Nineteenth Kansas Volunteer Cavalry.* Los Angeles, 1928.

Sutherland, R. Q., and R. L. Wilson. *The Book of Colt Firearms.* Kansas City, 1971.

Suydam, Charles R. *U.S. Cartridges and Their Handguns, 1795–1975.* N. Hollywood, Cal., 1977.

Taylerson, A. W. F. *The Revolver, 1865–1888.* New York, 1966.

———. *The Revolver, 1889–1914.* New York, 1971.

———. *Revolving Arms.* New York, 1967.

Tinker, George H. *A Land of Sunshine: Flagstaff and Its Surroundings.* Glendale, Cal., 1969.

Topping, E. S. *Chronicles of the Yellowstone.* Minneapolis, Minn., 1968.

Utley, Robert M. *Frontier Regulars: The United States Army and the Indian, 1866–1891.* New York, 1973.

Vaughn, J. W. *Indian Fights: New Facts on Seven Encounters.* Norman, Okla., 1966.

Waite, M. D., and B. D. Ernst. *Trapdoor Springfield.* N. Hollywood, Cal., 1980.

Watrous, George R. *The History of Winchester Firearms, 1866–1966.* 3rd ed. Edited by Thomas E. Hall and Pete Kuhlhoff. New Haven, Conn., 1966.

Webster, Donald B., Jr. *Suicide Specials.* Harrisburg, Pa., 1958.

Westerner's Brand Book, Denver Posse, 1946–70.

Williamson, Harold F. *Winchester, The Gun that Won the West.* Washington, D.C., 1952.

Wilson, R. L. *The Colt Heritage.* New York, n.d.

Young, Otis E. *The West of Philip St. George Cooke.* Glendale, Cal., 1955.

INDEX

References to illustrations are printed in boldface type.